Rick Steves'

LONDON

2012

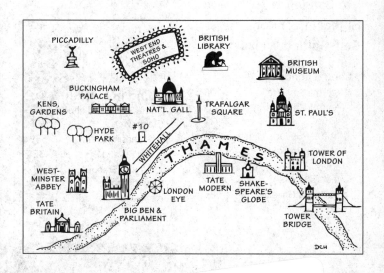

CONTENTS

CITY OF LONDON

London Map Overview

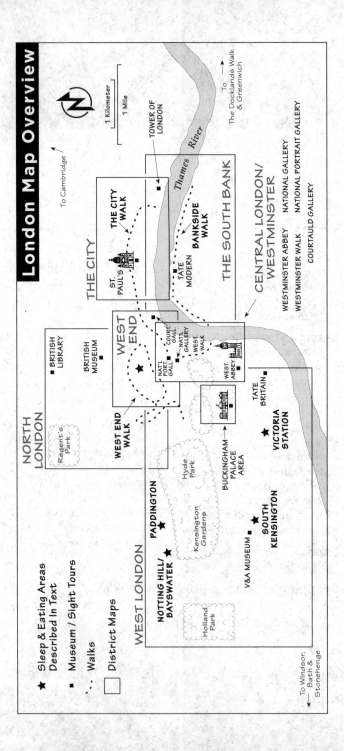

INTRODUCTION

Blow through the city on the open deck of a double-decker orientation tour bus, and take a pinch-me-I'm-in-London walk through the West End. Ogle the crown jewels at the Tower of London, hear the chimes of Big Ben, and see the Houses of Parliament in action. Cruise the Thames River, and take a spin on the London Eye. Hobnob with the tombstones in Westminster Abbey, and visit with Leonardo, Botticelli, and Rembrandt in the National Gallery. Enjoy Shakespeare in a replica of the Globe Theatre and marvel at a glitzy, fun musical at a modern-day theater. Whisper across the dome of St. Paul's Cathedral, then rummage through our civilization's attic at the British Museum. And sip your tea with pinky raised and clotted cream dribbling down your scone.

You can enjoy some of Europe's best people-watching at Covent Garden, and snap to at Buckingham Palace's Changing of the Guard. Just sit in Victoria Station, Piccadilly Circus, or a major Tube station and observe. Tip a pint in a pub with a chatty local, and beach-comb the Thames. Spend one evening at a theater and the other nights catching your breath.

London is more than its museums and landmarks. It's the L.A., D.C., and N.Y.C. of Britain—a living, breathing, thriving organism...a coral reef of humanity. The city has changed dramatically in recent years, and many visitors are surprised to find how "un-English" it is. ESL (English as a second language) seems like the city's first language, as white people are now a minority in major parts of the city that once symbolized white imperialism. Arabs have nearly bought out the area north of Hyde Park. Chinese takeouts outnumber fish-and-chips shops. Eastern Europeans pull pints in British pubs. Many hotels are run by people with foreign accents (who hire English chambermaids), while outlying suburbs are home to huge communities of Indians and Pakistanis. London

Map Legend

↳ Viewpoint	✈ Airport		)▭(	Tunnel
↑ Entry Arrow	⊤ Taxi Stand		▭	Pedestrian Zone
❶ Tourist Info	▣ Tram Stop		-------	Railway
WC Restroom	Ⓑ Bus Stop		·············	Ferry/Boat Route
♛ Castle	Ⓟ Parking		⊢—⊢—⊢	Tram
⛪ Church	)(Mtn. Pass		⊪⊪⊪⊪⊪	Stairs
▪ Statue/Point of Interest	⬚ Park		- - - -	Walk/Tour Route
			--------	Trail

Use this legend to help you navigate the maps in this book.

is a city of nearly eight million separate dreams, inhabiting a place that tolerates and encourages them. With the English Channel Tunnel and discount airlines making travel between Britain and the Continent easier than ever, London is learning—sometimes fitfully—to live as a microcosm of its formerly vast empire.

The city, which has long attracted tourists, seems perpetually at your service, with an impressive slate of sights, entertainment, and eateries, all linked by a great transit system. In anticipation of the 2012 Olympic Games and a greater onslaught of tourists than usual, the city is busy spiffing itself up, especially its rapidly developing Olympic Park in East London.

About This Book

Rick Steves' London 2012 is a personal tour guide in your pocket. Better yet, it's actually two tour guides in your pocket: The co-author of this book is Gene Openshaw. Since our first "Europe through the gutter" trip together as high school buddies in the 1970s, Gene and I have been exploring the wonders of the Old World. An inquisitive historian and lover of European culture, Gene wrote most of this book's self-guided museum tours and neighborhood walks. Together, Gene and I keep this book current and accurate (though, for simplicity, from this point "we" will shed our respective egos and become "I").

In this book, you'll find the following chapters:

Orientation to London includes specifics on public transportation, helpful hints, local tour options, easy-to-read maps, and tourist information. The "Planning Your Time" section suggests a schedule for how to best use your limited time.

Sights in London describes the top attractions and includes their cost and hours.

The **Self-Guided Walks** cover Westminster (from Big Ben to Trafalgar Square); the West End (it's the thee-ah-ter

Key to This Book

Updates
This book is updated every year—but things change. For the latest, visit www.ricksteves.com/update, and for a valuable list of reports and experiences—good and bad—from fellow travelers, check www.ricksteves.com/feedback.

Abbreviations and Times
I use the following symbols and abbreviations in this book:

Sights are rated:

▲▲▲	Don't miss
▲▲	Try hard to see
▲	Worthwhile if you can make it
No rating	Worth knowing about

When you see a ✪ in a sight listing, it means that the sight is covered in much more detail in one of the tour chapters.

Tourist information offices are abbreviated as **TI,** and bathrooms are **WC**s. To categorize accommodations, I use a **Sleep Code** (described on page 350).

Like Europe, this book uses the **24-hour clock.** It's the same through 12:00 noon, then keep going: 13:00, 14:00, and so on. For anything over 12, subtract 12 and add p.m. (14:00 is 2:00 p.m.).

When giving **opening times,** I include both peak season and off-season hours if they differ. So, if a museum is listed as "May-Oct daily 9:00-16:00," it should be open from 9:00 a.m. until 4:00 p.m. from the first day of May until the last day of October (but expect exceptions).

For **transit** or **tour departures,** I first list the frequency, then the duration. So, a train connection listed as "2/hour, 1.5 hours" departs twice each hour, and the journey lasts an hour and a half.

---

district, dahling, with restaurants and shops galore, from Leicester Square and Covent Garden to Soho, Regent Street, and Piccadilly Circus); The City (the financial district—banks, churches, and courts busy with barristers and baristas); Bankside (on the South Bank, through Shakespeare's world to the Tate Modern); and the Docklands (London's new and creatively planned urban district).

The **Self-Guided Tours** lead you through London's most fascinating museums and sights: Westminster Abbey, National Gallery, National Portrait Gallery, Courtauld Gallery, the British Museum, the British Library, St. Paul's Cathedral, the Tower of London, Tate Modern, Victoria and Albert Museum, and the Tate Britain.

Sleeping in London describes my favorite hotels, from good-value deals to cushy splurges.

Eating in London serves up a range of options, from inexpensive pubs to fancy restaurants.

London with Children includes my top recommendations for keeping your kids (and you) happy in London.

Shopping in London gives you tips for shopping painlessly and enjoyably, without letting it overwhelm your vacation or ruin your budget.

Entertainment in London is your guide to fun, including theater, music, walks, and cruises.

London Connections lays the groundwork for your smooth arrival and departure, covering transportation by train (including the Eurostar to Paris and Brussels) and by plane (with detailed information on London's major airports).

Day Trips include Greenwich, Windsor, Cambridge, Stonehenge, and Bath.

Great Britain: Past and Present gives the background of this country, including a timeline of London history, information about British architecture, and a rundown of contemporary events and current challenges.

The **appendix** is a traveler's tool kit, with telephone tips, useful phone numbers, recommended books and films, a festival list, a climate chart, a handy packing checklist, a hotel reservation form, and a fun British-Yankee dictionary.

Browse through this book and select your favorite sights. Then have a brilliant trip! Traveling like a temporary local, you'll get the absolute most out of every mile, minute, and dollar. As you visit places I know and love, I'm happy you'll be meeting my favorite Londoners.

Planning

This section will help you get started planning your trip—with notes on trip costs, when to go, and things to know before you take off.

Travel Smart

Your trip to London is like a complex play—easier to follow and really appreciate on a second viewing. While no one does the same trip twice to gain that advantage, reading this book in its entirety before your trip accomplishes much the same thing.

Design an itinerary that enables you to visit sights at the best possible times. Note festivals, holidays, street market days, and days when sights are closed. Visit The City (London's old center) during the day on weekdays, when it's lively, not at night or on weekends, when it's pretty dead. The two-hour orientation bus tour is best on Sunday morning (when some sights are closed anyway, and traffic doesn't slow down the bus) or evenings (when it's cheaper). There are almost no plays on Sundays, except for *The Lion King* and Shakespeare's Globe. Treat Saturday as a weekday, except for transportation connections outside of London (which can be less frequent than on Mon-Fri, and downright meager on Sun). A smart trip is a puzzle—a fun, doable, and worthwhile challenge.

Be sure to mix intense and relaxed periods in your itinerary. Every trip—and every traveler—needs slack time (laundry, picnics, people-watching, and so on). Pace yourself. Assume you will return.

Get online at Internet cafés or at your hotel, and buy a phone card or carry a mobile phone: You can get tourist information, learn the latest on sights (special events, tour schedules, etc.), book tickets and tours, make reservations, reconfirm hotels, research transportation connections, check weather, and keep in touch with your loved ones.

Enjoy the friendliness of the British people. Connect with the culture. Set up your own quest for the best pub, silly sign, or chocolate bar. Slow down and be open to unexpected experiences. You speak the language—use it! Ask questions—most locals are eager to point you in their idea of the right direction. Keep a notepad in your pocket for organizing your thoughts. Wear your money belt, and figure out how to estimate prices in dollars. Those who expect to travel smart, do.

Trip Costs

Five components make up your trip costs: airfare, surface transportation, room and board, sightseeing and entertainment, and shopping and miscellany.

Airfare: A basic round-trip flight from the US to London can cost $800-$1,300, depending on where you fly from and when (cheaper in winter).

Surface Transportation: For a typical one-week visit, allow about $45 for the Tube and buses (for a Seven-Day Travelcard transportation pass). The cost of round-trip train rides to day-trip destinations is about $30 for Windsor, $10 for Greenwich (two rides on a 1-2-zone pay-as-you-go Oyster card—see page 29), $60 for Cambridge, and $75 for Bath. You can save money by taking buses instead of trains. Add $90 if you plan to take a taxi ride between London's Heathrow Airport and your hotel (or save money by taking the Tube, train, bus, or airport shuttle).

Room and Board: London is one of Europe's most expensive major capitals. But if you're careful, you can manage comfortably in London on $130 a day per person for room and board. A $130-a-day budget allows $15 for lunch, $25 for dinner, and $90 for lodging (based on two people splitting the cost of a basic $180 double

London Almanac

Population: Approximately 7.75 million people

Currency: British pound (GBP)

City Layout: London is divided into the City of London (the main financial district), and 32 administrative boroughs—12 in inner London.

Tallest Building: The Shard London Bridge, still under construction, currently stands at 800 feet. When complete, it will reach 1,017 feet, making it the tallest building in the EU.

Tourist Tracks: Each year London hosts 26 million tourists, most of whom stop to take a photo at Trafalgar Square. London's most popular attraction, the British Museum, sees 5.9 million visitors annually.

Popular Misconception: "Big Ben" refers not to the clock, but instead to its 13-ton bell.

Culture Count: While the Queen's English is still the language of the land, fewer than half the residents of inner London speak English as their first language. Nearly 300 different languages are spoken in London's schools. About 58 percent of Londoners are white, 13.3 percent are South Asian, 10.6 percent are of African descent, and 6.6 percent are West Indian. Seven in ten British call themselves Christian (half of those are Anglican), but in any given week, more Londoners visit a mosque than an Anglican church.

Fun Food Facts: London's most popular take-away foods are fish-and-chips and minced-meat pie (the pies were originally filled with eels...so minced-meat is an improvement). But it's not all about meat; PETA recently named London the world's most vegan-friendly city.

Need a Restroom? Ask for the toilet, loo, lavatory, or bog.

Oldest Pub: The Lamb and Flag in Covent Garden. First licensed in 1623, it was once known as the Bucket of Blood, thanks to rowdy, bare-knuckle fights held there.

Average Londoner: The average Londoner is between 45 and 49 years old, has 1.7 children, and will live until the age of 80. He/she will drink 75,000 cups of tea in a lifetime and consumes less alcohol per week than the average Brit. He/she will commute 139 hours to work every year, riding the Tube four days a week.

room that includes breakfast). Students and tightwads can do it for as little as $70 a day ($45 for hostel bed, $25 for groceries).

Sightseeing and Entertainment: You'll pay more in London for sights that charge admission than you will anywhere else in Europe. Fortunately, most of London's best sights are free (although many request a donation), including the British Museum, National Gallery, National Portrait Gallery, Tate Britain, Tate Modern, British Library, and the Victoria and Albert Museum. (For a full list of free museums—and advice on saving money on sightseeing—see "Affording London's Sights," page 66.)

Figure on paying roughly $25-30 each for the major sights that charge admission (e.g., Westminster Abbey-$25, Tower of London-$29), $12-20 for guided walks, and $45 for bus tours and splurge experiences (plays range $25-100).

An overall average of $50 a day works for most people. Don't skimp here. After all, this category is the driving force behind your trip—you came to sightsee, enjoy, and experience London.

Shopping and Miscellany: Figure roughly $2 per postcard, $3 for tea or an ice cream cone, and $6 per pint of beer. Shopping can vary in cost from nearly nothing to a small fortune. Good budget travelers find that this category has little to do with assembling a trip full of lifelong and wonderful memories.

When to Go

July and August are peak season—my favorite time—with long days, the best weather, and the busiest schedule of tourist fun. Prices and crowds don't go up in summer as dramatically in Britain as they do in much of Europe, except for holidays and festivals (see page 565). Still, travel during "shoulder season" (May, early June, Sept, and early Oct) is easier and can be a bit less expensive. Shoulder-season travelers usually enjoy smaller crowds, decent weather, and the full range of sights and tourist fun spots.

Winter travelers find absolutely no crowds and soft room prices, but shorter sightseeing hours. The weather can be cold and dreary, and nightfall draws the shades on sightseeing well before dinnertime. While England's rural charm falls with the leaves, London sightseeing is fine in the winter, and is especially popular during the Christmas season. For more on planning a winter holiday visit, read "Winter Diversions" (at the end of the Entertainment in London chapter).

Plan for rain no matter when you go. Just keep traveling and take full advantage of "bright spells." The weather can change several times a day, but rarely is it extreme. As the locals say, "There's no bad weather, only inappropriate clothing." Bring a jacket and dress in layers. Temperatures below 32°F cause headlines, and days that break 80°F—while increasing in recent years—are still uncommon in London. (For more information, see the climate chart in the appendix.) July and August are not much better than shoulder months. May and June can be lovely. While sunshine may be rare, summer days are very long. The summer sun is up from 6:30 to 22:30. It's not uncommon to have a gray day, eat dinner, and enjoy hours of sunshine afterward.

Know Before You Go

Your trip is more likely to go smoothly if you plan ahead. Check this list of things to arrange while you're still at home.

You need a **passport**—but no visa or shots—to travel in Great Britain. You may be denied entry into certain European countries if your passport is due to expire within three to six months of your ticketed date of return. Get it renewed if you'll be cutting it close. It can take up to six weeks to get or renew a passport. (For more on passports, see www.travel.state.gov.) Pack a photocopy of your passport in your luggage in case the original is lost or stolen.

Book rooms well in advance if you'll be traveling during peak season and any major **holidays** (see page 565).

If you're planning to **stay in Bath** as well as London, consider doing it before London as the ideal small-town jet-lag pillow, then visit London afterward, when you're rested and accustomed to travel in Britain. Heathrow Airport has direct bus connections to Bath and other cities.

To book a **London play,** you can call from the US as easily as from London, using your credit-card number to pay for your tickets. For the current schedule and phone numbers, visit www .officiallondontheatre.co.uk. For simplicity, I book plays while in London. For more information, see the Entertainment in London chapter.

Call your **debit- and credit-card companies** to let them know the countries you'll be visiting, to ask about fees, and more (see page 11).

Do your homework if you want to buy **travel insurance.** Compare the cost of the insurance to the likelihood of your using it and your potential loss if something goes wrong. For more information, see www.ricksteves.com/insurance.

If you're bringing a mobile device, you can download free information from **Rick Steves Audio Europe,** featuring audio tours of London's major sights, hours of travel interviews on London, and more (via www.ricksteves.com/audioeurope, iTunes, or the Rick Steves Audio Europe smartphone app; for details, see page 559).

You won't want to drive in London because of the traffic and congestion charge (covered on page 38), but if you'll be **renting a car** for touring Britain, you'll need your driver's license.

If you'll be taking the **Eurostar train,** consider ordering a ticket in advance (or buy it in Britain); for details, see page 439.

Because **airline carry-on restrictions** are always changing, visit the Transportation Security Administration's website (www .tsa.gov/travelers) for an up-to-date list of what you can bring on the plane with you, and what you have to check. Some airlines may restrict you to only one carry-on (no extras like a purse or daypack); check Britain's website for the latest (www.dft.gov.uk).

Practicalities

Emergency and Medical Help: In Britain, dial 999 for police help or a medical emergency. If you get sick, do as the Brits do and go to a pharmacist for advice. Or ask at your hotel for help; they know of the nearest medical and emergency services.

Theft or Loss: To replace a passport, you'll need to go in person to a US embassy (see page 556). If your credit and debit cards disappear, cancel and replace them (see "Damage Control for Lost Cards" on page 13). File a police report, either on the spot or within a day or two; it's required to file an insurance claim for lost or stolen railpasses or travel gear, and can help with replacing your passport or debit and credit cards. For more information, see www .ricksteves.com/help.

Time Zones: Britain, which is one hour earlier than most of continental Europe, is five/eight hours ahead of the East/West Coasts of the US. The exceptions are the beginning and end of Daylight Saving Time: Britain and Europe "spring forward" the last Sunday in March (two weeks after most of North America) and "fall back" the last Sunday in October (one week before North America). For a handy online time converter, try www.timeand date.com/worldclock.

Business Hours: Most stores are open Monday through Saturday (roughly 10:00-17:00), with a late night on Wednesday or Thursday (until 19:00 or 20:00), depending on the neighborhood. On Sunday, when some stores are closed, street markets are lively with shoppers.

Watt's Up? Britain's electrical system is 220 volts, instead of North America's 110 volts. Most newer electronics (such as laptops, battery chargers, and hair dryers) convert automatically, so you won't need a "converter" plug, but you will need an "adapter" plug with three square prongs, sold inexpensively at travel stores in the US. Avoid bringing older appliances that don't automatically convert voltage; instead, buy a cheap replacement at a London department store (see the Shopping in London chapter).

Discounts: Discounts (called "concessions" or "concs" in Britain) are not listed in this book. However, many sights, buses, and trains offer discounts to youths (up to age 18), students (with proper identification cards, www.isic.org), families, seniors (loosely defined as retirees or those willing to call themselves seniors), and groups of 10 or more. Always ask. Some discounts are available only for EU citizens. For instance, you might see a "Gift Aid" admission price listed at sights, but US tourists are not eligible for it.

News: British papers cover global events, and Americans can also peruse the *International Herald Tribune* (published almost daily throughout Europe and online at www.iht.com). Another informative site is http://news.bbc.co.uk. Every Tuesday, editions of *Time* and *Newsweek* hit the stands with articles of particular interest to travelers in Europe. Sports addicts can get their daily fix online or from *USA Today*. Many hotels have BBC News (of course) and CNN television channels.

Money

This section covers advice on how to pay for purchases on your trip (including getting cash from ATMs and paying with plastic), dealing with lost or stolen cards, VAT (sales tax) refunds, and tipping.

What to Bring

Bring both a credit card and a debit card. You'll use the debit card at cash machines (ATMs) to withdraw pounds for most purchases, and the credit card to pay for larger items. Some travelers carry a third card as a backup, in case one gets demagnetized or eaten by a temperamental machine.

As an emergency backup, bring several hundred dollars in hard cash in easy-to-exchange $20 bills. Avoid using currency exchange booths (lousy rates and/or outrageous fees); if you have foreign currency to exchange, take it to a bank. Don't use traveler's checks—they're not worth the fees or the long lines at slow banks.

Cash

Cash is just as desirable in Britain as it is at home. Small businesses (hotels, restaurants, and shops) prefer that you pay your bills with cash. Some vendors will charge you extra for using a credit card, and some won't take credit cards at all. Cash is the best—and sometimes only—way to pay for bus fare, taxis, and local guides.

Throughout Britain, ATMs (which locals call "cashpoints") are the standard way for travelers to get cash. Most ATMs in London are located outside of a bank. Try to use the ATM when the branch is open; if your card is munched by a machine, you can immediately go inside for help.

To withdraw money from an ATM, you'll need a debit card (ideally with a Visa or MasterCard logo for maximum usability),

---

Exchange Rate

I list prices in pounds (£) throughout this book.

1 British pound (£1) = about $1.60

While the euro (€) is now the currency of most of Europe, Britain is sticking with its pound sterling. The British pound (£), also called a "quid," is broken into 100 pence (p). Pence means "cents." You'll find coins ranging from 1p to £2 and bills from £5 to £50. Fake pound coins are easy to spot (real coins have an inscription on their outside rims; the fakes look like tree bark).

London is so expensive that some travelers try to kid themselves that pounds are dollars. But when they get home, that £1,000-pound Visa bill isn't asking for $1,000...it wants around $1,600. (To get the latest rate and print a cheat sheet, see www.oanda.com.)

---

plus a PIN code. Know your PIN in numbers; there are only numbers—no letters—on European keypads. For security, it's best to shield the keypad when entering your PIN at an ATM. Although you can use a credit card for ATM transactions, it's generally more expensive because it's considered a cash advance rather than a withdrawal.

When using an ATM, try to withdraw large sums of money to reduce the number of per-transaction bank fees you'll pay. If the machine refuses your request, try again and select a smaller amount (some cash machines limit the amount you can withdraw—don't take it personally). If that doesn't work, try a different machine. It's easier to pay for purchases with smaller bills; if the ATM gives you big bills, try to break them at a bank or larger store.

Even in jolly olde England, you'll need to keep your cash safe. Use a money belt—a pouch with a strap that you buckle around your waist—and wear it under your clothes. Pickpockets target tourists. A money belt provides peace of mind, allowing you to carry lots of cash safely. Don't waste time every few days tracking down a cash machine—withdraw a week's worth of money, stuff it in your money belt, and travel!

Credit and Debit Cards

For purchases, Visa and MasterCard are more commonly accepted than American Express. Just like at home, credit or debit cards work easily at larger hotels, restaurants, and shops.

I typically use my debit card to withdraw cash to pay for most purchases. I use my credit card only in a few specific situations: to book hotel reservations by phone, to make major purchases (such as car rentals, plane tickets, and long hotel stays), and to pay for things near the end of my trip (to avoid another visit to the ATM). While you could use a debit card to make most large purchases, using a credit card offers you a greater degree of fraud protection (because debit cards draw funds directly from your account).

Ask Your Credit- or Debit-Card Company: Before your trip, contact the company that issued your debit or credit cards.

• Confirm your card will work overseas, and alert them that you'll be using it in Europe; otherwise, they may deny transactions if they perceive unusual spending patterns.

• Ask for the specifics on transaction **fees.** When you use your credit or debit card—either for purchases or ATM withdrawals—you'll often be charged additional "international transaction" fees of up to 3 percent (1 percent is normal) plus $5 per transaction. If your card's fees are too high, consider getting a card just for your trip: Capital One (www.capitalone.com) and most credit unions have low-to-no international fees.

• If you plan to withdraw cash from ATMs, confirm your daily **withdrawal limit** (£300 is usually the maximum). Some travelers prefer a high limit that allows them to take out more cash at each ATM stop, while others prefer to set a lower limit in case their card is stolen.

• Ask for your credit card's **PIN** in case you encounter Europe's "chip-and-PIN" system; since they're unlikely to tell you your PIN over the phone, allow time for the bank to mail it to you.

Chip and PIN: If your card is declined for a purchase in Europe, it may be because of chip and PIN, which requires cardholders to punch in a PIN instead of signing a receipt. Much of Europe, including Great Britain, Ireland, France, the Netherlands, and Scandinavia, is adopting this system. Chip and PIN is used by some merchants, and also at automated payment machines—such as those at train and subway stations, toll roads, parking garages, luggage lockers, bike-rental kiosks, and self-serve pumps at gas stations. If you're prompted to enter your PIN (but don't know it), ask if the cashier can swipe your card or print a receipt for you to sign instead. If not, just pay cash. If you're dealing with an automated machine that won't take your card, look for a cashier nearby who can make your card work. The easiest solution is to carry sufficient cash.

You can avoid potential hassles by getting your own chip-and-PIN card just for your trip, but I don't recommend it. Travelex offers US travelers a chip-and-PIN card, called "Cash Passport," preloaded with euros or British pounds (www.travelex.com). While handy, this service comes with exorbitant exchange rates; it's probably not worth it unless you're staying for several weeks in a country that's converted to chip-and-PIN cards, and you're willing to pay for the convenience.

Dynamic Currency Conversion: If merchants offer to convert your purchase price into dollars (called dynamic currency conversion, or DCC), refuse this "service." You'll pay even more in fees for the expensive convenience of seeing your charge in dollars.

Damage Control for Lost Cards

If you lose your credit, debit, or ATM card, you can stop people from using it by reporting the loss immediately to the respective global customer-assistance centers. Call these 24-hour US numbers collect: Visa (410/581-9994), MasterCard (636/722-7111), and American Express (623/492-8427). Diner's Club has offices in Britain (0870-1900-011) and the US (702/797-5532, call collect).

At a minimum, you'll need to know the name of the financial institution that issued the card, along with the type of card (classic, platinum, or whatever). Providing the following information will allow for a quicker cancellation of your missing card: full card number, whether you are the primary or secondary cardholder, the cardholder's name exactly as printed on the card, billing address, home phone number, circumstances of the loss or theft, and identification verification (your birth date, your mother's maiden name, or your Social Security Number—memorize this, don't carry a copy). If you are the secondary cardholder, you'll also need to provide the primary cardholder's identification-verification details. You can generally receive a temporary card within two or three business days in Europe (see www.ricksteves.com/help for more).

If you promptly report your card lost or stolen, you typically won't be responsible for any unauthorized transactions on your account, although many banks charge a liability fee of $50.

Tipping

Tipping in Britain isn't as automatic and generous as it is in the US, but for special service, tips are appreciated, if not expected. As in the US, the proper amount depends on your resources, tipping philosophy, and the circumstances, but some general guidelines apply.

Restaurants: At pubs where you order at the counter, you don't have to tip. (Regular customers ordering a round sometimes say, "Add one for yourself" as a tip for drinks ordered at the bar—but this isn't expected.) At a pub or restaurant with waitstaff, check the menu or your bill to see if the service is included; if not, tip about 10 percent. (For more information, see page 378 in the Eating in London chapter.)

Taxis: To tip the cabbie, round up. For a typical ride, round up your fare a bit (for instance, if the fare is £4.50, pay £5). If the cabbie hauls your bags and zips you to the airport to help you catch your flight, you might want to toss in a little more. But if you feel like you're being driven in circles or otherwise ripped off, skip the tip.

Special Services: Tour guides at public sites often hold out their hands for tips after they give their spiel. If I've already paid for the tour, I don't tip extra, unless they've really impressed me. At hotels, if you let the porter carry your luggage, it's polite to give them 50p for each bag (another reason to pack light). I don't tip the maid, but if you do, you can leave 50p per overnight at the end of your stay.

In general, if someone in the service industry does a super job for you, a small tip of a pound or two is appropriate...but not required.

When in doubt, ask. If you're not sure whether (or how much) to tip for a service, ask your hotelier or the TI; they'll fill you in on how it's done on their turf.

Getting a VAT Refund

Wrapped into the purchase price of your British souvenirs is a Value-Added Tax (VAT) of 20 percent. You're entitled to get most of that tax back if you purchase more than £30 (about $48) worth of goods at a store that participates in the VAT-refund scheme. Typically, you must ring up the minimum at a single retailer— you can't add up your purchases from various shops to reach the required amount.

Getting your refund is usually straightforward and, if you buy a substantial amount of souvenirs, well worth the hassle. If you're lucky, the merchant will subtract the tax when you make your purchase. (This is more likely to occur if the store ships the goods to your home.) Otherwise, you'll need to do the following:

Get the paperwork. Have the merchant completely fill out the necessary refund document, called a "Tax-Free Shopping Cheque." The newest ones look like a long receipt. You'll have to present your passport at the store.

Get your stamp at the border or airport. Process your cheque(s) at your last stop in the EU (e.g., at the airport) with the customs agent who deals with VAT refunds. Before checking in for your flight, find the local customs office, and be prepared to stand in line. It's best to keep your purchases in your carry-on for viewing, but if they're too large or dangerous (such as knives) to carry on, have your purchases easily accessible in the bag you're about to check, ready to show the customs agent. You're not supposed to use your purchased goods before you leave. If you show up at customs wearing your new Wellingtons, officials might look the other way—or deny you a refund.

Collect your refund. You'll need to return your stamped document to the retailer or its representative. Many merchants work with a service, such as Global Blue (www.global-blue.com) or Premier Tax Free (www.premiertaxfree.com), which have offices at major airports, ports, and border crossings (after check-in and security, probably strategically located near a duty-free shop). These services, which extract a 4 percent fee, can refund your money immediately in cash or credit your card (within two billing cycles). If the retailer handles VAT refunds directly, it's up to you to contact the merchant for your refund. Or you can mail the documents from your point of departure (using a stamped, self-addressed envelope or one that's been provided by the merchant). You'll then have to wait—it can take months.

Customs for American Shoppers

You are allowed to take home $800 worth of items per person duty-free, once every 30 days. You can also bring in, duty-free, a liter of alcohol. As for food, you can take home many processed and packaged foods: vacuum-packed cheeses, dried herbs, jams, chocolate, oil, vinegar, and honey. However, fresh fruits and vegetables and most meats are not allowed. Any liquid-containing foods must be packed in checked luggage, a potential recipe for disaster. To check customs rules and duty rates, visit www.cbp.gov.

Sightseeing

Sightseeing can be hard work. Use these tips to make your visits to London's finest sights meaningful, fun, efficient, and painless.

Plan Ahead

Set up an itinerary that allows you to fit in all your must-see sights. For a one-stop look at opening hours, see "London at a Glance" (page 52; also see "Daily Reminder" on page 26). Most sights keep stable hours, but you can easily confirm the latest by checking with the TI or visiting museums' websites.

Don't put off visiting a must-see sight—you never know when a place will close unexpectedly for a holiday, strike, or restoration. On holidays (see list on page 565), expect reduced hours or closures. Many museums have shorter hours off-season.

When possible, visit key museums first thing (when your energy is best), and save other activities for the afternoon. Hit the highlights first, then go back to other things if you have the stamina and time.

Going at the right time helps avoid crowds. This book offers tips on specific sights. Try visiting the sight very early, at lunch, or very late. Evening hours are usually peaceful, with fewer crowds.

INTRODUCTION

In addition to the London Eye, at least one major London sight is open late every night (see the "London for Early Birds and Night Owls" sidebar on page 74).

Study up. To get the most out of the sight descriptions in this book, read them before you visit. The British Museum rocks if you understand the significance of the Rosetta Stone.

At Sights

Here's what you can typically expect:

Some important sights have metal detectors or conduct bag searches that will slow your entry, while others require you to check daypacks and coats. They'll be kept safely. If you have something you can't bear to part with, stash it in a pocket or purse. To avoid checking a small backpack, carry it under your arm like a purse as you enter. From a guard's point of view, a backpack is generally a problem while a purse is not.

Flash photography is sometimes banned, but taking photos without a flash is usually OK. Look for signs or ask. Flashes damage oil paintings and distract others in the room. Even without a flash, a handheld camera will take a decent picture (or you can buy postcards or posters at the museum bookstore). If photos are permitted, video cameras are generally OK, too.

Museums may have special exhibits in addition to their permanent collections. Some exhibits are included in the entry price; others come at an extra cost (which you may have to pay even if you don't want to see the exhibit).

Expect changes—artwork can be on tour, on loan, out sick, or shifted at the whim of the curator. To adapt, pick up any available free floor plans as you enter, and ask museum staff if you can't find a particular item.

Many sights rent audioguides, which generally offer excellent recorded descriptions (about £4). If you bring along your own pair of headphones and a Y-jack, two people can sometimes share one audioguide and save money. I've produced free downloadable audio tours of the major sights; see page 559.

Guided tours are most likely to occur during peak season (usually £3-8 and widely ranging in quality). Some sights also run short films featuring their highlights and history. These are generally well worth your time. I make it standard operating procedure to ask if there is a film when I arrive at a sight.

Important sights often have an on-site café or cafeteria (usually a good place to rest and have a snack or light meal). The WCs are usually free and nearly always clean (it's smart to carry tissues in case a WC runs out of TP).

Many sights sell postcards that highlight their attractions.

Before you leave, scan the postcards and thumb through the biggest guidebook (or skim its index) to be sure you haven't overlooked something that you'd like to see.

Most sights stop admitting people 30-60 minutes before closing time, and some rooms close early (often about 45 minutes before the actual closing time). Guards usher people out, so don't save the best for last.

Every sight or museum offers more than what is covered in this book. Use this book as an introduction—not the final word.

Sightseeing Passes

The following three sightseeing passes are sold online and at the Britain and London Visitors Centre on Lower Regent Street (slated to move after March of 2012; see page 25).

To save any money with the pricey **London Pass,** you'd have to sightsee virtually nonstop (£43/1 day, £58/2 days, £71/3 days, £94/6 days; days are calendar days rather than 24-hour periods; comes with 160-page guidebook, also sold at major train stations and airports, toll tel. 0870-242-9988, www.londonpass.com). It lets you skip the lines and covers many sights, including the Tower of London, Westminster Abbey, and St. Paul's Cathedral, but not the London Eye or Madame Tussauds Waxworks. Think through your sightseeing plans, study their website to see what's covered, and do the math before you buy.

The **Great British Heritage Pass,** which covers your entry fees into more than 600 British Heritage and National Trust properties, doesn't make sense for a London visit, but can be worthwhile if you'll be traveling extensively throughout Britain. If you buy the pass online, you can pick it up at the TI near St. Paul's Cathedral (£39/3 days, £69/7 days, £89/15 days, £119/30 days; child passes available but note that kids already get discounts at sights, tel. 0870-242-9988, www.britishheritagepass.com).

The similar-sounding **English Heritage** society sells passes and memberships that include free entry to its 400 sights (which are exclusive to England but partly overlap the sights covered by the Great British Heritage Pass described above); again, they're worth it only if you'll be thoroughly exploring England, not just London. You can buy passes or memberships at any participating sight. For most travelers, the Overseas Visitor Pass is a better choice than the pricier one-year membership (Visitor Pass: £20/7 days, £24.50/14 days, discounts for couples and families, www.english-heritage.org.uk/ovp; Membership: £44 for one person, £77 for two, discounts for seniors and students, children under 19 free, www.english-heritage.org.uk/membership; toll tel. 0870-333-1182).

How Was Your Trip?

Were your travels fun, smooth, and meaningful? If you'd like to share your tips, concerns, and discoveries, please fill out the survey at www.ricksteves.com/feedback. I value your feedback. Thanks in advance—it helps a lot.

Traveling as a Temporary Local

We travel all the way to Europe to enjoy differences—to become temporary locals. You'll experience frustrations. Certain truths that we find "God-given" or "self-evident," such as cold beer, ice in drinks, bottomless cups of coffee, hot showers, and bigger being better, are suddenly not so true. One of the benefits of travel is the eye-opening realization that there are logical, civil, and even better alternatives. A willingness to go local ensures that you'll enjoy a full dose of British hospitality.

Europeans generally like Americans. But if there is a negative aspect to the image the British have of Americans, it's that we are big, loud, aggressive, impolite, rich, superficially friendly, and a bit naive.

Judging from all the happy feedback I receive from travelers who have used this book, it's safe to assume you'll enjoy a great, affordable vacation—with the finesse of an independent, experienced traveler.

Thanks, and have a brilliant holiday!

Back Door Travel Philosophy
From Rick Steves' Europe Through the Back Door

Travel is intensified living—maximum thrills per minute and one of the last great sources of legal adventure. Travel is freedom. It's recess, and we need it.

Experiencing the real Europe requires catching it by surprise, going casual..."Through the Back Door."

Affording travel is a matter of priorities. (Make do with the old car.) You can eat and sleep—simply, safely, and enjoyably—anywhere in Europe for $120 a day plus transportation costs (allow more for bigger cities). In many ways, spending more money only builds a thicker wall between you and what you traveled so far to see. Europe is a cultural carnival, and time after time, you'll find that its best acts are free and the best seats are the cheap ones.

A tight budget forces you to travel close to the ground, meeting and communicating with the people. Never sacrifice sleep, nutrition, safety, or cleanliness to save money. Simply enjoy the local-style alternatives to expensive hotels and restaurants.

Connecting with people carbonates your experience. Extroverts have more fun. If your trip is low on magic moments, kick yourself and make things happen. If you don't enjoy a place, maybe you don't know enough about it. Seek the truth. Recognize tourist traps. Give a culture the benefit of your open mind. See things as different, but not better or worse. Any culture has plenty to share.

Of course, travel, like the world, is a series of hills and valleys. Be fanatically positive and militantly optimistic. If something's not to your liking, change your liking.

Travel can make you a happier American, as well as a citizen of the world. Our Earth is home to nearly seven billion equally precious people. It's humbling to travel and find that other people don't have the "American Dream"—they have their own dreams. Europeans like us, but with all due respect, they wouldn't trade passports.

Thoughtful travel engages us with the world. In tough economic times, it reminds us what is truly important. By broadening perspectives, travel teaches new ways to measure quality of life.

Globetrotting destroys ethnocentricity, helping us understand and appreciate other cultures. Rather than fear the diversity on this planet, celebrate it. Among your most prized souvenirs will be the strands of different cultures you choose to knit into your own character. The world is a cultural yarn shop, and Back Door travelers are weaving the ultimate tapestry. Join in!

ORIENTATION TO LONDON

London is more than 600 square miles of urban jungle—a world in itself and a barrage on all the senses. On my first visit, I felt extremely small. To grasp London more comfortably, see it as the old town in the city center without the modern, congested sprawl. (Even from that perspective, it's still huge.)

The Thames River (pronounced "tems") runs roughly west to east through the city, with most of the visitor's sights on the north bank. Mentally, maybe even physically, use scissors to trim down your map to include only the area between the Tower of London (to the east), Hyde Park (west), Regent's Park (north), and the South Bank (south). This is roughly the area bordered by the Tube's Circle Line. This four-mile stretch between the Tower and Hyde Park (about a 1.5-hour walk) looks like a milk bottle on its side (see map on next page), and holds 80 percent of the sights mentioned in this book.

Sprawling London becomes much more manageable if you think of it as a collection of neighborhoods:

Central London: This area contains Westminster and what Londoners call the West End. The **Westminster** district includes Big Ben, Parliament, Westminster Abbey, and Buckingham Palace—the grand government buildings from which Britain is ruled. **Trafalgar Square,** London's gathering place, has many major museums. The **West End** is the center of London's cultural life, with bustling squares: Piccadilly Circus and Leicester Square host cinemas, tourist traps, and nighttime glitz. Soho and Covent Garden are thriving people-zones with theaters, restaurants, pubs, and boutiques. And Regent and Oxford streets are the city's main shopping zones.

North London: Neighborhoods in this part of town—including Bloomsbury, Fitzrovia, and Marylebone—contain such major

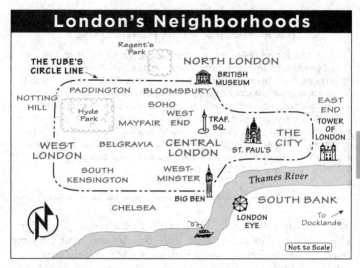

London's Neighborhoods

Regent's Park

THE TUBE'S CIRCLE LINE

NORTH LONDON

BRITISH MUSEUM

PADDINGTON   BLOOMSBURY

NOTTING HILL

Hyde Park

SOHO

WEST END   MAYFAIR

EAST END

TOWER OF LONDON

TRAF. SQ.

THE CITY

ST. PAUL'S

WEST LONDON   BELGRAVIA   CENTRAL LONDON

SOUTH KENSINGTON   WEST-MINSTER

Thames River

CHELSEA   BIG BEN   SOUTH BANK

LONDON EYE   To Docklands

ORIENTATION

Not to Scale

sights as the British Museum and the overhyped Madame Tussauds Waxworks. Nearby, along busy Euston Road, is the British Library plus a trio of train stations (one of them, St. Pancras International Station, is linked to Paris by the Eurostar "Chunnel" train).

The City: Today's modern financial district, called simply "The City," was a walled town in Roman times. Gleaming skyscrapers are interspersed with historical landmarks such as St. Paul's Cathedral, legal sights (Old Bailey), and the Museum of London. The Tower of London and Tower Bridge lie at The City's eastern border.

East London: Just east of The City is the **East End**—the increasingly gentrified former stomping ground of Cockney ragamuffins and Jack the Ripper. Even farther to the east is London's version of Manhattan, the **Docklands,** filling the area around Canary Wharf. Energized by big businesses, the Docklands shows you London at its most modern. Historic **Greenwich** lies just south of the Docklands/Canary Wharf area, across the Thames. And the **2012 Olympic Park** is being built in the once-dreary Stratford district, a short train ride to the north.

The South Bank: The South Bank of the Thames River offers major sights (Tate Modern, Shakespeare's Globe, London Eye) linked by a riverside walkway. Within this area, **Southwark** (SUTH-uck) stretches from the Tate Modern to London Bridge. Pedestrian bridges connect the South Bank with The City and Trafalgar Square.

West London: This huge area contains neighborhoods such as Mayfair, Belgravia, Chelsea, South Kensington, and Notting Hill. It's home to London's wealthy and has many trendy shops

> # Rick Steves' Free Audio Tours
>
> I've produced free, self-guided audio versions of my tours of the major sights in London (download them via www.rick steves.com/audioeurope, iTunes, or the Rick Steves Audio Europe free smartphone app). These user-friendly, easy-to-follow, fun, and informative audio tours are available for the British Museum, British Library, St. Paul's Cathedral, and the Westminster and City of London walks. Compared to live tours, these audio tours are hard to beat: No guide will stand you up, the quality is reliable, you can take the tour exactly when you like, and they're free.

and enticing restaurants. Here you'll find a range of museums (Victoria and Albert Museum, Tate Britain, and more), my top hotel recommendations, lively Victoria Station, and the vast green expanses of Hyde Park and Kensington Gardens.

With this neighborhood focus and a good orientation, you'll get a sampling of London's top sights, history, and cultural entertainment, and a good look at its ever-changing human face.

Planning Your Time

London is a super one-week getaway. Its sights can keep even the most fidgety traveler well entertained for seven days. After considering London's major tourist destinations, I've covered just my favorites in this book. You won't be able to see all of these, so don't try. You'll keep coming back to London. After dozens of visits myself, I still enjoy a healthy list of excuses to return.

For a one-week visit, buy the Seven-Day Travelcard (see page 30) and study up on "Affording London's Sights" (see page 66). Armed with this information and your Travelcard, you'll feel more like a Londoner, forget the high cost of sightseeing, and experience the city with a better attitude.

Here's a suggested schedule for London's best seven days:

Day 1

9:00 Tower of London (crown jewels first, then Beefeater tour, then White Tower; note that on Sun-Mon, the Tower opens at 10:00).

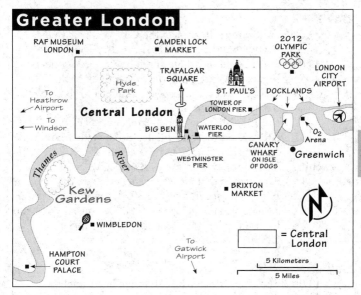

13:00	Grab a picnic, catch a boat at Tower Pier, and relax with lunch on the Thames while cruising to Westminster Pier.
14:30	Tour Westminster Abbey, and consider their evensong service (at 15:00 Sat-Sun, at 17:00 Mon-Fri and Sat in summer).
17:00 (or after evensong)	Follow my self-guided Westminster Walk. When you're finished, if it's a Monday or Tuesday, you could return to the Houses of Parliament and pop in to see the House of Commons in action (until 22:30).

Day 2

8:30	Take a double-decker hop-on, hop-off London sightseeing bus tour (from Green Park or Victoria) and hop off for the Changing of the Guard.
11:00	Buckingham Palace (guards change most days May-July at 11:30, alternate days Aug-April—confirm).
12:00	Walk through St. James's Park to enjoy London's delightful park scene.
13:00	After lunch, tour the Cabinet War Rooms and Churchill Museum.
16:00	Tour the National Gallery.
Evening	Have a pub dinner before a play, concert, or evening walking tour (for ideas, see the Entertainment in London chapter).

ORIENTATION

Day 3

9:00   Follow my self-guided The City Walk, as well as (a portion of) the St. Paul's Cathedral Tour.

15:00   Cross London Bridge and follow my self-guided Bankside Walk along the South Bank of the Thames. Tour Shakespeare's Globe or the Tate Modern if you're interested (or, if it's a day that the Tate Modern is open late, circle back here later). Then walk the Jubilee Promenade from the Millennium Bridge to the London Eye.

Evening   Cap your day with South Bank sights and experiences that are open late (a ride on the London Eye—last ascent 20:00-21:30, depending on season; a Shakespearean play at the Globe—usually at 19:30 in summer; or Tate Modern—open Fri-Sat until 22:00).

Day 4

10:00   Tour the British Museum, then have lunch.

14:00   Tube to Leicester Square to take my self-guided West End Walk to see Covent Garden and Soho, and browse the Regent Street shops.

17:00   Enjoy afternoon tea (at Fortnum & Mason or The Wolseley).

Day 5

Spend the morning exploring a street market (try to make today coincide with the day that your market of choice is busiest—see the Shopping in London chapter for details).

Spend the rest of your day at your choice of major sights. Depending on your interests, choose from the British Library, Tate Britain, Museum of London, Imperial War Museum, or Kew Gardens (consider a cruise to Kew, return to London by Tube).

Day 6

9:45   Cruise from Westminster Pier to Greenwich.

11:00   Tour the salty sights of Greenwich.

15:30   Ride the Docklands Light Railroad (DLR) to the Docklands for a look at London's emerging "Manhattan."

17:00   If you still have energy, ride the DLR to Pudding Mill Lane for a peek at the Olympics 2012 site.

18:00   Take the DLR or Tube back to London.

Day 7

10:00   Tour the Victoria and Albert Museum.

After lunch (or a picnic in the park), stroll through Hyde Park.

Spend the afternoon at Harrods or other shopping venues.

With More Time

Those with more than a week in London can spend a day or two side-tripping—Windsor, Cambridge, Stonehenge, and Bath each make a satisfying one-day visit.

Overview

Tourist Information

The **Britain and London Visitors Centre,** a block off Piccadilly Circus, is the best tourist information service in town. However, it is scheduled to move after March 2012 when its lease expires; check its website for its new location (Mon-Fri 9:30-18:00, Sat-Sun 10:00-16:00; 1 Lower Regent Street, toll tel. 0870-156-6366, www.visitbritain.com, www.visitlondon.com). Unfortunately, London's many "Tourist Information Centres" (which represent themselves as TIs at major train and bus stations, airports, and near major sights—including St. Paul's Cathedral) are now simply businesses, selling advertising space to companies with fliers to distribute.

The Britain and London Visitors Centre has many different departments. Along with getting tourist information, you can purchase advance tickets to big sights, buy sightseeing passes, arrange coach tours, get theater tickets (steep 20 percent booking fee), get online (£1/20 minutes, terminals upstairs), plan travel beyond London, and even book trains to the Continent. Bring your itinerary and a checklist of questions.

At the Tourist Information desk, pick up various free publications: the *London Planner* (a free monthly that lists all the sights, events, and hours), walking tours info, a theater guide, London bus map, and the *Guide to River Thames Boat Services*. The staff sells a good £1 map and all the various sightseeing passes (described on page 17).

The Hotels and Travel desk sells long-distance bus tickets and passes, train tickets (convenient for reservations), and Fast Track tickets to some of London's attractions. These tickets, which allow you to skip the queue at the sights at no extra cost, are worthwhile for places that can have long ticket lines, such as the Tower of London, the London Eye, and Madame Tussauds Waxworks. (If you're going to the Waxworks, buy tickets here, since—at £22.50—they're cheaper than at the sight itself.)

The Visitors Centre reserves hotel rooms, but you can avoid their £5 booking fee by contacting hotels on your own.

ORIENTATION

Daily Reminder

Sunday: The Tower of London and British Museum are both especially crowded today. The Speakers' Corner in Hyde Park rants from early afternoon until early evening. These places are closed: Banqueting House, Sir John Soane's Museum, and legal sights (Houses of Parliament, City Hall, and Old Bailey; the neighborhood called The City is dead). Westminster Abbey and St. Paul's are open during the day for worship but closed to sightseers. With all these closures, this morning is a good time to take a bus tour. Most big stores open late (around 11:30) and close early (18:00). Street markets are flourishing at Camden Lock, Spitalfields, Petticoat Lane, Brick Lane, and Greenwich, but Portobello Road and Brixton markets are closed (though the Brixton farmer's market is open 10:00-14:00). Because of all the market action, it's a good day to take the East End Walk (see page 83). Theaters are quiet, as most actors take today off. (There are a few exceptions, such as *The Lion King* and Shakespeare's Globe, which offer Sunday performances in summer.)

Monday: Virtually all sights are open except for Apsley House, Sir John Soane's Museum, Vinopolis, and a few others. The Courtauld Gallery is free until 14:00. The Houses of Parliament are usually open until 22:30.

Tuesday: Virtually all sights are open, except for Vinopolis and Apsley House. The British Library is open until 20:00. On the first Tuesday of the month, Sir John Soane's Museum is also open 18:00-21:00. The Houses of Parliament are usually open until 22:30.

Wednesday: Virtually all sights are open, except for Vinopolis.

Arrival in London

For more information on travel by train, bus, and plane, see the London Connections chapter.

By Train: London has nine major train stations, all connected by the Tube (subway). All have ATMs, and many of the larger stations also have shops, fast food, exchange offices, and luggage storage. From any station, you can ride the Tube or taxi to your hotel. For more info on train travel, see www.nationalrail.co.uk.

By Bus: The main intercity bus station is Victoria Coach Station, one block southwest of Victoria train station (and the Victoria Tube station). For more on bus travel, see www.national express.com.

By Plane: London has five airports. Most tourists arrive at Heathrow or Gatwick airports, although flights from elsewhere in Europe may land at Stansted, Luton, or London City airports. For specifics on getting from London's airports to downtown London,

Thursday: All sights are open, plus evening hours at the National Portrait Gallery (until 21:00) and Vinopolis (until 22:00).

Friday: All sights are open, except the Houses of Parliament. Sights open late include the British Museum (selected galleries until 20:30), National Gallery (until 21:00), National Portrait Gallery (until 21:00), Vinopolis (until 22:00), Victoria and Albert Museum (selected galleries until 22:00), and Tate Modern (until 22:00). The Tate Britain is open until 22:00 on the first Friday of the month. Best street market today: Spitalfields.

Saturday: Most sights are open except legal ones (Old Bailey, City Hall, Houses of Parliament; skip The City). Vinopolis and the Tate Modern are open until 22:00. Today's the day to hit the Portobello Road street market; the Camden Lock and Greenwich markets are also good.

Notes: The St. Martin-in-the-Fields church offers concerts at lunchtime (Mon, Tue, and Fri at 13:00) and in the evening (several nights a week at 19:30, jazz Wed at 20:00).

Evensong occurs daily at St. Paul's (Mon-Sat at 17:00 and Sun at 15:15), Westminster Abbey (Mon-Fri at 17:00—may be spoken on Wed, Sat-Sun at 15:00 except Sat in summer, when it's at 17:00), and Southwark Cathedral (weekdays at 17:30, Sat at 16:00, Sun at 15:00, no service on Wed or alternate Mon).

London by Night Sightseeing Tour buses leave from Victoria Station each evening (every 45 minutes from 19:15 to 21:30, only at 19:30 in winter).

The London Eye spins nightly (last departure between 20:00 and 21:30, depending on the season).

see the London Connections chapter; for hotels near Heathrow and Gatwick, see the Sleeping in London chapter.

Helpful Hints

Theft Alert: Wear your money belt. The Artful Dodger is alive and well in London. Be on guard, particularly on public transportation and in places crowded with tourists, who, considered naive and rich, are targeted. The Changing of the Guard scene is a favorite for thieves. And more than 7,500 purses are stolen annually at Covent Garden alone.

Pedestrian Safety: Cars drive on the left side of the road—which can be as confusing for foreign pedestrians as for foreign drivers. Before crossing a street, I always look right, look left, then look right again just to be sure. Most crosswalks are even painted with instructions, reminding foreign guests to "Look right" or "Look left."

Medical Problems: Local hospitals have good-quality 24-hour-a-day emergency care centers where any tourist who needs help can drop in and, after a wait, be seen by a doctor. Your hotel has details. St. Thomas' Hospital, immediately across the river from Big Ben, has a fine reputation.

Getting Your Bearings: London is well-signed for visitors. Through an initiative called Legible London, the city is erecting thoughtfully designed, pedestrian-focused maps around town. In this sprawling city—where predictable grid-planned streets are relatively rare—it's also smart to buy and use a good map. The *Benson's London Street Map* (£2.75), sold at many newsstands and bookstores, is my favorite for efficient sightseeing.

Internet Access: As nearly all hotels offer Internet access, and cafés all over town have free Wi-Fi, there are fewer actual Internet cafés. If you need to get online, you'll find Internet cafés near Trafalgar Square (456 Strand), on Oxford Street (at #358, opposite Bond Street Tube station), and near Victoria Station (at 164 Victoria Street).

Travel Bookstores: Located between Covent Garden and Leicester Square, the very good **Stanfords Travel Bookstore** stocks current editions of many of my books (Mon-Fri 9:00-19:30, Thu 9:00-20:00, Sat 10:00-20:00, Sun 12:00-18:00, 12-14 Long Acre, Tube: Leicester Square, tel. 020/7836-1321, www.stanfords.co.uk).

Two impressive **Waterstone's** bookstores have the biggest collection of travel guides in town: on Piccadilly (Mon-Sat 9:00-22:00, Sun 11:30-18:00, Costa Café, great views from top-floor bar—see sidebar on page 85, 203 Piccadilly, tel. 020/7851-2400) and on Trafalgar Square (Mon-Sat 9:00-21:00, Sun 11:30-18:00, Costa Café on second floor, tel. 020/7839-4411).

Baggage Storage: Train stations have replaced lockers with more secure baggage storage counters, known locally as "left luggage." Each bag must go through a scanner (just like at the airport), so lines can be slow. Expect long waits in the morning to check in (up to 45 minutes) and in the afternoon to pick up (each item-£8.50/24 hours, most stations daily 7:00-23:00). You can also store bags at the airports (similar rates and hours, www.excess-baggage.com). If leaving London and returning later, you may be able to store a box or bag at your hotel for free—assuming you'll be staying there again.

Time Zone Difference: Remember that Britain is one hour earlier than most of continental Europe (which makes it five/eight hours ahead of the east/west coasts of the US). British Summer Time (Daylight Saving Time) springs forward the last Sunday in March and falls back the last Sunday in October.

Getting Around London

To travel smart in a city this size, you must get comfortable with public transportation. London's excellent taxis, buses, and subway (Tube) system make a car unnecessary (see page 38 for details on driving in London—and why it's a bad idea).

Public-Transit Passes

London has the most expensive public transit in the world—save money on your Tube and bus rides using a multi-ride pass. You have three options: Pay double by buying individual tickets as you go; buy a £5 Oyster card and top it up as needed to travel like a local for about £1-2 per ride; or get a Travelcard for unlimited travel on either one or seven days.

The transit system has six zones. Since almost all of my recommended accommodations, restaurants, and sights are within Zones 1 and 2, those are the prices I've listed here—but you'll pay more to go farther afield. Specific fares and other details change constantly; for a complete and updated list of prices, check www.tfl.gov.uk.

Individual Transit Tickets

These days in London, individual paper tickets are obsolete; there's no point buying one unless you're literally taking just one ride your entire time in the city. Because individual fares (£4 per Tube ride, £2.20 per bus ride) are about double the cost of using a pay-as-you-go Oyster card (explained below), in just two or three rides you'll recoup the £5 added deposit for the Oyster. If you do buy a single ticket, avoid ticket-window lines in Tube stations by using the coin-op machines; practice on the punchboard to see how the system works (hit "Adult Single" and your destination). These tickets are valid only on the day of purchase.

Oyster Cards

A pay-as-you-go Oyster card (a plastic card embedded with a com-

puter chip) is the standard, smart way to economically ride the Tube, buses, Docklands Light Railway (DLR), and Overground. On each type of transport, you simply lay the card flat against the yellow card reader at the turnstile or entrance, it flashes green, and the fare is

ORIENTATION

automatically deducted. (You'll also touch your card again to exit the Tube and DLR turnstiles, but not to exit buses.)

With an Oyster card, rides cost about half the price of individual paper tickets (£1.90 or £2.50 per Tube ride—depending on time of day, £1.30 per bus ride). You buy the card itself at any Tube station ticket window for a £5 deposit, then load it up with as much credit as you want. (For extra peace of mind, ask about registering your card against theft or loss.) When your balance gets low, simply add credit—or "top up"—at a ticket window or machine (note that American credit cards will work at the ticketing window, but not at the automated "top-up" stations). A price cap on the pay-as-you-go Oyster card guarantees you'll never pay more than the One-Day Travelcard price within a 24-hour period.

You can see how much credit remains on your card or review the trips you've taken so far by swiping it at any automatic ticket machine. Oyster card balances never expire (though they need reactivating at a ticket window every two years), so you can use the card whenever you're in London, or lend it to someone else. If you're done with the card (and don't mind a short wait), you can turn it in to reclaim your £5 deposit at any ticket window.

Travelcards

Like the Oyster card, Travelcards are valid on the Tube, buses, Docklands Light Railway (DLR), and Overground. The difference is that Travelcards let you ride as many times as you want within a one- or seven-day period, for one fixed price.

Before you buy a card, estimate where you'll be going; there's a card for Zones 1 and 2, and another for Zones 1-6 (which includes Heathrow Airport). If Heathrow is the only ride you're taking outside Zones 1-2 (which is likely), you can pay a small supplement to make the Zones 1-2 Travelcard stretch to cover that one ride.

The **One-Day Travelcard** gives you unlimited travel for a day (Zones 1-2: £8, off-peak version £6.60; Zones 1-6: £15, off-peak version £8; off-peak cards are good for travel after 9:30 on weekdays and anytime on weekends). This Travelcard works like a traditional paper ticket: Buy it at any Tube station ticket window or machine, then feed it into a turnstile (and retrieve it) to enter and exit the Tube. On a bus, just show it to the driver when you get on.

The **Seven-Day Travelcard** is a great option if you're staying four or more days and plan to use the buses and Tube a lot. It's actually issued on a plastic Oyster card, but gives you unlimited travel anytime, anywhere in Zones 1 and 2 for a week (£27.60 plus the refundable £5 deposit for the Oyster card). As with an Oyster card, you'll touch it to the yellow pad when entering or exiting a Tube turnstile, or when boarding a bus.

Discounts

Groups: A gang of 10 or more adults can travel all day on the Tube for £4 each (but not on buses). Kids ages 11-17 pay £1.50 when part of a group of 10.

Families: A paying adult can take up to four kids (age 10 and under) for free on the Tube, Docklands Light Railway (DLR), and Overground all day, every day (kids 10 and under are always free on buses). At the Tube station, use the manual gate, rather than the turnstiles, to be waved in. Other child and student discounts are explained at www.tfl.gov.uk/tickets.

River Cruises: A Travelcard gives you a 33 percent discount on most Thames cruises (see "Cruises," later). If you pay for Thames Clippers (including the Tate-to-Tate museum boat) with your pay-as-you go Oyster card, you'll get a 10 percent discount.

Sightseeing Deal: Buy a paper One-Day Travelcard or rail ticket at a National Rail station, and you may qualify for two-for-one discounts at many popular sights (transport ticket must be used the same day as the sight discount; look for brochures with coupons at major train stations, or print vouchers at www.daysout guide.co.uk).

The Bottom Line

Struggling to choose which pass works best for your trip? First of all, skip the individual tickets. On a short visit (three days or fewer), if you think you'll be zipping around a lot, consider a One-Day Travelcard for each day you're here (or at least for your busiest days); if you'll be taking fewer, more focused rides, get an Oyster card and pay as you go. If you're in London four days or longer, the Seven-Day Travelcard will likely pay for itself.

By Tube

London's subway system (called the Tube or Underground—but never "subway," which refers to a pedestrian underpass) is one of  this planet's great people-movers and often the fastest long-distance transport in town (runs Mon-Sat about 5:00-24:00, Sun about 7:00-23:00). While technically not part of the Tube, two other commuter rail lines are tied into the network and use the same tickets: The Docklands Light Railway (called DLR, runs to the Docklands, 2012 Olympics site, and Greenwich) and the Overground.

Get your bearings by studying a map of the system. At the

front of this book, you'll find a Tube map of central London with color-coded lines and names. You can also pick up a free, more extensive Tube map at any station.

Each line has a name (such as Circle, Northern, or Bakerloo) and two directions (indicated by the end-of-the-line stops). Find the line that will take you to your destination, and figure out roughly which direction (north, south, east, or west) you'll need to go to get there.

You can use an Oyster card, Travelcard, or individual tickets (all explained earlier) to pay for your journey. At the Tube station, touch your Oyster card flat against the turnstile's yellow card reader, both when you enter and exit the station. If you have a regular paper ticket or a One-Day Travelcard, feed it into the turnstile, reclaim it, and hang on to it—you'll need it later.

Find your train by following signs to your line and the (general) direction it's headed (such as Central Line: east). Since some tracks are shared by several lines, double-check before boarding a train: First, make sure your destination is one of the stops listed on the sign at the platform. Also, check the electronic signboards that announce which train is next, and make sure the destination (the end-of-the-line stop) is the direction you want. Some trains, particularly

on the Circle and District lines, split off for other directions, but each train has its final destination marked above its windshield.

Trains run roughly every 3-10 minutes. If one train is absolutely packed and you notice another to the same destination is coming in three minutes, wait to avoid the sardine routine. Rush hours (8:00-10:00 and 16:00-19:00) can be packed and sweaty. Bring something to do to make your waiting time productive. If you get confused, ask for advice from a local, a blue-vested staff person, or at the information window located before the turnstile entry.

You can't leave the system without touching your Oyster card

to an electronic reader, or feeding your ticket or One-Day Travelcard into the turnstile. (If you have a single-trip paper ticket, the turnstile will eat your now-expired ticket; if it's a One-Day Travelcard, it will spit out your still-valid card.) Some stations, such as Hampton Court, do not have a turn-stile, so you'll have to locate a reader to validate your Oyster card. If you skip this step, the highest fare will be deducted from your card. When leaving a station, save walking time by choosing the best street exit—check the maps on the walls or ask any station personnel.

The system can be fraught with construction delays and breakdowns (the Circle Line is notorious for problems). This will be especially noticeable as London gears up for the 2012 Olympics. Most construction is scheduled for weekends. Closures are known and publicized in advance (online at www.tfl.gov.uk and with posters in the Tube). Pay attention to signs and announcements explaining necessary detours. Closed Tube lines are often replaced by temporary bus service, but it can be faster to figure out alternate routes on the Tube; since the lines cross each other constantly, there are several ways to make any journey. For help, check out the "Journey Planner" at www.tfl.gov.uk.

Tube Etiquette

- When your train arrives, stand off to the side and let riders exit the train before you try to board.
- Avoid using the hinged seats near the doors of some trains when the car is jammed; they take up valuable standing space.
- If you're blocking the door when the train stops, step out of the car and off to the side, let others off, then get back on.
- Talk softly in the cars. Listen to how quietly Londoners communicate and follow their lead.
- On escalators, stand on the right and pass on the left. But note that in some passageways or stairways, you might be directed to walk on the left (the direction Brits go behind the wheel).
- When leaving a station, it's polite to hold the door for the person behind you.
- Discreet eating and drinking are fine (nothing smelly); drinking alcohol and smoking are not.

By Bus

If you figure out the bus system, you'll swing like Tarzan through the urban jungle of London. Pick up a free bus map at a TI, transport office (located at major Underground stations such as Victoria), or some major museums. This map lists the best bus routes for sightseeing (see the sidebar for a quick run-down of these routes).

Buses are covered by Travelcards and Oyster cards. Or you can buy individual tickets from a machine at bus stops (no change given). Any bus ride in downtown London costs £2.20 for those paying cash, or £1.30 if using an Oyster card (with a cap of £4 per

ORIENTATION

Handy Bus Routes

Since London instituted a congestion charge for cars, the bus system has gotten faster, easier, and cheaper than ever. Tube-oriented travelers need to get over their tunnel vision, learn the bus system, and get around fast and easy. The best views are upstairs on a double-decker.

Here are some of the most useful routes:

Route #9: Knightsbridge (Harrods) to Hyde Park Corner to Piccadilly Circus to Trafalgar Square. This is one of two "Heritage Routes," using some old-style double-decker buses.

Routes #11 and #24: Victoria Station to Westminster Abbey to Trafalgar Square (#11 continues to St. Paul's and Liverpool Street Station).

Route #RV1 (a scenic South Bank joyride): Tower of London to Tower Bridge to Southwark Street (five-minute walk behind Tate Modern/Shakespeare's Globe) to London Eye/Waterloo Station/County Hall, then over Waterloo Bridge to Aldwych and Covent Garden.

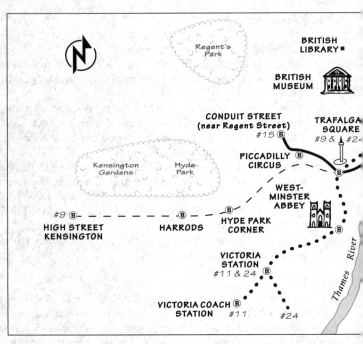

Route #15: Regent Street to Piccadilly Circus to TI to Trafalgar Square to Fleet Street to St. Paul's to Tower of London. This is the other "Heritage Route," using some old-style double-decker buses.

In addition, several buses (including #6, #13, #15, #23, #139, and #159) make the corridor run from Trafalgar, Piccadilly Circus, and Oxford Circus to Marble Arch. Check the bus stop closest to your hotel—it might be convenient to your sightseeing plans.

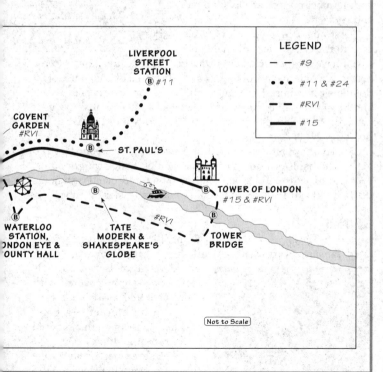

day). If you're staying longer, consider the £17.80 Seven-Day bus pass.

The first step in mastering London's bus system is learning how to decipher the bus stop signs (see photo). In the first column, find your destination on the list— e.g., Paddington. In the next column, find a bus that goes there—the #23. The final column has a letter within a circle (e.g., "M") that tells you exactly which bus stop you need to stand at to catch your bus. (You'll find the same letter marked on a neighborhood map nearby.) Make your way to that stop—you'll know it's yours because it will have the same letter on its pole—and wait for the bus with your number on it to arrive. Hop on, and you're good to go.

O		
Oakwood ⊖	N91	⓪ ⓪
Old Coulsdon	N68	Aldwych
Old Ford	N8	Oxford Circus
Old Kent Road Canal Bridge	53, N381	⓪
	453	⓪ ⓪
	N21	⓪
Old Street ⊖ ≷	243	Aldwych
Orpington ≷	N47	⓪
Oxford Circus ⊖	Any bus	⓪
	N18	⓪
P		
Paddington ⊖ ≷	23, N15	⓪ ⓪ ⓪
Palmers Green ≷	N29	⓪
Park Langley	N3	⓪ ⓪
Peckham	12	⓪ ⓪
	N89, N343	⓪
	N136	⓪ ⓪
	N381	⓪
Penge Pawleyne Arms	176	⓪
	N3	⓪ ⓪
Petts Wood ≷	N47	⓪
Pimlico Grosvenor Road	24	⓪ ⓪
Plaistow Greengate	N15	⓪ ⓪
Plumstead ≷	53	⓪
Plumstead Common	53	⓪

As you board, touch your Oyster card to the electronic card reader, or, if you have a paper ticket or a One-Day Travelcard, show it to the driver. On "Heritage Routes" #9 and #15 (some of which use older double-decker buses), you may still pay a conductor; take a seat, and he or she will come around to collect your fare or verify your pass. There's no need to tap your card or show your ticket when you hop off.

If you have an Oyster card or Travelcard, save your feet and get in the habit of hopping buses for quick little straight shots, even just to get to a Tube stop. During bump-and-grind rush hours (8:00-10:00 and 16:00-19:00), you'll usually go faster by Tube.

By Taxi

London is the best taxi town in Europe. Big, black, carefully regulated cabs are everywhere. (While historically known as "black

cabs," some of London's official taxis are now covered with wildly colored ads.) Some cabs now run on biofuels—a good way to dispose of all that oil used to fry fish-and-chips.

I've never met a crabby cabbie in London. They love to talk, and they know every nook and cranny in town. I ride in a taxi each day just to get my London questions answered (drivers must pass a rigorous test on "The Knowledge" of London geography to earn their license).

If a cab's top light is on, just wave it down. Drivers flash lights when they see you wave. They have a tight turning radius (on new cabs, the back tires actually pivot), so you can hail cabs going in either direction. If waving doesn't work, ask someone where you can find a taxi stand. Telephoning a cab will get you one in a few minutes, but costs a little more (toll tel. 0871-871-8710; £2 surcharge, plus extra fee to book ahead by credit card).

Rides start at £2.20. The regular tariff #1 covers most of the day (Mon-Fri 6:00-20:00), tariff #2 is during "unsociable hours" (Mon-Fri 20:00-22:00 and Sat-Sun 6:00-22:00), and tariff #3 is for night (22:00-6:00) and on holidays. Rates go up about 15-20 percent with each higher tariff. All extra charges are explained in writing on the cab wall. Tip a cabbie by rounding up (maximum 10 percent).

Connecting downtown sights is quick and easy, and will cost you about £6-8 (for example, St. Paul's to the Tower of London). For a short ride, three adults in a cab generally travel at close to Tube prices—and groups of four or five adults should taxi everywhere. All cabs can carry five passengers, and some take six, for the same cost as a single traveler.

Don't worry about meter cheating. Licensed British cab meters come with a sealed computer chip and clock that ensures you'll get the correct tariff. The only way a cabbie can cheat you is by taking a needlessly long route. Another pitfall is taking a cab when traffic is bad to a destination efficiently served by the Tube. On one trip to London, I hopped in a taxi at South Kensington for Waterloo Station and hit bad traffic. Rather than spending 20 minutes and £2 on the Tube, I spent 40 minutes and £16 in a taxi.

If you overdrink and ride in a taxi, be warned: Taxis charge £40 for "soiling" (a.k.a., pub puke). If you forget this book in a taxi, call the Lost Property office and hope for the best (toll tel. 0845-330-9882).

By Bike

London is keeping up its push to become more bike-friendly. The city continues to install bike lanes around town and in 2010, unveiled a citywide bike-rental program similar to ones in other major European cities.

Barclays Cycle Hire bikes, intended for quick point-to-point trips, are a snap to rent and a giddy joy to use, even for the most jaded London tourist. "Boris Bikes" (as they are affectionately called by locals, after cycle enthusiast and mayor Boris Johnson) are cruisers with big, cushy seats, a bag rack with elastic straps, and three gears.

ORIENTATION

Approximately 400 bike-rental stations are scattered through-out the city, each equipped with a computer kiosk. To rent a bike, you will need to pay an access fee (£1/day or £5/week). The first 30 minutes are free; if you hang on to the bike for longer, you'll be charged (£1 for 1 hour, £4 for 1.5 hours, £6 for 2 hours, and much steeper beyond that). When you are ready to ride, press "Hire a

Cycle" and insert your credit card when prompted. You'll then get a ticket with a five-digit code (using a combination of 1s, 2s, and 3s). Take the ticket to any bike and punch in the number on the panel by the front tire. After the yellow light blinks, a green light will appear; at that point, firmly pull the bike out of the slot.

When your ride is over, find a station with an empty slot, then push your bike in until it locks and the green light flashes. You can hire bikes as often as you like (which will start your free 30-minute period over again), as long as you wait five minutes between each use. A map of the docking stations is essential—pick one up at any major Underground station. It's also available online at www.tfl .gov.uk (click on the "Road Users" tab, then look for the "Barclays Cycle Hire" link) and as a free smartphone app (http://cyclehire app.com).

Helmets are not provided, so ride carefully. Stay to the far-left side of the road and watch closely at intersections for *left*-turning cars. If riding on crowded streets feels intimidating, stick to parks and quiet back lanes.

By Car

If you have a car, stow it—you don't want to drive in London. If you need convincing, here's one more reason: A £10 **congestion charge** is levied on any private car entering the city center during peak hours (Mon-Fri 7:00-18:00, no charge Sat-Sun and holidays, fee payable at gas stations, convenience stores, and self-service machines at public parking lots, or online at www.cclondon.com). Traffic cameras photograph and identify every vehicle that enters the fee zone; if you get spotted and don't pay up by midnight that day (or pay £12 before midnight of the following day), you'll get socked with at least a £60 penalty. The system has been effective in cutting down traffic jam delays and bolstering London's public transit. The revenue that's raised subsidizes the buses, which are now cheaper, more frequent, and even more user-friendly than before. Today, the vast majority of vehicles in the city center are buses, taxis, and service trucks.

Tours

▲▲▲Hop-on, Hop-off Double-Decker Bus Tours

Two competitive companies (Original and Big Bus) offer essentially the same two tours of the city's sightseeing highlights, with nearly 30 stops on each route. Big Bus tours are a little more expensive (£27), while Original tours are cheaper (£22 with this book) and nearly as good.

These two-to-three hour, once-over-lightly bus tours drive by all the famous sights, providing a stress-free way to get your bearings and see the biggies. They stop at a core group of sights regardless of which overview tour you're on: Piccadilly Circus, Trafalgar Square, Big Ben, St. Paul's, the Tower of London, Marble Arch, Victoria Station, and elsewhere. With a good guide and nice weather, I'd sit back and enjoy the entire tour. (If you don't like your guide, you can hop off and try your luck with the next departure.)

Each company offers at least one route with live (English-only) guides, and a second (sometimes slightly different route) comes with recorded, dial-a-language narration. In addition to the overview tours, both Original and Big Bus include the Thames River boat trip by City Cruises (similar to the River Red Rover ticket explained on page 48) and three 1.5-hour walking tours.

Pick up a map from any flier rack or from one of the countless salespeople, and study the complex system. Sunday morning—when the traffic is light and many museums are closed—is a fine time for a tour. Unless you're using the bus tour mainly for hop-on, hop-off transportation, consider saving time and money by taking a night tour (described on the next page).

Buses run about every 10-15 minutes in summer, every 20 minutes in winter, and operate daily. They start at about 8:30 and run until early evening in summer or late afternoon in winter. The last full loop usually leaves Victoria Station about 17:00 (confirm by checking the schedule or asking the driver).

You can buy tickets from drivers or from staff at street kiosks (credit cards accepted at kiosks at major stops such as Victoria, ticket good for 24 hours).

Original London Sightseeing Bus Tour—There are two versions of their basic highlights loop: **The Original Tour** (live guide, marked with a yellow triangle on the front of the bus) and the **City Sightseeing Tour** (essentially the same route but with recorded narration, a kids' soundtrack option, and a stop at Madame Tussauds; bus marked with a red triangle). Other routes include the blue-triangle **Museum Tour** (connecting far-flung museums and major shopping stops), and green, black, and purple triangle

Combining a London Bus Tour and the Changing of the Guard

For a grand and efficient intro to London, consider catching either of the bus companies' overview tours at 8:30, riding 90 percent of the loop (which takes just over two hours, depending on traffic), and hopping off at Buckingham Palace in time to catch the Changing of the Guard ceremony. Choose between the Big Bus Tour (catch it at the Green Park Tube station) or the Original Bus Tour (catch it at Grosvenor Gardens a block from Victoria Station). If you miss the 8:30 bus, there's generally another departure in 20 minutes that might get you to the ceremony a bit late (confirm with the driver).

routes (linking major train stations to the central route). All routes are covered by the same ticket. Keep it simple and just take one of the city highlights tours (£26, £22 with this book, limit four discounts per book, they'll rip off the corner of this page—raise bloody hell if the staff or driver won't honor this discount; also online deals, info center at 17 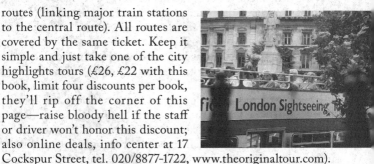 Cockspur Street, tel. 020/8877-1722, www.theoriginaltour.com).

Big Bus London Tours—For £27 (up to 30 percent discount online—requires printer), you get the same basic overview tours: Red buses come with a live guide, while the blue route has a recorded narration and a one-hour longer path that goes around Hyde Park. These pricier Big Bus tours tend to have better, more dynamic guides than the Original tours, and more departures as well—meaning shorter waits for those hopping on and off (daily 8:30-18:00, winter until 16:30, info center at 48 Buckingham Palace Road, tel. 020/7233-9533, www.bigbustours.com).

London by Night Sightseeing Tour—This tour offers a two-hour circuit, but after hours, with no extras (e.g., walks, river cruises), and at a lower price. While the narration can be pretty lame, the views at twilight are grand—though note that it stays light until late on summer nights, and London just doesn't do floodlighting as well as Paris (£16, £11 online, drivers accept cash only). From May through late September, open-top buses depart at 19:15, 20:00, 20:45, and 21:30 from Victoria Station (Jan-April and late Sept-late Dec departs at 19:30 only with closed-top bus, no tours between Christmas and New Year). Buses leave from the curb immediately in front of Victoria Station (closest to building at muster point C; or you can board at any stop, such as Paddington Station, Marble Arch, Trafalgar Square, London Eye, or Tower of London; tel. 020/8545-6109, www.london-by-night.net). For a memorable and economical evening, munch a scenic picnic dinner on the top deck. (There are plenty of take-away options within the train stations and near the various stops.)

▲▲Walking Tours

Several times a day, top-notch local guides lead (sometimes big) groups through specific slices of London's past. Look for brochures at TIs or ask at hotels, although the latter usually push higher-priced bus tours. *Time Out,* the weekly entertainment guide (£3 at newsstands), lists some, but not all, scheduled walks. Check with the various tour companies by phone or online to get their full picture.

To take a walking tour, simply show up at the announced location and pay the guide. Then enjoy two chatty hours of Dickens, Harry Potter, the Plague, Shakespeare, Legal London, the Beatles, Jack the Ripper, or whatever is on the agenda.

The Essential London Walk—Blue Badge Tourist Guides offer a basic two-hour walk for £5, 365 days a year at 10:00 (from the Eros statue on Piccadilly Circus—look for the guide with the Blue Badge umbrella, www.touristguides.org.uk). Tours go rain or shine, and there's no need to pre-book—just show up. This is the best deal going, as you know you'll get a well-trained guide leading you through the historic core of London (from Piccadilly, you walk to Trafalgar Square, Whitehall, Westminster Abbey, the Houses of Parliament, and the Thames, and end at Buckingham Palace—just in time for the last part of the Changing of the Guard).

London Walks—This leading company lists its extensive and creative daily schedule in a beefy, plain *London Walks* brochure. Pick it up at TIs, hotels, or St. Martin-in-the-Fields' Café in the Crypt on Trafalgar Square, or access it on their website. Just perusing their fascinating lineup of tours inspires me to stay longer in London. Their two-hour walks, led by professional guides and actors, cost £8 (cash only, walks offered year-round, private tours for groups-£120, tel. 020/7624-3978 for a live person, tel. 020/7624-9255 for a recording of today's or tomorrow's walks and the Tube station they depart from, www.walks.com).

London Walks also offers "Explorer Days" tours into the countryside, a good option for those with limited time and transportation (£14 plus £10-46 for transportation and any admission costs, cash only: Stonehenge/Salisbury, Oxford/Cotswolds, Cambridge, Bath, and so on). These are economical in part because everyone gets group discounts for transportation and admissions.

ORIENTATION

ORIENTATION

Sandemans New London "Free Royal London Tour"—This company employs English-speaking students (rather than licensed guides) who recite three-hour spiels covering the basic London sights. While the fast-moving, youthful tours are light and irreverent, and can be both entertaining and fun, it's misleading to call the tours "free," as tips are expected (the guides are unpaid). With the Essential London Walk (listed earlier) offered daily at a reasonable price by professional Blue Badge guides, taking this "free" tour makes no sense to me (daily at 11:00 and 13:00, meet at Wellington Arch, Tube: Hyde Park Corner, Exit 2). Sandemans also has other guided tours for a charge, including a Pub Crawl (£12, Tue-Sat at 19:30, meet at Belushi's at 9 Russell Street, Tube: Covent Garden, www.newlondon-tours.com).

Beatles Walks—Fans of the still-Fab Four can take one of three Beatles walks (London Walks has two that run 5 days/week; Big Bus includes a daily walk with their bus tour; both listed earlier). For more on Beatles sights, see page 76.

Jack the Ripper Walks—Each walking tour company seems to make most of its money with "haunted" and Jack the Ripper tours. Many guides are historians and would rather not lead these lightweight tours—but, in tourism as in journalism, "if it bleeds, it leads" (which is why the juvenile London Dungeon is one of the city's top sights).

Back in 1888—in the decade of Sherlock Holmes and Dr. Jekyll and Mr. Hyde, when London was still a Dickensian Tale of Two Cities—locals were terrorized by the murder of five prostitutes within a few weeks. In the wee hours, the murderer (who was given his name by local newspapers, which made a fortune on this sensational series of events) slit the throats and cut out the guts of his victims in the poor and wretched side of town. These were desperate women—so desperate they took their customers not to a bed, but up against a wall for a "four-penny knee trembler." While almost no hint of the dark and scary London of that period survives, guides do a good job of spinning the story. Think of this mile-long walk, starting at the Tower of London, as a cheap night out with a few laughs. It's still light out in summer, so the scary factor is limited to the tales of the victims' miserable lot in life and the gory way in which they were killed.

Two reliably good two-hour tours start every night at the Tower Hill Tube station exit. **Ripping Yarns** is guided by off-duty Yeoman Warders—the Tower of London "Beefeaters" (£7, pay at end, nightly at 18:45, no tours between Christmas and New Year, mobile 07813-559-301, www.jack-the-ripper-tours.com). **London Walks'** guides leave from the same spot later each night (£7, pay at the start, nightly at 19:30, tel. 020/7624-3978, recorded info tel.

020/7624-9255, www.jacktheripperwalk.com). After taking both, I found the London Walks tour more entertaining, informative, and with a better route (along quieter, once-hooker-friendly lanes, with less traffic), starting at Tower Hill and ending at Liverpool Street Station rather than returning to Tower Hill. Groups can be huge for both, but there's always room—just show up.

Private Walks with Local Guides—Standard rates for London's registered Blue Badge guides are about £127 for four hours and £200 or more for nine hours (tel. 020/7780-4060, www.tourist guides.org.uk or www.blue-badge.org.uk). I know and like four fine local guides: **Sean Kelleher** (tel. 020/8673-1624, mobile 07764-612-770, seankelleher@btinternet.com), **Britt Lonsdale** (£150/half-day, £250/day, great with families, tel. 020/7386-9907, mobile 07813-278-077, brittl@btinternet.com), and two others who work in London when they're not on the road leading my Britain tours, **Tom Hooper** (mobile 07986-048-047, tomh@ricksteves .net) and **Gillian Chadwick** (mobile 07889-976-598, gillianc@rick steves.net).

Driver-Guides—These two guides have cars or a minibus (particularly helpful for travelers with limited mobility) and charge around £290/half-day and £450/day for London tours (see websites and contact them for details): **Robina Brown** (tel. 020/7228-2238, www.driverguidetours.com, robina@driverguidetours.com) and **Janine Barton** (tel. 020/7402-4600, http://seeitinstyle.synthasite .com, jbsiis@aol.com).

London Duck Tours

A bright-yellow amphibious WWII-vintage vehicle (the model that landed troops on Normandy's beaches on D-Day) takes a gang of 30 tourists past some famous sights on land—Big Ben, Trafalgar Square, Piccadilly Circus—then splashes into the Thames for a cruise. All in all, it's good fun at a rather steep price. The live guide works hard, and it's kid-friendly to the point of goofiness (£20, April-Sept daily 10:30-18:00, shorter hours Oct-March, 1-4/ hour, 1.25 hours—45 minutes on land and 30 minutes in the river, £3 booking fee online, these book up in advance, departs from Chicheley Street—you'll see the big, ugly vehicle parked 100 yards behind the London Eye, Tube: Waterloo or Westminster, tel. 020/7928-3132, www.londonducktours.co.uk).

Bike Tours

London, like Paris, is committed to creating more bike paths, and many of its best sights can be laced together with a pleasant pedal through its parks. A bike tour is a fun way to see the sights and enjoy the city on two wheels.

London Bicycle Tour Company—Three tours covering London are offered daily from their base at Gabriel's Wharf on the south bank of the Thames. Sunday is the best, as there is less car traffic (**Central Tour**—£17, daily at 10:30, 6 miles, 2.5 hours, includes Westminster, Covent Garden, and St. Paul's; **Royal West Tour**—£20, April-Oct Sat-Sun at 12:00, Nov-March only on Sun, 9 miles, 3.5 hours, includes Westminster, Hyde Park, Buckingham Palace, and Covent Garden; **East Tour**—£20, April-Oct Sat-Sun at 14:00, Nov-March only on Sat at 12:00, 9 miles, 3.5 hours, includes south side of the river to Tower Bridge, then The City to the East End; book ahead for off-season tours). They also rent bikes (£3.50/hour, £20/day; office open daily 10:00-18:00, west of Blackfriars Bridge on the South Bank, 1a Gabriel's Wharf, tel. 020/7928-6838, www.londonbicycle.com).

Fat Tire Bike Tours—Daily bike tours cover the highlights of downtown London, on two different itineraries (£2 discount with this book): **Royal London** (£20, daily March-Nov at 11:00, June-Aug also at 15:30, 7 miles, 4 hours, meet at Queensway Tube station; includes Parliament, Buckingham Palace, Hyde Park, and Trafalgar Square) and **River Thames** (£30, mid-March-Nov Thu-Sat at 10:30, 5 hours, meet at Waterloo Tube station—exit 2; includes London Eye, St. Paul's, Tower of London, Trafalgar Square, Covent Garden, and boat trip on the Thames). The spiel is light and irreverent rather than scholarly, but the price is right. Reservations are easy online, and required for River Thames tours and kids' bikes (off-season tours can be arranged, mobile 078-8233-8779, www.fattirebiketourslondon.com). Confirm the schedule online or by phone.

▲▲Cruises

Boat tours with entertaining commentaries sail regularly from many points along the Thames. The options are plentiful, with several companies offering essentially the same trip. Your basic options are to use the boats either for a scenic joyride cruise within central London, or for transportation to an outlying sight (such as Greenwich or Kew Gardens).

Boats come and go from several docks in central London (see sidebar on the next page). The most popular places to embark are Westminster Pier (at the base of Westminster Bridge across the street from Big Ben) and Waterloo Pier (at the London Eye, across the river).

Buy boat tickets at the kiosks on the docks. While individual Tube and bus tickets don't work on the boats, a Travelcard can snare you a 33 percent discount on most cruises (just show the card when you pay for the cruise; no discount with the pay-as-you-go

Thames Boat Piers

While Westminster Pier is the most popular, it's not the only dock in town. Consider all the options (listed from west to east, as the Thames flows):

Millbank Pier (north bank), at the Tate Britain Museum, is used primarily by the "Tate to Tate" service (express connection to Tate Modern at Bankside Pier).

Westminster Pier (north bank), near the base of Big Ben, offers round-trip sightseeing cruises and lots of departures in both directions (though the Thames Clippers boats don't stop here). Nearby sights include Parliament and Westminster Abbey.

Waterloo Pier (a.k.a. **London Eye Pier,** south bank), right at the base of the London Eye, is a good, less-crowded alternative to Westminster, with many of the same cruise options (Waterloo Station is nearby).

Embankment Pier (north bank) is near Covent Garden, Trafalgar Square, and Cleopatra's Needle (the obelisk on the Thames). This pier is used mostly for special boat trips (such as some RIB—rigid inflatable boat—trips, and lunch and dinner cruises).

Festival Pier (south bank) is next to the Royal Festival Hall, just downstream from the London Eye.

Blackfriars Pier (north bank) is in The City, not far from St. Paul's.

Bankside Pier (south bank) is directly in front of the Tate Modern and Shakespeare's Globe.

London Bridge Pier (a.k.a. **London Bridge City Pier,** south bank) is near the HMS *Belfast* and the start of my Bankside Walk.

Tower Pier (north bank) is at the Tower of London, at the east edge of The City and near the East End.

St. Katharine's Pier (north bank) is just downstream from the Tower of London.

Canary Wharf Pier (north bank) is at the Docklands, London's new "downtown."

In outer London, you might also use the piers at **Greenwich, Kew Gardens,** and **Hampton Court.**

ORIENTATION

Oyster card except on Thames Clippers). Because different companies vary in the discounts they offer, always ask. Children and seniors generally get discounts. You can purchase drinks and scant, pricey snacks on board. Clever budget travelers pack a picnic and munch while they cruise.

Round-trip fares are only a bit more than one-way. Still, for pleasure and efficiency, consider combining a one-way cruise (to Kew, Greenwich, or wherever) with a Tube or train ride back.

Tourist-Oriented Cruises in Central London

London offers many made-for-tourist cruises, most on slow-moving, open-top boats accompanied by commentary about passing sights.

City Cruises runs boats from Westminster Pier across the river to Waterloo Pier, then downriver to Tower Pier and on to Greenwich (tel. 020/7740-0400, www.citycruises.com). If you

want just a sample, hop on their 30-minute cruise only as far as Tower Pier (£8 one-way, £10.50 round-trip, daily April-Oct roughly 10:00-19:00, until 18:00 in winter, 2/hour). City Cruises also offers a £13.50 River Red Rover ticket good for all-day hop-on, hop-off travel (also included with the bus tours described on page 39)—though the line's limited stops in central London make this a lesser deal than it might seem.

Thames River Services runs a similar trip with even fewer stops: Westminster to St. Katharine's Pier to Greenwich (tel. 020/7930-4097, www.thamesriverservices.co.uk). They have classic boats and feel a little friendlier and more old-fashioned. For more details, see the Greenwich section, later.

The **Circular Cruise** offered by Crown River Services is a handy hop-on, hop-off route with stops at the Westminster, Festival, Embankment, Bankside, London Bridge, and St. Katharine's piers (£3 to go one stop, £8.40 one-way for a longer trip, £11 for an all-day ticket, daily 11:00-18:30, every 30 minutes late May-early Sept, fewer stops and less frequent off-season, tel. 020/7936-2033, www.crownriver.com).

The **London Eye** operates its own river cruise, offering a 40-minute live-guided circular tour from Waterloo Pier. As it's much pricier than the alternatives for just a short loop, it's a poor value (£12, reservations recommended, 10 percent discount if you pre-book online, no Travelcard discounts, departures daily generally at :45 past the hour, April-Oct 10:45-18:45, Nov-March 11:45-16:45, closed mid-Jan-mid-Feb, toll tel. 0870-500-0600, www.londoneye.com).

Careening at Top Speed Along the Thames: Two competing companies invite you aboard a small, 12-person, high-speed rigid inflatable boat (RIB—similar to a Zodiac) for an adrenaline-fueled tour of the city (London RIB Voyages: stand-up comedian guides, £32.50/50 minutes, £45/1.25 hours, tel. 020/7928-8933, www.londonribvoyages.com; Thames RIB Experience: £32/50 minutes,

£45/1.5 hours, toll tel. 0870-224-4200, www.thamesribexperience
.com).

Away from the Thames, on Regent's Canal: Consider exploring London's canals by taking a cruise on historic Regent's Canal
in north London. The good ship *Jenny Wren* offers 1.5-hour guided
canal boat cruises from Walker's Quay in Camden Town through
scenic Regent's Park to Little Venice (£9.50; Aug daily at 10:30,
12:30, 14:30, and 16:30; April-July and Sept-Oct daily at 12:30 and
14:30, Sat-Sun also at 16:30; Walker's Quay, 250 Camden High
Street, 3-minute walk from Tube: Camden Town; tel. 020/7485-
4433, www.walkersquay.com). While in Camden Town, stop by
the popular, punky Camden Lock Market to browse through
trendy arts and crafts (daily 10:00-18:00, busiest on weekends, a
block from Walker's Quay, www.camdenlockmarket.com).

Commuting by Clipper

Thames Clippers, which uses fast, sleek, 220-seat catamarans,
is designed for commuters rather than sightseers. Think of the
boats as express buses on the river—they zip no-nonsense through
London every 20 minutes, stopping at most of the major docks en
route: Embankment, Waterloo, Blackfriars or Bankside, London
Bridge, Tower, Canary Wharf (Docklands), and Greenwich
(roughly 20 minutes from Embankment to Tower, 10 more minutes to Docklands, 10 more minutes to Greenwich). However, the
boats are less pleasant for joyriding than the cruises described earlier, with no commentary and no open deck up top (the only outside
access is on a crowded deck at the exhaust-choked back of the boat,
where you're jostling for space to take photos). Any one-way ride
costs £5.50, and a River Roamer all-day ticket costs £12.60 (33 percent discount with Travelcard, 10 percent off with a pay-as-you-go
Oyster card, tel. 020/7001-2222, www.thamesclippers.com).

Thames Clippers also offers two express trips. The **"Tate
to Tate"** boat service, which directly connects the Tate Britain
(Millbank Pier) and the Tate Modern (Bankside Pier), is made
for art-lovers (£5.50 one-way, covered by £12.60 River Roamer day
ticket; buy ticket at gallery desk, at kiosk by the dock, or on board;
for frequency and times, see the Tate Britain and Tate Modern tour
chapters or www.tate.org.uk/tatetotate). The **O2 Express** runs only
on nights when there are events going on at the O2 (formerly the
Millennium Dome; from Waterloo Pier, £6 one-way, £12 round-
trip, 30 minutes).

Cruising Downstream,
to Greenwich and the Docklands

Greenwich: Both of the big tour companies (City Cruises and
Thames River Services, described earlier) head to Greenwich

from Westminster Pier. The cruises are usually narrated by the captain, with most commentary given on the way to Greenwich. The companies' prices are the same (£10 one-way, £13 round-trip), though their itineraries are slightly different: **City Cruises** stops at Waterloo/London Eye Pier and Tower Pier on the way to Greenwich (if you buy their £13.50 River Red Rover ticket, you can hop on and off all day long; daily April-Oct generally 10:00-17:00, less off-season, 2/hour, 1.25 hours from Westminster to Greenwich; cheaper to go from Tower Pier to Greenwich—£8 one-way, £10.50 round-trip, only 30 minutes to Greenwich—but you miss all the scenery in central London). **Thames River Services** stops only at St. Katharine's Pier on the way to Greenwich, making the trip a little faster (April-Oct 10:00-16:00, July-Aug until 17:00, daily 2/hour; Nov-March shorter hours and runs every 40 minutes; 1 hour from Westminster to Greenwich).

The **Thames Clippers** boats, described earlier, are cheaper, faster, and make more stops downtown, but have no commentary and no seating up top (£5.50 one-way, £12.60 for an all-day pass, 3/hour, about 45 minutes to Greenwich).

To maximize both efficiency and sightseeing, I'd take a boat to Greenwich one way, and go the other way on the DLR (Docklands Light Railway), with a stop in the Docklands (Canary Wharf station; ✪ see The Docklands Walk chapter).

The Docklands: Thames Clippers connects the Docklands' Canary Wharf Pier to both central London and Greenwich (£5.50 one-way, £12.60 for an all-day pass, no commentary, 3/hour, roughly 10 minutes to Tower, 30 minutes to Waterloo, 10 minutes to Greenwich).

Cruising Upstream, to Kew Gardens and Hampton Court Palace

Boats operated by the Westminster Passenger Services Association leave for Kew Gardens from Westminster Pier (£12 one-way, £18 round-trip, cash only; 4/day, April-Oct daily at 10:30, 11:15, 12:00, and 14:00; 1.5 hours, about half the trip is narrated, tel. 020/7930-2062, www.wpsa.co.uk). Most boats continue on to Hampton Court Palace for an additional £3 (and another 1.5 hours). Because of the river current, you'll sometimes save 30 minutes cruising from Hampton Court back into town (depends on the tide—ask before you commit to the boat). Romantic as these rides sound, it can be a long trip...especially upstream.

SIGHTS IN LONDON

These sights are arranged by neighborhood for handy sightseeing. When you see a ✪ in a listing, it means the sight is covered in much more depth in a self-guided walk or in one of the tours.

For advice on keeping down your costs, see "Affording London's Sights" on page 66.

Central London

Westminster

These sights are listed roughly in geographical order from Westminster Abbey to Trafalgar Square, and are linked in the ✪ Westminster Walk chapter.

▲▲▲**Westminster Abbey**—The greatest church in the English-speaking world, Westminster Abbey is the place where England's kings and queens have been crowned and buried since 1066. Like a stony refugee camp huddled outside St. Peter's Pearly Gates,

Westminster Abbey has many stories to tell. The steep admission includes an excellent audioguide, worthwhile if you have the time and interest. To experience the church more vividly, take a live tour, or attend evensong or an organ concert.

Cost and Hours: £16, £32 family ticket (covers 2 adults and 1 child), includes cloisters, audioguide, and Abbey Museum; abbey—Mon-Fri 9:30-16:30, Wed until 19:00 (main church only), Sat 9:30-14:30, last entry one hour before closing, closed Sun to sightseers

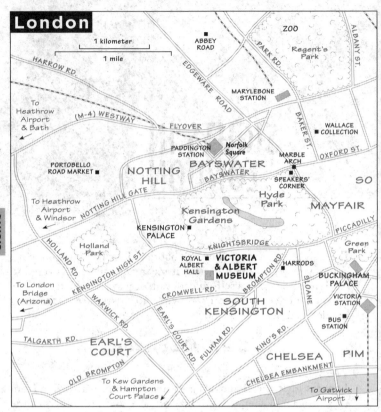

but open for services; museum—daily 10:30-16:00; cloisters—daily 8:00-18:00; Tube: Westminster or St. James's Park, tel. 020/7654-4834, www.westminster-abbey.org.

Music: The church hosts evensong performances daily (see page 126 for details). A free 30-minute organ recital is often held on Sunday at 17:45.

See the Westminster Abbey Tour chapter.

▲▲Houses of Parliament (Palace of Westminster)—This Neo-Gothic icon of London, the royal residence from 1042 to 1547, is now the meeting place of the legislative branch of government. The Houses of Parliament are located in what was once the Palace of Westminster—long the palace of England's medieval kings—until it was largely destroyed by fire in 1834. The

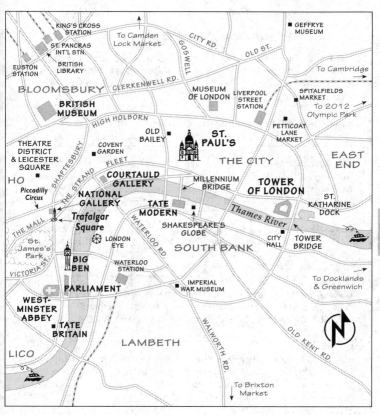

palace was rebuilt in the Victorian Gothic style (a move away from Neoclassicism back to England's Christian and medieval heritage, true to the Romantic Age) and completed in 1860.

Tourists are welcome to view debates in either the bickering House of Commons or the genteel House of Lords. You're only allowed inside when Parliament is in session, indicated by a flag flying atop the Victoria Tower at the south end of the building (generally Mondays through Thursdays). During the summer recess, when Parliament is not in session, visitors can take a guided tour. While the actual debates are generally quite dull, it is a thrill to be inside and see the British government inaction.

Cost and Hours: Free, both Houses usually open Mon-Tue 14:30-22:30, Wed-Thu 11:30-17:50, closed Fri-Sun and most of Aug-Sept, generally less action and no lines after 18:00, Tube: Westminster, tel. 020/7219-4272, see www.parliament.uk for schedule.

Visiting the Houses of Parliament (HOP): Enter the venerable HOP midway along the west side of the building (across the

London at a Glance

▲▲▲Westminster Abbey Britain's finest church and the site of royal coronations and burials since 1066. **Hours:** Mon-Fri 9:30-16:30, Wed until 19:00, Sat 9:30-14:30, closed Sun to sightseers except for worship. See page 49.

▲▲▲Churchill War Rooms Underground WWII headquarters of Churchill's war effort. **Hours:** Daily 9:30-18:00. See page 55.

▲▲▲National Gallery Remarkable collection of European paintings (1250-1900), including Leonardo, Botticelli, Velázquez, Rembrandt, Turner, Van Gogh, and the Impressionists. **Hours:** Daily 10:00-18:00, Fri until 21:00. See page 58.

▲▲▲British Museum The world's greatest collection of artifacts of Western civilization, including the Rosetta Stone and the Parthenon's Elgin Marbles. **Hours:** Daily 10:00-17:30, Fri until 20:30 (selected galleries only). See page 70.

▲▲▲British Library Impressive collection of the most important literary treasures of the Western world. **Hours:** Mon-Fri 9:30-18:00, Tue until 20:00, Sat 9:30-17:00, Sun 11:00-17:00. See page 70.

▲▲▲St. Paul's Cathedral The main cathedral of the Anglican Church, designed by Christopher Wren, with a climbable dome and daily evensong services. **Hours:** Mon-Sat 8:30-16:30, closed Sun except for worship. See page 77.

▲▲▲Tower of London Historic castle, palace, and prison housing the crown jewels and a witty band of Beefeaters. **Hours:** March-Oct Tue-Sat 9:00-17:30, Sun-Mon 10:00-17:30; Nov-Feb Tue-Sat 9:00-16:30, Sun-Mon 10:00-16:30. See page 82.

▲▲▲Victoria and Albert Museum The best collection of decorative arts anywhere. **Hours:** Daily 10:00-17:45, Fri until 22:00 (selected galleries only). See page 98.

▲▲Houses of Parliament London's Neo-Gothic landmark, famous for Big Ben and occupied by the Houses of Lords and Commons. **Hours:** Generally Mon-Tue 14:30-22:30, Wed-Thu 11:30-17:50, closed Fri-Sun and most of Aug-Sept. See page 50.

▲▲Trafalgar Square The heart of London, where Westminster, The City, and the West End meet. **Hours:** Always open. See page 58.

▲▲**National Portrait Gallery** A *Who's Who* of British history, featuring portraits of this nation's most important historical figures. **Hours:** Daily 10:00-18:00, Thu-Fri until 21:00, first and second floors open Mon at 11:00. See page 59.

▲▲**Covent Garden** Vibrant people-watching zone with shops, cafés, street musicians, and an iron-and-glass arcade that once hosted a produce market. **Hours:** Always open. See page 61.

▲▲**Changing of the Guard at Buckingham Palace** Hour-long spectacle at Britain's royal residence. **Hours:** Generally May-July daily at 11:30, Aug-April every other day. See page 68.

▲▲**London Eye** Enormous observation wheel, dominating—and offering commanding views over—London's skyline. **Hours:** Daily July-Aug 10:00-21:30, April-June 10:00-21:00, Sept-March 10:00-20:00. See page 87.

▲▲**Imperial War Museum** Examines the military history of the bloody 20th century. **Hours:** Daily 10:00-18:00. See page 90.

▲▲**Tate Modern** Works by Monet, Matisse, Dalí, Picasso, and Warhol displayed in a converted powerhouse. **Hours:** Daily 10:00-18:00, Fri-Sat until 22:00. See page 91.

▲▲**Shakespeare's Globe** Timbered, thatched-roofed reconstruction of the Bard's original wooden "O." **Hours:** Theater complex, museum, and actor-led tours generally daily 9:00-17:00; in summer, morning theater tours only. Plays are also held here. See page 92.

▲▲**Tate Britain** Collection of British painting from the 16th century through modern times, including works by William Blake, the Pre-Raphaelites, and J. M. W. Turner. **Hours:** Daily 10:00-18:00, first Fri of the month until 22:00. See page 96.

▲▲**Natural History Museum** Packed with stuffed creatures, engaging exhibits, and enthralled kids. **Hours:** Daily 10:00-17:50. See page 99.

▲**Courtauld Gallery** Fine collection of paintings filling one wing of the Somerset House, a grand 18th-century palace. **Hours:** Daily 10:00-18:00. See page 64.

SIGHTS

street from Westminster Abbey) through the Visitor Entrance (with the tourist ramp, next to the St. Stephen's Entrance—if lost, ask a guard). As you enter, you'll be asked if you want to visit the House of Commons or the House of Lords. The House of Lords has more pageantry, shorter lines, but less interesting debates (tel. 020/7219-3107 for schedule, visit www.parliament live.tv for a preview). Inquire about the wait—an hour or two is not unusual. If there's a long line for the House of Commons and you just want a quick look inside the grand halls of this majestic building, start with the House of Lords. Once inside, you can switch if you like.

Just past security (where you'll be photographed and given a badge to wear around your neck), you enter the vast and his-

toric **Westminster Hall,** which survived the 1834 fire. The cavernous hall was built in the 11th century, and its famous self-supporting hammer-beam roof was added in 1397. Racks of brochures here explain how the British government works, and plaques describe the hall. The Jubilee Café, open to the public, has live video feeds showing exactly what's going on in each house. Just seeing the café video is a fun experience (and can help you decide which house—if either—you'd like to see). Walking through the hall and up the stairs, you'll enter the busy world of government with all its high-powered goings-on.

Houses of Parliament Tours: Though Parliament is in recess during much of August and September, you can get a behind-the-scenes peek at the royal chambers of both houses during these months with a tour (£15, 1.25 hours, generally Mon-Fri, times vary, so confirm in advance; book ahead through www.ticket master.co.uk). The same tours are offered Saturdays year-round.

Jewel Tower: Across the street from the Parliament building's St. Stephen's Gate, the Jewel Tower is a rare remnant of the old Palace of Westminster, used by kings until Henry VIII. The crude stone tower (1365-1366) was a guard tower in the palace wall, overlooking a moat. It contains a fine little exhibit on Parliament and the tower (£3, daily March-Oct 10:00-17:00, Nov-Feb 10:00-16:00, tel. 020/7222-2219). Next to the tower (and free) is a quiet courtyard with picnic-friendly benches.

Big Ben: The 315-foot-high clock tower at the north end of the Palace of Westminster is named for its 13-ton bell, Ben. The light above the clock is lit when the House of Commons is sitting. The face of the clock is huge—you can actually see the minute hand moving. For a good view of it, walk halfway over Westminster Bridge.

▲▲▲**Churchill War Rooms**—This is a fascinating walk through the underground headquarters of the British government's fight against the Nazis in the darkest days of the Battle for Britain. The attraction includes two parts: the war rooms themselves and a top-notch museum dedicated to the man who steered the war from here, Winston Churchill. For details on all the blood, sweat, toil, and tears, pick up the excellent, essential, and included audioguide at the entry, and dive in.

Cabinet War Rooms: The 27-room, heavily fortified nerve center of the British war effort was used from 1939 to 1945. Churchill's room, the map room, and other rooms are just as

they were in 1945. As you follow the one-way route, be sure to take advantage of the audio-guide, which explains each room and offers first-person accounts of wartime happenings here (it takes about 45 minutes, not counting the Churchill Museum). Be patient—it's well worth it. While the rooms are spartan, you'll see how British gentility survived even as the city was bombarded—posted signs informed those working underground what the weather was like outside, and a cheery notice reminds you to turn off the light switch to conserve electricity.

Churchill Museum: Don't bypass this museum, which occupies a large hall about a half-dozen rooms into the war rooms. It dissects every aspect of the man behind the famous cigar, bowler hat, and V-for-victory sign. It's extremely well-presented and engaging, using artifacts, quotes, political cartoons, clear explanations, and high-tech interactive exhibits to bring the colorful statesman to life; this museum alone deserves an hour. You'll get a taste of Winston's wit, irascibility, work ethic, passion for painting, American ties, writing talents, and drinking habits. The exhibit shows Winston's warts as well: It questions whether his party-switching was just political opportunism, examines the basis for his opposition to Indian self-rule, and reveals him to be an intense taskmaster who worked 18-hour days and was brutal on his staffers (who deeply respected him nevertheless).

A long touch-the-screen timeline lets you zero in on events in his life from birth (November 30, 1874) to his first appointment as prime minister in 1940. Many of the items on display—such as a European map divvied up in permanent marker, which Churchill brought to England from the postwar Potsdam Conference—

Winston Churchill
(1874-1965)

As the 20th century dawned, 25-year-old Winston Churchill became famous. Working as a newspaper reporter embedded with British troops in South Africa, his train was attacked by Boers. Churchill was captured and held as a POW. Meanwhile, back home, the London papers were praising the young man's heroism for saving fellow train passengers. After two weeks, Churchill escaped from the Boer camp—he slipped through a bathroom window, scaled a wall, walked nonchalantly through an enemy town, hopped a freight train, and was smuggled out of the country. He emerged to find himself famous.

Churchill entered politics. He first followed in his father's (Lord Randolph Churchill) Conservative Party footsteps, but his desire for social reform drove him to switch to the Liberal Party. (He would later flip-flop back to Conservative.) For three decades, Churchill held numerous government posts, serving as Chancellor of This, Undersecretary of That, and Minister of The Other. He earned praise for prison reform and for developing newfangled airplanes for warfare; he was criticized for the heavy-handed way he broke labor strikes and for bungling the pacification of Iraq. During World War I, he took a break from

drive home the remarkable span of history this man lived through. Imagine: Churchill began his military career riding horses in the cavalry and ended it speaking out against the proliferation of nuclear armaments. It's all the more amazing considering that, in the 1930s, the man who would become my vote for greatest statesman of the 20th century was once considered a washed-up loony ranting about the growing threat of fascism.

Cost and Hours: £16 (includes small donation), daily 9:30-18:00, last entry one hour before closing; on King Charles Street, 200 yards off Whitehall, follow the signs, Tube: Westminster, tel. 020/7930-6961, http://cwr.iwm.org.uk. The museum's gift shop is great for anyone nostalgic for the 1940s.

Eating: If you're hungry, get your rations at the Switch Room café (in the museum), or for a nearby pub lunch, try the Westminster Arms (food served downstairs, on Storey's Gate, a couple of blocks south of the museum).

Horse Guards—The Horse Guards change daily at 11:00 (10:00 on Sun), and a colorful dismounting ceremony takes place daily

politics to personally command British troops on the Western Front.

In 1929, Churchill-the-career-bureaucrat retired from politics. He wrote books *(History of the English-Speaking Peoples)* and spoke out about the growing threat of fascist Germany. When World War II broke out, Prime Minister Chamberlain's appeasement policies were discredited, and—on the day that Germany invaded the Netherlands—the king appointed Churchill as prime minister. Churchill guided the nation through its darkest hour (see sidebar on page 258). His greatest contribution may have been his stirring radio speeches that galvanized the will of the British people.

Despite the Allies' victory over the Nazis, Churchill lost the 1945 election. Though considered the ideal man to lead Britain during war, many believed he and his Conservative Party colleagues were not the best choice to lead the country in peace and during rebuilding. Never one to be idle, he continued to be active in politics (especially in world affairs) as Leader of the Opposition. In 1946, he gave a speech at a Missouri college, which included the famous Cold War line, "From Stettin in the Baltic to Trieste in the Adriatic, an Iron Curtain has descended across the Continent." In 1951, Churchill was again elected prime minister and served for four years before he retired in 1955. When he died at the age of 90 in 1965, his state funeral in St. Paul's attracted leaders from around the world. Churchill, a legend in his own time, was buried northwest of Oxford in Bladon, a mile from Blenheim Palace, the place of his birth.

SIGHTS

at 16:00. The rest of the day, they just stand there—terrible for video cameras (on Whitehall, between Trafalgar Square and #10 Downing Street, Tube: Westminster, www.changing -the-guard.com). Buckingham Palace pageantry is canceled when it rains, but the Horse Guards change regardless of the weather.

▲**Banqueting House**—England's first Renaissance building (1619-1622) was designed by Inigo Jones. Built by King James I and decorated by his son Charles I, the Banqueting House came to symbolize the Stuart kings' "divine right" management style—the belief that God himself had anointed them to rule. The house is one of the few London landmarks spared by the 1698 fire and the only surviving part of the original Palace of Whitehall. Today it opens its doors to visitors, who enjoy a restful 20-minute audiovisual history, a 30-minute audioguide, and a look at the exquisite banqueting hall itself. As a tourist attraction, it's basically one big room—but what a grand room it is, with sumptuous ceiling paintings by Peter Paul Rubens. At Charles I's request, these paintings drove home the doctrine of the legitimacy of the divine right of kings. Ironically, in 1649—divine right ignored—King Charles I was famously executed right here.

Cost and Hours: £4.80, includes audioguide, Mon-Sat 10:00-17:00, closed Sun, last entry at 16:30, subject to closure for government functions, aristocratic WC, immediately across Whitehall from the Horse Guards, Tube: Westminster, tel. 020/3166-6155, www.hrp.org.uk.

For a brief self-guided tour of the Banqueting House—and more details about the history of the place—see page 119 in the Westminster Walk.

On Trafalgar Square

▲▲**Trafalgar Square**—London's recently renovated central square, the climax of most marches and demonstrations, is a

thrilling place to simply hang out. Lord Nelson stands atop his 185-foot-tall fluted granite column, gazing out toward Trafalgar, where he lost his life but defeated the French fleet. Part of this 1842 memorial is made from his victims' melted-down cannons. He's surrounded by spraying fountains, giant lions, hordes of people, and—until recently—even more pigeons. A former London mayor decided that London's "flying rats" were a public nuisance and evicted Trafalgar Square's venerable seed salesmen (Tube: Charing Cross).

For more on Trafalgar Square, see page 123 in the Westminster Walk.

▲▲▲**National Gallery**—Displaying Britain's top collection of European paintings from 1250 to 1900—including works by Leonardo, Botticelli, Velázquez, Rembrandt, Turner, Van Gogh, and the Impressionists—this is one of Europe's great galleries. Although the collection is huge, following the route suggested in my self-guided tour will give you the best quick visit. For a more thorough tour, the audioguide (£3.50) is excellent.

Cost and Hours: Free, but suggested donation of £2-3, temporary (optional) exhibits require an admission fee; daily 10:00-18:00, Fri until 21:00, last entry to special exhibits 45 minutes before closing; on Trafalgar Square, Tube: Charing Cross or Leicester Square, recorded info tel. 020/7747-2885, switchboard tel. 020/7839-3321, www.nationalgallery.org.uk. The excellent-but-pricey museum restaurant called the National Dining Rooms is a good spot to split afternoon tea (see page 398).

○ See the National Gallery Tour chapter.

▲▲**National Portrait Gallery**—Put off by halls of 19th-century characters who meant nothing to me, I used to call this "as interesting as someone else's yearbook." But a selective walk through this 500-year-long *Who's Who* of British history is quick and free, and puts faces on the story of England.

Some highlights: Henry VIII and wives; portraits of the "Virgin Queen" Elizabeth I, Sir Francis Drake, and Sir Walter Raleigh; the only real-life portrait of William Shakespeare; Oliver Cromwell and Charles I with his head on; portraits by Gainsborough and Reynolds; the Romantics (William Blake, Lord Byron, William Wordsworth, and company); Queen Victoria and her era; and the present royal family, including the late Princess Diana.

The collection is well-described, not huge, and in historical sequence, from the 16th century on the second floor to today's royal family on the ground floor.

Cost and Hours: Free, but suggested donation of £5, temporary exhibits extra; daily 10:00-18:00, Thu-Fri until 21:00, first and second floors open Mon at 11:00, last entry to special exhibits 45 minutes before closing; entry 100 yards off Trafalgar Square (around the corner from National Gallery, opposite Church of St. Martin-in-the-Fields), Tube: Charing Cross or Leicester Square, tel. 020/7306-0055, recorded info tel. 020/7312-2463, www.npg.org.uk.

○ See the National Portrait Gallery Tour chapter.

▲**St. Martin-in-the-Fields**—The church, built in the 1720s with a Gothic spire atop a Greek-type temple, is an oasis of peace on wild and noisy Trafalgar Square. St. Martin cared for the poor. "In the fields" was where the first church stood on this spot (in the 13th century), between Westminster and The City. Stepping inside, you

still feel a compassion for the needs of the people in this neighborhood—the church serves the homeless and houses a Chinese community center. The modern east window—with grillwork bent into the shape of a warped cross—was installed in 2008 to replace one damaged in World War II.

A freestanding glass pavilion to the left of the church serves as the entrance to the church's underground areas. There you'll find the concert ticket office, a gift shop, brass-rubbing center, and the recommended support-the-church Café in the Crypt.

Cost and Hours: Free, but donations welcome, £3.50 audio-guide at shop downstairs; hours vary but generally Mon-Fri 8:30-13:00 & 14:00-18:00, Sat 9:30-13:00 & 14:00-18:00, Sun 15:30-17:00; Tube: Charing Cross, tel. 020/7766-1100, www.smitf .org.

Music: The church is famous for its concerts. Consider a free lunchtime concert (suggested £3.50 donation; Mon, Tue, and Fri at 13:00), an evening concert (£8-26, several nights a week at 19:30), or Wednesday night jazz in the church's café (£5-10, at 20:00). See the website for the concert schedule.

The West End and Nearby

Most of these sights are linked (and further described) in the ✪ West End Walk chapter.

▲**Piccadilly Circus**—Although this square is slathered with neon billboards and tacky attractions (think of it as the Times Square of London), the surrounding streets are packed with great shopping opportunities and swimming with youth on the rampage. For overstimulation in a grimy mall that smells like teen spirit, drop by the extremely trashy Trocadero Center for its Funland arcade games, multiplex cinema, and 10-lane bowling alley (admission to Trocadero is free; individual attractions have separate admissions; located between Piccadilly and Leicester squares on Coventry Street).

Nearby Shaftesbury Avenue and Leicester Square teem with fun-seekers, theaters, Chinese restaurants, and street singers. To the northeast is London's Chinatown and, beyond that, the funky Soho neighborhood (described next). And curling to the northwest from Piccadilly Circus is genteel Regent Street, lined with the city's most exclusive shops.

▲**Soho**—North of Piccadilly, seedy Soho has become seriously trendy and is well worth a gawk (◐ see the West End Walk chapter). It's the epicenter of London's thriving and colorful youth...a fun and funky *Sesame Street* scene populated by people every color of the racial rainbow...straight, gay, and everything in between.

Soho is also London's red light district (especially near Brewer and Berwick Streets), where "friendly models" wait in tiny rooms up dreary stairways, and voluptuous con artists sell strip shows. Though venturing up a stairway to check out a model is interesting, anyone who goes into any one of the shows will be ripped off. Every time. Even a £5 show in a "licensed bar" comes with a £100 cover or minimum (as it's printed on the drink menu) and a "security man." You may accidentally buy a £200 bottle of bubbly. And suddenly, the door has no handle. While this all sounds creepy, it's easy to avoid trouble if you're not looking for it. In fact, the sleazy joints share the block with respectable pubs and restaurants, and elderly couples out for a stroll pass neon signs that flash *Licensed Sex Shop in Basement*.

Telephone sex ads are hard to avoid these days in London. Phone booths are littered with racy fliers of busty ladies "new in town." Some travelers gather six or eight phone booths' worth of fliers and take them home for kinky wallpaper.

▲▲**Covent Garden**—The centerpiece of this boutique-ish shopping district is an iron-and-glass arcade. The "Actors' Church" of St. Paul, the Royal Opera House, and the London Transport Museum (described next) all border the square, and venerable theatres are nearby. The area is a people-watcher's delight, with cigarette eaters, Punch-and-Judy acts, food that's good for you (but not your wallet), trendy crafts, sweet whiffs of marijuana, two-tone hair (neither natural), and faces that could set off a metal detector (Tube: Covent Garden). For better Covent Garden lunch deals, walk a block or two away from the eye of this touristic hurricane (check out the places north of the Tube station, along Endell and Neal Streets).

▲**London Transport Museum**—This modern, well-presented museum, located right at Covent Garden, is fun for kids and thought-provoking for adults (if a bit overpriced). Whether you're cursing or marveling at the buses and Tube, the growth of Europe's third-biggest city (after Moscow and Istanbul) has been made possible by its public transit system. Kids enjoy picking up the "stamp

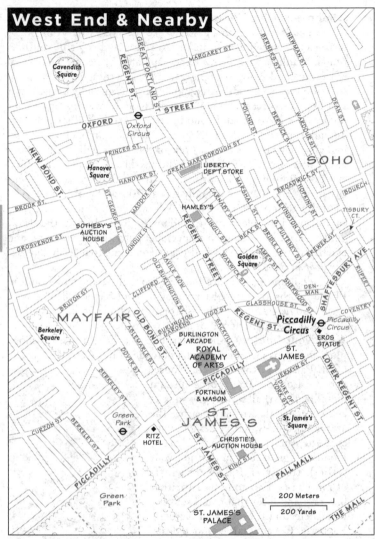

West End & Nearby

SIGHTS

card," then punching it with old-fashioned ticket punchers at the different exhibits.

After you enter, take the elevator up to the top floor...and the year 1800, when horse-drawn vehicles ruled the road. London invented the notion of a public bus traveling a set route that anyone could board without a reservation. Next, you descend to the first floor and the world's first underground Metro system, which used steam-powered locomotives (the Circle Line, c. 1865). On the ground floor, horses and trains are replaced by motorized vehicles

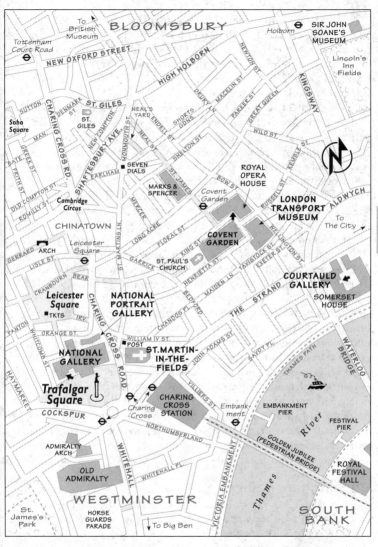

(cars, taxis, double-decker buses, streetcars), resulting in 20th-century congestion. How to deal with it? In 2003, car drivers in London were slapped with a congestion charge, and today, a half-billion people ride the Tube every year. Learn how city planners hope to improve efficiency with better tracks and more coverage of the expanding East End. Finally, an exhibit lets you imagine four different scenarios for the year 2055 depending on the choices you make today. Will fresh strawberries in December destroy the planet?

Cost and Hours: £13.50, ticket good for one year, Sat-Thu 10:00-18:00, Fri 11:00-18:00, last entry 45 minutes before closing, pleasant upstairs café with Covent Garden view, in southeast corner of Covent Garden courtyard, Tube: Covent Garden, switchboard tel. 020/7379-6344, recorded info tel. 020/7565-7299, www.ltmuseum.co.uk.

▲**Courtauld Gallery**—While less impressive than the National Gallery, this wonderful collection of paintings is still a joy. The gallery is part of the Courtauld Institute of Art, and the thoughtful description of each piece of art reminds visitors that the gallery is still used for teaching. You'll see medieval European paintings and works by Rubens, the Impressionists (Manet, Monet, and Degas), Post-Impressionists (such as Cézanne), and more. Besides the permanent collection, a quality selection of loaners and temporary exhibits are often included in the entry fee.

Cost and Hours: £6, free Mon until 14:00; open daily 10:00-18:00, last entry at 17:30, occasional late-night openings until 21:00—check website; at Somerset House along the Strand, Tube: Temple or Covent Garden, recorded info tel. 020/7848-2526, shop tel. 020/7848-2579, www.courtauld.ac.uk.

Somerset House: The Courtauld Gallery is located at Somerset House, a grand 18th-century civic palace that offers a marvelous public space (housing temporary exhibits) and a riverside terrace with several eateries (between the Strand and the Thames). The palace once held the national registry that recorded Britain's births, marriages, and deaths: "...where they hatch 'em, match 'em, and dispatch 'em." Step into the courtyard to enjoy the fountain. Go ahead...walk through it. The 55 jets get playful twice an hour. In the winter, this becomes a popular ice-skating rink with a toasty café for viewing (www.somerset-house.org.uk).

✪ See the Courtauld Gallery Tour chapter.

Buckingham Palace

Three palace sights require admission: the State Rooms (Aug-Sept only), Queen's Gallery, and Royal Mews. You can pay for each separately, or buy a combo-ticket. The combo-ticket for £31 admits you to all three sights; a cheaper version for £15.50 covers the Queen's Gallery and Royal Mews. Many tourists are more interested in the Changing of the Guard, which costs nothing at all to view.

▲**State Rooms at Buckingham Palace**—This lavish home has been Britain's royal residence since 1837. When the Queen's at

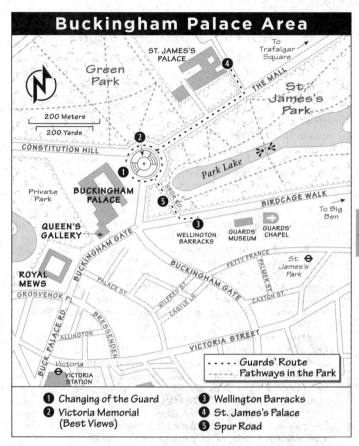

Buckingham Palace Area

ST. JAMES'S PALACE

To Trafalgar Square

THE MALL

Green Park

St. James's Park

N

200 Meters
200 Yards

CONSTITUTION HILL

Park Lake

Private Park

BUCKINGHAM PALACE

SPUR RD

BIRDCAGE WALK

To Big Ben

QUEEN'S GALLERY

BUCKINGHAM GATE

WELLINGTON BARRACKS

GUARDS' MUSEUM

GUARDS' CHAPEL

St. James's Park

ROYAL MEWS

GROSVENOR PL

PALACE ST.

BUCKINGHAM GATE

PETTY FRANCE

PALMER ST.

BRESSENDEN

ALLINGTON

BUCK. PALACE RD.

WILFRED ST.

CASTLE LN.

CAXTON ST.

VICTORIA STREET

Victoria
VICTORIA STATION

- - - - Guards' Route
- - - - Pathways in the Park

1 Changing of the Guard
2 Victoria Memorial (Best Views)
3 Wellington Barracks
4 St. James's Palace
5 Spur Road

SIGHTS

home, the royal standard flies (a red, yellow, and blue flag); otherwise, the Union Jack flaps in the wind. The Queen opens her palace to the public—but only in August and September, when she's out of town.

Cost and Hours: £17.50 for lavish State Rooms and throne room, includes audioguide; Aug-Sept only, daily 9:45-18:30, last admission 15:45; only 8,000 visitors a day by timed entry; come early to the palace's Visitor Entrance (opens 9:15), or book ahead in person, by phone, or online (£1.25 extra); Tube: Victoria, tel. 020/7766-7300, www.royalcollection.org.uk.

▲**Queen's Gallery at Buckingham Palace**—Queen Elizabeth's personal collection of art is on display in a wing adjoining the palace. Her 7,000 paintings make up the finest private art collection in the world, rivaling Europe's biggest national art galleries. It's actually a collection of collections, built on by each successive monarch since the 16th century. She rotates her paintings, enjoying some

Affording London's Sights

London is one of Europe's most expensive cities, with the dubious distinction of having some of the world's most expensive admission prices. Fortunately, many sights are free.

Free Museums: Many of the city's biggest and best museums won't cost you a dime. Free sights include the British Museum, British Library, National Gallery, National Portrait Gallery, Tate Britain, Tate Modern, Wallace Collection, Imperial War Museum, Victoria and Albert Museum, Natural History Museum, Science Museum, National Army Museum, Sir John Soane's Museum, the Museum of London, the Geffrye, and on the outskirts of town, the Royal Air Force Museum London.

About half of these museums request a donation of a few pounds, but whether you contribute or not is up to you. If I spend money for an audioguide, I feel fine about not otherwise donating. If that makes you uncomfortable, donate.

Free Churches: Smaller churches let worshippers (and tourists) in free, although they may ask for a donation. The big sightseeing churches—Westminster Abbey and St. Paul's—charge steep admission fees, but offer free evensong services daily (though you're not allowed to stick around afterward). Westminster Abbey also offers free organ recitals most Sundays at 17:45.

Other Freebies: London has plenty of free performances, such as lunch concerts at St. Martin-in-the-Fields (see page 421) and summertime movies at The Scoop amphitheater near City Hall (Tube: London Bridge, schedule at www.morelondon .com—click on "The Scoop"). For other freebies, check out www .freelondonlistings.co.uk. There's no charge to enjoy the pageantry of the Changing of the Guard, rants at Speaker's Corner in Hyde Park, displays at Harrods, the people-watching scene at Covent Garden, and the colorful streets of the East End. It's free to view the legal action at the Old Bailey and the legislature at work in the Houses of Parliament. And you can get into a bit of the Tower of London by attending Sunday services in the Tower's chapel (chapel access only).

Greenwich makes for a very cheap day out. Many of its sights are free, and the journey there is covered by a cheap Zones 1-2 Tube ticket.

Sightseeing Deals: If you buy a paper One-Day Travelcard or rail ticket at a National Rail station (such as Paddington or Victoria), you may be eligible for two-for-one discounts at many popular sights, such as the London Eye, Tower of London, Tate Modern, and Madame Tussauds Waxworks. This is a great deal if you can get it. To claim the discount, you must have a rail ticket that has been used and validated that day—for instance, if you are arriving by train into London (from elsewhere in England) or taking a short morning side-trip. Get details and print vouchers at www.daysoutguide.co.uk, or look for brochures with coupons at major train stations.

Good-Value Tours: The £5-8 city walking tours with professional guides are one of the best deals going. (Note that the guides for the "free" walking tours are unpaid and expect tips—I'd pay for a professionally guided tour instead.) Hop-on, hop-off big-bus tours, while expensive (£22-27), provide a great overview and include free boat tours as well as city walks. A one-hour Thames ride to Greenwich costs £10 one-way, but most boats come with entertaining commentary. A three-hour bicycle tour is about £20.

Pricey...but Worth It? Big-ticket sights worth their hefty admission fees are Kew Gardens (£14), Shakespeare's Globe (£11.50), and the Churchill War Rooms (£16).

The London Eye has become a London must-see—though if you're on a tight budget, it's difficult to justify its very high cost (£19). While Hampton Court Palace (£16) is expensive, it is well-presented and a reasonable value if you have an interest in royal history. The Queen charges royally to open her palace to the public: Buckingham Palace (£17.50, Aug-Sept only), and her art gallery and carriage museum (adjacent to the palace, £9 and £8, £15.50 for both) are expensive but interesting. Madame Tussauds Waxworks is pricey but still fun and popular (£29, £22.50 if purchased at TI, drops to £14 after 17:00 if booked online). The Vinopolis wine museum provides a way to get a buzz and call it museum-going (from £20, entry includes tastes of wine).

Many smaller museums charge low admission. My favorites include the Courtauld Gallery (£6, free on Mon until 14:00) and the Wellington Museum at Apsley House (£6.30, www.english-heritage.org.uk).

Totally Pants (Brit-speak for Not Worth It): The London Dungeon, at £23.50, is gimmicky, overpriced, and a terrible value...despite the long line at the door. It doesn't make sense to spend your pounds on Winston Churchill's Britain at War Experience (£13) when the Churchill War Rooms (£16) and the Imperial War Museum (free) cover the same themes much better.

Theater: Compared with Broadway's prices, London theater is a bargain. Seek out the freestanding "tkts" booth at Leicester Square to get discounts from 25 to 50 percent on good seats (though not necessarily for the hottest shows; see page 418). If you're willing to settle for the cheapest seats (possibly with obstructed views), ask the theater's box office for their best deal (even the most popular shows generally have some £10-25 tickets). A £5 "groundling" ticket for a play at Shakespeare's Globe is the best theater deal in town (see page 418). Tickets to the Open Air Theatre at north London's Regent's Park start at £12 (see page 419).

London doesn't come cheap. But with its many free museums and affordable plays, this cosmopolitan, cultured city offers days of sightseeing thrills without requiring you to pinch your pennies (or your pounds).

privately in her many palatial residences while sharing others with her subjects in public galleries in Edinburgh and London. Small, thoughtfully presented, and always exquisite displays fill the five rooms open to the public. As you're in "the most important building in London," security is tight.

In addition to the permanent collection, you'll see temporary exhibits and a small room glittering with the Queen's personal jewelry. Compared to the crown jewels at the Tower, it may be Her Majesty's bottom drawer—but it's still a dazzling pile of diamonds. Temporary exhibits change about twice a year and are lovingly described by the included audioguide. While admission tickets come with an entry time, this is only enforced during rare days when crowds are a problem.

Cost and Hours: £9, daily 10:00-17:30, last entry one hour before closing, Tube: Victoria, tel. 020/7766-7301—but Her Majesty rarely answers. Men shouldn't miss the mahogany-trimmed urinals.

Royal Mews—Located to the left of Buckingham Palace, the Queen's working stables, or "mews," are open to visitors. The visit is likely to be disappointing unless you follow the included audioguide or the hourly guided tour, in which case it's thoroughly entertaining—especially if you're interested in horses and/or royalty. The 40-minute tours show off a few of the Queen's 30 horses, a fancy car, and a bunch of old carriages, finishing with the Gold State Coach (c. 1760, 4 tons, 4 mph). Queen Victoria said absolutely no cars. When she died, in 1901, the mews got its first Daimler. Today, along with the hay-eating transport, the stable is home to five Bentleys and Rolls-Royce Phantoms, with one on display.

Cost and Hours: £8, April-Oct daily 11:00-17:00, Nov-March Mon-Fri 10:00-16:00, closed Sat-Sun, last entry 45 minutes before closing, guided tours on the hour, Buckingham Palace Road, Tube: Victoria, tel. 020/7766-7302.

▲▲Changing of the Guard at Buckingham Palace—This is the spectacle every visitor to London has to see at least once: stone-faced, red-coated, bearskin-hatted guards changing posts with much fanfare, in an hour-long ceremony accompanied by a brass band.

It's 11:00 at Buckingham Palace, and the on-duty guards are ready to finish their shift. Nearby at St. James's Palace (a half-mile northwest), a second set of guards is also ready for a break. Meanwhile, fresh replacement guards gather for a review and inspection at Wellington

Barracks, 500 yards east of the palace (on Birdcage Walk).

At 11:15, the tired St. James's guards head out to the Mall, and then take a right turn for Buckingham Palace. At 11:30, the replacement troops, led by the band, also head for Buckingham Palace. Meanwhile, a fourth group—the Horse Guard—passes by along the Mall on their way back to Hyde Park Corner from their own changing-of-the-guard ceremony on Whitehall (which just took place at Horse Guards Parade at 11:00, or 10:00 on Sun).

At 11:45, the tired and fresh guards converge on Buckingham Palace in a perfect storm of Red Coat pageantry. Everyone parades around, the guard changes (passing the regimental flag, or "color") with much shouting, the band plays a happy little concert, and then they march out. At noon, two bands escort two detachments of guards away: the tired guards to Wellington Barracks and the fresh guards to St. James's Palace. As the fresh guards set up at St. James's Palace and the tired ones dress down at the barracks, the tourists disperse.

Cost and Hours: Free, daily May-July at 11:30, every other day Aug-April, no ceremony in very wet weather; exact schedule subject to change—call 020/7766-7300 for the day's plan, or check www.changing-the-guard.com or www.royalcollection.org.uk (click "Visit," then "Changing the Guard"); Buckingham Palace, Tube: Victoria, St. James's Park, or Green Park. Or hop into a big black taxi and say, "Buck House, please."

Sightseeing Strategies: Most tourists just show up and get lost in the crowds, but those who know the drill will enjoy the event more. The action takes place in stages over the course of an hour, at several different locations. The main event is in the fore-court right in front of Buckingham Palace (between Buckingham Palace and the fence) from 11:30 to 12:00. To see it close up, you'll need to get here no later than 10:30 to get a place right next to the fence.

But there's plenty of pageantry elsewhere. Get out your map and strategize. You could see the guards mobilizing at Wellington Barracks or St. James's Palace (11:00-11:15). Or watch them parade with bands down The Mall and Spur Road (11:15-11:30). After the ceremony at Buckingham Palace is over (and many tourists have gotten bored and gone home), the parades march back along those same streets (12:10).

Pick one event and find a good, unobstructed place from which to view it. The key is to get either right up front along the road or fence, or find some raised elevation to stand or sit on—a balustrade or a curb—so you can see over people's heads.

For the best overall view, stake out the high ground on the circular Victoria Memorial (come before 11:00 to get a place). From the memorial, you have good views of the palace as well

SIGHTS

as the arriving and departing parades along The Mall and Spur Road. The actual changing of the guard in front of the palace is a nonevent. It is interesting, however, to see nearly every tourist in London gathered in one place at the same time.

If you arrive too late to get a good spot, or you just don't feel like jostling for a view, stroll down to St. James's Palace and wait near the corner for a great photo-op. At about 12:15, the parade marches up The Mall to the palace and performs a smaller changing ceremony—with almost no crowds. Afterward, stroll through nearby St. James's Park.

North London

▲▲▲**British Museum**—Simply put, this is the greatest chronicle of civilization...anywhere. A visit here is like taking a long hike through *Encyclopedia Britannica* National Park. While the vast British Museum wraps around its Great Court (the huge entrance hall), the most popular sections of the museum fill the ground floor: Egyptian, Assyrian, and ancient Greek, with the famous Elgin Marbles from the Parthenon in Athens. The museum's stately

Reading Room—famous as the place where Karl Marx hung out while formulating his ideas on communism and writing *Das Kapital*—sometimes hosts special exhibits.

Cost and Hours: Free but a £4, $5, or €5 donation requested; temporary exhibits usually extra; daily 10:00-17:30, Fri until 20:30 (selected galleries only), least crowded weekday late afternoons; Great Russell Street, Tube: Tottenham Court Road, general info tel. 020/7323-8299, ticket desk tel. 020/7323-8181, collection questions tel. 020/7323-8838, www.britishmuseum.org.

○ See the British Museum Tour chapter.

▲▲▲**British Library**—Here, in just two rooms, called "The Treasures of the British Library," are the literary treasures of Western civilization, from early Bibles, to the Magna Carta, to Shakespeare's *Hamlet*, to Lewis Carroll's *Alice's Adventures in Wonderland*. You'll see the Lindisfarne Gospels transcribed on an illuminated manuscript, as well as Beatles lyrics scrawled on the back of a greeting card. The British Empire built its greatest monuments out of paper; it's through literature that England made her most lasting and significant contribution to civilization and the arts.

Cost and Hours: Free but £2 suggested donation, admission

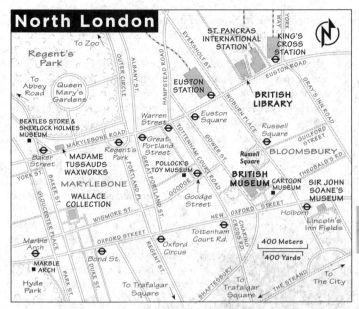

North London

To Zoo
Regent's Park
ST. PANCRAS INTERNATIONAL STATION
KING'S CROSS STATION
YORK WAY
EVERSHOLT ST.
ALBANY ST.
OUTER CIRCLE
HAMPSTEAD ROAD
EUSTON STATION
EUSTON ROAD
GRAY'S INN ROAD
To Abbey Road
Queen Mary's Gardens
WOBURN PLACE
BRITISH LIBRARY
Warren Street
Euston Square
Russell Square
GUILFORD STREET
BEATLES STORE & SHERLOCK HOLMES MUSEUM
MARYLEBONE ROAD
Great Portland Street
GOWER ST.
TOTTENHAM COURT ROAD
Russell Square
BLOOMSBURY
THEOBALD'S RD.
Baker Street
Regent's Park
MADAME TUSSAUDS WAXWORKS
POLLOCK'S TOY MUSEUM
GREAT PORTLAND ST.
PORTLAND PL.
BRITISH MUSEUM
CARTOON MUSEUM
SIR JOHN SOANE'S MUSEUM
YORK ST.
MARYLEBONE
GOODGE ST.
Goodge Street
WALLACE COLLECTION
WIGMORE ST.
NEW OXFORD STREET
Holborn
Lincoln's Inn Fields
GLOUCESTER PLACE
BAKER ST.
Marble Arch
OXFORD STREET
Bond St.
REGENT ST.
Tottenham Court Rd.
Oxford Circus
CHARING CROSS RD.
400 Meters
400 Yards
MARBLE ARCH
PARK ST.
DUKE ST.
SHAFTESBURY
To Trafalgar Square
To Trafalgar Square
THE STRAND
To The City
Hyde Park

SIGHTS

charged for some (optional) temporary exhibits, Mon-Fri 9:30-18:00, Tue until 20:00, Sat 9:30-17:00, Sun 11:00-17:00, 96 Euston Road, Tube: King's Cross St. Pancras or Euston, tel. 019/3754-6060 or 020/7412-7676, www.bl.uk.

○ See the British Library Tour chapter.

▲**Wallace Collection**—Sir Richard Wallace's fine collection of 17th-century Dutch Masters, 18th-century French Rococo, medi-

eval armor, and assorted aristocratic fancies fills the sumptuously furnished Hertford House on Manchester Square. From the rough and intimate Dutch lifescapes of Jan Steen to the pink-cheeked Rococo fantasies of François Boucher, a wander through this little-visited mansion

makes you nostalgic for the days of the empire. While this collection would be a big deal in a mid-sized city, it's small potatoes here in London...but enjoyable nevertheless.

Cost and Hours: Free, daily 10:00-17:00, £4 audioguide, free guided tours or lectures almost daily—call to confirm times, just north of Oxford Street on Manchester Square, Tube: Bond Street. Tel. 020/7563-9500, www.wallacecollection.org.

Touring the Museum: The manageable collection is displayed on three floors. As you enter the ground floor, on the right you'll find sumptuously furnished old drawing rooms, and to the left (through the gift shop) are the collections of Oriental and European armor. Then head up the red-carpeted grand staircase to the upper floor, devoted mostly to artwork.

In the Oval Drawing Room, look for the small but symbolism-packed Rococo masterpiece *The Swing* (1767), by Jean-Honoré Fragonard. The woman is being pulled on the swing by her husband. He's on the right, hidden in shadows, literally "in the dark"—unaware that his wife is having an affair with the man hiding in the bushes on the left. The rascal holds his arm erect as he peeps up this swinging lady's skirt and watches her shoe fly off, symbolizing sexual abandon.

Look for *The Laughing Cavalier* (1624) by Frans Hals (usually in the Great Gallery, which is under renovation in 2012—ask at the door for its current location). With his hat perched at a jaunty angle, the man smirks enigmatically with unhappy eyes...more of a polite chuckle or a bemused snort. As you view the canvas from multiple angles, notice his eyes following you.

Then head back down to the main floor and go out the door behind the staircase, into the building's gorgeous, glassed-in atrium, filled with light and an inviting café. The exhibit continues downstairs from the atrium, with a small collection of sculpture, porcelain, furniture, and other objects.

▲**Madame Tussauds Waxworks**—This waxtravaganza is gimmicky and expensive, but dang good...a hit with the kind of travelers who skip the British Museum. The original Madame Tussaud

did wax casts of heads lopped off during the French Revolution (such as Marie-Antoinette's). She took her show on the road and ended up in London in 1835. These days, they've dumped anything really historical (except for what they claim is the blade that beheaded Marie-Antoinette) because "there's no money in it and we're a business." Now it's all about squeezing Tom Cruise's bum, gambling with George Clooney, and partying with Beyoncé, Britney, and Brangelina. These wax dummies are eerily realistic. The gallery, which sprawls through several rooms of a huge building, is one giant photo-op—the whole point is jockeying for position to snap the best picture of your travel buddy with a famous "person." It's crowded and chaotic, as everyone clamors to press the wax with their heroes, while dodging tourist trinket kiosks and photographers standing by to overcharge you for a print. Count how many times you say "excuse me" after bumping into a wax figure.

Cost: £29, 10 percent discount and no waiting in line if you buy tickets on their website (also consider combo-deal with London Eye, sold cheaper online), £22.50 if purchased at TI, cheaper for kids. From 17:00 to closing, it's £14 if you buy in advance online. Children under 5 always free.

Hours: Mid-July-Aug and school holidays daily 9:00-21:00, Sept-mid-July Mon-Fri 9:30-19:30, Sat-Sun 9:00-20:00, last entry two hours before closing; Marylebone Road, Tube: Baker Street, toll tel. 0871-894-3000, www.madametussauds.com.

Crowd-Beating Tips: This popular attraction can be swamped with people. To avoid the hassle, buy your tickets and reserve an entry time in advance, either online (10 percent discount) or by phone (same price as box office). If you wait to buy tickets at the attraction, you'll discover that the ticket-buying line twists endlessly once inside the door (believe the posted signs warning you how long the wait will be—an hour or more is not unusual at busy times). If you buy your tickets at the door, try to arrive after 15:00.

Touring the Sight: First you'll join the paparazzi on the red carpet with A-list stars, from Johnny Depp to Will Smith to J-Lo. Then you'll head through several themed sections, featuring Hollywood stars new and old (Harrison Ford, John Wayne, Jim Carrey, Marilyn Monroe); sports heroes (Muhammad Ali, Tiger Woods, and some unfamiliar-to-Americans cricket players and footballers); the royal family (pose with the Queen...or settle for Camilla); scientists (Darwin, Einstein, Hawking); artists (Van Gogh, Picasso); writers (Shakespeare, Dickens); and musicians (Beatles, Michael Jackson).

The collection of world leaders includes everyone from the Pope to past PMs (Tony Blair) to the Dalai Lama. If camera flashes are any indication, Barack Obama wins the popularity contest. (Britain's previous prime minister, the unpopular Gordon Brown, was the first British PM in 150 years not to be immortalized in wax. His successor, David Cameron, got the wax treatment within a few weeks of his 2010

SIGHTS

London for Early Birds and Night Owls

Most sightseeing in London is restricted to the hours between 10:00 and 18:00. Here are a few exceptions:

Sights Open Early

Every day, several sights open at 9:45 or earlier.

Westminster Cathedral: Daily at 7:00.

St. Paul's Cathedral: Mon-Sat at 8:30.

Shakespeare's Globe: Daily at 9:00.

Madame Tussauds Waxworks: Daily mid-July-Aug at 9:00, Sept-mid-July Mon-Fri at 9:30, Sat-Sun at 9:00.

Tower of London: Tue-Sat at 9:00.

Churchill War Rooms: Daily at 9:30.

Kew Gardens: Daily at 9:30.

Westminster Abbey: Mon-Sat at 9:30.

British Library: Mon-Sat at 9:30.

Buckingham Palace: Aug-Sept daily at 9:45.

Sights Open Late

Every night in London, at least one sight is open late (in addition to the London Eye and Madame Tussauds). Here's the scoop from Monday through Sunday:

London Eye: Last ascent July-Aug daily at 21:30, April-June at 21:00, Sept-March at 20:00.

Madame Tussauds: Mid-July-Aug daily until 21:00; Sept-mid-July Mon-Fri until 19:30, Sat-Sun until 20:00.

Clink Prison Museum: July-Sept daily until 21:00, Oct-June Sat-Sun until 19:30.

Houses of Parliament (when in session, roughly Oct-July): Mon-Tue until 22:30.

British Library: Tue until 20:00.

Sir John Soane's Museum: First Tue of month from 18:00 to 21:00.

British Museum (some galleries): Fri until 20:30.

National Portrait Gallery: Thu-Fri until 21:00.

Vinopolis: Thu-Sat until 22:00.

National Gallery: Fri until 21:00.

Victoria and Albert Museum: Fri until 22:00 (selected galleries).

Tate Modern: Fri-Sat until 22:00.

Tate Britain: First Fri of the month until 22:00.

election.) In one sinister corner, Adolf Hitler, Saddam Hussein, and Fidel Castro conspire.

Downstairs is a hokey haunted-house exhibit called "Scream!", where you'll walk through a dark hallway while actors jump out and grab at you (a lame mini-version of the overrated London Dungeon, run by the same company). A small exhibit explains the history of Madame Tussaud and her waxy army, along with the process for casting a person in wax. Then you'll board a Disney-type people-mover and cruise through a kid-pleasing "Spirit of London" time trip, with a fun, once-over-lightly history of this city. The grand finale is the Marvel Super Heroes section, where you can pose with Spider-Man, the Hulk, and other favorites before heading into an auditorium for a nine-minute "4-D" show—a 3-D movie heightened by wind, "back ticklers," and other special effects.

▲**Sir John Soane's Museum**—Architects and fans of eclectic knickknacks love this quirky place, as do fans of interior decor

and lovers of Back Door sights. Tour this furnished home on a bird-chirping square and see 19th-century chairs, lamps, and carpets, wood-paneled nooks and crannies, and stained-glass skylights. (Note that some sections may be closed for restoration in 2012, but the main part of the house will be open.) The townhouse is cluttered with Soane's (and his wife's) collection of ancient relics, curios, and famous paintings, including Hogarth's series on *The Rake's Progress* (read the fun plot) and several excellent Canalettos. In 1833, just before his death, Soane established his house as a museum, stipulating that it be kept as nearly as possible in the state he left it. If he visited today, he'd be entirely satisfied. You'll leave wishing you'd known the man.

Cost and Hours: Free but donations much appreciated, Tue-Sat 10:00-17:00, open and candlelit the first Tue of the month 18:00-21:00, closed Sun-Mon, last entry 30 minutes before closing, long entry lines on Sat and first Tue, good £1 brochure, £5 guided tour Sat at 11:00, free, downloadable audio tours on their website, 13 Lincoln's Inn Fields, quarter-mile southeast of British Museum, Tube: Holborn, tel. 020/7405-2107, www.soane.org.

Cartoon Museum—This humble but interesting museum is located in the shadow of the British Museum. While its three rooms are filled with British cartoons unknown to most Americans, the satire of famous bigwigs and politicians—including Napoleon, Margaret Thatcher, the Queen, and Tony Blair—shows the power of parody to deliver social commentary. Upstairs, you'll see pages spanning from *Tarzan* to *Tank Girl,* and *Andy Capp* to the British *Dennis the Menace*—interesting only to comic-book diehards.

Cost and Hours: £5.50, Tue-Sat 10:30-17:30, Sun 12:00-17:30, closed Mon, 35 Little Russell Street—go one block south of the British Museum on Museum Street and turn right, Tube: Tottenham Court Road, tel. 020/7580-8155, www.cartoon museum.org.

Pollock's Toy Museum—This rickety old house, with glass cases filled with toys and games lining its walls and halls, is a time-warp experience that brings back childhood memories to people who grew up without batteries or computer chips. Though the museum is small, you could spend a lot of time here, squinting at the fascinating toys and dolls that entertained the children of 19th- and early 20th-century England. The included information is great. The story of Theodore Roosevelt refusing to shoot a bear cub while on a hunting trip was celebrated in 1902 cartoons, resulting in a new, huggable toy: the Teddy Bear. It was popular for good reason: It could be manufactured during World War I without rationed products; it coincided with the new belief that soft toys were good for a child's development; it was an acceptable "doll for boys"; and it was *the* toy children kept long after they'd grown up.

Cost and Hours: £5, kids-£2, generally Mon-Sat 10:00-17:00, closed Sun, last entry 30 minutes before closing, 1 Scala Street, Tube: Goodge Street, tel. 020/7636-3452, www.pollockstoy museum.com. A fun, retro toy shop is attached.

Beatles Sights—Central London is surprisingly devoid of sights associated with the famous '60s rock band. To see much of anything, consider taking a guided walk (see page 42).

For a photo op, go to **Abbey Road** and walk the famous crosswalk pictured on the *Abbey Road* album cover (Tube: St. John's Wood, get information and buy Beatles memorabilia at the small kiosk in the station). From the Tube station, it's a five-minute walk west down Grove End Road to the intersection with Abbey Road. The Abbey Road recording studio is the low-key, white building to the right of Abbey House (it's still a working studio, so you can't go inside). Ponder the graffiti on the low wall outside, and...imagine. To re-create the famous cover photo, shoot the crosswalk from the roundabout as you face north up Abbey Road. Shoes are optional.

Nearby is **Paul McCartney's current home** (7 Cavendish

Avenue): Continue down Grove End Road, turn left on Circus Road, and then right on Cavendish. Please be discreet.

The **Beatles Store** is at 231 Baker Street (Tube: Baker Street). It's small—some Beatles-logo T-shirts, mugs, pins, and old vinyl like you might have in your closet—and has nothing of historic value (open eight days a week, 10:00-18:30, tel. 020/7935-4464, www.beatlesstorelondon.co.uk; another rock memorabilia store is across the street).

Sherlock Holmes Museum—A few doors down from the Beatles Store, this meticulous re-creation of the (fictional) apartment of the (fictional) detective sits at the (real) address of 221b Baker Street. Fans will like it. Others might enjoy the Victorian-era furniture, clothes, pipes, paintings, and chamber pots, which give a glimpse at daily life from the time.

SIGHTS

Cost and Hours: £6, daily 9:30-18:00, last entry 30 minutes before closing, large gift shop for Holmes connoisseurs, Tube: Baker Street, tel. 020/7935-8866, www.sherlock-holmes.co.uk.

The City

When Londoners say "The City," they mean the one-square-mile business center in East London that 2,000 years ago was Roman Londinium. The outline of the Roman city walls can still be seen in the arc of roads from Blackfriars Bridge to Tower Bridge. Within The City are 23 churches designed by Sir Christopher Wren, mostly just ornamentation around St. Paul's Cathedral. Today, while home to only 7,000 residents, The City thrives with nearly 300,000 office workers coming and going daily. It's a fascinating district to wander on weekdays, but since almost nobody actually lives there, it's dull in the evenings and on Saturday and Sunday.

✪ See The City Walk chapter.

St. Paul's Cathedral and Nearby

▲▲▲**St. Paul's Cathedral**—Wren's most famous church is the great St. Paul's, its elaborate interior capped by a 365-foot dome. Since World War II, St. Paul's has been Britain's symbol of resistance. Despite 57 nights of bombing, the Nazis failed to destroy the cathedral, thanks to the St. Paul's volunteer fire watchmen, who stayed on the dome. Today you can climb the dome for a great city view. The crypt (included with admission) is a world of historic bones and memorials, including Admiral Nelson's tomb

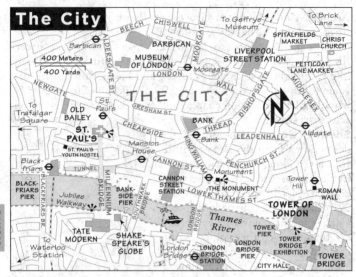

and interesting cathedral models.

Cost and Hours: £14.50, includes church entry and dome climb, Mon-Sat 8:30-16:30, last entry for sightseeing 16:00 (dome opens at 9:30, last entry at 16:15), closed Sun except for worship, Tube: St. Paul's, recorded info tel. 020/7236-4128, reception tel. 020/7246-8350, www.stpauls.co.uk.

Music: The evensong services are free, but nonpaying visitors are not allowed to linger afterward (see page 422 for details).

○ See the St. Paul's Tour chapter.

▲**Old Bailey**—To view the British legal system in action—lawyers in little blonde wigs speaking legalese with a British accent—spend a few minutes in the visitors' gallery at the Old Bailey, called the "Central Criminal Court." Don't enter under the dome; continue down the block about halfway to the modern part of the building—the entry is at Warwick Passage.

Cost and Hours: Free, generally Mon-Fri 9:45-13:00 & 14:00-16:30 depending on caseload, closed Sat-Sun, reduced hours in Aug; no kids under 14; no bags, mobile phones, cameras, iPods, or food, but small purses OK; Eddie, at Bailey's Café across the street at #27, stores bags for £2; 2 blocks northwest of St. Paul's on Old Bailey Street, follow signs to public entrance, Tube: St. Paul's, tel. 020/7248-3277.

▲**Museum of London**—This museum tells the fascinating story of London, taking you on a walk from its pre-Roman beginnings to the present. It features London's distinguished citizens through history—from Neanderthals, to Romans, to Elizabethans, to Victorians, to Mods, to today. The museum's displays are chronological, spacious, and informative without being overwhelming. Scale models and costumes help you visualize everyday life in the city at different periods. There are enough whiz-bang multimedia displays (including the Plague and the Great Fire) to spice up otherwise humdrum artifacts. This regular stop for the local school kids gives the best overview of London history in town.

Cost and Hours: Free, daily 10:00-18:00, galleries shut down 30 minutes before closing, see the day's events board for special talks and tours, on London Wall at Aldersgate Street, Tube: Barbican or St. Paul's plus a five-minute walk, tel. 020/7814-5660, www.museumoflondon.org.uk.

Touring the Museum: The first part of the tour zips quickly through a half-million years, when Britain morphed from peninsula to island, Neanderthals speared mammoths, and Stone Age humans huddled in crude huts on the South Bank of the Thames.

In 54 B.C., Julius Caesar invaded, and the Romans built "Londinium" on the North Bank. The settlement quickly became the hub of Britain and a river-trade town, complete with arenas, forums, baths, a bridge across the Thames, and a **city wall.** That wall—arcing from the present Tower of London to St. Paul's—defined the city's boundaries for the next 1,500 years. The Museum of London sits on the northwest perimeter of the city wall—look out the windows to see a crumbling remnant along the street, now called "London Wall."

When Rome could no longer defend the city (A.D. 410), it fell to the Saxons (becoming "Lundenburg") and, later, the Normans (in 1066), who built the Tower of London. Medieval London was devastated by the Black Death plague of 1348. As the city recovered and grew even bigger, it became clear to wannabe kings that

whoever controlled London controlled Britain.

When Queen Elizabeth I brought peace to the land, London thrived as a capital of theaters (the Globe and Rose), arts, and ideas. Then, just when things were going so well, the Great Fire of 1666 destroyed the city, leaving London a blank slate.

Next head downstairs to stroll through a multimedia "pleasure garden" and take a **"Victorian walk"** through a re-creation of a

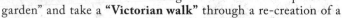

Harry Potter's London

Harry Potter's story is set in a magical Britain, and all of the places mentioned in the books, except London, are fictional, but you can visit many real film locations. Many of the locations are closed to visitors, though, or are an un-magical disappointment in person, unless you're a huge fan. For those diehards, here's a sampling.

Spoiler Warning: Information in this sidebar will ruin surprises for the three of you who haven't yet read or seen any of the Harry Potter *books or movies.*

Harry's story begins in suburban London, in the fictional town of Little Whinging. In the first film, *Sorcerer's Stone* (2001), the gentle giant Hagrid touches down on his flying motorcycle at #4 Privet Drive. There, baby Harry—who was orphaned by the murder of his wizard parents—is left on the doorstep to be raised by an anti-magic aunt and uncle. The scene was shot in the town of **Bracknell** (pop. 50,000, 10 miles west of Heathrow) on a street of generic brick rowhouses called Picket Close. Later, 10-year-old Harry first realizes his wizard powers when talking with a boa constrictor, filmed at the **London Zoo's Reptile House** in Regent's Park (Tube: Great Portland Street). Harry soon gets invited to Hogwarts School of Witchcraft and Wizardry, where he'll learn the magical skills he'll need to eventually confront his parents' murderer, Lord Voldemort.

Big Ben and **Parliament,** along the Thames, welcome Harry to the modern city inhabited by Muggles (non-magic folk). London bustles along oblivious to the parallel universe of wizards. Hagrid takes Harry shopping for school supplies. They enter the glass-roofed **Leadenhall Market** (Tube: Bank) and approach the **storefront** at 42 Bull's Head Passage—the entrance to The Leaky Cauldron pub (which, in the books, is placed among the bookshops of Charing Cross Road). The pub's back wall parts, opening onto the magical Diagon Alley (filmed at Leavesden Film Studios, 20 miles north of London near Watford), where Harry shops for wands, cauldrons, and wizard textbooks. He pays for them with gold Galleons from goblin-run Gringotts Wizarding Bank, filmed in the marble-floored and chandeliered Exhibition Hall of **Australia House** (Tube: Temple), home of the Australian Embassy.

Harry catches the train to Hogwarts at **King's Cross Station.**

London street, experiencing what it was like to live in the world's greatest city. The impressive costume section helps humanize all the history.

Two world wars and the car changed 20th-century London into a concrete jungle. But it remained a cultural capital of elegance (see an Art Deco elevator from Selfridge's) and a global trendsetter (Beatles-era memorabilia).

(The fanciful exterior shot in the *Chamber of Secrets* (2002) is actually nearby **St. Pancras International Station.**) Inside the glass-roofed train station, on a **pedestrian sky bridge** over the tracks, Hagrid gives Harry a train ticket.  Harry heads to platform 9¾, where he and his new buddy Ron magically push their luggage carts through a brick pillar between the platforms, emerging onto a hidden platform. (For a fun photo-op, find the *Platform 9¾* sign and the luggage cart that looks like it's disappearing into the wall. They're a little tricky to locate: Walk past Platform 8 toward the pedestrian bridge and turn left at the arch—or ask a staff member for help.)

A red steam train—the Hogwarts Express—speeds the boys through the (Scottish) countryside to Hogwarts, where Harry will spend the next seven years. Harry is taught how to wave his wand by tiny Professor Flitwick in a wood-paneled classroom filmed at **Harrow School** in Harrow on the Hill, eight miles northwest of London (Tube: Harrow on the Hill).

In the *Prisoner of Azkaban* (2004), Harry careens through London's lamp-lit streets on a purple three-decker bus that dumps him at The Leaky Cauldron. In this film, the pub's exterior was shot on rough-looking Stoney Street at the southeast edge of **Borough Market,** by The Market Porter pub, with trains rumbling overhead (Tube: London Bridge). In *the Half-Blood Prince* (2009), the **Millennium Bridge** collapses into the Thames.

For the *Order of the Phoenix* (2007) and the first *Deathly Hallows* (2010), the real government offices of **Whitehall** serve as exteriors for the Ministry of Magic. Other London scenes, such as the Ministry's interiors and Sirius Black's residence at Twelve Grimmauld Place, are fictional and, like Diagon Alley, only exist at Leavesden.

Finally, cinema buffs can visit **Leicester Square** (Tube: Leicester Square), where Daniel Radcliffe and other stars have strolled past paparazzi and down red carpets to the Odeon Theater to attend the movies' premieres.

SIGHTS

In the last room, you'll see the museum's prized possession—an example of the opulence of rebuilt Georgian London. The **Lord Mayor's Coach,** a golden carriage pulled by six white horses, looks as if it pranced right out of the pages of *Cinderella*. At the back of this room, a touching memorial to the victims of the terrorist bombings of July 7, 2005, weaves contemporary London into the tapestry of history.

The Monument—Wren's 202-foot-tall tribute to London's Great Fire was recently restored. Climb the 331 steps inside the column for a view of The City that is still monumental (£3, daily 9:30-17:30, last entry at 17:00, junction of Monument Street and Fish Street Hill, Tube: Monument, tel. 020/7626-2717, www.the monument.info).

Tower of London and Nearby

▲▲▲**Tower of London**—The Tower has served as a castle in wartime, a king's residence in peacetime, and, most notoriously, as the prison and execution site of rebels. You can see the crown jewels, take a witty Beefeater tour, and ponder the executioner's block that dispensed with troublesome heirs to the throne and a couple of Henry VIII's wives.

Note that lines can be long for this sight; see page 262 for tips on getting in quickly. After your visit, consider taking the boat to Greenwich from here (see cruise info on page 47).

Cost and Hours: £18, family-£50; March-Oct Tue-Sat 9:00-17:30, Sun-Mon 10:00-17:30; Nov-Feb Tue-Sat 9:00-16:30, Sun-Mon 10:00-16:30; last entry 30 minutes before closing; Tube: Tower Hill, switchboard toll tel. 0844-482-7777, www.hrp.org.uk.

✪ See the Tower of London Tour chapter.

Tower Bridge—The iconic Tower Bridge (often mistakenly called London Bridge) has been recently painted and restored. The hydraulically powered drawbridge was built in 1894 to accommodate the growing East End. While fully modern, its design was a retro Neo-Gothic look.

You can tour the bridge at the **Tower Bridge Exhibition,** with a history display and a peek at the Victorian engine room that lifts the span. It's overpriced at £8, though the city views from the walkways are spectacular (daily 10:00-18:00 in summer, 9:30-17:30 in winter, last entry 30 minutes before closing, enter at the northwest tower, Tube: Tower Hill, tel. 020/7403-3761, www .towerbridge.org.uk).

The bridge is most interesting when the drawbridge lifts to let ships pass, as it does a thousand times a year, but it's best viewed from outside the museum. For the bridge-lifting schedule, check the website or call (see above for contact info).

Nearby: The best remaining bit of London's **Roman Wall** is just north of the Tower (at the Tower Hill Tube station). The chic **St. Katharine Dock,** just east of Tower Bridge, has private yachts, mod shops, and the classic Dickens Inn, fun for a drink or pub lunch. Across the bridge is the South Bank, with the upscale Butlers Wharf area, City Hall, museums, and the Jubilee Walkway. Or you can head north to the Liverpool Street Tube station, and follow my **East End Walk** (described next).

East London

▲East End Walk: Markets, Banglatown, and Jack the Ripper

The East End—a formerly industrial area just beyond the Liverpool Street train and Tube stations—has turned into one of London's trendy spots. Take a walk around the Spitalfields Market neighborhood to see the colorful mix of bustling markets, late-night dance clubs, the Bangladeshi ghetto, and tenements of Jack the Ripper's London, all in the shadow of glittering new skyscrapers. This walk—which takes about an hour without stopping to slurp a curry or shop the markets—is best on Sunday afternoons, when the Spitalfields, Petticoat Lane, and Brick Lane markets thrive (for more on these markets, see page 412).

Ride the Tube to Liverpool Street. Exit the busy station by heading up the glassy escalator and emerging onto the street called Bishopsgate. Cross the street and turn left—you'll see Dirty Dick's Pub on the right (this is where we will end our walk). Continue another block ahead and turn right on Brushfield Street; from here you can see the steeple of Christ Church (described later).

Two blocks ahead on the left is the **Spitalfields Market** (pronounced "spittle-fields"). Explore this lively, inviting, modern-feeling market hall, boasting a combination of colorful restaurants, shops, and—on many days—market stalls selling upscale crafts. While the eateries here are tempting, consider waiting for the Bangladeshi curry joints coming up soon on this walk.

Exit the market at the far end through the "Spitfire" gate. Across busy Commercial Street (at the intersection with Brushfield/Fournier Street) is the rugged, working-class **Ten Bells Pub.** Established in 1753, it was the hangout of one of Jack the Ripper's victims. Across the street from the pub is **Christ Church,** with its impressive 225-foot steeple. Many Ripper witnesses could help pinpoint the time of the crimes by remembering the church bells' chimes.

Continuing alongside the church, head east one long block on **Fournier**

Street, which is lined with classic brick tenement houses. Despite the word's negative connotation, a "tenement" is simply an urban apartment building. In the distance, you'll see the big sign for BanglaCity supermarket. Head there.

When you reach Brick Lane, you're suddenly immersed in

"Banglatown," London's highest concentration of Bangladeshi residents. Immediately on your left is the neighborhood mosque, **Jamme Masjid**—also called the "Great London Mosque." This building has a history as dynamic as London's: It was built as a Huguenot chapel and then used as a Methodist chapel and a Jewish synagogue before being converted into a mosque in 1976. Notice the new, slender, metallic minaret.

Wander north (to the left) up **Brick Lane,** window-shopping for lunch or dinner. Here in "the curry capital of Europe," neon signs advertise cheap meals, and out front, pitchmen jockey for your business. The slightest hesitation on your part will result in an offer of a 20 percent discount. This is a great place to sample "Ruby Murray" (Cockney rhyming slang for "curry"—see page 244).

After two blocks is the former **Truman Brewery,** which now houses a Sunday market, trendy shops, and Café 1001 (good coffee). A half-block farther north, you'll find the old brewery smokestack. This is the epicenter of a youthful, trendy scene with several lively pub/café/nightclubs (including Vibe Bar and 93 Feet East).

Now turn around and backtrack south on Brick Lane, passing the mosque at Fournier Street (where you entered this street); continue another block and turn right (west) on **Fashion Street.** Though it twists around and changes names several times, this road leads straight back to the Liverpool Street Station. Along the way (on the left just after you start down Fashion Street), you'll pass the Islamic-looking **Abraham Davis' Moorish Market,** now housing high-tech businesses.

Where Fashion Street becomes White's Row, detour a block south (left) on Toynbee Street, then right on **Brune Street.** Here you'll see more Industrial Age tenements, the "Soup Kitchen for the Jewish Poor" (see engraved doorway on right, at #9), and a peek-a-boo view of the modern, bullet-shaped Swiss Re building. Notice the contrast between the new office tower at the end of this street and the old tenements. Modernization is changing this neighborhood. At the end of the block, turn right onto Tenter Ground, the street where weavers once dried cloth "on tenterhooks," giving us the phrase (meaning "uneasy").

London's Best Views

Though London is a height-challenged city, you can get lofty perspectives on it from several high-flying places. For some viewpoints, you need to pay admission (cheapest at The Monument) and at the bars or restaurants, you'll likely get a drink; the only truly free spot is the last (and farthest away), Primrose Hill.

London Eye: Ride the giant Ferris wheel for London's best, most expensive, and dizzying views. See page 87.

St. Paul's Dome: You'll earn a striking, unobstructed view by climbing hundreds of steps to the cramped balcony of the church's cupola. See the St. Paul's Tour chapter.

Tate Modern: Take in a classic vista across the Thames from the museum's seventh-floor restaurant and bar. See the Tate Modern Tour chapter.

The Monument: Though surrounded by modern buildings in the financial district, this 202-foot column memorializing the Great Fire of 1666 affords a nice view of The City. See page 82.

National Portrait Gallery: A mod top-floor restaurant peers over Trafalgar Square and the Westminster neighborhood. See the National Portrait Gallery Tour chapter.

Waterstone's Bookstore: Hip, low-key, top-floor café/bar has reasonable prices and sweeping views of the London Eye, Big Ben, and the Houses of Parliament (see page 28 for hours, 203 Piccadilly, Tube: Piccadilly Circus, tel. 020/7851-2433, www.5thview.co.uk).

OXO Tower: Perched high over the Thames River, the building's upscale restaurant/bar boasts views over London and St. Paul's, with al fresco dining in good weather (Barge House Street, Tube: Blackfriars, tel. 020/7803-3888, www.harveynichols.com/restaurants/oxo-tower-london).

London Hilton, Park Lane: You'll spot Buckingham Palace, Hyde Park, and the London Eye from Galvin at Windows, a 28th-floor restaurant/bar in an otherwise nondescript hotel (22 Park Lane, Tube: Hyde Park Corner, tel. 020/7208-4021, www.galvinatwindows.com).

Primrose Hill: For dramatic 360-degree city views, head to the huge grassy expanse at the summit of Primrose Hill, just north of Regent's Park (off Prince Albert Road, Tube: Chalk Farm or Camden Town, www.royalparks.gov.uk/The-Regents-Park).

Tenter Ground leads you back to White's Row (at the parking garage). Turn left onto White's Row, which soon becomes narrow **Artillery Lane,** then **Artillery Passage,** lined with tiny eateries—giving you an idea of how densely packed this neighborhood was when it was filled with grimy-faced 19th-century factory workers.

At the intersection with Sandy's Row are the **bollards** (black-white-red stakes in the pavement), alerting you that you're officially leaving the East End and entering the City of London.

Continue west one block on Widegate Street to busy Middlesex Street. Just to the left, along Middlesex Street, is the start of **Petticoat Lane Market.** One of the oldest markets in Britain, this one has existed here in some form for more than 400 years. Ahead at the corner is **Dirty Dick's Pub** (although the name has a history, the pub itself doesn't).

Heading right on Middlesex Street, you'll return to the **Liverpool Street** train and Tube stations. At 8:45 on July 7, 2005, a Tube train had just pulled out of Liverpool Street Station when it was rocked by a terrorist bomb—the first of four to hit London that day. But the next day, Londoners were back on the Tube.

Northeast of The City

▲**Geffrye Museum**—This low-key but well-organized museum—housed in an 18th-century almshouse—is located north of Liverpool Street Station in the trendy Shoreditch area. Walk past 11 English living rooms, furnished and decorated in styles from 1600 to 2000, then descend the circular stairs to see changing exhibits on home decor. In summer, explore the fragrant herb garden.

Cost and Hours: Free, Tue-Sat 10:00-17:00, Sun 12:00-17:00, closed Mon, garden open April-Oct, 136 Kingsland Road, tel. 020/7739-9893, www.geffrye-museum.org.uk.

Getting There: Take the Tube to Liverpool Street, then it's a 10-minute ride north on bus #149 or #242. Or take the East London line on the Overground to the Hoxton stop, which is right next to the museum (Tube tickets and Oyster cards also valid on Overground).

▲▲The Docklands

Once the primary harbor for the Port of London, the Docklands has been transformed into a vibrant business center, with ultra-tall skyscrapers, subterranean supermalls, trendy pubs, and peaceful parks with pedestrian bridges looping over canals. While not full of the touristy sights that many are seeking in London, the Docklands offers a refreshing look at the British version of a 21st-century city. It's best at the end of the workday, when it's lively with office workers. It's ideal on the way back from Greenwich, since both line up on the same train tracks. From the Docklands, it's also a relatively straightforward detour to see the Olympics 2012 sights (see page 104).

✪ See The Docklands Walk chapter (which contains a more thorough description of the museum mentioned below).

▲**Museum of London Docklands**—Illuminating the gritty and fascinating history of this site, this museum traces the story of what was London's primary harbor (free, daily 10:00-18:00, last entry 30 minutes before closing, West India Quay, Tube: West India Quay or Canary Wharf, tel. 020/7001-9844, www.museum indocklands.org.uk).

SIGHTS

The South Bank

▲**Jubilee Walkway**—The South Bank is a thriving arts and cultural center tied together by this riverside path, a popular, pub-crawling pedestrian promenade called the Jubilee Walkway. Stretching from Tower Bridge past Westminster Bridge, it offers

grand views of the Houses of Parliament and St. Paul's. On a sunny day, this is the place to see Londoners out strolling. The Walkway hugs the river except just east of London Bridge, where it cuts inland for a couple of blocks. Plans are under way to expand the path into a 60-mile "Greenway" circling the city, scheduled to open in 2012 for the Olympic Games and Elizabeth's 60th year as Queen (www.jubileewalkway.org.uk).

The following sights are all described here and connected by the ✪ Bankside Walk: Shakespeare's Globe, Tate Modern, Millennium Bridge, Old Operating Theatre Museum, Vinopolis, Southwark Cathedral, the *Golden Hinde* Replica, and the Clink Prison Museum.

▲▲**London Eye**—This giant Ferris wheel, towering above London opposite Big Ben, is the world's highest observational wheel and London's answer to the Eiffel Tower. While the experience is memorable, London doesn't have much of a skyline, and the price is borderline outrageous. But whether you ride or not, the wheel is a sight to behold.

Designed like a giant bicycle wheel, it's a pan-European

The South Bank

COURTAULD GALLERY
SOMERSET HOUSE
THE STRAND
Temple
THE TEMPLE
VICTORIA EMBANKMENT
Blackfriars
BLACKFRIARS PIER
BLACKFRIARS BRIDGE

Thames River

Jubilee Walkway

OXO TOWER

Trafalgar Square
CHARING CROSS
Charing Cross
CHARING CROSS STATION
Embank-ment
EMBANKMENT PIER
FESTIVAL PIER
WATERLOO BRIDGE
BFI SOUTHBANK
UPPER GROUND
STAMFORD ST.
SOUTHWARK ST.

SOUTH BANK

WHITEHALL
VICTORIA EMBANKMENT
GOLDEN JUBILEE BRIDGE

LONDON EYE
Jubilee Gardens
Waterloo
Southwark
BLACKFRIARS RD.

WATERLOO PIER
West-minster
WEST-MINSTER PIER
FORMER COUNTY HALL
WATERLOO STATION
BELVEDERE RD.
YORK RD.
WATERLOO RD.

WESTMINSTER

PARL ST.

BIG BEN & PARLIAMENT
ST. THOMAS' HOSPITAL
WESTMINSTER BRIDGE RD.
Lambeth North
THE BOROUGH
BOROUGH RD.

WEST-MINSTER ABBEY
MILLBANK
SOUTH PALACE RD.
Arch-Bishop's Park
LAMBETH RD.
IMPERIAL WAR MUSEUM
Harmsworth Park
ST. GEORGE'S RD.
LONDON RD.
Elephant & Castle

SIGHTS

undertaking: British steel and Dutch engineering, with Czech, German, French, and Italian mechanical parts. It's also very "green,"

running extremely efficiently and virtually silently. Twenty-five people ride in each of its 32 air-conditioned capsules for the 30-minute rotation (you go around only once). Each capsule has a bench, but most people stand. From the top of this 443-foot-high wheel— the highest public viewpoint in the city—even Big Ben looks small. Built to celebrate the new millennium, the Eye's original five-year lease has been extended, and it's become a permanent fixture on the London skyline.

After buying your ticket inside, you'll be aggressively ushered into *The London Eye 4-D Experience,* a brief (four-minute) and engaging show combining a 3-D movie with wind and water effects. It basically feels like a bombastic ad for the attraction you already bought a ticket for, and in some ways is more exciting than

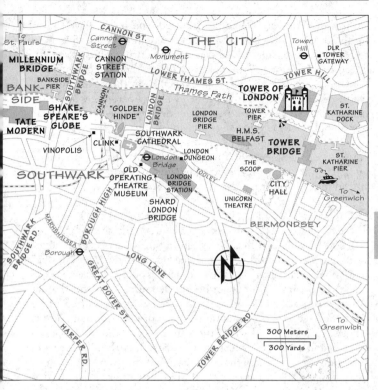

riding the Eye itself. You can politely skip the show if you just want to get on the wheel, and you have the option of coming back later to see the movie.

Cost: £19, or pay roughly twice as much for a combo-ticket with Madame Tussauds Waxworks (sold cheaper online), other packages are available. Buy tickets at the box office (in the corner of the County Hall building nearest the Eye), in advance by calling 0870-500-0600, or save 10 percent by booking online at www.londoneye.com.

Hours: Daily July-Aug 10:00-21:30, April-June 10:00-21:00, Sept-March 10:00-20:00, these are last-ascent times, closed Dec 25 and a few days in Jan for annual maintenance, Tube: Waterloo or Westminster. Thames boats come and go from Waterloo Pier at the foot of the wheel.

Crowd-Beating Tips: The London Eye is busiest between 11:00 and 17:00, especially on weekends year-round and every day in July and August. When it's crowded, you might have to wait up to 30 minutes to buy your ticket, then another 30-45 minutes to board your capsule. If you plan to visit during a busy time, call ahead or go online to pre-book your ticket, then punch your confirmation code into the automated machine in the ticket office (no wait to get the ticket, but you'll still wait to board the wheel). You can pay an extra £10 for a Fast Track ticket that lets you jump the queue, but the time you save is probably not worth the expense.

By the Eye: The area next to the London Eye has developed a cotton-candy ambience of kitschy, kid-friendly attractions. There's an aquarium, game arcade, and "Moviuem" dedicated to movies filmed in London, from *Harry Potter* to *Star Wars*.

Southwark

These sights are in Southwark (SUTH-uck), the core of the tourist's South Bank. Southwark was for centuries the place Londoners would go to escape the rules and decency of the city and let their hair down. Bearbaiting, brothels, rollicking pubs, and theater—you name the dream, and it could be fulfilled just across the Thames. A run-down warehouse district through the 20th century, it's been gentrified with classy restaurants, office parks, pedestrian promenades, major sights (such as the Tate Modern and Shakespeare's Globe), and a colorful collection of lesser sights. The area is easy on foot and a scenic—though circuitous—way to connect the Tower of London with St. Paul's. You'll find more information on these sights in the ✪ Bankside Walk chapter.

▲▲**Imperial War Museum**—This impressive museum covers the wars of the last century—from World War I biplanes, to the rise of fascism, to Montgomery's Africa campaign tank, to the Cold War, the Cuban Missile Crisis, the Troubles in Northern Ireland, the wars in Iraq, and terrorism. Allow plenty of time, as this powerful museum—with lots of artifacts and video clips—can be engrossing. War wonks love the place, as do general history buffs who enjoy patiently reading displays. For the rest, there are enough multimedia exhibits and submarines for the kids to climb in to keep it interesting.

Cost and Hours: Free, daily 10:00-18:00, last entry 17:45, temporary exhibits extra, £4 audioguide, often guided tours on weekends—ask at info desk, Tube: Lambeth North, bus #12 or #159, tel. 020/7416-5000, www.iwm.org.uk.

Touring the Museum: The core of the **permanent collection,** located downstairs, takes you step-by-step through World Wars I and II. A special exhibit called "Monty: Master of the Battlefield" celebrates Field Marshal Bernard Montgomery. Then you move on to conflicts since 1945. Most of the displays are low-tech—glass cases hold dummies in uniforms, weapons, newspaper clippings, ordinary objects from daily life—but have excellent explanations and video clips. The Trench Experience lets you walk through a dark, chaotic, smelly WWI trench. The Blitz Experience film assaults the senses with the noise and intensity of a WWII air raid on London. Also, the cinema shows a rotating selection of films.

In the entry hall are the **large exhibits**—including Monty's tank, several field guns, and, dangling overhead, vintage planes.

Imagine the awesome power of the 50-foot V-2 rocket, the kind the Nazis rained down on London, which could arrive silently and destroy a city block. Its direct descendant is the Polaris missile, capable of traveling nearly 3,000 miles in 20 minutes and obliterating an entire city.

Two other sections are not to be missed: The **"Secret War"** peeks into the intrigues of espionage in World Wars I and II and in conflicts since. The section on the **Holocaust,** one of the best on the subject anywhere, tells the story with powerful videos, artifacts, and fine explanations. Rather than glorify war, the museum does its best to shine a light on the 100 million deaths of the 20th century. It shows everyday life for people back home and never neglects the powerful human side of one of humankind's most persistent traits.

The museum (which sits in an inviting park equipped with an equally inviting café) is housed in what was the Royal Bethlam Hospital. Also known as "the Bedlam asylum," the place was so wild that it gave the world a new word for chaos. Back in Victorian times, locals—without reality shows and YouTube—paid admission to visit the asylum on weekends for entertainment.

▲▲**Tate Modern**—Dedicated in the spring of 2000, the striking museum across the river from St. Paul's opened the new century with art from the previous one. Its powerhouse collection of Monet, Matisse, Dalí, Picasso, Warhol, and much more is displayed in a converted powerhouse. Of equal interest are the many temporary exhibits featuring

SIGHTS

Crossing the Thames on Foot

You can cross the Thames on any of the bridges that carry car traffic over the river, but London's two pedestrian bridges are more fun. The Millennium Bridge (see photo) connects the sedate St. Paul's Cathedral with the great Tate Modern. The Golden Jubilee Bridge, well-lit and with a sleek, futuristic look, links bustling Trafalgar Square on the North Bank with the London Eye and Waterloo Station on the South Bank.

more current, cutting-edge art. Each year, the main hall features a different monumental installation by a prominent artist.

Cost and Hours: Free, but £3 donation appreciated, fee for special exhibitions, daily 10:00-18:00, Fri-Sat until 22:00—good times to visit, last entry to temporary exhibitions 45 minutes before closing; cross the Millennium Bridge from St. Paul's; Tube: Southwark, London Bridge, or Mansion House plus a 10-15-minute walk; or connect by "Tate to Tate" boat from Tate Britain—see page 47; tel. 020/7887-8888, www.tate.org.uk.

○ See the Tate Modern Tour chapter.

▲**Millennium Bridge**—The pedestrian bridge links St. Paul's Cathedral and the Tate Modern across the Thames. This is London's first new bridge in a century. When it first opened, the $25 million bridge wiggled when people walked on it, so it promptly closed for an $8 million, 20-month stabilization; now it's stable and open again. Nicknamed the "blade of light" for its sleek minimalist design (370 yards long, four yards wide, stainless steel with teak planks), its clever aerodynamic handrails deflect wind over the heads of pedestrians.

▲▲**Shakespeare's Globe**—A replica of the original Globe Theatre has been built, half-timbered and thatched, as it was in Shakespeare's time. (This is the first thatched roof constructed in

London since they were outlawed after the Great Fire of 1666.) The Globe originally accommodated 2,200 seated and another 1,000 standing. Today, slightly smaller and leaving space for reasonable aisles, the theater holds 800

seated and 600 groundlings. Its promoters brag that the theater melds "the three A's"—actors, audience, and architecture—with each contributing to the play. The working theater hosts authentic performances of Shakespeare's plays with actors in period costumes, modern interpretations of his works, and some works by other playwrights. For details on attending a play, see page 418.

The complex has three parts: the theater itself, the box office, and a museum. The Globe Exhibition ticket includes both a tour of the theater and the museum.

Museum: First, you browse on your own through displays of Elizabethan-era costumes, music, script-printing, and special effects. There are early folios and objects that were dug up on site. A video and scale models help put Shakespearean theater within the context of the times. (The Globe opened one year after England mastered the seas by defeating the Spanish Armada. The debut play was Shakespeare's *Julius Caesar*.)

Theater: You must tour the theater at the time stamped on your ticket, but you can come back to the museum afterward; tick-

ets are good all day. The guide (usually an actor) leads you into the theater to see the stage and the various seating areas for the different classes of people. You take a seat and learn how the new Globe is similar to the old Globe (open-air performances, standing-room by the stage, no curtain) and how it's different (female actors today, lights for night performances, concrete floor). It's not a backstage tour—you don't see dressing rooms or costume shops or sit in on rehearsals, though you may see workers building sets for a new production. You mostly sit and listen. The guides are energetic, theatrical, and knowledgeable, bringing the Elizabethan period to life.

When matinee performances are going on, you can't tour the theater. But you can see the museum, then tour the nearby (and less interesting) Rose Theatre instead.

Cost and Hours: £11.50 includes museum and 40-minute tour, £9 when only the Rose Theatre is available for touring, tickets good all day; complex open daily 9:00-17:00; exhibition and tours: May-Sept—Globe tours offered mornings only with Rose Theatre tours in afternoon; Oct-April—Globe tours run all day, tours start every 15-30 minutes; on the South Bank directly across Thames over Southwark Bridge from St. Paul's, Tube: Mansion House or London Bridge plus a 10-minute walk; tel. 020/7902-1400 or 020/7902-1500, www.shakespeares-globe.org.

Eating: The Swan at the Globe café offers a sit-down restaurant (for lunch and dinner, reservations recommended, tel. 020/7928-9444), a drinks-and-plates bar, and a sandwich-and-coffee cart (daily 9:00-closing, depending on performance times).

Vinopolis: City of Wine—While it seems illogical to have a huge wine museum in beer-loving London, Vinopolis makes a good case. Built over a Roman wine store and filling the massive vaults of an old wine warehouse, the museum offers an excellent audioguide with a light yet earnest history of wine to accompany your sips of various mediocre reds and whites, ports, and champagnes. Allow some time, as the audioguide takes an hour and a half—and the sipping can slow things down pleasantly. This place is popular. Booking ahead for Friday and Saturday nights is a must.

Cost and Hours: Self-guided tour options range from £20 to £40—each includes about five wine tastes and an audioguide. Other options are available for guided tours. Some packages also include whiskey (the new wine), other spirits, or a meal. Open Thu-Fri 14:00-22:00, Sat 12:00-22:00, Sun 12:00-18:00, closed Mon-Wed, last entry 2.5 hours before closing, between Shakespeare's Globe and Southwark Cathedral at 1 Bank End, Tube: London Bridge, tel. 020/7940-3000, www.vinopolis.co.uk.

The Clink Prison Museum—Proudly the "original clink," this was, until 1780, where law-abiding citizens threw Southwark troublemakers. Today, it's a low-tech torture museum filling grotty old rooms with papier-mâché gore. Unfortunately, there's little that seriously deals with the fascinating problem of law and order in Southwark, where 18th-century Londoners went for a good time.

Cost and Hours: Overpriced at £6; July-Sept daily 10:00-21:00; Oct-June Mon-Fri 10:00-18:00, Sat-Sun until 19:30; 1 Clink Street, Tube: London Bridge, tel. 020/7403-0900, www.clink.co.uk.

Golden Hinde Replica—This is a full-size replica of the 16th-century warship in which Sir Francis Drake circumnavigated the globe from 1577 to 1580. Commanding this ship, Drake earned his reputation as history's most successful pirate. The original is long gone, but this boat has logged more than 100,000 miles, including a voyage around the world. While the ship is fun to see, its interior is not worth touring.

Cost and Hours: £6, daily 10:00-17:30, sometimes closed for private events, Tube: London Bridge, tel. 020/7403-0123, www.goldenhinde.com.

Southwark Cathedral—While made a cathedral only in 1905, it's been the neighborhood church since the 13th century, and comes with some interesting history. The enthusiastic docents give impromptu tours if you ask.

Cost and Hours: Free, but £4 suggested donation, daily 8:00-18:00, last entry 30 minutes before closing, £2.50 guidebook, no photos without permission, Tube: London Bridge. Tel. 020/7367-6700, http://cathedral.southwark.anglican.org.

Music: The cathedral hosts evensong services (Mon-Tue and Thu-Fri at 17:30, Sat at 16:00, Sun at 15:00, no service on Wed or alternate Mon).

▲**Old Operating Theatre Museum and Herb Garret**—Climb a tight and creaky wooden spiral staircase to a church attic where you'll find a garret used to dry medicinal herbs, a fascinating exhibit on Victorian surgery, cases of well-described 19th-century medical paraphernalia, and a special look at "anesthesia, the defeat of pain." Then you stumble upon Britain's oldest operating theater, where limbs were sawed off way back in 1821. The museum occasionally offers "demonstrations." While fun and interesting to some, they can be distressing to those who are squeamish or have a vivid imagination.

Cost and Hours: £6, cash only, daily 10:30-16:45, closed Dec 15-Jan 5, 9a St. Thomas Street, Tube: London Bridge, tel. 020/7188-2679, www.thegarret.org.uk.

HMS *Belfast*—"The last big-gun armored warship of World War II" clogs the Thames just upstream from the Tower Bridge. This huge vessel—now manned with wax sailors—thrills kids who always dreamed of sitting in a turret shooting off their imaginary guns. If you're into WWII warships, this is the ultimate. Otherwise, it's just lots of exercise with a nice view of the Tower Bridge.

Cost and Hours: £13.50, includes audioguide, daily March-Oct 10:00-18:00, Nov-Feb 10:00-17:00, last entry one hour before closing, Tube: London Bridge, tel. 020/7940-6300, http://hmsbelfast.iwm.org.uk.

City Hall—The glassy, egg-shaped building near the south end of Tower Bridge is London's City Hall, designed by Sir Norman Foster, the architect who worked on London's Millennium Bridge and Berlin's Reichstag. City Hall houses the office of London's mayor—the blonde, flamboyant, conservative former journalist and author Boris Johnson.

He consults here with the Assembly representatives of the city's 25 districts. An interior spiral ramp allows visitors to watch and hear the action below in the Assembly Chamber—ride the lift to the second floor (the highest visitors can go) and spiral down. On the lower ground floor is a large aerial photograph of London, an information desk, and a handy cafeteria. Next to City Hall is the outdoor amphitheater called The Scoop.

Cost and Hours: Free, open to visitors Mon-Thu 8:30-18:00, Fri 8:30-17:30, closed Sat-Sun; Tube: London Bridge station plus 10-minute walk, or Tower Hill station plus 15-minute walk; tel. 020/7983-4000, www.london.gov.uk.

West London

▲▲Tate Britain—One of Europe's great art houses, Tate Britain specializes in British painting from the 16th century through modern times. The museum has a good representation of William Blake's religious sketches, the Pre-Raphaelites' realistic art, and J. M. W. Turner's swirling works.

Cost and Hours: Free, but £3 donation requested, admission fee for (optional) temporary exhibits; daily 10:00-18:00, first Fri of the month until 22:00, last entry to special exhibitions at 17:15 (or 21:00 when open late); on the Thames River, south of Big Ben and north of Vauxhall Bridge, Tube: Pimlico, "Tate to Tate" boat goes directly to the museum from Tate Modern—see page 47; switchboard tel. 020/7887-8888, recorded info tel. 020/7887-8008, www.tate.org.uk.

✪ See the Tate Britain Tour chapter.

▲Apsley House (Wellington Museum)—Having beaten Napoleon at Waterloo, Arthur Wellesley, the First Duke of Wellington, was once the most famous man in Europe. He was given a huge fortune with which he purchased London's ultimate address, #1 London. His refurbished mansion offers a nice interior, a handful of world-class paintings, and a glimpse at the life of the great soldier and two-time prime minister. Those who know something about Wellington ahead of time will

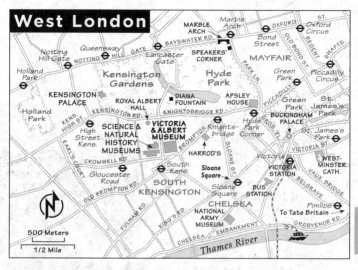

West London

MARBLE ARCH
Marble Arch
OXFORD ST.
Oxford Circus
ST.
Queensway
BAYSWATER RD.
Bond Street
OLD BOND ST.
REGENT ST.
SHAFTS.
Notting Hill Gate
NOTTING HILL GATE
Lancaster Gate
SPEAKERS' CORNER
PARK LN.
MAYFAIR
Kensington Gardens
Hyde Park
Green Park
Piccadilly Circus
Holland Park
KENSINGTON PALACE
DIANA FOUNTAIN
APSLEY HOUSE
PICCADILLY
Green Park
St. James's Park
Holland Park
ROYAL ALBERT HALL
KENSINGTON RD.
KNIGHTSBRIDGE RD.
Hyde Park Corner
BUCKINGHAM PALACE
KENS. HIGH ST.
SCIENCE & NATURAL HISTORY MUSEUMS
VICTORIA & ALBERT MUSEUM
Knights-bridge
BROMPTON RD.
GROS. PL.
St. James's Park
VICTORIA ST.
High Street Kens.
CROMWELL RD.
HARROD'S
SLOANE ST.
Victoria
VICTORIA STATION
WEST-MINSTER CATH.
Earl's Court
Gloucester Road
South Kens.
Sloane Square
BUS STATION
BELGRAVE
VAUX. BRIDGE
OLD BROMPTON RD.
SOUTH KENSINGTON
Sloane Square
Pimlico
FULHAM RD.
CHELSEA
To Tate Britain →
GROSVENOR RD.
N
KING'S RD.
NATIONAL ARMY MUSEUM
CHELSEA EMBANKMENT
500 Meters
1/2 Mile
Thames River

SIGHTS

appreciate the place much more than those who don't, as there's scarce biographical background. The place is well-described by the included audioguide, which has sound bites from the current Duke of Wellington (who still lives at Apsley).

An 11-foot-tall marble statue of Napoleon, clad only in a fig leaf, greets you. Napoleon commissioned the sculptor Canova to make it for him but didn't like it, and after Napoleon's defeat, it was eventually sold to Wellington as a war trophy. It's one of several images Wellington acquired of his former foe to have in his home. The two great men were polar opposites—Napoleon the daring general and champion of revolution, Wellington the play-it-safe strategist and conservative politician—but they're forever linked in history.

The core of the collection is a dozen first-floor rooms decorated with fancy wallpaper, chandeliers, a few pieces of furniture, and wall-to-wall paintings from Wellington's collection. You'll see fancy dinnerware and precious objects given to the Irish-born general by the crowned heads of Europe, who were eternally grateful to him for saving their necks from the guillotine. The highlight is the large ballroom, the Waterloo Gallery, decorated with Anthony van Dyck's *Charles I on Horseback* (over the main fireplace), Diego Velázquez's earthy *The Water-Seller of Seville* (to the left of Van Dyck), Jan Steen's playful *The Dissolute Household* (to the right), and a large portrait of Wellington by Francisco Goya (farther right).

Downstairs is a small gallery of Wellington memorabilia, including a pair of Wellington boots, which the duke popularized—Brits today still call rubber boots "wellies."

Cost and Hours: £6.30, free on June 18—Waterloo Day,

April-Oct Wed-Sun 11:00-17:00, Nov-March until 16:00, closed Mon-Tue, 20 yards from Hyde Park Corner Tube station, tel. 020/7499-5676, www.english-heritage.org.uk.

Nearby: Hyde Park's pleasant rose garden is picnic-friendly. **Wellington Arch,** which stands just across the street, is open to the public but not worth the £4 charge (elevator up, lousy views and boring exhibits).

▲Hyde Park and Speakers' Corner—London's "Central Park," originally Henry VIII's hunting grounds, has more than 600 acres of lush greenery, the huge man-made Serpentine Lake, the royal Kensington Palace and Orangery (described later), and the ornate Neo-Gothic Albert Memorial across from the Royal Albert Hall. The western half of the park is known as Kensington Gardens.

On Sundays, from just after noon until early evening, **Speakers' Corner** offers soapbox oratory at its best (northeast corner of the park, Tube: Marble Arch). Characters climb their stepladders, wave their flags, pound emphatically on their sandwich boards, and share what they are convinced is their wisdom. Regulars have resident hecklers who know their lines and are always ready with a verbal jab or barb. "The grass roots of democracy" is actually a holdover from when the gallows stood here and the criminal was allowed to say just

about anything he wanted to before he swung. I dare you to raise your voice and gather a crowd—it's easy to do.

The **Princess Diana Memorial Fountain** honors the "People's Princess," who once lived in nearby Kensington Palace. The low-key circular stream, great for cooling off your feet on a hot day, is in the south-central part of the park, near the Albert Memorial and Serpentine Gallery. (Don't be confused by signs to the Diana, Princess of Wales Memorial Playground, in the northwest corner of the park.)

▲▲▲Victoria and Albert Museum—The world's top collection of decorative arts (vases, stained glass, fine furniture, clothing, jewelry, carpets, and more) is a surprisingly interesting assortment of crafts from the West, as well as Asian and Islamic cultures. The British Galleries are grand, but there's much more to see, including Raphael's tapestry cartoons and a cast of Trajan's Column that depicts the emperor's conquests.

Cost and Hours: Free, but £5 donation requested, sometimes pricey fees for (optional) special exhibits, daily 10:00-17:45, some galleries open Fri until 22:00, free one-hour tours daily on the half-hour 10:30-15:30, on Cromwell Road in South Kensington, Tube: South Kensington, from the Tube station a long tunnel leads directly to museum, tel. 020/7942-2000, www.vam.ac.uk.

○ See the Victoria and Albert Museum Tour chapter.

▲▲**Natural History Museum**—Across the street from Victoria and Albert, this mammoth museum is housed in a giant and wonderful Victorian, Neo-Romanesque building. In the main hall,

above a big dinosaur skeleton and under a massive slice of sequoia tree, Charles Darwin sits as if upon a throne overseeing it all. Built in the 1870s specifically for the huge collection (50 million specimens), the building has two halves: the Life Galleries (creepy-crawlies, human biology, "our place in evolution," and awe-inspiring dinosaurs) and the Earth Galleries (meteors, volcanoes, earthquakes, and so on).

Exhibits are wonderfully explained, with lots of creative, interactive displays. Pop in, if only for the wild collection of dinosaurs and to hear English children exclaim, "Oh my goodness!" Get oriented by talking with one of the many "visit planners" (helpful guides scattered throughout the museum), review the "What's on Today" board for special events and tours, and note which sections are closed (rather than "renovating," they say "we are evolving"). While the dinosaur hall often has a long line, everything else is wide open. Don't miss the vault in the mineralogy section (top floor of the green zone), with rare and precious stones, including a meteorite from Mars and the Aurora Pyramid of Hope, displaying 296 diamonds showing their full range of natural colors.

Cost and Hours: Free, fees for special exhibits, daily 10:00-17:50, last entry at 17:30, occasional tours, long tunnel leads directly from South Kensington Tube station to museum, tel. 020/7942-5000, exhibit info and reservations tel. 020/7942-5011, www.nhm.ac.uk.

▲**Science Museum**—Next door to the Natural History Museum, this sprawling wonderland for curious minds is kid-perfect, with themes such as measuring time, exploring space, climate change, and the evolution of modern medicine. It offers hands-on fun, from moonwalks to deep-sea exploration, with trendy technology exhibits and a state-of-the-art IMAX theater (£10, kids-£8).

Cost and Hours: Free, daily 10:00-18:00, Exhibition Road, Tube: South Kensington, toll tel. 0870-870-4868, www.science museum.org.uk.

Kensington Palace—In 2012, this historic palace will reopen after a major renovation. A new permanent exhibit, "Victoria Revealed," will showcase the life and times of Britain's longest-ruling monarch. The palace was once the residence of King William and Queen Mary, who moved from Whitehall in central London in 1689 to the more pristine and peaceful village of Kensington (since engulfed by London). Sir Christopher Wren converted an existing house into the palace, which became the center of English court life until 1760, when the royal family moved into Buckingham Palace. Since then, lesser royals have bedded down in Kensington Palace. Princess Diana lived here from her 1981 marriage to Prince Charles until her death in 1997. Today it's home to three of Charles' cousins. If you visit before the renovations are finished, skip the temporary and cheesy "Enchanted Palace" theatrical show.

Cost and Hours: £12.50, discounts for booking online, daily 10:00-18:00, until 17:00 in winter, last entry one hour before closing, a 10-minute hike through Kensington Gardens from either Queensway or High Street Kensington Tube station, toll tel. 0870-751-5170 or 0844-482-7777, www.hrp.org.uk.

Nearby: Garden enthusiasts enjoy popping into the secluded Sunken Garden, 50 yards from the exit. Consider afternoon tea at the nearby Orangery (see page 398), built as a greenhouse for Queen Anne in 1704.

Victoria Station—From underneath this station's iron-and-glass canopy, trains depart for the south of England and Gatwick Airport. While Victoria Station is famous and a major Tube stop, few tourists actually take trains from here—most just come to take in the exciting bustle. It's a fun place to just be a "rock in a river" teeming with commuters and services. The station is surrounded by big red buses and taxis, travel agencies, and lousy eateries. It's next to the main intercity bus station (Victoria Coach Station) and the best inexpensive lodgings in town.

Westminster Cathedral—This cathedral, the largest Catholic church in England and just a block from Victoria Station, is strikingly Neo-Byzantine, but not very historic or important to visit. Opened in 1903, the church has an unfinished interior, with a spooky, blackened ceiling waiting for the mosaics that are supposed to be placed there. While it's definitely not Westminster

Abbey, half the tourists wandering around inside seem to think it is. Take the lift to the top of the 273-foot bell tower for a view of the glassy office blocks of Victoria Station.

Cost and Hours: Free entry, £5 for the lift, church—daily 7:00-19:00, tower—daily 9:30-17:00; 5-minute walk from Victoria Station, just off Victoria Street, Tube: Victoria, www.westminster cathedral.org.uk.

National Army Museum—This museum is not as awe-inspiring as the Imperial War Museum, but it's still fun, especially for kids who are into soldiers, armor, and guns. And while the Imperial War Museum is limited to wars of the 20th century, the National Army Museum tells the story of the British army from 1415 through the Bosnian conflict and Iraq, with lots of Redcoat lore and a good look at Waterloo. Kids enjoy trying on a Cromwellian helmet, seeing the skeleton of Napoleon's horse, and peering out from a World War I trench through a working periscope.

Cost and Hours: Free, daily 10:00-17:30, Royal Hospital Road, Chelsea, Tube: Sloane Square, tel. 020/7730-0717, www .national-army-museum.ac.uk.

Greater London

West of Central London

▲▲**Kew Gardens**—For a fine riverside park and a palatial green-house jungle to swing through, take the Tube or the boat to every

botanist's favorite escape, Kew Gardens. While to most visitors the Royal Botanic Gardens of Kew are simply a delightful opportunity to wander among 33,000 different types of plants, to the hardworking organization that runs the gardens, the gardens are a way to promote the understanding and preservation of the botanical diversity of our planet. The Kew Tube station drops you in an herbal little business community, a two-block walk from Victoria Gate (the main garden entrance). Pick up a map brochure and check at the gate for a monthly listing of best blooms.

Garden-lovers could spend days exploring Kew's 300 acres. For a quick visit, spend a fragrant hour wandering through three buildings: the Palm House, a humid Victorian world of iron, glass, and tropical plants that was built in 1844; a Waterlily House that Monet would swim for (see photo, next page); and the Princess of Wales Conservatory, a modern greenhouse with many different climate zones growing countless cacti, bug-munching

carnivorous plants, and more. With extra time, check out the Xstrata Treetop Walkway, a 200-yard-long scenic steel walkway that puts you high in the canopy 60 feet above the ground. Young kids will love the Climbers and Creepers indoor/outdoor playground and little zip line, as well as a slow and easy ride on the hop-on, hop-off Kew Explorer tram (£4 for narrated 40-minute ride, departs on the hour from 11:00 from near Victoria Gate).

Cost: £14, discounted to £11.50 45 minutes before greenhouses close, kids under 17 free, £5 for Kew Palace only.

Hours: April-Aug Mon-Fri 9:30-18:30, Sat-Sun 9:30-19:30, closes earlier Sept-March, last entry to gardens 30 minutes before closing, galleries and conservatories close at 17:30 in high season—earlier off-season, free one-hour walking tours daily at 11:00 and 14:00, Tube: Kew Gardens, boats run April-Oct between Kew Gardens and Westminster Pier—see page 48, switchboard tel. 020/8332-5000, recorded info tel. 020/8332-5655, www.kew.org.

Eating: For a sun-dappled lunch or snack, walk 10 minutes from the Palm House to the Orangery Cafeteria (£8-12 lunches, daily 10:00-17:30, until 16:30 in winter, closes early for events, tel. 0844-482-7777 www.hrp.org.uk).

▲**Hampton Court Palace**—Fifteen miles up the Thames from downtown, the 500-year-old palace of Henry VIII is worth ▲▲

for palace aficionados. Actually, it was originally the palace of his minister, Cardinal Wolsey. When Wolsey, a clever man, realized Henry VIII was experiencing a little palace envy, he gave the mansion to his king. The Tudor palace was also home to Elizabeth I and Charles I. Sections were updated by Christopher Wren for William and Mary. The stately palace stands overlooking the Thames and includes some impressive Tudor rooms, including a Great Hall with a magnificent hammer-beam ceiling. The industrial-strength Tudor kitchen was capable of keeping 600 schmoozing courtiers thoroughly—if not well—fed. The sculpted garden features a rare Tudor tennis court and a popular maze.

The palace tries hard to please, but it doesn't quite sparkle. From the information center in the main courtyard, you can pick up audioguides for self-guided tours of various wings of the palace (free but slow, aimed mostly at school-aged children). For more in-depth information, strike up a conversation with the costumed characters or docents posted in each room. The Tudor portions of the castle, including the rooms dedicated to the young Henry, are most interesting; the Georgian rooms are pretty dull. The maze in the nearby garden is a curiosity some find fun (maze free with palace ticket, otherwise £3.85).

Cost and Hours: £16, or £43.50 for families, online discounts, daily April-Oct 10:00-18:00, Nov-March 10:00-16:30, last entry one hour before closing, café, toll tel. 0844-482-7777, www.hrp .org.uk.

Getting There: The train (2/hour, 35 minutes, Oyster cards OK) from London's Waterloo Station drops you across the river from the palace (just walk across the bridge). Consider arriving at or departing from the palace by boat (connections with London's Westminster Pier, see page 48); it's a relaxing and scenic three- to four-hour cruise past two locks and a fun new/old riverside mix.

Kew Gardens/Hampton Court Blitz: Because these two sights are in the same general direction (about £20 for a taxi between the two), you can visit both in one day. Here's a game plan: Start your morning at Hampton Court, tour the palace and garden, and have a Tudor-style lunch in the atmospheric dining hall. After lunch, take bus #R68 from Hampton Court Station to Richmond (40 minutes), then transfer to bus #65, which will drop you off at the Kew Gardens gate (5 minutes). After touring the gardens, have tea in the Orangery, then Tube or boat back to London.

North of Central London

Royal Air Force Museum London—A hit with aviation enthusiasts, this huge aerodrome and airfield contain planes from World War II's Battle of Britain up through the Gulf War. You can climb inside some of the planes, try your luck in a cockpit, and fly with the Red Arrows in a flight simulator.

Cost and Hours: Free, daily 10:00-18:00, last entry 30 minutes before closing, café, shop, parking-£2.50, Grahame Park Way, 30-minute ride from central London, Tube: Colindale—top of Northern Line Edgware branch, tel. 020/8205-2266, www.raf museum.org.uk.

Highgate Cemetery—Located in the tea-cozy-cute village of Highgate, north of the city, this Victorian cemetery represents a fascinating, offbeat piece of London history. Built as a private cemetery, this was the fashionable place to bury the wealthy dead in the late 1800s. It has themed mausoleums, professional mourners, and several high-profile residents in its East Cemetery, including Karl Marx, George Eliot, and Douglas Adams. The tomb of "Godfather of Punk" Malcolm McLaren (former manager of the Sex Pistols) is often covered with rotten veggies.

Cost and Hours: East Cemetery—£3, Mon-Fri 10:00-17:00, Sat-Sun 11:00-17:00, closes one hour earlier in winter, last entry 30 minutes before closing; older, creepier West Cemetery—viewable by £7 guided tour only, Mon-Fri at 14:00, Sat-Sun hourly 11:00-16:00; Tube: Archway or bus #C2, tel. 020/8340-1834, www.high gate-cemetery.org.

2012 London Olympic Park, in Stratford

From July 27 to August 12, 2012, all eyes will be on London as it hosts athletes from 205 nations in the 30th Olympiad. Though events will take place throughout the city, festivities will center around Olympic Park, filling the Lea Valley, about seven miles northeast of central London. Lea Valley used to be the site of derelict factories, mountains of discarded tires, and Europe's biggest refrigerator dump. But now, this area glistens with gardens, greenery, and state-of-the-art construction.

London is the first city to host the modern games three times—first in 1908, then in 1948 (the first post-World-War-II Olympics, known as the "Austerity Games"). The city won the 2012 bid for its grand and green vision, including a promise to permanently improve the least desirable part of the city. The site's connection to the broader world will be extraordinary: During the games, it will take less than three hours to go from Paris to Olympic Park (ride the Eurostar to St. Pancras International Station in downtown London, and connect via a seven-minute bullet train to Stratford International Station, covered by your Eurostar ticket).

These will be the greenest games ever. There will be no public parking at the site—event tickets will include an all-day London Tube pass. About 90 percent of demolition material has been recycled. More than half of the deliveries will be by train or boat rather than by truck. Half a million trees have been planted, and 1.4 million tons of dirt have been cleansed of arsenic, lead, and other toxic chemicals—a reminder of this site's dirty industrial past. Locals whine about the cost—as locals have whined about big public building projects, I imagine, since the days great cities built great Gothic churches. But the $14 billion project is a stimulus plan, with 90 percent local investment and employment.

About 75 percent of the construction is "legacy building,"

2012 Olympics Venues

Although most of the Olympic Games will be held in London's East End, there will be sports and activities all over London and Britain. These are the main venues:

Olympic Park is the heart of the games. Here you'll find the 80,000-seat Olympic Stadium (for opening and closing ceremonies), the Olympic Village, where the athletes will stay, and a giant climbable sculpture called the Orbit. A new 12,000-seat basketball arena will be completely dismantled when the games are over. The Aquatics Center, with its swooping wave-like roofline, may become the architectural "face" of the games.

Central London will be the site of—really?—beach volleyball. Tons of sand will be spread across the parking lot behind #10 Downing Street and Horse Guards, creating an urban beach ringed with bleachers (see page 116 of the Westminster Walk). Triathletes will compete in **Hyde Park,** swimming in Serpentine Lake, then biking and running around the park. **Greenwich Park** (near the *Cutty Sark;* see page 449) will hold equestrian events, while the nearby **O2** arena (formerly the "Millennium Dome") hosts gymnastics and more basketball.

Farther afield, you'll find tennis at **Wimbledon** (of course), volleyball at **Earl's Court,** and football/soccer at **Wembley Stadium.** The Olympic torch will wend its way through various communities. And anywhere you go, you can't avoid the universally ridiculed Olympic mascots—those alien/Gumby/Cyclops-like creatures named Wenlock and Mandeville.

Tickets are being sold in phases through www.cosport .com (for residents of the US and Canada).

SIGHTS

giving these structures a practical life in a reinvigorated community after the games. Many of the buildings will be converted to housing, with half of these units designated for low-income people. Bridges leading to the site, built double-wide for huge crowds, will be scaled back. The commercial zone, Stratford City, will become the biggest shopping center in Europe. Between the bullet trains, Tube, regional rail services, and DLR, residents of post-Olympics Stratford will enjoy the best public transit in town, with multiple connections to central London. (Don't confuse it with Stratford-upon-Avon, the famous Warwickshire town where Shakespeare was born. That's two hours northwest of London.)

Suddenly, Stratford is a place with a future (and poor little grandmas who've called it home are now worth something to their relatives and developers...and chocolate and flowers appear on Sundays). It seems fitting that this most multiethnic part of London will host these famously multiethnic games.

Viewing the Olympic Park Site
Olympic Park is huge—bigger than Hyde Park/Kensington Gardens. It's also quite beautiful, laced with canals and tributaries of the Lea River. During the games, it will be closed except to ticket-holders. Following the games, the area will become a public park. But for now, the site is viewable from a spot called the View Tube, which you can visit on your own or via a guided tour.

On Your Own
You can see all the major landmarks—Olympic Stadium, the Orbit tower, and Aquatics Center—from the View Tube, a covered shelter with a lookout tower, café, WC, and maps (free, daily 9:00-17:00, café mobile 07834-275-687, www.theviewtube.co.uk). It sits at the park's southern perimeter, perched on a 500-yard-long berm called the Greenway. While you're there, you may see some of the legion of Nepali Gurkhas employed for security.

The View from the View Tube: Anchoring the complex is the big Olympic Stadium, which will host the opening and closing ceremonies. It's built with modular parts, so after the games, it may be partly dismantled and refitted to become a more intimate venue.

From the stadium, pan to the right to see the following:

On the far horizon, find the swooped wooden roofline of the bicycle track, or velodrome. To the right of that is the white ruffled exterior of the basketball arena. Immediately to the right of that are the Olympic Village apartments. After the 16,000 athletes move out at the end of the games, contractors will swoop in to install kitchens, turning these dorms into public housing.

In the near distance, the red, 350-foot viewing tower called the Orbit has been compared to a vertical roller coaster and a hubble bubble (a Middle-Eastern water pipe).

Pan to the right to see the Aquatics Center, with its roofline meant to suggest a dolphin. Behind it are Stratford Station and the east entrance to the park.

From the View Tube, you can stroll along the Greenway's 500-yard-long sidewalk, providing other viewpoints. At the far end of the stadium is the media center where 20,000 journalists (more than one per athlete) will be stationed.

Getting There: From central London, it's about a 25-minute ride on the Tube and/or DLR to one of the stations that ring Olympic Park.

To the View Tube Viewpoint: The closest stop is the Pudding Mill Lane DLR Station, which will only be open before the games start, and will close during the games. It sits on the southern edge of the park, only 200 yards from the viewpoint. From central London, ride the Tube to any station that allows you to transfer to the DLR to Pudding Mill Lane. Good change points are Bow Road/Bow Church, Stratford, and Canary Wharf.

To Tube Stations a Pleasant Stroll South of Olympic Park: The West Ham Tube Station is three-quarters of a mile south of Olympic Park. Though it's not close to the park, it's on the Tube line, so you can get there directly from, say, Victoria Station, on the District Line. Once at West Ham Station, you can walk along a bike path to the park. The Bromley-by-Bow Tube Station is also south of the park and also nearly a mile away; from the station, stroll the paths along the River Lea to the park.

To the East Entrance of Olympic Park: There are two similarly named stations, located 400 yards apart. The Stratford Station is both a Tube and DLR stop. The Stratford International Station serves the DLR and the new high-speed train. During the games, the Javelin bullet train will dart to Stratford International direct from St. Pancras International Station in seven minutes.

On a Tour

Blue Badge guides lead 1.5-hour guided walks of the area. It's a pleasant riverside stroll culminating at the View Tube. You'll learn about the Olympics, but you won't see any more of the park itself than you would on your own, plus it takes longer (£9, pay guide directly in cash, online reservations recommended but not required, daily at 11:00, www.toursof2012sites.com). Meet at the Bromley-by-Bow Tube Station (District or Hammersmith Line).

WESTMINSTER WALK

From Big Ben to Trafalgar Square

Just about every visitor to London strolls along historic Whitehall from Big Ben to Trafalgar Square. This quick nine-stop walk gives meaning to that touristy ramble. Under London's modern traffic and big-city bustle lie 2,000 fascinating years of history. You'll get a whirlwind tour as well as a practical orientation to London.

Orientation

Length of This Walk: Allow one hour for a leisurely walk, but figure on two or three hours if you drop by the Churchill War Rooms and the Banqueting House. (Other nearby sights include the Houses of Parliament, Westminster Abbey, National Gallery, National Portrait Gallery, and St. Martin-in-the-Fields.)

Getting There: Take the Tube to Westminster, then take the Westminster Pier exit. The walk ends at Trafalgar Square (nearest Tube stop: Charing Cross).

Churchill War Rooms: £16 (includes small donation), daily 9:30-18:00, last entry one hour before closing.

Supreme Court: Free, Mon-Fri 9:30-16:30, closed Sat-Sun, £2 audioguide, £5 guided tours on Fri, requires security check, tel. 020/7960-1900, www.supremecourt.gov.uk.

Banqueting House: £4.80, includes audioguide, Mon-Sat 10:00-17:00, closed Sun, last entry at 16:30, may close for government functions, aristocratic WC, immediately across Whitehall from the Horse Guards.

Audio Tour: You can download a free audio version of this tour for your mobile device via www.ricksteves.com/audioeurope, iTunes, or the Rick Steves Audio Europe smartphone app.

Services: You'll find several WCs along this walk: at Westminster

Pier (50p), at the intersection of Bridge Street and Whitehall (underground, 50p), and at Trafalgar Square (free WCs located in the square, at the National Gallery, and downstairs at St. Martin-in-the-Fields).

Eateries: See page 385 for a list of recommended eateries near Trafalgar Square, and page 126 for recommendations near Westminster Abbey.

The Walk Begins

• *Start halfway across Westminster Bridge.*

❶ On Westminster Bridge
Views of Big Ben and Parliament
• *First look upstream, toward the Parliament.*

Ding dong ding dong. Dong ding ding dong. Yes, indeed, you are in London. **Big Ben** is actually "not the clock, not the tower,

but the bell that tolls the hour." However, since the 13-ton bell is not visible, everyone just calls the whole works Big Ben. Named for a fat bureaucrat, Ben is scarcely older than my great-grandmother, but it has quickly become the city's symbol. The tower is 315 feet high, and the clock faces are 23 feet across. The 13-foot-long minute hand sweeps the length of your body every five minutes. For fun, call home from a pay phone near Big Ben at about three minutes before the hour to let your loved one hear the bell ring. You'll find four red phone booths lining the north side of Parliament Square (along Great George Street).

Big Ben hangs out in the north tower of a long building (the Houses of Parliament) that stretches along the Thames. Britain is ruled from this building, which for five centuries was the home of kings and queens. Then, as democracy was foisted on tyrants, a parliament of nobles was allowed to meet in some of the rooms. Soon, commoners were elected to office, the neighborhood was shot, and the royalty moved to Buckingham Palace. While most of the current building looks medieval with its prickly flamboyant spires, it was actually built after a fire gutted the old Westminster Palace in 1834.

Today, the House of Commons, which is more powerful than the Queen and prime minister combined, meets in one end of the building. The rubber-stamp House of Lords grumbles and snoozes in the other end of this 1,000-room complex, and provides a

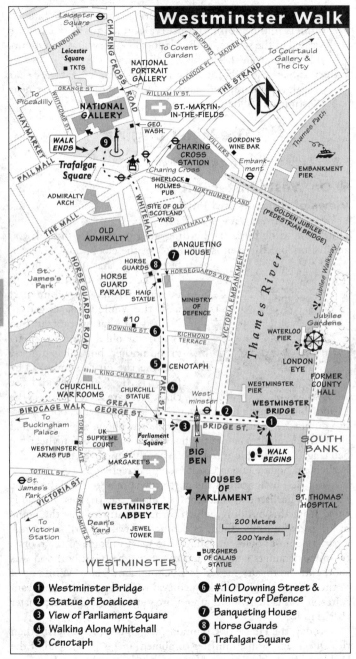

Westminster Walk

Leicester Square

Leicester Square
TKTS

CRANBOURN

CHARING CROSS ROAD

To Covent Garden

BEDFORD

CHANDOS PL.

MAIDEN LN.

THE STRAND

To Courtauld Gallery & The City

NATIONAL PORTRAIT GALLERY

ORANGE ST.

WILLIAM IV ST.

To Piccadilly

NATIONAL GALLERY

WHITCOMB ST.

HAYMARKET

ST.-MARTIN-IN-THE-FIELDS

GEO. WASH.

WALK ENDS

Trafalgar Square

PALL MALL

CHARING CROSS STATION

Charing Cross

VILLIERS

GORDON'S WINE BAR

Embankment

EMBANKMENT PIER

Thames Path

ADMIRALTY ARCH

SHERLOCK HOLMES PUB

NORTHUMBERLAND

SITE OF OLD SCOTLAND YARD

THE MALL

OLD ADMIRALTY

WHITEHALL

WHITEHALL PL.

BANQUETING HOUSE

GOLDEN JUBILEE (PEDESTRIAN BRIDGE)

St. James's Park

HORSE GUARDS

HORSEGUARDS AVE.

HORSE GUARD PARADE

HAIG STATUE

MINISTRY OF DEFENCE

Thames River

Jubilee Walkway

Jubilee Gardens

HORSE GUARDS ROAD

#10 DOWNING ST.

RICHMOND TERRACE

VICTORIA EMBANKMENT

WATERLOO PIER

CHURCHILL WAR ROOMS

CHURCHILL STATUE

KING CHARLES ST.

CENOTAPH

PARL. ST.

LONDON EYE

FORMER COUNTY HALL

BIRDCAGE WALK

GREAT GEORGE ST.

West-minster

WESTMINSTER PIER

WESTMINSTER BRIDGE

To Buckingham Palace

STOREY'S GATE

UK SUPREME COURT

Parliament Square

BRIDGE ST.

SOUTH BANK

WESTMINSTER ARMS PUB

ST. MARGARET'S

BIG BEN

WALK BEGINS

TOTHILL ST.

St. James's Park

VICTORIA ST.

GREAT SMITH ST.

WESTMINSTER ABBEY

HOUSES OF PARLIAMENT

ST. THOMAS' HOSPITAL

To Victoria Station

Dean's Yard

JEWEL TOWER

200 Meters

200 Yards

BURGHERS OF CALAIS STATUE

WESTMINSTER

1 Westminster Bridge
2 Statue of Boadicea
3 View of Parliament Square
4 Walking Along Whitehall
5 Cenotaph
6 #10 Downing Street & Ministry of Defence
7 Banqueting House
8 Horse Guards
9 Trafalgar Square

tempering effect on extreme governmental changes. The two houses are very much separate: Notice the riverside tea terraces with the color-coded awnings—royal red for lords, common green for commoners. Alluding to the traditional leanings of the two chambers, locals say, "Green for go...red for stop." If a flag is flying from the Victoria Tower, at the far south end of the building, Parliament is in session. The modern Portcullis Building (with the tube-like chimneys), across Bridge Street from Big Ben, holds offices for the 650 members of the House of Commons. They commute to the Houses of Parliament by way of an underground passage.

• *Now look north (downstream).*

Views of the London Eye, The City, and the Thames

Built in 2000 to celebrate the millennium, the London Eye—originally nicknamed "the London Eyesore," but now generally

appreciated by locals—stands 443 feet tall. It slowly spins 32 capsules, each filled with a maximum of 25 visitors, up to London's best viewpoint (with up to 25 miles' visibility on a rare clear day). Call the Eye a "Ferris wheel," and Londoners will set you straight, saying, "Technically, it's an *observation* wheel." Aside from Big Ben, Parliament, St. Paul's Cathedral (not visible from here), and the wheel itself, London's skyline is not overwhelming; it's a city that wows from within.

Next to the wheel sprawls the huge former County Hall building, now a hotel and tourist complex. The London Eye marks the start of the Jubilee Walkway, a pleasant one-hour riverside promenade along the South Bank of the Thames, through London's vibrant, gentrified new arts-and-cultural zone. Along the way, you have views across the river of St. Paul's stately dome and the financial district, called The City.

London's history is tied to the **Thames,** the 210-mile river linking the interior of England with the North Sea. The city got its start in Roman times as a trade center along this watery highway. As recently as a century ago, large ships made their way upstream to the city center to unload. Today, the major port is 25 miles downstream, and tourist cruise boats ply the waters.

Look for the **boat piers** on either bank of the Thames. Several tour-boat companies offer regular departures from Westminster Pier (on the left) or Waterloo Pier (on the right, near the London Eye). This is an efficient, scenic way to get from here

to the Tower of London or Greenwich (downstream) or Kew Gardens (upstream). For details, see page 47.

Lining the river, beneath the lampposts, are little green copper **lions' heads** with rings for tying up boats. Before the construction of the Thames Barrier in 1982 (the world's largest movable flood barrier, downstream near Greenwich), high tides from the nearby North Sea made floods a recurring London problem. The police kept an eye on these lions: "When the lions drink, the city's at risk."

Until 1750, only London Bridge crossed the Thames. Then a bridge was built here. Early in the morning of September 3, 1802, William Wordsworth stood where you're standing and described what he saw:

> *This City now doth, like a garment, wear*
> *The beauty of the morning; silent, bare,*
> *Ships, towers, domes, theatres, and temples lie*
> *Open unto the fields, and to the sky;*
> *All bright and glittering in the smokeless air.*

• *Near Westminster Pier is a big statue of a lady on a chariot (nicknamed "the first woman driver"...no reins).*

❷ Statue of Boadicea, Queen of the Iceni

Riding in her two-horse chariot, daughters by her side, this Celtic Xena leads her people against Roman invaders. Julius Caesar was the first Roman to cross the Channel, but even he was weirded out by the island's strange inhabitants, who worshipped trees, sacrificed virgins, and went to war painted blue. Later, Romans subdued and civilized them, building roads and making this spot on the Thames— "Londinium"—into a major urban center.

But Boadicea refused to be Romanized. In A.D. 60, after Roman soldiers raped her daughters, she rallied her people and "liberated" London, massacring its 60,000 Romanized citizens. However, the brief revolt was snuffed out, and she and her family took poison to avoid surrender.

• *There's a civilized public toilet down the stairs behind Boadicea. Cross the street to just under Big Ben and continue one block inland to the busy intersection of Parliament Square.*

❸ View of Parliament Square

To your left are the sandstone-hued **Houses of Parliament.** If Parliament is in session, the entrance (midway down the building) is lined with tourists, enlivened by political demonstrations, and staked out by camera crews interviewing Members of Parliament (MPs) for the evening news. Only the core part, Westminster Hall, survives from the circa-1090s original. While the Houses of Parliament are commonly described as "Neo-Gothic" (even in this book), this uniquely English style is more specifically called Neo-Perpendicular Gothic. For a peek at genuine Perpendicular Gothic (the fanciest and final stage of that style), simply look across the street at the section of Westminster Abbey closest to the Houses of Parliament—it dates from 1484.

Kitty-corner across the square, the two white towers of **Westminster Abbey** rise above the trees. The broad boulevard of Whitehall (here called Parliament Street) stretches to your right up to Trafalgar Square.

This square is the heart of what was once a suburb of London— the medieval City of Westminster. Like Buda and Pest (later

Budapest), London is two cities that grew into one. In Roman and medieval times, the city was centered farther east, near St. Paul's Cathedral. But in the 11th century, King Edward the Confessor moved his court here, and the center of political power shifted to this area. Edward built a palace and a church (minster) here in the west, creating the city of "West Minster." Over time, the palace evolved into a meeting place for debating public policy—a parliament. Today's Houses of Parliament sit atop the remains of Edward's original palace. To this day, the Houses of Parliament are known to Brits as the "Palace of Westminster."

Across from Parliament, the cute little church with the blue sundials, snuggling under the Abbey "like a baby lamb under a ewe," is **St. Margaret's Church.** Since 1480, this has been *the* place for politicians' weddings, including Winston and Clementine Churchill's.

Parliament Square, the expanse of green between West-minster Abbey and Big Ben, is filled with statues of famous

Brits (and sometimes with protesters). The statue of **Winston Churchill,** the man who saved Britain from Hitler, shows him in the military overcoat he was fond of wearing. According to tour guides, the statue has a current of electricity running through it to honor Churchill's wish that if a statue were made of him, his head wouldn't be soiled by pigeons. There are also a few non-Brits,

honored not for their contributions to Britain but to mankind. At the opposite corner of the square from Churchill, look for the newer statue of the leader who battled South African apartheid, **Nelson Mandela** (erected in 2007). And across the street and a bit to the right stands a man who opposed American apartheid, **Abraham Lincoln** (erected in 1920, patterned after a similar statue in Chicago's Lincoln Park).

The white building (flying the Union Jack) at the far end of the square houses Britain's new **Supreme Court.** You can wander the building, see a small exhibit on this recently sanctioned legal body, and observe any courts currently in session (it also has a café and WCs).

In 1868, the world's first traffic light was installed on the corner where Whitehall now spills double-decker buses into the square. Another reminder of a bygone era is the little yellow "Taxi" lantern atop the fence on the street corner closest to Parliament. In pre-mobile phone days, when an MP needed a taxi, this lit up to hail one.

• *Consider touring Westminster Abbey (❂ see the Westminster Abbey Tour chapter). Otherwise, turn right (north), walk away from the Houses of Parliament and the Abbey, and continue up Parliament Street, which becomes Whitehall.*

❹ Walking Along Whitehall

Today, Whitehall is choked with traffic, but imagine the effect this broad street must have had on out-of-towners a century ago. In your horse-drawn carriage, you'd clop along a tree-lined boule-

vard past well-dressed lords and ladies, dodging street urchins. Gazing left, then right, you'd try to take it all in, your eyes dazzled by the bone-white walls of this man-made marble canyon.

Whitehall is now the most important street in

Britain, lined with the ministries of finance, treasury, and so on. You may see limos and camera crews as important dignitaries enter or exit. Political demonstrators wave signs and chant slogans—sometimes about issues foreign to most Americans (Britain's former colonies still resent the empire's continuing influence), and sometimes about issues very familiar to us (wars in Iraq and Afghanistan, and the economy). Notice the security measures. Iron grates seal off the concrete ditches between the buildings and sidewalks for protection against explosives. The city has been on "orange alert" since long before September 2001, but Londoners refuse to be terrorized, as shown by their determination to continue with life as normal after the July 2005 Tube and bus bombings.

The black, ornamental arrowheads topping the iron fences were once colorfully painted. In 1861, Queen Victoria ordered them all painted black when her beloved Prince Albert ("the only one who called her Vickie") died. Possibly the world's most determined mourner, Victoria wore black for the standard two years of mourning—and tacked on 38 more.

• *Continue toward the tall, square, concrete monument in the middle of the road. On your right is a colorful pub, the Red Lion. Across the street, a 700-foot detour down King Charles Street leads to the Churchill War Rooms, the underground bunker of 27 rooms that was the nerve center of Britain's campaign against Hitler (see page 55 for details).*

❺ Cenotaph

This big, white stone monument (in the middle of the boulevard) honors those who died in the two events that most shaped modern Britain—World Wars I and II. The

monumental devastation of these wars helped turn a colonial superpower into a cultural colony of an American superpower.

The actual cenotaph is the slab that sits atop the pillar—a tomb. You'll notice no religious symbols on this memorial. The dead honored here came from many creeds and all corners of Britain's empire. It looks lost in a sea of noisy cars, but on each Remembrance Sunday (closest to November 11), Whitehall is closed off to traffic, the royal family fills the balcony overhead in the foreign ministry, and a memorial service is held around the cenotaph.

It's hard for an American to understand the impact of the Great War (World War I) on Europe. It's said that if the roughly one million WWI dead from the British Empire were to march four abreast past the cenotaph, the sad parade would last for seven days.

Eternally pondering the cenotaph (from *way* up the street) is an equestrian statue. Field Marshal Douglas Haig (marked with his honorary title, *Earl Haig*) was commander-in-chief of the British army from 1916 to 1918. He was responsible for ordering so many brave and not-so-brave British boys out of the trenches and onto the killing fields of World War I.

• *Just past the cenotaph, on the other (west) side of Whitehall, is an iron security gate guarding the entrance to Downing Street.*

❻ #10 Downing Street and the Ministry of Defence

Britain's version of the White House is where the prime minister and his family live, at #10 (in the black-brick building 300 feet down the blocked-off street, on the right; there's a lantern and usually a security guard).

Like the White House's Rose Garden, the black door marked #10 is a highly symbolic point of power, popular for photo ops to mark big occasions. This is where suffragettes protested in the early 20th century, where Neville Chamberlain showed off his regrettable peace treaty with Hitler, and where Winston Churchill made famous the V-for-Victory sign. In 2008, then-Prime Minister Gordon Brown and President George W. Bush posed here to bolster US-UK solidarity, and in 2009, President Barack Obama huddled here with Brown to consider solutions to the economic downturn. In 2010, newly elected Prime Minister David Cameron gave a short speech at a makeshift podium, posed for cameras with his pregnant wife, and then headed inside to assume control.

It looks modest, but #10's entryway does open up into fairly impressive digs—the prime minister's offices (downstairs), his residence (upstairs), and two large formal dining rooms. The PM's staff has offices here. Many on the staff are permanent bureaucrats, staying on to serve as prime ministers come and go. The cabinet meets at #10 on Tuesday mornings. This is where foreign dignitaries come for official government dinners, where the prime minister receives honored school kids and victorious soccer teams, and where he gives monthly addresses to the nation. Next door, at #11, the chancellor of the exchequer (finance minister) lives with his family, and #12 houses the PM's press office.

WESTMINSTER WALK

Prime Minister David Cameron

David Cameron succeeded Gordon Brown as prime minister in May of 2010, and lives at #10 Downing Street with his wife, Samantha, and their young children. At 43, Cameron is the youngest PM in two centuries. He heads the Conservative Party (the "Tories"), but he has never quite fit the stodgy Conservative image. Rumors still swirl of wild parties and illicit drugs in his student days at Oxford. He's known as "Dave" to his friends, and he developed a habit of riding his bike to work. Cameron rose quickly through the political ranks: He worked to reelect Conservative PM John Major (1992), assisted the finance minister at #11 Downing Street (1992-1994), and was himself elected to Parliament in 2001, becoming head of the Conservative Party in 2005. By 2008, he was on the cover of *Time* magazine, which hailed him as the future of conservatism.

In 2010, Cameron's Conservative Party came to power. The prime minister is not elected directly by popular vote (the way the American president is), but rules as leader of the party that garners the most votes in Parliamentary elections. The 2010 elections were hardly a sweeping Conservative mandate: Three parties split the vote, forcing Cameron's Conservatives to form a coalition with the (more left-leaning) Liberal Democrat Party. The Labour Party, which had held power in Britain for 13 years under Gordon Brown and Tony Blair, is the coalition's chief opposition.

Politically, Cameron is a moderate Conservative who is more pragmatic than ideological. Socially, he's "liberal" in the classical sense, advocating for personal freedoms—gay rights, decriminalization of drugs, allowing hunting and smoking, and ensuring citizens' privacy against government intrusion. Fiscally, he rails against big-government waste. In his early days as PM, he delivered a sober speech about a time of austerity looming on Britain's horizon, when belts would need to be tightened to get the budget under control. His most right-of-center stance is his support for distancing Britain from the euro and the European Union.

Despite his personal appeal, Cameron can't quite shake the Conservatives' image as the party of the upper class. Cameron was born rich, married rich, and has worked within the corporate culture. His colleagues form an old boys' network from his days at Eton, England's most exclusive prep school. The mayor of London, Boris Johnson, is not only an old Oxford frat buddy but also a distant cousin. As the Conservatives try to unite the country to solve Britain's severe economic and cultural problems, it remains to be seen whether David Cameron has brought a fresh enough approach to #10.

This has been the traditional home of the prime minister since the position was created in the early 18th century. But even before that, the neighborhood (if not the building itself) was a center of power, where Edward the Confessor and Henry VIII had palaces. The facade is, frankly, quite cheap, having been built as part of a middle-class cul-de-sac of homes by American-born George Downing in the 1680s. When the first PM moved in, the humble interior was combined with a mansion in back. During a major upgrade in the 1950s, they discovered that the facade's black bricks were actually yellow—but had been stained by centuries of Industrial Age soot. To keep with tradition, they now paint the bricks black.

The guarded metal gates were installed in 1989 to protect against Irish terrorists. Even so, #10 was hit and partly damaged in 1991 by an Irish Republican Army mortar launched from a van. These days, there's typically not much to see unless a VIP happens to drive up. Then the bobbies snap to and check credentials, the gates open, the car is inspected for bombs, the traffic barrier midway down the street drops into its bat cave, the car drives in, and... the bobbies go back to mugging for the tourists.

The huge building across Whitehall from Downing Street is the **Ministry of Defence** (MOD), the "British Pentagon." This bleak place looks like a Ministry of Defence should. In front are statues of illustrious defenders of Britain. "Monty" is **Field Marshal Bernard Law Montgomery** of World War II, who beat the Nazis in North Africa (defeating Erwin "The Desert Fox" Rommel at El Alamein), giving the Allies a jumping-off point to retake Europe. Along with Churchill, Monty breathed confidence back into a demoralized British army, persuading them they could ultimately beat Hitler. In 2005, a **memorial** honoring the women who fought and died in World War II was constructed. Its empty uniforms evoke the often-overlooked sacrifices of Britain's female war heroes.

THE WOMEN OF WORLD WAR II

You may be enjoying the shade of London's **plane trees.** They do well in polluted London: roots that work well in clay, waxy leaves that self-clean in the rain, and bark that sheds and regenerates so the pollution doesn't get into the trees' vascular systems.

• *At the equestrian statue, you'll be flanked by the Welsh and Scottish government offices. At the corner (same side as the Ministry of Defence), you'll find the...*

❼ Banqueting House

This two-story building is just about all that remains of what was once the biggest palace in Europe—Whitehall Palace, which once

stretched from Trafalgar Square to Big Ben. Henry VIII started building it when he moved out of the Palace of Westminster (now the Parliament) and into the residence of the archbishop of York. Queen Elizabeth I and other monarchs added on as England's worldwide prestige grew.

Today, the exterior of Greek-style columns and pediments looks rather ho-hum, much like every other white, marble building in London. But in 1620, it was a one-of-a-kind wonder—a big, white temple rising above small, half-timbered huts. Built by architect Inigo Jones, it sparked London's interest in the classical style. Within a century, London was awash in Georgian-style architecture, the English version of Neoclassical.

Facing the Banqueting House, look up at the first-floor windows—the site of one of the pivotal events of English history. On January 30, 1649, a man dressed in black appeared at one of the windows and looked out at a huge crowd that surrounded the building. He stepped out the window and onto a wooden platform. It was King Charles I. He gave a short speech to the crowd, framed by the magnificent backdrop of the Banqueting House. His final word was "Remember." Then he knelt and laid his neck on a block as another man in black approached. It was the executioner—who cut off the king's head.

Plop—the concept of divine monarchy in Britain was decapitated. But there would still be kings after Oliver Cromwell, the Protestant anti-monarchist who brought about Charles I's death and then became England's leader. Soon after, royalty was restored, and Charles' son, Charles II, got his revenge here in the Banqueting Hall...by living well. But, from then on, every king knew that he ruled by the grace of Parliament.

Charles I is remembered today with a statue at one end of Whitehall (in Trafalgar Square at the base of the tall column), while his killer, Oliver Cromwell, is given equal time with a statue at the other end (at the Houses of Parliament).

• *You can pop into the Banqueting House, following the self-guided tour below. Otherwise, skip to "Horse Guards."*

Banqueting House Interior

Start with the 20-minute video on the history of the House, which shows the place in banqueting action. History buffs might

WESTMINSTER WALK

The Banqueting House Through History

Imagine the many events this place has hosted over the centuries. Originally built as the royal dining hall for the sprawling Whitehall Palace, the Banqueting House also served as its de facto throne room. Picture ambassadors arriving here and walking the length of this hall lined with courtiers to pay homage to the king on his canopied throne. Loyal subjects knelt here to be made knights and nobles.

In the 1600s, the hall was famous throughout Europe as an occasional theater. Plays called "masques" were performed by torchlight and featured mask-wearing actors, singers and dancers, and elaborate costumes, sets, and special effects.

Picture the scene in 1622, when the brand-new Banqueting House was inaugurated with a performance of *The Masque of Augurs,* by Shakespeare protégé Ben Jonson (with set design by the hall's architect, Inigo Jones). King James and his courtiers crowded the balcony and tiered seats, and watched in awe as a parade of goofy commoners in masks entered the hall, singing and reveling, accompanied by two dancing bears. The comic chaos was suddenly interrupted by Greek gods who descended magically from the ceiling, eventually bringing harmony to the realm—just as a wise king does. And behind one of the masks, one of the actors was none other than 21-year-old Prince "I just can't wait to be king" Charles.

In 1649, the Banqueting House served a much more serious purpose—as an execution site for the public beheading of Charles I. Oliver Cromwell subsequently used this symbolic spot to legitimize his own leadership as Lord Protector. When Charles' son, Charles II, restored the monarchy in 1660, it was here that they celebrated.

In 1698, a massive fire destroyed Whitehall Palace, leaving only the name and the Banqueting House. The monarchs moved their residence elsewhere, eventually to Buckingham Palace. The Banqueting House became the Royal Chapel, complete with organ and pews.

Today, besides being a museum, the Banqueting House still functions much as it did in its heyday—hosting government receptions for foreign dignitaries or for parliament. World-renowned classical musicians perform for the paying public. And it's a rent-a-hall for parties and dinners. You could hold your daughter's wedding reception here, with 400 guests and full catering, for as little as $100,000.

consider the 30-minute audioguide. The low-ceilinged ground floor (or Undercroft) was King James I's personal wine cellar and tasting room. Climb to the first floor, passing a portrait of King Charles I in the stairwell.

The main hall is impressive—two stories high, white with gold trim, full of light, and topped with colorful paintings in a gold-coffered ceiling. At 55 feet wide, 55 feet high, and 110 feet long, it's a perfect double cube. The interior decoration echoes the exterior, with Ionic columns below and Corinthian pilasters above. The chandeliers can be raised and lowered to accommodate any event. The throne is a modern reconstruction, but it gives an idea of the king's canopied throne that once stood here.

Ceiling Paintings: Charles I, who inherited the Banqueting House from his father, commissioned the famed Peter Paul Rubens to complete the decor. Rubens planned the project during a visit in 1629, but he actually painted the huge canvases (the large ones are 28 feet by 20 feet) in his studio in Antwerp, Belgium. They were rolled up, shipped to England, put on frames, and hung from the ceiling in 1636.

The paintings glorify Charles' dad, James I, the man who built the Banqueting House and who once told Parliament: "Kings are called gods...even by God himself."

To view the large oval painting in the center, *The Apotheosis of James I,* approach from the entrance, like a visiting ambassador, and watch the scene unfold. King James I (in red robe, with gray beard) rests his foot on a globe, as king of the whole world. Lady Faith (with a torch) and Miss Justice (with scales) lead him up into heaven, where baby angels blow trumpets and the goddess Minerva crowns him with the laurel wreath of wisdom. Minerva sticks her foot in our face, a triumph of illusion three centuries before 3-D glasses.

The painting above the throne, *The Peaceful Reign of King James,* shows wise King James seated on his throne, flanked by corkscrew columns from the temple of wise King Solomon. To the left, Peace embraces Plenty. Two angels swoop down at dramatic angles to adorn James with laurels, while a cherub holds his royal crown. Below, the Greek gods—Hermes, Mars, Minerva—arrive to help James subdue the serpents of rebellion.

In the painting above the entrance, *The Union of the Crowns,* James points his scepter at two ladies—England and Scotland—warning them to get along. James united the two bickering countries, having been crowned both King of Scots (in 1567) and King of England (1603). Smoke clouds of peace rise in the background as Cupid (bottom left corner) torches the weapons of war. The ladies place a crown on a baby's head and lead him to the throne.

It's James' son, the future Charles I. When Charles grew up, he had this painting hung so that he could see it (right-side up) while seated on the Banqueting House throne.

• *When you're finished ogling the paintings, head back outside. Continue up Whitehall on the left (west) side, where you'll see (and smell) the building known as Horse Guards, guarded by traditionally dressed soldiers—who are also called Horse Guards.*

❽ Horse Guards

For 200 years, soldiers in cavalry uniforms have guarded this arched entrance along Whitehall that leads to Buckingham Palace and its predecessor as royal residence, St. James's Palace.

Two different squads alternate, so depending on the day you visit, you'll see soldiers in either red coats with white plumes in their helmets (the Life Guards), or blue coats with red plumes (the Blues and Royals). Together, they constitute the Queen's personal bodyguard. Besides their ceremonial duties here in old-time uniforms, these elite troops have fought in Iraq and Afghanistan. Both Prince William and Prince Harry have served in the Blues and Royals.

The Horse Guards building was the headquarters of the British army from the time of the American Revolution until the Ministry of Defence was created in World War II. Back when this archway was the only access point to The Mall (the street leading to Buckingham Palace), it was a security checkpoint. Anyone on horseback had to dismount before passing through. Today, by tradition, you must dismount your bicycle, Vespa, or Segway and walk it through. In 2012, it's worth passing through to check on the status of the Olympic event to be held here. The broad expanse of Horse Guards Parade will be covered in sand and ringed with seating to host the beach volleyball matches (Changing of the Guard Mon-Sat at 11:00, Sun at 10:00, dismounting ceremony daily at 16:00; the Horse Guards Museum offers a glimpse at the stables and a collection of uniforms and weapons).

• *Continue up Whitehall, passing the Old Admiralty (#26, on left), headquarters of the British navy that once ruled the waves. Across the street, behind the old Clarence Pub, stood the original Scotland Yard, headquarters of London's crack police force in the days of Sherlock Holmes. Finally, Whitehall opens up into the grand, noisy, traffic-filled Trafalgar Square.*

If you want to walk around in Trafalgar Square, you can cross two

Trafalgar Square

streets at the crosswalk, or—to avoid the traffic—use the pedestrian underpass (a.k.a. "subway" in British parlance, entrance to the left).

❾ Trafalgar Square

London's central meeting point bustles around the world's biggest Corinthian column, where **Admiral Horatio Nelson** stands 170 feet tall, looking over London in the direction of one of the greatest naval battles in history. Nelson saved England at a time as dark as World War II. In 1805, Napoleon was poised on the other side of the Channel, threatening to invade England. Meanwhile, more than 900 miles away, the one-armed, one-eyed, and one-minded Lord Nelson attacked the French fleet off the coast of Spain at Trafalgar. The French were routed, Britannia ruled the waves, and the

once-invincible French army was slowly worn down, then defeated at Waterloo. Nelson, while victorious, was shot by a sniper in the battle. He died, gasping, "Thank God, I have done my duty."

At the top of Trafalgar Square (north) sits the domed **National Gallery** with its grand staircase, and, to the right, the steeple of **St. Martin-in-the-Fields,** built in 1722, inspiring the steeple-over-the-entrance style of many town churches in New England (free lunch concerts—see page 421).

At the base of Nelson's column are bronze reliefs cast from melted-down enemy cannons, and four huggable lions dying to have their photo taken with you.
In front of the column, Charles I sits on horseback, with his head still on his shoulders. In the pavement just behind the statue is a plaque marking the center of London, from which all distances are measured. Of the many statues that dot the square, the ped-estal on the northwest corner (the "fourth plinth") is periodically topped with contemporary art. The newly restored fountains, lit by colored lights, can shoot water 80 feet in the air.

Trafalgar Square is the center of modern London, connecting Westminster, The City, and the West End. A recent remodeling of the square has rerouted car traffic, helping reclaim the area for London's citizens. Spin clockwise 360 degrees and survey the city:

To the south (down Whitehall) is the center of government, Westminster. Looking southwest, down the broad boulevard called The Mall, you see Buckingham Palace in the distance. (Down Pall Mall is St. James's Palace, where Prince Charles lives when in London.) A few blocks northwest of Trafalgar Square is Piccadilly Circus. Directly north (a block behind the National Gallery) sits Leicester Square, the jumping-off point for Soho, Covent Garden, and the West End theater district (❂ see the West End Walk chapter).

The boulevard called the Strand takes you past Charing Cross Station, then eastward to The City, the original walled town of London and today's financial center. In medieval times, when people from The City met with the Westminster government, it was here. And finally, Northumberland Street leads southeast to the Golden Jubilee pedestrian bridge over the Thames. Along the way, you'll pass the Sherlock Holmes Pub (just off Northumberland Street, on Craven Street), housed in Sir Arthur Conan Doyle's favorite watering hole, with an upstairs replica of 221b Baker Street.

Soak it in. You're smack-dab in the center of London, a thriving city atop two millennia of history.

WESTMINSTER ABBEY TOUR

Westminster Abbey is the greatest church in the English-speaking world, where the nation's kings and queens have been crowned and buried since 1066. The histories of Westminster Abbey and England are almost the same. A thousand years of English history—3,000 tombs, the remains of 29 kings and queens, and hundreds of memorials to poets, politicians, and warriors—lie within its stained-glass splendor and under its stone slabs.

Orientation

Cost: £16, £32 family ticket (covers 2 adults and 1 child), cash or credit cards accepted (line up in the correct queue to pay), includes fine audioguide and entry to the cloisters and Abbey Museum. Praying is free, thank God.

Hours: Abbey—Mon-Fri 9:30-16:30, Wed until 19:00 (main church only), Sat 9:30-14:30, last entry one hour before closing, closed Sun to sightseers but open for services; Abbey Museum—daily 10:30-16:00; cloisters—daily 8:00-18:00, free access to cloisters through Dean Court (near west entrance). Special events can shut down all or part of the Abbey.

When To Go: The place is most crowded every day at midmorning and on Saturdays and Mondays. Visit early, during lunch, or late to avoid tourist hordes. Weekdays after 14:30 are less congested; come then and stay for the 17:00 evensong. The main entrance, on the Parliament Square side, often has a sizable line. Of the two queues (cash or credit) at the admissions desk, the cash line is probably moving faster. There's talk of opening a "fast track" entry for London Pass holders; if you have the pass it's worth asking to see if that's happened yet.

Dress Code: There is none, even for services.

Getting There: Near Big Ben and the Houses of Parliament (Tube: Westminster or St. James's Park).

Information: Because special events and services can shut out sight-seers, check the website or call ahead to confirm that the Abbey is open, and ask about the schedule for guided tours, concerts, or services, depending on your interest (tel. 020/7654-4834, www.westminster-abbey.org). If you have questions about the cathedral, ask a marshal in red or any of the green-cloaked volunteer vergers (who also lead tours—see below).

Music and Services: Mon-Fri 7:30 (prayer), 8:00 (communion), 12:30 (communion), 17:00 evensong (on Wed the evensong may be spoken—no song); Sat 8:00 (communion), 9:00 (prayer), 12:30 (communion), 15:00 (evensong; June-Sept it's at 17:00); Sun services generally come with more music: 8:00 (communion), 10:00 (sung Matins), 11:15 (sung Eucharist), 15:00 (evensong), 18:30 (evening service). Services are free to anyone, though visitors who haven't paid church admission aren't allowed to linger afterward. Free organ recitals are often held Sun at 17:45 (30 minutes). For a schedule of services or recitals on a particular day, look for posted signs with schedules or check the Abbey's website.

Tours: The included **audioguide** is excellent, taking some of the sting out of the steep admission fee. To add to the experience, you can take an entertaining **guided tour** from a verger—the church equivalent of a museum docent (£3, see schedule just inside entry, up to 5/day in summer, 4/day in winter, 1.5 hours).

Length of This Tour: Allow 1.5 hours.

WCs: The nearest public WCs (50p) are in front of Methodist Central Hall, the domed building across the street from the Abbey's west entrance.

Photography: Photos are prohibited.

Cuisine Art: In good weather, kiosks in the cloister courtyard sell sandwiches, soups, and drinks. In bad weather, cross the street for reasonably priced cafeteria-style lunches in the basement of Methodist Central Hall (Wesley's Café, Mon-Fri 8:00-16:00, Sat-Sun 9:00-16:00, good free WC). Other options: The Supreme Court building (on Parliament Square) has a simple basement café and free WCs (Mon-Fri 9:30-16:30, closed Sat-Sun). The Westminster Arms pub (£9 fish and chips, food served daily 12:00-20:00, eat downstairs) is near Methodist Central Hall on Storey's Gate. Picnickers can find benches at the nearby Jewel Tower, a half-block south of the Abbey.

Starring: Edwards, Elizabeths, Henrys, Annes, Marys, and poets.

The Tour Begins

You'll have no choice but to follow the steady flow of tourists circling clockwise through the church—in through the north entrance, behind the altar, into Poets' Corner in the south transept, detouring through the cloisters, and, finally, back out through the west end of the nave. It's all one-way, and the crowds can be a real crush. Here are the Abbey's top 10 (plus one) stops.

• *Walk straight in, entering the north transept. Pick up the map flier that locates the most illustrious tombs, and walk into the center of the church.*

❶ North Transept and View of Nave

You're standing at the center of a cross-shaped church. The "high" (main) altar (which usually has a cross and candlesticks atop it) sits on the platform up the five stairs in front of you. This is the culminating point of the long, high-ceilinged nave. Nestled in the nave is the elaborately carved wooden seating of the choir (a.k.a. "quire" in British churchspeak), where monks once chanted their services and where, today, the Abbey boys' choir sings the evensong.

Look down the long and narrow center aisle of the church. Lined with the praying hands of the Gothic arches, glowing with light from the stained glass, it's clear that this is more than a museum. With saints in stained glass, heroes in carved stone, and the bodies of England's greatest citizens under the floor stones, Westminster Abbey is the religious heart of England.

The Abbey was built in 1065. Its name, Westminster, means Church in the West (west of St. Paul's Cathedral). For the next 250 years, the Abbey was redone and remodeled to become essentially the church you see today, notwithstanding an extensive resurfacing in the 19th century. Thankfully, later architects—ignoring building trends of their generation—honored the vision of the original planner, and the building was completed in one relatively harmonious style.

The Abbey's 10-story nave is the tallest in England. The chandeliers, 10 feet tall, look small in comparison (16 were given to the Abbey by the Guinness family).

The north transept (through which you entered) is nicknamed "Statesmen's Corner" and specializes in famous prime ministers. Find the rival prime ministers—proud William Gladstone and goateed Benjamin Disraeli, who presided over England's peak of

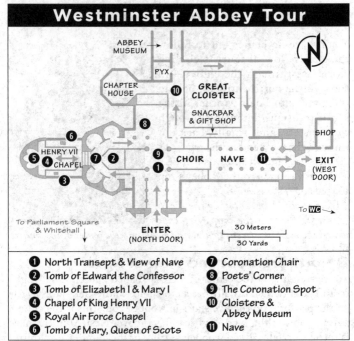

Westminster Abbey Tour

ABBEY MUSEUM

PYX

CHAPTER HOUSE

GREAT CLOISTER

SNACKBAR & GIFT SHOP

HENRY VII CHAPEL

CHOIR

NAVE

SHOP

EXIT (WEST DOOR)

To WC

To Parliament Square & Whitehall

ENTER (NORTH DOOR)

30 Meters

30 Yards

❶ North Transept & View of Nave
❷ Tomb of Edward the Confessor
❸ Tomb of Elizabeth I & Mary I
❹ Chapel of King Henry VII
❺ Royal Air Force Chapel
❻ Tomb of Mary, Queen of Scots

❼ Coronation Chair
❽ Poets' Corner
❾ The Coronation Spot
❿ Cloisters & Abbey Museum
⓫ Nave

WESTMINSTER ABBEY

power under Queen Victoria.

• *Now turn left and follow the crowd. Walk past Robert ("Bob") Peel, the prime minister whose policemen were nicknamed "bobbies," and stroll a few yards into the land of dead kings and queens. Stop at the wooden staircase on your right.*

❷ Tomb of Edward the Confessor

The holiest part of the church is the raised area behind the altar (where the wooden staircase leads—sorry, no tourist access except with verger tour). Step back and peek over the dark coffin of Edward I to see the tippy-top of the green-and-gold wedding-cake tomb of King Edward the Confessor—the man who built Westminster Abbey.

God had told pious Edward to visit St. Peter's Basilica in Rome. But with the Normans thinking conquest, it was too dangerous for him to leave England. Instead, he built this grand church and dedicated it to St. Peter. It was finished just in time to bury Edward and to crown his foreign successor, William the Conqueror, in 1066. After Edward's death, people prayed at his tomb, and, after getting good results, Pope Alexander III canonized him. This elevated, central tomb—which lost some of its luster when Henry VIII melted down the gold coffin-case—is surrounded by the tombs of eight kings and queens.

• *Continue on. At the top of the stone staircase, veer left into the private burial chapel of Queen Elizabeth I.*

❸ Tomb of Queen Elizabeth I and Mary I

Although there's only one effigy on the tomb (Elizabeth's), there are actually two queens buried beneath it, both daughters of Henry VIII (by different mothers). Bloody Mary—meek, pious, sickly, and Catholic—enforced Catholicism during her short reign (1553-1558) by burning "heretics" at the stake.

Elizabeth—strong, clever, and Protestant—steered England on an Anglican course. She holds a royal orb symbolizing that she's queen of the whole globe. When 26-year-old Elizabeth was crowned in the Abbey, her right to rule was questioned (especially by her Catholic subjects) because she was the bastard seed of Henry VIII's unsanctioned marriage to Anne Boleyn. But Elizabeth's long reign (1559-1603) was one of the greatest in English history, a time when England ruled the seas and Shakespeare explored human emotions. When she died, thousands turned out for her funeral in the Abbey. Elizabeth's face, modeled after her death mask, is considered a very accurate take on this hook-nosed, imperious "Virgin Queen."

The two half-sisters disliked each other in life—Mary even had Elizabeth locked up in the Tower of London for a short time. Now they lie side by side for eternity. The Latin inscription ends, "Here we lie, two sisters in hope of one resurrection."

• *Continue into the ornate, flag-draped room behind the main altar.*

❹ Chapel of King Henry VII (a.k.a. the Lady Chapel)

The light from the stained-glass windows; the colorful banners overhead; and the elaborate tracery in stone, wood, and glass give this room the festive air of a medieval tournament. The prestigious Knights of the Bath meet here, under the magnificent ceiling studded with gold pendants. The ceiling—of carved stone, not plaster (1519)—is the finest English Perpendicular Gothic and fan vaulting you'll see (unless you're going to King's College Chapel in Cambridge). The ceiling was sculpted on the floor in pieces, then jigsaw-puzzled into place. It capped the Gothic period

and signaled the vitality of the coming Renaissance.

The knights sit in the wooden stalls with their coats of arms on the back, churches on their heads, their banner flying above, and the graves of dozens of kings beneath their feet. When the Queen worships here, she sits in the southwest corner chair under the carved wooden throne with the lion crown.

Behind the small altar is an iron cage housing tombs of the old warrior Henry VII of Lancaster and his wife, Elizabeth of York. Their love and marriage finally settled the Wars of the Roses between the two clans. The combined red-and-white rose symbol decorates the top band of the ironwork. Henry VII, the first Tudor king, was the father of Henry VIII and the grandfather of Elizabeth I. This exuberant chapel heralds a new optimistic, post-war era as England prepares to step onto the world stage.

• Go to the far end of the chapel and stand at the banister in front of the modern set of stained-glass windows.

❺ Royal Air Force Chapel

Saints in robes and halos mingle with pilots in parachutes and bomber jackets. This tribute to WWII flyers is for those who earned their angel wings in the Battle of Britain (July-Oct 1940). Hitler's air force ruled the skies in the early days of the war, bombing at will, and threatening to snuff Britain out without a fight. But while determined Londoners hunkered down underground, British pilots in their Spitfires took advantage of newly invented radar to get the jump on the more powerful Luftwaffe. These were the fighters about whom Churchill said, "Never...was so much owed by so many to so few."

The Abbey survived the Battle and the Blitz, but this window did not. As a memorial, a bit of bomb damage has been preserved—the little glassed-over hole in the wall below the windows in the lower left-hand corner. The book of remembrances lists each of the 1,497 airmen (including one American) who died in the Battle of Britain.

You're standing on the grave of Oliver Cromwell, leader of the rebel forces in England's Civil War. Or, rather, what had been his grave, when Cromwell was buried here from 1658 to 1661. Then his corpse was exhumed, hanged, drawn, quartered, and decapitated, and the head displayed on a stake as a warning to anarchists.

• Exit the Chapel of Henry VII. Turn left into a side chapel with the tomb (the central one of three in the chapel).

❻ Tomb of Mary, Queen of Scots

Historians get dewy-eyed over the fate of Mary, Queen of Scots (1542-1587). The beautiful, French-educated queen was held under house arrest for 19 years by Queen Elizabeth I, who considered her a threat to her sovereignty. Elizabeth got wind of an assassination plot, suspected Mary was behind it, and had her first cousin (once removed) beheaded. When Elizabeth—who was called the "Virgin Queen"—died heirless, Mary's son, James VI, King of Scots, also became King James I of England and Ireland. James buried his mum here (with her head sewn back on) in the Abbey's most sumptuous tomb.

• *Exit Mary's chapel. Ahead of you, at the foot of the stairs, is the Coronation Chair. Behind the chair, again, is the tomb of the church's founder, Edward the Confessor.*

❼ Coronation Chair

The gold-painted oak chair waits here—with its back to the high altar—for the next coronation. For every English coronation since 1308 (except two), it's been moved to its spot before the high altar to receive the royal buttocks. The chair's legs rest on lions, England's symbol. The space below the chair originally held a big sandstone rock from Scotland called the Stone of Scone (pronounced "skoon"), symbolizing Scotland's unity with England's monarch. But in the 1990s, Britain gave Scotland more sovereignty, its own Parliament, and the Stone, which Scotland has agreed to loan to Britain for future coronations (the rest of the time, it's on display in Edinburgh Castle).

• *Continue on. Turn left into the south transept. You're in Poets' Corner.*

❽ Poets' Corner

England's greatest artistic contributions are in the written word. Here lie buried the masters of arguably the world's most complex and expressive language. (Many writers are honored with plaques and monuments; relatively few are actually buried here.)

• *Start with Chaucer, buried in the wall under the blue windows, marked with a white plaque reading* Qui Fuit Anglorum...

Geoffrey Chaucer (c. 1343-1400) is often considered the father of English literature. Chaucer's *Canterbury Tales* told of earthy people speaking everyday English, not French or Latin. He was the first great writer buried in the Abbey (thanks to his job as a Westminster clerk). Later, it became a tradition to bury other writers here, and Poets' Corner was built around his tomb. The blue windows have blank panels awaiting the names of future poets.

• *The plaques on the floor before Chaucer are gravestones and memorials to other literary greats.*

Lord Byron, the great lover of women and adventure: "Though the night was made for loving,/And the day returns too soon,/Yet we'll go no more a-roving/By the light of the moon."

Dylan Thomas, alcoholic master of modernism, with a Romantic's heart: "Oh as I was young and easy in the mercy of his means,/Time held me green and dying/Though I sang in my chains like the sea."

W. H. Auden, Brit-turned-American modernist on love, politics, and religion: "He was my North, my South, my East and West/My working week and Sunday rest/My noon, my midnight, my talk, my song/I thought that love would last forever: I was wrong."

Lewis Carroll, creator of *Alice's Adventures in Wonderland* and *Through the Looking-Glass:* "'Twas brillig, and the slithy toves/Did gyre and gimble in the wabe..."

T. S. Eliot, American-turned-British author of the influential *The Waste Land:* "April is the cruellest month, breeding/Lilacs out of the dead land, mixing/Memory and desire, stirring/Dull roots with spring rain."

Alfred, Lord Tennyson, conscience of the Victorian era: "'Tis better to have loved and lost/Than never to have loved at all."

Robert Browning: "Oh, to be in England/Now that April's there."

• *Farther out in the south transept, you'll find a statue of...*

William Shakespeare: Although he's not buried here, this greatest of English writers is honored by a fine statue that stands near the end of the transept, overlooking the others: "Life's but a walking shadow, a poor player that struts and frets his hour upon the stage and then is heard no more."

George Frideric Handel: High on the wall opposite Shakespeare is the German immigrant famous for composing the *Messiah* oratorio: "Hallelujah, hallelujah, hallelujah." The statue's features are modeled on Handel's death mask. Musicians can read the vocal score in his hands for "I Know That My Redeemer Liveth." His actual tomb is on the floor, next to...

Charles Dickens, whose serialized novels brought literature to the masses: "It was the best of times, it was the worst of times."

On the floor near Shakespeare, you'll also find the tombs of **Samuel Johnson** (who wrote the first English dictionary) and the great English actor **Laurence Olivier.** (Olivier disdained the "Method" style of experiencing intense emotions in order to portray them. When co-star Dustin Hoffman stayed up all night in order to appear haggard for a scene, Olivier said, "My dear boy, why don't you simply try acting?")

And finally, near the center of the transept, find the small, white floor plaque of **Thomas Parr** (marked *THO: PARR*). Check the dates of his life (1483-1635) and do the math. In his (reputed) 152 years, he served 10 sovereigns and was a contemporary of Columbus, Henry VIII, Elizabeth I, Shakespeare, and Galileo.

• *Return to the center of the church in front of the high altar.*

❾ The Coronation Spot

Here is where every English coronation since 1066 has taken place. Imagine the day when Prince William becomes king (or you can picture Prince Charles, who'll come first if his mother doesn't manage to outlive him):

The nobles in robes and powdered wigs look on from the carved wooden stalls of the choir. The Archbishop of Canterbury stands at the high altar (table with candlesticks, up five steps). The coronation chair is placed before the altar on the round, brown pavement stone representing the earth. Surrounding the whole area are temporary bleachers for 8,000 VIPs, going halfway up the rose windows of each transept, creating a "theater."

Long silver trumpets hung with banners sound a fanfare as the monarch-to-be enters the church. The congregation sings, "I will go into the house of the Lord," as William parades slowly down the nave and up the steps to the altar. After a church service, he sits in the chair, facing the altar, where the crown jewels are placed. William is anointed with holy oil, then receives a ceremonial sword, ring, and cup. The royal scepter is placed in his hands, and—dut, dutta dah—the archbishop lowers the Crown of St. Edward the Confessor onto his royal head. Finally, King William stands up, descends the steps, and is presented to the people. As cannons roar throughout the city, the people cry, "God save the king!"

Royalty are also given funerals here. Princess Diana's coffin was carried to this spot for her funeral service in 1997. The "Queen Mum" (mother of Elizabeth II) had her funeral here in 2002. This is also where most of the last century's royal weddings have taken place, including the unions of Queen Elizabeth II and Prince Philip (1947), her parents (1923), her sister Princess Margaret (1973), and her son Prince Andrew (to Sarah Ferguson, 1986). Most recently, of course, in April 2011, Prince William and Kate Middleton strolled up the nave, passed through the quire, climbed the five steps to the high altar, and became husband and wife—and the future King and Queen of the United Kingdom and its Commonwealth.

• *Exit the church (temporarily) at the south door, which leads to the...*

❿ Cloisters and Abbey Museum

The buildings that adjoin the church housed the monks. (The church is known as the "abbey" because it was the headquarters of the Benedictine Order until Henry VIII kicked them out in 1540.) Cloistered courtyards gave them a place to meditate on God's creations.

The Chapter House is where the monks had daily meetings. It features fine architecture and stained glass, some faded but well-described medieval art, and—in the corridor—Britain's oldest door. A few steps farther down the hall is the entrance to the Pyx Chamber. This old, thick-walled room once safeguarded the coins used to set the silver standard of the realm.

The small Abbey Museum, formerly the monks' lounge, is worth a peek for its fascinating and well-described exhibits. Look into the impressively realistic eyes of Elizabeth I, Charles II, Admiral Nelson, and a dozen others, part of a compelling series of wax-and-wood statues that, for three centuries, graced coffins during funeral processions. Also see exhibits on royal coronations, funerals, Abbey history, a close-up look at medieval stained glass, and replicas of the crown jewels used for coronation practice. The once-exquisite, now-fragmented Westminster Retable, which decorated the high altar in 1270, is the oldest surviving altarpiece in England. The image of Christ in the central panel is time-worn, but it retains the essentials: his face, the orb of power, and his blessing hand. Beyond the Abbey Museum, passageways lead to the Little Cloister and picturesque College Garden (open Tue-Thu).

As you return to the church, look back through the cloister courtyard to the church exterior, and meditate on the flying buttresses. These stone bridges that push in on the church walls allowed Gothic architects to build so high.

• Go back into the church for the last stop.

⓫ Nave

On the floor near the west entrance of the Abbey is the flower-lined Tomb of the Unknown Warrior, one ordinary WWI soldier buried in soil from France with lettering made from melted-down weapons from that war. Think about that million-man army from the empire and commonwealth, and all those who gave their lives. Their memory is so revered that, when Kate Middleton walked up the aisle on her wedding day, by tradition she had to step around the tomb (and her wedding bouquet was later placed atop this tomb, also in accordance with tradition). Hanging on a column next to the tomb is the US Congressional Medal of Honor, presented by General Pershing in 1921 to honor England's WWI dead. Closer to the door is a memorial to the hero of World War II, Winston Churchill.

To the left of the choir screen is "Scientists' Corner," with memorials to Isaac Newton, Michael Faraday, Charles Darwin, and others.

On that side of the nave, find the stained-glass window of St. Edward the Confessor (third bay from the end, marked *S: Edwardus rex...*), with crown, scepter, and ring. Thank him for the Abbey.

Finally, grab a seat in the center and look down the nave. Listen to and ponder this place, filled with the remains of the people who made Britain a world power—saints, royalty, poets, musicians, scientists, soldiers, politicians. Now step back outside into a city filled with modern-day poets, saints, and heroes who continue to make Britain great.

NATIONAL GALLERY TOUR

The National Gallery lets you tour Europe's art without ever crossing the Channel. With so many exciting artists and styles, it's a fine overture to art if you're just starting a European trip, and a pleasant reprise if you're just finishing. The "National Gal" is always a welcome interlude from the bustle of London sightseeing.

Orientation

Cost: Free, but suggested donation of £2-3. Temporary (optional) exhibits require an admission fee.

Hours: Daily 10:00-18:00, Fri until 21:00, last entry to special exhibits 45 minutes before closing.

Getting There: It's as central as can be, overlooking Trafalgar Square, a 15-minute walk from Big Ben and 10 minutes from Piccadilly. The closest Tube stop is Charing Cross or Leicester Square. Handy buses #9, #11, #15, and #24 (among others) pass by (see page 34).

Information: The information desk in the lobby has a helpful £1 floor plan and a schedule of upcoming events and lunchtime lectures. Info tel. 020/7747-2885, switchboard tel. 020/7839-3321, www.nationalgallery.org.uk.

Tours: Free one-hour **overview tours** leave from the Sainsbury Wing info desk daily at 11:30 and 14:30, plus Fri at 19:00.

The **audioguides** are excellent. Choose from the one-hour highlights tour, several theme tours, or a tour option that lets you dial up info on any painting in the museum (£3.50).

The Gallery's **ArtStart** computer terminals help you study any artist, style, or topic in the museum, and print out a tailor-made tour map. Find them on the first floor of the

Sainsbury Wing and in the comfy Espresso Bar (described below).

Length of This Tour: Allow 1.5 hours.

Cloakroom: Cloakrooms are at each entrance (free, but £1-2 suggested donation). You can take a small bag into the museum.

Photography: Photos are strictly forbidden.

Cuisine Art: There are three eateries in the Gallery. The National Dining Rooms restaurant—located on the first floor of the Sainsbury Wing—is cool, classy, and pricey for a sit-down meal (£15-20 entrées). The National Café—located near the Getty Entrance—has table service (£15-20 entrées) and an easier-on-the-budget sandwich/soup/salad/pastry buffet (£3-4). Both places offer afternoon tea (see page 398). The self-service Espresso Bar, near the Portico and Getty entrances, has soft couches, sandwiches, and ArtStart computers. Outside the Gallery, several options are on or near Trafalgar Square (see page 385 in the Eating in London chapter).

Starring: You name it—Leonardo da Vinci, Raphael, Titian, Rembrandt, Monet, and Van Gogh.

Overview

The recently remodeled National Gallery feels fresh and elegant, giving visitors a grand first impression of Britain's greatest collection of paintings. The museum is surprisingly family-friendly

(especially on Sunday mornings), with a variety of kids' activities. This tour gives you a quick overview of European art history. It requires a bit of map reading and navigating, but it's worthwhile for a chronological sweep through art history. We'll stay on one floor, working through medieval holiness, Renaissance realism, Dutch detail, Baroque excess, British restraint, and the colorful French Impressionism that leads to the modern world. Cruise like an eagle with wide eyes for the big picture, seeing how each style progresses into the next.

The Gallery has three entrances facing Trafalgar Square: The main Portico Entrance (under the dome, in the center), the low-key Getty Entrance (to the right), and the Sainsbury Entrance (to the left—in the smaller building to the left of the main entrance).

NATIONAL GALLERY

The Tour Begins

• Enter through the Sainsbury Entrance. Pick up the handy map (£1) and climb the stairs. At the top, turn left, then left again through Room 51, and enter Room 52.

Medieval and Early Renaissance (1260-1440)

In Rooms 52 and 53, shiny gold paintings of saints, angels, Madonnas, and crucifixions float in an ethereal gold never-never land. One thing is very clear: Medieval heaven was different from medieval earth. The holy wore gold plates on their heads. Faces were serene and generic. People posed stiffly, facing either directly out or to the side, never in between. Saints are recognized by the symbols they carry (a key, a sword, a book), rather than by their human features.

Art in the Middle Ages was religious, dominated by the Church. The illiterate faithful could meditate on an altarpiece and visualize heaven. It's as though they couldn't imagine saints and angels inhabiting the dreary world of rocks, trees, and sky they lived in.

• One of the finest medieval altarpieces is in a glass case in Room 53.

Anonymous—*The Wilton Diptych* (c. 1395-1399)

Two saint/kings and St. John the Baptist present King Richard II (left panel) to the Virgin Mary and her rosy-cheeked baby (right panel), who are surrounded by angels with flame-like wings.

Despite the gold-leaf background, a glimmer of human realism peeks through. The kings have distinct, down-to-earth faces. And the outside shows not a saint, not a god, but a real-life deer lying down in the grass of this earth.

But the anonymous artist is struggling with reality. John the Baptist is holding a "lamb of God" that looks more like a Chihuahua. Nice try. Mary's exquisite fingers hold an anatomically impossible little foot. The figures are flat, scrawny, and sinless, with cartoon features—far from flesh-and-blood human beings. Still, Richard II himself (king of England from 1377 to 1399) knelt before this portable altarpiece to inspire his personal devotions to the Virgin.

• Continuing into Room 54, you'll leave this gold-leaf peace and find...

Uccello—*Battle of San Romano* (c. 1438-1440)

This colorful battle scene shows the victory of Florence over Siena in 1432—and the battle for literal realism on the canvas. It's an

early Renaissance attempt at a realistic, nonreligious, three-dimensional scene.

Uccello challenges his ability by posing the horses and soldiers at every conceivable angle. The background of farmyards, receding hedges, and tiny soldiers creates an illusion of distance. The artist actually constructs a grid of fallen lances in the foreground, then places the horses and warriors within it. Still, Uccello hasn't quite worked out the bugs—the figures in the distance are far too big, and the fallen soldier on the left isn't much larger than the fallen shield on the right.

• *In Room 56, you'll find...*

Van Eyck—*The Arnolfini Portrait* (1434)

Called by some "The Shotgun Wedding," this painting was once thought to depict a wedding ceremony forced by the lady's swelling belly. Today it's understood as a

portrait of a solemn, well-dressed, well-heeled couple, the Arnolfinis of Bruges, Belgium. It is a masterpiece of down-to-earth details.

Van Eyck has built a medieval dollhouse, inviting us to linger over the furnishings. Feel the texture of the fabrics, count the terrier's hairs, trace the shadows generated by the window. Each object is painted at an ideal angle, with the details you'd see if you were standing directly in front of it. So the strings of beads hanging on the back wall are as crystal clear as the bracelets on the woman.

To top it off, look into the round mirror on the far wall—the whole scene is reflected backward in miniature, showing the loving couple and a pair of mysterious visitors. Is one of them Van Eyck himself at his easel? Or has the artist painted you, the home viewer, into the scene?

The surface detail is extraordinary, but the painting lacks true Renaissance depth. The tiny room looks unnaturally narrow, cramped, and claustrophobic.

MEDIEVAL &
EARLY RENAISSANCE
1 ANONYMOUS – The Wilton Diptych
2 UCCELLO – Battle of San Romano
3 VAN EYCK – The Arnolfini Portrait

ITALIAN RENAISSANCE
4 BOTTICELLI – Venus and Mars
5 CRIVELLI – The Annunciation, with Saint Emidius

HIGH RENAISSANCE
6 MICHELANGELO – The Entombment
7 RAPHAEL – Pope Julius II
8 HOLBEIN – The Ambassadors
9 DA VINCI – The Virgin of the Rocks; Virgin and Child with St. Anne and St. John the Baptist

VENETIAN RENAISSANCE
10 TINTORETTO – The Origin of the Milky Way
11 TITIAN – Bacchus and Ariadne

NORTHERN PROTESTANT ART
12 VERMEER – A Young Woman Standing at a Virginal
13 VAN HOOGSTRATEN – A Peepshow with Views of the Interior of a Dutch House
14 REMBRANDT – Belshazzar's Feast
15 REMBRANDT – Self-Portrait at the Age of 63

BAROQUE & FRENCH ROCOCO
16 RUBENS – The Judgment of Paris
17 VAN DYCK – Equestrian Portrait of Charles I
18 VELÁZQUEZ – The Rokeby Venus
19 CARAVAGGIO –The Supper at Emmaus
20 BOUCHER – Pan and Syrinx

BRITISH
21 CONSTABLE – The Hay Wain
22 TURNER – The Fighting Téméraire
23 DELAROCHE – The Execution of Lady Jane Grey

To Leicester Square ⊖
(5 min. walk)

SAINSBURY WING

ENTRANCE ON LEVEL 0

SELF-GUIDED TOUR
STARTS ON LEVEL 2

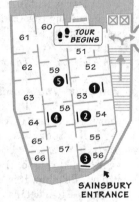

TOUR BEGINS

SAINSBURY ENTRANCE

NATIONAL GALLERY

In medieval times (this was painted only a generation after *The Wilton Diptych*), everyone could read the hidden meaning of certain symbols—the chandelier with its one lit candle (love), the fruit on the windowsill (fertility), the dangling whisk broom (the woman's domestic responsibilities), and the terrier (Fido—fidelity).

By the way, the woman likely is not pregnant. The fashion of the day was to gather up the folds of one's extremely full-skirted dress. At least, that's what they told her parents.

National Gallery Highlights

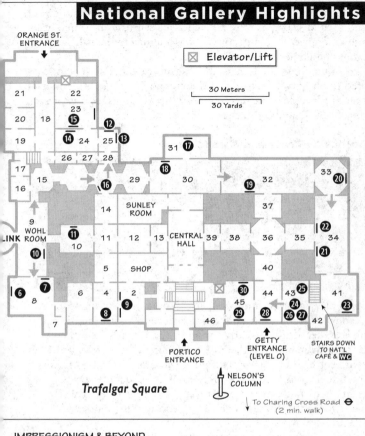

| | Elevator/Lift |

30 Meters

30 Yards

ORANGE ST. ENTRANCE

21 22 23 20 18 19 14 24 26 27 28 17 16 15 29 31 30 32 33

9 WOHL ROOM 11 10 5 SHOP 14 SUNLEY ROOM 12 13 CENTRAL HALL 39 38 36 37 35 34

LINK

6 8 7 4 2 6 9 8 45 46 30 44 43 41 42 40 29 28 26 27 24 25 23

PORTICO ENTRANCE

Trafalgar Square

GETTY ENTRANCE (LEVEL 0)

STAIRS DOWN TO NAT'L CAFÉ & WC

NELSON'S COLUMN

To Charing Cross Road ⊖ (2 min. walk)

IMPRESSIONISM & BEYOND

24 MONET – Gare St. Lazare
25 MONET – The Water-Lily Pond
26 MANET – Corner of a Café-Concert
27 RENOIR – The Skiff
28 SEURAT – Bathers at Asnières
29 VAN GOGH – Sunflowers
30 CÉZANNE – Bathers

• *Return to Room 55, turn left into Room 57, then turn right into Room 58.*

The Italian Renaissance (1400-1550)

The Renaissance—or "rebirth" of the culture of ancient Greece and Rome—was a cultural boom that changed people's thinking about every aspect of life. In politics, it meant democracy. In religion, it meant a move away from Church dominance and toward the assertion of man (humanism) and a more personal faith. Science and secular learning were revived after centuries of superstition and ignorance. In architecture, it was a return to the balanced columns and domes of Greece and Rome.

In painting, the Renaissance meant realism. Artists rediscovered the beauty of nature and the human body. With pictures of beautiful people in harmonious, 3-D surroundings, they expressed the optimism and confidence of this new age.

Botticelli—*Venus and Mars* (c. 1485)

Mars takes a break from war, succumbing to the delights of love (Venus), while impish satyrs play innocently with the discarded tools of death. In the early spring of the Renaissance, there was an optimistic mood in the air—the feeling that enlightened Man could solve all problems, narrowing the gap between mortals and the Greek gods. Artists felt free to use the pagan Greek gods as symbols of human traits, virtues, and vices. Venus has sapped man's medieval stiffness, and the Renaissance is coming.
• *Continue to Room 59.*

Crivelli—*The Annunciation, with Saint Emidius* (1486)

Mary, in green, is visited by the dove of the Holy Ghost, who beams down from the distant heavens in a shaft of light.

Like Van Eyck's wedding, this is a brilliant collection of realistic details. Notice the hanging rug, the peacock, the architectural minutiae that lead you way, way back, then bam!—you have a giant pickle in your face.

It combines meticulous detail with Italian spaciousness. The floor tiles and building bricks recede into the distance. We're sucked right in, accelerating through the alleyway, under the arch, and off into space. The Holy Ghost spans the entire distance, connecting heavenly background with earthly foreground. Crivelli creates an

Escheresque labyrinth of rooms and walkways that we want to walk through, around, and into—or is that just a male thing?

Renaissance Italians were interested in—even obsessed with—portraying 3-D space. Perhaps they focused their spiritual passion away from heaven and toward the physical world. With such restless energy, they needed lots of elbow room. Space, the final frontier.

• *Just two rooms ahead is Room 51, where we first entered. From Room 51, cross to the main building (the West Wing) and enter the large Room 9. We'll return to these big, colorful canvases—but first, turn right into Room 8.*

The High Renaissance (1500)

With the "Big Three" of the High Renaissance—Leonardo, Michelangelo, and Raphael—painters had finally conquered realism. But these three Florence-trained artists weren't content just to copy nature, cranking out photographs-on-canvas. Like Renaissance architects (which they also were), they carefully composed their figures on the canvas, "building" them into geometrical patterns that reflected the balance and order they saw in nature.

Michelangelo—*The Entombment* (c. 1500-1501)

Michelangelo, the greatest sculptor ever, proves it here in this "painted sculpture" of the crucified Jesus being carried to the tomb.

Like a chiseled Greek god, the musclehead in red ripples beneath his clothes. Christ's naked body, shocking to the medieval Church, was completely acceptable in the Renaissance world, where classical nudes were admired as an expression of the divine.

Renaissance balance and symmetry reign. Christ is the center of the composition, flanked by two equally leaning people who support his body with strips of cloth. They, in turn, are flanked by two others.

The painting is not damaged, but it is unfinished. Michelangelo, 25 years old at the time, moved on to other projects before he got around to adding crucial details, even leaving a blank space in the lower right where Mary would have been.

Regardless of the lack of detail, Michelangelo lets the bodies do the talking. The two supporters strain to hold up Christ's body, and in their tension we, too, feel the great weight and tragedy of their dead god. Michelangelo expresses the divine through the human form.

Raphael—*Pope Julius II* (1511)

The new worldliness of the Renaissance even reached the Church.

Pope Julius II, who was more a swaggering conquistador than a pious pope, set out to rebuild Rome in Renaissance style, hiring Michelangelo to paint the ceiling of the Vatican's Sistine Chapel.

Raphael gives a behind-the-scenes look at this complex leader. On the one hand, the pope is an imposing pyramid of power, with a velvet shawl, silk shirt, and fancy rings boasting of wealth and success. But at the same time, he's a bent and broken man, his throne backed into a corner, with an expression that seems to say, "Is this all there is?"

• *Exit Room 8 (opposite where you entered), and pass through several rooms until you reach Room 4.*

Holbein—*The Ambassadors* (1533)

Italian 3-D even shows up in this work by German-born Hans Holbein the Younger, who settled in England to create portraits

for Henry VIII. Two well-dressed, suave men flank a shelf full of books, globes, navigational tools, and musical instruments—objects that symbolize the secular knowledge of the Renaissance. Almost forgotten is the tiny crucifix in the upper-left corner. So what's with the gray, slanting blob at the bottom? If you view the blob from the right-hand edge of the painting (get real close, right up to the frame), the blob suddenly

becomes...a skull. In painting terms, the optical illusion is called an anamorphic projection. (For another example, see page 159.) Symbolically, the skull is a *memento mori*, a reminder that—despite the fine clothes, proud poses, and worldly knowledge—we will all die.

• *Continue into Room 2, with two works by Leonardo.*

Leonardo da Vinci—*The Virgin of the Rocks* (c. 1491-1508)

In this painting, Mary, the mother of Jesus, plays with her son and little Johnny the Baptist (with cross, at left) while an androgynous angel looks on. Leonardo brings this holy scene right down

Painting: From Tempera to Tubes

The technology of painting has evolved over the centuries.

1400s Artists used tempera (pigments dissolved in egg yolk) on wood.

1500s Still painting on wood, artists mainly used oil (pigments dissolved in vegetable oil, such as linseed, walnut, or poppy).

1600s Artists applied oil paints to canvases stretched across wooden frames.

1850 Paints in convenient, collapsible tubes are invented, making open-air painting feasible.

The Frames: Although some frames are original, having been chosen by the artist, most are selected by museum curators. Some are old frames from another painting, others are Victorian-era reproductions in wood, and still others are recent reproductions made of a composition substance to look like gilded wood.

to earth by setting it among rocks, stalactites, water, and flowering plants. But looking closer, we see that Leonardo has deliberately posed his people into a pyramid shape, with Mary's head at the peak, creating an oasis of maternal stability and serenity amid the hard rock of the earth. Leonardo, who was illegitimate, may have sought in his art the young mother he never knew. Freud thought so.

• *Also in Room 2, you'll find...*

NATIONAL GALLERY

Leonardo da Vinci—*Virgin and Child with St. Anne and St. John the Baptist* (c. 1499-1500)

At first glance, this chalk cartoon (a full-size preparatory drawing for a painting) looks like a simple snapshot of two loving moms and two playful kids. The two children play—oblivious to the violent deaths they'll both suffer—beneath their mothers' Mona Lisa smiles.

But follow the eyes: Shadowy-eyed Anne turns toward Mary, who looks tenderly down to Jesus, who blesses John, who

gazes back dreamily. As your eyes follow theirs, you're led back to the literal and psychological center of the composition—Jesus—the Alpha and Omega. Without resorting to heavy-handed medieval symbolism, Leonardo drives home a theological concept in a natural, human way. Leonardo the perfectionist rarely finished paintings. This sketch—pieced together from two separate papers (see the line down the middle)—gives us an inside peek at his genius.

• *The Renaissance—born in Florence and nurtured in Rome—soon shifted to Venice. Backtrack to the long Room 9.*

Venetian Renaissance (1510-1600)

Big change. The canvases are bigger, the colors brighter. Goddesses and heroes replace Madonnas and saints. And there are nudes—not Michelangelo's lumps of noble, knotted muscle, but smooth-skinned, sexy, golden centerfolds.

Venice got wealthy by trading with the luxurious and exotic East. Its happy-go-lucky art style shows a taste for the finer things in life.

Tintoretto—*The Origin of the Milky Way* (c. 1575)

In this scene from a classical myth, the god Jupiter places his illegitimate son, baby Hercules, at his wife's breast. Juno says, "Wait a

minute. That's not my baby!" Her milk spurts upward, becoming the Milky Way.

Tintoretto places us right up in the clouds, among the gods, who swirl around at every angle. Jupiter appears to be flying almost right at us. An X composition unites it all—Juno slants one way while Jupiter tilts the other.

• *Find a colorful, raucous parade in the adjoining Room 10. (The canvas is sometimes displayed in Room 12.)*

Titian—*Bacchus and Ariadne* (1520-1523)

Bacchus, the god of wine, leaps from his leopard-drawn chariot, his red cape blowing behind him, to cheer up Ariadne (far left), who has been jilted by her lover. Bacchus' motley entourage rattles cymbals, bangs on tambourines, and literally shakes a leg.

Man and animal mingle in this pre-Christian orgy, with leopards, a snake, a dog, and the severed head and leg of an ass ready for the barbecue. Man and animal also literally "mix" in the satyrs—part man, part goat. The fat, sleepy guy in the background has had too much.

Titian (see his "Ticianus" signature on the gold vase, lower left) uses a pyramid composition to balance an otherwise chaotic scene. Follow Ariadne's gaze up to the peak of Bacchus' flowing cape, then down along the snake handler's spine to the lower-right corner. In addition, the artist balances the picture with harmonious colors—blue sky on the left, green trees on the right, while the two main figures stand out with loud splotches of red.

• *Return to Room 9 and turn right. Exit this room at the far end and turn right, entering the long Room 29 (with mint-green wallpaper). Midway through Room 29, turn left and find Room 25.*

Northern Protestant Art (1600-1700)

We switch from CinemaScope to a tiny TV—smaller canvases, subdued colors, everyday scenes, and not even a bare shoulder.

Money shapes art. While Italy had wealthy aristocrats and the powerful Catholic Church to purchase art, the North's patrons were middle-class, hardworking, Protestant merchants. They wanted simple, cheap, no-nonsense pictures to decorate their homes and offices. Greek gods and Virgin Marys were out, hometown folks and hometown places were in—portraits, landscapes, still lifes, and slice-of-life scenes. Painted with great attention to detail, this is art meant not to wow or preach at you, but to be enjoyed and lingered over. Sightsee.

Vermeer—*A Young Woman Standing at a Virginal* (c. 1670)

Inside a simple but wealthy Dutch home, a prim virgin plays an early piano called a "virginal." We've surprised her, and she pauses to look up at us.

By framing off such a small world to look at—from the blue chair in the foreground to the wall in back—Vermeer forces us to appreciate the tiniest details, the beauty of everyday things. We can meditate on the tiles lining the floor, the subtle shades of the white wall, and the pale, diffused light that seeps in from the window. Amid straight lines and rectangles, the woman's billowing dress adds a soft touch. The painting of a nude cupid on the back wall only strengthens this virgin's purity.

• *Also in Room 25, you'll find...*

Van Hoogstraten—*A Peepshow with Views of the Interior of a Dutch House* (c. 1655-1660)

Look through the open end of this ingenious device to make the painting of a house interior come to three-dimensional life. Compare the twisted curves of the painting with the illusion it creates and appreciate the painstaking work of the dedicated artist.

• *Enter the adjoining Room 24.*

Rembrandt—*Belshazzar's Feast* (c. 1635)

Belshazzar, the wicked king of Babylon, has been feasting with God's sacred dinnerware when the meal is interrupted. The king turns to see the hand of God, burning an ominous message into the wall that Belshazzar's number is up. As he turns, he knocks over a goblet of wine. We see the jewels and riches of his decadent life.

Rembrandt captures the scene at the most ironic moment. Belshazzar is about to be ruined. We know it, his guests know it, and, judging by the look on his face, he's coming to the same conclusion.

Rembrandt's flair for the dramatic is accentuated by the strong contrast between light and dark. Most of his canvases are a rich, dark brown, with a few crucial details highlighted by a bright light.

• *Enter the adjoining Room 23.*

Rembrandt—*Self-Portrait at the Age of 63* (1669)

Rembrandt throws the light of truth on...himself. He made this craggy self-portrait in the year he would die, at age 63. Contrast

it with one done three decades earlier (hanging directly opposite). Rembrandt, the greatest Dutch painter, started out as the successful, wealthy young genius of the art world. But he refused to crank out commercial works. Rembrandt painted things that he believed in but no one would invest in—family members, down-to-earth Bible scenes, and self-portraits like these.

Here, Rembrandt surveys the

wreckage of his independent life. He was bankrupt, his mistress had just died, and he had also buried several of his children. We see a disillusioned, well-worn, but proud old genius.

• *Backtrack to the long, mint-green Room 29.*

Baroque (1600-1700)
Rubens

This room holds big, colorful, emotional works by Peter Paul Rubens and others from Catholic Flanders (Belgium). While

Protestant and democratic Europe painted simple scenes, Catholic and aristocratic countries turned to the style called Baroque. Baroque art took what was flashy in Venetian art and made it flashier, gaudy and made it gaudier, dramatic and made it shocking.

Rubens painted anything that would raise your pulse—battles, miracles, hunts, and, especially, fleshy women with dimples on all four cheeks. For instance, *The Judgment of Paris* (one of two versions by Rubens in this museum) is little more than an excuse for a study of the female nude, showing front, back, and profile all on one canvas.

• *Exit Room 29 at the far end. In Room 30 (with red wallpaper), turn left into the big, red Room 31, where you'll see a large canvas.*

Van Dyck—*Equestrian Portrait of Charles I* (c. 1637-1638)

King Charles sits on a huge horse, accentuating his power. The horse's small head makes sure that little Charles isn't dwarfed.

Charles was a soft-on-Catholics king in a hard-core Protestant country until England's Civil War (1648), when his genteel head was separated from his refined body by Cromwell and company.

Kings and bishops used the grandiose Baroque style to impress the masses with their power. Van Dyck's portrait style set the tone for all the stuffy, boring portraits of British aristocrats who wished to be portrayed as sophisticated gentlemen—whether they were or not.

• *For the complete opposite of a stuffy portrait, backpedal into Room 30 for...*

Velázquez—*The Rokeby Venus* (c. 1647-1651)

Like a Venetian centerfold, Venus lounges diagonally across the canvas, admiring herself, with flaring red, white, and gray fabrics to highlight her rosy white skin and inflame our passion. Horny Spanish kings loved Titianesque nudes despite Spain's strict Inquisition, the Church tribunal that rooted out bad behavior. This work by the king's personal court painter is a rare Spanish nude from that ultra-Catholic country. About the sole concession to Spanish modesty is the false reflection in the mirror—if it really showed what the angle should show, Velázquez would have needed two mirrors...and a new job.

• *Turning your left cheek to hers, tango into Room 32.*

Caravaggio—*The Supper at Emmaus* (1601)

After Jesus was crucified, he rose from the dead and appeared without warning to some of his followers. Jesus just wants a quiet

meal, but the man in green, suddenly realizing who he's eating with, is about to jump out of his chair in shock. To the right, a man spreads his hands in amazement, bridging the distance between Christ and us by sticking his hand in our faces.

The Baroque took reality and exaggerated it. Most artists amplified prettiness, but Caravaggio exaggerated grittiness, using real, ugly, unhaloed people in Bible scenes. Caravaggio's paintings look like how a wet dog smells. Reality.

We've come a long way since the first medieval altarpieces that wrapped holy people in gold foil. From the torn shirts to the five o'clock shadows, from the blemished apples to the uneven part in Jesus' hair, we are witnessing a very human miracle.

• *Leave Room 32 at the far end, and enter Room 33.*

French Rococo (1700-1800)

As Europe's political and economic center shifted from Italy to France, Louis XIV's court at Versailles became its cultural hub. Every aristocrat spoke French, dressed French, and bought French paintings. The Rococo art of Louis' successors was as frilly, sensual, and suggestive as the decadent French court. We see their rosy-cheeked portraits and their fantasies: lords and ladies at play

in classical gardens, where mortals and gods cavort together.
• *One of the finest examples is the tiny...*

Boucher—*Pan and Syrinx* (1759)

Curious Pan seeks a threesome, but to elude him, Syrinx eventually changes into reeds, leaving him all wet.

Rococo art is like a Rubens that got shrunk in the wash—smaller, lighter pastel colors, frillier, and more delicate than the Baroque style. Same dimples, though.
• *Enter Room 34. Take a hike around and enjoy the English country-garden ambience.*

British (1800-1850)

Constable—*The Hay Wain* (1821)

The reserved British were more comfortable cavorting with nature than with the lofty gods. Come-as-you-are poets like Wordsworth found the same ecstasy just in being outside.

John Constable set up his easel out-of-doors, making quick sketches to capture the simple majesty of billowing clouds, spreading trees, and everyday rural life. Even British portraits (by Thomas Gainsborough and others) placed refined lords and ladies amid idealized greenery.

This simple style—believe it or not—was considered shocking in its day. The rough, thick, earth-toned paint and crude country settings scandalized art lovers used to the highfalutin, prettified sheen of the Baroque and Rococo.

Turner—*The Fighting Téméraire* (1839)

Constable's landscape was about to be paved over by the Industrial Revolution. Soon, machines began to replace humans, factories belched smoke over Constable's hay cart, and cloud-gazers had to punch the clock. Romantics tried to resist it, lauding the forces of nature and natural human emotions in the face of technological "progress." But alas, here a modern steamboat symbolically drags a famous but obsolete sailing battleship off into the sunset to be destroyed.

Turner's messy, colorful style gives us our first glimpse into the modern art world—he influenced the Impressionists. Turner takes an ordinary scene (like Constable), captures the play of light with messy paints (like Impressionists), and charges it with mystery (like, wow).

• *To view more Constables, an enormous collection of Turners, and other British art, visit London's Tate Britain (❂ see the Tate Britain Tour). For now, enter Room 41.*

Delaroche—*The Execution of Lady Jane Grey* (1833)

It's 1554. The teenage queen's nine-day reign has reached its curfew. This innocent girl, manipulated into power politics by cunning advisors, is now sent to the  execution site in the Tower of London. As her friends swoon with grief, she's blindfolded and forced to kneel at the block. Legend has it that the confused, humiliated girl was left kneeling on the scaffold. She crawled around, groping for the chopping block, crying out, "Where is it? What am I supposed to do?" The executioner in scarlet looks on with as much compassion as he can muster.

Britain's distinct contribution to art history is this Pre-Raphaelite style, showing medieval scenes in luminous realism with a mood of understated tragedy.

• *Exit Room 41 and enter Room 43. The Impressionist paintings are scattered throughout Rooms 43–46.*

Impressionism and Beyond (1850-1910)

For 500 years, a great artist was someone who could paint the real world with perfect accuracy. Then along came the camera and, click, the artist was replaced by a machine. But unemployed artists refused to go the way of *The Fighting Téméraire*.

They couldn't match the camera for painstaking detail, but they could match it—even beat it—in capturing color, the fleeting moment, the candid pose, the play of light and shadow, the quick impression. A new breed of artists burst out of the stuffy confines of the studio. They donned scarves and berets and set up their canvases in farmers' fields or carried their notebooks into crowded cafés, dashing off quick sketches in order to catch a momentary... impression.

• *Start with the misty Monet train station.*

Monet—*Gare St. Lazare* (1877)

Claude Monet, the father of Impressionism, was more interested in the play of light off his subject than the subject itself. He uses smudges of white and gray paint to capture how sun filters through the glass roof of the train station and is refiltered through the clouds of steam.

Monet—*The Water-Lily Pond* (1899)

We've traveled from medieval spirituality to Renaissance realism to Baroque elegance and Impressionist colors. Before you spill out into the 21st-century hubbub of London, relax for a second in Monet's garden at Giverny, near Paris. Monet planned an artificial garden, rechanneled a stream, built a bridge, and planted these water lilies— a living work of art, an oasis of order and calm in a hectic world.

Manet—*Corner of a Café-Concert* (1878-1880)

Imagine just how mundane (and therefore shocking) Manet's quick "impression" of this café must have been to a public that was raised on Greek gods, luscious nudes, and glowing Madonnas.

Renoir—*The Skiff* (*La Yole,* 1875)

It's a nice scene of boats on sun-dappled water. Now move in close. The "scene" breaks up into almost random patches of bright colors. The "blue" water is actually separate brushstrokes of blue, green, pink, purple, gray, and white. The rower's hat is a blob of green, white, and blue. Up close, it looks like a mess, but when you back up to a proper distance, *voilà!* It shimmers. This kind of rough, coarse brushwork (where you can actually see the brushstrokes) is one of the telltale signs of Impressionism. Renoir was not trying to paint the water itself, but the reflection of sky, shore, and boats off its surface.

• *In Room 44, you'll find...*

Seurat—*Bathers at Asnières* (1884)

Viewed from about 15 feet away, this is a bright, sunny scene of people lounging on a riverbank. Up close it's a mess of dots, showing the Impressionist color technique taken to its logical extreme. The "green" grass is a shag rug of green, yellow, red, brown, purple, and white brushstrokes. The boy's "red" cap is a collage of red, yellow, and blue.

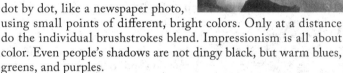

Seurat has "built" the scene dot by dot, like a newspaper photo, using small points of different, bright colors. Only at a distance do the individual brushstrokes blend. Impressionism is all about color. Even people's shadows are not dingy black, but warm blues, greens, and purples.

• *In Room 45, you'll see...*

Van Gogh—*Sunflowers* (1888)

In military terms, Van Gogh was the point man of his culture. He went ahead of his cohorts, explored the unknown, and caught a bullet young. He added emotion to Impressionism, infusing his love of life even into inanimate objects. These sunflowers, painted with characteristic swirling brushstrokes, shimmer and writhe in

either agony or ecstasy—depending on your own mood.

Van Gogh painted these during his stay in southern France, a time of frenzied creativity, when he hovered between despair and delight, bliss and madness. A year later, he shot himself.

In his day, Van Gogh was a penniless nobody, selling only one painting in his whole career. In 1987, a different *Sunflowers* painting (he did a half-dozen versions) sold for $40 million (a salary of about $2,500 a day for 45 years), and that's not even his highest-priced painting. Hmm.

Cézanne—*Bathers* (*Les Grandes Baigneuses,* c. 1894-1905)

These bathers are arranged in strict triangles à la Leonardo—the five nudes on the left form one triangle, the seated nude on the right forms another, and even the background trees and clouds are triangular patterns of paint.

Cézanne uses the Impressionist technique of building a fig-
ure with dabs of paint (though his "dabs" are often larger-sized "cube" shapes) to make solid, 3-D geometrical figures in the style of the Renaissance. In the process, his cube shapes helped inspire a radical new art style— Cubism—bringing art into the 20th century.

• *Exiting Room 45, you find yourself in the stairwell of the Gallery's main entrance (under the dome) on Trafalgar Square. If you want to return to the Sainsbury Entrance, cross the stairwell and pass through several familiar rooms (with Leonardo,* The Ambassadors, *etc.); in Room 9, turn left to reach the Sainsbury Wing.*

After perusing 700 years of art—from gold-backed Madonnas to Cubistic bathers—you've earned a well-deserved break.

NATIONAL PORTRAIT GALLERY TOUR

Rock groupies, book lovers, movie fans, gossipmongers, and even historians all can find at least one favorite celebrity here. From Elizabeth I to Elizabeth II, Byron to Bowie, the National Portrait Gallery puts a face on 500 years, making "history" the simple story of flesh-and-blood people. Consider that, for the most part, these portraits were painted in the presence of their subjects—providing us with a tangible link to the real person in the painting. The Gallery is a great rainy-day museum for serious students, or a quick (and free) peek at the eccentric inhabitants of the British Isles.

Orientation

Cost: Free, but suggested donation of £5. Temporary (optional) exhibits require an admission fee.

Hours: Daily 10:00-18:00, Thu-Fri until 21:00—often with music and drinks offered in the evening, first and second floors open Mon at 11:00, last entry to special exhibits 45 minutes before closing, tel. 020/7306-0055, recorded info tel. 020/7312-2463, www.npg.org.uk.

Getting There: It's at St. Martin's Place, 100 yards off Trafalgar Square (around the corner from the National Gallery and opposite the Church of St. Martin-in-the-Fields). The closest Tube stops are Charing Cross and Leicester Square.

Tours: The £3 audioguide lets you choose among several theme tours, or you can dial up any of 300 individual works. "Portrait Explorer" computers on the mezzanine give info on virtually any portrait or artist in the extensive collection.

Length of This Tour: Allow 1.5 hours.

Photography: Photos are not allowed.

Cuisine Art: The elegant Portrait Restaurant on the top floor is pricey but has a fine view over the rooftops of Westminster (£15-20 entrées, reservations smart, tel. 020/7312-2490). The Portrait Café in the basement (take the elevator down) is cheaper and offers sandwiches, salads, and pastries. For more eateries near Trafalgar Square, see page 385.

Starring: Royalty (Henry VIII, Elizabeth I, Victoria), writers (Shakespeare, the Brontës), scientists (Newton, Darwin), politicians (Churchill), and musicians (Handel, McCartney). As 2012 marks the Queen's Diamond Jubilee (her 60th year on the throne), expect to see numerous portraits of her during the summer months.

Overview

The Gallery covers 500 years of history from top to bottom—literally. Start on the top (second) floor and work chronologically down to modern times on the ground floor. Historians should linger at the top; celebrity hunters will lose elevation quickly and head to the contemporary section. There are many, many famous people from all walks of life, so use this chapter as an overview, then follow your interests, either with an audioguide or by reading the museum's informative labels.

The Tour Begins

• *Ride the long escalator up to the second floor and start in Room 1, marked The Early Tudors. Find the large black-and-white sketch (cartoon) of Henry VIII with his hands on his hips.*

Second Floor

1500s—Debut

The small, isolated island of Britain (pop. four million) enters the world stage. The Tudor kings—having already settled family feuds (the Wars of the Roses), balanced religious factions, and built England's navy—bring wealth from abroad.

• *Enter Room 1.*

❶ Henry VIII (1491-1547), The Whitehall Mural Cartoon

Young, athletic, intense, and charismatic, with jeweled hands, gold dagger, and bulging codpiece (the very image of kingly power), Henry VIII carried England on his broad shoulders from political isolation to international power.

National Portrait Gallery— Second Floor

ST. MARTIN'S PLACE
ENTRANCE (BELOW)

ELEV.

ORANGE
STREET
ENTRANCE
(BELOW)

REST.

TOUR BEGINS

STAIRS TO
FIRST FLOOR

ROOM
20

1 Henry VIII & Wives
2 Edward VI
3 Elizabeth I (3 Versions)
4 William Shakespeare
5 James I
6 Charles I
7 Oliver Cromwell
8 Charles II
9 Isaac Newton & John Locke
10 Christopher Wren
11 George Frideric Handel
12 James Watt
13 King George III
14 George Washington
15 Admiral Horatio Nelson & Emma, Lady Hamilton
16 The Romantics

In middle age, he divorced his older, dull-eyed, post-child-bearing queen, Catherine of Aragon (see her portrait opposite Henry), for younger, shrewd, sparkling-eyed Anne Boleyn (near Catherine; see photo), in search of love, sex, and a male heir. Nine months later, the future Elizabeth I was born, and the pope excommunicated adulterous Henry. Defiant, Henry started the (Protestant) Church of England, sparking a century-plus of religious strife between the country's Protestants and Catholics.

By the time Henry died—400 pounds of stinking, pus-ridden paranoia—he had wed six wives (see the sixth, sweet young Catherine Parr, opposite Henry), executed

several of them (including Anne Boleyn), killed trusted advisors, pursued costly wars, and produced one male heir, Edward VI.
• *Also in Room 1 is the looooong picture of...*

❷ Edward VI (1537-1553)
Nine-year-old Edward (son of Henry's third wife, Jane Seymour) ruled for only six years before dying young, leaving England in religious and economic turmoil. (View the optical illusion through the hole at the right end to put the enigmatic boy king into perspective.)
• *Go to Room 2.*

❸ Elizabeth I (1533-1603),
Three Different Portraits on Three Different Walls
Elizabeth I was pale, stern-looking, red-haired (like her father, Henry VIII), and wore big-shouldered power dresses. During her

reign, she kept Protestant/Catholic animosity under control and made England a naval power and cultural capital. Find three different portraits that span her life. The smallest of the three shows her coronation at age 26, with the crown, scepter, and orb. At age 42 (see photo), she exudes a regal bearing. The largest painting (*The Ditchley Portrait*) captures her at age 60. She looks ageless, always aware of her public image, resorting to makeup, dye, wigs, showy dresses, and pearls to dazzle courtiers.

The "Virgin Queen" was married only to her country, but she flirtatiously wooed opponents to her side. ("I know I have the body of a weak and feeble woman," she'd coo, "but I have the heart and stomach of a king.") When England's navy sank 72 ships of the Spanish Armada in a single, power-shifting battle (1588), Britannia ruled the waves, feasting on New World spoils. Elizabeth surrounded herself with intellectuals, explorers, and poets.
• *Pass through Room 3, through the stairwell, and into Room 4.*

❹ William Shakespeare (1564-1616)
Though famous in his day, Shakespeare's long hair, beard, earring, untied collar, and red-rimmed eyes make him look less the celebrity and more the bohemian barfly he likely was (for more on Shakespeare's life and influence, see the sidebar on page 222). This unassuming portrait (reportedly one of only two done in his lifetime) captures 45-year-old Shakespeare just before he retired from his career as actor, poet, and world's greatest playwright. The

shiny, domed forehead is a beacon of intelligence. (I suspect Shakespeare liked this plain-spoken portrait.)

The museum attributes this portrait to a Shakespeare contemporary, John Taylor, but other scholars insist it was done long after the writer's death. One recently discovered portrait (not in the museum) depicts a 46-year-old Shakespeare looking like a matinee idol, with a full head of hair. The search goes on for the "real" Will.

• *Also in Room 4, find the portrait of James I that marks the end of the Elizabethan Age and the beginning of the...*

1600s—Religious and Civil Wars

Catholic kings bickered with an increasingly vocal Protestant Parliament until Civil War erupted (1642-1651), killing thousands, decapitating the king, and eventually establishing Parliament as the main power.

❺ James I (1566-1625) of England and VI of Scotland

When the "Virgin Queen" died childless, her cousin—an arrogant Scotsman—moved to genteel London and donned the royal robes. Deeply religious, he launched the "King James" translation of the Bible, but he alienated Anglicans (Church of England), harder-line Protestants (Puritans), and democrats everywhere by insisting that he ruled by divine right, directly from God. He passed on this attitude to his son, Charles.

• *Enter Room 5, with portraits of Civil War veterans.*

❻ Charles I (1600-1649)

Picture Charles' sensitive face (with scholar's eyes and artist's long hair and beard) severed from his elegant body (in horse-riding finery), and you've arrived quickly at the heart of the Civil War.

The short, shy, stuttering Charles angered Protestants and democrats by dissolving Parliament, raising taxes, and marrying a Catholic. Parliament formed an army, fought the king's supporters, arrested and tried Charles, and—outside the Banqueting House on Whitehall—beheaded him.

• *The man responsible was...*

❼ Oliver Cromwell (1599-1658)

Cromwell, with armor, sword, command baton, and a determined look, was the Protestant champion and military leader. The Civil

War pitted Parliamentarians (Parliament, Protestant Puritans, industry, and urban areas) against Royalists (King, Catholics, nobles, traditionalists, and rural areas). After Charles' execution, Cromwell led kingless England as "Lord Protector."

Stern Cromwell hated luxury and ordered a warts-and-all portrait (see wart on his left temple and scar between his eyebrows). He has a simple, bowl-cut hairstyle adorning his 82-ounce brain (49 is average). Speaking of heads, three years after Cromwell's death, vengeful Royalists exhumed his body, cut off the head, stuck it on a stick, and placed it outside Westminster Abbey, where it rotted publicly for 24 years.

• *Pass through Room 6 and into Room 7. Facing you is...*

❽ Charles II (1630-1685)

After two decades of wars, Cromwell's harsh rule, and Puritanical excesses (no dancing, theater, or political incorrectness), Parliament welcomed the monarchy back (with tight restrictions) under Charles II. England was ready to party.

Looking completely ridiculous, with splayed legs, puffy face, big-hair wig, garters, and ribbons on his shoes, Charles II became a king with nothing to do, and he did it with grace and a sense of humor. Charles' picture is sandwiched between portraits of his devoted wife, Catherine of Braganza, and one of his well-known mistresses, the actress Nell Gwyn.

• *Make a U-turn right, entering Room 8. In the right corner are the bewigged and unamused...*

❾ Isaac Newton (1642-1727) and John Locke (1632-1704)

The 1600s, the Age of Enlightenment, saw scientific discoveries suggesting that the world operates in an orderly, rational way. Isaac Newton explained the universe's motion with the simplest of formulas ($f = ma$, etc.), and John Locke used human reason to plan a democratic utopia, coining phrases like "life, liberty..." that would

inspire America's revolutionaries.
• *Walk straight ahead to Room 10. Along the right wall, find...*

❿ Christopher Wren (1632-1723)

Christopher Wren—leaning on blueprints with a compass in hand—designed St. Paul's Cathedral, a glorious demonstration of mathematics in stone.
• *In Room 11, make a U-turn left, entering Room 12, with painters, writers, actors, and musicians of the 1700s.*

1700s—Domestic Stability, Wars with France

Blossoming agriculture, the first factories, overseas colonization, and political stability from German-born kings (George I, II, III) allowed the arts to flourish. Overseas, England financed wars against Europe's No. 1 power, France.

⓫ George Frideric Handel (1685-1759)

In London, an old form of art became something new—modern theater. Handel, a German who wrote Italian operas in England, had several smash hits in London (especially with the oratorio *Messiah*, on his desk), making musical theater popular with ordinary folk. Hallelujah.
• *Walk on, to Room 13, for the portrait of...*

⓬ James Watt (1736-1819)

Deep-thinking Watt pores over plans to turn brainpower into work power. His steam engines (with a separate condenser to capture formerly wasted heat energy) soon powered gleaming machines, changing England's economy from grain and ships to iron and coal.
• *Head to Room 14, where you'll find George III over your left shoulder and George Washington along the right wall.*

⓭ King George III (1738-1820) and
⓮ George Washington (1732-1799)

Just crowned at 23, King George III gives little hint in this portrait that he will lead England into the drawn-out, humiliating "American War" (Revolutionary War) against a colony demanding independence. George III, perhaps a victim of an undiagnosed disease, closed out the stuffy "Georgian" era (in Percy Shelley's words) "an old, mad, blind, despised, dying king."

Perhaps it was the war that drove him mad, or perhaps it was that his enemy, George

Washington (portrait nearby), had the same hairdo. Washington was born in British-ruled Virginia and fought for Britain in the French and Indian War, but sided with the colonies in what the British called the "American War." This famous portrait of Washington is one of several versions of a 1796 portrait by Gilbert Stuart.

1800s—Colonial and Industrial Giant

Britain defeated France (Napoleon) and emerged as the world's top power. With natural resources from overseas colonies (Australia, Canada, India, West Indies, China), good communications, and a growing population of seven million, Britain became the first industrial powerhouse, dotted with smoke-belching factories and laced with railroads.

• *Exit Room 14 into Room 8 and turn right, ending up in the bright aqua Room 17, featuring a red-jacketed man flanked by portraits of brave Brits who battled Napoleon.*

⓯ Admiral Horatio Nelson (1758-1805) and Emma, Lady Hamilton (1761-1815)

While the Duke of Wellington fought Napoleon on land (the final victory at Waterloo, near Brussels, 1815), Admiral Nelson battled France at sea (Battle of Trafalgar, off Spain, 1805).

At Nelson's side is Emma, Lady Hamilton, dressed in white, with her famously beautiful face turned coyly. She first met dashing Nelson on his way to fight the French in Egypt. She used the influence of her husband, Lord Hamilton, to restock Nelson's ships. Nelson's daring victory at the Battle of the Nile made him an instant celebrity, though the battle cost him an arm and an eye. The hero—a married man—returned home to woo, bed, and impregnate Lady H., with sophisticated Lord Hamilton's patriotic tolerance.

• *Go to Room 18.*

⓰ The Romantics

Not everyone worshipped industrial progress. Romantics questioned the clinical detachment of science, industrial pollution, and the personal restrictions of modern life. They reveled in strong emotions, non-Western cultures, personal freedom, opium, and the beauties of nature.

• *Scattered around the room, you'll see...*

John Keats (1795-1821) broods over his just-written "Ode to a Nightingale." ("My heart aches, and a drowsy numbness pains/My sense, as though of hemlock I had drunk.")

Samuel Taylor Coleridge (1772-1834), at 23, is open-eyed, open-mouthed, and eager. ("And all should cry, Beware! Beware!/

NAT'L PORTRAIT GALLERY

His flashing eyes, his floating hair!/...For he on honey-dew hath fed,/And drunk the milk of Paradise."—from "Kubla Khan")

Mary Wollstonecraft Shelley (1797-1851), in telling ghost stories with husband Percy Shelley and friend Lord Byron, conceived a tale of science run amok—*Frankenstein*—imitated by many. ("Ahhhhhhh, sweet mystery of life, at last I've found you!")

William Wordsworth (1770-1850): "The world is too much with us.../Little we see in Nature that is ours;/We have given our hearts away, a sordid boon!"

Percy Bysshe Shelley (1792-1822), political radical, sexual explorer (involving Mary and Claire Clairmont), traveler, and poet. ("O wild West Wind, thou breath of Autumn's being,.../If Winter comes, can Spring be far behind?")

George Gordon, **Lord Byron** (1788-1824), was athletic, exotic, and passionate about women and freedom. Famous and scandalous in his day, he became a Kerouacian symbol of the Romantic movement. ("She walks in beauty, like the night/Of cloudless climes and starry skies...")

• *After browsing Rooms 19 and 20, backtrack to Room 15 and head downstairs one flight to the first floor. Turn right at the bottom of the stairs, and enter a long hall lined with busts (Room 22). Go to the far end of the hall to Room 21, where you'll find a statue of a happy couple, titled* Queen Victoria and Prince Albert in Anglo-Saxon Dress.

First Floor

1837-1901—The Victorians

As the wealthiest nation on earth with a global colonial empire, Britain during Queen Victoria's long reign embraced modern technology, contributing to the development of power looms, railroads, telephones, motorcars, and electric lights. It was a golden age of science, literature, and middle-class morality, though pockets of extreme poverty and vice lurked in the heart of London itself.

• *In Room 21, on either side of the statue,* Queen Victoria and Prince Albert in Anglo-Saxon Dress, *you'll find paintings of...*

NAT'L PORTRAIT GALLERY

National Portrait Gallery— First Floor

ST. MARTIN'S PLACE
ENTRANCE (BELOW)

17 21 ELEV.

19 **18**

24 23 STAIRS TO
MEZZANINE
& GROUND
FLOOR
22
26 25 ROOM
32

27 STAIRS TO
SECOND FLOOR
20 & GROUND FLOOR

TOUR BEGINS

21 30

22

31

17 Queen Victoria
& Prince Albert

18 Florence Nightingale

19 Brontës, Dickens
& Tennyson

20 Charles Darwin
& Michael Faraday

21 World War I
Statesmen

22 20th-Century
Luminaries

17 Queen Victoria (1819-1901) and Prince Albert (1819-1861)

Crowned at 18, the short (5 feet), plump, bug-eyed, quiet girl inherited a world empire. The next year, she proposed marriage (the

custom) to the German Prince Albert. They were a perfect match—lovers, friends, and partners—a model for middle-class couples. (See the white statue of the pair as genteel knight and adoring lady.) Albert co-ruled, especially when "Vickie" was pregnant with their nine kids. "Bertie" promoted

NAT'L PORTRAIT GALLERY

education, science, public works, and the Great Exhibition of 1851 in Hyde Park. When Albert died at 42, a heartbroken Victoria moped for 40 years.

• *Double back through the long hall lined with stuffy busts of starched shirts (Room 22), browsing around the rooms branching off it. These rooms are filled with many prominent Victorians. Start with Room 23 and...*

⑱ Florence Nightingale (1820-1910)

Known as "the Lady with the Lamp" for her nightly nursing visits (though she's standing lampless here, in the center, with a

piece of paper), Nightingale traveled to Turkey in 1854 to tend to Crimean War victims. In fact, her forte was not hands-on nursing but efficient hospital administration (sanitation, keeping supplies stocked, transporting wounded), which ended up saving lives and raising public awareness about health issues. To learn more about her, you can visit the Florence Nightingale Museum, just across the Thames from Big Ben (in Gassiot House at 2 Lambeth Palace Road, Tube: Westminster, Waterloo, or Lambeth North).

• *Across the hall, in Room 24, you'll find several...*

⑲ Writers

Anne, Emily, and Charlotte Brontë (left to right, youngest to oldest, painted by brother Branwell), three teenage country girls, grew

up to write novels such as *Wuthering Heights* (Emily, 1818-1848) and *Jane Eyre* (Charlotte, 1816-1855), about the complex family and love lives of England's rural gentry.

To the left of the Brontës is a youthful **Charles Dickens** (1812-1870). He was only 12 years old when his dad was sent to a debtor's prison, forcing young Charles to work in a factory. The experience gave him a working-class perspective on British society. He became phenomenally successful writing popular novels (*Oliver Twist*, *A Tale of Two Cities*, *A Christmas Carol*) for Britain's educated middle class.

To the right of the Brontës is **Alfred, Lord Tennyson** (1809-1892), the poet laureate of Victorian earnestness. ("Theirs not to

NAT'L PORTRAIT GALLERY

reason why,/Theirs but to do and die;/Into the Valley of Death/ Rode the six hundred.")
• *Head to Room 27.*

⓴ Science and Technology
Charles Darwin (1809-1882), with basset-hound eyes and long white beard, looks tired after a lifetime of reluctantly defending his controversial theory of evolution that shocked an entire generation. **Michael Faraday** (1791-1867), across from Darwin, shocked himself from time to time, harnessing electricity as the work force of the next century.

• *The long hall (Room 22) leads into Room 30, dedicated to World War I.*

1900s—World Wars
Two devastating world wars and an emerging US superpower shrank Britain from global empire to island nation. But the country remained a cultural giant, producing writers, actors, composers, painters, and Beatles.

㉑ World War I Statesmen
Fighting Germans from trenches in France and Belgium, the British Army lost nearly a million men. In the big group portrait titled *Some Statesmen of the Great War,* find a bored-looking Winston Churchill.
• *The large Room 31 contains 20th-century portraits. These exhibits change frequently, and some of the portraits mentioned here may not be on display during your visit. Be prepared to put the book aside and browse.*

㉒ 20th-Century Luminaries
Find the painting of the **Duchess of Windsor** (see photo, next page) and the small statue of **Edward, Duke of Windsor.** The Duchess' smug smile tells us she got her man.

Edward VIII (1894-1972), great-grandson of Queen Victoria, became king in 1936 as a bachelor dating a common-born (gasp),

twice-divorced (double gasp) American (oh no!) named Wallis Simpson (1896-1986). Rather than create a constitutional stink, Edward quietly abdicated, married Wallis, and the two moved to the Continent, living happily ever after. They hosted cocktail parties, played golf, and listened to servants call them "Your Majesty"—though they were now just plain Duke and Duchess of Windsor. (As depicted in the Oscar-winning movie *The King's Speech*, his brother "Bertie" took over as King George VI, and George VI's daughter became Queen Elizabeth II. Elizabeth—and all the other royals—essentially snubbed their disgraced aunt and uncle for the rest of their lives.)

George Bernard Shaw (1856-1950)—playwright, critic, and political thinker—brought socialist ideas into popular discussion with plays such as *Man and Superman* and *Major Barbara*. **Virginia Woolf** (1882-1941) wrote feminist essays ("A woman must have money and a room of her own if she is to write fiction") and experimental novels (*Mrs. Dalloway* jumps back and forth in time) before filling her pockets with stones and drowning herself in a river to silence the voices in her head.

In the darkest days at the beginning of the war, with Nazi bombs raining on a wounded London, Sir **Winston Churchill** (1874-1965) rallied his people with stirring speeches from the Houses of Parliament. ("We shall fight on the beaches...We shall never surrender!") Britain's military chief, Field Marshall **Bernard Montgomery, 1st Viscount** (1887-1976, known as "Monty") points out the D-Day beaches of the decisive Allied assault.

Sir **Laurence Olivier** (1907-1989), movie and stage actor, played everything from romantic leads and Shakespeare heavies to character parts with funny accents. Sir **Noel Coward** (1899-1973) continued the British tradition of writing witty, sophisticated comedies about the idle rich. **Henry Moore** (1898-1986), the most famous 20th-century sculptor, combined the grandeur of Michelangelo, the raw stone of primitive carvings, and the simplified style of abstract art. **Dylan**

Thomas (1914-1953) wrote abstract imagery with a Romantic's heart ("Do not go gentle into that good night..."). American-born poet **T. S. Eliot** (1888-1965; see photo, previous page) captured the quiet banality of modern life: "This is the way the world ends/Not with a bang but a whimper."

• *Backtrack to the stairs, and head down to the ground floor.*

Ground Floor

1990 to the Present

London since the Swinging '60s has been a major exporter of pop culture. The contemporary collection, located in Rooms 32-42,

changes often depending on who's hot, but you'll likely find royalty (Queen Elizabeth II, Prince Charles, the late Princess Diana, newlyweds William and Kate, and Prince Harry), politicians (Tony Blair), entrepreneurs (Sir Richard Branson), classic-rock geezers (Sir Paul McCartney, Sir Elton John, David Bowie), and actors (Sir Michael Caine, Dame Judi Dench), as well as those in lower-profile professions—writers (Sir Salman Rushdie, Doris Lessing, Germaine Greer), scientists (Stephen Hawking), composers, painters, and intellectuals.

We've gone from battles to Beatles, seeing Britain's history in the faces of its major players.

WEST END WALK

*From Leicester Square
to Piccadilly Circus*

The West End, the area just west of the original walled City of London, is London's liveliest neighborhood. It's easy to get caught up in fantasies of jolly olde England, but the West End is where you'll feel the pulse of the living, breathing London of today, from genteel shopping to raunchy red light districts, and everything in between. Theaters, pubs, restaurants, bookstores, ethnic food, markets, and boutiques attract rock stars, gay people, punks, tourists, and ladies and gentlemen stepping from black cabs for a night on the town.

Most of this book's walks and tours focus on history, art, and museums. But this walk is about appreciating the London lifestyle: the entertainment energy at Leicester Square; the thriving popular hum of Covent Garden; the rock-and-roll history of Denmark Street; the bohemian, creative, hedonistic groove of Soho; the once-swingin', now corporate Carnaby Street; the bustling neon hub of Piccadilly Circus; and the distinctive shopping boulevards of Regent Street and Piccadilly Street.

The walk is divided into two parts. The first takes you through the colorful heart of this area (lively and a bit seedy), while the second part—for those who still have energy (and pounds) left—is more focused on swanky shopping (or window-shopping) zones.

Orientation

Length of This Walk: Allow three hours to lace together these highlights (or much more if you go beyond window-shopping).

Getting There: Take the Tube to the Leicester Square stop, which is actually a long block from the square itself. From the Tube, head for the square (either on Irving Street or on Cranbourn

Street, depending on which exit you use) and stand near the "tkts" booth, where the walk begins.

When to Go: Take your pick—shopping by day, or nightlife after dark. The many shops in this walk are generally open Mon-Sat 10:00-18:00 or 20:00, and Sun 12:00-18:00. If you'd like to stop for afternoon tea at The Wolseley or Fortnum & Mason, plan on arriving between 15:30 and 18:30. Early evenings are ideal, since most shops stay open at least until 18:00 (and many later). After that, you join the bustle of people grabbing dinner or a show.

Finding Your Way: I've provided walking instructions, but as this area has a maze of irregular streets, a map is particularly useful here (the one I've provided should work fine, but if you have a more detailed version, it could be helpful if you're tempted off course).

The Walk Begins

• *Start at Leicester Square. Stand at the top of the square and take in the scene.*

Part 1: Leicester Square, Covent Garden, and Soho

❶ Leicester Square

Leicester (LESS-ter) Square is a tranquil park surrounded by glitzy cinema houses (although much of it may be fenced off for renovation when you visit). It also sits smack in the middle of the theater district—ground zero for London's enticing offerings of flashy musicals, intimate plays starring big-name actors, and much more (for details, see the Entertainment in London chapter). Here, at the entertainment center of London, a statue of Shakespeare looks out, as if pondering the quote chiseled into his pedestal: "There is no darkness but ignorance." Charlie Chaplin, facing the bard, was a Londoner, the child of music-hall performers.

The square's **movie theaters**—the Odeon (Britain's largest

cinema), Empire, and Vue—are famous for hosting red-carpet movie premieres. When Tom Cruise, Angelina Jolie, or Brad Pitt needs a publicity splash, it'll likely be here. (Search online for "London film premieres" to find upcoming events.) On any given night, this entire area is a mosh-pit of clubs and partying teens in

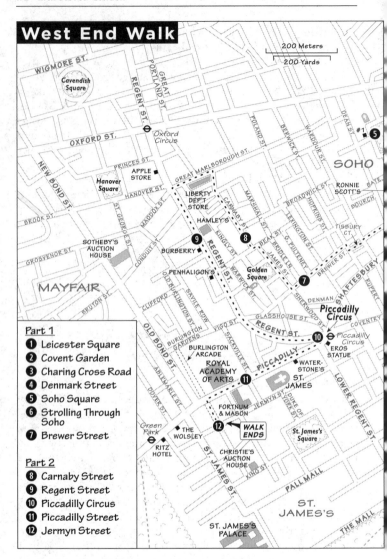

West End Walk

200 Meters
200 Yards

WIGMORE ST.

Cavendish
Square

REGENT ST.

GREAT PORTLAND ST.

OXFORD ST.   Oxford
Circus

SOHO

PRINCES ST.

NEW BOND ST.

Hanover
Square

APPLE
STORE

GREAT MARLBOROUGH ST.

POLAND ST.

BERWICK ST.

WARDOUR ST.

DEAN ST. #1 **5**

RONNIE
SCOTT'S

HANOVER ST.

LIBERTY
DEP'T
STORE

BROADWICK ST.

TISBURY
CT.

BROOK ST.

MADDOX ST.

ST. GEORGE ST.

HAMLEY'S

CARNABY ST.

MARSHALL ST.

LEXINGTON ST.

G. HOPKINS ST.

BREWER ST.

SOTHEBY'S
AUCTION
HOUSE

CONDUIT ST.

9 BURBERRY

KINGLY ST.

WARWICK ST.

BEAK ST.

BRIDLE LN.

JAMES ST.

8

GROSVENOR ST.

MAYFAIR

BRUTON ST.

PENHALIGON'S

Golden
Square

SHERWOOD ST.

DENMAN

7

SHAFTESBURY

RUPERT

**Piccadilly
Circus**

GLASSHOUSE ST.

COVENTRY

OLD BOND ST.

CLIFFORD ST.

SAVILE ROW

OLD BURLINGTON ST.

BURLINGTON GARDENS

VIGO ST.

REGENT ST.

10 Piccadilly
Circus
EROS
STATUE

Part 1

1 Leicester Square
2 Covent Garden
3 Charing Cross Road
4 Denmark Street
5 Soho Square
6 Strolling Through
Soho
7 Brewer Street

Part 2

8 Carnaby Street
9 Regent Street
10 Piccadilly Circus
11 Piccadilly Street
12 Jermyn Street

BURLINGTON
ARCADE

ROYAL
ACADEMY
OF ARTS

SACKVILLE ST.

ALBEMARLE ST.

DOVER ST.

PICCADILLY

WATER-
STONE'S

ST.
JAMES

LOWER REGENT ST.

JERMYN ST.

DUKE OF YORK ST.

11

Green
Park

THE
WOLSELEY

RITZ
HOTEL

FORTNUM
& MASON

12 WALK
ENDS

St. James's
Square

CHRISTIE'S
AUCTION
HOUSE

KING ST.

ST. JAMES ST.

PALL MALL

ST.
JAMES'S

THE MALL

ST. JAMES'S
PALACE

town from the suburbs.

Leicester Square is the central clearinghouse for daytime theater ticket sales. Check out the half-price **"tkts" booth** (see page 418) and ignore all the other establishments that bill themselves as "half-price" (they're just normal booking agencies). It's usually cheaper still to buy tickets directly from one of the theaters we'll pass on this walk.

Capital Radio London (next to the Odeon) plays a role in

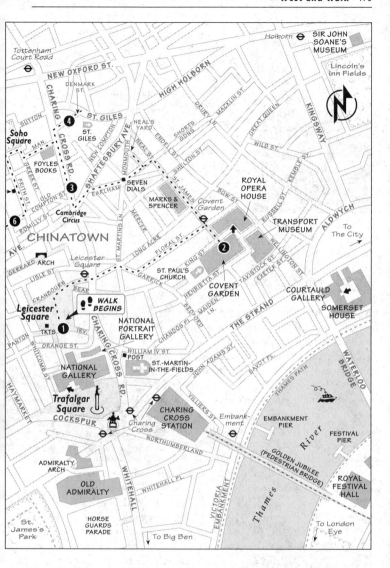

British rock-and-roll history. Back in the 1960s, the BBC was the only radio station in town, and it was mostly talk and Bach, with a smattering of pop. The British Invasion was in full swing—Beatles, Rolling Stones, the Who—but Brits couldn't hear much of it on the BBC. They had to resort to "pirate" radio stations, beamed from Luxembourg or from ships at sea. Capital Radio was one of the first commercial stations allowed to play rock and roll—and that was in 1973! Ironically, within a few years, Capital had itself

become mainstream, refusing to play punk acts like the Clash or Ramones. The Clash struck back with their song "Capital Radio," which starts, "Yes, it's time for the Dr. Goebbels Show..." Today, FM 95.8 carries on as a major top-40 broadcasting power.

• *Exit Leicester Square from its top corner, heading east (past the Vue cinema) on Cranbourn Street. Cross Charing Cross Road and continue along Cranbourn to the six-way intersection, then angle right onto Garrick Street. Shortly afterward, turn left onto calm, brick-lined Floral Street, with its tidy assortment of fashion boutiques. When Floral Street opens up onto traffic-free James Street, turn right and head for...*

❷ Covent Garden

Covent Garden (only tourists pluralize the name) is a large square teeming with people and street performers—jugglers, sword swallowers, and guitar players. London's buskers (including those in the Tube) are auditioned, licensed, and assigned times and places where they are allowed to perform.

The square's centerpiece is a covered marketplace. A market has been here since medieval times, when it was the "convent" garden owned by Westminster Abbey. In the 1600s, it became a housing development with this courtyard as its center, done in the Palladian style by Inigo Jones. Today's fine iron-and-glass structure was built in 1830 (when such buildings were all the

Industrial Age rage) to house the stalls of what became London's chief produce market.

A market still thrives here today (for details, see page 413). Go inside the market hall and poke around. As you enter through the brick passage, notice the posted diagram on the right identifying shops. Inside the market, you'll hit the so-called Apple Market zone. Picture it in full Dickensian color, lined with fruit and vegetable stalls. Covent Garden remained a produce market

WEST END WALK

until 1973, when its venerable arcades were converted to boutiques, cafés, and antiques shops.

Back out on Covent Garden square, across from the west end of the market hall, stands **St. Paul's Church** (not the famous cathedral), with its Greek temple-like facade and blue clock face. Known as the Actors' Church, it's long been a favorite of nervous performers praying for success. To go inside, pass through one of the gates on either side of the facade, and find the entrance around back (irregular hours, generally daily 8:30-17:30, often later for special events, sometimes closed Mon in winter). Inside, the walls are lined with memorials to theater folk, some of whom (Chaplin, Karloff) you might recognize.

At the bottom (southeast) corner of the square is the **London Transport Museum,** which gives a well-presented look at the evolution of this city's famously well-planned mass transit (see page 61).

Tucked into the top (northeast) corner of the square is the **Royal Opera House,** which showcases top-notch opera and ballet. For such a high-profile building, it has a surprisingly low-profile entrance (through the revolving door in the corner of the square).
• *Now browse your way northwest, along some lively and colorful streets.*

❸ From Covent Garden to Charing Cross Road

First backtrack two blocks up James Street, jog right, then continue straight (along the side of Marks & Spencer) up narrow Neal Street. Head two blocks up Neal Street, enjoying the pretty back streets. Turn left on Shorts Gardens, and find the tight alley (on the right) leading to the cozy, funky courtyard called **Neal's Yard,** with a thriving veggie restaurant scene (see page 390 in the Eating in London chapter).

Back on Shorts Gardens, Neal's Yard Dairy (at #17) sells a wide variety of cheeses from the British Isles. This is the original shop of what is now a thriving chain. Everything is well-described,

and they'll slice off a sample if you ask nicely.

Continue along Shorts Gardens to the next intersection—called **Seven Dials**—where seven sundials atop a pole mark the meeting of seven small streets. Continue more or less straight ahead onto Earlham Street.

Then, bearing left, you'll spill out into **Cambridge Circus**— the busy intersection of Shaftesbury Avenue and Charing Cross

Road—with its fine red-brick Victorian architecture and classic theaters. Charing Cross Road is the traditional home of London's bookstores. Turn right up Charing Cross to reach one of the biggest, **Foyles Books,** which puts on free events several nights a week—from book signings to jazz in their upstairs café (usually around 18:00, bookstore is on left at 113 Charing Cross Road, www.foyles.co.uk).

• *A few steps up from Foyles, turn right onto Denmark Street.*

❹ Denmark Street

This seemingly nondescript little street is a musician's mecca. In the 1920s, it was known as "Britain's Tin Pan Alley"—the center of the UK's music-publishing industry, when songwriters here cranked out popular tunes printed as sheet music.

Later, in the 1960s, Denmark Street was ground zero for rock and roll's British Invasion, which brought so much great pop music to the US. Regent Sound Studio (at #4, on the right) was a low-budget recording studio.

It was here in 1964 that the Rolling Stones recorded the song that raised them from obscurity, "Not Fade Away" ("I'm gonna tell you how it's gonna be..."). Denmark Street recorded music from the Kinks (who wrote a song called "Denmark Street"), to the Beatles ("Fixing a Hole"), to the Who ("I Can See for Miles"). Today, Regent is a music store.

The storefront at #20 (on the left, now Wunjo Guitars) was formerly a music publishing house that employed a lowly office boy named Reginald Dwight. In 1969, on the building's rooftop, he wrote "Your Song" and went on to become famous as Sir Elton John. In the 1970s, the Sex Pistols lived in apartments above #6 (on the right). The 12 Bar Café (at #25, on the left) features live music, and helped launch the careers of more recent acts: Damien Rice, KT Tunstall, Jeff Buckley, and Keane.

Today, Denmark Street offers one-stop-shopping for the modern musician. Without leaving this short street, you could buy a vintage Rickenbacker guitar, get your sax repaired, take piano lessons, lay down a bass track, have a few beers, or tattoo your name across your fist like Ozzy Osbourne. Notice the bulletin board in the alley alongside the 12 Bar Café (through the doorway marked #27). If you're a musician looking for a band to play in, this could be your connection.

• *From Denmark Street, go back across Charing Cross Road and head down Manette Street (alongside Foyles). After a short block on the right (down the lane called Orange Yard), you'll see The Borderline, where R.E.M. and Oasis have played. Continue down Manette Street and under the "Pillars of Hercules" passage, then turn right up Greek Street to...*

❺ Soho Square

The Soho neighborhood is London's version of New York City's Greenwich Village. It's a ritzy, raffish, edgy, and colorful area. Because of its eccentric 1970s landlord, porn publisher Paul Raymond, the Soho district escaped late-20th-century development. So, rather than soulless office towers, it retains its characteristic charm. And because the square has no real through-roads, it's almost traffic-free—strangely quiet and residential-feeling for being in the center of such a huge city.

Soho Square Gardens is a favorite place on a sunny afternoon. The little house in the middle of the square is the gardener's hut. At #1, on the west (left) side of the square, the MPL building (McCartney Publishing Limited) houses offices of the 120th richest man in Britain, Sir Paul McCartney.

• *At the bottom of the square, wander down Frith Street.*

❻ Strolling Through Soho

The restaurants and boutiques here and on adjoining streets (e.g., Greek, Dean, and Wardour Streets) are trendy and gay, the kind that attract high society when they feel like slumming it. Bars with burly, well-dressed bouncers abound. Private clubs, like the low-profile Groucho Club (a block over, at #45 Dean Street), cater to the late-night rock crowd.

Ronnie Scott's Jazz Club (#47 Frith Street) has featured big-name acts for more than 50 years. In 1970, Jimi Hendrix jammed here with Eric Burdon and War; it was the last performance before his death in a London apartment a few days later.

Frith Street hits **Old Compton Street** at the center of the neighborhood. Stroll a block to the right on Old Compton Street to take in the eclectic variety of people going by. You're surrounded by the buzz of Soho.

At the corner of Dean Street, look for the pagoda-style arch down the street. South of here, on the other side of Shaftesbury

Avenue, is London's underwhelming **Chinatown.** With Gerrard Street as its spine, it occupies what was once just more of Soho, with the same Soho artsy vibe. In the 1960s, the Chinese community gathered here, eventually dominated this zone, and non-Asian businesses moved out. The Chinese population swelled when the former British colony of Hong Kong was returned to China in 1997, but the neighborhood's identity is now threatened by developers eyeing this high-rent real estate.

• *Continue along Old Compton Street to where it squeezes down into a narrow alley (Tisbury Court). Penetrate this sleazy passage of sex shows and blue-video shops, tolerate the barkers' raunchy come-ons, then jog a half-block right and turn left on Brewer Street.*

❼ Brewer Street: Sleaze, Porn Shops, and Prostitutes

Soho was a bordello zone in the 19th century. A bit of that survives today in this area. Sex shops, video arcades, and prostitution min-

gle with upscale restaurants here in west Soho. While it's illegal in Britain to sell sex on the street, well-advertised "models" entertain (profitably) in their tiny apartments. Berwick Street hosts a daily produce market.

• *The first half of our walk is nearly finished. When you reach the intersection of Brewer Street and Sherwood Street (also called Lower James Street), it's time to plan your next move.*

If you're ready to call it quits, you can head straight down to Piccadilly Circus for a grand finale: Turn left onto Sherwood Street, walk one block, and turn to page 180 to finish up at Piccadilly Circus.

Better yet, stick with me for...

Part 2: Shopping Streets and Piccadilly Circus

The mile-long second half of this walk—along Regent Street to Piccadilly Circus, then up the street called Piccadilly and down Jermyn Street—takes you by the most typically London stores and shops. While useful for true shoppers, this walk is also a lot of fun for window-shoppers.

• *At Sherwood/Lower James Street, turn right (north on Upper James Street) and walk two blocks. Then jog left at Beak Street to find...*

❽ Carnaby Street

In the Swinging '60s, when Pete Townshend needed a paisley shirt, John Lennon a Nehru jacket, or Twiggy a miniskirt, they came here—where those mod fashions were invented. Today, there's not a hint of hippie. For the most part, Carnaby Street looks like everything else from the '60s does now—sanitized and co-opted by upscale franchises. At least the upper end of the street retains a whiff of funkiness.

Walk north, the length of Carnaby Street, which leads to the back entrance of the venerable **Liberty** department store. Pop in. Liberty is a big, stately, local-favorite department store established in 1875, now housed in this distinctive faux-Tudor building (built in the 1920s from the timbers of two Royal Navy ships). Liberty is known for its fine design and "Liberty Print" patterned cloth.

• *From Liberty, continue west (hook left on Great Marlborough Street) to Regent Street.*

❾ The Shops of Regent Street

You're in the heart of London's shopping neighborhood. This intersection also marks a sort of class divide among London shoppers. (A couple of blocks to the north is the mid-range shopping area, **Oxford Street,** which is lined by less-distinguished chains and department stores and seems scruffier than Regent Street).

But this walk focuses on **Regent Street,** with London's high-class, top-dollar shopping outlets. This street has wide sidewalks, fine architecture, and royal-family connections. Most of its shops call the Queen their landlord, as she owns much of the land here.

While it's the local shops and boutiques that make Regent Street famous, American chains are certainly part of the scene. For example, the **Apple Store** is in a building that looks more like a palace (between Liberty and

Oxford Circus, on the left as you walk to your right up Regent Street, at #235). It's popular with Londoners, who are astounded by its service. The English are capable of good service too, but, as a Londoner put it to me, "not the obsequious butt-kissing some Americans expect, because that makes you feel like a servant."

Also on Regent Street (just downhill from Liberty, left side, at #188-196), follow the giddy kids to **Hamleys,** Britain's biggest toy store. In 2010 it marked its 250th anniversary of delighting children. Seven floors buzz with 28,000 toys, managed by a staff of 200. Employees, some dressed in playful costumes, give demos of the latest gadgets. At the Build-a-Bear Factory, kids can pick out a made-to-order teddy bear and watch while it's stuffed and sewn.

On this stretch of Regent Street, fine bits of old England class dominate. **Burberry** (on the right, at #167) was once dowdy—the queen's choice—but is hip again. **Hackett** (right, at #143-147) is the place to go for preppy young English menswear. **Mappin and Webb** (left, at #132) is the Queen's jeweler. **Penhaligon's** (right, at #125) is the quintessential English perfumery, where royals shop (note the coat of arms at the door) for classic English scents like lavender and rose (fine sampler gift packs and free sniff samples).

• *Regent Street arcs seductively into the ever-vibrant...*

❿ Piccadilly Circus

London's most touristy square got its name from the fancy ruffled shirts—*picadils*—made in the neighborhood long ago. To measure how dramatically things have changed, look no further than the gargantuan Ripley's Believe-It-or-Not Museum to capture the gimmicky flavor of today's Piccadilly.

Until just a couple of years ago, this was a famously busy traffic circle, with cars and big red buses spinning around the tipsy-but-perfectly-balanced Eros statue in the center. (You may see some construction, as guardrails are removed to make the inter-section more pedestrian-friendly.) At night, when neon pulses, the 20-foot-high Coke ads paint the classic Georgian facades pink. Black cabs honk, tourists crowd the attractions, and Piccadilly shows off big-city London at its glitziest.

Piccadilly Circus is where common tastes steamroll the elegance of Regent Street. **Lillywhites** (at the bottom of the square, near the Eros fountain) is a sports store popular as a place to buy the jersey of your favorite football (soccer) team. Farther left (at the start of Coventry Street) is **Cool Britannia,** a tacky palace of English kitsch and a Union Jack fantasy for anyone needing to buy a Brit-themed gift.

• *For some more characteristic London shops—and a chance for a tea break—we'll do a little loop to the west. From Piccadilly Circus, turn right and wander down the busy...*

⓫ Piccadilly Street

After a block on your left (at #203), escape from the frenzy of Piccadilly into the quiet of **Waterstone's,** Europe's largest bookshop and the flagship store of its widespread chain. Page through seven orderly floors. The fifth floor offers a hip bar with minimalist furniture and great views (see sidebar on page 85).

Next you'll pass Christopher Wren's **St. James's Church** (with free lunchtime concerts at 13:10) and a tiny all-day flea market (antiques Tue 10:00-18:00, crafts Wed-Sat 11:00-18:00, closed Sun-Mon). One block farther (on the left, at #181) is the **Fortnum & Mason** department store, which eschews the glitz of bigger stores and revels in understated, old-school elegance. At the top of the hour the fancy clock on the facade is the scene of a low-key spectacle, as the venerable store's founders—Fortnum and Mason—come out and bow to each other (best viewed from across the street). This reminds shoppers of the store's humble beginnings 300 years ago, when it was started by these two footmen of Queen Anne. With rich displays and deep red carpet, Fortnum's feels classier and more relaxed than Harrods.

Across the street from Fortnum & Mason is the delightful covered shopping street of **Burlington Arcade** (at #51, just beyond the entrance to the Burlington House).

An elegant way to cap your shopping stroll (we'll finish just a block from here) is with a traditional **afternoon tea.** While pricey, many consider this ritual an essential part of any London visit.

My two favorite places in town for a traditional afternoon tea are within a block of here: **St. James's Restaurant,** on the fourth floor of Fortnum & Mason; and, a block farther down Piccadilly Street, **The Wolseley,** the grand 1920s former showroom of a now defunct car manufacturer (where couples are allowed to split a £21 tea in sumptuous surroundings; on the left at #160). Beyond that is the original **Ritz Hotel,** where the tea is much fancier. For more on this ritual, see "Taking Tea in London" on page 397.

• *But before we part ways, we'll stroll a block south of big and busy*

Piccadilly Street. Opposite the Burlington Arcade, the Piccadilly Arcade leads to quiet...

⓬ Jermyn Street

A statue of *Beau Brummell,* the ultimate dandy, meets you as if to say, "Within a block in either direction are numerous fine gentleman's shirtmakers and many other delightful small shops."

Stand by the statue and survey your menswear shopping options (all to the right): **Bates Hats** (#73) still sells bowlers and top hats, as it has for a century. **Turnbull & Asser** (#71) has dressed Winston Churchill, Prince Charles, and James Bond with its "bespoke" (custom-made) shirts and suits. **John Lobb** (#88) has sold boots to Princes William and Harry. **Tricker's** (#67) has been making shoes for the gentleman since the days of Beau Brummell.

It was Brummell (1778-1840) who popularized the understated jacket-trousers-and-tie ensemble that men still wear today. As the quote on his statue reads, "To be truly elegant, one should not be noticed."

• *Our walk is finished. From here, you have several nearby options. If you're ready for* **teatime,** *cut back through the block to Piccadilly Street and the places I mentioned earlier.*

Or, to head back to **Piccadilly Circus** *(and its handy Tube stop), walk east down Jermyn Street, pausing at Floris (at #89) and Paxton & Whitfields (#93), which has served exceptional cheese since 1797, with generous tastings. On the little Duke of York Street (behind St. James's Church) is an old-fashioned barbershop called Trumpers (selling top-quality shaving gear) and the classic Red Lion Pub. If all of this is just too elegant, dip into Piccadilly Square's Cool Britannia and buy some Union Jack underwear.*

COURTAULD GALLERY TOUR

The Courtauld Gallery (part of the Courtauld Institute of Art) is just small enough that you can see it all in a single visit, which makes for a pleasant experience. The collection spans the history of Western painting, from medieval altarpieces through Italian Renaissance to the 20th century. But its highlight is Impressionist and Post-Impressionist works, some of which you'll recognize. Besides the pieces I've featured, you'll likely see many other well-known Post-Impressionist, Fauvist, and early modern paintings, part of the museum's rotating collection of loaners. For some, the Van Gogh self-portrait alone is worth the price of admission.

Orientation

Cost: £6 (free Mon until 14:00). Admission includes temporary exhibits.

Hours: Daily 10:00-18:00, last entry 30 minutes before closing. There are occasional late-night openings until 21:00—check their website.

Getting There: The Courtauld is part of the museum/temporary exhibit complex at Somerset House along the Strand. It's a 10-minute walk from Trafalgar Square. Tube: Temple or Covent Garden, or catch bus #6, #9, #11, #13, #15, or #23 from Trafalgar Square.

Information: Lunchtime art talks are generally offered Mon and Fri at 13:15. Recorded info tel. 020/7848-2526, gallery shop tel. 020/7848-2579, www.courtauld.ac.uk.

Length of This Tour: Allow one hour.

Services: Free coin-op lockers (you get your £1 coin back) and WCs are in the basement.

Photography: Permitted without flash.

Cuisine Art: The café (serving soups, salads, sandwiches, pastries, and drinks), with the same hours as the gallery, is in the basement.

Starring: Van Gogh, Manet, Cézanne, Degas, and many other artists spanning the centuries.

Overview

The museum is not arranged chronologically, but by collector—namely the wealthy people who created this museum by donating their personal collections. Samuel Courtauld (1876-1947), a philanthropist, industrialist, and wealthy great-nephew of a textile magnate, gave his paintings (Van Gogh, Manet, Cézanne, and others on the first floor) and his name to the budding museum.

Occasionally, the paintings described in this tour are lent out to other museums. If there's a piece you really want to see, check with a guard or at the front desk (the ticket seller has a notebook that lists which pieces are currently out on loan).

This tour covers just enough to introduce you to the wide range of art in the collection. Take time to explore the gallery's many other masterpieces.

The Tour Begins

• *Start on the ground floor, in Room 1 (a.k.a. Gallery I, directly across from the ticket counter), filled with religious paintings.*

Robert Campin—*The Seilern Triptych—The Entombment* (c. 1425)

As the earliest known work of this pioneering artist, the altarpiece is a mix of medieval piety and proto-Renaissance techniques. Christ's followers prepare to lower him into the tomb. In medieval fashion, it's set on a gold-leaf background with intricate vines and flowers hammered in. Christ's body is spindly, weightless, and presented at an unnatural angle. But the faces! With knit brows, they bear their sorrow solemnly. Even the angels are choked up. The man kneeling at left (who donated the money for the altarpiece) has a day's growth of beard—that's spot-on realism.

• *Upstairs on the first floor, in Room 3, you'll find...*

Edouard Manet—*A Bar at the Folies-Bergère* (1881-1882)

While we look at the barmaid and her wares, Manet also shows us the barmaid's-eye view of the crowded nightclub, reflected in the (slightly tilted) mirror behind

her. We see the glittering chandeliers rendered in Impressionist smudges, the bottles of wine, the swirl of activity, and even a trapeze artist (upper left). From the barmaid's own reflection, we see that she's facing a mustachioed man in a top hat. This may be a self-portrait, but whoever he is, he's standing right where we are.

Manet, in his last major painting, places us in the center of the scene, surrounded with glitter. Reflected in the mirror, the gaiety all looks a bit fake, and, judging from her blank expression, that's the way the barmaid sees it.

Edouard Manet—*Le Dejeuner sur l'Herbe* (1863)

This is a smaller, cruder version Manet did of his famous painting (now in Paris' Orsay Museum) that launched the Impressionist revolution. The nude woman in a classical pose wasn't shocking. It was the presence of the fully clothed men in everyday dress that suddenly made the nude naked. Manet and the Impressionists rejected goddesses and romance for the landscapes, café scenes, and still lifes of the real world.

Paul Cézanne—*La Montagne Sainte-Victoire* (c. 1887)

Cézanne could look out his studio window at this 3,300-foot-high mountain in Provence. Over a 20-year span, he painted the same mountain 60 different ways, each with its own color scheme and mood. This one—with a windblown branch framing the mountain from above—may reflect the turmoil of the fortysomething's life (father's death, stalled Impressionist career, shuttling between Paris and hometown Aix-en-Provence, the recent humiliation of having his childhood friend Emile Zola parody him in a novel).

The mountain is realistic, but the scene is carefully composed. The tree branch echoes the curving ridgeline, uniting foreground and background. A patch of paint forming a house (in the

foreground) is the same size as a patch depicting a rock forma-
tion (in the background), further flattening this "distant" scene
into a wall of brushstrokes. (Cézanne's "cube"-shaped brushstrokes
inspired the Cubists, a decade later, to build figures using geometric shapes, to mix foreground and background, and to empha-
size style over realism.) Cézanne juggles many technical balls of
modern painting—a roughed-up surface texture done with thick
brushwork, a self-imposed color scheme, abstract composition—
and still manages to stay true to his Impressionist roots, painting
the mountain he sees.

Paul Gauguin—*Nevermore* (1897)

A nude Tahitian woman lies daydreaming. The curves of her body
and of the headboard soften the horizontal lines of the bed and the
verticals of the wall.

Gauguin—who quit his
stockbroker job, abandoned
his wife and family, and
moved to Tahiti—paints
in the "primitive" style he
found there. Like a child, he
draws the girl with a thick
outline (so different from Impressionists who "built" a figure with
a mosaic of brushstrokes) and then fills it in with solid Crayola colors. Gauguin emphasizes only the two dimensions of height and
width, so that the women and clouds in the "background" blend
into the flowery wallpaper in the "foreground." Gauguin rejected
the camera-eye literalness of Western art. His is a simpler style
that requires the viewer's imagination to fill in the blanks, perhaps
evoking the romance of a bygone world that is...nevermore.

By the way, Gauguin insisted that the title and the raven were
not from Poe's poem, but "a bird of the devil who watches." Hmm.
• *In Room 4, you'll see...*

Vincent van Gogh—*Self-Portrait with Bandaged Ear* (1888-1889)

On the night of December 23, 1888, Vincent van Gogh went bal-
listic. Drunk, self-doubting, clinically insane, and enraged at his
friend Gauguin's smug superiority, he waved a knife in Gauguin's
face, then cut off a piece of his own ear and gave it to a prostitute.
Gauguin hightailed it back to Paris, and the locals in Arles per-
suaded the mad Dutchman to get help. A week later, just released
from the hospital, Vincent stood in front of a blank canvas and
looked at himself in the mirror.

What he saw looking back was a calm man with an unflinching gaze, dressed in a heavy coat (painted with thick, vertical

strokes of blue and green) and fur-lined hat. The slightly stained bandage over his ear is neither hidden in shame nor worn as a badge of honor—it's just another accessory. The scene is evenly lit, with no melodramatic shadows.

Vincent must have been puzzled and unnerved by his "artist's fit," as he called it. Does this man suspect it would only be the first of many he'd suffer over the next year and a half before finally taking his own life?

• *Pass through Room 5 and into Room 6.*

Lucas Cranach the Elder—*Adam and Eve* (1526)

Eve takes a bite of Knowledge, gazes into the distance, and passes the forbidden fruit to a puzzled Adam, standing in a lush garden amid peaceful animals. Strategic branches fuzz their genitals, but otherwise they're nude, with the pale, thin bodies of the aristocrats for whom Cranach painted. (Adam, beware of antlers.) Though the subject is biblical, it captures the worldly spirit of Germany's Renaissance. The northern version of humanism saw humans not as noble Greek gods (as the Italian Renaissance did), but as fallible, lusty, and even a bit cynical.

Peter Paul Rubens—*The Family of Jan Brueghel the Elder* (c. 1613-1615)

Rubens paints his close friend and occasional collaborator, along with his wife and two kids. Rubens and Brueghel, Antwerp's two best painters, tag-teamed a couple of dozen works. Brueghel focused on his specialty—background, flowers, animals, and garlands—and Rubens did the people. Also in Room 6 is Rubens' dreamy *Landscape by Moonlight* (c. 1637-1638).

• *Upstairs on the second floor is the sculpture gallery in Room 8.*

Edgar Degas—*Study in the Nude for Dressed Ballet Dancer* (1879-1917)

The naked 14-year-old girl splays her feet out (fourth position), bends her arms back, and turns her face up, exuding the sheer joy of dancing. Like a stripped Barbie doll, this is a smaller-scale, nude version of the famous statue Edgar Degas exhibited in Paris in 1881. The original was made of wax and plaster over a wire frame. (The Courtauld's version is a bronze cast of a wax statue, done after Degas' death.) Degas dressed his original wax statue in a cloth tutu and ballet slippers and attached real human hair to the wax head, creating a modern collage of materials that shocked and intrigued the Parisians. Critics of the day both praised its modernism and lambasted the angular, adolescent body and "ugly" face.

The model for the statue was an aspiring dancer who, like so many adolescent girls then and now, dreamed of finding a career on stage. Degas sketched and painted her many times. But this well-known painter was also a closet sculptor, fashioning dozens of small-scale statues in the privacy of his studio, especially in his later years as his eyesight failed and painting became more difficult. Only *The Little Fourteen-Year-Old Dancer* was exhibited.

The Rest of the Courtauld

Rooms 9-14 contain late 19th- and early 20th-century paintings by Derain, Dufy, Kandinsky, Jawlensky, and more. Many have the bright, bold colors and thick brushstrokes of the Fauvist style, from the time when Impressionism was merging into abstract. The museum rotates its large collection, so you may see a different mix. Temporary exhibits also occupy the second floor.

You'll also see works by members of Britain's own Bloomsbury Group—Roger Fry, Vanessa Bell, and Duncan Grant. This group of intellectual friends also included Virginia Woolf (Bell's sister), E. M. Forster, and the economist John Maynard Keynes. During the 1910s and 1920s, they met for cocktails, flirting, and high-minded discussions in their Bloomsbury neighborhood (east of the British Museum), and went on to fame in their respective fields.

BRITISH MUSEUM TOUR

In the 19th century, the British flag flew over one-fourth of the world. London was the world's capital, where women in saris walked the streets with men in top hats. And England collected art as fast as it collected colonies.

The British Museum is *the* chronicle of Western civilization. History is a modern invention. Three hundred years ago, people didn't care about crumbling statues and dusty columns. Nowadays, we value a look at past civilizations, knowing that "those who don't learn from history are condemned to repeat it."

The British Museum is the only place I can think of where you can follow the rise and fall of three great civilizations—Egypt, Assyria, and Greece—in a few hours with a coffee break in the middle. And, while the sun never set on the British Empire, it will on you, so on this tour we'll see just the most exciting two hours.

Orientation

Cost: Free (but a £4, $5, or €5 donation is requested). If you can afford it, donate. Interesting temporary exhibits usually require a separate admission.

Hours: The museum is open daily 10:00-17:30, Fri until 20:30 (not all galleries are open Fri night, but most of our tour is). Rainy days and Sundays always get me down, because they're most crowded. (The museum is least crowded late on weekday afternoons.)

The **Great Court**—the grand entrance with eateries, gift shops, an exhibit gallery, and the Reading Room—is open daily 9:00-18:00, Fri until 23:30.

Getting There: The main entrance is on Great Russell Street. From the Tottenham Court Road Tube stop, take exit #3 and

BRITISH MUSEUM

British Museum Overview

MONTAGUE PLACE

MONTAGUE PLACE ENTRANCE

Russell Square

CAFÉ

BLOOMSBURY ST.

G R E E C E

A S S Y R I A

ROSETTA STONE

E G Y P T

READING ROOM

THE GREAT COURT

THE KING'S GALLERY

MONTAGUE ST.

INFO

INFO

WINGED LIONS

SHOP

CLOAKROOM

CAFÉ

COLUMNS

MAIN ENTRANCE

GREAT RUSSELL ST.

To Tottenham Court Road ⊖ (10 min. walk)

To Holborn ⊖ (10 min. walk)

walk four blocks to the museum. The Holborn and Russell Square Tube stops are also nearby. Buses #168 and #24 are among the many that stop here (see page 34).

Information: Information desks are just inside the Great Court. Choose between a standard museum map (£1 suggested donation) and a £2 version that highlights important pieces. The main bookstore

is tucked behind the Reading Room. The "Visitor's Guide" (£3.50) offers 15 different tours and skimpy text. General info tel. 020/7323-8299, ticket desk tel. 020/7323-8181, collection questions tel. 020/7323-8838, www.britishmuseum.org.

Tours: Free 30-minute **eyeOpener tours** are led by volunteers, who focus on select rooms (daily 11:00-15:45, generally every 15 minutes). The 1.5-hour **Highlights tours,** led by licensed guides, are expensive but meaty, giving an introduction to the museum's masterpieces (£9, daily at 10:30, 13:00, and 15:00). Free 45-minute gallery talks on specific subjects are offered Tue-Sat at 13:15.

The £5 **multimedia guide** offers dial-up audio commentary and video on 200 objects, as well as several theme tours (for example, 1.5-hour Highlights tour or Parthenon Sculptures tour). They're substantial and cerebral (must leave photo ID). There's also a fun children's audioguide (£3.50).

You can download a free **audio version** of this tour for your mobile device via www.ricksteves.com/audioeurope, iTunes, or the Rick Steves Audio Europe smartphone app.

Length of This Tour: Allow at least two hours.

Cloakroom: £1.50 per item. You can carry a day bag in the galleries, but big backpacks must be checked. The cloakroom can get very crowded on rainy days; if the line is long and not moving, it may be full.

No-Nos: No eating, drinking, smoking, or gum-chewing in the galleries.

Photography: Photos allowed without flash or tripod.

Cuisine Art: You have three choices inside the complex. The self-service Court Café (£4-5 sandwiches and salads) is in the Great Court ground floor. The pricier Court Restaurant (£15-20 entrées) is on the upper level atop the Reading Room. The cafeteria-style Gallery Café (£8 hot dishes) is deeper into the museum, near the Greek art in Room 12.

Near the museum, there are lots of fast, cheap, and colorful cafés, pubs, and markets along Great Russell Street and Museum Street. No picnicking is allowed inside the Great Court or the museum, except on weekends and holidays, when the museum opens a family area in the basement under the Great Court. Karl Marx picnicked on the benches near the museum entrance and in nearby Russell Square.

Starring: Rosetta Stone, Egyptian mummies, Assyrian lions, and Elgin Marbles.

The Tour Begins

The main entrance on Great Russell Street spills you into the Great Court, a glass-domed space with the round Reading Room in the center. From the Great Court, doorways lead to all wings. To the left are the exhibits on Egypt, Assyria, and Greece—our tour. You'll notice that this tour does not follow the museum's numbered sequence of rooms. Instead, we'll try to hit the highlights as we work chronologically.

Enjoy the Great Court, Europe's largest covered square, which is bigger

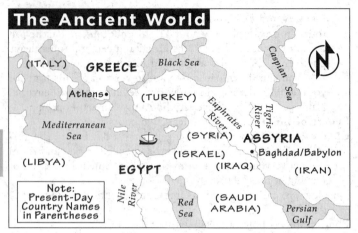

than a football field. This people-friendly court—delightfully spared from the London rain—was for 150 years one of London's great lost spaces...closed off and gathering dust. Since the year 2000, it's been the 140-foot-wide hub of a two-acre cultural complex.

When the stately Reading Room is not being used for special exhibitions, it's open and free to the public. In years past, it was a study hall for Oscar Wilde, Arthur Conan Doyle, Rudyard Kipling, T. S. Eliot, Virginia Woolf, W. B. Yeats, Mark Twain, V. I. Lenin. Karl Marx formulated his ideas on communism and wrote *Das Kapital* here.

• *The Egyptian Gallery is in the West Wing, to the left of the round Reading Room. Enter the Egyptian Gallery. The Rosetta Stone is directly in front of you.*

Egypt (3000 B.C.- A.D. 1)

Egypt was one of the world's first "civilizations"—a group of people with a government, religion, art, free time, and a written language. The Egypt we think of—pyramids, mummies, pharaohs, and guys who walk funny—lasted from 3000 to 1000 B.C. with hardly any change in the government, religion, or arts. Imagine two millennia of Eisenhower.

❶ The Rosetta Stone (196 B.C.)

When this rock was unearthed in the Egyptian desert in 1799, it was a sensation in Europe. This black slab caused a quantum leap in the study of ancient history. Finally, Egyptian writing could be decoded.

The writing in the upper part of the stone is known as hieroglyphics, which was indecipherable for a thousand years. Did a

British Museum—Egypt

ASSYRIA

WINGED LIONS

8

7 **1** **2** **4**
3

5 To & **6**

11 **10** **9**

CLOAKROOM

GREAT COURT & READING ROOM

1 Rosetta Stone
2 Upper Half of Ramesses II
3 Egyptian Gods as Animals
4 Monumental Granite Scarab
5 Up to Nebamun Hunting in the Marshes
6 Up to Mummies, Coffins, Etc.

7 Red Granite Head
8 Four Black Granite Figures
9 Limestone Fragment of Sphinx Beard
10 Limestone False Door & Architrave of Ptahshepses
11 Statue of Nenkheftka

picture of a bird mean "bird"? Or was it a sound, forming part of a larger word, like "burden"? As it turned out, hieroglyphics

are a complex combination of the two, surprisingly more phonetic than symbolic. (For example, the hieroglyph that looks like a mouth or eye is the letter "R.")

The Rosetta Stone allowed scientists to break the code. It contains a single inscription repeated in three languages. The bottom third is plain old Greek (find your favorite frat or sorority), while the middle is medieval Egyptian. By comparing the two known languages with the one they didn't know, translators figured out the hieroglyphics.

The breakthrough came when they discovered that the large ovals (e.g., in the sixth line from the top) represented the name of the ruler, Ptolemy. Simple.

• *The Rosetta Stone sits in the middle of the long Egyptian Gallery. In the gallery to the right of the Stone, find the huge head of Ramesses.*

❷ Upper Half of Colossal Statue of Ramesses II of Granite (c. 1270 B.C.)

When Moses told the king of Egypt, "Let my people go!" this was the stony-faced look he got. Ramesses II ruled for 66 years

(c. 1290-1223 B.C.) and may have been in power when Moses cursed Egypt with plagues, freed the Israeli slaves, and led them out of Egypt to their homeland in Israel (according to the Bible, but not exactly corroborated by Egyptian chronicles).

This seven-ton statue, made from two different colors of granite, is a fragment from a temple in Thebes. It shows Ramesses with the traditional features of a pharaoh—goatee, cloth headdress, and cobra diadem on his forehead. Ramesses was a great builder of temples, palaces, tombs, and statues of himself. There are probably more statues of him in the world than there are cheesy fake *David*s. He was so concerned about achieving immortality that he even chiseled his own name on other people's statues. Very cheeky.

Picture what the archaeologists saw when they came upon this: a colossal head and torso separated from the enormous legs and toppled into the sand—all that remained of the works of a once-great pharaoh. Kings, megalomaniacs, and workaholics, take note.

• Say, "Ooh, heavy," and climb the ramp behind Ramesses, looking for animals.

❸ Egyptian Gods as Animals

Before technology made humans the alpha animal on earth, it was easier to appreciate our fellow creatures. Animals were stronger, swifter, and fiercer than puny *Homo sapiens*. The Egyptians worshipped animals as incarnations of the gods.

The powerful ram is the god Amun (king of the gods), protecting a puny pharaoh under his powerful chin. The falcon is Horus, the god of the living. The speckled, standing hippo (with lion head) is Tawaret, protectress of childbirth. Her stylized breasts and pregnant belly are supported by ankhs, symbols of life. (Is Tawaret grinning or grimacing in labor?) Finally, the cat (with ear- and nose-rings) served Bastet, the popular goddess of stress relief.

Scattered around the floor are huge stone boxes. The famous mummies of ancient Egypt were wrapped in linen and then encased in finely decorated wooden coffins, which were then placed in these massive stone outer coffins.

• *At the end of the Egyptian Gallery is a big stone beetle.*

❹ Monumental Granite Scarab (c. 200 B.C.)

This species of beetle would burrow into the ground, then reappear—like the sun rising and setting, or dying and rebirth, a symbol of resurrection. Scarab amulets were placed on mummies' chests to protect the spirit's heart from acting impulsively. Pharaohs wore the symbol of the beetle, and tombs and temples were decorated with them. The hieroglyph for scarab meant "to come into being."

Like the scarab, Egyptian culture was buried—first by Greece, then by Rome. Knowledge of the ancient writing died, condemning the culture to obscurity. But since the discovery of the Rosetta Stone, Egyptology has boomed, and Egypt has come back to life.

• *You can't call Egypt a wrap until you visit the mummies upstairs. Continue to the end of the gallery past the giant stone scarab and up the West Stairs (four flights; an elevator is in the works). At the top, take a left into Room 61, with objects and wall-paintings from the tomb of Nebamun.*

❺ Painting of Nebamun Hunting in the Marshes (c. 1425 B.C.)

Nebamun stands in a reed boat, gliding through the marshes. He raises his arm, ready to bean a bird with a snakelike hunting

stick. On the right, his wife looks on, while his daughter crouches between his legs, a symbol of fatherly protection.

This nobleman walks like Egyptian statues look—stiff and flat, like he was just run over by a pyramid. We see the torso from the front and everything else—arms, legs, face—in profile, creating the funny walk that has become an Egyptian cliché. (Like an early version of Cubism, we see various perspectives at once.)

But the stiffness is softened by a human touch. It's a family snapshot of loved ones from a happy time. The birds, fish, and plants are painted realistically, like encyclopedia entries. (The first "paper" came from papyrus plants like the bush on the left.) The only unrealistic element is the house cat (thigh-high, in front of the man) acting as a retriever—possibly the only cat in history that ever did anything useful.

When Nebamun passed into the afterlife, his awakening soul could look at this painting on the tomb wall and think of his wife and daughter—doing what they loved for all eternity.

• *Browse through Rooms 61-64, filled with displays in glass cases.*

❻ Rooms 61-64: Mummies, Coffins, Canopic Jars, and Statuettes—The Egyptian Funeral

To mummify a body, disembowel it (but leave the heart inside), pack the cavities with pitch, and dry it with natron, a natural form

of sodium carbonate (and, I believe, the active ingredient in Twinkies). Then carefully bandage it head to toe with hundreds of yards of linen strips. Let it sit 2,000 years, and...*voilà!* Or just dump the corpse in the desert and let the hot, dry, bacteria-killing Egyptian sand do the work—you'll get the same results.

The mummy was placed in a wooden coffin, which was put in a stone coffin, which was placed in a tomb. (The pyramids were supersized tombs for the rich and famous.) The result is that we now have Egyptian bodies that are as well-preserved as Joan Rivers.

The internal organs were preserved alongside in canopic jars, and small-scale statuettes of the deceased *(shabtis)* were scattered around. Written in hieroglyphs on the coffins and the tomb walls were burial rites from the Book of the Dead. These were magical spells to protect the body and crib notes for the waking soul, who needed to know these passwords to get past the guardians of eternity.

Many of the mummies here are from the time of the Roman occupation, when they painted a fine portrait in wax on the wrapping. X-ray photos in the display cases tell us more about these people.

Don't miss the animal mummies. Cats (Room 62) were popular pets. They were also considered incarnations of the goddess Bastet. Worshipped in life as the sun god's allies, preserved in death, and memorialized with statues, cats were given the adulation they've come to expect ever since.

• Linger in Rooms 62 and 63, but remember that eternity is about the amount of time it takes to see this entire museum. In Room 64, in a glass case, you'll find what's left of a visitor who tried to see it all. (Actually, it's the body of a man called...)

"Ginger" (Typical Egyptian Grave Containing a Naturally Preserved Body)

This man died 5,400 years ago, a thousand years before the pyramids. His people buried him in the fetal position, where he could "sleep" for eternity. The hot sand naturally dehydrated and protected the body. With him are a few of his possessions: bowls, beads, and the flint blade next to his arm. His grave was covered with stones. Named "Ginger" by scientists for his wisps of red hair, this man from a distant time seems very human.

• Backtrack to Room 61 and head back down the stairs to the Egyptian Gallery and the Rosetta Stone. Just past the Rosetta Stone, find a huge head (facing away from you) with a hat like a bowling pin.

❼ Red Granite Head from a Colossal Figure of a King (c. 1350 B.C.)

Art also served as propaganda for the pharaohs, kings who called themselves gods on earth. Put this head on top of an enormous body (which still stands in Egypt), and you have the intimidating image of an omnipotent ruler who demands servile obedience. Next to the head is, appropriately, the pharaoh's powerful fist—the long arm of the law.

The crown is actually two crowns in one. The pointed upper half is the royal cap of Upper Egypt. This rests on the flat, fez-like crown symbolizing Lower Egypt. A pharaoh wearing both crowns together is bragging that he rules a combined Egypt. As both "Lord of the Two Lands" and "High Priest of Every Temple," the pharaoh united church and state.

• Along the wall to the left of the red granite head (as you're facing it) are four black lion-headed statues.

❽ Four Black Granite Figures of the Goddess Sakhmet (1400 B.C.)

This lion-headed goddess Sakhmet looks pretty sedate here, but she could spring into a fierce crouch when crossed. She was the pharaoh's personal bodyguard, who could burn his enemies to a crisp with flaming arrows.

The gods ruled the Egyptian cosmos like dictators in a big banana republic (or the US Congress). Egyptians bribed their gods for favors, offering food, animals, or money, or by erecting statues like these to them.

Sakhmet holds an ankh. This key-shaped cross was the hieroglyph meaning "life" and was a symbol of eternal life. Later, it was adopted as a Christian symbol because of its cross shape and religious overtones.

• *Continuing down the Egyptian Gallery, a few paces directly in front of you and to the left, find a glass case containing a...*

❾ Limestone Fragment of the Beard of the Sphinx

The Great Sphinx—a statue of a pharaoh-headed lion—crouches in the shadow of the Great Pyramids in Cairo. Time shaved off the sphinx's soft-sandstone, goatee-like beard, and a piece is now preserved here in a glass case. This hunk of stone is only a whisker—about three percent of the massive beard—giving an idea of the scale of the six-story-tall, 250-foot-long statue.

The Sphinx is as old as the pyramids (c. 2500 B.C.), built during the time known to historians as the Old Kingdom (2686-2181 B.C.), but this beard may have been added later, during a restoration (c. 1420 B.C., or perhaps even later under Ramesses II).

• *Ten steps past the Sphinx's soul patch is a 10-foot-tall, red-tinted "building" covered in hieroglyphics.*

❿ Limestone False Door and Architrave of Ptahshepses (c. 2400 B.C.)

This "false door" was a ceremonial entrance (never meant to open) for a sealed building, called a *mastaba*, that marked the grave of a man named Ptahshepses. The hieroglyphs of eyes, birds, and rabbits serve as his epitaph, telling his life story, how he went to school with the pharaoh's kids, became an honored vizier, and married the pharaoh's daughter.

The deceased was mummified, placed in a wooden coffin that was encased in a stone coffin, then in a stone sarcophagus (like

the **red-granite sarcophagus with paneled exterior surfaces** in front of Ptahshepses' door), and buried 50 feet beneath the *mastaba* in an underground chamber (see the diagram of "Old Kingdom Tombs," on a nearby wall).

BRITISH MUSEUM

Mastabas like Ptahshepses' were decorated inside and out with statues, stelas, and frescoes like those displayed nearby. These pictured the things that the soul could find useful in the next life—magical spells, lists of the deceased's accomplishments, snapshots of the deceased and his family while alive, and secret passwords from the Egyptian Book of the Dead. False doors like this allowed the soul (but not grave robbers) to come and go.

• *Just past Ptahshepses' false door is a glass case with a statue.*

⓫ Statue of Nenkheftka (2400 b.c.)

Originally standing in a "false door" of his *mastaba,* this statue represented the soul of the deceased still active, going in and out of the burial place. This was the image of the departed that greeted his loved ones when they brought food offerings to the *mastaba* to place at his feet to nourish his soul. (In the mummification rites, the mouth was ritually opened, to prepare it to eat soul food.)

In ancient Egypt, you *could* take it with you. They believed that after you died, your soul lived on, enjoying its earthly possessions—sometimes including servants, who might be walled up alive with their dead master. (Remember that even the great pyramids were just big tombs for Egypt's most powerful.)

Statues functioned as a refuge for the soul on its journey after death. The rich scattered statues of themselves everywhere, just in case. Statues needed to be simple and easy to recognize, mug shots for eternity: stiff, arms down, chin up, nothing fancy. This one has all the essential features, like the simplified human figures on international traffic signs. To a soul caught in the fast lane of astral travel, this symbolic statue would be easier to spot than a detailed one.

With their fervent hope for life after death, Egyptians created calm, dignified art that seems built for eternity.

• *Relax. One civilization down, two to go. Near the end of the gallery*

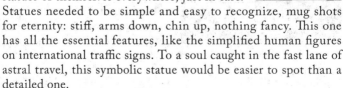

are two huge, winged Assyrian lions (with bearded human heads) standing guard over the Assyrian exhibit halls.

Assyria (900-600 B.C.)

Long before Saddam Hussein, Iraq was home to other palace-building, iron-fisted rulers—the Assyrians.

Assyria was the lion, the king of beasts of early Middle Eastern civilizations. These Semitic people from the agriculturally challenged hills of northern Iraq became traders and conquerors, not farmers. They conquered their southern neighbors and dominated the Middle East for 300 years (c. 900-600 B.C.).

Their strength came from a superb army (chariots, mounted cavalry, and siege engines), a policy of terrorism against enemies ("I tied their heads to tree trunks all around the city," reads a royal inscription), ethnic cleansing and mass deportations of the vanquished, and efficient administration (roads and express postal service). They have been called "The Romans of the East."

⑫ Two Human-Headed Winged Lions (c. 865-860 B.C.)

These lions guarded an Assyrian palace. With the strength of a lion, the wings of an eagle, the brain of a man, and the beard of ZZ Top, they protected the king from evil spirits and scared the heck out of foreign ambassadors and left-wing newspaper reporters. (What has five legs and flies? Take a close look. These quintupeds, which appear complete from both the front and the side, could guard both directions at once.)

Carved into the stone between the bearded lions' loins, you can see one of civilization's most impressive achievements—writing. This wedge-shaped **(cuneiform)** script is the world's first written language, invented 5,000 years ago by the Sumerians (of southern Iraq) and passed down to their less-civilized descendants, the Assyrians.

• *Walk between the lions, glance at the large reconstructed wooden gates from an Assyrian palace, and turn right into the long, narrow red gallery (Room 7) lined with brown relief panels.*

⑬ Nimrud Gallery (Ninth Century B.C.)— Palace of Ashurnasirpal II

This gallery is a mini version of the throne room of King

British Museum—Assyria

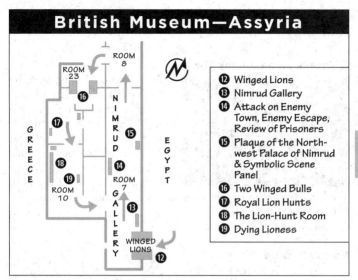

12 Winged Lions
13 Nimrud Gallery
14 Attack on Enemy Town, Enemy Escape, Review of Prisoners
15 Plaque of the Northwest Palace of Nimrud & Symbolic Scene Panel
16 Two Winged Bulls
17 Royal Lion Hunts
18 The Lion-Hunt Room
19 Dying Lioness

Ashurnasirpal II's palace at Nimrud. Entering, you'd see the king on his throne at the far end, surrounded by these pleasant, sand-colored, gypsum relief panels (which were, however, originally painted and varnished).

That's Ashurnasirpal himself in the **first panel on your right,** with braided beard, earring, and fez-like crown, flanked by his supernatural hawk-headed henchmen, who sprinkle incense on him with pine cones. The bulging forearms tell us that Ashurnasirpal II (r. 883-859 B.C.) was a conqueror's conqueror who enjoyed his reputation as a merciless warrior, using torture and humiliation as part of his distinct management style. The room's panels chronicle his bloody career.

Under Ashurnasirpal's reign, the Assyrians dominated the Mideast from their capital at Nineveh (near modern Mosul). Ashurnasirpal II proved his power by building a brand-new palace in nearby Nimrud (called "Calah" in the Bible).

The cuneiform inscription running through the center of the panel is Ashurnasirpal's résumé: "The king who has enslaved all mankind, the mighty warrior who steps on the necks of his enemies, tramples all foes and shatters the enemy; the weapon of the gods, the mighty king, the King of Assyria, the king of the world, B.A., M.B.A., Ph.D., etc...."

• *A dozen paces farther down, on the left wall, you'll find an upper panel labeled...*

⓮ Attack on an Enemy Town

Many "nations" conquered by the Assyrians consisted of little more than a single walled city. Here, the Assyrians lay siege with a crude "tank" that shields them as they advance to the city walls to smash down the gate with a battering ram. The king stands a safe distance away behind the juggernaut and bravely shoots arrows.

• *In the next panel to the right, you'll find...*

Enemy Escape

Soldiers flee the slings and arrows of outrageous Assyrians by swimming across the Euphrates, using inflated animal bladders as life preservers. Their friends in the castle downstream applaud their ingenuity.

• *Below, you'll see...*

Review of Prisoners

The Assyrian economy depended on booty. Here, a conquered nation is paraded before the Assyrian king, who is shaded by a parasol. Ashurnasirpal II sneers and tells the captured chief, "Drop

and give me 50." Above the prisoners' heads, we see the rich spoils of war—elephant tusks, metal pots, and so on. The Assyrians depopulated conquered lands by slavery and ethnic cleansing, then repopulated with Assyrian settlers.

• *On the opposite wall, a few steps farther along, is an artist's rendering of what the palace would have looked like.*

⓯ Plaque of the Northwest Palace of Nimrud and Symbolic Scene Panel

The plaque shows the king at the far end of the throne room, shaded by a parasol and flanked by winged lions. (In the diagram of the palace's floor plan, the throne room is Room B.) The 30,000-square-foot palace was built atop a 50-acre artificial mound. The new palace was inaugurated with a 10-day banquet (according to an inscription), where the king picked up the tab for 69,574 of his closest friends.

The relief panel (immediately to the right) labeled **Symbolic Scene** stood behind the throne. It shows the king (and his double) tending the tree of life while reaching up to receive the ring of kingship from the winged sun god.

• *Exit the Nimrud Gallery at the far end, then hang a U-turn left. Pause at the entrance of Room 10c to see the impressive...*

⑯ Two Winged Bulls from Khorsabad, the Palace of Sargon (c. 710-705 b.c.)

These marble bulls guarded the entrance to the city of Dur-Sharrukin ("Sargonsburg"), a new capital (near Nineveh/Mosul)

with vast palaces built by Sargon II (r. 721-705 b.c.). The 30-ton bulls were cut from a single block, tipped on their sides, then dragged to their place by POWs. (In modern times, when the British transported them here, they had to cut them in half; you can see the horizontal cracks through the bulls' chests.)

Sargon II gained his reputation as a general by subduing the Israelites after a three-year siege of Jerusalem (2 Kings 17:1-6). He solidified his conquest by ethnically cleansing the area and deporting many Israelites (inspiring legends of the "Lost" Ten Tribes).

In 710 b.c., while these bulls were being carved for his palace, Sargon II marched victorious through the streets of Babylon (near modern Baghdad), having put down a revolt there against him. His descendants would also have to deal with the troublesome Babylonians.

• *Sneak between these bulls and veer right (into Room 10), where horses are being readied for the big hunt.*

⑰ Royal Lion Hunts from the Palace of Ashurbanipal

Lion hunting was Assyria's sport of kings. On the right wall are horses, on the left are the hunting dogs. And next to them, lions, resting peacefully in a garden, unaware that they will shortly be rousted, stampeded, and slaughtered.

Lions lived in Mesopotamia up until modern times, and it was the king's duty to keep the lion population down to protect farmers and herdsmen. This duty soon became sport, with staged hunts and zoo-bred lions, as the kings of men proved their power by taking on the king of beasts.

• *Continue ahead into the larger lion-hunt room. Reading the panels like a comic strip, start on the right and gallop counterclockwise.*

🔞 The Lion-Hunt Room (c. 650 B.C.)

They release the lions from their cages, then soldiers on horseback herd them into an enclosed arena. The king has them cor-

nered. Let the slaughter begin. The chariot carries King Ashurbanipal, the great-grandson of Sargon II (not to be confused with Ashurnasirpal II, who ruled 200 years earlier, mentioned previously).

The last of Assyria's great kings, Ashurbanipal has reigned now for 50 years. Having left a half-dozen corpses in his wake, he moves on, while spearmen hold off lions attacking from the rear.

• *At about the middle of the long wall...*

The fleeing lions, cornered by hounds, shot through with arrows, and weighed down by fatigue, begin to fall. The lead lion carries on even while vomiting blood.

This low point of Assyrian cruelty is, perhaps, the high point of their artistic achievement. It's a curious coincidence that civilizations often produce their greatest art in their declining years. Hmm.

• *On the wall opposite the vomiting lion is the...*

🔞 Dying Lioness

A lioness roars in pain and frustration. She tries to run, but her body is too heavy. Her muscular hind legs, once the source of her power, are now paralyzed.

Like these brave, fierce lions, Assyria's once-great warrior nation

was slain. Shortly after Ashurbanipal's death, Assyria was conquered, and their capital at Nineveh was sacked and looted by an
ascendant Babylon (612 B.C.). The mood of tragedy, dignity, and
proud struggle in a hopeless cause makes this dying lioness simply
one of the most beautiful of human creations.

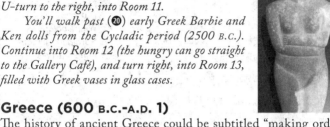

• Exit the lion-hunt room at the far end and make
your way back to the huge, winged lions at the start
of the Assyrian exhibit. To reach the Greek section,
exit Assyria between the winged lions and make a
U-turn to the right, into Room 11.

*   You'll walk past (❷⓪) early Greek Barbie and*
Ken dolls from the Cycladic period (2500 B.C.).
Continue into Room 12 (the hungry can go straight
to the Gallery Café), and turn right, into Room 13,
filled with Greek vases in glass cases.

BRITISH MUSEUM

Greece (600 B.C.-A.D. 1)

The history of ancient Greece could be subtitled "making order
out of chaos." While Assyria was dominating the Middle East,
"Greece"—a gaggle of warring tribes roaming the Greek peninsula—was floundering in darkness. But by about 700 B.C., these
tribes began settling down, experimenting with democracy, forming self-governing city-states, and making ties with other city-
states. Scarcely two centuries later, they would be a relatively
united community and the center of the civilized world.

    During its Golden Age (500-430 B.C.), Greece set the tone for
all of Western civilization to follow. Democracy, theater, literature,
mathematics, philosophy, science, gyros, art, and architecture, as
we know them, were virtually all invented by a single generation of
Greeks in a small town of maybe 80,000 citizens.

• Roughly in the middle of Room 13 is a Z-shaped glass case marked #8.
On the upper shelf, find a...

❷① Black-Figured Amphora (Jar): Achilles and Penthesileia (540-530 B.C.)

Greeks poured wine from jars like this one,
painted with a man stabbing a woman, a
legend from the Trojan War. The Trojan
War (c. 1200 B.C.)—part fact but mostly
legend—symbolized Greece's long struggle
to rise above war and chaos.

    Achilles of Greece faces off against the
Queen of the Amazons, Penthesileia, who
was fighting for Troy. (The Amazons were a
legendary race of warrior women who cut off
one breast to facilitate their archery skills.)

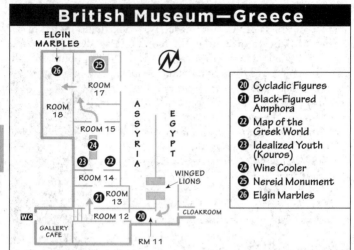

British Museum—Greece

ELGIN
MARBLES

26 25
ROOM
17
ROOM
18
ROOM 15
24
23 22
ROOM 14
21 ROOM
13
WC ROOM 12 20
GALLERY
CAFE
RM 11
ASSYRIA
EGYPT
WINGED
LIONS
CLOAKROOM

20 Cycladic Figures
21 Black-Figured
   Amphora
22 Map of the
   Greek World
23 Idealized Youth
   (Kouros)
24 Wine Cooler
25 Nereid Monument
26 Elgin Marbles

BRITISH MUSEUM

Achilles bears down, plunging a spear through her neck, as the blood spurts. In her dying moment, Penthesileia looks up and her gaze locks on Achilles. His eyes bulge wide, and he falls instantly in love with her. She dies, and Achilles is smitten.

Pottery like this (and many others in the room), usually painted red and black, was a popular export product for the sea-trading Greeks. The earliest featured geometric patterns (eighth century B.C.), then a painted black silhouette on the natural orange clay, then a red figure on a black background. On this jar, see the names of the two enemies/lovers ("AXILEV" and "PENOESIIEA") as well as the signature of the craftsman, Exekias.

• Continue to Room 15, then relax on a bench and read, surrounded by statues and vases in glass cases. On the entrance wall, find a...

22 Map of the Greek World (500-430 B.C.)

After Greece drove out Persian invaders in 480 B.C., the city of Athens became the most powerful of the city-states and the center of the Greek world. Golden Age Greece was never really a full-fledged empire, but more a common feeling of unity among Greek-speaking people.

A century after the Golden Age, Greek culture was spread still farther by Alexander the Great, who conquered the Mediterranean world and beyond (including Persia). By 300 B.C., the "Greek" world stretched from Italy and Egypt to India (including most of what used to be the Assyrian Empire). Two hundred years later, this Greek-speaking "Hellenistic Empire" was conquered by the Romans.

• There's a nude male statue on the left side of the room.

㉓ Idealized Youth (Kouros, 490 B.C.)

The Greeks saw their gods in human form...and human beings were godlike. With his perfectly round head, symmetrical pecs, and navel in the center, the youth exemplifies the divine orderliness of the universe. The ideal man was geometrically perfect, a balance of opposites, the "Golden Mean." In a statue, that meant finding the right balance between movement and stillness, between realistic human anatomy (with human flaws) and the perfection of a Greek god. He's still a bit uptight, stiff as the rock from which he's carved. But—as we'll see—in just a few short decades, the Greeks would cut loose and create realistic statues that seemed to move like real humans.

• *Two-thirds of the way down Room 15 (on the left) is a glass case containing a vase.*

㉔ Wine Cooler (Psykter) Signed by Douris as Painter (490 B.C.)

This clay vase, designed to float in a bowl of cooling water, shows satyrs at a symposium, or drinking party. These half-man/half-animal creatures (notice their tails) had a reputation for lewd behavior, reminding the balanced and moderate Greeks of their rude roots.

The reveling figures painted on this jar (red on black) are more realistic, more three-dimensional, and suggest more natural movements than even the literally three-dimensional but quite stiff kouros. The Greeks are beginning to conquer the natural world in art. The art, like life, is more in balance. And speaking of "balance," if that's a Greek sobriety test, revel on.

• *Carry on into Room 17 and sit facing the Greek temple at the far end.*

㉕ Nereid Monument from Xanthos (c. 390-380 B.C.)

Greek temples (like this reconstruction of a temple-shaped tomb; see photo, next page) housed a statue of a god or goddess. Unlike Christian churches, which serve as meeting places, Greek temples were the gods' homes. Worshippers gathered outside, so the most impressive part of the temple was its exterior. Temples were rectangular buildings surrounded by rows of columns and topped by slanted roofs.

The triangle-shaped roof, filled in with sculpture, is called the "pediment." The cross beams that support the pediment are called

"metopes" (MET-uh-pees). Now look through the columns to the building itself. Above the doorway is another set of relief panels running around the building (under the eaves), called the "frieze."

The statues between the columns (and three more facing the monument) are dubbed Nereids—friendly sea nymphs—because of their dramatic wave-like poses and wind-blown clothes, and because some appear to be borne aloft by sea animals. Notice the sculptor's delight in capturing the body in motion, and the way the wet clothes cling to the figures' anatomy.

Next, we'll see pediment, frieze, and metope decorations from Greece's greatest temple.

• *Leave the British Museum. Take the Tube to Heathrow and fly to Athens. In the center of the old city, on top of the high, flat hill known as the Acropolis, you'll find...*

The Parthenon (447-432 B.C.)

The Parthenon—the temple dedicated to Athena, goddess of wisdom and the patroness of Athens—was the crowning glory of an enormous urban-renewal plan during Greece's Golden Age. After Athens was ruined in a war with Persia, the city—under the bold leadership of Pericles—constructed the greatest building of its day. The Parthenon was a model of

balance, simplicity, and harmonious elegance, the symbol of the Golden Age. Phidias, the greatest Greek sculptor, decorated the exterior with statues and relief panels.

While the building itself remains in Athens, many of the Parthenon's best sculptures are right here in the British Museum—the so-called Elgin Marbles, named for the shrewd British ambassador who had his men hammer, chisel, and saw them off the Parthenon in the early 1800s. Though the Greek government complains about losing its marbles, the Brits feel they rescued and preserved the sculptures. The often-bitter controversy continues.

• *Enter through the glass doors labeled* The Parthenon Galleries. *(The rooms branching off the entryway usually have helpful exhibits that reconstruct the Parthenon and its once-colorful sculpture.)*

British Museum—Elgin Marbles

METOPES

FRIEZE

PEDIMENT

ROOM 18

FRIEZE

TOUR BEGINS

ROOM 17   NEREID MONUMENT

To Egypt

㉖ Elgin Marbles (450 B.C.)

The marble panels you see lining the walls of this large hall are part of the frieze that originally ran around the exterior of the

Parthenon (under the eaves). The statues at either end of the hall once filled the Parthenon's triangular-shaped pediments. Near the pediment sculptures, we'll also find the relief panels known as metopes.

The Frieze: These 56 relief panels show Athens' "Fourth of July" parade, celebrating the birth of the city. On this day, citizens marched up the Acropolis to symbolically present a new robe to the 40-foot-tall gold-and-ivory statue of Athena housed in the Parthenon.

• *Start at the panels by the entrance (#136) and work counterclockwise.*

Men on horseback, chariots, musicians, children, animals for sacrifice, and young maidens with offerings are all part of the grand parade, all heading in the same direction—uphill. Prance on.

Notice the muscles and veins in the horses' legs and the intricate folds in the cloaks and dresses. Some panels have holes drilled

Centaurs Slain Around the World

Dateline 500 B.C.—Greece, China, India: Man no longer considers himself an animal. Bold new ideas are exploding simultaneously around the world. Socrates, Confucius, Buddha, and others are independently discovering a nonmaterial, unseen order in nature and in man. They say man has a rational mind or soul. He's separate from nature and different from the other animals.

in them, where gleaming bronze reins were fitted to heighten the festive look. Of course, all these panels were originally painted in realistic colors. As you move along, notice that, despite the bustle of figures posed every which way, the frieze has one unifying element—all the people's heads are at the same level, creating a single ribbon around the Parthenon.

• *Cross to the opposite wall.*

A three-horse chariot (#67), cut out of only a few inches of marble, is more life-like and three-dimensional than anything the Egyptians achieved in a freestanding statue.

Enter the girls (five yards to the left, #61), the heart of the procession. Dressed in pleated robes, they shuffle past the parade marshals, carrying incense burners and jugs of wine and bowls to pour out an offering to the thirsty gods.

The procession culminates (#35) in the presentation of the robe to Athena. A man and a child fold the robe for the goddess while the rest of the gods look on. There are Zeus and Hera (#29), the king and queen of the gods, seated, enjoying the fashion show and wondering what length hemlines will be this year.

• *Head for the set of pediment sculptures at the far right end of the hall.*

The Pediment Sculptures: These statues were originally nestled nicely in the triangular pediment above the columns at

the Parthenon's main (east) entrance. The missing statues at the peak of the triangle once showed the birth of Athena. Zeus had his head split open, allowing Athena, the goddess of wisdom, to rise from his brain fully grown and fully armed, inaugurating the Golden Age of Athens.

The other gods at this Olympian banquet slowly become aware of the amazing event. The first to notice is the one closest to them, Hebe, the cup-bearer of the gods (tallest surviving fragment). Frightened, she runs to tell the others, her dress whipping behind her. A startled Demeter (just left of Hebe) turns toward Hebe.

The only one who hasn't lost his head is laid-back Dionysus (the cool guy farther left). He just raises another glass of wine to his lips. Over on the right, Aphrodite, goddess of love, leans back in to her mother's lap, too busy admiring her own bare shoulder to even notice the hubbub. A chess-set horse's head screams, "These people are nuts—let me out of here!"

The scene had a message. Just as wise Athena rose above the lesser gods, who were scared, drunk, or vain, so would her city, Athens, rise above her lesser rivals.

This is amazing workmanship. Compare Dionysus, with his natural, relaxed, reclining pose, to all those stiff Egyptian statues standing eternally at attention.

Appreciate the folds of the clothes on the female figures (on the right half), especially Aphrodite's clinging, rumpled robe. Some sculptors would first build a nude model of their figure, put real clothes on it, and study how the cloth hung down before actually sculpting in marble. Others found inspiration at the *taverna* on wet T-shirt night.

Even without their heads, these statues, with their detailed anatomy and expressive poses, speak volumes.

Wander behind. The statues originally sat 40 feet above the ground. The backs of the statues, which were never intended to be seen, are almost as detailed as the fronts.

• *The metopes are the panels on the walls to either side. Start with the three South Metope panels on the right wall.*

The Metopes: In #XXXI (the central panel of the three), a centaur grabs a man by the throat while the man pulls his hair. The humans have invited some centaurs—wild half-man/half-horse creatures—to a wedding feast. All goes well until the brutish centaurs, the original party animals, get too drunk and try to carry off the women. A battle ensues. In #XXX, the centaur does the hair-pulling, and begins to drive the man to his knees.

The Greeks prided themselves on creating order out of chaos. Within just a few generations, they went from nomadic barbarism to the pinnacle of early Western civilization. These metopes tell the story of this struggle between the forces of human civilization and animal-like barbarism.

In #XXVIII (opposite wall, center, see photo at left), the centaurs have taken control of the party, as one rears back and prepares to trample the helpless man. The leopard skin draped over the centaur's arm roars a taunt. The humans lose face.

In #XXVII (to the left—see photo next page), the humans finally rally and drive off the brutish centaurs. A centaur tries to run, but the man grabs him by the neck and raises his right hand (missing) to run him through. The man's folded cloak sets off his smooth skin and graceful figure.

The centaurs have been defeated. Civilization has triumphed over barbarism, order over chaos, and rational man over his half-animal alter ego.

Why are the Elgin Marbles so treasured? The British of the 19th century saw themselves as the new "civilized" race, subduing "barbarians" in their far-flung empire. Maybe these carved stones made them stop and wonder—will our great civilization also turn to rubble?

BRITISH MUSEUM

The Rest of the Museum

You've toured only the foundations of Western civilization on the ground floor, West Wing. Upstairs you'll find still more artifacts from these ancient lands, plus Rome and the medieval civilization that sprang from it. Pick up the free map, locate the rooms with themes you find interesting (Etruscan, Persian, Roman Britain, Dark Age Europe, and so on) and explore. Some highlights:

- Lindow Man (a.k.a. the "Bog Man") in Room 50 (upper floor, via east stairs). This victim of a Druid human-sacrifice ritual, with wounds still visible, was preserved for 2,000 years in a peat bog.
- The seventh-century Anglo-Saxon Sutton Hoo Burial Ship (Room 41, upper floor, via East Stairs).
- Treasures of the Persian civilization. The collection here is far better than what remains to be seen in Iran (Room 52, upper floor).
- The only existing, complete cartoon (preliminary sketch) by Michelangelo (Room 90, Level 4, accessed via the North Stairs or from the top of the Reading Room).
- The King's Library—which once held the British Library's treasures—now houses the delightful Enlightenment Gallery, created to give you the feeling of this grand museum when it was founded in 1753. Back then it was a place of both learning and wonder (Room 1; the long hall to the right of the main entry).

And, of course, history doesn't begin and end in Europe. Look for remnants of the sophisticated, exotic cultures of Asia and the Americas (in North Wing, ground floor) and Africa (lower floor)—all part of the totem pole of the human family.

BRITISH LIBRARY TOUR

The British Empire built its greatest monuments out of paper. It's with literature that England has made her lasting contribution to history and the arts. These national archives of Britain include more than 12 million books, 180 miles of shelving, and the deepest basement in London.

But everything that matters for your visit is in a delightful room labeled "Sir John Ritblat Gallery: Treasures of the British Library" and an adjacent room containing the Magna Carta. We'll concentrate on a handful of documents—literary and historical—that changed the course of history. Start with these top stops, then stray according to your interests.

Orientation

Cost: Free (£2 suggested donation); admission charged for some (optional) temporary exhibits.

Hours: Mon-Fri 9:30-18:00, Tue until 20:00, Sat 9:30-17:00, Sun 11:00-17:00.

Getting There: From the King's Cross St. Pancras Tube station, exit to Euston Road, turn right, and walk a block west to 96 Euston Road, where you'll see a humble brick building dating from 1998. Euston Tube station is also nearby. Buses #10, #30, #59, #63, #73, and #91 (among others) also stop nearby.

Rotating Exhibits: Exhibits change often, and many of the museum's old, fragile manuscripts need to "rest" periodically in order to stay well-preserved. Even some of the major items I describe here could be napping out of view. If your heart's set on seeing that one particular rare Dickens book or letter penned by Gandhi, call ahead to make sure it's on display (tel. 019/3754-6060; for questions on the collection, call 020/7412-7676, www.bl.uk).

Tours: There are no guided tours or audioguides for the permanent collection. There are, however, **guided tours** of the building itself—the archives and reading rooms (for details, call 020/7412-7639 or see the website). **Touch-screen computers** in the permanent collection let you page virtually through some of the rare books.

You can also download a free **audio version** of this tour for your mobile device via www.ricksteves.com/audioeurope, iTunes, or the Rick Steves Audio Europe smartphone app.

Length of This Tour: Allow one hour.

Cloakroom: Free. Lockers require £1 coin deposit (no large bags). For security, bags may be searched at the library entrance.

Photography: No photos allowed.

Cuisine Art: The upper-level restaurant has good hot meals. The ground-floor café (sandwiches and drinks) is next to the vast and fun pull-out stamp collection. From either café, you'll see the 50-foot-tall wall of 65,000 books, a present to the people from King George IV in 1823. The high-tech bookshelf is behind glass and has movable lifts.

Starring: Bibles, Shakespeare, English Lit 101, Magna Carta, and—ladies and gentlemen—the Beatles.

The Tour Begins

Entering the library courtyard, you'll see a big statue of a naked Isaac Newton bending forward with a compass to measure the universe. The statue symbolizes the library's purpose: to gather all knowledge and promote humanity's endless search for truth.

Stepping inside, you'll find the information desk and shop. The cloakroom and WC are down a short staircase to the right. The reading rooms upstairs are not open to the general public. The PACCAR Gallery, down a few steps to the left, houses temporary exhibits (sometimes requiring an admission charge).

Our tour is of the tiny but exciting area to the left. It's variously called "The Sir John Ritblat Gallery," "Treasures of the British Library," or just "The Treasures." This priceless literary and historical collection is held in one large, carefully designed, dimly lit room.

Enter and let your eyes adjust. The room has display cases grouped according to themes: maps, sacred texts, music, and so on. Focus on the big picture, and don't be too worried about locating every specific exhibit in this tour.

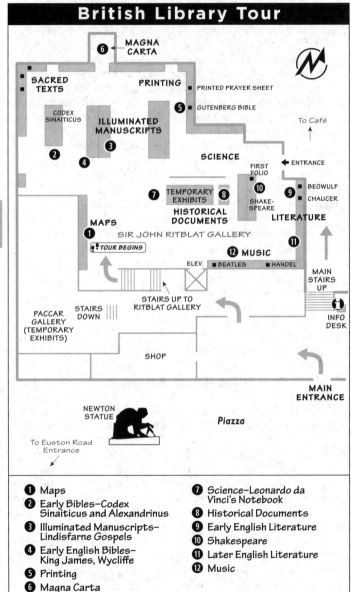

British Library Tour

MAGNA CARTA

SACRED TEXTS

PRINTING

PRINTED PRAYER SHEET

CODEX SINAITICUS

ILLUMINATED MANUSCRIPTS

GUTENBERG BIBLE

To Café

SCIENCE

ENTRANCE

FIRST FOLIO

BEOWULF

TEMPORARY EXHIBITS

CHAUCER

SHAKE-SPEARE

HISTORICAL DOCUMENTS

LITERATURE

MAPS

SIR JOHN RITBLAT GALLERY

TOUR BEGINS

MUSIC

ELEV.

BEATLES

HANDEL

MAIN STAIRS UP

STAIRS UP TO RITBLAT GALLERY

STAIRS DOWN

INFO DESK

PACCAR GALLERY (TEMPORARY EXHIBITS)

SHOP

MAIN ENTRANCE

NEWTON STATUE

Piazza

To Euston Road Entrance

1 Maps
2 Early Bibles–Codex Sinaiticus and Alexandrinus
3 Illuminated Manuscripts–Lindisfarne Gospels
4 Early English Bibles–King James, Wycliffe
5 Printing
6 Magna Carta
7 Science–Leonardo da Vinci's Notebook
8 Historical Documents
9 Early English Literature
10 Shakespeare
11 Later English Literature
12 Music

❶ Maps

The historic maps show how humans' perspective of the world expanded over the centuries. These pieces of paper, encoded with information gleaned from travelers, could be passed along to future generations—each building upon the knowledge of the last.

The collection changes year to year, but you may see maps similar to these: A crude 13th-century map of Britain put medieval man in an unusual position—looking down on his homeland from 50 miles in the air. A few centuries later, maps of Britain were of such high quality they could be used today to plan a trip. And only a few generations after Columbus' first journey, the entire globe was fairly well-mapped, except for the mysterious expanse of unknown land that lay beyond America's east coast—"Terra Incognita."

• *Move into the area dedicated to sacred texts from several cultures— the Hebrew Torah, Muslim Quran, Buddhist sutras, and Hindu Upanishads. Start by browsing the different versions of the sacred text of Christians, the Bible.*

❷ Early Bibles— Codex Sinaiticus and Alexandrinus

My favorite excuse for not learning a foreign language is "If English was good enough for Jesus Christ, it's good enough for me!" I don't know what that has to do with anything, but obviously Jesus didn't speak English—nor did Moses or Isaiah or Paul or any other Bible author or character. As a result, our present-day English Bible came not directly from the mouths and pens of these religious figures, but is instead the fitful product of centuries of evolution and translation.

The Bible is not a single book; it's an anthology of books by many authors from different historical periods writing in various languages (usually Hebrew or Greek). So there are three things that editors must do in compiling the most accurate Bible: 1) decide which books actually belong, 2) find the oldest and most accurate version of each book, and 3) translate it accurately.

The **Codex Sinaiticus,** from 350 A.D., is one of the oldest complete Bibles in existence ("codex" means it's an ancient, bound manuscript). It's one of the first attempts to collect various books by different authors into one authoritative anthology. The parchment is made from animal skin. It's in Greek, the language in which most of the New Testament was written. The Old Testament

portions are Greek translations from the original Hebrew. This particular Bible, and the nearby **Codex Alexandrinus** (A.D. 425), contain some books not included in most modern English Bibles. (Even today, Catholic Bibles contain books not found in Protestant Bibles.)

These accounts of Jesus of Nazareth are about as old as any in existence, but even so, they weren't written down until several generations after Jesus' death. Today, Bible scholars pore diligently over every word in the New Testament, trying to separate Jesus' authentic words from those that seem to have been added later.

❸ Illuminated Manuscripts— Lindisfarne Gospels

After the fall of Rome, the Christian message was preserved by monks, who reproduced ancient Bibles by hand. This was a pains-taking process, usually done for a rich patron. The Bibles were often beauti-fully illustrated, or "illuminated," and are some of the finest works of art from what we call the Dark Ages. The little intimate details offer a rare and fascinating peek into medieval life.

The Lindisfarne version of the four Gospels (A.D. 698) is the most magnifi-cent of medieval British monk-uscripts. The text is in Latin, the language of scholars ever since the Roman Empire, but the illustrations—with elaborate tracery and interwoven decoration—mix Irish, classical, and even Byzantine forms. (Read an electronic copy using the touch-screen computers.)

These Gospels are a reminder that Christianity almost didn't make it in Europe. After the fall of Rome (which had established Christianity as the Empire's official religion), much of Europe reverted to its pagan ways. People worshipped woodland spirits and terrible Teutonic gods.

Lindisfarne was an obscure monastery of Irish monks on an island off the east coast of England. In that chaotic era, it was one of the few beacons of light, tending the embers of civilization through the long night of the Dark Ages. It took 500 years before Christianity was fully re-established in Europe.

❹ Early English Bibles— King James Version, Wycliffe Bible, etc.

By the year 1400, England was mostly Christian. But the Bible was still written in Latin, even though only a small percentage of the population understood that language. A few brave reformers risked death to translate the sacred books into English and print them using Gutenberg's new invention, the printing press. Within two centuries, English translations were both legal and popular.

These Bibles are written in the same language you speak, but try reading them. The strange letters and archaic words clearly show how quickly languages evolve. Jesus spoke Aramaic, a form of Hebrew. His words were written down in Greek. Greek manuscripts were translated into Latin, the language of medieval monks and scholars. In the 1400s, English scholars began translating the Greek and Latin into the King's English.

The King James version (made during his reign) has been the most widely used English translation. Fifty scholars worked for four years, borrowing heavily from previous translations, to produce the work. Its impact on the English language was enormous. It made Elizabethan English something of the standard, even after ordinary people had long since stopped saying "thee," "thou," and "verily, verily."

Recent translations are not only more readable but also more accurate, based on better scholarship and original manuscripts. But scholars still encounter problems when trying to translate old phrases to fit contemporary viewpoints (case in point: our generation's debate over whether the God of the Bible should be a he or a she).

❺ Printing

Printing was invented by the Chinese (what wasn't?). The **Printed Prayer Sheet** (c. 618-907) was made seven centuries before the printing press was "invented" in Europe. A bodhisattva (an incarnation of Buddha) rides a lion, surrounded by a prayer in Chinese characters. The faithful gained a blessing by saying the prayer, and so did the printer by reproducing it. Texts such as this were printed using wooden blocks carved with Chinese characters, then dipped into paint or ink.

The Gutenberg Bible (c. 1455)

It looks like just another monk-made Latin manuscript, but it was the first book printed in Europe using movable type. Printing is one of the most revolutionary inventions in history.

Johann Gutenberg (c. 1397-1468), a German silversmith, devised a convenient way to reproduce written materials quickly, neatly, and cheaply—by printing with movable type. You scratch each letter onto a separate metal block, then arrange them into words, ink them up, and press them onto paper. When one job was done you could reuse the same letters for a new one.

This simple idea had immediate and revolutionary consequences. Suddenly, the Bible was available for anyone to read, fueling the Protestant Reformation. Knowledge became cheap and accessible to a wide audience, not just the rich. Books became the mass medium of Europe, linking people by a common set of ideas.

❻ Magna Carta (1215)

Duck into the Magna Carta Room to answer this question: How did Britain, a tiny island with a few million people, come to rule a quarter of the world? Not by force, but by law. The Magna Carta was the basis for England's constitutional system of government. Though historians talk about *the* Magna Carta, several different versions of the document exist, some of which are kept in this room.

The Articles of the Barons (labeled *King John*): In 1215, England's barons rose in revolt against the slimy King John. (The same King John appears as a villain in the legends of Robin Hood.) After losing London, John was forced to negotiate. The barons presented him with this list of demands. John, whose rule was worthless without the barons' support, had no choice but to affix his seal to it.

Magna Carta: A few days after John agreed to this original document, it was rewritten in legal form, and some 35 copies of the final version of the "Great Charter" were distributed around the kingdom.

This was a turning point in the history of government. Before, kings had ruled by God-given authority, above the laws of men. Now, for the first time, there were limits—in writing—on how a king could treat his subjects. More generally, it established the idea of "due process"—the notion that a government can't infringe on citizens' freedom without a legitimate legal reason. This small step became the basis for all constitutional governments, including yours.

So what did this radical piece of paper actually say? Not much, by today's standards. The specific demands had to do with things such as inheritance taxes, the king's duties to widows and orphans, and so on. It wasn't the specific articles that were important, but the simple fact that the king had to abide by them as law.

• *Now return to the main room to find...*

➐ Science—Leonardo da Vinci's Notebook

Books also spread secular knowledge. During the Renaissance, men turned their attention away from heaven and toward the nuts

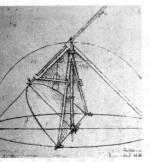

and bolts of the material world around them. These pages from Leonardo's notebook show his powerful curiosity, his genius for invention, and his famous backward and inside-out handwriting, which makes sense only if you know Italian and have a mirror. Leonardo's restless mind pondered diverse subjects, from how birds fly, to the flow of the Arno River, to military fortifications, to an early helicopter, to the "earthshine"

reflecting onto the moon.

One person's research inspired another's, and books allowed knowledge to accumulate. Galileo championed the counter-commonsense notion that the earth spun around the sun, and Isaac Newton later explained the mathematics of those moving celestial bodies.

➑ Historical Documents

Nearby are many more historical documents. The displays change frequently, but you may see letters by Henry VIII, Queen Elizabeth I, Darwin, Freud, Gandhi, and others. But for now, let's trace the evolution of...

➒ Early English Literature

Four out of every five English words have been borrowed from other languages. The English language, like English culture (and London today), is a mix derived from foreign invaders. Some of the historic ingredients that make this cultural stew:

- The original Celtic tribesmen
- Latin-speaking Romans (A.D. 1-500)
- Germanic tribes called Angles and Saxons (English is a Germanic language, and the name England comes from "Angle-land"—island of the Angles)
- Vikings from Denmark (A.D. 800)
- French-speaking Normans under William the Conqueror (1066-1250)

Beowulf (c. 1000)

Ponder this first English literary masterpiece. The Anglo-Saxon epic poem, written in Old English (the earliest version of our language), almost makes the hieroglyphics on the Rosetta Stone look easy. The manuscript is from A.D. 1000, although the story

William Shakespeare
(1564-1616)

William Shakespeare is the greatest author in any language, period. He expanded and helped define modern English. In one fell swoop, he made the language of everyday people as important as Latin. In the process, he gave us phrases like "one fell swoop," which we quote without knowing they're Shakespeare.

Shakespeare was born in Stratford-upon-Avon in 1564 to John Shakespeare and Mary Arden. Though his parents were probably illiterate, Shakespeare is thought to have attended Stratford's grammar school, finishing his education at age 14. When he was 18, he married a 26-year-old local girl, Anne Hathaway, who was three months pregnant at the time with their daughter Susanna.

The next few years are a blank—following his marriage, Shakespeare disappeared from any historical record, not turning up again until seven years later. By this point, he was a budding poet and playwright in London. He soon hit the big time, writing and performing for royalty, founding (along with his troupe) the Globe Theatre (a replica of which now sits along the Thames' South Bank—see page 92), and raking in enough dough to buy New Place, a swanky mansion back in his hometown. Around 1611, the rich-and-famous playwright retired from the theater, moving back to Stratford, where he died at the age of 52.

With plots that entertained both the highest and the lowest minds, Shakespeare taught the play-going public about human nature. His tool was an unrivaled mastery of the English language. Using borrowed plots, outrageous puns, and poetic language, Shakespeare wrote comedies (c. 1590—*Taming of the Shrew, As You Like It*), tragedies (c. 1600—*Hamlet, Othello, Macbeth, King Lear*), and fanciful combinations (c. 1610—*The Tempest*), explor-

itself dates to about 750. In this epic story, the young hero Beowulf defeats two half-human monsters threatening the kingdom. Beowulf symbolizes England's emergence from the chaos and barbarism of the Dark Ages.

The Canterbury Tales (c. 1410)

Six hundred years later, England was Christian, but it was hardly the pious, predictable, Sunday-school world we might imagine. Geoffrey Chaucer's bawdy collection of stories, told by pilgrims on their way to Canterbury, gives us the full range of life's expe-

ing the full range of human emotions and reinventing the English language.

Perhaps as important was his insight into humanity. His father was a glove maker and wool merchant, and his mother was the daughter of a landowner from a Catholic family. Some scholars speculate that Shakespeare's parents were closet Catholics, practicing their faith during the rise of Protestantism. It is this tug-of-war between two worlds, some think, that helped enlighten Shakespeare's humanism. Think of his stock of great characters and great lines: Hamlet ("To be or not to be, that is the question"), Othello and his jealousy ("It is the green-eyed monster"), ambitious Mark Antony ("Friends, Romans, countrymen, lend me your ears"), rowdy Falstaff ("The better part of valor is discretion"), and the star-crossed lovers Romeo and Juliet ("But soft, what light through yonder window breaks"). Shakespeare probed the psychology of human beings 300 years before Freud. Even today, his characters strike a familiar chord.

The scope of his brilliant work, his humble beginnings, and the fact that no original Shakespeare manuscripts survive raise a few scholarly eyebrows. Some have wondered if maybe Shakespeare had help on several of his plays. After all, they reasoned, how could a journeyman actor with little education have written so many masterpieces? And he was surrounded by other great writers, such as his friend and fellow poet, Ben Jonson. Most modern scholars, though, agree that Shakespeare did indeed write the plays and sonnets attributed to him.

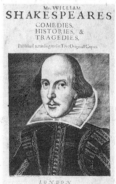

His contemporaries had no doubts about Shakespeare—or his legacy. As Jonson wrote in the preface to the First Folio, "He was not of an age, but for all time!"

riences—happy, sad, silly, sexy, and devout. (Late in life, Chaucer wrote an apology for those works of his "that tend toward sin.")

While most serious literature of the time was written in scholarly Latin, the stories in *The Canterbury Tales* were written in Middle English, the language that developed after the French invasion of 1066 added a Norman twist to Old English.

❿ Shakespeare—The First Folio (1623)

Shakespeare wrote his plays to be performed, not read. He published a few, but as his reputation grew, unauthorized "bootleg" versions began to circulate. Some of these were written by actors who were trying (with faulty memories) to re-create plays they had appeared in years before. Publishers also put out different versions of his plays.

It wasn't until seven years after his death, in 1623, that a complete collection of Shakespeare's plays was published, commonly known as the First Folio. Of the 700 printed, about 150 survive (most are in the US). Western literature owes much to this folio, which collects 36 of the 37 known Shakespeare plays (*Pericles* missed out). If the First Folio is not out, the library should have other Shakespeare items on display.

The engraving of Shakespeare on the title page is reportedly one of only two portraits done during his lifetime. Is this what he really looked like? No one knows. The best answer probably comes from Ben Jonson, in the introduction on the facing page. Jonson concludes, "Reader, look not on his picture, but his book."

⓫ Later English Literature

The rest of the *"Beowulf*/Chaucer wall" is a greatest-hits sampling of literature in English, featuring works that have enlightened and brightened our lives for centuries.

The displays rotate frequently, but there's always a tasty selection of famous works, from Austen to Kipling to Woolf to Joyce to Dickens, whose novels were as popular in his time as blockbuster movies are today. Often on display is the original *Alice's Adventures in Wonderland* by Lewis Carroll. Carroll (whose real name was Charles L. Dodgson) was a stutterer, which made him uncomfortable around everyone but children. For them he created a fantasy world, where grown-up rules and logic were turned upside down. In the 21st century, Britain continues to be a powerful force in the world of ideas and imagination.

⓬ Music

The Beatles

Bach, Beethoven, Brahms, Bizet...Beatles. Future generations will have to judge whether this musical quartet ranks with such artists, but no one can deny their historical significance. The Beatles burst onto the scene in the early 1960s to unheard-of popularity. With their long hair and loud music, they brought counterculture and revolutionary ideas to the middle class, affecting the values of a whole generation. Touring the globe, they served as a link between young people everywhere. Look for photos of John Lennon, Paul

McCartney, George Harrison, and Ringo Starr before and after their fame.

Most interesting are the manuscripts of song lyrics written by Lennon and McCartney, the two guiding lights of the group. "I Want to Hold Your Hand" was the song that launched them to superstardom in America. "A Hard Day's Night" and "Help" were title songs of two films capturing the excitement and chaos of their hectic touring schedule. Some call "Ticket to Ride" the first heavy-metal song. "Michelle," with a line in French, seemed oh-so-sophisticated. "Yesterday," by Paul, was recorded with guitar and voice backed by a string quartet—a touch of class from producer George Martin. Also, glance at the rambling, depressed, and cynical but humorous "untitled verse" by a young John Lennon. Is that a self-portrait at the bottom?

Handel's *Messiah* (1741) and Other Music Manuscripts

Kind of an anticlimax after the Fab Four, I know, but here are

manuscripts by Mozart, Beethoven, Schubert, and others. George Frideric Handel's famous oratorio, the *Messiah*, was written in a flash of inspiration— three hours of music in 24 days. Here are the final bars of its most famous tune. Hallelujah.

THE CITY WALK

From Trafalgar Square to London Bridge

In Shakespeare's day, London consisted of a one-square-mile area surrounding St. Paul's. Today, that square mile, the neighborhood known as "The City," is still the financial heart of London, densely packed with history and bustling with business.

This two-mile walk from Trafalgar Square to London Bridge parallels the Thames, on the same main road that's been used for centuries. Along the way, you'll see sights from The City's storied past, such as St. Paul's Cathedral, the steeples of other Wren churches, historic taverns, a Crusader church, and narrow alleyways with faint remnants of the London of Shakespeare and Dickens.

But you'll also catch The City in action today, especially if you visit on a weekday at lunchtime, when workers spill out onto the streets and The City is at its liveliest. See lawyers and judges in robes and wigs taking cigarette breaks, brokers in pin-striped power suits buying newspapers from Cockneys, and the last of a dying breed—elderly gentlemen with bowler hats and brollies (umbrellas) browsing for tailored shirts and Cuban cigars. Sip a pint in the same pub where Dickens did, and eavesdrop on a power lunch. Use this walk to help resurrect the London that was, then let The City of today surprise you with what is.

Orientation

Length of This Walk: Allow three or more hours, depending on what you visit.

Getting There: Start at Trafalgar Square (Tube: Charing Cross or Embankment). You'll head east on the Strand and end at London Bridge (where the Bankside Walk begins). Handy buses #15 and #11 (see page 34), travel along the Strand and

Fleet Street from Trafalgar Square.

Tourist Information: A TI is located next to St. Paul's (Mon-Sat 9:30-17:30, Sun 10:00-16:00, tel. 020/7606-3030).

Audio Tour: You can download a free audio version of this tour for your mobile device via www.ricksteves.com/audioeurope, iTunes, or the Rick Steves Audio Europe smartphone app.

Courtauld Gallery: £6, free on Mon until 14:00, daily 10:00-18:00, last entry at 17:30, in Somerset House. ✪ See the Courtauld Gallery Tour chapter.

St. Clement Danes: Free, daily 9:00-16:00, closed to sightseers during worship (generally Sun at 11:00, Wed and Fri at 12:30), on the Strand.

Royal Courts of Justice: Free, Mon-Fri 10:00-16:30, closed Sat-Sun, no photos, on the Strand, www.hmcourts-service.gov.uk.

Temple Church: £3, visiting hours vary, generally open for a few hours Sun-Fri (likely 11:00-16:00), closed most Sat, Middle Temple Lane.

Dr. Johnson's House: £4.50, Mon-Sat 11:00-17:30, closed Sun, closes at 17:00 Oct-April, audioguide-£2, 17 Gough Square, tel. 020/7353-3745, www.drjohnsonshouse.org.

St. Bride's Church: Free, Mon-Fri 8:00-18:00, Sat hours generally 11:00-15:00, Sun 10:00-18:30; free lunch concerts usually Tue and Fri at 13:15; Sun choral Eucharist at 11:00 and evensong at 17:30, just off Fleet Street, www.stbrides.com.

Old Bailey: Free, public galleries only; opening hours depend on court schedule, but generally Mon-Fri 9:45-13:00 & 14:00-16:30, closed Sat-Sun, reduced hours in Aug, no kids under 14, on Old Bailey Street. No bags, mobile phones, cameras, iPods, or food, but small purses OK; Eddie, at Bailey's Café across the street at #27, stores bags for £2.

St. Paul's Cathedral: £14.50, includes church entry and dome climb; Mon-Sat 8:30-16:30, last entry for sightseeing at 16:00; dome opens at 9:30, last entry at 16:15; closed Sun except for worship—when it's free; free evensong Mon-Sat at 17:00, Sun at 15:15—visitors who haven't paid admission aren't allowed to linger after the service. ✪ See the St. Paul's Tour chapter.

St. Mary-le-Bow: Free, Mon-Wed 7:00-18:00, Thu 7:00-18:30, Fri 7:00-16:00, closed Sat-Sun, Cheapside.

The Monument: £3 to climb the steps for the view, daily 9:30-17:30, last entry at 17:00, junction of Monument Street and Fish Street Hill.

Services: Public WCs are in front of the Royal Courts of Justice (in a traffic island) and in the basement of St. Paul's (free entry, around the left side).

Overview

The City stretches from Temple Church (near Blackfriars Bridge) to the Tower of London. This was the London of the ancient Romans, William the Conqueror, Henry VIII, Shakespeare, and Elizabeth I.

But The City has been stripped of its history by the Great Fire (1666), the WWII Blitz (1940-1941), and modern economic realities. Today, it's a neighborhood of modern bank buildings and retail stores. Only about 7,000 people actually live here, but The City is a hive of business activity on workdays—packed with hundreds of thousands of commuting bankers, legal assistants, and coffee-shop baristas. At night and on weekends, it's a ghost town.

The route is simple—a two-mile walk east along a single street that changes names as you go. The Strand becomes Fleet Street, which becomes Cannon Street.

The Walk Begins

• *From Trafalgar Square (Tube: Charing Cross or Embankment), head east on the Strand. (Some may wish to skip a mile's worth of the Strand by taking the Tube directly to Temple, picking up the walk at St. Clement Danes.)*

The Strand—
From Trafalgar Square to The City

This busy boulevard, home to theaters and retail stores, was formerly a high-class riverside promenade, back before the Thames was tamed with retaining walls in the 19th century.

The venerable **Charing Cross Station** still has a terminus hotel (a standard part of station design in the early days of rail travel) and remains a busy transportation hub.

The station is named for the **Charing Cross monument,** which stands quietly out of place amid all the commotion in front of the station. This monument is a Victorian Age replacement of the original, medieval "Eleanor Cross." When Queen Eleanor died in 1290, her body was carried from Nottingham to Westminster Abbey. King Edward I had a memorial "Eleanor Cross" built at each of the 12 places his wife's funeral procession spent the night during that long, sad trek. Charing Cross marks the final overnight stop.

A few blocks up the Strand on the left is Southampton Street, which leads to **Covent Garden** (described on page 61).

Ahead on the right is the drive-up entrance to the **Savoy Hotel and Savoy Theatre.** The hotel sparkles after a recent £100 million renovation. Its shiny gold knight represents the Earl of Savoy, who built the original riverside palace here in 1245. This is one of London's ritziest locales, with Rolls-Royces, fancy shops, Simpson's Restaurant, Donald Trump luxury, and the doorman in top hat and tails. Everyone has stayed here. Monet painted the Thames at the Savoy; Oscar Wilde romanced Lord Douglas; Chaplin, Sinatra, and Burton-and-Taylor made the scene; as did The Beatles, The Who, and Bob Dylan, who filmed his cue-card-flipping film for *Subterranean Homesick Blues* in an alley around back—one of the earliest examples of a music video. Step inside to see the spiffy foyer under the pretext of asking about their (over-priced) afternoon tea under the glass cupola.

At the next intersection, a side-trip out onto **Waterloo Bridge** affords one of the best London views, overlooking the city in both directions.

A half-block farther is **Gibraltar House** (at 150 Strand), a quasi-embassy and visitors center for one of Britain's last little "colonies," located on the southern tip of Spain.

Next up is **Somerset House,** the last of the many great river-side mansions that once lined the Strand. Today, it has a people-friendly courtyard with playful fountains, a riverside terrace, an exhibition hall, and the **Courtauld Gallery**—a fine art collection including Impressionist and Post-Impressionist gems (❂ see the Courtauld Gallery Tour chapter).

You'll encounter two different churches left Strand-ed in the middle of traffic when the road was widened around them. **St. Mary-le-Strand,** with its clean, white interior lit by blue-and-green stained glass, is an oasis of quiet (see photo). Charles Dickens' parents were married here. To the right of the church (in the ugly concrete building) is **King's College,** one of the world's top universities, with 20,000 current students and a distinguished list of former students that includes John Keats, Florence Nightingale, and Desmond Tutu.

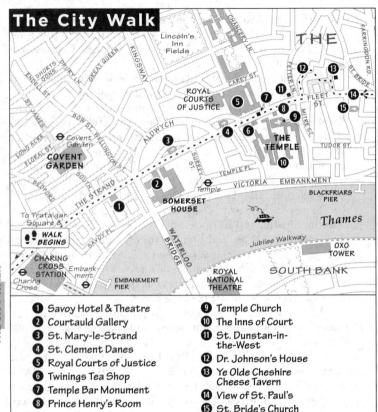

The City Walk

THE CITY WALK

1. Savoy Hotel & Theatre
2. Courtauld Gallery
3. St. Mary-le-Strand
4. St. Clement Danes
5. Royal Courts of Justice
6. Twinings Tea Shop
7. Temple Bar Monument
8. Prince Henry's Room
9. Temple Church
10. The Inns of Court
11. St. Dunstan-in-the-West
12. Dr. Johnson's House
13. Ye Olde Cheshire Cheese Tavern
14. View of St. Paul's
15. St. Bride's Church

To the left is **Bush House,** home of BBC's World Service. And just beyond is **Australia House,** a kind of embassy for that member of the British Commonwealth. It's most famous for its role as the goblin-run Gringotts Wizarding Bank in the *Harry Potter* movies. (Though it's not open to visiting Muggles, you can peek into the chandeliered lobby from the door.) The building sits on a multi-branched intersection where the flow of traffic is a marvel to watch.

St. Clement Danes, built by Christopher Wren (1682), was blitzed heavily in World War II. Today, it's a busy Royal Air Force chapel and a memorial to the 125,000 RAF servicemen who gave their lives in both world wars. Outside stand statues of brave airmen. Inside, hundreds of gray medallions in the stone floor are dedicated to various squadrons, and Books of Remembrance—10 thick volumes, with a page respectfully turned each day—line the walls, including one for Americans (on back wall, first book on left side). This is the first of several Wren-built churches (steeple added

#			#	
16	St. Martin-within-Ludgate		23	Bow Lane
17	Old Bailey		24	Bank Junction
18	St. Paul's Cathedral		25	Royal Exchange
19	Paternoster Square		26	Bank of England & Museum
20	Cheapside		27	Mansion House
21	Mermaid Tavern Site		28	The Monument
22	St. Mary-le-Bow		29	London Bridge

THE CITY WALK

later) we'll see on the walk. Of the 50-some he originally built, 23 Wren churches still dot London.

• *Past St. Clement Danes, on the left side of street are the...*

Royal Courts of Justice

When former Spice Girls sue tabloids for libel, when *The Da Vinci Code* author gets sued for plagiarism, or when ex-Beatles pay $50 million divorce settlements to gold diggers, the trial is likely to be held here, at Britain's highest civil court. (Criminal cases are heard down the street at the Old Bailey.) Paparazzi often litter the entrance, awaiting a celeb or a lawyer (many of whom are celebrities themselves). The 76 courtrooms in this Neo-Gothic complex are open to the public. At least step into the lobby to see the vast Gothic entry hall (submit to a security check to go farther in). This is just one of several legal buildings in the neighborhood.

• *Across the street is...*

Twinings Tea Shop (216 Strand)

When this narrow store first opened its doors ("established 1706"), tea was an exotic concoction from newly explored lands.

(The Chinese statues at the entrance remind us that tea came first from China, then India.) This store has been in the Twining family for nearly 300 years (Mon-Fri 9:00-17:00, Sat 10:00-16:00, closed Sun, tel. 0844-324-5000). The Twinings shop is narrow, but explore its depths—there's a tea-tasting room in the back (sessions by appointment, so call ahead).

In the 1700s, London was in the grip of a coffee craze, and "coffee houses" were everywhere. These were rather seedy places, where "gentlemen" went for coffee, tobacco, and female companionship. Tea offered a refreshing change of pace, and the late-in-the-day "cuppa" (as well as "afternoon tea") soon became a national institution. These days—as you'll see on this walk—coffee has made a comeback in London in the form of modern Starbucks-style coffee shops.

• *Up ahead, in the middle of the street, is a small statue of a winged creature.*

Temple Bar Monument

A statue of a griffin, a mythological beast with an eagle's wings and a lion's body, marks the official border between the City of

Westminster and The City of London. The Queen, who presides over Westminster, does not pass this point without ceremonial permission of The City's Lord Mayor. The relief at its base shows Queen Victoria submitting to this ritual in 1837.

• *Cross the border, leaving Westminster and entering The City. Ahead on the left (194 Fleet Street) is The Old Bank of England pub—a former bank with a lavish late Victorian interior that serves lunches to the 9-to-5 crowd. (To imagine a fancy 19th-century bank, pop inside.) Up a few storefronts, on the right side of the street, look above a beauty shop to find an old building with black-framed, stained-glass bay windows.*

Prince Henry's Room (17 Fleet Street)

This half-timbered, three-story, Tudor-style building (1610) is one of the few to survive the Great Fire. In Shakespeare's day, the

entire City was packed, rooftop to rooftop, with wood and plaster buildings like this. Many were five and six stories high, with narrow frontage. Little wonder that a small fire could spread so quickly and become the Great Fire of 1666.

The top floor of the house is "Prince Henry's Room," once an office for King Charles I's son. It's likely closed in 2012 for restoration, but if it's open, admire the elaborate plaster ceiling and stained glass, and check out any temporary exhibitions (free, Mon-Fri 11:00-14:00, closed Sat-Sun, tel. 020/7332-1097, www.cityoflondon.gov.uk).

• *Pass underneath the house, through the passageway called Inner Temple Lane that leads a half-block to the exotic...*

Temple Church

Exterior: The round, crenellated, castle-turret roof and tiny statue of a knight on horseback (on a pillar in the courtyard) mark this as a Crusader church (1185) from the days of King Richard the Lionhearted. The church was the headquarters of the Knights Templar, a band of heavily armed, highly trained monks who

dressed in long white robes (decorated with red crosses) beneath heavy armor. In their secret rituals, the knights were sworn to chastity and to the protection of pilgrims on their way to the Muslim-held Holy Land.

Interior: Inside, some honored knights lie face-up on the floor under the rotunda of the circular "nave," patterned after the Church of the Holy Sepulchre in Jerusalem. A knight's crossed legs indicate that he probably died peacefully at home. Surrounding the serene knights are grotesque faces, perhaps the twisted expressions seen in distant wars.

Fans of the novel *The Da Vinci Code* will recognize the Temple Church as a place the protagonist comes to find clues leading to a special tomb. For the film version, some footage was shot here.

By 1300, the Knights Templar's mission of protecting pilgrims had become a corrupt "protection" racket, and they'd grown rich loaning money to kings and popes. Those same kings and popes condemned the monks as heretics and sodomites, and confiscated their lands (1312). The Temple Church was rented to lawyers, who built the Inns of Court around it.

• *Abutting, surrounding, and extending from the Temple Church is a vast complex of buildings covering a full city block between the Strand/Fleet Street and the Thames, known collectively as...*

The Inns of Court

Wander through the peaceful maze of buildings, courtyards, narrow lanes, nooks, gardens, fountains, and century-old gas lamps, where lawyers take a break from the Royal Courts. The complex is a self-contained city of lawyers, with offices, lodgings, courtrooms, chapels, and dining halls. Law students must live here (and are even required to eat a number of meals on the premises) to complete their legal internship.

You'll see barristers in modern business suits and ties, plus a few in traditional wigs and robes, as they prepare to do legal battle. The wigs are a remnant of French manners of the 1700s, when every self-respecting European gentleman wore one.

• *Get lost. Don't worry—you'll eventually spill back out onto the busy street. Return to the building that houses Prince Henry's Room, which marks the spot where the Strand becomes...*

Fleet Street

"The Street" was the notorious haunt of a powerful combination—lawyers and the media. (You just passed a pub called "The Wig and Pen.") In 1500, Wynkyn de Worde moved here with a new-fangled invention, a printing press, making this area the center of an early Information Age. In 1702, the first daily newspaper appeared. Soon you had the *Tatler,* the *Spectator,* and many others pumping out both hard news and paparazzi gossip for the hungry masses. Just past St. Dunstan Church, you'll see a building decorated with mosaic signs with the names of some bygone newspapers: the *Dundee Evening Telegraph,* the *People's Journal,* and so on.

London became the nerve center of a global, colonial empire, and Fleet Street was where every twitch found expression. Hard-drinking, ink-stained reporters gathered in taverns and coffeehouses, pumping lawyers for juicy pretrial information, scrambling for that choice bit of must-read gossip that would make their paper number one. They built an industry that still endures: Britain supports close to a dozen national newspapers, selling more than 10 million papers a day.

Today, busy Fleet Street bustles with almost every business *except* newspapers. The industry made a mass exodus in the 1980s for offices elsewhere, replaced by financial institutions. As you walk along, you'll see the former offices of the *Daily Telegraph* (135 Fleet Street) and the *Daily Express* (#121-128—peek into the lobby to see its classic 1930s Art Deco interior). The last major institution to leave (in the summer of 2005) was the Reuters news agency (#85, opposite the *Daily Express*).

• *Heading 50 yards east along Fleet Street, you'll find...*

St. Dunstan-in-the-West—
The Great Fire of 1666

This church stands where the Great Fire of September 1666 finally ended. The fire started near London Bridge. For three days it

swept westward, fanned by hot and blustery weather, leveling everything in its path. As it approached St. Dunstan, 40 theology students battled the blaze, holding it off until the wind shifted, and the fire slowly burned itself out.

From here to the end of our walk (1.5 miles), we'll be passing through the fire's path of destruction. It left London a Sodom-and-Gomorrah wasteland so hot it couldn't be walked on for weeks. (For more on the fire, ✪ see the end of the Bankside Walk chapter.)

Today, St. Dunstan is one of the few churches with a thriving congregation (of Orthodox Romanians) in this now depopulated and secularized district. An unbroken line of vicars dating back

The Great Fire

The stones of St. Paul's flew from the building, the lead melting down the streets in a stream.... God grant mine eyes may never behold the like.... Above 10,000 homes all in one flame, the noise and crackling and thunder of the impetuous flames, the shrieking of women and children, the hurry of the people, the fall of the towers, houses, and churches was like an hideous storm.

—John Evelyn, eyewitness

to 1237 is listed in the vestibule. The clock on the bell tower outside (1670) features London's first minute hand and has two slaves gonging two bells four times an hour.

Alongside the church is a rare contemporary statue of Queen Elizabeth. Surviving from her reign, this 1586 depiction of Elizabeth is as accurate as anything we have. The scepter and orb symbolize her religious and secular authority.

• *Continue east on Fleet Street. A half-block past Fetter Lane, turn left through a covered alleyway (at #167, immediately across from #54). Follow signs through the narrow lanes directing you to* Dr. Johnson's House.

Narrow Lanes—1700s London

"Sir, if you wish to have a just notion of the magnitude of this city, you must...survey the innumerable little lanes and courts," said the writer Samuel Johnson in 1763 to his young friend and biographer, James Boswell. These twist-ing alleyways and cramped buildings that house urban hobbits give a faint glimpse of rebuilt 1700s London, a crowded city of half a million people. After the Great Fire, London was resurrected in brick and stone instead of wood, but they stuck to the same medieval street plan, resulting in narrow lanes of brick buildings like these.

• *The narrow lanes eventually spill out onto Gough Square, about a block north of Fleet Street, where you'll find...*

Dr. Johnson's House (17 Gough Square)

"When a man is tired of London, he is tired of life," wrote Samuel Johnson, "for there is in London all that life can afford." Johnson

(1709-1784) loved to wander these twisting lanes, looking for pungent slices of London street life that he could pass along in his weekly col-umns called "The Rambler" and "The Idler."

At age 28, Johnson arrived in London with one of his former students, David Garrick, who went on to revolutionize London theater. Dr. Johnson prowled the pubs, brothels, coffeehouses, and illicit gaming pits where terriers battled cornered rats while men bet on the outcome. Johnson—described as "tall, stout," and "slovenly in his dress"—became a well-known eccentric and man-about-town, though he always seemed to live on the fringes of poverty. At the far end of Gough Square is a statue of Johnson's beloved cat Hodge, who dined on oysters.

Johnson inhabited this house from 1748 to 1759. He prayed at St. Clement Danes, drank in Fleet Street pubs, and, in the attic of the house, produced his most famous work, *A Dictionary of the English Language*. Published in 1755, it was the first great English-language dictionary, starring Johnson's 42,773 favorite words culled from all the books he'd read. It took Johnson and six assistants more than six years to sift through all the alternate spellings and Cockney dialects of the world's most complex language. He stan-dardized spelling and pronunciation, explained each word's ety-mology, and occasionally put his own droll spin on words. ("Oats: a grain, which is generally given to horses, but in Scotland sup-ports the people.")

London's Great Plague of 1665

The Grim Reaper—in the form of the bacteria *Yersinia pestis* (bubonic plague)—rode through London on fleas atop a black rat. It killed one in six people, while leaving the buildings standing. (The next year, the Great Fire consumed the buildings.) It started in the spring as "the Poore's Plague," neglected until it spread to richer neighborhoods. During the especially hot summer, 5,000 died each week. By December, St. Bride's congregation was 2,111 souls fewer.

Victims passed through several days of agony: headaches, vomiting, fever, shivering, swollen tongue, and swollen buboes (lumps) on the groin glands. After your skin turned blotchy black (the "Black Death"), you died. "Searchers of the Dead" carted them off to mass graves, including one near St. Bride's. Both the victims and their families were quarantined under house arrest, with a red cross painted on the door and a guard posted nearby, and denied access to food, water, or medical attention for 40 days—a virtual death sentence even for the uninfected.

The disease was blamed on dogs and cats, and paid dog-killers destroyed tens of thousands of pets—which brought even more rats. People who didn't die tried to leave. The Lord Mayor quarantined the whole city within the walls, so the only way out was to produce (or purchase) a "certificate of health."

By fall, London was a ghost town, and throughout England, people avoided Londoners like the Plague. It took the Great Fire of 1666 to fully cleanse the city of the disease. Some scholars have suggested that a popular nursery rhyme refers to the dreaded disease (while others brush this off as bunk):

> *Ring around the rosie* (flower garlands to keep the Plague away)
> *A pocket full of posies* (buboes on the groin)
> *Ashes, ashes* (your skin turns black)
> *We all fall down* (dead).

Today, the house is a museum. While the exhibits are fascinating for hard-core Johnson fans (I met one once), the old house is interesting in itself, even for the casual visitor. See a video and climb four stories through period furniture, passing a first edition of Johnson's dictionary and pictures of Johnson, Garrick, and Boswell. Nothing is roped off or behind glass, and you can browse at will. Finally you arrive in the top-floor garret where literary history was made—the birthplace of the dictionary that standardized our English language.

• *At the other end of Gough Square, turn right at the statue of Hodge*

and head back toward Fleet Street, noticing the lists of barristers (trial lawyers) on the doorways (e.g., next to the door at 9 Gough Square). They work not as part of a firm, but as freelancers sharing offices and clerks. Stay to the left as you wind downhill through the alleys, and look near Fleet Street for the entrance of...

Ye Olde Cheshire Cheese Tavern

Johnson often—and I do mean often—popped 'round here for a quick one, sometimes with David Garrick and his sleazy actor friends.

"The Cheese" dates from 1667, when it was rebuilt after the Great Fire, but it's been a tavern since 1538. It's a four-story warren of small, smoky, wood-lined rooms, each offering different menus, from pub grub to white-tablecloth meals. A traditional "chop house," it serves hearty portions of meats to power-lunching businessmen.

Sit in Charles Dickens' favorite seat, next to a coal fireplace (in the "Chop Room," main floor) and order a steak-and-kidney pie and some spotted dick (sponge pudding with currants). Sip a pint of Samuel Smith (the house beer of the current owners) and think of Samuel Johnson, who drank here pondering various spellings: "pint" or "pynte," "color" or "colour," "theater" or "theatre." Immerse yourself in a world largely unchanged for centuries, a world of reporters scribbling the news over lunch, of Alfred Lord Tennyson inventing rhymes and Arthur Conan Doyle solving crimes, of W. B. Yeats, Teddy Roosevelt, and Mark Twain.

• *Back out on Fleet Street, you're met with a cracking...*

View of St. Paul's—the Blitz, the Great Fire, the Plague, and Christopher Wren

If you were standing here on December 30, 1940, the morning after a German Luftwaffe firebomb raid, you'd see nothing but a flat, smoldering landscape of rubble, with St. Paul's rising above it almost miraculously intact. (For more on the Blitz, see the sidebar on page 258.)

Standing here in September 1666, you'd see nothing but smoke and ruins. The Great Fire razed everything, including the original St. Paul's Cathedral. And standing here a year earlier, in September 1665, you'd hear "Bring out yer dead!" as they carted away 70,000 victims of the bubonic plague. After the double-whammy of plague and fire, the architect Christopher Wren was hired to rebuild St. Paul's and The City.

Even today, we see the view that Wren intended—a majestic dome hovering above the hazy rooftops, surrounded by the thin spires of his lesser churches. In the foreground below St. Paul's is the slender, lead-covered steeple of St. Martin-within-Ludgate, perfectly offsetting the more massive dome. Wren's 23 surviving churches are more than plenty for today's secular ghost town of a city.

• *A half-block east of Ye Olde Cheshire Cheese, and a half-block down St. Bride's Avenue, is the stacked-tier steeple of...*

St. Bride's Church (1671-1675)

The 226-foot steeple, Wren's tallest, is stacked in layers as it tapers to a point. It's said to have inspired the wedding cake. Supposedly,

a Fleet Street baker named Mr. Rich gazed out his shop window at St. Bride's as he made the first multi-tiered cake. (By the way, the word "Bride" in St. Bride's is only coincidental. The church was dedicated to St. Bridgit—or Bride—of Kildare long before the steeple or any wedding cakes.)

St. Bride's was one of the first of Wren's churches to open its doors after the Fire. St. Bride's is nicknamed both "The Cathedral of Fleet Street" and "The Printer's Church." Notice that the pews bear the names of departed journalists. It has been home to newspaper reporters, scholars, and literati ever since 1500, when Wynkyn de Worde set up his printing press here on church property. De Worde's press first served the literate clergy of St. Bride's, but was soon adopted by secular scholars, bookmakers, and newspapers, as Fleet Street became a global center for printed information.

During World War II, St. Bride's suffered terribly in the Blitz. (Today's structure was largely rebuilt after the war.) But thanks to Hitler's bombs, St. Bride's was instantly excavated down to its

Christopher Wren
(1632-1723)

After London burned, King Charles II turned to his childhood friend, Christopher Wren, to rebuild it. The 33-year-old Wren was not an architect, but he'd proven his ability in every field he'd touched: astronomy (mapping the moon and building a model of Saturn), medicine (using opium as a general anesthetic, making successful blood transfusions between animals), mathematics (a treatise on spherical trigonometry), and physics (his study of the laws of motion influenced Newton's "discovery" of gravity). Wren also invented a language for the deaf, studied refraction and optics, and built weather-watching instruments.

Though domed St. Paul's is Wren's most famous church, the smaller churches around it better illustrate his distinctive style: a steeple over the west entrance; an uncluttered, well-lit interior; Neoclassical (Greek-style) columns; a curved or domed plaster ceiling; geometrical shapes (e.g., round rosettes inside square frames); and fine carved woodwork, often by his favorite whittler, Grinling Gibbons.

THE CITY WALK

sixth-century Saxon foundations. Layers of previously unknown history were revealed from six previous churches that stood on this spot, including items such as Roman coins, medieval stained glass, and 17th-century tobacco pipes.

Also in the crypt is a wedding dress—worn by the wife of the Fleet Street baker whose wedding cake was inspired by St. Bride's steeple.

• *A block past St. Bride's Church on Fleet Street is* The Punch Tavern, *draped with memories of the venerable London political magazine famous for its satirical cartoons. Peek in to see Punch and his twin wife Judy looking down on a perfectly Victorian scene. These characters from a popular puppet show came onto the London scene 350 years ago—the anniversary is celebrated in 2012. The characters gave the magazine its name, and the pub became the magazine staff's hangout*

(open daily, good lunches, 99 Fleet Street, tel. 020/7353-6658). The valley between St. Bride's and St. Paul's is the...

Fleet River and Ludgate

The Fleet River—now covered over by Farringdon Road—still

flows southward, crossing underneath Fleet Street on its way to the Thames at Blackfriars Bridge. In medieval times, the river formed the western boundary of the walled city. Between you and the towering dome of St. Paul's stands Wren's steeple-topped church of **St. Martin-within-Ludgate.** It incorporates the old city wall into its west wall, at the old city entrance known as Ludgate.

• *After crossing Farringdon Road, look left down Old Bailey Street to see a dome crowned by a golden statue of justice, which marks the...*

Old Bailey—Central Criminal Court

England's most infamous criminals—from the king-killers of

the Civil War to the radically religious William Penn, from the "criminally homosexual" Oscar Wilde to the Yorkshire Ripper—were tried here, in Britain's highest criminal court. On top of the copper dome stands the famous golden Lady who weighs and executes Justice with scale and sword. The Old Bailey is built on the former site of Newgate Prison, with its notorious execution-by-hanging site. Inside, you can visit courtrooms and watch justice doled out the old-fashioned way (see page 78). Bewigged barristers argue before stern judges while the accused sit in the dock.

• *Continue up Ludgate Hill to...*

St. Paul's Cathedral

The greatest of Wren's creations is the rebuilt St. Paul's, England's national church and the heart of The City. Wren labored for over 40 years on the church, both designing and overseeing construction of what was then the second-largest

dome in the world. Unlike many church architects, Wren lived long enough to see his masterpiece completed. (❂ See the St. Paul's Tour chapter.)

If you're not paying to enter the great church, you can pop into the basement (entry to left of front) for a café, fine WCs, a shop, and a peek at the memorials in the crypt. Belly up to the iron Churchill Gates. Standing on a plaque honoring Churchill, you can see the tomb of Admiral Lord Nelson directly below the dome.

• *A right turn at St. Paul's would take you to the Millennium Bridge, leading across the Thames. Instead, look for the Temple Bar gate—a white stone archway—directly to the left of the church. The gate was once the west entrance to the city of London. Relocated here, it now welcomes you to...*

Paternoster Square

This gate originally stood a half-mile west of here. It marked "Temple Bar," the boundary between the City of London and Westminster, where the griffin monument now stands (see page 232). The original Temple Bar gate was built of stone by St. Paul's architect, Christopher Wren, in 1672. But given the increase in traffic and new construction around it, the gate didn't "fit" at Temple Bar anymore. It was disassembled in 1878 and carted off to ornament the rural estate of a brewery owner. Finally, in 2004, the 2,700 stones were brought back to The City and painstakingly rebuilt here in Paternoster Square.

Enjoy a view of the dome from behind the church's red-brick Chapter House (a good example of Wren's Neoclassicism). This square was designed in the early 21st century to save views of the church, while allowing maximum modern development here in the city center.

• *Stride right past the Shepherd and Sheep statue to the pedestrian walkway behind the statue, then bear right onto the busy, noisy street called...*

Cheapside—Shakespeare's London

This was the main east-west street of Shakespeare's London, which had a population of about 200,000. The wide street hosted The City's marketplace ("cheap" meant market), seen today in the names of the streets that branch off from it: Bread, Milk, Honey. Rebuilt after the war, Cheapside is now the home of cheap mobile

244 Rick Steves' London

THE CITY WALK

Cockney Rhyming Slang

The East End (specifically, the area around the Church of St. Mary-le-Bow) is known as the traditional home of the Cockneys. This colorful, working-class group spoke in a quirky pastiche that was the opposite of the Queen's English...think Audrey Hepburn as Eliza Doolittle in *My Fair Lady*, Dick van Dyke as the chimney-sweep in *Mary Poppins*, or Don Cheadle in *Ocean's Eleven*.

One colorful Cockney invention that survives from the mid-19th century is their unique rhyming slang. According to urban legend, the Cockneys devised this secret way of talking to confuse policemen who might be listening. Another theory suggests that it was used between market vendors in order to rip off customers. Either way, Cockney rhyming slang helped create a sort of neighborhood pride for this downtrodden community.

Here's how it works: Simply replace an everyday word with a nonsensical phrase that rhymes with it. Instead of stairs, it's "apples and pears"—often shortened to simply "apples," as in, "I'm walking up the apples." For teeth, it's "Hampstead Heath" (or just "hampstead": "The dentist took a bloody good whack at me hampsteads").

Some Cockney rhyming slang words have become integrated into everyday speech. For example, "blow a raspberry" comes from the slang "raspberry tart" for fart. And did you ever notice that "getting down to brass tacks" rhymes with "facts"? Many others—including several on the list on the next page—remain widely used as slang throughout the UK (if not in the US).

The tradition has continued into the 21st century—though these days it's done as a fun bit of irony, rather than as an actual secret language. For curry, they might say "Ruby Murray"—also the name of an Irish pop singer from the 1950s. Someone might suggest, "After work, let's head to the pub for some Britneys" (Britney Spears = beers), or "Go wash yer Chevy" (Chevy Chase = face).

phones, concrete-and-glass offices, clothing stores, and Ye Olde Starbucks. It's also swamped in construction projects, as redeveloping London tears down the cheap buildings of its postwar decades.

If you were to detour two blocks south on Bread Street (to the corner of Bread and Cannon streets), you would not see even a trace of the **Mermaid Tavern**, Shakespeare's favorite haunt—but that's where it stood. In the early 1600s, "Sweet Will" would meet

Cockney Rhyming Slang (and abbreviation, if used)	Translation
a la mode	code
Adam and Eve	believe
Barnet Fair (barnet)	hair (hairstyle)
bubble and squeak (bubble)	Greek
butcher's hook (butcher's)	look
china plate (china)	mate (friend)
deep sea diver	fiver (£5 note)
loaf of bread (loaf)	head
Mutt and Jeff (mutton)	deaf
plates of meat (plates)	feet
porkpies (porkies)	lies
rabbit and pork (rabbit)	talk
Scapa Flow (scarper)	go
septic tank (septic, seppo)	Yank (American)
tea leaf	thief
trouble and strife	wife
whistle and flute	suit

So the next time you find yourself 'avin' a rabbit with a Cockney, slip the bartender a deep sea diver to buy him a Britney and ask him about his trouble and strife's new barnet. Or take a butcher's at his fancy whistle and flute, and try out the local a la mode. Maybe he'll tap his loaf and say, "Not bad fer a septic."

THE CITY WALK

Ben Jonson, Sir Walter Raleigh, and John Donne at the Mermaid for food, ale, and literary conversation. Francis Beaumont, one of the group, wrote: "What things have we seen/Done at the Mermaid! heard words that have been/So nimble, and so full of subtle flame..."

• *A little farther east along Cheapside is...*

St. Mary-le-Bow

From London's earliest Christian times, a church has stood here. The steeple of St. Mary-le-Bow, rebuilt after the Fire, is one of Wren's most impressive. He incorporated the ribbed-arch design of the former church (a "bow" is an arch) in the steeple's midsection. In the courtyard is a statue of a smiling Captain John Smith, who in 1607 established an English colony in Jamestown, Virginia,

USA, before retiring here near the church. Inside the church, see not one but two pulpits, used today for point-counterpoint debates of moral issues.

This is the very center of old London, where, in medieval times, the church's bells rang each evening, calling Londoners safely back in to the walled town before the gates were locked. To be born "within the sound of Bow bells" long defined a true local, or "Cockney."

This is also the "Cockney" neighborhood of plucky streetwise urchins, where a distinctive Eliza Doolittle dialect is sometimes still spoken. Today's Cockney is the hard accent of rough-and-tumble, working-class Londoners—and the Geico gecko on American TV ads. There are no Hs. "Are you 'appy, 'arry?" "Where's your 'orse? ...'urry up now." (Another fun element of the Cockney dialect—its creative rhyming slang—is described in the sidebar.) Nineteenth-century social climbers added extra Hs in order not to sound Cockney. "I hunderstand you are hinterested in renting my hattic."

These days, few people actually live within the sound of Bow bells. The City's population, while 300,000 during working hours, falls to about 7,000 at night.

• *Just past St. Mary-le-Bow is...*

Bow Lane

Today, pedestrian-only Bow Lane features smart clothing shops, sandwich bars, and pubs. The entire City once had narrow lanes like Bow, Watling, and Bread Streets. Explore this area between Cheapside and Cannon Street.

When Shakespeare bought his tights and pointy shoes in Bow Lane, the shops were wooden, the streets were dirt, and the bathroom was a ditch down the middle of the road. (The garbage brought rats, and rats brought plagues, like the one in 1665.) You bought your water in buckets carted up from the Thames. And at night, the bellman walked the streets, ringing the hour.

(For more Shakespearean ambience, it's a three-block walk south from St. Paul's to the river, where the Millennium Bridge crosses the Thames to Shakespeare's Globe, a reconstruction of the theater where many of Shakespeare's plays premiered. See page 92.)

• *Continue east on Cheapside a few blocks to the long, wide intersection where nine streets meet, called Bank Junction (Tube: Bank). Looking east, survey the buildings before you. There may be a historical plaque at the street corner with a helpful diagram of Bank Junction's buildings. A good place to view it all is from the front of Mansion House, the building with the six-columned (not eight-columned) entrance, standing where Victoria Street empties onto Bank Junction.*

Bank Junction

You're at the center of financial London. The Square Mile hosts 500 foreign and British banks. London, centrally located amid the  globe's time zones, can find someone around the world to trade with 24 hours a day. In 2009, thousands of protesters packed this square, smashing bank windows in anger over Britain's severe financial downturn.

• *Look across the square at the eight-columned entrance to the...*

Royal Exchange: When London's original stock exchange opened, "stock" meant whatever could be loaded and unloaded onto a boat in the Thames. Remember, London got its start as a river-trading town. Soon, they were gathering here, trading slips of paper and "futures" in place of live goats and chickens. Traders needed money-changers, who needed bankers...and London's financial district boomed. Today, you can step inside under the *Trading Since 1571* sign to a skylight-covered courtyard lined with traders of retail goods.

• *To the left of the Royal Exchange is the city-block-sized Bank of England (main entrance just across Threadneedle Street from the Royal Exchange entrance).*

Bank of England: This 3.5-acre, two-story complex houses the country's national bank. In 1694, it loaned £1.2 million to King William III at 8 percent interest to finance a war with France; it's managed the national debt ever since. It's an investment bank (a banker's bank), loaning money to other financial institutions. Working in tandem with the government (nationalized 1946, independent 1997), "The Old Lady of Threadneedle Street" sets interest rates, prints pound notes, and serves as the country's Fort Knox, housing stacks of gold bars.

The complex has a **Bank Museum** inside (free, Mon-Fri 10:00-17:00, closed Sat-Sun, enter from far side, on St. Bartholomew Lane). See banknotes from 1699, an old safe, account books, and mannequins of CPAs in powdered wigs. Also see current pound notes—with a foil hologram and numbers visible under UV light (to stay one step ahead of counterfeiters). The museum's highlight is under the rotunda, displaying 59 fake gold bars and one real one. The real gold is worth more than $400,000 (check today's rates nearby) and weighs 28 pounds. Try lifting it.

• *Rising up behind the Bank of England is...*

Tower 42: The black-capped skyscraper at 600 feet is The City's tallest (but not London's tallest, which is at Canary Wharf, far to the east of here).

• *Rising to the right is the tip of the bullet-shaped, spiral-ribbed, glass building called...*

30 St. Mary Axe: Built in 2003, the 40-story building houses the London office of a Swiss re-insurance company (an insurer's insurer). The building, nicknamed "The Gherkin" (pickle), is ventilated by natural air entering the balconies spiraling around the perimeter.

• *You're standing in front of...*

Mansion House: This is the official residence of The City's Lord Mayor. The Lord Mayor governs not all of London but just this neighborhood. In the year 2000, a new post was created—"Mayor of London"—overseeing all of London. But the "Lord Mayor of the City" still carries out the old traditions, presiding from this palatial building. Once a year, he rides the streets in the Lord Mayor's Coach, a gilded carriage pulled by six white horses that looks like something right out of *Cinderella*.

• *From Bank Junction, turn right on Lombard Street, which turns into King William Street, and head southeast toward London Bridge. Near the northeast corner of the bridge, look to your left and find a lone column poking its bristly bronze head above the modern rooftops.*

The Monument

The 202-foot hollow column is Wren's tribute to the Great Fire

that gave him a blank canvas on which to create modern London. At 2:00 in the morning of September 2, 1666, a small fire broke out in a baker's oven in nearby Pudding Lane. Supposedly, if you tipped the Monument over (to the east), its top would fall on the exact spot. Fanned by hot, blustery weather, the fire swept westward, leaping from house to house until The City was a square mile of flame.

You can climb the Monument's 311 steps for a view that's still pretty good, despite modern buildings.

• *From here, hike out over the river on...*

London Bridge

End our walk at The City's beginning. (For the history of London Bridge, see page 279.)

The City was born as a river-trading town. The Thames flows east to west, from the interior of England to the open sea. It's a tidal river from here to the sea, so ancient boats hitched rides on the tide in both directions. London Bridge, first built by the ancient Romans, established a north-south axis. Soon, goods from every corner of the world were pouring into this, one of the modern world's first great urban centers. Surviving plagues, fires, blitzes, economic changes, and even the Great Recession, with its world-wide financial network and cultural heritage, The City thrives.

• *From here, the **Tower of London** (◒ see the Tower of London Tour chapter) is a seven-minute walk east, down either Eastcheap or Lower Thames Street. The **Bankside Walk** (◒ see the Bankside Walk chapter) begins across London Bridge. The **East End Walk** (see page 83 in the Sights in London chapter) begins a 20-minute walk (up Gracechurch/ Bishopsgate) or one Tube stop to the north, at Liverpool Street Station. Or you can return to **Trafalgar Square** on the Tube (Monument stop nearby) or bus #15 (from Cannon Street).*

ST. PAUL'S TOUR

No sooner was Sir Christopher Wren selected to refurbish Old St. Paul's Cathedral than the Great Fire of 1666 incinerated it. Within a week, Wren had a plan for a whole new building...and for the city around it, complete with some 50 new churches. For the next four decades he worked to achieve his vision—a spacious church, topped by a dome, surrounded by a flock of Wrens.

St. Paul's is England's national church. There's been a church on this spot since 604. It was the symbol of London's rise from the Great Fire of 1666 and of the city's survival of the Blitz of 1940. Today, it's the center of the Anglican faith. Military buffs will find memorials to many great wars and their war heroes. Dome-climbers will be rewarded with expansive views over London's skyline.

Orientation

Cost: £14.50 (includes church entry, dome climb, tour, and audioguide). Free on Sun but officially open only to worshippers.

Hours: Mon-Sat 8:30-16:30, last entry for sightseeing at 16:00 (dome opens at 9:30, last entry at 16:15), closed Sun except for worship. Sometimes closed for special events. The church is also open Mon-Sat 16:00-18:00 for evensong worship; during this time you can enter the church for free, but unless you're here for the service, your visit is restricted to the back of the nave.

Getting There: Located in The City; Tube: St. Paul's (other nearby Tube stops include Mansion House, Cannon Street, and Blackfriars). You can take handy buses #15 and #11 (see page 34), as well as #4, #23, or #26. Careful: Don't head for tiny St. Paul's Church near Covent Garden; your destination is St. Paul's Cathedral, in The City.

Information: Recorded info tel. 020/7236-4128, reception tel. 020/7246-8350, www.stpauls.co.uk.

Music and Services: Communion is Mon-Sat at 8:00 and 12:30. Sunday services are held at 8:00, 10:15 (Matins), 11:30 (sung Eucharist), 15:15 (evensong), and 18:00. Additional evensong services are held Mon-Sat at 17:00 (40 minutes, free to anyone—though visitors who haven't paid admission aren't allowed to linger after the service). If you're here for evensong worship and sitting under the dome, at 16:45 you may be able to grab a big wooden stall in the choir, next to the singers.

Tours: Guided 1.5-hour tours (included in admission) are offered Mon-Sat at 10:45, 11:15, 13:30, and 14:00 (confirm schedule at church or call 020/7246-8357). Free 15-minute talks are offered throughout the day. The **audioguide** (included in admission) contains video clips that show the church in action. You can download a free **audio version** of this tour for your mobile device via www.ricksteves.com/audioeurope, iTunes, or the Rick Steves Audio Europe smartphone app.

Climbing the Dome: It's 530 steps to the top and a mere 257 to the first viewing level (elevator only for people with disabilities). Allow an hour to go up and down. The tower has three levels, called galleries. The climb gets steeper, narrower, and more claustrophobic as you go higher. It's a one-way system, so you can't come back down until you reach the next level.

Length of This Tour: Allow one hour, two if you climb the dome.

Photography: No photography allowed.

Cuisine Art: Good café (£5 soups and sandwiches) and pricier restaurant (afternoon tea) in the crypt; free access from north side of church. There are several places to get a quick bite in Paternoster Square; for other choices, see page 397 of the Eating in London chapter.

Nearby: A helpful TI is located to the right of the church. Millennium Bridge is a five-minute walk south, leading to the South Bank (Tate Modern and Shakespeare's Globe).

Starring: Sir Christopher Wren, Wellington, and World War II.

The Tour Begins

Even now, as skyscrapers encroach, the 365-foot-high dome of St. Paul's rises majestically above the rooftops of the neighborhood.

The tall dome is set on classical columns, capped with a lantern, topped by a six-foot ball, and iced with a cross. As the first Anglican cathedral built in London after the Reformation, it is Baroque: St. Peter's in Rome filtered through clear-eyed English reason.

Viewing St. Paul's facade from in front of the church, you can see the story of Paul's conversion told in the stone pediment. A blinding flash leaves Saul sightless on the road to Damascus (see cityscape, lower left). When his sight was restored he became Paul, the Christian. This was the pivotal moment in the life of the man who established Christianity as a world religion through his travels, writing, and evangelizing.

While Paul stands on the top, Peter (with the annoying cock that crowed three times, symbolizing his betrayal of Jesus) is to the left and James is on the right. The four evangelists at the towers' bases each carry the gospel they wrote. As Queen Anne was on the throne when the church was finished in 1710, the statue in front portrays her.

• *Enter, buy your ticket, pick up the free visitor's map, and stand at the far back of the nave, near the font.*

❶ Nave

Look down the nave through the choir stalls to the stained glass at the far end. This big church feels big. At 515 feet long and 250 feet wide, it's Europe's fourth largest, after Rome (St. Peter's), Sevilla, and Milan. The spaciousness is accentuated by the relative lack of decoration. The simple, cream-colored ceiling and the clear glass in the windows light everything evenly. Wren wanted this: a simple, open church with nothing to hide. Unfortunately, only this entrance area keeps his original vision—the rest was encrusted with 19th-century Victorian ornamentation.

A diamond-shaped plaque on the floor honors the guards ("St.

St. Paul's Tour

E
N
T
E
R

STAIRS

DOME

NAVE

CHOIR

HIGH
ALTAR

BISHOP'S
CHAIR

To
St. Paul's ⊖

To
Millennium
Bridge

30 Meters
30 Yards

❶ Nave
❷ Wellington Monument
❸ Dome
❹ Choir & High Altar
❺ HUNT—The Light of the World
❻ MOORE—Mother and Child
❼ American Memorial Chapel
❽ John Donne Statue
❾ Nelson & Cornwallis Monuments
❿ Climb the Dome (2 Entrances)
⓫ Crypt Entrance

Paul's Watch") who worked so valiantly from 1939 until 1945 to save the church from WWII destruction. On the wall next to the door a dirty panel of stone remains, reminding visitors how dark the entire church was before undergoing a huge cleaning (2004-2008) in preparation for the 300th anniversary of the first service held in the church. Remarkably, this is the first great church completed in the lifetime of its architect (built 1675-1710).

• *Glance up and behind. The organ trumpets say, "Come to the evensong and hear us play." Ahead and on the left is the towering, black-and-white...*

❷ Wellington Monument

It's so tall that even Wellington's horse has to duck to avoid bumping its head. Wren would have been appalled, but his church has become so central to England's soul that many national heroes are buried here (in the basement crypt). General Wellington, Napoleon's conqueror at Waterloo (1815) and the embodiment of British stiff-upper-lippedness, was honored here in a funeral packed with 13,000 fans. The church is littered with memorials. While all the monuments are upstairs, all the tombs are downstairs.

• *Stroll up the same nave Prince Charles and Lady Diana walked on their 1981 wedding day. Imagine how they felt making the hike to the altar with the world watching. Grab a chair underneath the impressive dome.*

❸ The Dome

The dome you see, painted with scenes from the life of St. Paul, is only the innermost of three. From the painted interior of the first dome, look up through the opening to see the light-filled lantern of the second dome. Finally, the whole thing is covered on the outside by the third and final dome, the shell of lead-covered wood that you see from the street. Wren's ingenious three-in-one design was psychological as well as functional—he wanted a low, shallow inner dome so worshippers wouldn't feel diminished.

You'll see tourists walking around the base of the dome in the Whispering Gallery. The dome is constructed with such acoustic precision that secrets whispered from one side of it are heard on the opposite side, 170 feet away.

Christopher Wren (1632-1723) was the right man at the right time. Though the 31-year-old astronomy professor had never built a major building in his life when he got the commission for St. Paul's, his reputation for brilliance and his unique ability to work with others carried him through. The church has the clean lines and geometric simplicity of the age of Newton, when reason was holy and God set the planets spinning in perfect geometrical motion.

For more than 40 years, Wren worked on this site, overseeing every detail of St. Paul's and the 65,000-ton dome. It's estimated that the dome cost $850 million (in today's dollars). At age 75, Wren got to look up and see his son place the cross on top of the dome, completing the masterpiece.

On the floor directly beneath the dome is a brass grate—part of a 19th-century attempt to heat the church. Encircling it is Christopher Wren's name and epitaph, written in Latin: *Lector, si monumentum requiris circumspice* (Reader, if you seek his monument, look around you).

Now review the ceiling: Behind is Wren simplicity and ahead is Victorian ornateness.

• *The choir area blocks your way, but you can see the altar at the far end under a golden canopy.*

❹ The Choir and High Altar

English churches, unlike most in Europe, often have a central choir area (a.k.a. a "quire" or "chancel"), where church officials and

the singers sit. (You can see the human quire in action at the daily evensong service.) St. Paul's—a cathedral since 604—is home to the local Anglican bishop, who presides in the chair nearest the altar on the south or right side (the carved bishop's hat hangs over the chair).

The ceiling above the choir is a riot of glass mosaics, representing God (above the altar) and his creation. The mosaics are very Victorian. In fact, Queen Victoria complained that the earlier ceiling was "dreary and undevotional." The Dean and chapter wisely took note and had it spiffed up with this brilliant mosaic work...textbook late Victorian. In separate spheres, eight "Angels of the Morning" hold up creatures of the earth, sea, and sky.

The high altar (the marble slab with crucifix and candlesticks—you'll get a close look later) sits under a huge canopy with corkscrew columns. The canopy looks ancient, but it only dates from 1958, when it was rebuilt after being heavily damaged in October 1940 by the bombs of Hitler's Luftwaffe. For regular services, the priest stands beneath the dome on the low wooden platform.

• *In the north transept (to your left as you face the altar), find the big painting of Christ, in a golden wood altarpiece. Glare? Try walking side-to-side to find the best viewing angle.*

❺ *The Light of the World* (1904), by William Holman Hunt

In the dark of night, Jesus—with a lantern, halo, jeweled cape, and crown of thorns—approaches an out-of-the-way home in the woods, knocks on the door, and listens for an invitation to come in. A Bible passage on the picture frame says: "Behold, I stand at the door and knock..." (Revelation 3:20).

In his early twenties, William Holman Hunt (1827-1910) was in the dark night of a spiritual crisis when he heard this verse knocking in his head. He opened his soul to Christ, his life changed forever, and he tried to capture the experience in paint. As one of the Pre-Raphaelites who adored medieval art, he used symbolism, but only images the average Brit-on-the-street could understand. The door is the closed mind, the weeds the neglected soul, the darkness is malaise, while Christ carries the lantern of spiritual enlightenment.

In 1854, Hunt debuted *The Light of the World* (not this version, but a smaller one now at Oxford). The critics savaged it—"syrupy," "too Catholic," "simple"—but the masses lapped it up. It became

ST. PAUL'S

The Anglican Communion

St. Paul's Cathedral is the symbolic (but not official) nucleus of earth's 70 million Anglicans. The Anglican Communion is a loose association of churches—including the Church of England and the Episcopal Church in the US—with common beliefs. The rallying point is *The Book of Common Prayer,* their handbook for worship services.

Forged in the fires of Europe's Reformation, Anglicans see themselves as a "middle way" between Catholics and Protestants. They retain much of the pomp and ceremony of traditional Catholic worship but with Protestant elements such as married priests (and, recently, female priests); attention to Scripture; and a less hierarchical, more consensus-oriented approach to decision making. Among Anglicans there are divisions, from Low Church congregations (more evangelical and "Protestant") to High Church (more traditional and "Catholic").

The Church of England, the largest single body, is still the official religion of the state, headed by the Archbishop of Canterbury (who presides in Canterbury but lives in London). In 1982, Pope John Paul II and the then Archbishop of Canterbury met face to face. In 2010, Pope Benedict XVI visited London and joined the Archbishop in prayer. These symbolic gestures signal a new ecumenical spirit.

the most famous painting in Victorian England, a pop icon that inspired sermons, poems, hymns, and countless Christ-at-the-door paintings in churches and homes. Hunt's humble-hippie image of Christ was stamped forever on the minds of generations of school kids. It was so popular that late in life Hunt was asked to do this larger version specifically for St. Paul's. Nearly blind, he needed an assistant. (*The Guardian* newspaper once published a list of "Britain's Ten Worst Paintings." They honored *The Light of the World* as number seven, comparing it to a plastic crucifix.)

• *Return to the area underneath the dome and walk toward the altar, along the left side of the choir, pausing at a modern statue.*

❻ Mother and Child, by Henry Moore

Britain's (and perhaps the world's?) greatest modern sculptor, Henry Moore, rendered a traditional subject in an abstract, minimalist way. This Mary and baby Jesus was inspired by the sight of British moms nursing babies in WWII bomb shelters. Moore intended the viewer to touch and interact with the art. It's OK.

• *Continue to the altar at the far end of the church. The area behind it has three bright and modern stained-glass windows.*

❼ American Memorial Chapel

This special spot in St. Paul's honors the Americans who sacrificed their lives to save Britain in World War II. An inscription on

the floor reads: "To the American Dead of the Second World War, From the People of Britain."

Each of the three windows has a central core of religious scenes, but the brightly colored panes that arch around them have some unusual iconography: American. Spot the American eagle (center window, to the left of Christ), George Washington (right window, upper-right corner), and symbols of all 50 states (find your state seal). In the carved wood beneath the windows, you'll see birds and foliage native to the US. And

at the very far right of the paneling, check out the tiny tree "trunk" (amid foliage, below the bird)—it's a US rocket ship circa 1958, shooting up to the stars.

Britain is very grateful to its WWII saviors, the Yanks, and remembers them religiously with the Roll of Honor (immediately behind the altar). This 500-page book under glass lists the names of 28,000 US servicemen and women based in Britain who gave their lives during the war.

• *Take a close look at the high altar and the view back to the entrance from here. Look up and enjoy the Victorian mosaic ceiling above the choir. Then continue around the altar and head back toward the entrance. On the left wall of the aisle, standing white in a black niche, is a statue of...*

❽ John Donne (1573-1631)

John Donne, shown here wrapped in a burial shroud, was a passionate preacher in old St. Paul's (1621-1631), as well as a great poet. Donne personally chose to be portrayed here in a shroud to capture the melancholy he felt after his wife's death. The statue is one of the few treasures to survive the Great Fire of 1666. You can still see the dark scorch marks on the urn beneath Donne's feet.

Imagine hearing Donne deliver a funeral

St. Paul's, the Blitz, and the Battle of Britain

Nazi planes mercilessly firebombed London in 1940. While the city around it burned to the ground, St. Paul's survived, giving hope to the citizens. The church took two direct hits, crumbling the altar and collapsing the north transept. On December 29, 1940, some 28 bombs fell on the church. The surrounding neighborhood was absolutely flattened, while the church rose above it, nearly intact. Some swear that many bombs bounced miraculously off Wren's dome, while others credit the heroic work of local firefighters. (There's a memorial chapel to the firefighters who kept watch over St. Paul's with hoses cocked.) Still, it's clear from the damage that St. Paul's was not fully Blitz-proof.

Often used synonymously, the Blitz and the Battle of Britain are actually two different phases of the Nazi air raids of 1940-1941. The Battle of Britain (June-Sept 1940) pitted Britain's Royal Air Force against German planes trying to soften up Britain for a land-and-sea invasion. The Blitz (Sept 1940-May 1941) was Hitler's punitive terror campaign against civilian London.

In the early days of World War II, the powerful, technologically superior Nazi army quickly overran Poland, Belgium, and France. The British army hightailed it out of France, crossing the English Channel from Dunkirk, and Britain hunkered down, waiting to be invaded. Hitler bombed R.A.F. airfields while his

sermon here, with the huge church bell tolling in the background: "No man is an island....Any man's death diminishes me, because I am involved in Mankind. Therefore, never wonder for whom the bell tolls—it tolls for thee."

• *And also for dozens of people who lie buried beneath your feet, in the crypt where you'll end your tour. But first, in the south transept, find the...*

❾ Horatio Nelson Monument and Charles Cornwallis Monument

Admiral Horatio Nelson (1758-1805) leans on an anchor, his coat draped discreetly over the arm he lost in battle.

In October 1805, England trembled in fear as Napoleon—bent on world conquest—prepared to invade from across the Channel. Meanwhile, hundreds of miles away, off the coast of Spain, the daring Lord Nelson sailed the HMS *Victory* into battle against the

ground troops massed along the Channel. Britain was hopelessly outmatched, but Prime Minister Winston Churchill vowed, "We shall fight on the beaches...We shall fight in the fields and in the streets...We shall never surrender."

Britain fought back. Though greatly outgunned, they had a new and secret weapon—radar—that allowed them to get the jump on puzzled Nazi pilots. Speedy Spitfires flown by a new breed of young pilots shot down 1,700 German planes. By September 1940, the German land invasion was called off, Britain counterattacked with a daring raid on Berlin...and the Battle of Britain was won.

A frustrated Hitler retaliated with a series of punishing air raids on London itself, known as the Blitz. All through the fall, winter, and spring of 1940-1941, including 57 consecutive nights, Hermann Göring's Luftwaffe pummeled a defenseless London, killing 20,000 and leveling half the city (mostly from St. Paul's eastward). Residents took refuge deep in the Tube stations. From his Whitehall bunker, Churchill made radio broadcasts exhorting his people to give their all, their "blood, toil, sweat, and tears."

Late in the war (1944-1945), Hitler ordered another round of terror-inducing attacks on London (sometimes called the "second Blitz") using car-sized V-1 and V-2 bombs, an early type of cruise missile. But Britain's resolve had returned, the United States had entered the fight, and the pendulum shifted. Churchill could say that even if the empire lasted a thousand years, Britons would look back and say, "This was their finest hour."

After the war, Churchill's state funeral was held at St. Paul's in a bittersweet remembrance of Britain's victory.

French and Spanish navies. His motto: England expects that every man shall do his duty.

Nelson's fleet smashed the enemy at Trafalgar, and Napoleon's

hopes for a naval invasion of Britain sank. Unfortunately, Nelson took a sniper's bullet in the spine and died, gasping, "Thank God I have done my duty." The lion at Nelson's feet groans sadly, and two little boys gaze up—one at Nelson, one at Wren's dome. You'll find Nelson's tomb directly beneath the dome, downstairs in the crypt.

Opposite Nelson is a monument to another great military man, Charles Cornwallis (1738-1805), honored here for his service as Governor General of

Bengal (India). Yanks know him better as the general who lost the American Revolutionary War (or "American War," as it's known here) when George Washington—aided by French ships—forced his surrender at Yorktown in 1780.

• *There are several entrances to the dome and its Galleries, but only one is open to the public at any given time, so check the free visitor's map.*

❿ Climb the Dome

The 530-step climb is worthwhile, and each level (or Gallery) offers something different.

First you get to the Whispering Gallery (257 steps, with views of the church interior). Whisper sweet nothings into the wall, and

your partner (and anyone else) standing far away can hear you. Exactly how it works is debated (some even question *if* it works). Most likely, the sound does not travel up and over the dome to the diametrically opposite side (as it would in a perfect sphere). Rather, it goes around the curved wall horizontally, so you don't have to stand in any particular spot. For best effects, try whispering (not talking) with your mouth close to the wall, while your partner stands a few dozen yards away with his or her ear to the wall.

After another set of stairs, you're at the Stone Gallery, with views of London. If you're exhausted, claustrophobic, or wary of heights, this middle level might be high enough. (The top level has very little standing room for tourists.)

Finally a long, tight, metal staircase takes you to the very top of the cupola, the Golden Gallery. (Just before the final dozen stairs to the top, there's a tiny window at your feet that allows

you to peek directly down—350 feet— to the church floor.) Once at the top, you emerge to stunning unobstructed views of the city. Looking west, you'll see the London Eye and Big Ben. To the south,  across the Thames, is the rectangular smokestack of the Tate Modern, with Shakespeare's Globe nestled nearby. To the east is the 600-foot-tall, black-topped Tower 42 and the bullet-shaped

30 St. Mary Axe building (nicknamed "The Gherkin"). Looking farther into the distance, you'll see London's future—the teeming, fast-growing expanse of the East End and the Docklands. The cluster of skyscrapers marks Canary Wharf. Just north of that is the site of the 2012 Olympic Games.

• *Descend the dome to church level, then follow signs directing you downstairs to the...*

⓫ Crypt

Many famous people are buried here. Start by locating the central tomb of Horatio Nelson, who wore down Napoleon. It's a big

coffin-on-a-pedestal in a round alcove at the center of the crypt, directly beneath the dome. Nearby is the granite tomb of the Duke of Wellington (who finished Napoleon off). The flags near the tomb were carried at his funeral procession.

Continuing up the central axis of the crypt, you enter a chapel. At the chapel's altar, turn right to reach Christopher Wren's tomb—a simple black slab with no statue. Next to it is a hunk of rough Portland stone quarried but unused by Wren while building St. Paul's; see his triangle brand on the left end. These few stones are not much of an honor for the man who built this great church. "If you seek his monument..." you'll be disappointed.

Use the free visitor's map to find other tombs and memorials: of painters Turner and Reynolds (located near Wren); of Florence Nightingale (near Wellington); and a memorial to George Washington, who lies buried back in old Virginny.

Temporary exhibits (they change frequently) often chronicle important events that have been held at the cathedral—for instance, Queen Victoria's funeral, services for the victims of the tsunami in 2004, or remembrances of the "7/7" terrorist bombings in London in 2005. There are also models of previous churches that stood on this spot. A multimedia room features the church through history.

The crypt contains a fine gift shop, a WC, a restaurant, and the grim-sounding Crypt Café, which nevertheless serves tasty food.

ST. PAUL'S

TOWER OF LONDON TOUR

William I, still getting used to his new title of "the Conqueror," built the stone "White Tower" (1077-1097) to keep the Londoners in line. The Tower also served as an effective lookout for seeing invaders coming up the Thames. His successors enlarged it to its present 18-acre size. Because of the security it provided, the Tower served over the centuries as a royal residence, the Royal Mint, the Royal Jewel House, and, most famously, as the prison and execution site of those who dared oppose the Crown.

The Tower's hard stone and glittering jewels represent the ultimate power of the monarch. So does the executioner's block. You'll find more bloody history per square inch in this original tower of power than anywhere else in Britain. Today, though its military purpose is history, it's still home to the Yeoman Warders, a.k.a. the "Beefeaters," who host three million visitors a year.

Your visit has four parts: the lively Beefeater tour (included in admission price, 1 hour), the White Tower (a serious museum and armory, which many rush and under-appreciate), the crown jewels (best in Europe, generally with a bit of a wait), and the grounds and walls (a simple and enjoyable stroll).

Orientation

Cost: £18, family ticket £50.

Hours: March-Oct Tue-Sat 9:00-17:30, Sun-Mon 10:00-17:30; Nov-Feb Tue-Sat 9:00-16:30, Sun-Mon 10:00-16:30; last entry 30 minutes before closing.

Advance Tickets: To avoid the long ticket-buying lines at the Tower, you have several options. The easiest is to buy your ticket at the Trader's Gate gift shop, located down the steps from the Tower Hill Tube stop; at the Tower Welcome Centre to the left of the normal ticket lines (credit card only); or at any London TI at no extra cost. It's also easy to book online (www.hrp.org.uk, £1 discount, no fee) or by phone (tel. 0844-482-7799 within UK or tel. 011-44-20-3166-6000 from the US; £2 fee), then pick up your tickets at the Tower.

More Crowd-Beating Tips: It's most crowded in summer, on weekends (especially Sundays), and during school holidays. Any time of year, the line for the crown jewels—the best on earth—can be just as long as the line for tickets. For fewer crowds, arrive before 10:00 and go straight for the jewels, then tour the rest of the Tower. Crowds die down after 16:30.

Getting There: The Tower is located in East London (Tube: Tower Hill). For speed, take the Tube there; for romance, take the boat. Thames Clippers boats make the trip between the Tower of London and Westminster Pier near Big Ben in 30 minutes; the boat continues on to Greenwich from the Tower Pier. For details about these cruises, see page 47. Buses #15 and #RV1 make the trip from Trafalgar Square (see map on page 34).

Information: Upon arrival, pick up the free map/guide, and check the schedule of the day's events and special demonstrations (such as knights in armor explaining medieval fighting techniques). Everything inside is well-described, so skip the audioguide (£4, plus £40 deposit or ID) and the Tower guidebook. Switchboard toll tel. 0844-482-7777, www.hrp.org.uk.

Yeoman Warder (Beefeater) Tours: The free, worthwhile, 1-hour Beefeater tours leave every 30 minutes from inside the gate (last one at 15:30, 14:30 in winter, they take a midday lunch break). The boisterous Beefeaters are great entertainers. While groups can be huge, the guides are easy to hear. Their talks include lots of bloody anecdotes about the Tower and its history. Check the clock inside the gate. If you just missed a tour, you can join it in progress (just a bit ahead). Tips are not expected, but if you want, slip your Beefeater a coin (not a bill) at the end of the tour.

Sunday Worship: On Sunday morning, visitors are welcome on the grounds for free to worship in the Chapel Royal of St. Peter ad Vincula. You get in without the lines, but you can only see the chapel—no sightseeing (9:15 Communion or 11:00 service with fine choral music, meet at west gate 30 minutes early, dress for church, may be closed for ceremonies—call ahead).

Length of This Tour: Allow two hours.

Photography: Photos are allowed, except of the jewels and in chapels.

Cuisine Art: The New Armouries Café, inside the Tower, is a big, efficient cafeteria (large, splittable meals for £8). Outside the

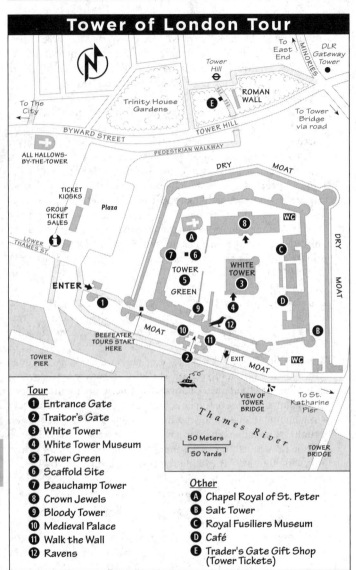

Tower of London Tour

To East End

To DLR Gateway Tower

Tower Hill

Trinity House Gardens

ROMAN WALL

To The City

BYWARD STREET

TOWER HILL

To Tower Bridge via road

ALL HALLOWS-BY-THE-TOWER

PEDESTRIAN WALKWAY

DRY   MOAT

TICKET KIOSKS

GROUP TICKET SALES

Plaza

WC

8

A

WHITE TOWER

C

DRY   MOAT

LOWER THAMES ST.

7   6

TOWER GREEN

5

3

ENTER

1

9

4

D

12

B

BEEFEATER TOURS START HERE

MOAT

10

11

2

EXIT   MOAT

WC

TOWER PIER

VIEW OF TOWER BRIDGE

To St. Katharine Pier

Thames River

50 Meters
50 Yards

TOWER BRIDGE

Tour
1. Entrance Gate
2. Traitor's Gate
3. White Tower
4. White Tower Museum
5. Tower Green
6. Scaffold Site
7. Beauchamp Tower
8. Crown Jewels
9. Bloody Tower
10. Medieval Palace
11. Walk the Wall
12. Ravens

Other
A. Chapel Royal of St. Peter
B. Salt Tower
C. Royal Fusiliers Museum
D. Café
E. Trader's Gate Gift Shop (Tower Tickets)

TOWER OF LONDON

Tower, there's Paul along the river (£4 sandwiches); the big, modern EAT, uphill from the ticket lines; and various take-out stands. Picnicking is allowed on Tower grounds but not inside the buildings.

Nearby: The Tower is close to three of my self-guided walks: If you're not in a hurry to get to the Tower from central London (i.e., Trafalgar Square), consider following ✪ The City Walk.

Across the river is the ✪ Bankside Walk (begins at London Bridge, upstream). And just to the north, near Liverpool Street Station, is the ✪ East End Walk (see page 83).

Starring: Crown jewels, Beefeaters, William the Conqueror, and Henry VIII.

The Tour Begins

❶ Entrance Gate

Even an army the size of the ticket line couldn't storm this castle. After the drawbridge was pulled up and the iron portcullis

slammed down, you'd have to swim a 120-foot moat; cross an island prowled by wild animals; then toss a grappling hook onto a wall and climb up while the enemy poured boiling oil on you. If you made it this far, you'd only be halfway there. You'd still have to swim a second moat (eventually drained to make the grassy parade ground we see today), then, finally, scale a second, higher wall. In all, the central keep (tower) was surrounded by two concentric rings of complete defenses. Yes, it was difficult to get into the Tower (if you were a foreign enemy)...but it was almost as impossible to get out (if you were an enemy of the state).

• *Show your ticket, enter, and check the posted daily event schedule. The entertaining one-hour tours by the Yeoman Warders (the Beefeaters) begin just inside the entrance gate. The information booth is nearby. Make sure to get a free map (you may have to ask for it at the bookstore up ahead). WCs are 100 yards ahead.*

When you're all set, go 50 yards straight ahead to the...

❷ Traitor's Gate

This was the boat entrance to the Tower from the Thames. Princess Elizabeth, who was a prisoner here before she became Queen Elizabeth I, was carried down the Thames and through this gate on a barge, thinking about her mom, Anne Boleyn, who had been decapitated inside just a few years earlier. Many English leaders who

fell from grace entered through here—Elizabeth was one of the lucky few to walk out.

The Beefeaters

The original duty of the Yeoman Warders (called "Beefeaters") was to guard the Tower, its prisoners, and the jewels. Their nickname may come from an original perk of the job—large rations of the king's beef. The Beefeaters dress in blue knee-length coats with red trim and a top hat. The "ER" on the chest stands for the monarch they serve—Queen Elizabeth II (Elizabetha Regina in Latin). On special occasions, they wear red. All are retired non-commissioned officers from the armed forces with distinguished service records.

These days, the Yeoman Warders are no longer expected to protect the tower. Instead, they've evolved into great entertainers, leading groups of tourists through the Tower. At night, they ritually lock up the Tower in the Ceremony of the Keys. There are 35 Yeoman Warders, including one woman. They and their families make for a Beefeating community of 120 that live inside the Tower.

• *Pass underneath the "Bloody Tower" into the inner courtyard. The big, white tower in the middle is the...*

❸ White Tower

This square, 90-foot-tall tower was the original structure that gave this castle complex of 20 towers its name. William the Conqueror built it more than 900 years ago to put 15 feet of stone between himself and those he conquered. Over the centuries, the other walls and towers were built around it.

The keep was a last line of defense. The original entry (on the south side) is above ground level so that the wooden approach (you'll climb its modern successor to get in, and lots more stairs once you're inside) could be removed, turning the tower into a safe refuge. Originally, there were even fewer windows—the lower windows were added during a Christopher Wren-ovation in 1660. In the 13th century, the tower was painted white (hence the name).

Standing high above the rest of old London, the White

Tower provided a gleaming reminder of the monarch's absolute power over subjects. If you made the wrong move here, you could be feasting on roast boar in the banqueting hall one night and chained to the walls of the prison the next. Torture ranged from stretching on the rack to the full monty: hanging by the neck until nearly dead, then "drawing" (cut open to be gutted), and finally quartering, with your giblets displayed on the walls as a warning. (Guy Fawkes, who tried to blow up Parliament with 36 barrels of gunpowder, received this treatment after being tortured here.) Any cries for help were muffled by the thick stone walls—15 feet at the base, a mere 11 feet at the top.

• *Either now or later, find time to go inside the White Tower for its excellent museum.*

❹ White Tower Museum

Inside the White Tower, a one-way route winds through exhibits re-creating medieval life and the Tower's bloody history of torture and executions.

In the Royal Armory, you'll see some *suits of armor* of Henry VIII—slender in his youth (c. 1515), heavy-set by 1540—with

his bigger-is-better codpiece. There's memorabilia of two army veterans, Princes William and Harry. The Line of Kings is a colorful row of painted wooden horses (some carved in the 17th century by revered sculptor Grinling Gibbons, the "King's Carver"), which once held the suits-of-armor of the monarchs who rode them. (The Tower curators are currently restoring this venerable three-centuries-old exhibit.)

Upstairs, the rare and lovely St. John's Chapel (1080) is where Lady Jane Grey (described later) offered up a last unanswered prayer. The oldest surviving part of the original Tower—and the oldest church in London—the chapel's round Norman (Romanesque) arches and column capitals decorated with the T-shaped Tau cross evoke the age of William the Conqueror.

Moving on, the Arsenal displays the suits of armor of a 6' 8" giant and a 3' 1" midget (more likely a child), as well as various weapons used through the ages, including machine guns and the jeweled "Tiffany Revolver."

On the top floor, see the Tower's actual *execution ax* and

chopping block. In 1747, this seven-pound ax sliced through the neck of Lord Lovat, a Scottish supporter of Bonnie Prince Charlie's claim to the throne. With his death, the ax was retired.

• *Back outside, find the courtyard to the left of the White Tower, called...*

❺ Tower Green

In medieval times, this spacious courtyard within the walls was the "town square" for those who lived in the castle. Knights exercised and jousted here, and it was the last place of refuge in troubled times. The Tower is still officially a royal residence, and the Queen's lodgings are on the south side of the green, in the white half-timbered buildings where a soldier stands guard.

The north side of the Green is bordered by the stone Chapel Royal of St. Peter ad Vincula. The current structure was built by Henry VIII, and his most famous victims are buried here (among them his wives Anne Boleyn and Catherine Howard).

• *About in the middle of the Tower Green is a granite-paved square marked* Site of Scaffold.

❻ Scaffold Site

The actual execution site looks pleasant enough today; the chopping block has been moved to inside the White Tower, and a modern sculpture encourages visitors to ponder those who died.

It was here that enemies of the crown would kneel before the king for the final time. With their hands tied behind their backs, they would say a final prayer, then lay their heads on a block, and—*shlit*—the blade would slice through their necks, their heads tumbling to the ground. The headless corpses were buried in unmarked graves in the Tower Green or under the floor of the Chapel Royal of St. Peter ad Vincula. The heads were stuck on a stick and displayed at London Bridge. Passersby did not really see the heads, they saw spheres of insects and parasites.

Tower Green was the most prestigious execution site at the Tower. Common criminals were hanged outside the Tower. More prominent evil-doers were decapitated before jeering crowds atop Tower Hill (near today's Tube station). Inside the Tower walls was reserved for the most heinous traitors.

Henry VIII axed a couple of his ex-wives here (divorced readers can insert their own cynical joke). Anne Boleyn was the appealing young woman Henry had fallen so hard for that he broke with the Catholic Church in order to divorce his first wife and marry her. But when Anne failed to produce a male heir, the court turned against her. She was locked up in the Tower, tried in a kangaroo court, branded an adulteress and traitor, and decapitated.

Henry's fifth wife, teenage Catherine Howard, was beheaded and her body laid near Anne's in the church. Jane Boleyn (Anne's sister-in-law) was also executed here for arranging Catherine's adulterous affair behind Henry's back. Next.

Henry even beheaded his friend Thomas More (a Catholic) because he refused to recognize (Protestant) Henry as head of the Church of England. (Thomas died at the less-prestigious Tower Hill site near the Tube stop.)

The most tragic victim was 17-year-old Lady Jane Grey, who was manipulated into claiming the crown for nine days during the scramble for power after Henry's death and the six-year reign and death of his sickly young son, Edward VI. When Bloody Mary (Mary I, Henry's daughter) took control, she forced her Protestant cousin Jane to kneel before the executioner. Young Jane bravely blindfolded herself, but then couldn't find the block. She crawled around the scaffolding pleading "Where is it?!" (The scene is depicted, beautifully if not entirely accurately, in sharp Pre-Raphaelite detail in one of the National Gallery's most popular paintings; see page 152.)

Years ago, a Beefeater, tired of what he called "Hollywood coverage" of the Tower, grabbed my manuscript, read it, and told me that in more than 900 years as a fortress, palace, and prison, the place held 8,500 prisoners. But only 120 were executed, and, of those, only six were executed inside it. Stressing the hospitality of the Tower, he added, "Torture was actually quite rare here."

❼ The Beauchamp Tower—Prisoners

The Beauchamp Tower (pronounced "BEECH-um") was one of several places in the complex that housed Very Important Prisoners. In an upstairs room, you can read graffiti carved into the stone by bored and despondent inmates.

Picture Philip Howard, the Earl of Arundel (c. 1555-1595), warming himself by this fireplace and glancing out at the execution site during his 10-year incarceration. Having lived a devil-may-care life of pleasure in the court of Queen Elizabeth, the pro-Catholic Arundel was charged with treason by the Protestant government. He pleaded with the queen—his former friend—to at least let him see his wife and young children. She refused, unless he would renounce his faith. On June 22, 1587, he carved his family name "Arundell" into the chimney (graffiti #13) and wrote in Latin: "*Quanto plus afflictionis...*" ("The more we suffer for Christ in this world, the more glory with Christ in the next.") Arundel suffered  faithfully another eight years here before he wasted away and died at age 40.

Graffiti #85 belongs to Lady Jane Grey's young husband, Lord Guilford Dudley. Locked in the Beauchamp Tower and executed the same day as his wife, Dudley vented his despair by scratching "IANE" into the stone. Cynics claim he was actually whining for his mommy, who was also named Jane.

Read other pitiful graffiti, like the musings of James Typping (#18). Imprisoned for three years "in great disgrace," he wonders what will happen to him: "I cannot tell but be death." Consider the stoic cry of Thomas Miagh (#29), an Irish rebel, who writes: "By torture straynge my truth was tried," having suffered some form of the rack. Thomas Clarke (#28), a Catholic priest who later converted to Protestantism, wrote pathetic poetry: "Unhappy is that man whose acts doth procure/the misery of this house in prison to endure." Many held onto their sense of identity by carving their family's coats of arms.

The last enemy of state imprisoned in the Tower complex was one of its most infamous: the renegade Nazi Rudolf Hess. In 1941, Hitler's henchman secretly flew to Britain with a peace proposal (Hitler denied any such plan). He parachuted into a field, was arrested and held for four days in the Tower, and was later given a life sentence.

• *Join the line leading to...*

❽ The Crown Jewels

• *Like a line for a Disney ride, the queue is still quite long even once you've made it in the door. But great videos help pass the time pleasantly. Don't let the crowd flow rush you through these instructive warm-up videos—just step aside.*

First, you'll pass through a room of wooden chairs and coats of arms—one for every monarch who wore jewels like these, from William I the Conqueror (1066), to Henry VIII, to his daughter Elizabeth I (with her lion-and-dragon crest), to the current Queen Elizabeth II.

Next, you'll see a film of the latter Elizabeth's 1953 coronation, which gives you a chance to see the jewels in use.

In the next room, you'll see video close-ups of the jewels. After pass–

ing a hallway of ceremonial maces, swords, and trumpets, you finally reach the jewels.

The first displays show the royal regalia. The monarch-to-be is dressed in the 20-pound gold robe, anointed with holy oil poured from the eagle-beak flask, and handed the jeweled sword. The 12th-century coronation spoon, last used in 1953 to anoint the head of Queen Elizabeth, is the most ancient object here. Most of the original crown jewels from medieval times were lost during Cromwell's 1648 revolution.

After being dressed and anointed, the new monarch prepares for the "crowning" moment.

• *Five glass cases display the various crowns, orbs, and scepters used in various royal ceremonies. Ride the moving sidewalk that takes you past them. You're welcome to circle back and glide by again (I did, several times) or hang out on the elevated viewing area with the guard. Chat with the guards—they're actually here to provide information (and to keep you from taking photos, which aren't allowed).*

Case #1: St. Edward's Crown is the coronation crown, the one placed by the archbishop upon the head of each new monarch on coronation day in Westminster Abbey. It's worn for 20 minutes, then locked away until the next coronation. The original crown, destroyed by Cromwell, was older than the Tower itself and dated back to 1061, the time of King Edward the Confessor, "the last English king" before William the Conqueror invaded from France (1066). This 1661 remake is said to contain some of the original's gold amid its 443 precious and semiprecious stones. Because the crown weighs nearly five pounds, weak or frail monarchs have opted not to wear it.

Case #2: After being crowned, the new monarch is handed the scepter and orb. The **Sovereign's Scepter** is encrusted with the world's largest cut diamond—the 530-carat Star of Africa, beefy as a quarter-pounder. This was one of nine stones cut from the original 3,106-carat (1.37-pound) Cullinan diamond. The **orb** symbolizes how Christianity rules over the earth, a reminder that even a "divine monarch" is not above God's law. The coronation is a kind of marriage between the church and the state in Britain, since the king or queen is head of both, and the ceremony celebrates the monarch's power to do good for the whole of the nation.

Case #3: Several crowns illustrate a bit of regalia symbolism. Kings and queens get four arches on their crowns, emperors get eight arches (e.g., the Imperial Crown of India you'll see in the case at the exit), and princes get only two (Charles has a two-arch crown that he keeps in Wales).

Case #4: The **Queen Victoria Small Diamond Crown** is tiny. Victoria had a normal-sized head, but this was designed to sit atop the widow's veil she insisted on wearing for decades after the death of her husband, Prince Albert. This four-ounce job was made in 1870 for £50,000—personally paid for by the queen.

The **Crown of the Queen Mother** (Elizabeth II's famous mum, who died in 2002), the highest crown in the case, has the 106-carat Koh-I-Noor diamond glittering on the front. The Koh-I-Noor diamond is considered unlucky for male rulers and, therefore, only adorns the crown of the king's wife. If Charles becomes king, Camilla might wear this. This crown was remade in 1937 and given an innovative platinum frame.

Case #5: The **Imperial State Crown** is what the Queen wears for official functions such as the annual opening of Parliament. When Victoria was queen, she insisted on wearing her small crown, but by law, this State Crown had to be carried next to her on a pillow, as it represents the sovereign. Among its 3,733 jewels are Queen Elizabeth I's former earrings (the hanging pearls, top center), a stunning 13th-century ruby look-alike in the center, and Edward the Confessor's ring (the blue sapphire on top, in the center of the Maltese cross of diamonds). When Edward's tomb was exhumed—a hundred years after he was buried—his body was "incorrupted." The ring on his saintly finger featured this sapphire and ended up on the crown of all future monarchs. This is the stylized crown you see representing the royalty on Britain's coins and stamps. It's even depicted on the pavement at the end of the sliding walk.

• *Leave the jewels by exiting through the thick vault doors. Back near the Traitor's Gate you'll find sights #9 and #10.*

❾ Bloody Tower

Not all prisoners died at the block. The 13-year-old future king Edward V and his kid brother were kidnapped in 1483 during the Wars of the Roses by their uncle Richard III ("Now is the winter of our discontent...") and locked in the Bloody Tower, never to be seen again (until two centuries later, when two children's skeletons were discovered).

Sir Walter Raleigh—poet, explorer, and political radical—was imprisoned here for 13 years. In 1603, the English writer and adventurer was accused of plotting against King James and sentenced to death. The king commuted the sentence to life imprisonment in the Bloody Tower. While in prison, Raleigh wrote the first volume of his *History of the World*. Check out his rather cushy bedroom, study, and walkway (courtesy of the powerful tobacco lobby?). Raleigh promised the king a wealth of gold if he would release him to search for El Dorado. The expedition was a failure. Upon Raleigh's return, the displeased king had him beheaded in 1618.

❿ Medieval Palace

The Tower was a royal residence as well as a fortress. These rooms were built around 1240 by Henry III, the king most responsible for the expansive Tower of London complex we see today. The well-described rooms are furnished as they might have been during the reign of his son, Edward I ("Longshanks"). You'll see his re-created bedroom and throne room, both with massive fireplaces to keep this cold stone palace cozy. After Cromwell temporarily deposed the monarchy (in the 17th century), the Tower ceased to be a royal residence except in name.

• *Near where you leave the Medieval Palace, enter to...*

⓫ Walk the Wall

The Tower was defended by state-of-the-art walls and fortifica-

tions in the 13th century. This walk offers a good look. From the walls, you also get a fine view of the famous bridge straddling the Thames, with the twin towers and blue spans. It's not London Bridge (which is the nondescript bridge just upstream), but **Tower Bridge.** Although it looks somewhat medieval, this drawbridge was built in 1894, of steel and concrete. Sophisticated steam engines raise and lower the bridge, allowing tall-masted ships to squeeze through.

Gaze out at the bridge, the river, City Hall (the egg-shaped glass building across the river, see page 95), and life-filled London.

• *Between the White Tower and the Bloody Tower are cages housing the...*

⓬ Ravens

According to goofy tradition, London is only safe as long as the ravens are at the Tower. Their wings are clipped so they'll stay, and about ten are kept in the cage. World War II bombing raids reduced the population to one. In recent years, with their clipped

wings, the birds had trouble mat-
ing, so a slide was built to help
them get a bit of lift to mate.
Happily, that worked, and a baby
raven was born. A children's TV
show sponsored a nationwide contest to come up with a name. The
winner: "Ronald Raven." As you
leave through the riverside exit,

look into the moat on the right for the tiny raven graveyard. There
lie Cedric (2003), Gundolf (2005), and Hardey (2006). RIP.

Other Sights

Get out your Tower-issued map to check out other areas you can
visit. The **Salt Tower** has graffiti by Henry Walpole, a staunch
Catholic who was imprisoned here by Queen Elizabeth I, tortured on the rack, and had a finger torn off. At the **Royal Fusiliers
Regimental Museum** you can see the uniforms, swords, and fusils
(flintlock rifles) of the army of Redcoats who've fought Napoleon,
the American War of Independence, two World Wars ("Monty"—
Field Marshal Bernard Montgomery of D-Day fame—was a
Fusilier), and wars in the Persian Gulf.

Take one final look at the stern stone walls of the Tower. Be
glad you can leave.

TOWER OF LONDON

BANKSIDE WALK

*Along the South Bank
of the Thames*

Bankside—the neighborhood between London Bridge and Blackfriars Bridge—is the historic heart of the revamped southern bank of the Thames. In ancient times "greater London" consisted of two Roman settlements straddling the easiest place to ford the river: one settlement was here, and the other was across the river—in the financial district known today as "The City."

From the Roman era until recently, the south side of the river was the wrong side of the tracks. For centuries, it was London's red light district. In the 20th century, it became an industrial wasteland of empty warehouses and street crime. Today, the prostitutes and pickpockets are gone, replaced by a riverside promenade dotted with pubs, cutesy shops, and historic tourist sights.

This half-mile Bankside Walk gives you plenty of history and sights to choose from—you can see it all, design your own plan, or just enjoy the view of London's skyline across the river.

Orientation

Length of This Walk: One hour (or up to an entire day if you tour Vinopolis, Shakespeare's Globe, and the Tate Modern).

Getting There: Take the Tube to the London Bridge stop to begin the walk. (The Monument stop, on the Circle Line, is also nearby.)

    The walk ends near Blackfriars Bridge (closest Tube stop: Blackfriars—or Southwark is several blocks south of the bridge on the South Bank). Bus #RV1 stops along Southwark Street behind the Tate Modern, and runs east to Tower Bridge or west to Covent Garden.

Old Operating Theatre Museum and Herb Garret: £6, cash only, daily 10:30-16:45, closed Dec 15-Jan 5, 9a St. Thomas Street.

Southwark Cathedral: Free but £4 donation requested (you'll likely be approached about the donation, so be prepared with at least £1 or a simple "No"); daily 8:00-18:00, last entry 30 minutes before closing; £2.50 guidebook, evensong services weekdays at 17:30, Sat at 16:00, Sun at 15:00, no service on Wed or alternate Mon; no photos without permission.

Borough Market: Thu 11:00-17:00, Fri 12:00-18:00, Sat 8:00-17:00, closed Sun-Wed.

Golden Hinde **Replica:** £6, daily 10:00-17:30, sometimes closed for private events.

The Clink Prison Museum: Overpriced at £6; July-Sept daily 10:00-21:00; Oct-June Mon-Fri 10:00-18:00, Sat-Sun until 19:30; 1 Clink Street.

Vinopolis: £20-40 self-guided tour packages, even more expensive packages include a meal; Thu-Fri 14:00-22:00, Sat 12:00-22:00, Sun 12:00-18:00, closed Mon-Wed; last entry 2.5 hours before closing; between Shakespeare's Globe and Southwark Cathedral at 1 Bank End. Tour prices depend on when you go, how many tastes you want, and whether you'd like a meal.

Shakespeare's Globe: The complex is open daily 9:00-17:00. To see the theater interior, you must either take a 40-minute guided tour (£11.50, includes "Globe Exhibition" museum; £9 when only the Rose Theatre is open for touring; see page 93) or buy a ticket to a performance (see Entertainment in London chapter).

Tate Modern: Free, but £3 donation appreciated (fee for special exhibitions), daily 10:00-18:00, Fri-Sat until 22:00, last entry to temporary exhibits 45 minutes before closing, view café on top floor. ○ See the Tate Modern Tour chapter.

Starring: Shakespeare's world, London Bridge, historic pubs, and views of the London skyline.

The Walk Begins

• *Start at the south end of London Bridge. From the London Bridge Tube stop, take the "Borough High Street east" exit and turn right (north), walking 100 yards to the bridge.*

❶ London Bridge

The City (across the river) is to the north, Tower Bridge is east, and the Thames flows from west to east (left to right). Looking to the east (downstream) and turning counterclockwise, you'll see the following:

BANKSIDE WALK

Downstream

- Tower Bridge (the Neo-Gothic-towered drawbridge that many Americans mistakenly call London Bridge).
- The HMS *Belfast* (in the foreground, docked on the southern bank), a WWII cruiser that's open to tourists.
- Rising up on the South Bank is London's newest skyscraper, the Shard London Bridge, nicknamed "the Shard." Upon completion, it'll reach 1,017 feet and become the tallest building in the UK and the EU.
- Canary Wharf Tower (the distant 800-foot skyscraper with pyramid top and blinking light), built in 1990 on the Isle of Dogs. It will lose its standing as the UK's tallest to "the Shard."
- The "Pool of London." This is the stretch of river between Tower Bridge (a drawbridge) and London Bridge, which marks the farthest point seagoing vessels can sail inland. In the 18th century this was the busiest port in the world.

North Bank

- The Tower of London (four domed spires and a flag rising above the trees on the North Bank).
- The Monument (north end of London Bridge but almost completely buried among modern buildings), a column topped with a shiny bronze knob, marking the start of the 1666 Great Fire.
- St. Paul's Cathedral (to the northwest, with a dome like a state capitol and twin spires).
- St. Bride's Church, the pointed, stacked steeple (nestled among office buildings) that supposedly inspired the wedding cake.
- A radio/TV tower.
- Southwark Bridge (the next bridge upstream).

South Bank

- The Tate Modern art museum (square brick smokestack tower on the South Bank).
- Southwark Cathedral (on South Bank, 100 yards away, may not be visible from where you're standing).
- Borough High Street, the busy street that London Bridge spills onto.
- The small griffin statues (winged lions holding shields) at the

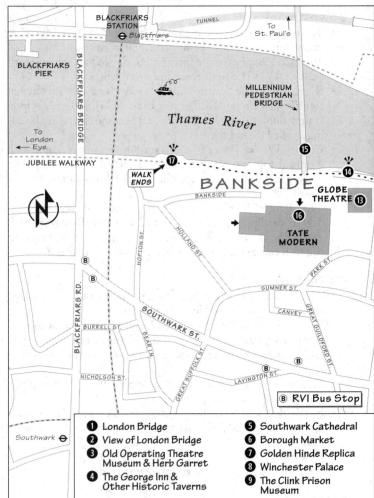

BANKSIDE WALK

south end of London Bridge guard the entrance to The City. They marked the jurisdiction of The City to include both sides of the all-important river. For centuries, they said, "Neener neener" to late-night partiers who got locked out of town when the gates shut tight at curfew.

• *The best view of London Bridge is not from the bridge itself, but from the riverbank, 50 yards west, reached by a staircase leading down from the bridge. Find the staircase next to the southwest griffin, by the building marked Two London Bridge. These stairs will impress fans of Charles Dickens'* Oliver Twist—*they're the setting of the infamous* "Meeting on the Bridge."

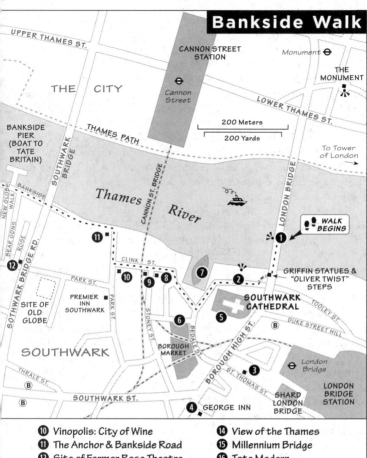

Bankside Walk

BANKSIDE PIER (BOAT TO TATE BRITAIN)

THE CITY

CANNON STREET STATION

Cannon Street

Monument

THE MONUMENT

UPPER THAMES ST.

LOWER THAMES ST.

THAMES PATH

200 Meters

200 Yards

To Tower of London

Thames River

SOUTHWARK BRIDGE

CANNON ST. BRIDGE

LONDON BRIDGE

WALK BEGINS

❶

❷

GRIFFIN STATUES & "OLIVER TWIST" STEPS

NEW GLOBE WALK

BEAR GDNS. WALK

BANKSIDE

RUSE

❷

❶❶

CLINK ST.

PARK ST.

PARK ST.

STONEY ST.

BEDALE ST.

❶❶

❶❶

❾

❽

❼

❺

❻

SOUTHWARK CATHEDRAL

TOOLEY ST.

DUKE STREET HILL

SITE OF OLD GLOBE

PREMIER INN SOUTHWARK

BOROUGH MARKET

BOROUGH HIGH ST.

ST. THOMAS ST.

London Bridge

SOUTHWARK

THRALE ST.

SOUTHWARK ST.

❸

❹

GEORGE INN

SHARD LONDON BRIDGE

LONDON BRIDGE STATION

❿ Vinopolis: City of Wine
⓫ The Anchor & Bankside Road
⓬ Site of Former Rose Theatre & Bear Gardens
⓭ Shakespeare's Globe

⓮ View of the Thames
⓯ Millennium Bridge
⓰ Tate Modern
⓱ View of 1666 Great Fire Area

❷ View of London Bridge

The bridge of today—three spans of boring, traffic-clogged con-

crete, built in 1972—is (at least) the fourth incarnation of this 2,000-year-old river crossing. The Romans (A.D. 50) built the first wooden footbridge to Londinium (rebuilt many times), which was pulled down by boatmen in 1014 to retake London from Danish invaders.

(They celebrated with a song passed down to us as "London Bridge is falling down, my fair lady.")

The most famous version—crossed by everyone from Richard the Lionhearted, to Henry VIII, to Shakespeare, to Newton, to Darwin—was built around 1200 and stood for more than six centuries, the only crossing point into this major city. Built of stone on many thick pilings, stacked with houses and shops that arched over the roadway and bulged out over the river, with its own chapel and a fortified gate at each end, it was a neighborhood unto itself (pop. 300). Picture Mel Gibson's head boiled in tar and stuck on a spike along the bridge (like the Scots rebel William Wallace in 1305, depicted in Gibson's movie *Braveheart*), and you'll capture the local color of that time.

In 1823, the famous bridge was replaced with a more modern (but less impressive) brick one. In 1967, that brick bridge was sold to an American, dismantled, shipped to Arizona, and reassembled (all 10,000 bricks) in Lake Havasu City. (Humor today's Brits, who'd like to believe the Yank thought he was buying Tower Bridge.)

• *This walk is a pick-and-choose collection of sights. If you're interested in visiting the Old Operating Theatre Museum and Borough High Street inns, described next, see those sights first before heading west: Hike 150 yards south of the bridge (along the left-hand side of Borough High Street) to the Old Operating Theatre Museum (turn left on St. Thomas Street) and The George Inn.*

❸ Old Operating Theatre Museum and Herb Garret

Back when the common cold was treated with a refreshing bloodletting, the Old Operating Theatre—a surgical operating room from the 1800s—was a shining example of "modern" medicine. Today a museum, this is a quirky, sometimes gross, look at that painful transition from folk remedy to clinical health care. Originally part of a larger hospital complex, the Old Operating Theatre was boarded up when the hospital relocated, lying untouched for 100 years until its chance discovery in 1956. The location alone—in a long-forgotten attic above a church, reached by a steep spiral staircase—makes this odd place worth a visit.

The first room, the Herb Garret, was used to dry herbs for the former hospital. Today, it displays healing plants used for millennia—different ones for each of the traditional four ailments (melancholic, choleric, sanguine, phlegmatic), supposedly caused by an imbalance in the body's traditional four substances, or "humours" (black bile, yellow bile, blood, and phlegm), corresponding to the earth's traditional four elements (earth, wind, fire, and Ringo). You'll also learn that Florence Nightingale, the nurse famed for saving so many Crimean War soldiers wounded in Russia, worked here to improve sanitation and to turn nurses from low-paid domestics into trained doctors' assistants.

The small hallway displays crude anesthetics (ether, chloroform, three pints of ale), surgical instruments by Black & Decker (knives, saws, drills), and a glaring lack of antiseptics—that is, until young Dr. Joseph Lister discovered carbolic acid, which reduced the high rates of mortality (and halitosis).

The Old Operating Theatre is the highlight—a semicircular room surrounded by railings for 150 spectators (truly a "theater"),

where doctors operated on patients while med students observed.

The patients were often poor women, blindfolded for their own modesty. The doctors donated their time to help, practice, and teach (see the motto *Miseratione non Mercede:* "Out of compassion, not for profit"). The surgeries, usually amputations, were performed under very crude working conditions—under the skylight or by gaslight, with no sink, and only sawdust to sop up blood. The wood still bears bloodstains. Nearly one in three patients died. There was a fine line between Victorian-era surgeons and Jack the Ripper.

• *Farther down Borough High Street (on the left-hand side), you'll find...*

❹ The George Inn and (Faint Echoes of) Other Historic Taverns

The George is the last of many "coaching inns" that lined the main highway from London to all points south. Like Greyhound bus stations, each inn was a terminal for far-flung journeys, since coaches were forbidden inside The City. They offered food, drink, beds, and entertainment for travelers—Shakespeare, as a young actor, likely performed in The George's courtyard.

Along Borough High Street are plaques locating the alleyway ("yard") of long-gone taverns known to book lovers. **The Queen's Head** (north of The George) was owned by the mother of John Harvard, of university fame. **The White Hart** (also north of The George) was where Shakespeare and Dickens drank and set scenes. At **The Tabard** (now called "Talbot," south of The George), Chaucer's band began its fictional trip south in *The Canterbury Tales*—"Befell that in that season on a day/In Southwark at The Tabard as I lay/Ready to wander on my pilgrimage/To Canterbury with full courage."

• *Walk back toward the bridge. Southwark Cathedral is near the southwest corner of the structure.*

❺ Southwark Cathedral

This neighborhood parish church is where Shakespeare prayed while brother Edmund rang the bells. The Southwark (SUTH-uck) church dates back to 1207, though the site has had a church for at least a thousand years, and inhabitants for 2,000.

❶ **View down the Nave:** Clean and sparse, with warm golden stone, the church was revamped, a symbol of the urban renewal of the whole Bankside/Southwark area. Its WWII damage has been repaired, with replacement windows of unstained glass on the right side. The nave bends slightly to the left (the chandelier, ceiling arches, and altar don't line up until you take two baby steps left) as a medieval tribute to Christ's bent body on the cross.

❷ **Shakespeare Monument:** William reclines in front of a backdrop of the 16th-century Bankside skyline (view look-

ing north). Find (left to right) the original Globe Theatre, Winchester Palace, Southwark Cathedral, and the old London Bridge with its arched gate. Shakespeare seems to be dreaming about the many characters of his plays, depicted in the stained-glass window above (see Hamlet addressing a skull, right window). To the right is a plaque to the American actor Sam Wanamaker, who spearheaded the building of a replica of Shakespeare's Globe Theatre (explained later in this chapter). Shakespeare's brother Edmund is buried in the church, possibly under a marked slab on the floor of the choir area, near the very center of the church. (The Bard lies buried in his hometown of Stratford-upon-Avon.)

❸ **The Retro-Choir:** The 800-year-old crisscross arches and stone tracery in the windows are some of the oldest parts of this historic church. Located in the heart of the industrial district, the church was heavily bombed during World War II.

❹ **Model of Church:** Near a reclining stone corpse and a reclining wooden knight, find a model (marked *Church and Priory of St. Mary Overy*) of the church and old Winchester Palace—a

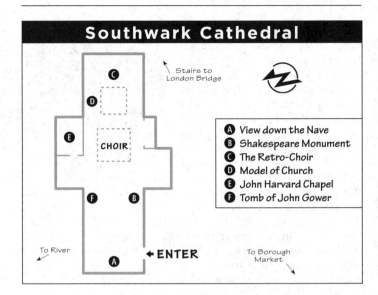

Southwark Cathedral

Stairs to London Bridge

CHOIR

A View down the Nave
B Shakespeare Monument
C The Retro-Choir
D Model of Church
E John Harvard Chapel
F Tomb of John Gower

To River

To Borough Market

← ENTER

helpful reconstruction before we visit the paltry Winchester Palace ruins.

E John Harvard Chapel: The Southwark-born son of an innkeeper (see the record of baptism near the window) inherited money from the sale of The Queen's Head tavern, got married, and sailed to Boston (1637), where he soon died. The money and his 400-book library funded the start of Harvard University.

F Tomb of John Gower: The poet and friend of Chaucer (c. 1400) rests his head on his three books, one written in Middle English, one in French, and one in Latin—the three languages from which modern English soon emerged.

• *Just south of Southwark Cathedral, you'll find the...*

6 Borough Market

The first trading starts at 2:00 in the morning at this open-air wholesale produce market. Workers can knock off by sunrise for a pint at the specially licensed Market Porter tavern (on Park Street).

On Thursday and Friday afternoons and all day Saturday, the colorful market opens for retail sales to Londoners seeking trendy specialty and organic foods. It's great for gathering a picnic on a sunny day. Of the many market stalls, the Ginger Pig is *the* place for serious English sausage and bacon, while Maria's Market Café is a colorful eatery popular with market workers.

First started a thousand years ago on London Bridge, where country farmers brought fresh goods to the city gates, the market now sits here under a Victorian arcade. The railroad rumbling overhead, knifing right through dingy apartment houses (and the Globe Tavern), only adds to the color of London's oldest vegetable market and public gathering spot.

A detour westward through the market leads to Park Street, with an old 19th-century ambience that makes it popular as a filming location. Check out the colorful pub and the fragrant cheese shop at Neal's Yard Dairy.

• *Walk to the river along Cathedral Street, veering left at the Y.*

❼ *Golden Hinde* Replica

As we all learned in school, "Sir Francis Drake circumcised the globe with a hundred-foot clipper." Or something like that...

Imagine a hundred men on a boat this size (yes, this replica is full-size) circling the globe on a three-year voyage, sleeping on the wave-swept decks, suffering bad food, floggings, doldrums, B.O., and attacks from foreigners. They explored unknown waters and were paid only from whatever riches they could find or steal along the way. (I took a bus tour like that once.)

The *Golden Hinde* (see the female deer, or hind, on the prow and stern) was Sir Francis Drake's flagship as he circumnavigated the globe (1577-1580). Drake, a farmer's son who followed the lure of the sea, hated Spaniards. So did Queen Elizabeth I, who hired him to plunder rich Spanish vessels and New World colonies in England's name.

With 164 men on five small ships (the *Hinde* was the largest, at 100 tons and 18 cannons), he sailed southwest, dipping around South America, raiding Spanish ships and towns in Chile, and inching up the coast perhaps as far as Canada. By the time it continued across the Pacific to Asia and beyond, the *Hinde* was so full of booty that its crew replaced the rock ballast with gold ingots

and silver coins. Three years later, Drake—with only one remaining ship and 56 men—sailed the *Hinde* up the Thames, unloading a fabulously valuable hoard of gold, silver, emeralds, diamonds, pearls, silks, cloves, and spices before the Queen. A grateful Elizabeth knighted Drake on the main deck and kissed him on his *Golden Hinde*.

The *Hinde* was retired gloriously, but rotted away from neglect. Drake received a large share of the wealth, became enormously famous, and later gained more glory defeating the Spanish Armada (aided by "the winds of God") in the decisive battle in the English Channel, off Plymouth (1588), making England ruler of the waves.

The galleon replica, a working ship that has itself circled the globe, is berthed at St. Mary Overie Dock ("St. Mary's over the river"), a public dock available for free to all Southwark residents. A victim of WWII bombing and container ships that require big berths and deep water, the Thames river trade that used to thrive even this far upstream is now concentrated east of Tower Bridge. Only a few brick warehouses remain (just west of here), waiting to be leveled or yuppified.

• *There's a fine view (with a handy chart to identify things) from the riverside. The beach below is fun for beachcombing—old red roof tiles and little chunks of disposable clay tobacco pipes litter the rocks at low tide. From here, the Monument is visible across London Bridge, poking its bristly bronze head above the ugly postwar buildings. Beyond that is the bullet-shaped tip of the modern 30 St. Mary Axe Tower (also known as the "Swiss Re Tower" as well as "The Gherkin" and "Towering Innuendo" for its unusual design). Now turn left, and head west along Pickfords Wharf. About 25 yards ahead on the left are the excavated ruins of...*

❽ Winchester Palace

All that remains today is a wall with a medieval rose window, but this was once a lavish 80-acre estate stretching along 200 feet of waterfront. It had a palace, gardens, fountains, stables, tennis courts, a working farm, and a fish-stocked lake. The wall marks the west end of the Great Hall (134 feet by 29 feet), the banquet room for receptions held by the palace's owner, the Bishop of Winchester.

Bishops from 1106 to 1626 lived here as wealthy, worldly rulers of the Bankside area, outside the jurisdiction of The City. They profited from activities illegal across the river, such as prostitution and gambling. They were a law unto themselves, with their own courts and prisons. One famous prison—the Clink—built by the bishops remained, even after its creators were ousted by a Puritan Parliament.

• *Fifty yards farther west (along what is now called Clink Street) is...*

❾ The Clink Prison Museum

The prison—now an overpriced and disappointing museum—gave us our expression "thrown in the Clink" from the sound of prisoners' chains. It burned down in 1780, but the underground cells remain, featuring historical information on wall plaques, many torture devices, and a generally creepy, claustrophobic atmosphere.

Originally part of Winchester Palace, it housed troublemakers who upset the smooth running of the bishop's 22 licensed brothels (called "the stews"), gambling dens, and taverns. Bouncers delivered drunks who were out of control, johns who couldn't pay, and prostitutes ("women living by their bodies") who tried to go freelance or cheated loyal customers. Offending prostitutes had their heads shaved and breasts bared, and were carted through the streets and whipped while people jeered. They might share cells side by side with "heretics"—namely, priests who'd crossed their bishops.

In 1352, debtors (who'd maxed out their Visa cards) became criminals, housed here among harder criminals in harsh conditions. Prisoners were not fed. They had to bribe guards to get food, to avoid torture, or even to gain their release. (The idea was that you'd brought this on yourself.) Prisoners relied on their families for money, prostituted themselves to guards and other inmates, or reached through the bars at street level, begging from passersby. Murderers, debtors, Protestants, priests, and many innocent people experienced this strange brand of justice...all part of the rough crowd that gave Bankside such a seedy reputation.

• *Continuing west and crossing under the Cannon Street Bridge, you'll find...*

❿ Vinopolis: City of Wine

This warehouse of wine—with a splash of France, a dash of ancient Rome, and a taste of Italian *vino*—seems out of place in

London, but no one's complaining. For more on this wine-tasters' Disneyland, see page 94.

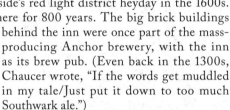

• *Switching from wine to beer, across the street is...*

⑪ The Anchor and Bankside Road

The Anchor is the last of the original 22 licensed "inns" (tavern/brothel/restaurant/night-club/casino) of Bankside's red light district heyday in the 1600s. A tavern has stood here for 800 years. The big brick buildings behind the inn were once part of the mass-producing Anchor brewery, with the inn as its brew pub. (Even back in the 1300s, Chaucer wrote, "If the words get muddled in my tale/Just put it down to too much Southwark ale.")

ANCHOR TAP

In the cozy, maze-like interior are memories of greats who've drunk here (I have) or indulged in a new drug that hit London in the 1560s—tobacco. Shakespeare, who may have lived along Clink Street, may have tippled here, especially because the original Globe Theatre was right behind The Anchor (see map on page 278). Dr. Samuel Johnson also worked here while writing the famous dictionary that helped codify the English language and spelling (for more on Dr. Johnson, see page 237).

The Anchor marks the start of once-notorious Bankside Road that runs along a river retaining wall. In Elizabethan times (16th century), the street was lined with "inns" offering one-stop shopping for addictive personalities. The streets were jammed with sword-carrying punks in tights looking for a fight, prostitutes, gaping tourists from the Borough High Street coaching inns, pickpockets, river pirates, highwaymen, navy recruiters kidnapping drunks, and many proper ladies and gentlemen who ferried across from The City for an evening's entertainment. And then there were the really seedy people—yes, actors.

• *Crossing under the green-and-yellow Southwark Bridge, notice the metal reliefs depicting London's "Frost Fair" of 1564. Because the old London Bridge was such a wall of stone, the swift-flowing Thames would back up and even freeze over during cold winters.*

Emerging from under the bridge, head farther west on Bankside to Shakespeare's Globe ⑫*.*

Possible Detour: Die-hard theater fans may wish to detour inland to the site of the former Rose Theatre. It's not recommended, since the Rose is rarely open (though tours are offered through Shakespeare's Globe), and, if it is, there's not much to see. But if I can't talk you out of it, here's how to get there: Emerging from under the bridge, turn at the first left (Bear Gardens Lane), then go left on Park Street. Go one block to the gray-granite modern building located on the site of the former Rose Theatre.

⓬ Site of the Former Rose Theatre and Bear Gardens

When the 2,200-seat Rose first raised its curtain in 1587, it signaled four decades of phenomenal popularity (centered in Bankside) for a rapidly evolving form of entertainment—theater. Soon there were four great theaters in the area: the Rose, the Hope, the Swan, and the Globe. (Theatrical types can find the unimpressive plaque marking the site of the original Globe Theatre—a half-block east of the Rose—and be as disappointed as Sam Wanamaker, who was inspired to build the replica of Shakespeare's Globe. More on the Globe when we arrive at the replica.)

It's thought that the young Will Shakespeare, recently arrived from the country, got his start at the Rose tending theatergoers' horses ("What?" he said, "and give up show business?!"). Soon, though, the struggling actor saw his first play *(Henry VI, Part I)* come to life on the Rose stage.

Closer to the river was a theatrical venue called the Bear Gardens (only a plaque marks the spot today). Bankside theaters presented everything from serious drama, to light comedy, to vaudeville, to circus acts, to...animal fights. Bearbaiting was the most popular. A bear was chained to a stake while a pack of dogs (mastiffs) attacked, and spectators bet on the winner. The bears, often with teeth filed down or jaws wired shut, fought back with their paws, sweeping dogs into the crowd. Now, that's entertainment.

⓭ Shakespeare's Globe— 1997 Replica of the Original Globe Theatre

All the world's a stage,
And all the men and women merely players.
They have their exits and their entrances,
And one man, in his time, plays many parts.
                                        —As You Like It

By 1599, 35-year-old William Shakespeare was a well-known actor, playwright, and businessman in the booming theater trade (see sidebar on page 222). His acting company, the Lord Chamberlain's

Men, built the 3,000-seat Globe Theatre, by far the largest of its day (200 yards from today's replica, where only a plaque stands now).

The Globe premiered Shakespeare's greatest works—*Hamlet, Othello, King Lear, Macbeth*—in open-air summer afternoon performances, though occasionally at night by the light of torches and buckets of tar-soaked ropes.

In 1612, it featured Shakespeare's *All Is True (Henry VIII)*. During Scene 4, a stage cannon boomed, announcing the arrival of King Henry, who started flirting with Anne Boleyn. As the two actors generated sparks onstage, play-watchers smelled fire. Some stray cannon wadding had sparked a real fire off-stage. Within an hour, the wood-and-thatch building had burned completely to the ground, but with only one injury: A man's pants caught fire and were quickly doused with a tankard of ale.

Built in 1997, the new Globe—round, half-timbered, thatched, with wooden pegs for nails—is a quite realistic replica, though slightly smaller (seating 1,500 spectators), located a block away from the original site, and constructed with fire-repellent materials. Performances are staged almost nightly in summer—check at the box office (at the east end of the complex).

Bankside's theater scene vanished in the 1640s, closed by a Parliament dominated by hard-line Puritans. Drama seemed to portray and promote immoral behavior, and actors—men who also played women's roles—parodied and besmirched fair womanhood. Bearbaiting was also outlawed by the outraged moralists (to paraphrase the historian Thomas Macaulay)—not because it caused bears pain, but because it gave people pleasure.

⓮ View of the Thames

From the Cotswolds to the North Sea, the river winds eastward a total of 210 miles. London is close enough to the estuary to be affected by the North Sea's tides, so the river level does indeed rise and fall twice a day. In fact, one of the reasons Romans found this a practical location—even though it was about 40 miles inland—was that their boats could hitch a free ride with the tides between the sea and the town twice a day. But tides also mean floods.

After centuries of periodic flooding (spring rains plus high tides), barriers to regulate the tides were built in 1982, east of Tower Bridge. The barriers also slow down the once fast-moving river.

The Thames is still a major commercial artery (east of Tower Bridge). In the previous two centuries, it ran brown with Industrial Revolution pollution. Today it's brown because of estuary silt—the Thames is now one of the cleanest rivers in the industrialized world.

• *Fifty yards west of the Globe, spanning the river, is the...*

⑮ Millennium Bridge

This pedestrian bridge was built in 2000 to connect the Tate Modern with St. Paul's Cathedral and The City. For its first two

glorious days, Londoners made the pleasant seven-minute walk across...before the $25 million "bridge to the next millennium" started wobbling dangerously (insert your own ironic joke here) and was closed for rethinking. After much work, 20 months, and $8 million, the bridge reopened. Nicknamed the "blade of light," it was designed (partly by Lord Norman Foster, who also did the 30 St. Mary Axe Tower and City Hall downstream) to allow a wide-open view of St. Paul's. Now stabilized, it links two revitalized sections of London.

⑯ Tate Modern

London's large, impressive modern art collection is housed in a former power station—typical of the move to renovate empty,

ugly Industrial Age hulks on the South Bank. Even if you don't tour the collection, pop inside the north entrance (free) to view the spacious interior, decorated each year with a new industrial-sized sculptural installation by one of the world's top contemporary artists.

❂ See the Tate Modern Tour chapter.

• *Bankside—maybe at The Founder's Arms pub along the river—is a great place to contemplate...*

⓱ The Great Fire of 1666

On Sunday, September 2, 1666, stunned Londoners quietly sipped beers in Bankside pubs and watched The City across the river go up in flames. ("When we could endure no more upon the water," wrote Samuel Pepys in his diary, "we went to a little alehouse on the Bankside.") Started in a bakery shop near the Monument (north end of London Bridge) and fanned by strong winds, the fire swept westward, engulfing the mostly wooden city, devouring Old St. Paul's, and moving past what is now Blackfriars Bridge and St. Bride's to Temple Church (near the pointy, black, gold-tipped steeple of the Royal Courts of Justice).

In four days, 80 percent of The City was incinerated, including 13,000 houses and 89 churches. The good news? Incredibly, only nine people died, the fire cleansed a plague-infested city, and Christopher Wren was around to rebuild London's skyline.

The fire also marked the end of Bankside's era as London's naughty playground. Having recently been cleaned up by the Puritans, it now served as a temporary refugee camp for those displaced by the fire. And, with the coming Industrial Age, businessmen demolished the inns and replaced them with brick warehouses, docks, and factories to fuel the economy of a world power.

• *From here, the closest* **Tube** *stops are Southwark (a several-block walk to the south) and Blackfriars (just over Blackfriars Bridge, to the north).*

If you're footsore, you may want to skip the walk to the Tube and instead catch handy **bus #RV1,** *which stops about a five-minute walk away, along Southwark Street behind the Tate (Lavington Street stop); from there, the bus heads west to the London Eye, Waterloo Station (Tube stop), then across Waterloo Bridge to Covent Garden; or east, to London Bridge Station (Tube stop), City Hall, and over Tower Bridge to the Tower of London (and Tower Hill Tube stop).*

To continue by **foot,** *follow the Jubilee Walkway along the South Bank of the Thames to the London Eye and Big Ben. (The 20-minute stroll is particularly enjoyable in the evening.) Or you can cross the Thames on the Millennium Bridge, where a pedestrian mall leads past the glassy Salvation Army headquarters (good café and small, free Salvation Army history display in daylight basement) to St. Paul's Cathedral and Tube station.*

TATE MODERN TOUR

Remember the 20th century? Accelerated by technology and fragmented by war, it was an exciting and chaotic time, with art as turbulent as the world that created it. The Tate Modern lets you walk through the explosive last century with a glimpse at its brave new art.

The Tate Modern is (controversially) displayed by concept—"Poetry and Dream," for example—rather than by artist and chronology. Unlike the museum, this chapter is neatly chronological. It's not intended as a painting-by-painting tour. Read through this chapter for a general introduction, use it as a reference, then take advantage of the Tate's excellent audioguides to focus on specific works. With this background in 20th-century art, you'll appreciate the Tate's even greater strength: art of the 21st century.

Orientation

Cost: Free for the permanent collection (but £3 donations are appreciated). Varying costs for temporary exhibits.

Hours: Daily 10:00-18:00, Fri-Sat until 22:00, last entry to temporary exhibitions 45 minutes before closing. This popular place is especially crowded on weekend days (crowds thin out on Fri and Sat evenings).

Getting There: Located on the South Bank, across from St. Paul's and near the Globe Theatre. You can get here by Tube, ferry, or foot:

By Tube: Take the Tube to Southwark, London Bridge, or Mansion House; then walk 10-15 minutes. ✪ See the Bankside Walk chapter.

By Ferry: Catch Thames Clippers' "Tate to Tate" ferry service from the Tate Britain (£5.50 one-way or £12.60 for day ticket, 33 percent discount with Travelcard, buy ticket on board, departs every 40 minutes from 9:55 to 17:00, 18 minutes, check schedule at www.tate.org.uk/tatetotate).

> **On Foot:** Walk across the Millennium Bridge from St. Paul's Cathedral.

Information: The ground floor (Level 1) and Level 2 have the basic services: info desks, baggage check, bookstores, audioguide rentals, and tickets for temporary exhibits. The helpful staff at the info desk can tell you the location of specific works. In addition, several **touch-screen computers** are scattered throughout the museum (particularly on Level 5). Tel. 020/ 7887-8888, www.tate.org.uk.

The Future: The Tate is constructing an expansion wing to the south, which will double its exhibition space. Some parts may open in 2012.

Tours: The £3.50 **audioguide** (with photos, video, and interactive features) covers the entire permanent collection, and includes a tour geared for kids ages 8-12. Free 45-minute **guided tours** are offered daily on Level 3 at 11:00 and 12:00, and on Level 5 at 14:00 and 15:00 (confirm at info desk).

Length of This Tour: Read this chapter ahead of time, then browse according to your tastes.

Cloakroom: Level 1 (free, £2 suggested donation).

Photography: Photos are only permitted in the entrance hall.

Cuisine Art: View coffee shops with food are on Levels 2 and 4. On Level 7, there's a table-service restaurant (plus a few stools at the casual bar), with stunning views of St. Paul's—see photo. Some trendy restaurants are several blocks southwest of the Tate, along the street named "the Cut" (near Southwark Tube stop).

Starring: Picasso, Matisse, Dalí, and all the "classic" modern artists, plus the Tate Modern's specialty—British and American artists of the last half of the 20th century.

Overview

To see the core of the permanent collection—and the artwork described in this tour—visit Levels 3 and 5. Paintings are arranged according to theme, not artist. Paintings by Picasso, for example, are scattered all over the building. Temporary exhibits are on Level 4.

Even though the layout of the Tate Modern changes constantly, the collection's focus is the same: the postwar period. Don't just come to see the Old Masters of modernism (Matisse, Picasso, Kandinsky, and so on). Push your mental envelope with works by Pollock, Miró, Bacon, Picabia, Beuys, Twombly, and others. If you're here in summer 2012, you'll also be able to see a major exhibition of one of Britain's towering contemporary artists, Damien Hirst.

More modern art from British artists is on display at the Tate Britain museum (✪ see the Tate Britain Tour chapter).

The Tour Begins

Entrance Hall

The grandest entry is from the west entrance. The massive empty space of the former industrial powerhouse dwarfs the art it houses.

(A metaphor for the triumph of 20th-century technology, perhaps?) The Turbine Hall displays major art installations by contemporary artists—always one of the highlights of the art world. During the Olympics, the Hall will display a new work by Tino Sehgal. It may prove quite interesting—Sehgal is known not so much for creating art objects as for staging situations where the viewer interacts with live actors.

From the Turbine Hall, you can reach Level 3 (start of permanent collection) via the escalator near the ground-floor cloakroom.

Reminder: The following is not a painting-by-painting tour but rather a chronological overview of modern art.

1900—Victoria's Legacy

Anno Domini 1900, a new century dawns. Europe is at peace, Britannia rules the world. Technology is about to usher in a golden age.

Claude Monet (1840-1926)

Monet captures the relaxed, civilized spirit of belle époque France and Victorian England with Impressionist snapshots of peaceful landscapes and middle-class family picnics. But the true subject is the shimmering effect of reflected light, rendered with rough brushstrokes and bright paints that look messy up close but blend at a distance. The newfangled camera made camera-eye realism obsolete. Artists began placing more importance on *how* something was painted rather than on *what* was painted.

1905—Colonial Europe

Europe ruled a global empire, tapping its dark-skinned colonials for raw materials, cheap labor, and bold new ways to look at the world. The cozy Victorian world was shattering. Nietzsche murdered God. Darwin stripped off Man's robe of culture and found a naked ape. Primitivism was modern. Ooga-booga.

Henri Matisse (1869-1954)

Matisse was one of the Fauves, or "wild beasts," who tried to inject a bit of the jungle into civilized European society. Inspired by  "primitive" African and Oceanic masks and voodoo dolls, the Fauves made modern art that looked primitive: long, mask-like faces with almond eyes; bright, clashing colors; simple figures; and "flat," two-dimensional scenes.

Matisse simplifies. A man is a few black lines and blocks of paint. A snail is a spiral of colored paper. A woman's back is an outline. Matisse's colors are unnaturally bright. The "distant" landscape is as crisp and clear as close objects, and the slanted lines meant to suggest depth are crudely done.

Traditionally, the canvas was like a window that you looked "through" to see a slice of the real world stretching off into the horizon. With Matisse, you look "at" the canvas, like wallpaper, to appreciate the decorative pattern of colors and shapes.

Though his style is modern, Matisse builds on 19th-century art—the bright colors of Van Gogh, the primitive figures of Gauguin, the colorful designs of Japanese woodblock prints, and the Impressionist patches of paint that blend together only at a distance.

Paul Cézanne (1839-1906)

Cézanne brings Impressionism into the 20th century. Whereas Monet uses separate dabs of different-colored paint to "build" a figure, Cézanne "builds" a man with somewhat larger slabs of paint, giving him a kind of 3-D chunkiness. It's not hard to see the progression from Monet's dabs to Cézanne's slabs to Picasso's cubes—Cubism.

1910—The Moderns

The modern world was moving fast, with automobiles, factories, and mass communication. Motion pictures captured the fast-moving world, while Einstein explored the fourth dimension: time.

Cubism: Pablo Picasso (1881-1973)

Born in Spain, Picasso moved to Paris as a young man. He worked with painter and sculptor Georges Braque in poverty so dire they often didn't know where their next bottle of wine was coming from.

Picasso's Cubist works show the old European world shattering to bits. He pieces the fragments back together in a whole new way, showing several perspectives at once (for example, looking up the left side of a woman's body and, at the same time, down at her right).

Whereas newfangled motion pictures capture several perspectives in succession, Picasso achieves it on a canvas with overlapping images. A single "cube" might contain an arm (in the foreground) and the window behind (in the background), both painted the same color. The foreground and background are woven together so that the subject dissolves into a pattern.

Picasso, the most famous and—OK, I'll say it—the greatest artist of the 20th century, constantly explored and adapted his style to new trends. He made collages, tried his hand at "statues" out of wood, wire, or whatever, and even made art out of everyday household objects. These multimedia works, so revolutionary at the time, have become stock-in-trade today. Scattered throughout the museum are works from the many periods of Picasso's life.

Futurism: Férnand Leger (1881-1955) and Umberto Boccioni (1882-1916)

The Machine Age is approaching, and the whole world gleams with promise in cylinder shapes ("Tubism"), like an internal-combustion engine. Or is it the gleaming barrel of a cannon?

1914—World War I

A soldier—shivering in a trench, ankle-deep in mud, waiting to be ordered "over the top," to run through barbed wire, over fallen comrades, and into a hail of machine-gun fire, only to capture a few hundred yards of meaningless territory that would be lost the next day. This soldier was not thinking about art.

World War I left nine million dead. (At times, England lost more men per month than America lost during the entire Vietnam War.) The war also killed the optimism and faith in humankind that had guided Europe since the Renaissance.

Expressionism: Grosz, Kirchner, Beckmann, Soutine, Dix, and Kokoschka

Cynicism and decadence settled over postwar Europe. Artists "expressed" their disgust by showing a distorted reality that emphasized the ugly. Using the lurid colors and simplified figures of the Fauves, they slapped paint on in thick brushstrokes, depicting a hypocritical, hard-edged, dog-eat-dog world—a civilization watching its Victorian moral foundations collapse.

Dada: Duchamp's Urinal (1917)

When they could grieve no longer, artists turned to grief's giddy twin, laughter. The war made all old values a joke, including artistic ones. The Dada movement, choosing a purposely childish name, made art that was intentionally outrageous: a moustache on the *Mona Lisa*, a shovel hung on the wall, or a modern version of a Renaissance "fountain"—a urinal (by Marcel Duchamp...or was it I. P. Freeley?).

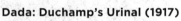

It was a dig at all the pompous pre-war artistic theories based on the noble intellect of Rational Women and Men. While the experts ranted on, Dadaists sat in the back of the class and made cultural fart noises.

Hey, I love this stuff. My mind says it's sophomoric, but my heart belongs to Dada.

1920s—Anything Goes

In the Jazz Age, the world turned upside-down. Genteel ladies smoked cigarettes. Gangsters laid down the law. You could make a fortune in the stock market one day and lose it the next. You could dance the Charleston with the opposite sex, and even say the word "sex" while talking about Freud over cocktails. It was almost...surreal.

Surrealism: Dalí, Ernst, and Magritte

Artists caught the jumble of images on a canvas. A telephone made from a lobster, an elephant with a heating-duct trunk, Venus sleepwalking among skeletons. Take one mixed bag of reality, jumble it in a blender, and serve on a canvas—Surrealism.

The artist scatters seemingly unrelated things on the canvas, leaving us to trace the connections in a kind of connect-the-dots without numbers.

Further complicating the modern world was Freud's discovery of the "unconscious" mind, which thinks dirty thoughts while we sleep. Surrealists let the id speak. The canvas is an uncensored, stream-of-consciousness "landscape" of these deep urges, revealed in the bizarre images of dreams.

Salvador Dalí (1904-1989)

Salvador Dalí, the most famous Surrealist, combines an extraordinarily realistic technique with an extraordinarily twisted mind. He paints "unreal" scenes with photographic realism, making us believe they could really happen. Dalí's images—crucifixes, political and religious figures, and naked bodies—pack an emotional punch.

1930s—Depression

As capitalism failed around the world, governments propped up their economies with vast building projects. The architecture style was modern, stripped-down (i.e., cheap), and functional. Propagandist campaigns championed noble workers in the heroic Social Realist style.

Piet Mondrian (1872-1944)

Like blueprints for modernism, Mondrian's T-square style boils painting down to its basic building blocks: a white canvas, black lines, and the three primary colors—red, yellow, and blue—arranged in orderly patterns. (When you come right down to it, that's all painting ever has been. A schematic drawing of, say, the *Mona Lisa* shows that it's less about a woman than

Abstract Art

Abstract art simplifies. A man becomes a stick figure. A squiggle is a wave. A streak of red expresses anger. Arches make 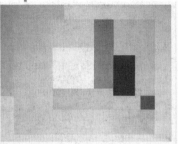 you want a cheeseburger. These are universal symbols that everyone from a caveman to a banker understands. Abstract artists capture the essence of reality in a few lines and colors, boldly capturing objects and ideas that even a camera can't—emotions, abstract concepts, musical rhythms, and spiritual states of mind.

With abstract art, you don't look "through" the canvas to see the visual world, but "at" it to read the symbolism of lines, shapes, and colors. Most 20th-century paintings are a mix of the real world (representation) and colorful patterns (abstraction).

about the triangles and rectangles she's composed of.)

Mondrian started out painting realistic landscapes of the orderly fields in his native homeland of Holland. Increasingly, he simplified his style into horizontal and vertical patterns. For Mondrian, who was heavily into Eastern mysticism, "up versus down" and "left versus right" were the perfect metaphors for life's dualities: good versus evil, body versus spirit, fascism versus communism, man versus woman. The canvas is a bird's-eye view of Mondrian's personal landscape.

1940s—World War II

World War II was a global war (involving Europe, the Americas, Australia, Africa, and Asia) and a total war (saturation bombing of civilians and ethnic cleansing). It left Europe in ruins.

Alberto Giacometti (1901-1966)

Giacometti's skinny statues have the emaciated, haunted, and faceless look of concentration-camp survivors. In the sweep of world war and overpowering technology, man is frail and fragile. All he can do is stand at attention and take it like a man.

Francis Bacon (1909-1992)

Bacon's caged creatures speak for all of war-torn Europe when they scream, "Enough!" (For more on Bacon, see page 334.)

1950s—America, the Global Superpower

As converted war factories turned swords into kitchen appliances, America helped rebuild Europe while pumping out consumer goods for its own booming population. Prosperity, a stable government, national television broadcasts, and a common fear of Soviet communism threatened to turn America into a completely homogeneous society.

Some artists, centered in New York, rebelled against conformity and superficial consumerism. (They'd served under Eisenhower in war and now had to in peace, as well.) They created art that was the very opposite of the functional, mass-produced goods of the American marketplace.

Art was a way of asserting your individuality by creating a completely original and personal vision. The trend was toward bigger canvases, abstract designs, and experimentation with new materials and techniques. It was called "Abstract Expressionism"— expressing emotions and ideas using color and form alone.

Jackson Pollock (1912-1956)

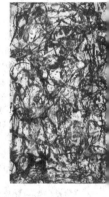

"Jack the Dripper" attacks convention with a can of paint, dripping and splashing a dense web onto the canvas. Picture Pollock in his studio, jiving to the hi-fi, bouncing off the walls, throwing paint in a moment of enlightenment. Of course, the artist loses some control this way—over the paint flying in midair and over himself in an ecstatic trance. Painting becomes a whole-body activity, a "dance" between the artist and his materials.

The intuitive act of creating is what's important, not the final product. The canvas is only a record of that moment of ecstasy.

Big, Empty Canvases

With all the postwar prosperity, artists could afford bigger canvases. But what reality are they trying to show?

In the modern world, we find ourselves insignificant specks in a vast and indifferent universe. Every morning, each of us must confront that big, blank, existential canvas, and decide how we're going to make our mark on it.

Another influence was the simplicity of Japanese landscape painting. A Zen master studies and meditates for years to achieve the state of mind in which he can draw one pure line. These canvases, again, are only a record of that state of enlightenment. (What is the sound of one brush painting?)

On more familiar ground, postwar painters were following in the footsteps of artists such as Mondrian. The geometrical forms here reflect the same search for order, but these artists painted to the musical 5/4 asymmetry of the Dave Brubeck Quartet's jazzy *Take Five*.

Patterns and Textures

Enjoy the lines and colors, but also a new element: texture. Some works have very thick paint piled on, where you can see the brush-strokes clearly. Some have substances besides paint applied to the canvas, or the canvas is punctured so the fabric itself (and the hole) becomes the subject. Artists show their skill by mastering new materials. The canvas is a tray, serving up a delightful buffet of different substances with interesting colors, patterns, shapes, and textures.

Mark Rothko (1903-1970)

Rothko makes two-toned rectangles, laid on their sides, that seem to float in a big, vertical canvas. The edges are blurred, so if you get close enough to let the canvas fill your field of vision (as Rothko intended), the rectangles appear to rise and sink from the cloudy depths like answers in a Magic 8 Ball.

Serious students appreciate the subtle differences in color between the rectangles. Rothko experimented with different bases for the same color and used a single undercoat (a "wash") to unify them. His early works are warmer, with brighter reds, yellows, and oranges; his later works are maroon and brown, approaching black.

Still, these are not intended to be formal studies in color and form. Rothko was trying to express the most basic human emotions in a pure language. (A "realistic" painting of a person is inherently fake because it's only an illusion of the person.) Staring into these windows onto the soul, you can laugh, cry, or ponder, just as Rothko did when he painted them.

Rothko, the previous century's "last serious artist," believed

in the power of art to express the human spirit. When he found out that his nine large Seagram canvases were to be hung in a corporate restaurant, he refused to sell them, and they ended up in the Tate. (A 2010 Tony Award-winning play called *Red* deals with Rothko's anguished decision.)

In his last years, Rothko's canvases—always rectangles—got bigger, simpler, and darker. When Rothko finally slashed his wrists in his studio, one nasty critic joked that what killed him was the repetition. Minimalism was painting itself into a blank corner.

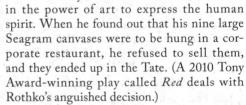

20th-Century British Artists

Since 1960, London has rivaled New York as a center for the visual arts. You'll find British artists displayed in both the Tate Modern and the Tate Britain. Check out the Tate Britain Tour chapter for more on the following artists: David Hockney, Stanley Spencer, Jacob Epstein, Gilbert and George, Henry Moore, Francis Bacon, and Barbara Hepworth.

1960s—The Sixties

The decade began united in idealism—young John F. Kennedy pledged to put a man on the moon, newly launched satellites signaled a united world, the Beatles sang exuberantly, peaceful race demonstrations championed equality, and the Vatican II Council preached liberation. By decade's end, there were race riots, assassinations, student protests, and America's floundering war in distant Vietnam. In households around the world, parents screamed, "Turn that down...and get a haircut!"

Culturally, every postwar value was questioned by a rising wealthy and populous baby-boom generation. London—producer of rock-and-roll music, film actors, mod fashions, and Austin Powers' joie de vivre—once again became a world cultural center.

Though government-sponsored public art was dominated by big, abstract canvases and sculptures, other artists pooh-poohed the highbrow seriousness of abstract art. Instead, they mocked lowbrow, popular culture by embracing it in a tongue-in-cheek way (Pop Art), or they attacked authority with absurd performances to make a political statement (conceptual art).

Pop Art: Andy Warhol (1928-1987)

America's postwar wealth made the consumer king. Pop Art is created from the popular objects of that throwaway society—soup cans, car fenders, tacky plastic statues, movie icons. Take a Sears product, hang it in a museum, and you have to ask: Is this art? Are mass-produced objects beautiful? Or crap? Why do we work so hard to acquire them? Pop Art, like Dadaism before it, questions our society's values.

Andy Warhol (who coined "15 minutes of fame") concentrated on another mass-produced phenomenon: celebrities. He took publicity photos of famous people and reproduced them. The repetition—like the constant bombardment we get from recurring images on TV—cheapens even the most beautiful things.

Roy Lichtenstein (1923-1997)

Take a comic strip, blow it up, hang it on a wall, and charge a mil-

lion bucks—wham, Pop Art. Lichtenstein supposedly was inspired by his young son, who challenged him to do something as good as Mickey Mouse. The huge newsprint dots never let us forget that the painting—like all commercial art—is an illusionistic fake. The work's humor comes from portraying a lowbrow subject (comics and ads) on the epic scale of a masterpiece.

Op Art: Bridget Riley (b. 1931)

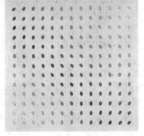

Optical illusions play tricks with your eyes, the way a spiral starts to spin when you stare at it. These obscure scientific experiments in color, line, and optics suddenly became trendy in the psychedelic '60s.

1970s—The "Me Decade"

All forms of authority—"The Establishment"—seemed bankrupt. America's president resigned in the Watergate scandal, corporations were polluting the earth, and capitalism nearly ground to a halt when Arabs withheld oil.

Artists attacked authority and institutions, trying to free individuals to discover their full human potential. Even the concept of "modernism"—that art wasn't good unless it was totally original and progressive—was questioned. No single style could dictate in this postmodern period.

Earth Art
Fearing for the health of earth's ecology, artists rediscovered the beauty of rocks, dirt, trees, even the sound of the wind, using them to create natural art. A rock placed in a museum or urban square is certainly a strange sight.

Joseph Beuys (1921-1986)
The Tate Modern's collection of "sculptures" by Beuys—assemblages of steel, junk, wood, and, especially, felt and animal fat—only hint at his greatest artwork: Beuys himself.

Imagine Beuys ("boyss") walking through the museum, carrying a dead rabbit, while he explains the paintings to it. Or taking off his clothes, shaving his head, and smearing his body with fat.

This charismatic, ex-Luftwaffe art shaman did ridiculous things to inspire others to break with convention and be free. He choreographed "Happenings"—spectacles where people did absurd things while others watched—and pioneered performance art, in which the artist presents himself as the work of art. Beuys inspired a whole generation of artists to walk on stage, cluck like a chicken, and stick a yam up themselves. Beuys will be Beuys.

New Media
Minimalist painting and abstract sculpture were old hat, and there was an explosion of new art forms. Performance art was the most controversial, combining music, theater, dance, poetry, and the visual arts. New technologies brought video, assemblages, installations, artists' books (paintings in book form), and even (gasp!) realistic painting.

Conceptual Art
Increasingly, artists are not creating an original work (painting a canvas or sculpting a stone) but assembling one from premade objects. The *concept* of which object to pair with another to produce maximum effect ("Let's stick a crucifix in a jar of urine," to cite one notorious example) is the key.

1980s—Material Girl
Ronald Reagan in America, Margaret Thatcher in Britain, and corporate executives around the world ruled over a conservative and materialistic society. On the other side were starving Ethiopians, gays with the new disease AIDS, people of color, and women—all demanding power. Intelligent, peaceful, straight white males assumed a low profile.

The art world became big business, with a Van Gogh fetching $54 million. Corporations paid big bucks for large, colorful, semi-abstract canvases. Marketing became an art form. Gender and sexual orientation were popular themes. Many women picked up paintbrushes, creating bright-colored abstract forms hinting at vulva and penis shapes. Visual art fused with popular music, bringing us installations in dance clubs and fast-edit music videos. The crude style of graffiti art demanded to be included in corporate society.

1990s—Multicultural Diversity

The communist-built Berlin Wall was torn down, ending four decades of a global Cold War between capitalism and communism. The new battleground was the "Culture Wars," the struggle to include all races, genders, and lifestyles within an increasingly corporate-dominated, global society.

Artists looked to Third World countries for inspiration and championed society's outsiders against government censorship and economic exclusion. A new medium, the Internet, arose, allowing instantaneous multimedia communication around the world through electronic signals carried by satellites and telephone lines.

2000—?

A new millennium dawned, with Europe and America at a peak of prosperity unmatched in human history....

VICTORIA AND ALBERT MUSEUM TOUR

With one of the biggest, most eclectic collections of objects anywhere, the Victoria and Albert (V&A) has something for everyone. It bills itself as a museum for the decorative arts, and Martha Stewart types will be in hog heaven. You'll see furniture, glassware, clothing, jewelry, and carpets from every corner of the world. Throw in historical artifacts, a few fine-arts masterpieces (painting and sculpture), and a bed that sleeps seven, and you have a museum built for browsing.

The V&A grew out of the Great Exhibition of 1851, that ultimate celebration of the Industrial Revolution. Now "art" could be brought to the masses through modern technology and mass production. The museum was founded on the idealistic Victorian notion that anyone can be continually improved by education and example. After much support from Queen Victoria and Prince Albert, the museum was renamed for the royal couple, and its present building was opened in 1909.

You could spend days in this place. The museum is large and gangly, with 150 rooms and more than 12 miles of corridors. My quick tour gives you a sample of the V&A's range, covering fine art, historical objects, interior design, fashion, and beautiful objects from around the globe. Use this tour to get your bearings, then pick up a museum map and wander at will.

The V&A is in the midst of a 10-year update and expansion. Changes so far include a new café, sculpture gallery, Islamic Art room, and refurbished Medieval and Renaissance galleries. During this chaotic time, exhibits may be rearranged, so check with the information desk for current room closures, carry a copy of the museum's detailed map, and ask a nearby guard if you can't find one of the objects in this tour.

Orientation

Cost: Free (£5 donation requested), sometimes pricey fees for (optional) special exhibits.

Hours: Daily 10:00-17:45, some galleries open Fri until 22:00 (note that Tube tunnel may be closed at this time).

Getting There: The Grand Entrance—where our tour begins—is on Cromwell Road in the South Kensington neighborhood (Tube: South Kensington). You can also reach the Grand Entrance via a tunnel that leads directly from the Tube station to a lower level of the museum (Level 0). Once inside, go upstairs to Level 1, following signs to *Galleries, Information, and Tickets*. You'll pass through a few rooms before emerging at the Grand Entrance lobby.

Information: Pick up the much-needed museum map (£1 suggested donation). The fine £5 *V&A Guide Book* outlines five self-guided, speedy tours. The V&A's helpful website lists its current exhibitions. Tel. 020/7942-2000, www.vam.ac.uk.

Tours: Free one-hour orientation tours leave from the Grand Entrance lobby daily on the half-hour from 10:30 to 15:30. Additional tours and lectures are offered sporadically; check the website for details.

Length of This Tour: Allow 1.5 hours (not counting the British Galleries).

Cloakroom: Free, mandatory for large bags.

Photography: Permitted in most of the gallery without flash or tripod, but not for the Raphael room, the Jewel gallery, special exhibits, and works on loan.

Cuisine Art: The V&A Café offers self-service lunch and tea in the elegant Morris, Gamble, and Poynter rooms (£11 meals, £5 sandwiches and salads). In summer, a self-service café (£5 sandwiches) sets up in the Madejski Garden—grab a bite there or bring a picnic. For a list of recommended eateries in the neighborhood, see page 396.

Starring: A little of everything—and all of it beautiful.

The Tour Begins

• *Start at the Grand Entrance lobby, on Level 1. Look up into the rotunda.*

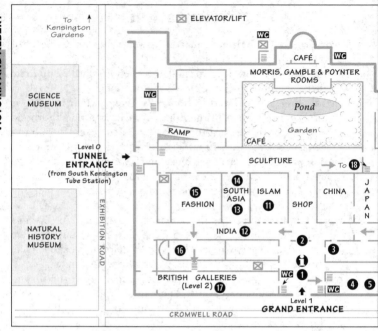

❶ Dale Chihuly Chandelier

This modern chandelier/sculpture by this American glass artist epitomizes the spirit of the V&A's collection—beautiful manu-

factured objects that demonstrate technical skill and innovation, wedding the old with the new, and blurring the line between arts and crafts.

Each blue-and-yellow strand of the chandelier is tied with a wire to a central spine. When the chandelier first went up in 2001, Chihuly said "Too small," had it disassembled, and fired up still more glass bubbles.

Dale Chihuly (b. 1941)—face-famous for the eye-patch he's worn since

a car accident—studied glassmaking in Venice, then set up his own studio/factory in Seattle, making art as the director of a creative team. He makes an old medium seem fresh and modern...and the V&A keeps his chandelier looking fresh with a long feather duster.

• *From the lobby, look up to the balcony and see the pointed arches of the...*

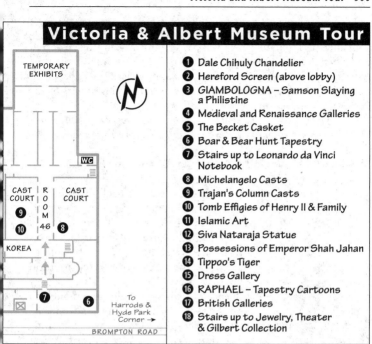

Victoria & Albert Museum Tour

TEMPORARY
EXHIBITS

WC

CAST
COURT
❾

❿

CAST
COURT

R
O
O
M
46

❽

KOREA

❼

❻

To
Harrods &
Hyde Park
Corner →

BROMPTON ROAD

❶ Dale Chihuly Chandelier
❷ Hereford Screen (above lobby)
❸ GIAMBOLOGNA – Samson Slaying
   a Philistine
❹ Medieval and Renaissance Galleries
❺ The Becket Casket
❻ Boar & Bear Hunt Tapestry
❼ Stairs up to Leonardo da Vinci
   Notebook
❽ Michelangelo Casts
❾ Trajan's Column Casts
❿ Tomb Effigies of Henry II & Family
⓫ Islamic Art
⓬ Siva Nataraja Statue
⓭ Possessions of Emperor Shah Jahan
⓮ Tippoo's Tiger
⓯ Dress Gallery
⓰ RAPHAEL – Tapestry Cartoons
⓱ British Galleries
⓲ Stairs up to Jewelry, Theater
   & Gilbert Collection

❷ Hereford Screen (1862)

In the 1800s, just as Britain was steaming into the future on the cutting edge of the Industrial Revolution, the public's taste went

retro. This 35-by-35-foot, eight-ton rood screen (built for the Hereford Cathedral's sacred altar area) looks medieval, but it was created with the most modern materials the Industrial Revolution could produce. The metal parts were not hammered and hand-worked as in olden days, but are made of electroformed copper. The parts were first cast in plaster, then bathed in molten copper with an electric current running through it, leaving a metal skin around the plaster. The entire project—which might have taken years in medieval times—was completed in five months.

George Gilbert Scott (1811-1878), who built the screen, redesigned all of London in the Neo-Gothic style, restoring old churches such as Westminster Abbey, renovating the Houses of Parliament, and building new structures like St. Pancras Station and the Albert Memorial—some 700 buildings in all.

The world turns, and a century later (1960s), the Gothic style was "out" again, modernism was in, and this screen was neglected and ridiculed. Considering that the V&A was originally called the Museum of Manufactures (1857), it's appropriate that the screen was brought here, where it shows off the technical advances of the Industrial Revolution.

• *To the right of the Grand Entrance lobby, look into a large hall of statues (Room 50a), including a spiraling statue of two battling men.*

❸ Samson Slaying a Philistine, by Giambologna (c. 1562)

Carved from a single block of marble, the statue shows the testy

Israelite warrior rearing back, brandishing the jawbone of an ass, preparing to decapitate a man who'd insulted him. Samson pauses to make sure the Philistine looks him in the eye so he can see what's coming. Circle the statue and watch it spiral around its axis. Giambologna was clearly influenced by Michelangelo, who pioneered both the theme of the fallen enemy and the spiral-shaped pose that many artists imitated. The V&A has (arguably) the best collection of Italian Renaissance sculpture outside Italy.

• *From the Grand Entrance lobby (near the main doorway), head down a few steps, into the rooms labeled* Medieval and Renaissance, *300-1500 (on Level 0, Rooms 8-10).*

❹ Medieval and Renaissance Galleries, A.D. 300-1500

Walk through 1,200 years of decorative arts, seeing how the mix of pagan-Roman and medieval-Christian elements created modern Europe.

It's A.D. 300, and Rome's Europe-wide empire is beginning to unravel. Within two centuries, its political dominance would be over, but Rome's culture lived on in the Christian faith. Rooms 8-10 show how traditional Roman media (mosaics, carved ivory, column-and-arch building techniques) were adapted to make Christian-themed art and churches.

• *About three-fourths of the way down the long Room 8 is a glass case displaying the...*

❺ The Becket Casket (c. 1180)

The blue-and-gold box contains the mortal remains (or relics) of St. Thomas Becket, who was brutally murdered. Look at the scene depicted along the side—the Archbishop of Canterbury is about to grab a chalice from the altar, when knights tiptoe up, draw their

swords, and slice off his head. Two shocked priests throw up their hands.

Becket's soul (upper right) is borne aloft on a sling by two angels. His body is laid to rest (upper left) and blessed by the new bishop. Mourners kneel at the tomb, just as the man behind Becket's murder—King Henry II—is said to have done in remorse.

Henry II had handpicked his good friend Thomas Becket (1118-1170) for the job of archbishop, assuming he'd follow the king's orders. In two days, Thomas was made a priest, a bishop, then archbishop—the head of all England's Christians. But when Becket proved loyal to the Church and opposed Henry's policies, the king, in a rash fit of anger, said he wanted Becket dead. Remorseful after his knights murdered the archbishop, Henry had 80 monks whip him, and then he spent all night at the foot of the tomb.

Just three years after his death, Becket was made a saint. Pieces of Becket's DNA—valuable relics—were conserved in this enamel-and-metal work box, a specialty of Limoges, France.

• *Continue to the far end of this long set of rooms. In Room 10a, you'll run right into...*

❻ The Boar and Bear Hunt Tapestry (c. 1425-1430)

Though most medieval art depicted the Madonna and saints, this colorful wool tapestry—woven in Belgium—provides a secular slice of life.

"Read" it from right to left: The nobles want to go hunting, so they hire some professional guides. One pro (in red) enters with his dogs and hunting horn, leading two nobles. His colleague (above) rousts bear cubs from their den, so the mama and papa bears can be flushed out into the open. Men and dogs (in the center) surround a bear, while another is lanced by a nobleman on horseback. Below, well-dressed ladies look on.

Continuing to the left, the hunt turns to wild boar, as two dogs flush one out of hiding. Finally (far left, bottom corner), the boar has been caught, and they begin to skin him for dinner.

In the nearby Room 10c, you'll find a **world map** (c. 1300) showing Christ sitting at the center of the known universe: Jerusalem. Try a little **brass rubbing** at the hands-on station.

• *Backtrack 20 more paces and find the nearby staircase (or use the elevator). Head upstairs two flights to Level 2 to see how the foundation of civilization that was laid in medieval times would launch the Renaissance. You'll spill out into Rooms 62–64b, labeled* Medieval and Renaissance, 1400-1600. *In Room 64, find...*

❼ Notebook by Leonardo da Vinci *(Codex Forster III)*, 1490-1493

Leonardo da Vinci—painter, sculptor, engineer, musician, and scientist—epitomized the merging of art, knowledge, and science we call the Renaissance. He recorded his observations and inventions in tiny notebooks like this. This particular codex (or bound book) dates from years when he was living in Milan, shortly before undertaking his famous *Last Supper* fresco. He was always busy, but completed little from this time.

The book's contents are all over the map. See meticulous sketches of the human head, diagrams illustrating nature's geometrical perfection, a horse's leg for a huge equestrian statue, and even drawings of the latest ballroom fashions. The adjacent computer lets you flip his backwards handwriting to make the secret code legible.

In Room 64a, the *Donatello and the Making of Art* exhibit shows works by the sculptor who blazed the artistic path followed by his fellow Florentine, Michelangelo. This all leads (in room 63) to *A World of Goods—Splendor and Society,* showing the new wealth of Europe as it enters the modern age.

• *Get out your V&A map to find our next destination, in Room 46b. To get there, go back down the stairs one flight to the ground floor (Level 1). Cross the big sculpture hall and find Rooms 46a and 46b, labeled* The Cast Courts. *Start in Room 46b (to the right, may be closed for renovation). It contains replicas of many famous statues, including some...*

❽ Michelangelo Casts

These plaster-cast versions of famous Renaissance statues by Michelangelo and others allowed 19th-century art students who couldn't afford a railpass to go study the classics.

The statues were made by coating the original with a non-stick substance, then laying wet plaster strips over it that dried to form a mold, from which a plaster cast was made. They look solid but are very fragile. In a single glance, you can follow Michelangelo's career, from youthful optimism *(David),* to

his never-finished masterpiece (statues from the tomb of Julius II, including *Moses* and two *Slaves*), to full-blown midlife crisis (while sculpting the brooding Medici Tomb statues of Lorenzo and Giuliano). Compare Michelangelo's monumental *David* with Donatello's girlish *David* (at the other end of the room), and see Ghiberti's bronze Baptistery doors, which inspired the Florentine Renaissance.

David was a gift from Tuscany to Queen Victoria, who immediately donated it to the museum. Circle behind *David* to see the clip-on fig leaf that was hung on him when modest aristocrats visited (this was "the Victorian Age," after all).

• *Across the hall, in Room 46a, you can't miss the two halves of...*

❾ Trajan's Column Casts

Rising 140 feet and decorated with a spiral relief of 2,500 figures trumpeting the exploits of the Roman Emperor Trajan (c. A.D.

100), this is a copy of the world's grandest column from antiquity. The original column still stands in Rome, but the V&A's version was cast from a copy in Paris. In fact, they had to cut it in half to fit it here.

The column's relief unfolds like a scroll, telling the story of Trajan's conquest of Dacia (modern-day Romania). It starts at the bottom (the half with the pedestal) with a trickle of water that becomes a river and soon picks up boats full of supplies. Then come the soldiers themselves, who spill out from the gates of the city. A river god surfaces to bless the journey. Along the way (second band), they build roads and forts to sustain the vast enterprise. Trajan himself (fourth band, in military skirt with toga over his arm) mounts a podium to fire up the troops. They hop into a Roman galley (fifth band) and head off to fight the valiant Dacians in the middle of a forest (eighth band). Finally, at the very top, the Romans hold a sacrifice to give thanks for the victory, while the captured armor is displayed on the pedestal.

Originally, the entire story was painted in bright colors. If you unwound the scroll, it would stretch the length of two football fields—it's far longer than the frieze around the Greek Parthenon.

• *Near Trajan's column, find several casts of knights and ladies on their backs, staring at the ceiling (in faded hues of red, gold, and blue). Some of these are the...*

⓾ Tomb Effigies of Henry II and Family (Plaster cast, French, Fontevrault)

This was a remarkable and dysfunctional royal family. King Henry II (1133-1189)—Becket's murderer—lies alongside his wife and

their children. Henry's wife, Eleanor of Aquitaine (the one reading a book while dead), was the ex-wife of the King of France and was renowned as Europe's most sophisticated lady. The wedding of Henry and Eleanor united their two families' large land holdings, creating an "England" that stretched as far down as southern France. It would eventually take the Hundred Years' War (1336-1453) to sort out the current border between England and France.

As king, Henry placed church courts under secular control, causing the rift that led to Becket's bloody murder. In Henry's old age, his children rebelled, taking arms against him for their slice of the royal pie. Henry's heir, Richard the Lionhearted, famous as the good guy in the Robin Hood legend, was actually an absentee monarch—a French-speaking dandy allied with the King of France. Younger son John, the "evil" King John of the Robin Hood legend, became a tyrant, prompting English nobles to make him sign the document called the Magna Carta, which established the principle that even kings must follow the law. (The British Library has a copy of the Magna Carta—☼ see the British Library Tour chapter.)

• *Backtrack toward the Grand Entrance lobby, heading down the long hallway past Asian art in Rooms 47g, 47f, 47e, etc. Turn right into Room 42, which contains art of the Islamic Middle East.*

⓫ Islamic Art (c. 8th and 9th Centuries)

Rather than making paintings and statues, Islamic artists expressed themselves with beautiful but functional objects.

In the center of the room is the 630-square-foot Ardabil Carpet (1539-1540). Its silk-thread underpinnings are topped by a dense wool pile made of 304 knots per square inch. (Carpet connoisseurs will nod approvingly at this impressively high KPI number.) Woven on a huge standing loom, it likely took a dozen workers years to make. In the center of the design is a yellow medallion ringed with ovals, supporting two hanging lamps. If you sat on the carpet near the smaller of the two lamps, you'd have

The British in India

December 31, 1600—The British East India Company—a multinational trading company owned by stockholders—is founded with a charter from Queen Elizabeth I. They're given a virtual monopoly on trade with India.

1600s—The British trade peacefully with Indian locals on the coast, competing with France, Holland, and Portugal for access to spices, cotton, tea, indigo, and jute (for rope-making).

1700s—As the Mughal (Islamic) Empire breaks down, Britain and France vie for trade ports and inland territory. By the 1750s, Britain is winning. Britain establishes itself in Bombay, Madras, and Calcutta. First they rule through puppet Mughal leaders, then dump local leaders altogether.

1800s—By midcentury, two-thirds of the subcontinent is under British rule, exporting opium and tea (transplanted from its native China) and importing British-made cloth. Britain tries to reform Indian social customs (e.g., outlawing widow suicides) with little long-lasting effect. They build railways, roads, and irrigation systems.

1857-1858—The "Indian Mutiny"—sparked by high taxes, British monopoly of trade, and a chafing against foreign rule—is the first of many uprisings that slowly erode British rule.

1900s—Two world wars drain and distract Britain while Indians lobby for self-rule.

August 15, 1947—After a decade of peaceful protests led by Mahatma Gandhi, India gains its independence.

the illusion of a symmetrical pattern.

Also in the room are more carpets, ceramics (mostly blue-and-white or red-and-white), and glazed tile—all covered top to bottom in similarly complex patterns. The intricate interweaving, repetition, and unending lines suggest the complex, infinite nature of God (Allah).

You'll likely see only a few pictures of humans or animals—the Islamic religion is wary of any "graven images," or idols forbidden by God. However, secular art for homes and palaces was not bound by this, and you may see realistic depictions of men and women enjoying a garden paradise, a symbol of the Muslim heaven.

Notice floral patterns (twining vines, flowers, arabesques) and geometric designs (stars, diamonds). But the most common pattern is calligraphy—elaborate lettering of an inscription in Arabic, the language of the Quran (and the lettering used even in non-Arabic languages). A quote from the Quran on a vase or lamp combines the power of the message with the beauty of the calligraphy.

• *Return to the hall and continue on. In the hallway (technically "Room" 47b) is a glass case with a statue of...*

⓬ Siva Nataraja (12th Century)

Life is a dance.

The Hindu god Siva (SHEE-vah)—one of the hundreds, if not thousands, of godlike incarnations of Hinduism's eternal being, Brahma—steps lively and creates the world by dancing. His four arms are busy creating, and he treads on the sleepy dwarf of ignorance.

This bronze statue, one of Hinduism's most popular, is loaded with symbolism, summing up where humans came from and where we're going. Surrounded by a ring of fire, he crosses a leg in time to the music. Smiling serenely, he blesses with one hand, while another beats out the rhythm of life with a hand drum. The cobra draped over his arm symbolizes the *Kundalini Sakti,* the cosmic energy inside each of us that can, with the right training, uncoil and bring us to enlightenment.

As long as Siva keeps dancing, the universe will continue. But Siva also holds a flame, a reminder that, at the end of time, he will transform into his female alter ego, Kali, and destroy the world by fire, clearing the slate for another round of existence.

• *Head through the doorway into the adjoining Room 41 (labeled* South Asia*). You'll run right into a glass case in the center of the room containing small items that were the...*

⓭ Possessions of Emperor Shah Jahan (r. 1628-1658)

Look at the cameo portrait, thumb ring, and wine cup (made of white nephrite jade, 1657) that belonged to one of the world's most powerful men.

Shah Jahan—or "King of the World"—ruled the largest empire of the day, covering northern India, Pakistan, and Afghanistan. His

Mughal Empire was descended from Genghis Khan and the Mongol horde, who conquered and then settled in central Asia and converted to Islam.

Shah Jahan was known for his building projects, especially the Taj Mahal (see a picture of it nearby), built as a mausoleum for his favorite wife, Mumtaz, who bore him 14 children before dying in childbirth.

His unsuccessful attempts to expand the empire drained the treasury. In his old age, his sons quarreled over the inheritance. Imprisoned by his sons in the Agra fort, Shah Jahan died gazing across the river at the Taj Mahal, where he, too, would be buried. India's glory days were ending.

Then came the British.

• *At the far end of Room 41 is the huge wood-carved...*

⑭ Tippoo's Tiger (1790s)

This life-size robotic toy, once owned by an oppressed Indian sultan (see Tipu's portrait and belongings nearby), is perhaps better  called "India's revenge." The Bengal tiger has a British redcoat down, sinking its teeth into his neck. When you turned the crank, the Brit's left arm would flail, and both he and the tiger would roar through organ pipes. (The mechanism still works.)

Tipu, the Sultan of Mysore (1750-1799), called himself "The Tiger of Mysore." He was well educated in several languages and collected a library of 2,000 books. An enlightened ruler, he built roads and dams and promoted new technology. Tipu could see that India was being swallowed up by the all-powerful British East India Company. He allied himself with France and fought several successful wars against the British, but he was eventually defeated and forced to give up half his kingdom to them. Tipu was later killed by the Brits in battle (1799), his palace ransacked, and his possessions—including this toy—were taken, like much of India, by the British East India Company.

• *Backtrack out of Room 41 and turn right, then right again into Room 40. Here you'll find the...*

⑮ Dress Gallery

Nearly 400 years of English fashion are corseted into 40 display cases. The cases around the perimeter show the evolution of a particular article of clothing. You'll see ladies' underwear through the ages, formal wear, men's suits, and so on. The inner ring of displays contains designer dresses, and the four freestanding cases in the corners have wedding dresses. Temporary exhibits here usually enliven the displays. For more on old English fashion, visit the British Galleries (described below).

• *Directly across the hall from Room 40 is Room 48a, filled with...*

⑯ Raphael's Tapestry Cartoons

For Christmas in 1519, Pope Leo X unveiled 10 new tapestries in the Sistine Chapel, designed by the famous artist Raphael. The project was one of the largest ever undertaken by a painter—it cost far more than Michelangelo's Sistine ceiling—and when it was done, the tapestries were a hit, inspiring princes across Europe to decorate their palaces in masterpieces of cloth.

The V&A owns seven of the full-size designs by Raphael that were used to produce the tapestries (approximately 13 feet by 17 feet, done in tempera on paper, now mounted on canvas). The cartoons were sent to factories in Brussels, cut into strips (see the lines), and placed on the looms. The scenes are the reverse of the final product—lots of left-handed saints.

Raphael (1483-1520) chose scenes from the Acts of the Apostles—particularly of Peter and Paul, the two early saints most associated with Rome, the seat of the popes. Knowing where the tapestries were to be hung, Raphael was determined to top Michelangelo's famous Sistine ceiling, with its huge, dramatic figures and subtle color effects. He matched Michelangelo's body-builder muscles (e.g., the fishermen in *The Miraculous Draught of Fishes*), dramatic gestures, and reaction shots (e.g., the busy crowd scenes in *St. Paul Preaching in Athens*), and he exceeded Michelangelo in the subtleties of color.

Unfortunately, it was difficult to reproduce Raphael's painted nuances in the tapestry workshop. Traditional tapestries were simple, depicting either set patterns or block figures on a neutral background. Raphael challenged the Flemish weavers. Each brushstroke had to be reproduced by a colored thread woven horizontally. The finished tapestries (which are still in the Vatican) were glorious, but these cartoons capture Raphael's original vision.

• In the Raphael Room (48a), a staircase leads up. At the top of the stairs (on Level 2), turn left into Room 57. This is the heart of the British Galleries, featuring the Great Bed of Ware and Elizabethan miniatures.

⑰ British Galleries

Room 57 covers the era of Queen Elizabeth I. Find rare miniature portraits—a popular item of the day—including Hilliard's oft-reproduced *Young Man Among Roses* miniature, capturing the romance of a Shakespeare sonnet. Also in the room are musical instruments and suits of armor— a love-and-war combination appropriate to the Elizabethan Age. Finally, there's the Great Bed of Ware. Built as a tourist-attracting gimmick by an English inn around 1600, this four-poster bed still wows. You and six of your favorite friends could bed down here, taking a well-earned rest after this eclectic tour.

Continue into the next room (Room 58), dedicated to *Birth, Marriage and Death,* and displaying swaddling clothes, a wedding portrait, and a

casket pall. Continuing on, you'll pass through a couple of alcoves with Tudor-era tapestries. The far end of Room 58, devoted to Henry VIII, has a portrait of him; his writing box (with quill pens, ink, and sealing wax); and a whole roomful of fancy furniture, tapestries, jewelry, and dinnerware that may have decorated his palaces.

If you're interested, there's much more to the British Galleries, which sweep chronologically through 400 years of British high-class living (1500-1900)—all laid out over two floors and beautifully described.

• For now, pop out the doorway of Room 58. You'll notice we've come full circle: You're overlooking the Grand Entrance lobby. This tour is officially over. But if you'd like more suggestions, there's great stuff upstairs.

⑱ Upstairs to Level 3

• From the Grand Entrance lobby, pass through the shop, turn right into Room 24, and climb the staircase to Level 3.

Jewelry (Rooms 90-93): This collection is understandably popular. In one long glittering gallery, you can trace the evolution of jewelry from ancient Egyptian, Greek, and Roman to the 20th century. The Art Nouveau style of Parisian jeweler Rene Lalique is hard not to love.

• *Exit the jewelry rooms at the far end and turn right to find...*

Theater and Performance (Rooms 103-106): With artifacts from Hamlet skulls to rock-and-roll tour posters, this exhibit records the history of live perfor-

mance in the UK. Kids will enjoy the dress-up costume box. Nearby, aging boomers will see Mick Jagger's jumpsuit...and marvel that he used to fit into it.

• *Exit the collection where you entered, turn right (into "Prints and Drawings"), then left, pass through the lo-o-o-ong Silver Collection (Rooms 65-69), and enter...*

Gold, Silver, and Mosaics (Rooms 70-73): The exquisite Gilbert Collection features treasures so tiny you'd need magnifying glasses to fully appreciate them (fortunately, they're available—look around).

The supreme luxury of the 18th century was a jeweled snuff box. Bewigged gentlemen used them to carry tobacco powder, which they pinched and snorted for a stimulating jolt. Ladies used them as candy tins. These extravagant little cases were the ultimate gifts between kings, nobles, and art lovers, who were enamored with their tiny scale. With 200 such boxes, this is the finest collection in existence. Frederick the Great's snuff boxes (from the mid-1700s) are particularly dazzling.

Among the snuff boxes are the Gilbert Collection's micromosaics. Artists pieced together literally thousands of teeny-tiny pieces of glass and precious stones to create a dog, a bird, a cupid. These eye-boggling works of art were popular souvenirs for 18th- and 19th-century aristocratic tourists on the Grand European Tour.

• *I'll leave you here (find exit stairs at the far right end of Room 74), but there's plenty left to see. If you have stamina, use your V&A map to plot the rest of your Grand Tour of this museum.*

TATE BRITAIN TOUR

The "National Gallery of British Art" (a.k.a. the Tate Britain) features the world's best collection of British art—sweeping you from 1500 until today. This is people's art, with realistic paintings rooted in the people, landscape, and stories of the British Isles. Its walls contain Hogarth's stage sets, Gainsborough's ladies, Blake's angels, Constable's clouds, Turner's tempests, the swooning realism of the Pre-Raphaelites, and the camera-eye portraits of Hockney and Freud. Even if these names are new to you, don't worry. You'll likely see a few "famous" works you didn't know were British and exit the Tate Britain with at least one new favorite artist.

Renovation in 2012: While renovation work on the main entrance, rotunda, and several galleries is underway, much of the permanent collection has been stored. Fortunately, a few paintings are on display in a single room, labeled "Key Works from the Historic Collection." Find it about halfway down the main hallway, on the left.

Orientation

Cost: Free (£3 donation requested), but optional temporary exhibits require separate admission.

Hours: Daily 10:00-18:00, first Fri of each month until 22:00, last entry to special exhibitions at 17:15 (or 21:00 when open late).

Getting There: It's on the Thames River, south of Big Ben and north of Vauxhall Bridge. The museum has two entrances: the main entrance on Millbank, facing the Thames, and the newer Manton entrance on Atterbury Street (wheelchair-accessible).

You can reach the museum by Tube, ferry, bus, or on foot:

By Tube: Take the Tube to Pimlico, then walk seven minutes.

By Ferry: Hop on Thames Clippers' "Tate to Tate" ferry from the Tate Modern (£5.50 one-way, £12.60 day ticket, 33 percent discount with a Travelcard, buy ticket on board, departs every 40 minutes from 10:00 to 17:00, 18 minutes, www.tate.org.uk/tatetotate).

By Bus: Take bus #87 (leaves from National Gallery, drops off in front of museum) or bus #88 (leaves from Oxford Circus, drops off behind museum).

On Foot: Walk 25 minutes south along the Thames from Big Ben.

Information: Pick up a £1 map at the information desk. The museum's two bookstores are great for cultural information and trinkets. Switchboard tel. 020/7887-8888, recorded info tel. 020/7887-8008, www.tate.org.uk.

Tours: Free tours are offered Mon-Fri at 11:00 (art from 1500 to 1800), 12:00 (art from 1800 to 1900), 14:00 (Turner), and 15:00 (art from the 20th century). Weekend tours cover the collection's highlights (Sat-Sun 12:00 and 15:00); call to confirm schedule. The £3.50 audioguide, with photos and video clips, is useful (covered by London Pass). The museum also hosts games, activities, and art projects for children (Sat-Sun 11:00-17:00 plus other times as scheduled).

Length of This Tour: Allow one hour.

Cloakroom: Bag and coat check are free (£2 suggested donation).

Photography: Photos are not allowed, unless you've requested permission at least a week in advance.

Cuisine Art: Your options are a café with an affordable gourmet buffet line (£5 sandwiches or salads) or a pricey-but-delightful restaurant (£7 small plates; lunch daily 11:30-15:00, afternoon tea daily 15:15-17:00).

Starring: Hogarth, Gainsborough, Reynolds, Blake, Constable, Pre-Raphaelites, and Turner.

Orien-Tate: Gallery in Motion

While the huge renovation project is on, it's hard to predict which of the Tate Britain's large collection of paintings will be on display, or where you might find them. I've designed this tour as a roughly chronological walk through British paintings from 1500 to 1901 (normally found in the west half of the building), the works of J. M. W. Turner in the Clore Gallery (still there and intact), and British paintings from the 20th century (normally in the east half). Ask at the front desk for the latest—if the current configuration bears no resemblance to this order, it may be easiest to head to the café, give your feet a rest, and read this chapter over a cup of tea—then go enjoy what's currently on display in whatever order you find it. Temporary exhibitions (usually requiring an entrance fee) are likely to be in the east wing and in the basement.

Note: There are two separate Tate museums in London. The Tate Britain, which this chapter describes, features British art. The Tate Modern (at Bankside, on the South Bank of the Thames across from St. Paul's Cathedral) features modern art (✪ see the Tate Modern Tour chapter).

The Tour Begins

British artists painted people, countrysides, and scenes from daily life, realistically and without the artist passing judgment (substance over style). What you won't see here are the fleshy goddesses, naked baby angels, and Madonna-and-child altarpieces so popular elsewhere in Europe. The largely Protestant English abhorred the "graven images" of the wealthy Catholic world; many such images were destroyed during the 16th-century Reformation. They preferred portraits of flesh-and-blood English folk.

1500-1700—Portraits of Lord and Lady Whoevertheyare

Stuffy portraits of a beef-fed society try to turn crude country nobles into refined men and delicate women. Men in ruffled collars clutch symbols of power. Women in ruffled collars, puffy sleeves, and elaborately patterned dresses display their lily-white complexions, turning their pinkies out.

English country houses often had a long hall built specially to hang family portraits. You could stroll along and see your noble forebears looking down their noses at you. Britain's upper crust had little interest in art other than as a record of themselves along with their possessions—their wives, children, jewels, furs, ruffled collars, swords, and guns.

You'll see plenty more portraits in the Tate Britain, right up to modern times. Each era had its own style. Portraits from the 1500s are stern and dignified. The 1600s brought a more relaxed and elegant style and more décolletage.

1700s—Art Blossoms

With peace at home (under three King Georges), a strong overseas economy, and a growing urban center in London, England's artistic life began to bloom. As the English grew more sophisticated, so

TATE BRITAIN

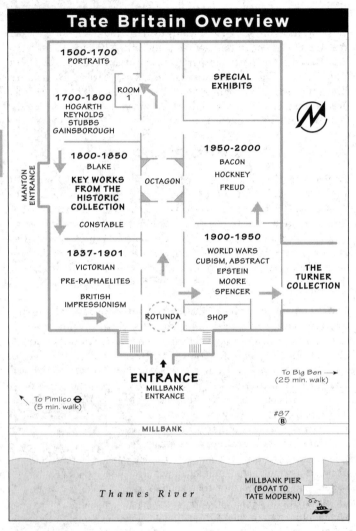

Tate Britain Overview

1500-1700
PORTRAITS

ROOM 1

1700-1800
HOGARTH
REYNOLDS
STUBBS
GAINSBOROUGH

SPECIAL EXHIBITS

1800-1850
BLAKE

KEY WORKS FROM THE HISTORIC COLLECTION

CONSTABLE

MANTON ENTRANCE

OCTAGON

1950-2000
BACON
HOCKNEY
FREUD

1837-1901
VICTORIAN

PRE-RAPHAELITES

BRITISH IMPRESSIONISM

ROTUNDA

1900-1950
WORLD WARS
CUBISM, ABSTRACT
EPSTEIN
MOORE
SPENCER

SHOP

THE TURNER COLLECTION

ENTRANCE
MILLBANK ENTRANCE

To Pimlico ⊖
(5 min. walk)

To Big Ben →
(25 min. walk)

#87
Ⓑ

MILLBANK

Thames River

MILLBANK PIER
(BOAT TO TATE MODERN)

did their portraits. Painters branched out into other subjects, capturing slices of everyday life. The Royal Academy added a veneer of classical Greece to even the simplest subjects.

William Hogarth (1697-1764)

Hogarth loved the theater. "My picture is my stage," he said, "and my men and women my players." The curtain goes up, and we see one scene that tells a whole story, often satirizing English high society. The London theater scene came into its own (after post-Shakespeare censorship) during Hogarth's generation. He often

painted series based on popular plays of the time.

A born Londoner, Hogarth loved every gritty aspect of the big city. You'd find him in seedy pubs and brothels, at the half-price ticket booth in Leicester Square, at prize-fights, cockfights, duels, and public executions—all with sketchbook in hand. An 18th-century Charles Dickens, he exposed the hypocrisy of fat-bellied squires, vain ladies, and gluttonous priests. He also gave the upper classes a glimpse into the hidden poverty of "merry olde England"—poor soldiers with holes in their stockings, overworked servants, and unwed mothers.

Hogarth's portraits (and self-portraits) are unflinchingly honest, quite different from the powdered-wig fantasies of his contemporaries. Hogarth was an accomplished engraver; his works were mass-produced, giving Londoners a sense of their city and themselves.

Sir Joshua Reynolds and the "Grand Manner" (1723-1792)

Real life wasn't worthy of a painting. So said Sir Joshua Reynolds, the pillar of Britain's Royal Academy. Instead, people, places, and things had to be gussied up with Greek columns, symbolism, and great historic moments, ideally from classical Greece.

In his portraits, he'd pose Lady Bagbody like the Medici Venus, or Lord Milquetoast like Apollo Belvedere. In landscapes you get Versailles-type settings of classical monuments amid perfectly manicured greenery. Inspired by Rembrandt, Reynolds sometimes used dense, clotted paint to capture the look of the Old Masters.

This art was meant to elevate the viewer, to appeal to his rational nature and fill him with noble sentiment. Sir Joshua Reynolds, the pillar of England's art establishment, stood for all that was upright, tasteful, rational, brave, clean, reverent, and...zzzzzzz....

George Stubbs—Horses (1724-1806)

Stubbs was the Michelangelo of horse painters. He understood these creatures from the inside out, having dissected them in his studio. He even used machinery to prop the corpses up into lifelike poses. He painted the horses first on a blank canvas, then filled in the background landscape around them (notice the heavy outlines that make them stand out clearly from the countryside). The result is both incredibly natural—from the veins in their noses to their freshly brushed coats—and geometrically posed.

Thomas Gainsborough (1727-1788)

Gainsborough showcased the elegant, educated women of his generation. He portrayed them as they wished to see themselves: a

feminine ideal, patterned after fashion magazines. The cheeks are rosy, the poses relaxed and S-shaped, the colors brighter and more pastel, showing the influence of the refined French culture of the court at Versailles. His ladies tiptoe gracefully toward us, with clear, Ivory-soap complexions that stand out from the swirling greenery of English gardens. (Though he painted portraits, he longed to do landscapes.) Gainsborough worked hard to prettify his subjects, but the results were always natural and never stuffy.

1800-1850—The Industrial Revolution

Newfangled inventions were everywhere. Railroads laced the land. You could fall asleep in Edinburgh and wake up in London, a trip that used to take days or weeks. But along with technology came factories coating towns with soot, urban poverty, regimentation, and clock-punching. Machines replaced honest laborers, and once-noble Man was viewed as a naked ape.

Strangely, you'll see little of the modern world in paintings of the time—except in reaction to it. Many artists rebelled against "progress" and the modern world. They escaped the dirty cities to commune with nature (Constable and the Romantics). Or they found a new spirituality in intense human emotions (dramatic scenes from history or literature). Or they left the modern world altogether.

William Blake (1757-1827)

At the age of four, Blake saw the face of God. A few years later, he ran across a flock of angels swinging in a tree. Twenty years later, he was living in a run-down London flat with an illiterate wife, scratching out a thin existence as an engraver. But even in this squalor, ignored by all but a few fellow artists, he still had his heavenly visions, and he described them in poems, paintings, drawings, and prints.

One of the original space cowboys, Blake also was a unique artist, often classed with the Romantics because he painted in a fit of ecstatic inspiration rather than by studied technique. He painted angels, not the dull material world. While Britain was conquering the world with guns and nature with machines, and while his fellow Londoners were growing rich, fat, and self-important, Blake turned his gaze inward, illustrating the glorious visions of the soul.

Blake's work hangs in a darkened room to protect his watercolors from deterioration. Enter his mysterious world and let your pupils dilate opium-wide.

His pen and watercolor sketches glow with an unearthly aura. In visions of the Christian heaven or Dante's hell, his figures have superhero musculature. The colors are almost translucent.

Blake saw the material world as bad, trapping the divine spark inside each of our bodies and keeping us from true communion with God. Blake's prints illustrate his views on the ultimate weakness of material, scientific man. Despite their Greek-god anatomy, his men look noble but tragically lost.

A famous poet as well as painter, Blake summed up his distrust of the material world in a poem addressed to "The God of this World"—that is, Satan:

> *Tho' thou art Worship'd by the Names Divine*
> *Of Jesus and Jehovah, thou art still*
> *The Son of Morn in weary Night's decline,*
> *The lost Traveller's Dream under the Hill.*

"Romantic" Landscapes—Art and the Sublime

Artists in the Romantic style saw the most intense human emotions reflected in the drama and mystery of nature. Some of them mixed landscapes with intense human emotion to produce huge, colorful canvases depicting storms, burning sunsets, towering clouds, and crashing waves, all dwarfing puny humans.

History paintings reflected great moments from the past, from ancient Greece to medieval knights,

Napoleon to Britain's battles abroad. These were seen as the classiest form of art, combining the high drama of heroic acts with refined technique.

Other artists made supernatural, religious fantasy-scapes. God is found within nature, and nature is charged with the grandeur and power of God.

John Constable (1776-1837)

Constable brought painting back into the real world. Although the Royal Academy thought Nature needed makeup, Constable

thought she was just fine. He painted the English landscape as it was—realistically, without idealizing it. With simple earth tones he caught leafy green trees, gathering gray skies, brown country lanes, and rivers the color of the clouds reflected in them. Many details came from actual landscapes and villages from his childhood roots in Suffolk.

Clouds are Constable's trademark. Appreciate the effort involved in sketching ever-changing cloud patterns for hours on end—the mix of dark clouds and white clouds, cumulus and stratus, the colors of sunset. A generation before the Impressionists, he actually set up his easel outdoors and painted on the spot, a painstaking process before the invention of ready-made paints-in-a-tube (about 1850).

It's rare to find a Constable (or any British) landscape that doesn't have the mark of man in it—a cottage, hay cart, field hand, or a country road running through the scene. For him, the English countryside and its people were one.

In his later years, Constable's canvases became bigger, the style more "Impressionistic" (messier brushwork), and he worked more from memory than observation.

Constable's commitment to unvarnished nature wasn't fully recognized in his lifetime, and he was forced to paint portraits for his keep. The neglect caused him to ask a friend, "Can it therefore be wondered at that I paint continual storms?"

1837-1901—The Victorian Era

In the world's wealthiest nation, the prosperous middle class dictated taste in art. They admired paintings that were realistic (showcasing the artist's talent and work ethic), depicting Norman Rockwell-style slices of everyday life.

We see families and ordinary people eating, working, and

relaxing. Some paintings tug at the heartstrings, with scenes of parting couples, the grief of death, or the joy of families reuniting. Dramatic scenes from classical (Chaucer and Shakespeare) and popular literature get the heart beating. There's the occasional touching look at the plight of the honest poor, reminiscent of Dickens. Many paintings warn us to be good little boys and girls by showing the consequences of a life of sin. And then there are the puppy dogs with sad eyes.

Pre-Raphaelites: Millais, Rossetti, Holman Hunt, Waterhouse, Burne-Jones, etc.

You'll see medieval damsels in dresses and knights in tights, legendary lovers from poetry, and even a very human Virgin Mary as a delicate young woman. The women wear flowing dresses and have long, wavy hair and delicate, elongated, curving bodies. Beautiful.

Overdosed with the gushy sentimentality of their day, a band of 20-year-old artists said "Enough!" and dedicated themselves to creating less saccharine art. Their "Pre-Raphaelite Brotherhood" (you may see the initials P. R. B. by the artist's signature) returned to a style "pre-Raphael"—that is, "medieval" in its simple style, in its melancholy mood, and often in its subject matter.

"Truth to Nature" was their slogan. Like the Impressionists who followed them, they donned their scarves, barged out of the stuffy studio, and set up outdoors, painting trees, streams, and people, like scientists on a field trip. Still, they often captured nature with such a close-up clarity that it's downright unnatural.

And despite the Pre-Raphaelite claim to paint life just as it is, this is so beautiful it hurts.

This is art from the cult of femininity, worshipping Woman's haunting beauty, compassion, and depth of soul (proto-feminism or nouveau-chauvinism?). The artists' wives and lovers were their models and muses, and the art echoed their love lives. The people are surrounded by nature at its most beautiful, with every detail painted crystal clear. Even without the people, there is a mood of melancholy.

The Pre-Raphaelites hated overacting. Their subjects—even

in the face of great tragedy, high passions, and moral dilemmas—barely raise an eyebrow. Outwardly, they're reflective, accepting their fate. But sinuous postures—with lovers swooning into each other, and parting lovers swooning apart—speak volumes. These volumes are footnoted by the small objects with symbolic importance placed around them: red flowers denoting passion, lilies for purity, pets for fidelity, and so on.

The colors—greens, blues, and reds—are bright and clear, with everything evenly lit, so that we see every detail. To get the lumi-

nous color, some painted a thin layer of bright paint over a pure white, still-wet undercoat, which subtly "shines" through. These canvases radiate a pure spirituality, like stained-glass windows.

Stand for a while and enjoy the exquisite realism and human emotions of these Victorian-era works...flesh-and-blood people painted realistically. Get your fill, because beloved Queen Victoria is about to check out, the modern world is coming, and, with it, new art to express modern attitudes.

British Impressionism

Realistic British art stood apart from the modernist trends in France, but some influences drifted across the Channel. John

Singer Sargent (American-born) studied with Parisian Impressionists, learning the thick, messy brushwork and play of light at twilight. James Tissot used Degas' snapshot technique to capture a crowded scene from an odd angle. And James McNeill Whistler (born in America, trained in Paris, lived in London) composed his paintings like music—see some of his paintings' titles. These collages of shapes and colors please the eye like a song tickles the ear. Whistler signed his paintings with his initials in the shape of a butterfly. You may also see sophisticated works by London's own "Bloomsbury Group," who put a British spin on French Post-Impressionism.

• *Before moving on to 20th-century art, first visit the Turner Collection. Pass through the rotunda to the east side of the gallery (near the bookshop) and just keep going through a few rooms (Rooms 19-20) till you enter The Clore Gallery/The Turner Collection.*

The Turner Collection—
J. M. W. Turner (1775-1851)

The Tate Britain has the world's best collection of Turners. Walking through his life's work, you can trace his progression from a painter of realistic historical scenes, through his wandering years, to Impressionist paintings of color-and-light patterns.

• *Start a few rooms into the collection, in Room T-7. This room and the adjoining rooms often contain biographical info on Turner, some of his early works, or displays of his notebooks, paints, and brushes. From Room T-7, explore the rest of the collection, watching Turner's style evolve from clear-eyed realism to hazy proto-Impressionism. You'll also see how Turner dabbled in different subjects: landscapes, seascapes, Roman ruins, snapshots of Venice, and so on.*

Self-Portrait as a Young Man

At 24, Turner has just been elected the youngest Associate of the Royal Academy. The son of a Covent Garden barber now dresses like a gentleman. His clear, realistic painting style caught the public's fancy. The full-frontal pose and intense gaze of this portrait show a young man ready to take on the world.

The Royal Academy Years

Trained in the Reynolds school of grandiose epics, Turner painted the obligatory big canvases of great moments in history—*The Destruction of Sodom, Hannibal and His Army Crossing the Alps, The Lost ATM Card, Jason and the Argonauts,* and various shipwrecks. Not content to crank them out in the traditional staid manner, he sets them in expansive landscapes. Nature's stormy mood mirrors the human events, but is so grandiose it dwarfs them.

This is a theme we'll see throughout his works: The forces of nature—the burning sun, swirling clouds, churning waves, gathering storms, and the weathering of time—overwhelm men and wear down the civilizations they build.

Travels with Turner

Turner's true love was nature—he was a born hobo. Oblivious to the wealth and fame that his early paintings gave him, he set out traveling—mostly on foot—throughout England and the Continent, with a rucksack full of sketch pads and painting gear. He sketched the English countryside—not green, leafy, and placid as so many others had done, but churning in motion, hazed over by a burning sunset.

He found the "sublime" not in the studio or in church, but in the overwhelming power of nature. The landscapes throb with life and motion. He sets Constable's clouds on fire.

Italy's Landscape and Ruins

With a Rick Steves guidebook in hand, Turner visited the great museums of Italy, drawing inspiration from the Renaissance masters. He painted the classical monuments and Renaissance architecture. He copied masterpieces, admired the works of the French classicist Claude Lorrain, and fused a great variety of styles—a true pan-European vision. Turner's Roman ruins are not grand; they're dwarfed by the landscape around them and eroded by swirling, misty, luminous clouds.

Stand close to a big canvas of Roman ruins, close enough so that it fills your whole field of vision. Notice how the buildings seem to wrap around you. Turner was a master of using multiple perspectives to draw the viewer in. On the one hand, you're right in the thick of things, looking "up" at the tall buildings. Then again, you're looking "down" on the distant horizon, as though standing on a mountaintop.

Venice

I know what color the palazzo is. But what color is it at sunset? Or through the filter of the watery haze that hangs over Venice? Can I paint the glowing haze itself? Maybe if I combine two different colors and smudge the paint on....

Venice stoked Turner's lust for reflected, golden sunlight. You'll see both finished works and unfinished sketches...uh, which is which?

Seascapes

The ever-changing sea was his specialty, with waves, clouds, mist, and sky churning and mixing together, all driven by the same forces.

Turner used oils like many painters use watercolors. First, he'd lay down a background (a "wash") of large patches of color, then he'd add a few dabs of paint to suggest a figure. (Some artists might use pencil lines to sketch out their figures, but Turner avoided that.) The final product lacked photographic clarity, but showed the power and constant change in the forces of nature. He was perhaps the most prolific painter ever, with some 2,000 finished paintings and 20,000 sketches and watercolors.

Late Works

The older Turner got, the messier both he and his paintings became. He was wealthy, but he died in a run-down dive, where  he'd set up house with a prostitute. Yet the colors are brighter and the subjects less pessimistic than in the dark and brooding early canvases. His last works—whether landscape, religious, or classical scenes—are a blur and swirl of colors in motion, lit by the sun or a lamp burning through the mist. Even Turner's own creations were finally dissolved by the swirling forces of nature.

These paintings are "modern" in that the subject is less important than the style. You'll have to read the title to "get" it. You could argue that an Englishman helped invent Impressionism a generation before Monet and his ilk boxed the artistic ears of Paris in the 1880s. Turner's messy use of paint to portray reflected light "Chunneled" its way to France to inspire the Impressionists.

• *Now, back to where we left off: the beginning of the 20th century.*

1900-1950—World Wars

As two world wars whittled down the powerful British Empire, it still remained a major cultural force.

British art mirrored many of the trends and "-isms" pioneered in Paris. You'll see Cubism like Picasso's, abstract art like Mondrian's, and so on. But British artists also continued the British tradition of realistic paintings of people and landscapes. (Note: You'll find 20th-century artists' work both here in the Tate Britain and in the Tate Modern—◎ see also the Tate Modern Tour chapter.)

World War I, in which Britain lost a million men, cast a long shadow over the land. Artists expressed the horror of war, particularly of dehumanizing battles pitting powerful machines against puny human pawns. Jacob Epstein's (1880-1959) gleaming, abstract statues suggest mangled half-human/half-machine forms.

Henry Moore (1898-1986)

Twice a week, young Henry Moore went to the British Museum to sketch ancient statues, especially reclining ones (as in the Parthenon pediment or the Mayan god, Chac Mool, which he saw in a photo). His statues—mostly female, mostly reclining—catch the primitive power of carved stone. Moore almost always carved with his own hands (unlike, say, Rodin, who modeled a small clay figure and let assistants chisel the real thing), capturing the human body in a few simple curves, with minimal changes to the rock itself.

The statues do look vaguely like what their titles say, but it's the stones themselves that are really interesting. Notice the texture and graininess of these mini-Stonehenges; feel the weight, the space they take up, and how the rock forms intermingle.

During World War II, Moore passed time in the bomb shelters sketching mothers with babes in arms, a theme found in later works.

Moore carves the human body with the epic scale and restless poses of Michelangelo but with the crude rocks and simple lines of the primitives.

Stanley Spencer (1891-1959)

Spencer paints unromanticized landscapes, portraits, and hometown scenes. Even the miraculous *Resurrection of the Dead* is portrayed absolutely literally, with the dead climbing out of their Glasgow graves. In fully modern times, Spencer carried on the British tradition of sober realism.

Francis Bacon (1909-1992)

With a stiff upper lip, Britain survived the Blitz, World War II, and the loss of hundreds of thousands of men—but at war's end, the bottled-up horror came rushing out. Bacon's 1945 exhibition, opening just after Holocaust details began surfacing, stunned London with its unmitigated ugliness.

His deformed half-humans/half-animals—caged in a claustrophobic room, with twisted hunk-of-meat bodies and quadriplegic, smudged-mouth helplessness—can do nothing but scream in anguish and frustration. The scream becomes a blur, as though it goes on forever.

Bacon, largely self-taught, uses "traditional" figurativism, painting somewhat recognizable people and things. His subjects

express the existential human predicament of being caught in a world not of your making, isolated and helpless to change it.

1950-2000—Modern World

No longer a world power, Britain in the Swinging '60s became a major exporter of pop culture. British art's traditional strengths—realism, portraits, landscapes, and slice-of-life scenes—were redone in the modern style.

David Hockney (b. 1937)

The "British Andy Warhol"—who is bleach-blonde, horn-rimmed, gay, and famous—paints "pop"-ular culture with photographic realism. Large, airy canvases of L.A. swimming pools, double

portraits of his friends in their stylish homes, or mundane scenes from the artist's own life capture the superficial materialism of the 1970s and 1980s. (Is he satirizing or glorifying it by painting it on a monumental scale with painstaking detail?)

Hockney saturates the canvas with bright (acrylic) paint, eliminating any haze, making distant objects as clear and bright as close ones. This technique, combined with his slightly simplified "cutout" figures, gives the painting the flat look of a billboard.

Lucian Freud (b. 1922)

Sigmund's grandson (who emigrated from Nazi Germany as a boy) puts every detail on the couch for analysis, then reassembles them into works that are still surprisingly realistic. His subjects

look you right in the eye, slightly on edge. Even the plants create an ominous mood. Everything is in sharp focus (unlike in real life, where you concentrate on one thing while your peripheral vision is blurred). Thick brushwork is especially good at capturing the pallor of British flesh.

In the great tradition of British portrait painting, Freud recently did an unflinching (and controversial) portrait of Queen Elizabeth.

Bridget Riley (b. 1931)

The pioneer of Op Art paints patterns of lines and alternating colors that make the eye vibrate (the way a spiral will "spin") when you stare at them. These obscure, scientific experiments in human optics suddenly became trendy in the psychedelic, cannabis-fueled 1960s. Like, wow.

Barbara Hepworth (1903-1975)

Hepworth's small-scale carvings in stone and wood—like "mini-Moores"—make even holes look interesting. Though they're not exactly realistic, it isn't hard to imagine them being inspired by, say, a man embracing a woman (she called it "sex harmony"), or the shoreline encircling a bay near her Cornwall-coast home, or a cliff penetrated by a cave—that is, two forms intermingling.

Gilbert (b. 1943) and George (b. 1942)

The Siegfried and Roy of art satirize the "Me Generation" and its shameless self-marketing by portraying their nerdy, three-piece-suited selves on the monumental scale normally dedicated to kings, popes, and saints.

The Rest of the Museum

We've covered 500 years, with social satire from Hogarth to Hockney, from Constable's placid landscapes to Turner's churning scenes, from Blake's inner visions to Pre-Raphaelite fantasies, from realistic portraits to...realistic portraits.

But the Tate's great strength is championing contemporary British art in special exhibitions. There are two exhibition spaces: one in the northeast corner of the main floor, and another downstairs (each usually requiring separate admission). Explore the cutting-edge art from one of the world's thriving cultural capitals: London.

Enough Tate? Great. It's late.

THE DOCKLANDS WALK

Survey London's skyline (or a Tube map), and it becomes clear that London is shifting east. The thundering heart of this new London is the Docklands. Nestled around a hairpin bend in the Thames, this area was London's harbor and warehouse district back in the 19th century, when Britannia ruled the waves. Today it's been gentrified into a futuristic, skyscraper-filled landscape rising from the canals and docks.

The heart of the Docklands is the Isle of Dogs, a marshy peninsula in the river's curve. From the Isle rises the 800-foot-tall Canary Wharf Tower (officially the "One Canada Square" building) surrounded by a cluster of other office buildings.

Don't expect Jolly Olde England here. The Docklands has more of a Chicago vibe. You'll find gleaming skyscrapers, glitzy shopping malls, businessmen in suits, creatively planned parks, art-filled plazas, and trendy cafes. But there are also traces of its rugged dockworker past. You'll see the canals, former docks, brick warehouses, and a fine history museum. Most impressive of all—there's not a tourist in sight.

For most people, the Docklands is probably not worth a special trip if your London visit is brief and focused on the big, famous sights. But a short stroll through the Docklands can easily be combined with a trip to Greenwich (to the south) or Olympic Park (to the north). If you want to say you've seen today's London, visit the Docklands.

Orientation

Length of This Walk: 1.5 hours, including museum tour.
When to Go: As it's now a financial district, the Docklands bustles Mon-Fri. On weekends, it can either be laid-back and

Docklands Area

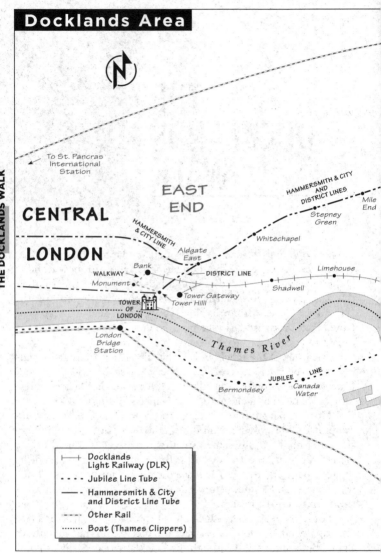

To St. Pancras
International
Station

EAST
END

CENTRAL

LONDON

HAMMERSMITH & CITY
AND
DISTRICT LINES

Mile
End

Stepney
Green

HAMMERSMITH
& CITY LINE

Whitechapel

Aldgate
East

WALKWAY   Bank   ← DISTRICT LINE →   Limehouse

Monument ●   Shadwell

TOWER   Tower Gateway ●
OF   Tower Hill!
LONDON

London   *Thames River*
Bridge
Station

JUBILEE   LINE
Bermondsey   Canada
Water

├─┤ Docklands
    Light Railway (DLR)

- - - Jubilee Line Tube

—— - Hammersmith & City
    and District Line Tube

-·-·- Other Rail

········ Boat (Thames Clippers)

festive (if sunny) or empty and dead (if rainy). It's liveliest at the end of the workday.

Getting There: Start at the Canary Wharf Tube station. You can get there via the Tube, Docklands Light Rail (DLR), or boat.

By Tube: Take the Jubilee Line to the Canary Wharf station (15 minutes from Westminster, frequent departures).

By Docklands Light Rail: From central London, riding the DLR to the Canary Wharf station probably isn't as

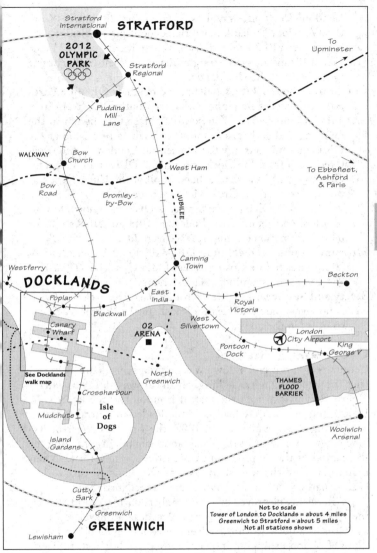

convenient as just taking the Tube (unless you're already near a DLR stop; the Bank/Monument stops are the most central). But if you're returning from Greenwich, the DLR's the way to go (described later). The DLR works like the Tube, and accepts the Oyster card; be sure to touch your card to the reader on the platform before and after your journey, or risk being fined. For more on the DLR, see page 31.

By Boat: Catch the Thames Clippers boat from central

London (£5.50 one-way; boats leave every 20 minutes from the Waterloo, Embankment, Bankside, London Bridge, and Tower piers; 10-30-minute trip). You arrive at Canary Wharf Pier, a 10-minute walk straight ahead on West India Avenue to the heart of the Docklands.

Combining the Docklands with Greenwich or Olympic Park: All three places lie along the north-south DLR train line, a few minutes apart. You could sightsee Greenwich in the morning and early afternoon, then make a brief stop at the Docklands on your way back to central London. Or, to reach Greenwich from the Docklands, hop a DLR train bound for Greenwich or Lewisham, then get off at the Cutty Sark station (for coverage of Greenwich, see page 446).

To reach Olympic Park, catch a DLR train north toward Stratford and get off at the Pudding Mill Lane DLR stop. For more information on this area, see page 104.

Museum of London Docklands: Free, daily 10:00-18:00, last entry 30 minutes before closing, West India Quay, tel. 020/7001-9844, www.museumindocklands.org.uk.

Safety and Services: Despite its rough past, the area we'll visit is now very safe and clean (almost sterile). Public WCs are plentiful in the malls.

Overview

Centuries ago, this end of town was notorious for its smelly industries (bone boiling, glue making, chemical works). It was conveniently downwind from the rest of London. By the late 1700s, 13,000 ships a year were loaded and unloaded in central London, congesting the Thames. So in 1802, the world's largest-of-its-kind harbor was built in the Docklands, organizing shipping for the capital of the empire upon which the sun never set. When Britannia ruled the waves, the Isle of Dogs hosted the world's leading harbor, with direct connections to the North Sea.

After being destroyed by Nazi bombers during World War II, the Docklands struggled for several decades and never regained its status as a port. With the advent of container shipping in the 1960s, London's shipping industry moved farther east, to deepwater docks. The old Docklands became a derelict and dangerous wasteland. Until a generation ago, local surveys ranked it as one of the least desirable places to call home. It's said that for every Tube stop you lived east of central London, your life expectancy dropped one year.

But all of this misfortune paid off in the 1980s, when investors realized that the Docklands were ripe for redevelopment... the perfect place to host a new and vibrant economic center. Over the past few decades, Britain's new Information Age industries—

banking, finance, publishing, and media—have vacated downtown London and set up shop here. You'll still see remnants of the past—those 1802 West India warehouses survive, but rather than trading sugar and rum, today they house the excellent Museum of London Docklands and a row of happening restaurants.

Our walk takes us from the heart of the modern Docklands (the plaza by the Canary Wharf Tower and Tube stop), through some pleasant squares, and ends at the Museum of London Docklands.

The Walk Begins

• *Start at the Canary Wharf Tube station. If arriving by Tube, ride up the escalators to the west exit. If coming on the DLR, exit the Canary Wharf station toward Cabot Place East, go down the escalator and straight ahead into the underground mall, and turn right at the little HSBC bank kiosk. Either way, you'll wind up in...*

❶ Canada Square

Stand in the square and take it all in. You're surrounded by towering skyscrapers, three glitzy shopping malls, trendy cafés, and hurried businesspeople. One section of Canada Square, called Thomson Reuters Plaza, has a playful display of clocks on lampposts and red ticker-tape data streaming across the wall on workdays.

Standing in this busy square, it can seem like continual rush hour—with the young high-tech workforce coursing through the battery of turnstiles. Flash back 200 years, to this area's heyday as a shipping harbor. "Canary Wharf"—the name for the whole neighborhood—is a reminder of the trading connection London had with distant ports such as the Canary Islands, off the western coast of Africa. Where sailors once drank grog while stevedores unloaded cargo, today thousands of office workers (the stevedores of the Information Age) populate a forest of skyscrapers, towering high above the remnants of the Industrial Age.

Docklands Walk

MUSEUM OF
LONDON
DOCKLANDS

To London

100 Meters
100 Yards

To Stratford
(Olympic Park site)
& London City
Airport

Poplar

BILLINGSGATE
FISH MARKET

MARRIOTT

West India
Quays

8

7 WEST INDIA DOCK

CANARY WHARF
TOWER

Westferry
Cross

Cabot Square

6

Canary
Wharf
DLR

2

THAMES
CLIPPERS
BOAT DOCK

5

WALK BEGINS

To
London

MIDDLE DOCK

1

Canary Wharf Tube

3

Jubilee
Place
Park

WESTFERRY RD.

Heron
Quays

4

SOUTH DOCK

Thames
River

South
Quay

To
Greenwich

1 Canada Square
2 Canary Wharf
Tower
3 Jubilee Place Park
4 South Quay, with
View of the O2

5 Mackenzie Walk
6 Cabot Square
7 West India Dock
8 Museum of
London Docklands

Docklands Light
Railway (DLR)

• Of the many skyscrapers, the tallest one, in the center, is the...

❷ One Canada Square
(a.k.a. Canary Wharf Tower)

The 800-foot, 50-story building is known throughout London for
its distinctive pyramid cap. (You can't see
the top from this angle—we'll get views
later.) Once the tallest building in the UK,
and, for a time, in Europe, it will be topped
by "The Shard," which is being constructed
in central London.

Canary Wharf Tower is filled with big
banks, and financial and media companies.
If you like modern art, enter the lobby from
street level and poke around to see what's
on display. Flanking skyscrapers are owned
by HSBC (Hong Kong Shanghai Banking
Corporation) and Citigroup.

• *Behind the Tube station is a grassy park. You can reach it by a path to the right of the Tube entrance.*

❸ Jubilee Place Park

Opened in 2002 on the 50th anniversary ("Golden Jubilee") of Queen Elizabeth's rule, this delightful little park is an example

of how the new Canary Wharf was designed with a futuristic people-friendliness. Workers and residents enjoy plenty of green spaces, waterways, public art, and good public-transit service. The entire ensemble sits upon an underground shopping mall. (The entrance to the mall is in the middle of the park.) Stroll through the park past meandering fountains, picnicking workers, and outdoor art displays.

• *Return to Canada Square. Head south (directly away from the Canary Wharf Tower), pass through the glassy building marked* Jubilee Place: shops and restaurants, *and exit out the far end. Cross the canal over the curvy, modernistic footbridge, reaching the...*

❹ South Quay, with View of the O2

Gazing across the water, in the distance, you see Greenwich. The

prickly white dome pierced with crane-like projections is the O2 (a.k.a. "the Dome," described on page 452), a costly and long-unpopular edifice that's now primarily the locus of sports matches, arena concerts, and Londoners' habitual disdain.

• *Return to Canada Square. Once there, face the water (so that Canary Wharf Tower is to your right). Start walking along the right side of the canal, along the promenade called...*

❺ Mackenzie Walk

Stroll along the canal, called Middle Dock, past All Bar One and other inviting eateries, and under the train bridge. The canal is a surviving remnant of the many artificial harbors and canals from the Docklands' 19th-century shipping heyday. The land here on the Isle of Dogs was marshy, flooded by the Thames, and unsuitable for farming or habitation. But it was perfect for accommodating

large sea-going vessels. Beginning around 1800, industrious Londoners channeled the water into canals, and lined them with docks. Picture the lively scene: burly men off-loading goods from ships at anchor, while an army of poor laborers bustled between storage warehouses, dry docks for ship repair, and various ship-building enterprises. Each dock specialized in a particular product to ship—spices, coal, whatever. By the mid-1800s, the Docklands had siphoned away shipping from London's traditional port (near London Bridge) and was the world's busiest port.

• *Cross under the DLR bridge and keep going. When you reach the arched footbridge, turn right and hike up Cubitt Steps, into...*

❻ Cabot Square

Enjoy its playful modern art, big fountain, and views of domineering skyscrapers. From the west end of the square, you have the iconic photo-op of Canary Wharf Tower with the fountain in the foreground. Many newlyweds come here for their wedding photos.

• *Exit the square at the north side, where steps lead down to a footbridge that crosses another canal to the...*

❼ West India Dock

This row of 19th-century brown-brick warehouses typifies today's Docklands. Standing side-by-side are elements of the old

Docklands (the warehouses, canal, a few barges) and the new (the esplanade of umbrella-shaded restaurants, the futuristic Marriott skyscraper). Back in the 19th century, the water originally lapped up right against those buildings. You can still see the rustic gates to the lofts. Imagine heavily laden cargo boats off-loading there.

The Docklands thrived as a shipping port until the mid-20th

century; two big gray cranes-on-tracks are reminders of the two events that eventually doomed the area. First, the Blitz of World War II obliterated the Docklands—it was hit by more than 2,000 bombs. Of course, Hitler's aim was to wipe out this vital industrial area.

Though it survived the Blitz, the Docklands couldn't survive the next hit—when the shipping industry converted to containers. The large container ships couldn't make it this far up the shallow Thames, and almost overnight, the industry rapidly shifted to seaports. In the 1970s, the Docklands became London's poorest area.

• *In the left part of the row of warehouses you'll find the...*

❽ Museum of London Docklands

This fine museum, which fills an old sugar warehouse, gives the Docklands historic context. In telling the story of the world's leading 19th-century port, it also conveys the story of London. Ride the elevator up to the third floor, then work your way down, going on a 2,000-year walk through the story of commerce on the Thames.

Third Floor: You start out in old London, back when London's port was at London Bridge, and the Docklands was a barely-inhabited swamp far to the east. See fascinating models of Old London Bridge, crammed with little houses and shops—not unlike how Florence's Ponte Vecchio still looks.

Continuing on, you see how the Docklands rapidly developed in the 1800s. There's a reconstruction of a "Legal Quay," where cargo was processed. You'll see a life-size mannequin in a hamster-wheel contraption for lifting cargo from ships. Crime and punishment were brutal in those days: Executed pirates were displayed publicly, suspended in metal cages called "gibbets." The next, thought-provoking section analyzes the connection between sugar and slavery—a frank and sober look at the terrible human toll taken by several centuries of transatlantic trade.

Second Floor: This section explores London's growth after 1800—its population was more than one million by 1810. Stroll through a gritty reconstruction of "Sailortown," listening to the salty voices of those who lived and worked in quarters like this. A painted banner from the 1889 Dock Strike is a reminder that the Industrial Revolution first exploited workers, then provoked them to rise up.

During World War II, the Docklands were a prime target for Nazi bombers bent on crippling British shipping. Find the claustrophobic, dome-shaped "consul shelter," where dockworkers could take cover in case of attack. There's also a re-creation of the fuel pipeline that was laid under the English Channel to supply the Allies on the Continent.

The final section, "New Port, New City," traces the Docklands' post-WWII rebuilding. In the 1980s, a combination of government and private investors remade the area into an office zone. The area has prospered, but not without controversy—there's still tension between the yuppie newcomers and the blue-collar old-timers.

When you're finished, step out into today's Docklands and take in this combination of old and new.

• *Our walk is over. You have several options from here:*

Return to Central London:
The Tube is your fastest way back
into the city—to take it, retrace your
steps to the Canary Wharf Tube
station.

To catch a boat (slower but very
scenic), return to Cabot Square, turn
right, and walk five minutes along
West India Avenue to the round
Westferry Circus park; the Thames Clippers dock is just beyond (see
"Orientation" at the top of this chapter).

Shopping and Eating: Three different subterranean shopping
malls all flow into each other via underground corridors. There's Cabot
Place shopping mall (enter at Cabot Square), a mall beneath Canary
Wharf Tower, and Jubilee Place (enter from Jubilee Park).

Waterside restaurants abound—at the West India Dock, along
Mackenzie Walk, and elsewhere. Or enjoy a picnic in Jubilee Park.

Visiting Greenwich or Olympic Park: Catch a DLR train south
to Greenwich or north to Olympic Park.

SLEEPING IN LONDON

I've chosen several favorite neighborhoods (Victoria Station, South Kensington, Notting Hill, and Paddington Station, among others) convenient to your sightseeing activities and recommended the best accommodations values for each. I've also listed big, good-value, modern hotels scattered throughout London.

I like places that are clean, central, relatively quiet at night, reasonably priced, friendly, small enough to have a hands-on owner and stable staff, run with a respect for British traditions, and not listed in other guidebooks. (In London, for me, six out of these eight criteria means it's a keeper.) I'm more impressed by a handy location and a fun-loving philosophy than by flat-screen TVs and shoeshine machines.

London is an expensive city for lodging. Cheaper rooms are relatively dumpy. Don't expect £130 cheeriness in an £80 room. For £70, you'll get a double with breakfast in a safe, cramped, and dreary place with minimal service and the bathroom down the hall. For £90, you'll get a basic, clean, reasonably cheery double with a private bath in a usually cramped, cracked-plaster building, or a soulless but comfortable room without breakfast in a huge Motel 6-type place. My London splurges, at £160-290, are spacious, thoughtfully appointed places good for entertaining or romancing.

I've described my recommended accommodations using a Sleep Code (see sidebar). Prices listed are for one-night stays in peak season, include a hearty breakfast unless otherwise noted, and assume you're booking directly (not through a TI or online hotel-booking engine). London's stiff 20 percent Value-Added Tax (VAT) is usually included in the quoted rates, but it's sometimes added on—especially at pricier hotels. Ask in advance.

Staying in B&Bs and small hotels can sometimes be a great way to save money over sleeping in big hotels, but lately the big, impersonal chain hotels are offering rooms even cheaper than the mom-and-pop places (but without breakfast); see "Big, Good-Value, Modern Hotels" on page 367. When comparing prices between these chain hotels and B&Bs, remember you're getting two breakfasts (about a £25 value) for each double room at a B&B. Some fancy hotels rent for a third off if you arrive late on a slow day and ask for a deal. Official "rack rates" (the highest rates a hotel charges) can be misleading, because they often omit cheaper oddball rooms and special promo deals.

Given the economic downturn, hoteliers are willing and eager to make a deal. I'd suggest emailing several hotels to ask for their best price. Comparison-shop and make your choice. In general, prices can soften if you do any of the following: offer to pay cash, stay at least three nights, or mention this book. You can also try asking for a cheaper room or a discount, or offer to skip breakfast.

As you look over the listings, you'll notice that some accommodations promise special prices to my readers who book direct (without using a room-finding service or hotel-booking website, which take a commission). To get these rates, you must mention this book when you reserve, and then show the book upon arrival. Some readers with ebooks have reported difficulty getting a Rick Steves discount. If this happens to you, please show this to the hotelier: Rick Steves discounts apply to readers with ebooks as well as printed books.

For tips on making reservations, see page 352.

Looking for Hotel Deals Online

Given London's high hotel prices, using the Internet can help you score a deal. Various websites list rooms in high-rise, three- and four-star business hotels. You'll give up the charm and warmth of a family-run establishment, and breakfast probably won't be included, but you might find that the price is right.

Start by browsing the websites of several chains to get a sense of typical rates and online deals. For listings of no-frills, Motel 6-type places, see "Big, Good-Value, Modern Hotels," on page 367.

Pricier London hotel chains include Millennium/Copthorne (www.millenniumhotels.com), Thistle (www.thistle.com), Intercontinental/Holiday Inn (www.ichotelsgroup.com), Radisson (www.radisson.com), Hilton (www.hilton.com), and Red Carnation (www.redcarnationhotels.com).

Auction-type sites (such as www.priceline.com or www.hotwire.com) match flexible travelers with empty hotel rooms, often at prices well below the hotel's normal rates.

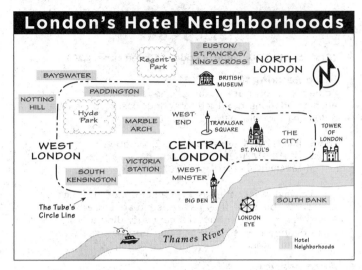

My readers report good experiences with these accommodation discount sites: www.londontown.com (an informative site with a discount booking service), http://athomeinlondon.co.uk and www.londonbb.com (both list central B&Bs), www.lastminute.com, www.visitlondon.com, http://roomsnet.com, and www.eurocheapo.com.

Travel Review Websites: TripAdvisor (www.tripadvisor.com) and similar review websites are popular tools for finding hotels, but have drawbacks. To write a review, people need only an email address—making it easy to hide their true identity. If a hotel is well-reviewed in a guidebook or two, and also gets good ratings on TripAdvisor, it's probably a safe bet—but I wouldn't stay at a hotel based solely on a TripAdvisor recommendation.

Types of Accommodations

Hotels

Many of my recommended hotels have three floors of rooms and steep stairs. Elevators are rare except in the larger hotels. If you're concerned about stairs, call and ask about ground-floor rooms or pay for a hotel with a lift (elevator). Air-conditioning is rare (I've noted which of my listings have it), but most places have fans. On hot summer nights, you'll want your window open—and unfortunately, in this big city, street noise is a fact of life. If concerned, request a room on the back side.

"Twin" means two single beds, and "double" means one double bed. If you'll take either one, let them know, or you might be needlessly turned away. Most hotels offer family deals, which

Sleep Code

(£1 = about $1.60, country code: 44, area code: 020)

Price Rankings

To help you sort through these listings easily, I've divided the accommodations into three categories based on the price for a double room with bath:

$$$ Higher Priced—Most rooms £125 or more.
$$ Moderately Priced—Most rooms between £75-125.
$ Lower Priced—Most rooms £75 or less.

I always rate hostels as $, whether or not they have double rooms, because they have the cheapest beds in town. Prices can change without notice; verify the hotel's current rates online or by email. For other updates, see www.ricksteves.com/update.

Abbreviations

To give maximum information in a minimum of space, I use the following code to describe accommodations listed in this book. Prices are listed per room, not per person. When a price range is given for a type of room (such as double rooms listing for £80-120), it means the price fluctuates with the season, size of room, or length of stay; expect to pay the upper end for peak-season stays.

S = Single room, or price for one person in a double.
D = Double or twin room. (I specify double- and twin-bed rooms only if they are priced differently, or if a place has only one or the other. You should specify when reserving.)
T = Three-person room (generally a double bed with a single).
Q = Quad (usually two double beds; adding an extra child's bed to a T is usually cheaper).
b = Private bathroom with toilet and shower or tub.
s = Private shower or tub only (the toilet is down the hall).

According to this code, a couple staying at a "Db-£90" hotel would pay a total of £90 (about $144) per night for a double room with a private bathroom. Unless otherwise noted, breakfast is included and credit cards are accepted. For most places, the rates I list include the 20 percent VAT tax—but it's smart to ask when you book your room.

If I mention "Internet access" in a listing, there's a public terminal in the lobby for guests to use. If I use the terms "Wi-Fi" or "cable Internet," you can access it in your room, but only if you have your own laptop.

means that parents with young children can easily get a room with an extra child's bed or a discount for larger rooms. Call to negotiate the price. Teenagers are generally charged as adults. Kids under five sleep almost free.

Be careful of the terminology: An "en suite" (pronounced "on sweet") room has a bathroom (toilet and shower/tub) actually inside the room; a room with a "private bathroom" can mean that the bathroom is all yours, but it's across the hall; and a "standard" room has access to a bathroom down the hall that's shared with other rooms. Figuring there's little difference between "en suite" and "private" rooms, some places charge the same for both. If you want your own bathroom inside the room, request "en suite."

If money's tight, ask for a standard room. You'll almost always have a sink in your room, and as more rooms go "en suite," the hallway bathroom is shared with fewer standard rooms.

Confusingly, pricey hotels might call an en suite room "standard" to differentiate it from a fancier "superior" or "deluxe" room—if you're not sure, ask for clarification.

Note that to be called a "hotel," a place technically must have certain amenities, including a 24-hour reception (though this rule is loosely applied). TVs are standard in rooms, but may come with only the traditional five British channels (no cable). Note that all of Britain's accommodations are now non-smoking.

If you're arriving on an early flight or an overnight train, your room probably won't be ready first thing in the morning. You should be able to safely check your bag at the hotel and dive right into sightseeing.

Hoteliers can be a great help and source of advice. Most know their city well, and can assist you with everything from public transit and airport connections to finding a good restaurant, the nearest launderette, or an Internet café. But even at the best places, mechanical breakdowns occur: Air-conditioning malfunctions, sinks leak, hot water turns cold, and toilets gurgle and smell. Report your concerns clearly and calmly at the front desk. For more complicated problems, don't expect instant results.

To guard against theft in your room, keep valuables out of sight. Some rooms come with a safe, and other hotels have safes at the front desk. Use them if you're concerned.

Checkout can pose problems if surprise charges pop up on your bill. If you settle up your bill the night before you leave, you'll have time to discuss and address any points of contention (before 19:00, when the night shift usually arrives).

Above all, keep a positive attitude. Remember, you're on vacation. If your hotel is a disappointment, spend more time out enjoying the city you came to see.

Making Reservations

Given the quality of the accommodations I've found for this book, I'd recommend that you reserve your rooms in advance, particularly if you'll be traveling during peak season. Book several weeks ahead, or as soon as you've pinned down your travel dates. Note that some national holidays jam things up and merit your making reservations far in advance (see "Holidays and Festivals" on page 565).

Phoning: To call London from the US or Canada, dial 011-44-20 and then the local number. (The 011 is our international access code, 44 is Britain's country code, and 20 is London's area code without its initial zero.) If you're calling London from another European country, dial 00-44-20-local number. (The 00 is Europe's international access code.) To make calls within London, drop the area code (020) and dial only the local number. For more tips on calling, see page 552.

Requesting a Reservation: To make a reservation, contact hotels directly by email, phone, or fax (email is the clearest and most economical way). Or go straight to the hotel's website—many have secure online reservation forms and you can instantly check availability and any special deals. But be sure you use the hotel's official site and not a booking agency's site—otherwise you may pay higher rates than you should.

The hotelier wants to know these key pieces of information about your stay (also included in the sample request form in the appendix):

- number and type of rooms
- number of nights
- date of arrival
- date of departure
- any special needs (e.g., bathroom in the room or down the hall, twin beds vs. double bed, air-conditioning, quiet, view, ground floor, etc.)

When you request a room, use the European style for writing dates: day/month/year. For example, for a two-night stay in July, I would request: "1 double room for 2 nights, arrive 16/07/12, depart 18/07/12." Consider carefully how long you'll stay; don't just assume you can extend your reservation for extra days when you arrive. Make sure you mention any discounts—for Rick Steves readers or otherwise—when you make the reservation.

Confirming a Reservation: If the hotel's response tells you its room availability and rates, it's not a confirmation. You must tell them that you want that room at the given rate. Most hoteliers will request your credit-card number to hold the room. While you can email your credit-card information (I do), it's safer to share that confidential info via phone call, fax, split between two emails, or via a secure online reservation form (if the hotel has one on its website).

Canceling a Reservation: If you must cancel your reservation, it's courteous to do so with as much advance notice as possible. Simply make a quick phone call or send an email. Family-run hotels and B&Bs lose money if they turn away customers while holding a room for someone who doesn't show up. Understandably, many places bill no-shows for one night.

Cancellation policies can be strict: For example, you might lose a deposit if you cancel within two weeks of your reserved stay, or you might be billed for the entire visit if you leave early. Internet deals may require prepayment, with no refunds for cancellations. Ask about cancellation policies before you book.

If canceling in an email, request confirmation that your cancellation was received to avoid being billed accidentally.

Reconfirming Your Reservation: Always call to reconfirm your room reservation a few days in advance from the road. (Don't have a TI call for you; they may take a commission.) Smaller hotels and B&Bs appreciate knowing your time of arrival, especially if you'll be arriving late (after 17:00). On the small chance that a hotel loses track of your reservation, bring along a hard copy of their emailed or faxed confirmation.

Reserving Rooms as You Travel: If you'll be traveling beyond London, you may want to make reservations as you go, calling hotels or B&Bs a few days to a week before your visit. If everything's full, don't despair. Call a day or two in advance and fill a cancellation. If you'd rather travel without any reservations at all, you'll have greater success snaring rooms if you arrive at your destination early in the day. When you anticipate crowds (weekends are worst), call hotels at about 9:00 or 10:00 on the day you plan to arrive, when the hotel clerk knows who'll be checking out and just which rooms will be available.

Small Hotels and B&Bs

Places with "townhouse" or "house" in their name (such as "London House") are like big B&Bs or small family-run hotels—with fewer amenities but more character than a hotel. Places named "B&B"—rare in big and bustling London—typically have six rooms or fewer.

Small hotels and B&Bs come with their own etiquette and quirks. Keep in mind that owners are at the whim of their guests—if you're getting up early, so are they; and if you check in late, they'll wait up for you. Be considerate. It's polite to call ahead to confirm your reservation the day before, and give them a rough estimate of your arrival time.

Small places usually serve a hearty fried breakfast of eggs and much more (for details on breakfast, see page 378 in the Eating in London chapter). Because your B&B or small hotel owner is often also the cook, there's usually a quite-limited time span when breakfast is served (typically about an hour—make sure you know when it is before you turn in for the night). It's an unwritten rule that guests shouldn't show up at the very end of the breakfast period and expect a full cooked breakfast. If you do arrive late (or if you need to leave before breakfast is served), most establishments are happy to let you help yourself to cereal, fruit or juice, and coffee; ask politely if it's possible.

Most places stock rooms with an electric kettle, along with cups, tea bags, and coffee packets (if you prefer decaf, buy a jar at a grocery and dump the contents into a baggie for easy packing).

Electrical outlets sometimes have switches that turn the current on or off; if your electrical appliance isn't working, flip the switch at the outlet. When you unplug your appliance, don't forget your adapter—most B&Bs have boxes of various adapters and converters that guests have left behind (which is handy if you left yours at the last place).

You're likely to encounter unusual bathroom fixtures. The "pump toilet" has a flushing handle or button that doesn't kick in unless you push it just right: too hard or too soft, and it won't go. (Be decisive but not ruthless.) There's also the "dial-a-shower," an electronic box under the shower head where you'll turn a dial to select the heat of the water and (sometimes with a separate dial or button) turn on or shut off the flow of water. If you can't find the switch to turn on the shower, it may be just outside the bathroom.

Many B&Bs and small hotels come with thin walls and doors that can make for a noisy night. If you're a light sleeper, bring earplugs. And please be quiet in the halls and in your rooms at night (talk softly, and keep the TV volume low)...those of us getting up early will thank you for it.

Hostels and Dorms

London hostels charge about £20-30 per bed. Travelers of any age are welcome if they don't mind sleeping in dorm-style accommodations and meeting other travelers. Cheap meals are sometimes available, and kitchen facilities are usually provided for do-it-yourselfers. Hostelling International hostels (also known as "official" hostels and run by the YHA in Britain) charge a few extra pounds a night for nonmembers. If you'll be staying for several days in an official hostel, consider buying a membership card before you go (www.hihostels.com). Hostels that have no such requirements are called "independent" hostels.

Many London colleges rent out their dorms during school holidays, most notably during July, August, and early September. Types of accommodations vary, but are usually somewhat spartan (no phones or TVs in the rooms) and come with single or twin beds. For listings, see "Dorms" on page 371.

Apartments

It's easy, though not necessarily cheap, to rent a furnished apartment in London. Consider this option if you're traveling with a family or staying a week or longer. For listings, see "For Longer Stays" at the end of this chapter.

Accommodations

Victoria Station Neighborhood (Belgravia)

The streets behind Victoria Station teem with little, moderately priced-for-London B&Bs. It's a safe, surprisingly tidy, and decent area without a hint of the trashy, touristy glitz of the streets in

front of the station. I've divided these accommodations into two broad categories: west or east of the station. Decent eateries abound in both areas (see page 393). All the recommended hotels are within a five-minute walk of the Victoria Tube, bus, and train stations. On hot summer nights, request a quiet back room.

Near the hotels on the west side is the 400-space Semley Place NCP **parking garage** (£34/day, possible discounts with hotel voucher, just west of the Victoria Coach Station at Buckingham Palace Road and Semley Place, toll tel. 0845-050-7080, www.ncp.co.uk). The best laundry options are on the east side: The handy **Pimlico Launderette** is about five blocks southwest of Warwick Square (daily 8:00-19:00, self- or

Victoria Station Neighborhood

① Lime Tree Hotel
② Cartref House
③ Morgan House
④ Lynton Hotel B&B
⑤ Luna Simone Hotel
⑥ New England Hotel
⑦ Best Western Victoria Palace
⑧ Cherry Court Hotel
⑨ Jubilee Hotel
⑩ Bakers Hotel
⑪ easyHotel Victoria
⑫ Vandon House Hotel
⑬ Ebury Wine Bar
⑭ Jenny Lo's Tea House
⑮ La Bottega Deli
⑯ To The Duke of Wellington Pub
⑰ The Thomas Cubitt Pub
⑱ Grumbles Restaurant
⑲ Seafresh Fish Restaurant
⑳ The Jugged Hare Pub
㉑ St. George's Tavern
㉒ Grocery Stores (4)
㉓ Launderettes (2)
㉔ Bus Tours – Day (2)
㉕ Bus Tours – Night
㉖ Tube, Taxis, City Buses
㉗ Green Line Coach Terminal
㉘ Buses to Luton & Stansted Airports
㉙ Apollo Victoria Theatre
㉚ Victoria Palace Theatre

200 Meters
200 Yards

full-service, south of Sutherland Street at 3 Westmoreland Terrace, tel. 020/7821-8692), and **Launderette Centre** is a block northeast of Warwick Square (Mon-Fri 8:00-21:00, Sat 8:00-19:00, Sun 9:00-20:00, last wash 2 hours before closing, about £7 wash and dry, £9 full-service, 31 Churton Street, tel. 020/7828-6039).

West of Victoria Station

Here in Belgravia, the prices are a bit higher and your neigh-

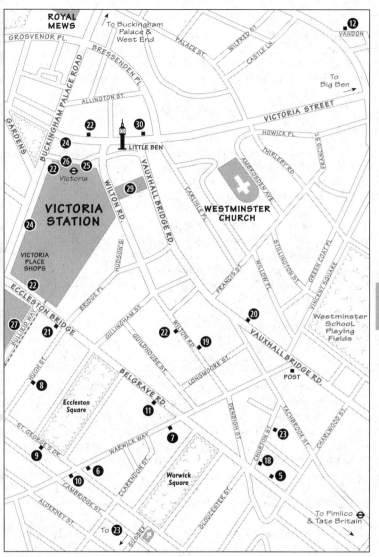

bors include Andrew Lloyd Webber and Margaret Thatcher (her policeman stands outside 73 Chester Square). All of these places line up along tranquil Ebury Street, two blocks over from Victoria Station.

$$$ Lime Tree Hotel, enthusiastically run by Charlotte and Matt, comes with 25 spacious, stylish, comfortable, thoughtfully decorated rooms and a fun-loving breakfast room (Sb-£85-95, Db-£145, larger superior Db-£165, Tb-£190, family room-£205, free Internet access and Wi-Fi, small lounge opens onto quiet garden, 135 Ebury Street, tel. 020/7730-8191, www.limetreehotel.co.uk, info@limetreehotel.co.uk, trusty Alan covers the night shift).

$$ Cartref House B&B offers rare charm on Ebury Street, with 10 delightful rooms and a warm welcome (Sb-£82, Db-£115, Tb-£151, Qb-£185, fans, free Wi-Fi, 129 Ebury Street, tel. 020/7730-6176, www.cartrefhouse.co.uk, info@cartrefhouse .co.uk, Sharon and Derek).

$$ Morgan House, a great budget choice in this neighborhood, has 11 rooms and is entertainingly run, with lots of travel tips and friendly chat from owner Rachel Joplin and her staff (S-£58, D-£78, Db-£98, T-£98, family suites-£138-148 for 3-4 people, Wi-Fi, 120 Ebury Street, tel. 020/7730-2384, www.morganhouse .co.uk, morganhouse@btclick.com).

$$ Lynton Hotel B&B is a well-worn, steep-stairs kind of place renting 13 inexpensive rooms with small prefab WCs. It's a decent value run by brothers Mark and Simon Connor (D-£85, Db-£105, these prices with this book in 2012, free Wi-Fi, 113 Ebury Street, tel. 020/7730-4032, www.lyntonhotel.co.uk, mark -and-simon@lyntonhotel.co.uk).

East of Victoria Station

This area is a bit less genteel-feeling than the neighborhood west of the station, but still plenty inviting. Most of these places are on or near Warwick Way, the main drag through this area.

$$ Luna Simone Hotel rents 36 fresh, spacious, nicely remodeled rooms with modern bathrooms. It's a smartly managed place, run for more than 40 years by twins Peter and Bernard and son Mark, and they still seem to enjoy their work (Sb-£75, Db-£105, Tb-£130, Qb-£160, these prices with cash and this book in 2012, free Internet access and Wi-Fi, near the corner of Charlwood Street and Belgrave Road at 47 Belgrave Road, handy bus #24 to Victoria Station and Trafalgar Square stops out front, tel. 020/7834-5897, www.lunasimonehotel.com, stay@lunasimone hotel.com).

$$ New England Hotel, run by Jay and the Patel family, has slightly worn public spaces but tidy, well-priced rooms in a tight old corner building (small Sb-£59, Db-£89, Tb-£119, Qb-£129, prices soft during slow times, pay Internet access and Wi-Fi, 20 Saint George's Drive, tel. 020/7834-8351, fax 020/7834-9000, www.newenglandhotel.com, mystay@newenglandhotel.com).

$$ Best Western Victoria Palace offers modern business-class comfort compared to the other creaky old hotels listed here. Choose between the 43 rooms in the main building (Db-£120, includes breakfast, elevator, 60-64 Warwick Way), or 22 rooms in the annex a half-block away (Db-£89, breakfast-£12.50, no elevator, 17 Belgrave Road, reception at main building). Both places have been recently renovated (air-con, free Wi-Fi, tel. 020/7821-7113, fax 020/7630-0806, www.bestwesternvictoriapalace.co.uk, info@bestwesternvictoriapalace.co.uk). Another 20-room annex may open by the time you visit.

$ Cherry Court Hotel, run by the friendly and industrious Patel family, rents 12 very small but bright and well-designed rooms in a central location (Sb-£50, Db-£58, Tb-£85, Qb-£100, Quint/b-£115, these prices with this book in 2012, 5 percent fee to pay with credit card, fruit-basket breakfast in room, air-con, free Internet access and Wi-Fi, laundry, peaceful garden patio, 23 Hugh Street, tel. 020/7828-2840, fax 020/7828-0393, www.cherry courthotel.co.uk, info@cherrycourthotel.co.uk).

$ Jubilee Hotel is a well-run slumbermill with 24 tiny, simple rooms and many tiny, neat beds (S-£39-45, Sb-£59-65, tiny D-£55-59, Db-£69-79, Tb-£79-95, Qb-£99-109, higher prices are for Fri-Sun, 5 percent Rick Steves discount if you book direct, Internet access and Wi-Fi, 31 Eccleston Square, tel. 020/7834-0845, www .jubileehotel.co.uk, stay@jubileehotel.co.uk, Bob Patel).

$ Bakers Hotel shoehorns 11 brightly painted rooms into a small building, but it's conveniently located and offers near-youth-hostel prices and a small breakfast (S-£40, D-£55, Db-£65, T-£65, Tb-£75, family room-£85, less for longer stays and on weeknights, pay Wi-Fi, 126 Warwick Way, tel. 020/7834-0729, www.bakers hotel.co.uk, reservations@bakershotel.co.uk, Amin Jamani).

$ easyHotel Victoria, at 36 Belgrave Road, is part of the budget chain described on page 370.

"South Kensington," She Said, Loosening His Cummerbund

To stay on a quiet street so classy it doesn't allow hotel signs, surrounded by trendy shops and colorful restaurants, call "South Ken" your London home. Shoppers like being a short walk from Harrods and the designer shops of King's Road and Chelsea. When I splurge, I splurge here. Sumner Place is just off Old Brompton Road, 200 yards from the handy South Kensington Tube station (on Circle Line, two stops from Victoria Station; and on Piccadilly Line, direct from Heathrow). A handy **launderette** is on the corner of Queensberry Place and Harrington Road (Mon-Fri 7:30-21:00, Sat 9:00-20:00, Sun 10:00-19:00, bring 50p and £1 coins).

$$$ Number Sixteen, for well-heeled travelers, packs over-the-top formality and class into its 41 rooms, plush lounges, and tranquil garden. It's in a labyrinthine building, with modern decor—perfect for an urban honeymoon (Db-from £215—but soft, ask for discounted "seasonal rates," especially on weekends and in Aug—subject to availability, does not include 20 percent VAT,

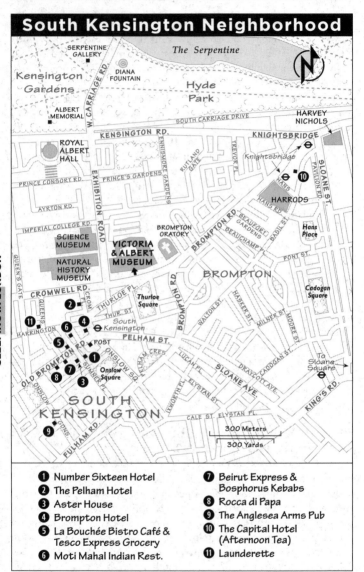

South Kensington Neighborhood

- **1** Number Sixteen Hotel
- **2** The Pelham Hotel
- **3** Aster House
- **4** Brompton Hotel
- **5** La Bouchée Bistro Café & Tesco Express Grocery
- **6** Moti Mahal Indian Rest.
- **7** Beirut Express & Bosphorus Kebabs
- **8** Rocca di Papa
- **9** The Anglesea Arms Pub
- **10** The Capital Hotel (Afternoon Tea)
- **11** Launderette

breakfast buffet in the garden-£18, elevator, 16 Sumner Place, tel. 020/7589-5232, fax 020/7584-8615, US tel. 800-553-6674, www .firmdalehotels.com, sixteen@firmdale.com).

$$$ The Pelham Hotel, a 52-room business-class hotel with a pricey mix of pretense and style, is not quite sure which investment company owns it. It's genteel, with low lighting and a pleasant drawing room among the many perks (Db-£190-290, breakfast extra, does not include 20 percent VAT, lower prices on weekends and in Aug, Web specials can include free breakfast, air-con, elevator, free Internet access, pay Wi-Fi, gym, 15 Cromwell Place, tel. 020/7589-8288, fax 020/7584-8444, US tel. 1-888-757-5587, www .pelhamhotel.co.uk, reservations@pelhamhotel.co.uk).

$$$ Aster House, run by friendly and accommodating Simon and Leonie Tan, has a cheerful lobby, lounge, and breakfast room. Its rooms are comfy and quiet, with TV, phone, and air-conditioning. Enjoy breakfast or just lounging in the whisper-elegant Orangery, a glassy greenhouse. Simon and Leonie offer free loaner mobile phones to their guests (Sb-£125, Db-£190, bigger Db-£235, does not include 20 percent VAT, 20 percent discount with this book in 2012 if you book three or more nights, 25 percent discount for five or more nights, additional 5 percent off with cash, check website for specials, free Wi-Fi, 3 Sumner Place, tel. 020/7581-5888, fax 020/7584-4925, www.asterhouse .com, asterhouse@btinternet.com).

$$ Brompton Hotel is a humble, borderline-dreary place with 17 rooms above a jumble of cafés and clubs. There's a noisy bar and some street noise, so ask for a room in the back if you want quiet. It has old carpet and no public spaces, and they serve breakfast in your room. In spite of all this, it's cheap for London and very well-located (Sb-£95, Db-£100, Tb-£140, "deluxe" rooms are just like the others but with a tub, save a little by booking via their website, includes continental breakfast, Wi-Fi, across from the South Kensington Tube station at 30 Brompton Road, tel. 020/7584-4517, fax 020/7823-9936, www.bromhotel.com, book @bromhotel.com).

Notting Hill and Bayswater Neighborhoods

Residential Notting Hill has quick bus and Tube access to downtown, and, for London, is very "homely" (Brit-speak for cozy). It's also peppered with trendy bars and restaurants, and is home to the famous Portobello Road Market (see the Shopping in London chapter).

Popular with young international travelers, Bayswater's Queensway street is a multicultural festival of commerce and eateries (see the Eating in London chapter). The neighborhood does its dirty clothes at **Galaxy Launderette** (£6 self-service, £8-10 full-service, daily 8:00-20:00, staff on hand with soap and coins, 65 Moscow Road, at corner of St. Petersburgh Place and Moscow Road, tel. 020/7229-7771). For **Internet access,** you'll find several stops along busy Queensway, and a self-serve bank of computer terminals on the food-circus level—third floor—of Whiteleys Shopping Centre (daily 8:30-24:00, corner of Queensway and Porchester Gardens).

SLEEPING IN LONDON

Notting Hill & Bayswater Neighborhoods

1. Vancouver Studios
2. Garden Court Hotel
3. Phoenix Hotel
4. Kensington Gardens Hotel
5. Princes Square Guest Accommodation
6. Westland Hotel
7. London Vicarage Hotel
8. The Gate Hotel
9. To Norwegian YWCA
10. Maggie Jones Restaurant
11. The Churchill Arms Pub & Thai Kitchen
12. The Prince Edward Pub
13. Café Diana
14. Royal China Restaurant
15. Whiteleys Shopping Centre (Food Court, Grocery, Internet)
16. Tesco Grocery
17. Spar Market
18. The Orangery (Afternoon Tea)
19. Launderette

Near Kensington Gardens Square

Several big, old hotels line quiet Kensington Gardens Square (not to be confused with the much bigger Kensington Gardens adjacent to Hyde Park), a block west of bustling Queensway, north of Bayswater Tube station. These hotels are quiet for central London, but the area feels a bit sterile, and the hotels here tend to be impersonal.

$$$ Vancouver Studios offers 45 modern rooms with fully equipped kitchenettes (utensils, stove, microwave, and fridge) rather than breakfast (Sb-£92, Db-£135, Tb-£175, extra bed-£20, can be more at busy times, 10 percent discount for seven or more nights, pay Internet access, free Wi-Fi, welcoming lounge and wonderful garden, near Kensington Gardens Square at 30 Prince's Square, tel. 020/7243-1270, fax 020/7221-8678, www.vancouver studios.co.uk, info@vancouverstudios.co.uk).

$$$ Garden Court Hotel is homey and understated, with 32 simple beige rooms and a peaceful garden in back. Edward takes pride in the hotel his family has run for more than 50 years (S-£50, Sb-£80, D-£80, Db-£130, Tb-£160, Qb-£180, these prices when booked direct with this book in 2012, elevator, free Wi-Fi, 30-31 Kensington Gardens Square, tel. 020/7229-2553, fax 020/7727-2749, www.gardencourthotel.co.uk, info@gardencourthotel.co.uk).

$$ Phoenix Hotel, a Best Western modernization of a 125-room hotel, offers American business-class comforts; spacious, plush public spaces; and big, fresh, modern-feeling rooms. Its prices—which range from fine value to rip-off—are determined by a greedy computer program, with huge variations according to expected demand. Book online to save money (flexible prices, but usually Sb-£65, Db-£100, elevator, free Wi-Fi, 1-8 Kensington Gardens Square, tel. 020/7229-2494, fax 020/7727-1419, US tel. 800-528-1234, www.phoenixhotel.co.uk, info@phoenixhotel .co.uk).

$$ Kensington Gardens Hotel, which has the same owners as the Phoenix Hotel down the street (see above), laces 17 pleasant rooms together in a tall, skinny building with lots of stairs and no elevator (Ss-£57, Sb-£64, Db-£88, Tb-£110; book by phone or email for these special Rick Steves prices, rather than through the pricier website; continental breakfast served at Phoenix Hotel, free Wi-Fi, 9 Kensington Gardens Square, tel. 020/7243-7600, fax 020/7792-8612, www.kensingtongardenshotel.co.uk, info @kensingtongardenshotel.co.uk, Rowshanak).

$$ Princes Square Guest Accommodation is a big 50-room place that's well-located, practical, and a good value, especially with its online discounts (Sb-£65-70, Db-£80-90, Tb-£90-100, elevator, pay Wi-Fi, 23-25 Princes Square, tel. 020/7229-9876, www.princessquarehotel.co.uk, info@princessquarehotel.co.uk).

Near Kensington Gardens

$$$ **Westland Hotel,** conveniently located on a busy street a five-minute walk from the Notting Hill neighborhood, feels like a wood-paneled hunting lodge with a fine lounge. The 32 spacious rooms are comfortable, with old-fashioned charm. Their £130 doubles are the best value, but check their website for specials. It's been run by the Isseyegh family for three generations (Sb-£112, deluxe Sb-£127, Db-£133, deluxe Db-£155, cavernous premier Db-£176, sprawling Tb-£169-197, gargantuan Qb-£190-225, Quint/b-£239, elevator, pay Wi-Fi, garage-£12/day, between Notting Hill Gate and Queensway Tube stations at 154 Bayswater Road, tel. 020/7229-9191, fax 020/7727-1054, www.westlandhotel.co.uk, reservations@westlandhotel.co.uk, Shirley and Bertie).

$$$ **London Vicarage Hotel** is family-run, understandably popular, and elegantly British in a quiet, classy neighborhood. It has 17 rooms furnished with taste and quality, a TV lounge, a grand staircase, and facilities on each floor. Mandy and Monika maintain a homey atmosphere (S-£60, Sb-£102, D-£102, Db-£130, T-£130, Tb-£170, Q-£140, Qb-£185, 20 percent less in winter—check website, free Wi-Fi; 8-minute walk from Notting Hill Gate and High Street Kensington Tube stations, near Kensington Palace at 10 Vicarage Gate; tel. 020/7229-4030, fax 020/7792-5989, www.londonvicaragehotel.com, vicaragehotel@btconnect.com).

$$ **The Gate Hotel** has seven cramped but decent rooms on a delightful curved street near the start of the Portobello Road Market, in the heart of the characteristic Notting Hill neighborhood. While the lodgings are basic, the romantic setting might be worth it for some (Sb-£60, Db-£85, bigger "luxury" Db-£95, Tb-£115, each room £10 more Fri-Sat, 5 percent fee to pay with credit card, continental breakfast in room, no elevator, pay Wi-Fi, 6 Portobello Road, Tube: Notting Hill Gate, tel. 020/7221-0707, fax 020/7221-9128, www.gatehotel.co.uk, bookings@gatehotel.co.uk, Jasmine).

Near Holland Park

$ **Norwegian YWCA (Norsk K.F.U.K.)**—where English is definitely a second language—is open to any Norwegian woman, and to non-Norwegian women under 30. (Men must be under 30 with a Norwegian passport.) Located on a quiet, stately street, it offers a study, TV room, piano lounge, and an open-face Norwegian ambience (goat cheese on Sundays!). They have mostly quads, so those willing to share with strangers are most likely to get a bed (July-Aug: Ss-£41, shared double-£39/bed, shared triple-£34/bed, shared quad-£30.50/bed, includes breakfast year-round plus sack lunch and dinner Sept-June, £20 key deposit and £2 membership fee required, pay Wi-Fi, 52 Holland Park, Tube: Holland Park, tel. 020/7727-9346 or 020/7727-9897, www.kfukhjemmet.org.uk, kontor@kfukhjemmet.org.uk). With each visit, I wonder which is easier to get—a sex change or a Norwegian passport?

Paddington Station Neighborhood

The neighborhood near Paddington Station—while much less charming than the other areas I've recommended—is pleasant enough, and very convenient to the Heathrow Express airport train. The area is flanked by the Paddington and Lancaster Gate Tube stops. Most of my recommendations circle Norfolk Square, just two blocks in front of Paddington Station, yet are still quiet and comfortable. The main drag, London Street, is lined with handy eateries—pubs, Indian, Italian, Greek, Lebanese, and more—plus convenience stores and an Internet café. To reach this area, exit the station toward Praed Street (with your back to the tracks, it's to the left). Once outside, continue straight across Praed Street and down London Street; Norfolk Square is a block ahead on the left.

On Norfolk Square

These places (and many more on the same street) are similar; all offer small rooms at a reasonable price, in tall buildings with lots of stairs and no elevator. I've chosen the ones that offer the most reasonable prices and the warmest welcome.

$$ St. David's Hotels, run by the hospitable and energetic Neokleous family, has 60 fine rooms in several adjacent buildings (S-£60, Sb-£70, D-£70, Db-£90, Tb-£100, free Wi-Fi, 14-20 Norfolk Square, tel. 020/7723-3856, fax 020/7402-9061, www.stdavidshotels.com, info@stdavidshotels.com).

$$ Tudor Court Hotel has 38 colorful rooms run by the Gupta family (S-£40, Sb-£85, Db-£95, Tb-£115, family room-£135, 10-12 Norfolk Square, tel. 020/7723-5157, fax 020/7723-0727, www.tudorcourtpaddington.co.uk, reservations@tudorcourtpaddington.co.uk).

$$ Ashley Hotel is a peeling-wallpaper kind of place with 54 rooms (S-£35-40, Sb-£50-60, Db-£70-80, pay Wi-Fi, 15-17 Norfolk Square, tel. 020/7723-3375, fax 020/7723-0173, www.ashleyhotellondon.com, info@ashleyhotellondon.com).

$ easyHotel, the budget chain described on page 370, has a branch at 10 Norfolk Place.

Elsewhere near Paddington Station

To reach these hotels, follow the directions on the previous page, but continue past Norfolk Square to the big intersection with Sussex Gardens; the Royal Park is a couple of blocks to the right, and the Springfield Hotel is immediately to the left.

$$$ The Royal Park is the neighborhood's classy splurge, with 48 plush rooms, polished service, a genteel lounge (free champagne for guests nightly 19:00-20:00), and all the little extras (standard Db-£139-149, bigger "executive" Db-£169-179, prices vary with demand, does not include 20 percent VAT or breakfast, free Internet access and Wi-Fi, 3 Westbourne Terrace, tel. 020/7479-6600, fax 020/7479-6601, www.theroyalpark.com, info @theroyalpark.com).

$$ Springfield Hotel is efficiently run and simple, with 17 updated rooms. It sits on the wide, busy street called Sussex Gardens (request a quieter back room), with several other similar hotels nearby if you're in a pinch (Sb-£60, Db-£80-90, Tb-£100, extra fee to pay with credit card, 154 Sussex Gardens, tel. 020/7723-9898, fax 020/7723-0874, www.springfieldhotellondon .co.uk, info@springfieldhotellondon.co.uk).

Other Neighborhoods

North of Marble Arch: **$$$ The 22 York Street B&B** offers a casual alternative in the city center, renting 10 traditional, hardwood, comfortable rooms (Sb-£95, Db-£129, free Internet access and Wi-Fi, inviting lounge; from Baker Street Tube station, walk 2 blocks down Baker Street and take a right to 22 York Street—since there's no sign, just look for #22; tel. 020/7224-2990, www.22yorkstreet.co.uk, mc@22yorkstreet.co.uk, energetically run by Liz and Michael Callis).

$$$ The Sumner Hotel, renting 19 rooms in a 19th-century Georgian townhouse, is located a few blocks north of Hyde Park and Oxford Street, a busy shopping destination. Decorated with fancy modern Italian furniture, this swanky place packs in all the extras (Db-£170-220 depending on size, 20 percent discount with this book in 2012, extra bed-£50, air-con, elevator, free Wi-Fi, 54 Upper Berkeley Street just off Edgware Road, Tube: Marble Arch, tel. 020/7723-2244, fax 0870-705-8767, www.thesumner .com, hotel@thesumner.com).

Near Buckingham Palace: **$$ Vandon House Hotel,** run by Central College in Iowa, is packed with students most of the year, but rents its 32 rooms to travelers from late May through August at great prices. The rooms, while institutional, are comfy, and the location is excellent (S-£48, D-£75, Db-£95, Tb-£105, Qb-£125, apartment for up to 4 people-£125, only twin beds, a few rooms available year-round, elevator, pay Internet access and Wi-Fi; 3-minute walk west of St. James's Park Tube station or 7-minute walk from Victoria Station, near west end of Petty France Street on a tiny road, 1 Vandon Street; tel. 020/7799-6780, www.vandon house.com, info@vandonhouse.com).

Near Euston Station and the British Library: The **$$$ Methodist International Centre (MIC),** a modern, youthful Christian hotel and conference center, fills its lower floors with international students and its top floor with travelers. The 28 rooms are modern and sleek yet comfortable, with fine bathrooms, phones, and desks. The atmosphere is friendly, safe, clean, and controlled; it also has a spacious lounge and game room (Sb-£119 Fri-Sun, £139 Mon-Thu; Db-£130 Fri-Sun, £149 Mon-Thu; pricier "deluxe" rooms also available, buying a £100 annual membership saves you £20-40 per night—do the math to see if it's worth paying for, check website for specials, elevator, pay Wi-Fi, on a quiet street a block west of Euston Station, 81-103 Euston Street—not Euston Road, Tube: Euston, tel. 020/7380-0001, www.micentre .com, reservations@micentre.com). In addition to the rooms in the main building, they have several "annex" rooms—three rooms in one house that share a single bathroom—which could work well for families (S-£85, D-£95). In June-August, when the students are gone, they also rent simpler twin rooms in the main building (S or D-£75, includes one breakfast, extra breakfast-£15).

Big, Good-Value, Modern Hotels

These places—popular with budget tour groups—are well-run and offer elevators, 24-hour reception, and all the modern comforts in a no-frills, practical package. If you can score a double for £90-100 (or less—often possible with promotional rates) and don't mind a modern, impersonal, American-style hotel, one of these can be a decent value for London. It's especially worth considering for families, as kids generally stay for free (but check details on the websites). However, keep in mind that for about the same price, you can get a basic room at a budget hotel or B&B that has less predictable comfort, but more funkiness and friendliness in a more characteristic neighborhood.

Midweek prices are generally higher than weekend rates, and Sunday nights can be shockingly cheap. Breakfast is always extra. I've listed wide price ranges, as the specific rates vary dramatically with demand. In fact, the rates for a particular room for a specific date can change from day to day or week to week (like airline tickets), making it difficult to know when to book. On the hotel's website, punch in the dates you're considering to see what the going rate is, or look for special online offers. For the best deals, book at least three weeks in advance, prepay in full...and hope you don't have to change your plans (since these promotional rates are nonrefundable).

These hotels are often located on busy streets in dreary train-station neighborhoods, so use common sense after dark and wear your money belt.

North London Accommodations

❶ The 22 York Street B&B
❷ The Sumner Hotel
❸ Methodist International Centre
❹ Hotel Ibis London Euston
   St. Pancras & Drummond
   St. Eateries
❺ Premier Inn London
   Kings Cross St. Pancras

❻ Premier Inn London Euston
❼ Travelodge London Kings Cross
❽ To Jurys Inn Islington
❾ London Central Youth Hostel
❿ Oxford Street Youth Hostel
⓫ Salumeria Dino Italian Deli &
   Lantana OUT Take-Away

Premier Inn

For any of these, call their reservations toll line at 0870-242-8000 or—the best option—book online at www.premierinn.com. Premier Inn offers a "Premier Offer" non-flexible booking option on certain dates, but you have to book at least three weeks in advance and prepay for your room in its entirety (not changeable or refundable). The rates can be far lower than the ones I've listed below. If your dates are unlikely to change, check the website for details.

$$ Premier Inn London County Hall, literally down the hall from a $400-a-night Marriott Hotel, fills one end of London's massive former County Hall building. This family-friendly place is wonderfully located near the base of the London Eye and across the Thames from Big Ben. Its 313 efficient rooms come with all the necessary comforts, though it's quite impersonal—rather than a real reception desk, you'll find self-service check-in kiosks with a couple of clerks standing by to help (Db-£109-170 for 2 adults and up to 2 kids under age 16, elevator, pay Wi-Fi, some accessible rooms, 500 yards from Westminster Tube stop and Waterloo Station, Belvedere Road, central reservations toll tel. 0870-242-8000, reception desk toll tel. 0870-238-3300, easiest to book online at www.premierinn.com).

$$ Premier Inn London Southwark, with 59 rooms, is near Shakespeare's Globe on the South Bank (Db for up to 2 adults and 2 kids-£99-169, elevator, pay Wi-Fi, Bankside, 34 Park Street, Tube: London Bridge, toll tel. 0871-527-8676, www.premierinn .com).

$$ Premier Inn London Kings Cross St. Pancras, with 276 rooms, is across the street from the east end of King's Cross Station and near the Eurostar terminus at St. Pancras Station (Db-£96-160, air-con, elevator, pay Wi-Fi, 26-30 York Way, Tube: King's Cross St. Pancras, toll tel. 0871-527-8672, www.premierinn.com).

Other **$$ Premier Inns** charging £90-170 per room include **London Euston** (big, blue Lego-type building packed with vacationing families, on handy but noisy street at corner of Euston Road and Dukes Road, Tube: Euston, toll tel. 0870-238-3301), **London Kensington Earl's Court** (11 Knaresborough Place, Tube: Earl's Court or Gloucester Road, toll tel. 0870-238-3304), **London Victoria** (82-83 Eccleston Square, Tube: Victoria, toll tel. 0870-423-6494), and **London Putney Bridge** (farther out, 3 Putney Bridge Approach, Tube: Putney Bridge, toll tel. 0870-238-3302). Avoid the **Tower Bridge** location, which is an inconvenient 15-minute walk from the nearest Tube stop.

Other Chains

Travelodge: This chain has a nonrefundable "Saver" rate, where you prepay for your stay at least three weeks in advance (changes possible for a small fee until up to a week ahead). In general, it's cheapest to book online and in advance. **$$ Travelodge London Kings Cross** is another typical chain hotel with 140 cookie-cutter rooms, just 200 yards south (in front) of King's Cross Station (Db-usually £85, family rooms, can be noisy, elevator, pay Wi-Fi, Grays Inn Road, Tube: King's Cross St. Pancras, toll tel. 0871-984-6256). Other convenient Travelodge London locations are nearby **Kings Cross Royal Scot, Euston, Marylebone, Covent Garden, Liverpool Street,** and **Farringdon.** For details on all Travelodge hotels, see www.travelodge.co.uk.

Ibis: **$$$ Hotel Ibis London Euston St. Pancras** rents 380 rooms on a quiet street a block west of Euston Station (Db-£89-149, usually £139, no family rooms, elevator, pay Internet access and Wi-Fi, 3 Cardington Street, Tube: Euston, tel. 020/7388-7777, fax 020/7388-0001, www.ibishotel.com, h0921@accor.com). There's also an **Ibis London City** (5 Commercial Street, Tube: Aldgate East, tel. 020/7422-8400), but the other Ibis locations are far from the center.

Jurys Inn: **$$ Jurys Inn Islington** rents 200-plus compact, comfy rooms near King's Cross Station (Db/Tb-£109-169, some discounted rooms available online, 2 adults and 2 kids under age 12 can share one room, 60 Pentonville Road, Tube: Angel, tel. 020/7282-5500, fax 020/7282-5511, www.jurysinns.com). You'll also find Jurys Inns at **Chelsea** (Imperial Road, Tube: Imperial Wharf, tel. 020/7411-2200) and near **Heathrow Airport** (see "Heathrow and Gatwick Airports," later).

easyHotel

With several hotels in good neighborhoods around London, easy-Hotel is a radical concept—offering what you need to sleep well and safely, and nothing more. Most of them are fitted into old buildings, so the rooms are all odd shapes, from tiny windowless closets to others that are quite spacious. All rooms are well-ventilated and come with an efficient "bathroom pod" that looks like it was popped out of a plastic mold—just big enough to take care of business. While they do have a 24-hour reception, everything else is spartan: you get two towels, liquid soap, and a clean bed—no breakfast, no fresh towels, and no daily cleaning. The base rate ranges from £21-65, depending on the room size and when you book—"The earlier you book, the less you pay." Prices are the same for one person or two, but then you're nickel-and-dimed with optional charges for the TV, Wi-Fi, luggage storage, and so on.

If you go with the basic package, it's like hosteling with privacy—a hard-to-beat value. But you get what you pay for; in my experience, easyHotels are cheap in every sense of the word (no elevator, thin walls, noisy halls filled with loud travelers seeking bargain beds, flimsy construction that often results in broken things in the room). And they're only a good deal if you book far enough ahead to get a good price, and skip the many extras...which can add up fast.

$ easyHotel Victoria is well-located in an old building near Victoria Station (77 rooms, 36 Belgrave Road—for location, see map on page 356, Tube: Victoria, tel. 020/7834-1379, enquiries @victoria.easyhotel.com). They also have branches at **South Kensington** (34 rooms, 14 Lexham Gardens, Tube: Earl's Court or Gloucester Road, tel. 020/7136-2870, enquiries@southken.easy hotel.com), **Earl's Court** (80 rooms, 44-48 West Cromwell Road, Tube: Earl's Court, tel. 020/7373-4546, enquiries@earlscourt .easyhotel.com), **Paddington** (47 rooms, 10 Norfolk Place, Tube: Paddington, tel. 020/7706-9911, enquiries@paddington.easyhotel .com), and **Heathrow** and **Luton** airports (Heathrow location described on next page). Regardless of the location, reserve through their website (www.easyhotel.com).

Hostels

$ London Central Youth Hostel is the flagship of London's hostels, with 300 beds and all the latest in security and comfortable efficiency. Families and travelers of any age will feel welcome in this wonderful facility. You'll pay the same price for any bed in a 4- to 8-bed single-sex dorm—with or without private bathroom—so try to grab one with a bathroom (£20-30 per bunk bed—fluctuates with demand, £3/night extra for nonmembers, breakfast-£4; includes sheets, towel and locker; families welcome to book an entire room, pay Wi-Fi, members' kitchen, laundry, book long in advance, between Oxford Circus and Great Portland Street Tube stations at 104 Bolsover Street—see map on page 368, toll tel. 0870-770-6144 or 0845-371-9154, www.yha.org.uk, londoncentral@yha.org.uk).

$ Oxford Street Youth Hostel, newly opened, is right in the shopping and clubbing zone in Soho (£17-30 per bunk, 14 Noel Street, Tube: Oxford Street, toll tel. 0845-371-9133, www.yha.org.uk, oxfordst@yha.org.uk).

$ St. Paul's Youth Hostel, near St. Paul's Cathedral, is clean, modern, friendly, and well-run. Most of the 190 beds are in shared, single-sex 3- to 11-bunk rooms (bed-around £20 depending on demand, twin D-£60, includes locker and sheets but not breakfast, nonmembers pay £3 extra, cheap meals, open 24 hours, 36 Carter Lane, Tube: St. Paul's, tel. 020/7236-4965 or toll tel. 0845-371-9012, www.yha.org.uk, stpauls@yha.org.uk).

$ A cluster of three **St. Christopher's Inn** hostels, south of the Thames near London Bridge, have cheap dorm beds; one branch is for women only. All have loud and friendly bars attached (£22-32, must be over 18 years old, 161-165 Borough High Street, Tube: Borough or London Bridge, reservations tel. 020/8600-7500, www.st-christophers.co.uk).

Dorms

$$ The **University of Westminster** opens its dorm rooms to travelers during summer break, from mid-June through late September. Located in several high-rise buildings scattered around central London, the rooms—some with private bathrooms, others with shared bathrooms nearby—come with access to well-equipped kitchens and big lounges (S-£35, Sb-£60, D-£54, Db-£106, tel. 020/7911-5181, www.westminster.ac.uk/business/summer-accommodation, summeraccommodation@westminster.ac.uk).

$ University College London also has rooms for travelers, from mid-June until mid-September (S-£31-43, pay Internet access, tel. 020/7278-3895, www.ucl.ac.uk/residences).

$$ The **London School of Economics** has openings in its dorms from July through September (S-£33-43, Sb-£59-65, D-£52-60, Db-£76-94, tel. 020/7955-7575, www.lsevacations .co.uk, vacations@lse.ac.uk).

Heathrow and Gatwick Airports
At or near Heathrow Airport

It's so easy to get to Heathrow from central London, I see no reason to sleep there. But if you do, here are some options. The Yotel is actually inside the airport, while the rest are a short bus or taxi ride away. In addition to public buses, the cleverly named £4 "Hotel Hoppa" shuttle buses connect the airport to many nearby hotels (different routes serve the various hotels and terminals—may take a while to spot your particular bus at the airport).

$$ Yotel, at the airport inside Terminal 4, has small sleep dens that offer a popular place to catch a quick nap (four hours-£37-64), or to stay overnight (tiny "standard cabin"—£65/8 hours, "premium cabin"—£87/8 hours; cabins sleep 1-2 people; price is per cabin—not person, reserve online for free or by phone for small fee). Prices vary by day, week, and time of year, so check their website. All rooms are only slightly larger than a double bed, and have private bathrooms and free Internet access and Wi-Fi. These windowless rooms have oddly purplish lighting (tel. 020/7100-1100, www.yotel.com, customer@yotel.com).

$ easyHotel, your cheapest bet, is in a low-rent residential neighborhood a £5 taxi ride from the airport. Its 53 no-frills, pod-like rooms are on two floors. Before booking at this very basic place, read the explanation on page 370 (Db-£25-50, no breakfast, no elevator, pay Internet access and Wi-Fi, Brick Field Lane; take local bus #140 from airport's Central Bus Station or the "Hotel Hoppa" #H8 from Terminals 1 or 3, or the hotel can arrange a taxi to the airport; tel. 020/8897-9237, www.easyhotel.com, enquiries @heathrow.easyhotel.com).

$$ Hotel Ibis London Heathrow is a chain hotel offering predictable value (Db-£80 Mon-Thu, Db-£60 Fri-Sun, check website for specials as low as £35, breakfast-£7, pay Internet access and Wi-Fi; 112-114 Bath Road, take local bus #105, #111, #140, #285, #423, or #555 from airport's Central Bus Station or Terminal 4, or the "Hotel Hoppa" #H6 from Terminals 1 or 3, or #H56 from Terminals 4 or 5; tel. 020/8759-4888, fax 020/8564-7894, www .ibishotel.com, h0794@accor.com).

$$ Jurys Inn, another hotel chain, tempts tired travelers with 300-plus cookie-cutter rooms (Db-£89-105, check website for deals, breakfast extra; on Eastern Perimeter Road, Tube: Hatton Cross plus 5-minute walk; take the Tube one stop from Terminals

1, 2, or 3; or two stops from Terminals 4 or 5; or the "Hotel Hoppa" #H9 from Terminals 1 or 3, or #H53 from Terminals 4 or 5; or buses #285, #482, #490, or #555; tel. 020/8266-4664, fax 020/8266-4665, www.jurysinns.com).

At or near Gatwick Airport

$$ Yotel, with small rooms, has a branch right at the airport (Gatwick South Terminal; see prices and contact info in Heathrow listing, previous page).

$ Gatwick Airport Central Premier Inn rents cheap rooms 350 yards from the airport (Db-£40-75, breakfast-£8, £2 shuttle bus from airport—must reserve in advance, Longbridge Way, North Terminal, toll tel. 0871-527-8406, frustrating phone tree, www.premierinn.com). Four more Premier Inns are within a five-mile radius of the airport.

$$ Barn Cottage, a converted 16th-century barn flanked by a tennis court and swimming pool, sits in the peaceful countryside, with a good pub just two blocks away. Its two wood-beamed rooms, antique furniture, and large garden makes you forget Gatwick is 10 minutes away (S-£60, D-£80, cash only, Church Road, Leigh, Reigate, Surrey, tel. 01306/611-347, warmly run by Pat and Mike Comer). Don't confuse this place with others of the same name. A taxi from Gatwick to here runs about £15; the Comers can take you back to the airport or train station for about £10.

$ Gatwick Airport Travelodge has budget rooms about two miles from the airport (Db-£39-57, breakfast extra, pay Wi-Fi, Church Road, Lowfield Heath, Crawley, £3 shuttle bus from airport, toll tel. 0871-984-6031, www.travelodge.co.uk).

For Longer Stays

Staying a week or longer? Consider the advantages that come with renting a furnished apartment—or "flat," as the British say. Complete with a small, equipped kitchen and living room, this option can also work for families or groups on shorter visits. Among the many organizations ready to help, the following have been recommended by local guides and readers: www.perfectplaces.com, www.homefromhome.co.uk, www.london33.com, www.london-house.com, www.gowithit.co.uk, www.aplacelikehome.co.uk, www.regentsuites.com, and www.airbnb.com/travel/london/gb.

Sometimes you can save money by renting directly from the apartment owner (check www.vrbo.com). Readers also report success using Craigslist (http://london.craigslist.co.uk; search within "vacation rentals").

Read the rental conditions carefully and ask lots of questions.

If a certain amenity is important to you (such as Wi-Fi or a washing machine in the unit), ask specifically about it and what to do if it stops working. Plot the location carefully (plug the address into http://maps.google.com), and remember to factor in travel time and costs from outlying neighborhoods to central London. Finally, it's a good idea to buy trip cancellation/interruption insurance, as many weekly rentals are nonrefundable.

SLEEPING IN LONDON

EATING IN LONDON

England's reputation for miserable food, while once well-deserved, is now dated. The British cuisine scene is lively, trendy, and pleasantly surprising. (Unfortunately, it's also expensive.) Even the basic, traditional pub grub has gone "upmarket," with gastropubs that serve fresh vegetables rather than soggy fries and mushy peas.

In London, the sheer variety of foods—from every corner of its former empire and beyond—is astonishing. You'll be amazed at the number of hopping, happening new restaurants of all kinds.

If you want to dine (as opposed to eat), drop by a London newsstand to get a weekly entertainment guide or an annual restaurant guide (both have extensive restaurant listings). Visit www.london-eating.co.uk or www.squaremeal.co.uk for more options.

The thought of a £50 meal in Britain generally ruins my appetite, so my London dining is limited mostly to easygoing, fun, moderately priced alternatives. I've listed places by neighborhood—handy to your sightseeing or hotel. Considering how expensive London can be, if there's any good place to cut corners to stretch your budget, it's by eating cheaply.

When restaurant-hunting, choose a spot filled with Londoners, not tourists. Venturing even a block or two off the main drag leads to higher-quality food for less than half the price of the tourist-oriented places. Londoners eat better at lower-rent locales.

London (and all of Britain) is smoke-free. Expect restaurants and pubs that sell food to be non-smoking indoors, with smokers occupying patios and doorways outside.

Budget Eating Tips

You have plenty of inexpensive £8-10 choices: pub grub, daily lunch and early-bird dinner specials, ethnic restaurants, cafeterias, fast food, picnics, fish-and-chips, greasy-spoon cafés, or pizza.

I've found that portions are huge, and with locals feeling the pinch of their recession, **sharing plates** is generally just fine. Ordering two drinks, a soup or side salad, and splitting a £10 meat pie can make a good, filling meal. If you are on a limited budget, I'd recommend sharing a main course in a more expensive place for a nicer eating experience.

Pub grub is the most atmospheric budget option. Many of London's 7,000 pubs serve fresh, tasty buffets under ancient timbers, with hearty lunches and dinners priced reasonably at £6-10 (see "Pubs," later).

Classier restaurants have some affordable deals. Lunch is usually cheaper than dinner; a top-end £25-for-dinner-type restaurant often serves the same quality two-course lunch deals for £10. Look for early-bird dinner specials, allowing you to eat well and affordably (generally two courses-£15, three courses-£20), but early (about 17:30-19:00, last order by 19:00).

Ethnic restaurants from all over the world add spice to London's cuisine scene. Eating Indian, Bangladeshi, Chinese, or Thai is cheap (even cheaper if you do takeout). Middle Eastern stands sell gyros, falafel, and *shwarmas* (lamb in pita bread). An Indian samosa (greasy, flaky meat-and-vegetable pie) costs £2, can be microwaved, and makes a very cheap, if small, meal. You'll find all-you-can-eat Chinese and Thai places serving £6 meals and offering £3.50 take-away boxes. While you can't "split" a buffet, you can split a take-away box. Stuff the box full, and you and your partner can eat in a park for under £2 each—making this London's cheapest hot meal.

Most large **museums** (and many historic **churches**) have handy, moderately priced cafeterias.

Fast-food places, both American and British, are everywhere.

Cheap chain restaurants, such as steak houses and pizza places, serve no-nonsense food in a family-friendly setting (steak-house meals about £10, all-you-can-stomach pizza around £5). For specific chains to keep an eye out for, see "Good Chain Restaurants," on the next page.

Bakeries sell yogurt, cartons of "semi-skimmed" milk, pastries, and pasties (PASS-teez). Pasties are hearty, savory meat pies that originated in the Cornish mining country; they had big crimped edges so miners with filthy hands could eat them and toss the dirty crust. The most traditional filling is beef stew, but you'll also find them with chicken, vegetable, lamb and mint, and even Indian flavors inside.

Picnicking saves time and money. Fine park benches and polite pigeons abound in most neighborhoods. You can easily get prepared food to go. Munch a relaxed "meal on wheels" picnic dur-

ing your open-top bus tour or river cruise to save 30 precious minutes for sightseeing.

Good **sandwich shops** and corner **grocery stores** are a hit
with local workers eating on the
run. Try boxes of orange juice
(pure, by the liter), fresh bread,
tasty English cheese, meat, a tube
of Colman's English mustard,
local eatin' apples, bananas, small
tomatoes, a small tub of yogurt
(drinkable), trail mix, nuts, plain
or chocolate-covered digestive
biscuits (cookies), and any local specialties. At **open-air markets**
and **supermarkets,** you can get fruit and veggies in small quan-
tities. Supermarkets often have good deli sections, even offering
Indian dishes, and sometimes salad bars. Decent packaged sandwiches are sold everywhere (£3-4).

Good Chain Restaurants

I know—you're going to London to enjoy characteristic little hole-
in-the-wall pubs, so mass-produced food is the furthest thing
from your mind. But several excellent chains with branches around
London (and across the UK) can be a nice break from pub grub.

Sit-Down Chains

Wagamama Noodle Bar, serving up fresh and reliably delicious
pan-Asian cuisine, is stylish, youthful, and mod. There's one in
almost every midsize city in the UK, and after you've sampled
their udon noodles, fried rice, or curry dishes, you'll know why.
They're usually in a sprawling, loud, and modern hall filled with
long shared tables and busy servers who scrawl your order on the
placemat. Portions are huge enough for light eaters on a tight budget to share (typically £7-10 main dishes, good vegetarian options).
For locations in London, see page 391.

At **Yo! Sushi,** freshly prepared sushi dishes trundle past on
a conveyor belt. Color-coded plates tell you how much each dish
costs (£1.75-5), and a picture-filled menu explains what you're eating. Just help yourself. For locations in London, see page 390.

Gourmet Burger Kitchen (GBK) offers burgers that are, if
not quite gourmet, very good. Choices range from a simple cheeseburger to more elaborate options, such as Jamaican (£7-8 burgers).
Choose a table and order at the counter—they'll bring the food to
you.

Loch Fyne Fish Restaurant, a Scottish chain, serves up fish,
oysters, and mussels in a lively, upscale-but-unpretentious setting
(£10-15 main dishes, early-bird deals).

Tipping

Tipping is an issue only at restaurants and fancy pubs that have waiters and waitresses. If you order food at a counter, don't tip.

If the menu states that service is included, there's no need to tip beyond that. If service isn't included, tip about 10 percent by rounding up. Leave the tip on the table, or hand it to your server with your payment for the meal and say, "Keep the rest, please." Most restaurants in London now add a 12.5 percent "optional" tip onto the bill—read your bill carefully, and tip only what you think the service warrants.

Ask and **Pizza Express** serve quality pasta and pizza in a pleasant, sit-down atmosphere that's family-friendly. **Jamie's Italian** (from celebrity chef Jamie Oliver) is hipper and pricier, and feels more upmarket.

Carry-Out Chains

While the following places might have some seating, they're an easy place to grab some prepackaged food on the run.

Major supermarket chains have smaller, offshoot branches that specialize in sandwiches, salads, and other prepared foods to go. These can be a picnicker's dream come true. Some shops are stand-alone, while others are located inside a larger store. The most prevalent—and best—is **M&S Simply Food** (an offshoot of the Marks & Spencer department-store chain; one is inside Victoria Station). **Sainsbury's Local** grocery stores also offer some decent prepared food; **Tesco Express** and **Tesco Metro** run a distant third.

Some "cheap and cheery" chains, such as **Pret à Manger** and **Eat,** provide office workers with good, healthful sandwiches, salads, and pastries to go.

West Cornwall Pasty Company sells a variety of these traditional savory pies for around £3—as do many smaller, independent bakeries.

Breakfast

The traditional "fry," or "full English breakfast," is famous as a hearty way to start the day. Also known as a "heart attack on a plate," the breakfast is especially feast-like if you've just come from the land of the skimpy continental breakfast across the Channel.

Your standard fry gets off to a healthy start with juice and cereal or porridge. (Try Weetabix, a soggy British cousin of Shredded Wheat and perhaps the most absorbent material known to man.) Next, with tea or coffee, you get a heated plate with a fried egg, Canadian-style bacon or a sausage, a grilled tomato, sautéed mushrooms, baked beans, and toast. Toast comes in a rack (to cool quickly and crisply) with butter and marmalade. This protein-stuffed meal is great for stamina, and tides many travelers over until dinner (or at least afternoon tea). You'll be asked which elements of the full fry you want; your host appreciates it if you order only what you'll eat. There's nothing wrong with skipping some or all of the fry—few locals actually start their day with this heavy breakfast. Many progressive B&B owners offer vegetarian, organic, or other creative variations on the traditional breakfast.

Pubs

Pubs are a basic part of the British social scene, and, whether you're a teetotaler or a beer-guzzler, they should be a part of your travel here. "Pub" is short for "public house." It's an extended living room where, if you don't mind the stickiness, you can feel the pulse of London. Smart travelers use the pubs to eat, drink, get out of the rain, watch sporting events, and make new friends.

Though hours vary, pubs generally serve beer Monday-Saturday 11:00-23:00 and Sunday 12:00-22:30, though many are open later, particularly on Friday and Saturday. As it nears closing time, you'll hear shouts of "Last orders." Then comes the 10-minute warning bell. Finally, they'll call "Time!" to pick up your glass, finished or not, when the pub closes.

A cup of darts is free for the asking. People go to a public house to be social. They want to talk. Get vocal with a local. This is easiest at the bar, where people assume you're in the mood to talk (rather than at a table, where you're allowed a bit of privacy). The pub is the next best thing to having relatives in town. Cheers!

Pub Grub

Pub grub gets better each year. It's London's best indoor eating value. For £6-10, you'll get a basic budget hot lunch or dinner in friendly surroundings. (For something more refined, try a gastropub, which serves higher-quality meals for £12-18.) The *Good Pub Guide* is an excellent resource (www.thegoodpubguide.co.uk). Pubs that are attached to restaurants, advertise their food, and are crowded with locals are more likely to have fresh food and a chef—and less likely to be the kind of pub that sells only lousy microwaved snacks.

Pubs generally serve traditional dishes, such as fish-and-chips, vegetables, "bangers and mash" (sausages and mashed potatoes), roast beef with Yorkshire pudding (batter-baked in the oven), and assorted meat pies, such as steak-and-kidney pie or shepherd's pie (stewed lamb topped with mashed potatoes). Sunday afternoons at

Pub Appreciation

The pub is the heart of the people's England, where all manner of folks have, for generations, found their respite from work and a home-away-from-home. England's classic pubs are national treasures, with great cultural value and rich history, not to mention good beer and grub.

The Golden Age for pub-building was in the late Victorian era (c. 1880-1905), when pubs were independently owned and land prices were high enough to make it worthwhile to invest in fixing up pubs. The politics were pro-pub as well: Conservatives, backed by Big Beer, were in, and temperance-minded Liberals were out.

Especially in class-conscious Victorian times, traditional pubs were divided into sections by elaborate screens (now mostly gone), allowing the wealthy to drink in a more refined setting, while commoners congregated on the pub's rougher side. These were really "public houses," featuring nooks (snugs) for groups and clubs to meet, friends and lovers to rendezvous, and families to get out of the house at night. Because many pub-goers were illiterate, pubs were simply named for the picture hung outside (e.g., The Crooked Stick, The Queen's Arms—meaning her coat of arms).

Historic pubs still dot the London cityscape. The only place to see the very oldest-style tavern in the "domestic tradition" is at **Ye Olde Cheshire Cheese,** which was rebuilt in 1667 (after the Great Fire) from a 16th-century tavern (see description on page 239; £6-7 pub grub, £9-12 meals in the restaurant, open daily, 145 Fleet Street, Tube: Blackfriars, tel. 020/7353-6170). Imagine this place in the pre-Victorian era: With no bar, drinkers gathered around the fireplaces, while tap boys shuttled tankards up from the cellar. (This was long before barroom taps were connected to casks in the cellar. Oh, and don't say "keg"—that's a gassy modern thing.)

Late-Victorian pubs, such as the lovingly restored 1897 **Princess Louise** (Mon-Fri 11:00-23:00, Sat 12:00-23:00, closed Sun, 208 High Holborn, see map on page 387, Tube: Holborn, tel. 020/7405-8816), are more common. These places are fancy, often with heavy embossed wallpaper ceilings, decorative tile work, fine-etched glass, ornate carved stillions (the big central hutch for storing bottles and glass), and even urinals equipped with a place to set your glass.

London's best Art Nouveau pub is **The Black Friar** (c. 1900-1915), with fine carved capitals, lamp holders, and quirky phrases worked into the decor (£7-12 meals, open daily, outdoor seating, 174 Queen Victoria Street, Tube: Blackfriars, tel. 020/7236-5474).

The "former-bank pubs" represent a more modern trend in pub-building. As banks increasingly go electronic, they're mov-

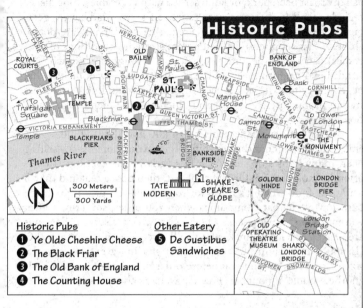

Historic Pubs

THE CITY

ROYAL COURTS
OLD BAILEY
BANK OF ENGLAND
NEWGATE
PETER LN.
ST. BRIDE
CHANCERY LANE
THE TEMPLE
FLEET ST.
LUDGATE
WARWICK
NEW CHANGE
ST. PAUL'S
St. Paul's
CHEAPSIDE
Bank
Mansion House
CORNHILL
KING WILLIAM ST.
CARTER LN.
QUEEN VICTORIA ST.
UPPER THAMES ST.
CANNON ST.
Cannon St.
EASTCHEAP
To Tower of London
To Trafalgar Square
Blackfriars
Monument
LOWER THAMES ST.
THE MONUMENT
VICTORIA EMBANKMENT
Temple
BLACKFRIARS PIER
BLACKFRIARS BRIDGE
MILLENNIUM BRIDGE
BANKSIDE PIER
SOUTHWARK BRIDGE
GOLDEN HINDE
LONDON BRIDGE
LONDON BRIDGE PIER
Thames River
300 Meters
300 Yards
TATE MODERN
SHAKE-SPEARE'S GLOBE
London Bridge Station
OLD OPERATING THEATRE MUSEUM
SHARD LONDON BRIDGE
NEWCOMEN ST.
ST. THOMAS ST.
SNOWFIELDS

Historic Pubs
❶ Ye Olde Cheshire Cheese
❷ The Black Friar
❸ The Old Bank of England
❹ The Counting House

Other Eatery
❺ De Gustibus Sandwiches

ing out of lavish, high-rent old buildings. Many of these former banks are being refitted as pubs with elegant bars and freestanding stillions, which provide a fine centerpiece. Three such pubs are **The Old Bank of England** (Mon-Fri 11:00-23:00, closed Sat-Sun, 194 Fleet Street, Tube: Temple, tel. 020/7430-2255), **The Jugged Hare** (open daily, 172 Vauxhall Bridge Road—see map on page 356, Tube: Victoria, tel. 020/7828-1543, also see listing on page 394), and **The Counting House** (Mon-Fri 11:00-23:00, closed Sat-Sun, 50 Cornhill, Tube: Bank, tel. 020/7283-7123, also see listing on page 397).

Go pubbing in the evening for a lively time, or drop by during the quiet late morning (from 11:00), when the pub is empty and filled with memories. For a guided tour, check out Bob Steel's London Heritage pub walks (about £50/group for a leisurely half-day private walk, www.aletrails.com, tel. 020/715-4815, info @aletrails.com).

most pubs are reserved for a traditional favorite, "Sunday Roast," usually roast beef, pork, or lamb served with vegetables. Side dishes include salads (sometimes even a nice self-serve salad bar), vegetables, and—invariably—"chips" (French fries). "Crisps" are potato chips. A "jacket potato" (baked potato stuffed with fillings of your choice) can almost be a meal in itself. A "ploughman's lunch" is a "traditional English meal" of bread, cheese, and sweet pickles that nearly every tourist tries...once. These days, you'll likely find more Italian pasta, curried dishes, and quiche on the menu than traditional fare.

Meals are usually served 12:00-14:00 and 18:00-20:00—generally not throughout the day. Since they make more money selling beer, many pubs stop serving meals early in the evening. There's often no table service. Order at the bar, then take a seat and they'll bring the food when it's ready (or sometimes you pick it up at the bar). Pay at the bar (sometimes when you order, sometimes after you eat). Don't tip unless it's a place with full table service. Servings are hearty, service is quick, and you'll rarely spend more than £10. (If you're on a tight budget, consider sharing a meal—note the size of portions around you before ordering.) A beer or cider adds another couple of pounds. (Free tap water is always available.)

Beer

The British take great pride in their beer. Many Brits think that drinking beer cold and carbonated, as Americans do, ruins the taste.

Most pubs will have **lagers** (cold, refreshing, American-style beer), **ales** (amber-colored, cellar-temperature beer), **bitters** (hop-flavored ale, perhaps the most typical British beer), and **stouts** (dark and somewhat bitter, like Guinness). At pubs, long-handled pulls are used to pull the traditional, rich-flavored "real ales" up from the cellar. These are the connoisseur's favorites: fermented naturally, varying from sweet to bitter, often with a hoppy or nutty flavor. Notice the fun names. Short-handled pulls at the bar mean colder, fizzier, mass-produced, and less interesting keg beers. Mild beers are sweeter, with a creamy malt flavoring. Irish cream ale is a smooth, sweet experience. Try the draft cider (sweet or dry)...carefully.

Order your beer at the bar and pay as you go, with no need to tip. An average beer costs £3. Part of the experience is standing before a line of "hand pulls," or taps, and wondering which beer to choose.

Drinks are served by the pint (20-ounce imperial size) or the half-pint. (It's almost feminine for a man to order just a half; I order mine with quiche.) Proper English ladies enjoy a half-beer and half-7-Up **shandy.**

Besides beer, many pubs have a good selection of wines by the glass, a fully stocked bar for the gentleman's "G and T" (gin and tonic), and the increasingly popular bottles of alcohol-plus-sugar (such as Bacardi Breezers) for the younger working-class set. **Pimm's** is a refreshing and fruity summer cocktail, traditionally popular during Wimbledon. It's an upper-class drink…a rough bloke might insult a pub by claiming it sells more Pimm's than beer. Teetotalers can order from a wide variety of soft drinks. Children are served food and soft drinks in pubs, but you must be 18 to order a beer.

Indian Food

Eating Indian food is "going local" in cosmopolitan, multiethnic London. Take the opportunity to sample food from Britain's former colony. Indian cuisine is as varied as the country itself. In general, they use more exotic spices than British or American cuisine—some hot, some sweet. Indian food is very vegetarian-friendly, offering many meatless dishes to choose from on any given menu.

For a simple meal that costs about £10-12, order one dish with rice and naan (Indian flatbread that can be served plain, with garlic, or other ways). Many restaurants offer a fixed-price combination called a *thali* that offers more variety, and is simpler and cheaper than ordering à la carte. For about £20, you can make a mix-and-match platter out of several sharable dishes, including dal (lentil soup) as a starter, one or two meat or vegetable dishes with sauce (e.g., chicken curry, chicken *tikka masala* in a creamy tomato sauce, grilled fish tandoori, chickpea *chana masala*, or the spicy vindaloo dish), *raita* (a cooling yogurt that's added to spicy dishes), rice, naan, and an Indian beer (wine and Indian food don't really mix) or chai (a cardamom- and cinnamon-spiced tea, usually served with milk).

Desserts (Sweets)

To the British, the traditional word for dessert is "pudding," although it's also referred to as "sweets" these days. Sponge cake, cream, fruitcake, and meringue are key players.

Trifle is the best-known British concoction, consisting of sponge cake soaked in brandy or sherry (or orange juice for children), then covered with jam and/or fruit and custard cream. Whipped cream can sometimes put the final touch on this "light" treat.

British Chocolate

My chocoholic readers are enthusiastic about British choco-lates. As with other dairy products, chocolate seems richer and creamier here than it does in the US, so even the basics like Kit Kat and Twix have a different taste. Some favor-ites include Cadbury Gold bars (filled with liquid caramel), Cadbury Crunchie bars, Nestle's Lion bars (layered wafers covered in caramel and chocolate), Cadbury's Boost bars (a shortcake biscuit with caramel in milk chocolate), Cadbury Flake (crumbly folds of melt-in-your-mouth chocolate), and Galaxy chocolate bars (especially the ones with hazelnuts). Thornton shops (in larger train stations) sell a box of sweets called the Continental Assortment, which comes with a tast-ing guide. (The highlight is the mocha white-chocolate truf-fle.) British M&Ms, called Smarties, are better than American ones. Many Brits feel that the ultimate treat is a box of either Nestlé Quality Street or Cadbury Roses—assortments of filled chocolates in colorful wrappers. At ice-cream vans, look for the beloved traditional "99p"—a vanilla soft-serve cone with a small Flake bar stuck right into the middle.

Castle puddings are sponge puddings cooked in small molds and topped with Golden Syrup (a popular brand and a cross between honey and maple syrup). Bread-and-butter pudding con-sists of slices of French bread baked with milk, cream, eggs, and raisins (similar to the American preparation), served warm with cold cream. Hasty pudding, supposedly the invention of people in a hurry to avoid the bailiff, is made from stale bread with dried fruit and milk. Queen of puddings is a breadcrumb pudding topped with warm jam, meringue, and cream. Treacle pudding is a popular steamed pudding whose "sponge" mixture combines flour, suet (animal fat), butter, sugar, and milk. Christmas pud-ding (also called plum pudding) is a dense mixture with dried and candied fruit served with brandy butter or hard sauce. Sticky toffee pudding is a moist cake made with dates, heated and drizzled with toffee sauce, and served with ice cream or cream. Banoffee pie is the delicious British answer to banana cream pie.

The English version of custard is a smooth, yellow liquid. Cream tops most everything that custard does not. There's single cream for coffee. Double cream is really thick. Whipped cream is familiar, and clotted cream is the consistency of whipped butter.

Fool is a dessert with sweetened pureed fruit (such as rhubarb, gooseberries, or black currants) mixed with cream or custard and chilled. Elderflower is a popular flavoring for sorbet.

Flapjacks here aren't pancakes, but are dense, sweet oatmeal cakes (a little like a cross between a granola bar and a brownie).

They come with toppings such as toffee and chocolate.

Scones are tops, and many inns and restaurants have their secret recipes. Whether made with fruit or topped with clotted cream, scones take the cake.

Restaurants

Central London

Near Trafalgar Square

These places are within about 100 yards of Trafalgar Square.

St. Martin-in-the-Fields Café in the Crypt is just right for a tasty meal on a monk's budget—maybe even on a monk's tomb. You'll dine sitting on somebody's gravestone in an ancient crypt. Their enticing buffet line is kept stocked all day, serving breakfast, lunch, and dinner (£6-10 cafeteria plates, hearty traditional desserts, free jugs of water). They also serve a restful cream tea (£6, daily 14:00-17:00). You'll find it directly under the St. Martin-in-the-Fields Church, facing Trafalgar Square (Mon-Tue 8:00-20:00, Wed 8:00-22:30, Thu-Sat 8:00-21:00, Sun 11:00-18:00, profits go to the church, Tube: Charing Cross, tel. 020/7766-1158 or 020/7766-1100). Wednesday evenings at 20:00 come with a live jazz band (£6-9 tickets). While here, check out the concert schedule for the busy church upstairs (or visit www.smitf.org).

The Chandos Pub's Opera Room floats amazingly apart from the tacky crush of tourism around Trafalgar Square. Look for it opposite the National Portrait Gallery (corner of William IV Street and St. Martin's Lane) and climb the stairs (to the right of the pub entrance) to the Opera Room. This is a fine Trafalgar rendezvous point and wonderfully local pub. They serve traditional, plain-tasting £6-7 pub meals—meat pies and fish-and-chips are their specialty. The ground-floor pub is stuffed with regulars and offers snugs (private booths), the same menu, and more serious beer drinking. Chandos proudly serves the local Samuel Smith beer at £2 a pint (kitchen open daily 11:00-19:00, order and pay at the bar, 29 St. Martin's Lane, Tube: Leicester Square, tel. 020/7836-1401).

Gordon's Wine Bar, with a simple, steep staircase leading into a candlelit 15th-century wine cellar, is filled with dusty old bottles, faded British memorabilia, and nine-to-fivers. At the "English rustic" buffet, choose a hot meal or cold meat dish with a salad, or a hearty (and splittable) plate of cheeses, bread, and pickles (£7.75)—or share four plates for £12. Then step up to the wine bar and consider the many varieties of wine and port available by the glass (this place is passionate about port). The low carbon-crusted vaulting deeper in the back seems to intensify the Hogarth-painting atmosphere. Although it's crowded, you can normally corral two chairs and grab the corner of a table. On hot

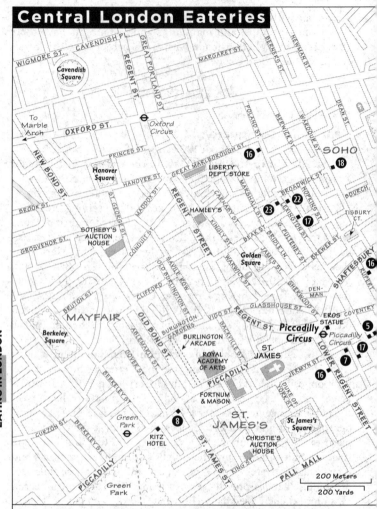

Central London Eateries

① St. Martin-in-the-Fields Café in the Crypt

② The Chandos Pub's Opera Room

③ Gordon's Wine Bar

④ The Lord Moon of the Mall Pub

⑤ Stockpot & Woodlands South Indian Vegetarian Restaurant

⑥ West End Kitchen

⑦ Criterion Restaurant

⑧ The Wolseley

⑨ Joe Allen

⑩ Loch Fyne Fish Restaurant

⑪ Sofra Turkish Restaurant

⑫ Sitar Indian Restaurant

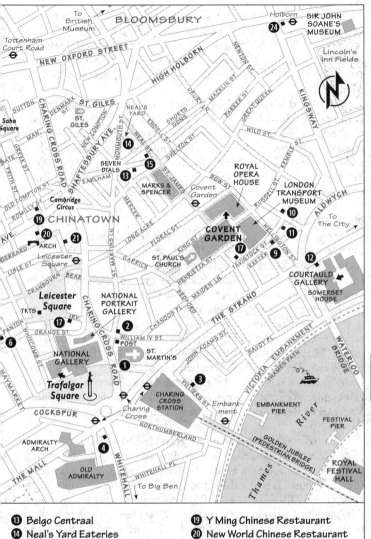

13 Belgo Centraal
14 Neal's Yard Eateries
15 Food for Thought Café
16 Yo! Sushi (3)
17 Wagamama Noodle Bar (4)
18 Busaba Eathai Thai Rest.
& Côte Restaurant

19 Y Ming Chinese Restaurant
20 New World Chinese Restaurant
21 Jen Café
22 Andrew Edmunds Restaurant
23 Mildred's Vegetarian Rest.;
Fernandez & Wells
24 The Princess Louise Pub

days, the crowd spills out onto a leafy back patio, where a barbecue cooks for a long line of tables (arrive before 17:00 to get a seat, Mon-Sat 11:00-23:00, Sun 12:00-22:00, 2 blocks from Trafalgar Square, bottom of Villiers Street at #47, Tube: Embankment, tel. 020/7930-1408, www.gordonswinebar.com, manager Gerard Menan).

The Lord Moon of the Mall pub, with real ales on tap and cheap pub grub such as fish-and-chips, is a good place to experience retro English cuisine from the days when it had a horrible reputation. The pub fills a great old former Barclays Bank building a block down Whitehall from Trafalgar Square (daily 9:00-22:00, kid-friendly menu but no kids after 20:00, 16-18 Whitehall, Tube: Charing Cross or Embankment, tel. 020/7839-7701).

Near Piccadilly

Hungry and broke in the theater district? Head for Panton Street (off Haymarket, two blocks southeast of Piccadilly Circus), where several hardworking little places compete, all seeming to offer a three-course meal for about £9. Peruse the entire block (vegetarian, Pizza Express, Moroccan, Thai, Chinese, and two famous diners) before making your choice.

Stockpot is a meat, potatoes, gravy, and mushy-peas kind of place, famous and rightly popular for its edible, cheap English meals (Mon-Sat 7:00-23:00, Sun 7:00-22:00, 38-40 Panton Street, cash only). The **West End Kitchen** (across the street at #5, same hours and menu) is a direct competitor that's also well-known and just as good. Vegetarians may prefer the **Woodlands South Indian Vegetarian Restaurant,** which serves an impressive £18 *thali* (37 Panton Street).

The palatial **Criterion** offers grand-piano ambience beneath gilded tiles and chandeliers in a dreamy Byzantine church setting from 1880. It's right on Piccadilly Circus but a world away from the punk junk. It's a deal for the visual experience during lunch and before 19:00—but after 19:00, the menu becomes really expensive...and, at any hour, the service could care less. Anyone can drop in for coffee or a drink (£17-20 fixed-price meals, daily 12:00-14:30 & 17:30-19:00 & 22:00-23:30, 224 Piccadilly, tel. 020/7930-0488).

The Wolseley is the grand 1920s showroom of a long-defunct British car. The last Wolseley drove out with the Great Depression, but today this old-time bistro bustles with formal waiters serving traditional Austrian and French dishes in an elegant black-marble-and-chandeliers setting fit for its location next to the Ritz. Although the food can be unexceptional, prices are reasonable, and the presentation and setting are grand. Reservations are a must (£18 plates; cheaper soup, salad, and sandwich menu available; Mon-Fri 7:00-24:00, Sat 8:00-24:00, Sun 8:00-23:00, 160

Piccadilly—for exact location, see map on page 386, tel. 020/7499-6996). They're popular for their fancy cream or afternoon tea (for details, see page 397).

Near Covent Garden

Covent Garden bustles with people and touristy eateries. The area feels overrun, but if you must eat around here, there are some good options.

Joe Allen, tucked in a basement a block away, serves modern international and American cuisine with both style and hubbub. Downstairs off a quiet street with candles and white tablecloths, it's comfortably spacious and popular with the theater crowd (meals for about £30, £16 two-course specials and £18 three-course specials Mon-Wed and Sun, open daily 11:30-23:00, piano music after 21:00, 13 Exeter Street, tel. 020/7836-0651).

Loch Fyne Fish Restaurant is part of a Scottish chain that grows its own oysters and mussels. It offers an inviting atmosphere with a fine fishy energy and no pretense (£10-15 main dishes, £12.50 two-course special served 12:00-19:00, open daily, a couple of blocks behind Covent Garden at 2 Catherine Street, tel. 020/7240-4999).

Sofra Turkish Restaurant is good for quality Turkish with a touch of class. They have several menus: *meze* (Turkish tapas), vegetarian, and set (£8 before 19:00, £11 after 18:00, open long hours daily, 36 Tavistock Street, tel. 020/7240-3773).

Sitar Indian Restaurant is a well-respected Indian/Bangladeshi place serving dishes from many regions, fine fish, and a tasty £17 vegetarian *thali*. It's small and dressy, with snappy service (£15 main dishes, Mon-Fri 12:00-24:00, Sat-Sun 14:30-24:00, next to Somerset House at 149 Strand—see map on page 386, tel. 020/7836-3730).

Belgo Centraal serves hearty Belgian specialties in a vast 400-seat underground lair. It's a mussels, chips, and beer emporium dressed up as a mod-monastic refectory—with noisy acoustics and waiters garbed as Trappist monks. The classy restaurant section is more comfortable and less rowdy, but usually requires reservations. It's often more fun just to grab a spot in the boisterous beer hall, with its tight, communal benches (no reservations accepted). Both sides have the same menu and specials. Belgians claim they eat as well as the French and as heartily as the Germans. This place, which offers a stunning array of dark, blonde, and fruity Belgian beers, actually makes Belgian things trendy—a formidable feat (£10-14 meals, open daily 12:00-23:00; Mon-Fri £5-6.30 "beat the clock" meal specials 17:00-18:30—the time you order is the price you pay—including main dishes and fries; no meal-splitting after 18:30, and you must buy food with

The Soho "Food Is Fun" Three-Course Dinner Crawl

For a multicultural, movable feast, consider enjoying a drink and eating (or splitting) one course at each of these places. Start around 17:30 to avoid lines, get in on early-bird specials, and find waiters willing to let you split a meal. Prices, though reasonable by London standards, add up. Servings are large enough to share. All are open nightly. Arrive at 17:30 at **Belgo Centraal** and split the early-bird dinner special: a kilo of mussels, fries, and dark Belgian beer. At **Yo! Sushi,** have beer or sake and a few dishes, then head to **Fernandez & Wells** for a glass of wine and a meat-and-cheese plate. For dessert, people-watch at Leicester Square.

beer; daily £8 lunch special 12:00-17:00; 1 kid eats free for each parent ordering a regular entrée; 1 block north of Covent Garden Tube station at 50 Earlham Street, tel. 020/7813-2233).

Neal's Yard is *the* place for cheap, hip, and healthy eateries near Covent Garden. The neighborhood is a tabouli of fun, hippie-type cafés. One of the best is the venerable and ferociously vegetarian **Food for Thought,** packed with local health nuts (good £5 vegetarian meals, £8 dinner plates, Mon-Sat 12:00-20:30, Sun 12:00-17:30, 2 blocks north of Covent Garden Tube station at 31 Neal Street, near Neal's Yard, tel. 020/7836-0239).

Near Soho and Chinatown

London has a trendy scene that most Beefeater-seekers miss entirely. These restaurants are scattered throughout the hipster, gay, and strip-club district, teeming each evening with fun-seekers and theatergoers. Even if you plan to have dinner elsewhere, it's a treat just to wander around this lively area. (For a guided visit, see my West End Walk.)

Beware of the extremely welcoming women standing outside the strip clubs (especially on Great Windmill Street). Enjoy the sales pitch—but only fools fall for the "£5 drink and show" lure. They don't get back out without emptying their wallet...literally.

Yo! Sushi is a futuristic Japanese-food-extravaganza experience, complete with thumping rock, Japanese cable TV, and a 195-foot-long conveyor belt. For £1.25, you get unlimited green tea or water. Snag a bar stool and grab dishes as they rattle by (priced by color of dish; check the chart: £1.75-5 per dish, daily 12:00-23:00, 2 blocks south of Oxford Street, where Lexington Street becomes Poland Street, 52 Poland Street, tel. 020/7287-0443). If you like

Yo!, there are about 40 other locations around town, including a handy branch a block from the London Eye on Belvedere Road, as well as outlets within Selfridges, Harvey Nichols department stores, Victoria Station, and Whiteleys Shopping Centre on Queensway.

Wagamama Noodle Bar is a noisy, pan-Asian, organic slurp-athon. As you enter, check out the kitchen and listen to the roar of the basement, where benches rock with happy eaters. Everybody sucks. Portions are huge and splitting is allowed (£7-10 meals, Mon-Sat 11:30-23:00, Sun 12:00-22:00, crowded after 19:00, 10A Lexington Street, tel. 020/7292-0990 but no reservations taken). If you like this place, handy branches are all over town, including one near the British Museum (4 Streatham Street), Kensington (26 High Street), in Harvey Nichols (109 Knightsbridge), Covent Garden (1 Tavistock Street), Leicester Square (14 Irving Street), Piccadilly Circus (8 Norris Street), Fleet Street (#109), and next to the Tower of London (Tower Place).

Busaba Eathai Thai Restaurant is a hit with locals for its snappy service, casual-yet-high-energy ambience, and good, inexpensive Thai cuisine. You'll sit communally around big, square 16-person hardwood tables or in two-person tables by the window—with everyone in the queue staring at your noodles. They don't take reservations, so arrive by 19:00 or line up (£7-10 meals, Mon-Thu 12:00-23:00, Fri-Sat 12:00-23:30, Sun 12:00-22:00, 106 Wardour Street, tel. 020/7255-8686). They have three other handy locations: on nearby Panton Street, just below Piccadilly Circus; at 22 Store Street, near the British Museum and Goodge Street Tube; and at 8-13 Bird Street, just off Oxford Street and across from the Bond Street Tube.

Côte Restaurant is a contemporary French bistro chain with no pretense, serving good-value French cuisine at the right prices (£9-13 mains, £12 three-course early dinner specials if you order by 19:00, open Mon-Wed 8:00-23:00, Thu-Fri 8:00-24:00, Sat 9:00-24:00, Sun 9:00-22:30, 124-126 Wardour Street, tel. 020/7287-9280).

Y Ming Chinese Restaurant—across Shaftesbury Avenue from the ornate gates, clatter, and dim sum of Chinatown—has dressy European decor, serious but helpful service, and authentic Northern Chinese cooking (good £11 meal deal offered 12:00-18:00, £7-11 plates, open Mon-Sat 12:00-23:45, closed Sun, 35-36 Greek Street, tel. 020/7734-2721).

New World Chinese Restaurant is a sprawling old-fashioned Chinese diner that just feels real. It's a fixture in Chinatown, serving cheap Cantonese food, including dim sum and a similar dinner menu with an array of little £3 dishes (daily 11:00-24:00, dim sum daily 12:00-18:00, 1 Gerrard Place, tel. 020/7734-0677).

Jen Café, across the street, is a humble Chinese corner eatery much loved for its homemade dumplings. It's just stools and simple seating, with fast service, a fun, inexpensive menu, and a devoted following (£3-5 plates, long hours daily, 4 Newport Place, tel. 020/7287-9708).

On Lexington Street, in the Heart of Soho

Andrew Edmunds Restaurant is a tiny, candlelit place where you'll want to hide your camera and guidebook and not act like a tourist. This little place—with a jealous and loyal clientele—is the closest I've found to Parisian quality in a cozy restaurant in London. The modern European cooking and creative seasonal menu are worth the splurge (£6-8 starters, £10-20 main dishes, Mon-Sat 12:30-15:00 & 18:00-22:45, Sun 13:00-15:30 & 18:00-22:30, come early or call ahead, request ground floor rather than basement, 46 Lexington Street, tel. 020/7437-5708).

Mildred's Vegetarian Restaurant, across from Andrew Edmunds, has cheap prices, an enjoyable menu, and a pleasant interior filled with happy eaters (£7-9 meals, Mon-Sat 12:00-23:00, closed Sun, vegan options, 45 Lexington Street, tel. 020/7494-1634).

Fernandez & Wells is a delightfully simple little wine, cheese, and ham bar. Drop in and grab a stool as you belly up to the big wooden bar. Share a plate of top-quality cheeses and/or Spanish, Italian, or French hams with fine bread and oil, while sipping a nice glass of wine (Mon-Sat 11:00-22:00, Sun 12:00-19:00, quality sandwiches at lunch, wine/cheese/ham bar after 16:00, 43 Lexington Street, tel. 020/7734-1546).

Near the British Museum

Tiny Charlotte Place is lined with small eateries. It's a short walk from the Goodge Street Tube station and convenient to the British Museum and Pollock's Toy Museum (see map on page 368).

Salumeria Dino serves up hearty sandwiches, pasta, and Italian coffee. Dino, a native of Naples, has run his little shop for 30 years and has managed to create a classic Italian deli that's so authentic, you'll walk out singing "O Sole Mio" (£3-5 sandwiches, £1 take-away cappuccinos, Mon-Fri 9:00-17:00, closed Sat-Sun, #15, tel. 020/7580-3938).

Lantana OUT, next door to Salumeria Dino, sells modern soups, sandwiches, and salads at their take-away window. Their changing menu features a soup-salad-sweet combo deal for £5.50 (£3-7 meals, pricier sit-down café next door, Mon-Fri 7:30-15:00, café open Sat-Sun 9:00-15:00, #13, tel. 020/7637-3347).

West London
Near Victoria Station Accommodations

These restaurants are within a few blocks of Victoria Station—and all are places where I've enjoyed eating. As with the accommodations in this area, I've grouped them by location: east or west of the station (see the map on page 356).

Cheap Eats: For groceries, a handy **M&S Simply Food** is inside Victoria Station (Mon-Sat 7:00-24:00, Sun 8:00-22:00), along with a **Sainsbury's Market** (daily 6:00-23:00, at rear entrance, on Eccleston Street). A second Sainsbury's is just north of the station on Victoria Street, and a larger Sainsbury's is on Wilton Road near Warwick Way, a couple of blocks southeast of the station (Mon-Fri 7:00-23:00, Sat 7:00-22:00, Sun 11:00-17:00). A string of good ethnic restaurants lines Wilton Road (near the recommended Seafresh Fish Restaurant). For affordable if forgettable meals, try the row of cheap little eateries on Elizabeth Street.

West of Victoria Station

Ebury Wine Bar, filled with young professionals, provides a cut-above atmosphere, delicious £13-18 entrées, and an £18 two-course and £23 three-course special anytime (three-course meal includes a glass of champagne that you're welcome to swap for wine). In the delightful back room, the fancy menu features modern European cuisine with a French accent; at the wine bar, find a cheaper bar menu that's better than your average pub grub. This is emphatically a "traditional wine bar," with no beers on tap (daily 11:00-23:00, reservations smart, at intersection of Ebury and Elizabeth Streets, 139 Ebury Street, tel. 020/7730-5447).

Jenny Lo's Tea House is a simple budget place serving up reliably tasty £7-9 eclectic Chinese-style meals to locals in the know. While the menu is small, everything is high quality. Jenny clearly learned from her father, Ken Lo, one of the most famous Cantonese chefs in Britain, whose fancy place is just around the corner (Mon-Fri 12:00-15:00 & 18:00-22:00, closed Sat-Sun, cash only, 14 Eccleston Street, tel. 020/7259-0399).

La Bottega is an Italian delicatessen that fits its upscale Belgravia neighborhood. It offers tasty, freshly cooked pastas (£6), lasagnas, and salads (lasagna and salad meal-£8), along with great sandwiches (£3) and a good coffee bar with pastries. While not cheap, it's fast (order at the counter), and the ingredients would please an Italian chef. Grab your meal to go, or enjoy the Belgravia good life with locals, either sitting inside or on the sidewalk (Mon-Fri 8:00-19:00, Sat 9:00-18:00, Sun 10:00-17:00, on corner of Ebury and Eccleston Streets, tel. 020/7730-2730).

The Duke of Wellington Pub is a classic neighborhood place with forgettable grub, woodsy sidewalk seating, and an inviting interior (dinner served Mon-Sat 18:00-21:00, 63 Eaton Terrace, tel. 020/7730-1782).

The Thomas Cubitt Pub, packed with young professionals, is a trendy neighborhood gastropub, great for a drink or pricey meal (44 Elizabeth Street, tel. 020/7730-6060).

East of Victoria Station

Grumbles brags it's been serving "good food and wine at nonscary prices since 1964." Offering a delicious mix of "modern eclectic French and traditional English," this unpretentious little place with cozy booths inside (on two levels, including a cellar) and four nice sidewalk tables is *the* spot to eat well in this otherwise workaday neighborhood. Their traditional dishes are their forte (£9-18 plates, £11 early-bird specials 18:00-19:00, open daily 12:00-14:30 & 18:00-23:00, reservations wise, half a block north of Belgrave Road at 35 Churton Street, tel. 020/7834-0149, Alex).

Seafresh Fish Restaurant is the neighborhood place for plaice—and classic and creative fish-and-chips cuisine. You can either take out on the cheap or eat in, enjoying a white fish ambience. Though Mario's father started this place in 1965, it feels like the chippie of the 21st century (meals-£6 to go, £10-15 to sit, Mon-Sat 12:00-15:00 & 17:00-22:30, closed Sun, 80-81 Wilton Road, tel. 020/7828-0747).

The Jugged Hare pub, a 10-minute walk from Victoria Station, sits in a lavish old bank building, with vaults replaced by tankards of beer and a fine kitchen. They have a fun, traditional menu with more fresh veggies than fries, and a plush, vivid pub scene good for a meal or just a drink (£6.25 sandwiches, £8-10 meals, food served daily 12:00-21:30, drinks served daily 11:00-23:00, 172 Vauxhall Bridge Road, tel. 020/7828-1543).

St. George's Tavern is *the* pub for a meal in this neighborhood. They serve dinner from the same fun menu in three zones: on the sidewalk to catch the sun and enjoy some people-watching, in the sloppy pub, and in a classier back dining room. They're proud of their sausages and "toad in the hole." The scene is inviting for just a beer, too (£7-10 meals, Mon-Sat 10:00-22:00, Sun until 21:30, corner of Hugh Street and Belgrave Road, tel. 020/7630-1116).

Near Notting Hill and Bayswater Accommodations

For locations, see the map on page 362.

Maggie Jones, a Charles Dickens-meets-Ella Fitzgerald splurge, is exuberantly rustic and very English, with a 1940s-jazz soundtrack. You'll get solid English cuisine, including huge plates of crunchy vegetables, served by a young and casual staff.

It's pricey, but the portions are huge (especially the meat-and-fish pies, their specialty). You're welcome to save lots by splitting your main course. The candlelit upstairs is the most romantic, while the basement is kept lively with the kitchen, tight seating, and lots of action. If you eat well once in London, eat here—and do it quick, before it burns down (lunch—£5 starters, £7 main dishes; dinner—£6-9 starters, £10-23 main dishes; Mon-Sat 12:00-15:00 & 18:30-23:00, Sun 12:30-16:00 & 18:30-22:30, reservations recommended, 6 Old Court Place, just east of Kensington Church Street, near High Street Kensington Tube stop, tel. 020/7937-6462).

The Churchill Arms pub and **Thai Kitchen** (same location) are local hangouts, with good beer and a thriving old-English ambience in front, and hearty £8 Thai plates in an enclosed patio in the back. You can eat the Thai food in the tropical hideaway (table service) or in the atmospheric pub section (order at the counter and they'll bring it to you). They also serve basic English pub food at lunch (£3 sandwiches, £6 meals). The place is festooned with Churchill memorabilia and chamber pots (including one with Hitler's mug on it—hanging from the ceiling farthest from Thai Kitchen—sure to cure the constipation of any Brit during World War II). Arrive by 18:00 or after 21:00 to avoid a line. During busy times, diners are limited to an hour at the table (daily 12:00-22:00, 119 Kensington Church Street, tel. 020/7792-1246).

The Prince Edward serves good grub in a quintessential pub setting (£7-12 meals, Mon-Wed 10:00-23:00, Thu-Sat 10:00-23:30, Sun 10:00-22:30, plush-pubby indoor seating or sidewalk tables, family-friendly, pay Wi-Fi, 2 blocks north of Bayswater Road at the corner of Dawson Place and Hereford Road, 73 Prince's Square, tel. 020/7727-2221).

Café Diana is a healthy little eatery serving sandwiches, salads, and Middle Eastern food. It's decorated—almost shrine-like—with photos of Princess Diana, who used to drop by for pita sandwiches. You can dine in the simple interior, or order some food from the counter to go (£3-5 sandwiches, £6-8 meat dishes, daily 8:00-23:00, 5 Wellington Terrace, on Bayswater Road, opposite Kensington Palace Garden Gates, where Di once lived, tel. 020/7792-9606, Abdul).

On Queensway: The road called Queensway is a multiethnic food circus, lined with lively and inexpensive eateries—browse the options along here and choose your favorites. For a cut above, head for **Royal China Restaurant**—filled with London's Chinese, who consider this one of the city's best eateries. It's dressed up in black, white, and gold, with candles and brisk waiters. While it's pricier than most neighborhood Chinese restaurants, the food is noticeably better (£9-13 dishes, Mon-Thu 12:00-23:00, Fri-Sat 12:00-23:30, Sun 11:00-22:00, dim sum until 17:00, 13 Queensway, tel.

020/7221-2535). For a lowbrow alternative, **Whiteleys Shopping Centre Food Court**—at the top end of Queensway—offers a fun selection of ethnic and fast-food chain eateries among Corinthian columns, and a multiscreen theater in a delightful mall (daily 9:00-23:00; options include Yo! Sushi, good salads at Café Rouge, pizza, Starbucks, and a coin-op Internet place; third floor, corner of Porchester Gardens and Queensway).

Supermarkets: **Tesco** is a half-block from the Notting Hill Gate Tube stop (Mon-Sat 7:00-23:00, Sun 12:00-18:00, near intersection with Pembridge Road, 114-120 Notting Hill Gate). The smaller **Spar Market** is at 18 Queensway (Mon-Sat 7:00-24:00, Sun 9:00-24:00), and **Marks & Spencer** can be found in Whiteleys Shopping Centre (Mon-Sat 9:00-20:00, Sun 12:00-18:00).

South Kensington

Popular eateries line Old Brompton Road and Thurloe Street (Tube: South Kensington), and a good selection of cheap eateries are clumped around the Tube station. For locations, see the map on page 360.

La Bouchée Bistro Café is a classy hole-in-the-wall touch of France. This candlelit and woody bistro, with very tight seating, serves a two-course, £11.50 special on weekdays during lunch and from 17:30-18:30, and £17 *plats du jour* all *jour*. Reservations are smart in the evening (daily 12:00-15:00 & 17:30-23:30, 56 Old Brompton Road, tel. 020/7589-1929).

Moti Mahal Indian Restaurant, with minimalist-yet-classy mod ambience and attentive service, serves mostly Bangladeshi cuisine that's delicious. Consider chicken *jalfrezi* if you like spicy food, and buttery chicken if you don't (£10 dinners, daily 12:00-14:30 & 17:30-23:00, 3 Glendower Place, tel. 020/7584-8428).

Beirut Express has fresh, well-prepared Lebanese cuisine. In the front, you'll find take-away service as well as barstools for quick service (£4 sandwiches). In the back is a sit-down restaurant with £14 plates (daily 12:00-23:00, 65 Old Brompton Road, tel. 020/7591-0123).

Bosphorus Kebabs is the student favorite for a quick, fast, and hearty Turkish dinner. While mostly for take-away, they have a few tight tables indoors and on the sidewalk (£5 meals, Turkish kebabs, daily until 24:00, 59 Old Brompton Road, tel. 020/7584-4048).

Rocca di Papa is a bright and dressy Italian place with a heated terrace (£8 pizza, pasta, and salads; open daily, 73 Old Brompton Road, tel. 020/7225-3413).

The Anglesea Arms, with a great terrace surrounded by classy South Kensington buildings, is a destination pub that feels like the classic neighborhood favorite. It's a thriving and happy place, with a woody ambience and a mellow back dining room a world away from any tourism. Chef Julian Legge freshens up traditional English cuisine and prints up a daily menu listing his creative meals. While it'd be a shame to miss his cooking, this is also a fine place to just have a beer (£6 starters, £13 main dishes, meals served daily 12:00-15:00 & 18:00-22:00; from Old Brompton Road, turn right at Onslow Gardens and go down a few blocks to 15 Selwood Terrace; tel. 020/7373-7960).

Supermarket: **Tesco Express** is handy for picnics (daily 7:00-24:00, 50-52 Old Brompton Road).

Elsewhere in London

Between St. Paul's and the Tower: **The Counting House,** formerly an elegant old bank, offers great £8-10 meals, nice homemade meat pies, fish, and fresh vegetables. The fun "nibbles menu" is available starting in the early evening until 22:00 (or until 21:00 on Mon-Tue; open Mon-Fri 11:00-23:00, gets really busy with the buttoned-down 9-to-5 crowd after 12:15 especially Thu-Fri, closed Sat-Sun, near Mansion House in The City, 50 Cornhill—see map on page 381, tel. 020/7283-7123).

Near St. Paul's: **De Gustibus Sandwiches** is where a top-notch artisan bakery meets the public, offering fresh, you-design-it sandwiches, salads, and soups. Just one block below St. Paul's, it has simple seating or take-out picnic sacks for lugging to one of the great nearby parks (Mon-Fri 7:00-17:00, closed Sat-Sun, from church steps follow signs to youth hostel a block downhill—see map on page 381, 53-55 Carter Lane, tel. 020/7236-0056; another outlet is inside the Borough Market in Southwark).

Near the British Library: Drummond Street (running just west of Euston Station—see map on page 368) is famous in London for cheap and good Indian vegetarian food (£5-10 dishes, £7 lunch buffet). Consider **Chutneys** (124 Drummond, tel. 020/7388-0604) and **Ravi Shankar** (133-135 Drummond, tel. 020/7388-6458) for a good *thali* (both open long hours daily).

Taking Tea in London

Once the sole province of genteel ladies in fancy hats, afternoon tea has become more democratic in the 21st century. While some tearooms—such as the wallet-draining £40-a-head tea service at the Ritz and the finicky Fortnum & Mason—still require a jacket and tie (and a bigger bank account), most happily welcome tourists in jeans and sneakers.

Tea Terms

The cheapest "tea" on the menu is generally a "cream tea"; the most expensive is the "champagne tea." **Cream tea** is simply a pot of tea and a homemade scone or two with jam and thick clotted cream. (For maximum pinkie-waving taste per calorie, slice your scone thin like a miniature loaf of bread.) **Afternoon tea**—what Americans usually call "high tea"—generally is a cream tea plus a tier of three plates holding small finger foods (such as cucumber sandwiches) and an assortment of small pastries. **Champagne tea** includes all of the goodies, plus a glass of champagne. **High tea** to the English generally means a more substantial late-afternoon or early-evening meal, often served with meat or eggs.

Tearooms, which often also serve appealing light meals, are usually open for lunch and close about 17:00, just before dinner. At all the places listed below, it's perfectly acceptable for two people to order one afternoon tea and one cream tea (at about £5) and share the afternoon tea's goodies.

Places to Sip Tea

The Wolseley serves a good afternoon tea in between their meal service. Split one with your companion and enjoy two light meals at a great price in classic elegance (£10 cream tea, £21 afternoon tea, served Sun-Fri 15:30-18:30, Sat 15:30-17:30, see full listing on page 388).

The Orangery at Kensington Palace serves four different varieties of tea meals, from the £15 "Orangery tea" to the £35 "Tregothnan tea" in its bright white hall near Princess Di's former residence. You can also order treats à la carte. The portions aren't huge, but who can argue with eating at a princess' orangery or on the terrace? (Tea served 12:00-18:00, no reservations taken; a 10-minute walk through Kensington Gardens from either Queensway or High Street Kensington Tube stations to the orange brick building, about 100 yards from Kensington Palace—see map on page 362; tel. 020/3166-6113, www.hrp.org.uk.)

The National Dining Rooms, a restaurant and café within the National Gallery on Trafalgar Square, are convenient and have a nondescript modern ambience. Although the restaurant can book up in advance, you can generally waltz in for afternoon tea at the café. To play it safe, arrive in the early afternoon to reserve a tea time, then take the self-guided National Gallery Tour (page 136) before or after your appointed time (£4 cakes and tarts, £5.75 cream tea, £17 afternoon tea, tea served 15:00-17:00, located in Sainsbury Wing of National Gallery, Tube: Charing Cross or Leicester Square, tel. 020/7747-2525, www.peytonandbyrne.co.uk). **The National Café,** at the other end of the building (across the street from St. Martin-in-the-Fields), also serves tea in a more appealing, old-fashioned atmosphere—and their afternoon tea is a bit cheaper (£6 cream tea, £15 afternoon tea, tea served 15:00-17:30).

The Café at Sotheby's, located on the ground floor of the auction giant's headquarters, is manna for shoppers taking a break from fashionable New Bond Street. There are no windows—just a long leather bench, plenty of mirrors, and a dark-wood room where waiters serve sweet treats and the £6.50 mix-and-match Neal's Yard cheese plate to locals in the know (£3 cakes and creams, £7 "small tea," £12 afternoon tea, £18.75 champagne tea, café open Mon-Fri only 9:30-11:30 & 12:00-16:45, afternoon tea served 15:00-16:45, reservations recommended, 34-35 New Bond Street—see map on page 172, Tube: Bond Street or Oxford Circus, tel. 020/7293-5077, www.sothebys.com/cafe).

The Capital Hotel, a luxury hotel a half-block from Harrods, caters to weary shoppers with its intimate five-table, linen-tablecloth tearoom. It's where the ladies-who-lunch meet to decide whether to buy that Versace gown they've had their eye on. Even so, casual clothes, kids, and sharing plates are all OK (£20.50 afternoon tea, daily 14:30-17:30, call to book ahead—especially on weekends, 22 Basil Street—see map on page 360, Tube: Knightsbridge, tel. 020/7589-5171, www.capitalhotel.co.uk).

Fortnum & Mason's St. James's Restaurant, on the fourth floor, offers plush seats under the elegant tearoom's chandeliers. You'll get the standard three-tiered silver tea tray: finger sandwiches on the bottom, fresh scones with jam and clotted cream on the first floor, and decadent pastries and "tartlets" on the top floor, with unlimited tea. At this price, consider it dinner (about £34-38, Mon-Sat 12:00-18:30, Sun 12:00-16:30, dress up a bit for this—no shorts, "children must be behaved," 181 Piccadilly—see map on page 172, reserve in advance online or at tel. 0845-602-5694, www.fortnumandmason.com).

Harrods' Georgian Restaurant is where you (along with 200 of your closest friends) can enjoy a fancy tea under a skylight as a pianist tickles the keys of a Bösendorfer, the world's most expensive piano (£26 afternoon tea, includes finger sandwiches and pastries with free refills, tea served Mon-Fri from 15:00, Sat-Sun from 15:45, last order at 17:15, on Brompton Road, Tube: Knightsbridge, reservations tel. 020/7225-6800, www.harrods.com).

Cheaper Options: Taking tea is not just for tourists and the wealthy—it's a true English tradition. If you want the teatime experience but are put off by the price, most department stores on Oxford Street (including those between Oxford Circus and Bond Street Tube stations) offer an afternoon tea (some more affordable than others). For example, **John Lewis** has a mod third-floor brasserie that serves a nice £10 afternoon tea platter from 15:00 (on Oxford Street one block west of the Bond Street Tube station, tel. 020/3073-0626, www.johnlewis.com). Many museums and bookstores have cafés serving afternoon tea goodies à la carte, where you can put together a spread for less than £10—**Waterstone's**

fifth-floor café and the **Victoria and Albert Museum** café are two of the best. **Teapod,** a modern option near the Tower Bridge, advertises the "best-value afternoon tea in London," serving cream tea for £5.50 and afternoon tea for £14, along with sandwiches, soups, salads, and pastries (Mon-Fri 8:00-18:00, Sat 9:00-19:00, Sun 10:00-19:00, 31 Shad Thames, 200 yards from the Tower Bridge on the South Bank, tel. 020/7407-0000; another branch at 22 Wellington Street in Covent Garden; www.teapodtea.co.uk).

In Bath: **The Pump Room** is reason enough to put off tea in London—assuming you'll be visiting the city of Bath. This historic, elegant Georgian hall with live music lets anyone enjoy the ritual of tea in grand style (see page 498).

EATING IN LONDON

LONDON WITH CHILDREN

The key to a successful family trip to London is making everyone happy, including the parents. My family-tested recommendations have this objective in mind. Consider these tips:

- Take advantage of the local newsstand guides. *Time Out*'s family monthly is called *Kids Out,* and the weekly version of *Time Out* has handy kids' calendars listing activities and shows. The *Time Out* guidebook, *London for Children* (£8, www.timeout.com/london/kids, available in bookstores and many newsstands), is chockablock with ideas for the serious parent tour guide in London.

- Most of the big museums—such as the Tate Modern, Tate Britain, and National Gallery—schedule children's activities on weekends. Some museums also offer "backpacks" with activities to make the visit more interesting. Ask at museum information desks.

- London's big, budget chain hotels generally allow kids to sleep for free (see page 367).

- Eat dinner early (around 18:00) to miss the romantic crowd. Skip the famous places. Look instead for relaxed cafés, pubs (kids are welcome, though sometimes restricted to the restaurant section or courtyard area), or even fast-food restaurants where kids can move around. Picnic lunches and dinners work well.

- Public WCs can be hard to find. Try department stores, museums, and restaurants, particularly fast-food places.

- Follow this book's crowd-beating tips. Kids get antsy standing in line for a museum. At each sight, ask about a kids' guide or flier.

- Hamleys is the biggest toy store in Britain, with seven floors of toys (Mon-Fri 10:00-20:00, Sat 9:00-20:00, Sun 12:00-18:00,

188-196 Regent Street, Tube: Oxford Circus, tel. 0871-704-1977, www.hamleys.com). It's also included in the shopping-oriented second half of my West End Walk (see page 180). Hamleys has branches at Heathrow, Gatwick, and Stansted airports, and at St. Pancras International Station.

• Harry Potter fans (and Muggle parents) enjoy visiting places in London where scenes from the movies were filmed (see page 80).

Sights and Activities

East London

Tower of London—The crown jewels are awesome, and the Beefeater tour plays off kids in a memorable and fun way. Avoid the long ticket lines by buying your ticket in advance (must use within seven days) at any London TI, at the gift shop just below the Tower Hill Tube station ticket office, or online at a slight discount (£18, families-£50, audioguide-£4, March-Oct Tue-Sat 9:00-17:30, Sun-Mon 10:00-17:30; Nov-Feb Tue-Sat 9:00-16:30, Sun-Mon 10:00-16:30; last entry 30 minutes before closing, the long but fast-moving ticket lines are worst on Sun, no photography allowed of jewels or in chapels, Tube: Tower Hill, recorded info tel. 0844-482-7777, booking tel. 0844-482-7799 from within UK or tel. 020/3166-6000 from overseas, www.hrp.org.uk).

☺ See the Tower of London Tour.

Museum of London—The museum has a very kid-friendly presentation that takes you from prehistoric times to the present. The events guide at the entrance lists kids' activities (free, daily 10:00-18:00, last entry 30 minutes before closing, café, Tube: Barbican or St. Paul's, tel. 020/7814-5660, recorded info tel. 020/7001-9844, www.museumoflondon.org.uk, see page 79).

Unicorn Theatre—This modern complex presents professional theater for children on two stages (show tickets: £10-15, kids-£8-10, families-£30-50, check play's recommended ages before booking; café, on the South Bank just behind City Hall, 147 Tooley Street; Tube: London Bridge; tel. 020/7645-0560, www.unicorntheatre.com).

Central London

Covent Garden—This is a great area for people-watching and candy-licking. Kids like the **London Transport Museum**, with its interactive zone (£13.50, kids under 16 free, Sat-Thu 10:00-18:00, Fri 11:00-18:00, some Fri until

22:00, last entry 45 minutes before closing, in southeast corner of Covent Garden courtyard, Tube: Covent Garden, switchboard tel. 020/7379-6344, recorded info tel. 020/7565-7299, www.ltmuseum .co.uk, see page 61).

Trafalgar Square—The grand square is fun for kids (Tube: Charing Cross). Climb the lions, munch a meal in a crypt (at St. Martin-in-the-Fields, see below), and tour the National Gallery (below).

National Gallery—Begin your visit in the "ArtStart" multi-media room. Your child can list his or her interests (cats, naval battles, and so on) and print out a tailor-made tour map for free. Ask about their children's printed guides, audioguide programs, and events—Sunday mornings are especially kid-friendly (free, but suggested £2-3 donation; daily 10:00-18:00, Fri until 21:00, no photography, cafés, on Trafalgar Square, Tube: Charing Cross or Leicester Square, switchboard tel. 020/7839-3321, recorded info tel. 020/7747-2885, www.nationalgallery.org.uk).

   ✪ See the National Gallery Tour.

St. Martin-in-the-Fields—Next to the church on Trafalgar Square is a glass pavilion with a brass-rubbing center below that's fun for kids who'd like a souvenir to show for their efforts (£4.50 and up, Mon-Wed 10:00-18:00, Thu-Sat 10:00-20:00, Sun 11:30-17:00, tel. 020/7766-1122 or 020/7766-1100; for details on the church, see page 59). The affordable Café in the Crypt has just the right spooky tables-on-gravestones ambience (£6-8 cafeteria plates, Mon-Tue 8:00-20:00, Wed 8:00-22:30, Thu-Sat 8:00-21:00, Sun 11:00-18:00, Tube: Charing Cross, tel. 020/7766-1158 or 020/7766-1100, www.smitf.org).

London Eye—The grand observation wheel is a delight for the whole family (£19, families-£56, 10 percent discount for booking online, daily July-Aug 10:00-21:30, April-June 10:00-21:00, Sept-March 10:00-20:00, closed Dec 25 and in mid-Jan for annual maintenance, Tube: Waterloo or Westminster, www.londoneye .com). For more specifics, including crowd avoidance, see page 87).

Sealife Aquarium—Part of the London Eye complex and run by the same company as Madame Tussauds, this small but entertaining aquarium resembles an overpriced theme park. Even though there are far better aquariums elsewhere, this place packs in school groups and families looking for a break from museums (£19, online combo-ticket deals, Mon-Thu 10:00-18:00, Fri-Sun 10:00-19:00, last entry one hour before closing, Tube: Waterloo or Westminster, tel. 0871-663-1678, www.visitsealife.com).

Changing of the Guard—Kids enjoy the bands and pageantry of the Buckingham Palace Changing of the Guard, but little ones get a better view at the inspection; guards assemble daily May-July (every other day Aug-April) at 11:00 at Wellington Barracks, and march out at 11:30 for Buckingham Palace (see page 68). For horse-lovers, the Horse Guards change daily at 11:00 (10:00 on Sun) and have a colorful dismounting ceremony daily at 16:00 (on Whitehall, between Trafalgar Square and #10 Downing Street, Tube: Westminster, www.changing-the-guard.com, see page 56).

Piccadilly Circus—This titillating district has lots of Planet Hollywood-type amusements, such as the Trocadero Center. Be careful of fast-fingered riffraff. (For more information on the district, see page 60.) Hamleys toy store is just two blocks up Regent Street at 188-196 (hours listed earlier in this chapter).

Shopping—If your teenager wants to bring home a few chic and cheap London fashions, Oxford Street (at the intersection of Regent Street) is a good place to start. Take the Tube to the Oxford Circus stop, and you'll be surrounded by lots of shops selling inexpensive, trendy clothes for teens. Stores include Top Shop (36-38 Great Castle Street), Miss Selfridge (334-348 Oxford Street), Zara (118 Regent Street), two H&M shops (174-176 and 261-271 Regent Street), and music stores like HMV (150 Oxford Street). Sandwich-to-go shops and coffeehouses (including a half-dozen Starbucks) offer easy rest stops for families. Also see Part 2 of my West End Walk ("Shopping Streets and Piccadilly Circus" on page 179), which goes down Regent Street. Harrods in Knightsbridge, with its over-the-top toy and food departments, can be fun for kids of all ages (see page 409). Markets, particularly the Camden Lock Market, will hit the spot for finicky teenagers in need of loud music, cool clothes, and plenty of food choices (see page 411).

Theater—Long-running shows are kid- and parent-pleasers (see Entertainment in London chapter).

West London

Hyde Park—London's backyard is the perfect place for muse-umed-out kids to play and run free. For older kids, the park has a tennis court, a putting green, and trails for running or biking. Young children will enjoy the Diana, Princess of Wales Memorial Playground in adjacent Kensington Gardens, with its Peter Pan-themed climbing equipment (including a huge wooden pirate ship). Events such as music, plays, and clown acts are scheduled throughout the summer. The Serpentine Lake offers paddleboat rentals and a swimming area with a playground and a shallow kid-die pool (Lido swimming entrance-£4, kids-£1, families-£9, less after 16:00, daily June-mid-Sept 10:00-18:00 plus Sat-Sun only in May, last entry 30 minutes before closing, closed Oct-April, Tube: Knightsbridge or South Kensington, tel. 020/7706-3422). The park is open daily from 5:00 in the morning until midnight (www.royalparks.org.uk).

Natural History Museum—This wonderful world of dinosaurs, volcanoes, meteors, and creepy-crawlies offers creative interactive displays (free, fee for special exhibits, daily 10:00-17:50, last entry 20 minutes before closing, a long tunnel leads directly from South Kensington Tube station to museum, tel. 020/7942-5000, exhibit info and reservations tel. 020/7942-5011, www.nhm.ac.uk, see page 99).

Science Museum—This museum, next door to the Natural History Museum, offers lots of hands-on fun and IMAX movies (free entry, charge for special exhibits; IMAX shows: £10, kids-£8; daily 10:00-18:00, Exhibition Road, Tube: South Kensington, tel. 0870-870-4868, www.sciencemuseum.org.uk, see page 99).

Both the Natural History and Science museums are kid-friendly and can be clogged with school groups during the school year. Check for special events and exhibits (noted at each museum's entry and on their websites).

North London

Madame Tussauds Waxworks—Despite the lines, the waxworks are popular with kids for gory stuff, pop and movie stars, everyone's favorite royals, and more (£29, kids-£25; save money and skip the line by purchasing tickets in advance on their website; open Mon-Fri 9:30-19:30, Sat-Sun 9:00-20:00, mid-July-Aug and school holidays daily 9:00-21:00, last entry two hours before closing; Marylebone Road, Tube: Baker Street, www.madame tussauds.com, see page 72).

London Zoo—This venerable animal habitat features more than 8,000 creatures and a fine petting zoo (£20.50, kids-£16.40, prices include £1.90 suggested donation, less off-season, daily mid-July-Sept 10:00-18:00, March-mid-July and Sept-Oct 10:00-17:30, closes earlier in winter, last entry one hour before closing, in Regent's Park, Tube: Camden Town, then bus #274, tel. 020/7722-3333, www.zsl.org). Call for feeding and event times. For a scenic treat that also happens to be a good value, take the London Waterbus down Regent's Canal to the zoo. They drop you off right at the entry (£21, kids-£17, price includes admission to the zoo; board at Camden Lock Market, Tube: Camden Town, or at Little Venice, Tube: Warwick Avenue; tel. 020/7482-2660, www.londonwaterbus.com).

Pollock's Toy Museum—Kids will wonder how their grandparents ever survived without PlayStation, as they wander through this rickety old house filled with toys that predate batteries and microchips. Be aware, though, there's a neat toy shop you must exit through (£5, kids-£2, generally Mon-Sat 10:00-17:00, closed Sun, last entry 30 minutes before closing, 1 Scala Street, Tube: Goodge Street, tel. 020/7636-3452, www.pollockstoymuseum .com, see page 76).

LONDON WITH CHILDREN

Sports—Older kids may enjoy attending a Premier League soccer game (expensive but memorable and nontouristy; see schedule at www.premierleague.com).

South London

The Bankside Walk (see page 275) links several sights children might enjoy: The *Golden Hinde* ship, Clink Prison, and Old Operating Theatre. Nearby, kids get a kick out of this sight:

HMS *Belfast*—Older kids might enjoy scrambling across the decks of this World War II warship (£13.50, kids under 15 free, includes audioguide, daily March-Oct 10:00-18:00, Nov-Feb 10:00-17:00, last entry one hour before closing, Tube: London Bridge, tel. 020/7940-6300, http://hmsbelfast.iwm.org.uk, see page 95).

Greater London

Kew Gardens—These famous 300-acre gardens include the Rhizotron and Xstrata Treetop Walkway, which lets kids explore the canopy 60 feet above the ground on a 200-yard-long scenic steel walkway. Younger children will love the Climbers and Creepers indoor play area, as well as the Treehouse Towers playground with its climbing structures and a kid-size zip line (£14, discounted 45 minutes before closing to £11.50, kids under 17 free; April-Aug Mon-Fri 9:30-18:30, Sat-Sun 9:30-19:30; closes earlier Sept-March, last entry to gardens 30 minutes before closing, galleries and conservatories close at 17:30 in high season—earlier off-season, free one-hour walking tours daily at 11:00 and 14:00; £4 narrated 40-minute hop-on, hop-off joyride on little Kew Explorer tram departs on the hour from 11:00 from near Victoria Gate; Tube: Kew Gardens, boats run April-Oct between Kew Gardens and Westminster Pier; switchboard tel. 020/8332-5000, recorded info tel. 020/8332-5655, www.kew.org, see page 101).

Fun Transportation

Thames Cruise—Young sailors delight in boats. Westminster Pier (near Big Ben) offers a lot of action, with round-trip cruises and boats to the Tower of London, Greenwich, and Kew Gardens. For details, see page 44.

Hop-on, Hop-off London Bus Tours—These two-hour double-decker bus tours, which drive by all the biggies, are fun for kids and stress-free for parents. You can stay on the bus the entire time, or hop on and hop off at any of the nearly 30 stops and catch a later bus (every 10-15 minutes in summer, every 20 minutes in winter, see page 39). The Original London Sightseeing Tour's "City Sightseeing Tour" bus (marked with a red triangle) has a kids' soundtrack on the earphones, although your kids might get more entertaining commentary from Big Bus's live guides.

Day Trip

Legoland Windsor—If your kids are loopy over Legos, they'll love a day trip to Legoland Windsor. While older kids will probably enjoy it, the park is really aimed at the 10-and-under crowd (see page 462 for cost, hours, and other details, tel. 0871-222-2001, www.lego land.co.uk).

What to Avoid

The **London Dungeon**'s popularity with teenagers makes it one of London's most-visited sights. I enjoy gore and torture as much as the next boy, but this is lousy gore and torture, and I would not waste the time or money on it with my child. **The London Bridge Experience** (not to be confused with the Tower Bridge Exhibition) and **The London Tombs** are also to be avoided. They are copycat rip-offs of the London Dungeon.

SHOPPING IN LONDON

London is great for shoppers—and, thanks to the high prices, perhaps even better for window-shoppers. This chapter will tell you where to get essentials, where to get souvenirs, where to browse through colorful street markets, and where to gawk at some high-end stores in this major fashion capital.

Most stores are open Monday through Saturday from roughly 10:00 to 18:00, and many close Sundays. Large department stores stay open later during the week (until 20:00 or 21:00) and are open shorter hours on Sundays. If you're looking for bargains, you can visit one of the city's many street markets.

Consider these five ways to shop in London:

1. If all you need are souvenirs, a surgical strike at any souvenir shop will do.
2. Large department stores offer relatively painless one-stop shopping. Consider the down-to-earth Marks & Spencer (Mon-Sat 9:00-20:00, Thu until 21:00, Sun 12:00-18:00, 173 Oxford Street, Tube: Oxford Circus; another at 458 Oxford Street, Tube: Bond Street or Marble Arch; see www.marks andspencer.com for more locations).
3. Connect small shops with a pleasant walk (❂ see the West End Walk chapter, particularly "Part 2").
4. For flea-market fun, try one of the many street markets.
5. Gawkers as well as serious bidders can attend auctions.

Warning: Refuse any offers to charge your credit card in dollars. This is called dynamic currency conversion, or DCC, and it's offered by some stores (including Harrods) as a "convenience." The very bad exchange rate they use is convenient only for increasing the store's profits.

For information on VAT refunds and customs regulations, see page 14.

Shopping Streets

London is famous for its shopping. The best and most convenient shopping streets are in the West End and West London (roughly

between Soho and Hyde Park). You'll find mid-range shops along **Oxford Street** (running east from Tube: Marble Arch), and fancier shops along **Regent Street** (stretching south from Tube: Oxford Circus to Piccadilly Circus) and **Knightsbridge** (where you'll find Harrods and Harvey Nichols, described later; Tube: Knightsbridge). Other streets are more specialized, such as **Jermyn Street** for old-fashioned men's clothing (just south of Piccadilly Street) and **Charing Cross Road** for books.

The second half of my ◐ West End Walk chapter is designed to connect several shopping areas, including Regent Street and Jermyn Street; even if you're not taking the entire walk, consider riding the Tube to Oxford Circus, walking south two blocks to Liberty department store, and starting the walk with "Part 2" on page 179.

Fancy Department Stores in West London

Harrods—Harrods is London's most famous and touristy department store. With more than four acres of retail space covering seven floors, it's a place where some shoppers could spend all day. (To me, it's still just a department store.) Big yet classy, Harrods has everything from elephants to toothbrushes (Mon-Sat 10:00-20:00, Sun 11:30-18:00, mandatory storage for big backpacks-£3, on Brompton Road, Tube: Knightsbridge, tel. 020/7730-1234, www.harrods.com).

While the store is famous partly for its Egyptian theme and its memorials to Princess Diana and her boyfriend, Dodi Fayed, those were the pet projects of Harrods' former owner, Mohamed Al Fayed (Dodi's Egyptian father). Al Fayed sold the store in 2010 to a Qatari investment group, so it's possible some of these features (especially the Di and Dodi stuff) could change.

Sightseers should pick up the free *Store Guide* at any info post. Here's what I enjoy: On the ground floor, find the Food Halls, with their Edwardian tiled walls, creative and exuberant displays, and staff in period costumes—not quite like your local supermarket back home.

Descend to the lower ground floor and follow signs to the Egyptian Escalator (in the center of the store), where you'll likely find a memorial to Dodi Fayed and Princess Diana. Photos and flowers honor the late Princess and her lover, who both died in a car crash in Paris in 1997. Inside a small, clear pyramid, you can see a wine glass still dirty from their last dinner and the engagement ring that Dodi purchased the day before they died. True Di-hards can go back up one level to the ground floor and follow signs to Door #3 in Menswear (near Men's Designer and Men's Tailoring, at the escalator). A huge (and more than a little creepy) bronze statue shows Di and Dodi releasing a symbolic albatross.

Back in the center of the store, ride the Egyptian Escalator—lined with pharaoh-headed sconces, papyrus-plant lamps, and hieroglyphic balconies—to the fourth floor. From the escalator, make a U-turn left and head to the far corner of the store (toys) to find child-size luxury pedal cars. If you have £10,000 to spare, these are the perfect gift for the child who has everything.

Also on the fourth floor is **The Georgian Restaurant,** where you can enjoy a fancy afternoon tea (see page 399). For non-tea drinkers, 27 other eateries are scattered throughout the store, including a sushi bar, kosher deli, pizzeria, classic pub, and—for the truly homesick—a Krispy Kreme.

Many of my readers report that Harrods is overpriced, snooty, and teeming with American and Japanese tourists. It's the only shopping mall I've seen with its own gift store. Still, it's the palace of department stores. The nearby Beauchamp Place is lined with classy and fascinating shops.

Harvey Nichols—Once Princess Diana's favorite, "Harvey Nick's" remains the department store *du jour* (Mon-Sat 10:00-20:00, Sun 11:30-18:00, near Harrods, 109-125 Knightsbridge, Tube: Knightsbridge, tel. 020/7235-5000, www.harveynichols.com). Want to pick up a little £20 scarf for the wife? You won't do it here, where they're more like £200. The store's fifth floor is a veritable food fest, with a gourmet grocery store, a fancy restaurant, a Yo! Sushi bar, and a lively café. Consider a take-away tray of sushi to eat on a bench in the Hyde Park rose garden two blocks away.

Fortnum & Mason—The official department store of the Queen, Fortnum & Mason embodies old-fashioned, British upper-class taste. While some may find it too stuffy, you won't find another store with the same storybook atmosphere (Mon-Sat 10:00-20:00, Sun 12:00-18:00, elegant tea served in St. James's Restaurant—see page 399, 181 Piccadilly, Tube: Green Park, tel. 020/7734-8040, www.fortnumandmason.com, also see ✪ West End Walk).

Liberty—Known for its gorgeous floral fabrics and well-stocked crafts department, Liberty is fun to stroll through just for a look at its hip, artful displays and castle-like interior (Mon-Sat 10:00-21:00, Sun 10:00-18:00, Great Marlborough St, Tube: Oxford Circus, tel. 020/7734-1234, www.liberty.co.uk, also see ✪ West End Walk).

Street Markets

Antiques buffs, people-watchers, and folks who brake for garage sales love London's street markets. There's good early-morning market activity somewhere any day of the week. The best markets—which combine lively stalls and a colorful neighborhood with cute and characteristic shops of their own—are Portobello Road and Camden Lock Market. Any London TI has a complete, up-to-date list. If you like to haggle, there are no holds barred in London's street markets.

Warning: Markets attract two kinds of people: tourists and pickpockets.

In Notting Hill

Portobello Road Market—Arguably London's best street market, Portobello Road stretches for several blocks through the delightful, colorful, funky-yet-quaint Notting Hill neighborhood (immortalized by the Hugh Grant/Julia Roberts film of the same name). Already charming streets lined with pastel-painted houses and offbeat antiques shops are enlivened on Saturdays with 2,000 additional stalls (5:30-17:00), plus food, live music, and more. (It's also extremely crowded.) If you start at Notting Hill Gate and work your way north, you'll find these general sections: antiques, new goods, produce, more new goods, and a flea market. While Portobello Road is best on Saturdays, it's enjoyable to stroll this street on most other days as well, since the characteristic shops are fun to explore—but skip it on Sundays, when virtually everything is closed (Tube: Notting Hill Gate, near recommended accommodations, tel. 020/7229-8354, www.portobelloroad.co.uk).

In Camden Town

Camden Lock Market—This huge, trendy arts-and-crafts festival is divided into three areas, each with its own vibe. The main market, set alongside the picturesque canal, features a mix of shops and stalls selling boutique crafts and artisanal foods. The market to the opposite side of Chalk Farm Road is edgier, with cheap ethnic food and punk crafts. The Stables, a sprawling, incense-scented complex, is more low-brow with cheap clothes, junk jewelry, and loud music (daily 10:00-18:00, busiest on weekends, Tube: Chalk

Farm, tel. 020/7485-7963, www.camdenlockmarket.com). Avoid the tacky, crowded area between the market and the Camden Town Tube station by getting off at the Chalk Farm stop; better yet, consider arriving via a scenic waterbus ride from Little Venice (tel. 020/7482-2660, www.londonwaterbus.com).

In the East End
All three of these East End markets are busiest and most interesting on Sundays. For a walk tying together these three markets—and a lot more in this neighborhood, which combines Cockney memories with London's biggest Bangladeshi community—see page 83.

Spitalfields Market—This huge, mod-feeling market hall (pronounced "spittle-fields") combines a shopping mall with old brick buildings and sleek modern ones, all covered by a giant glass roof. While the shops and a rainbow of restaurant options are open every day, the open space between them is filled with stalls during the week. It's best on Sundays (9:00-17:00), when all stalls and shops are open; you'll find a lively organic food market, many ethnic eateries, crafts, trendy clothes, bags, and an antique-and-junk market. Thursdays are for antiques, Fridays specialize in cutting-edge fashion and art, and the first and third Wednesday of every month feature a record and book fair (all 10:00-16:00). It's quietest on Saturdays, Mondays, and Tuesdays, when only the shops are open—no stalls (shops open daily 11:00-19:00, Tube: Liverpool Street; from the Tube stop, take Bishopsgate East exit, turn left, walk to Brushfield Street, and turn right; tel. 020/7375-2963, www.visitspitalfields.com).

Petticoat Lane Market—Just a block from Spitalfields Market, this line of stalls sits on the otherwise dull, glass-skyscraper-filled Middlesex Street; adjoining Wentworth Street is grungier and more characteristic. Expect budget clothing, leather, shoes, watches, jewelry, and crowds (Sun 9:00-14:00, sometimes later; smaller market Mon-Fri 10:00-16:30 on Wentworth Street only; closed Sat; Middlesex Street and Wentworth Street, Tube: Liverpool Street). The Columbia Road flower market is nearby (Sun 8:00-15:00, http://columbiaroad.info).

Brick Lane Market—Housed in the former Truman Brewery, this market is in the heart of the "Banglatown" Bangladeshi community. Of the three East End markets, Brick Lane is the grittiest and most avant-garde, selling handmade clothes and home decor, as well as ethnic street food (Sun 10:00-17:00, 91 Brick Lane, Tube: Liverpool Street or Aldgate East, tel. 020/7770-6028, www.brick lanemarket.com).

In the West End
Covent Garden Market—Originally the convent garden for Westminster Abbey, the iron-and-glass market hall hosted a produce market until the 1970s (earning it the name "Apple Market"). Yesteryear's produce stalls are now open 10:00-18:00 daily with antiques (Mon); clothes, gifts, and foods (Tue-Fri); and handmade crafts (Sun; Tube: Covent Garden, tel. 020/7836-9136, www.coventgardenlondonuk.com, also see ○ West End Walk). The **Jubilee Hall Market** to the south follows a similar schedule (antiques Mon 5:00-16:00, general market Tue-Fri 9:30-18:30, handcrafts Sat-Sun 9:30-17:30, tel. 020/7836-2139, www.jubilee market.co.uk).

In South London
Brixton Market—This seedy neighborhood south of the Thames features yet another thriving market. Here the food, clothing, records, and hair-braiding throb with an Afro-Caribbean beat (stalls open Mon-Sat 8:00-18:00, Wed until 15:00, farmer's market Sun 10:00-14:00 but otherwise dead on Sundays; Tube: Brixton, www.brixtonmarket.net).

Borough Market—The Southwark neighborhood hosts a carnival of food under the Borough Bridge, with stalls selling produce, baked goods, cheeses, and other delicacies (Thu 11:00-17:00, Fri 12:00-18:00, Sat 8:00-17:00, closed Sun-Wed, Tube: London Bridge, tel. 020/7407-1002, www.boroughmarket.org.uk, also see ○ Bankside Walk).

In Greenwich
Greenwich—With several sightseeing treats just a quick DLR ride from central London, Greenwich has its share of great markets. They're especially lively on weekends. For details, see page 447.

Famous Auctions
London's famous auctioneers welcome the curious public for viewing and bidding. You can preview estate catalogs or browse auction calendars online. To ask questions or set up an appointment, contact **Sotheby's** (Mon-Fri 9:00-16:30, closed Sat-Sun, café, 34-35 New Bond Street—see map on page 172, Tube: Oxford Circus, tel. 020/7293-5000, www.sothebys.com) or **Christie's** (Mon-Fri 9:00-17:00, Sat-Sun usually 12:00-17:00 but weekend hours vary—call ahead, 8 King Street, Tube: Green Park, tel. 020/7839-9060, www.christies.com).

ENTERTAINMENT IN LONDON

London bubbles with top-notch entertainment seven days a week: plays, movies, concerts, exhibitions, walking tours, shopping, and children's activities.

For the best list of what's happening and a look at the latest London scene, pick up a current copy of *Time Out* (£3, www.timeout.com). The TI's free monthly *London Planner* covers sights, events, and plays at least as well as *Time Out* does.

Choose from classical, jazz, rock, and far-out music, Gilbert and Sullivan, tango lessons, comedy, Baha'i meetings, poetry readings, spectator sports, theater, and the cinema. In Leicester Square, you'll sometimes find movies that have yet to be released in the States—if Colin Firth is attending an opening-night premiere in London, it will likely be at one of the big movie houses here.

There are plenty of free performances, such as lunch concerts at St. Martin-in-the-Fields (at Trafalgar Square) and summertime events at The Scoop amphitheater near City Hall (see "Summer Evenings Along the South Bank").

Theater (a.k.a. "Theatre")

London's theater rivals Broadway's in quality and usually beats it in price. Choose from 200 offerings—Shakespeare, musicals, comedies, thrillers, sex farces, cutting-edge fringe, revivals starring movie celebs, and more. London does it all well. I prefer big, glitzy—even bombastic—musicals over serious chamber dramas, simply because London can deliver the lights, sound, dancers, and multimedia spectacle I rarely get back home. (If you're a regular visitor to Broadway or Las Vegas—where you have access to similar spectacles—you might prefer some of London's more low-key offerings.) For a rundown of what's hot right now, see the "What's On in the West End" sidebar.

There are also plenty of enticing plays to choose from, ranging from revivals of classics to cutting-edge works by the hottest young playwrights. Many star huge-name celebrities (you'll see the latest offerings advertised all over the Tube and elsewhere). London is a magnet for movie stars who want to stretch their acting chops. For example, since 2003, Kevin Spacey has been the artistic director of the Old Vic theater. He has directed and appeared in several productions, and has enlisted many big-name film directors and actors for others (www.oldvictheatre.com).

Most theaters, marked on tourist maps, are found in the West End between Piccadilly and Covent Garden. Box offices, hotels, and TIs offer a handy free *Official London Theatre Guide* and *Entertainment Guide*. From home, you can look online at www.officiallondontheatre.co.uk for the latest on what's currently playing in London.

Performances are nightly except Sunday, usually with one or two matinees a week (Shakespeare's Globe is the rare theater that does offer performances on Sun, late April-early Oct). Tickets range from about £15 to £60. Matinees are generally cheaper and rarely sell out.

Buying Theater Tickets

To book a seat, simply call the theater box office (which may ring through to a central ticketing office), ask about seats and available dates, and buy a ticket with your credit card. You can call from the US as easily as from England. Arrive about 30 minutes before the show starts to pick up your ticket and avoid lines.

For a booking fee, you can reserve online. Most theater websites link you to a preferred ticket vendor, usually www.ticketmaster.co.uk or www.seetickets.com. In the US, Keith Prowse Ticketing is also handy by phone or online (US tel. 212/398-4175, http://www.keithprowse.com/tickets/slink.buy).

Although booking through an agency is quick and easy, prices are inflated by a standard 25 percent fee. Ticket agencies (whether in the US, at London's TIs, or scattered throughout the city) are just scalpers with an address. If you're buying from an agency, look at the ticket carefully (your price should be no more than 30 percent over the printed face value; the 20 percent VAT is already included in the face value), and understand where you're sitting according to the floor plan (if your view is restricted, it will state this on the ticket; for floor plans of the various theaters, see www.theatremonkey.com).

Agencies are worthwhile only if a show you've just got to see is sold out at the box office. They scarf up hot tickets, planning to make a killing after the show is sold out. US booking agencies get their tickets from another agency, adding even more to your

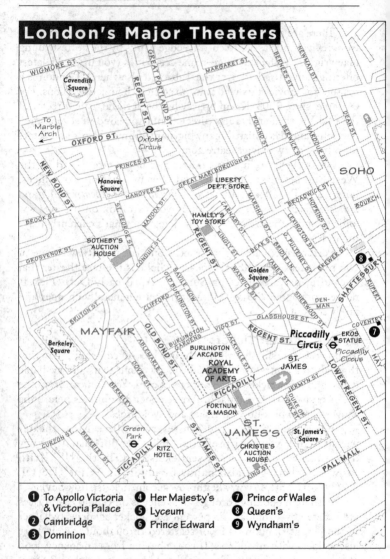

London's Major Theaters

① To Apollo Victoria & Victoria Palace
② Cambridge
③ Dominion
④ Her Majesty's
⑤ Lyceum
⑥ Prince Edward
⑦ Prince of Wales
⑧ Queen's
⑨ Wyndham's

expense by involving yet another middleman. Many tickets sold on the street are forgeries. Although some theaters use booking agencies to handle their advance sales, you'll stand a good chance of saving money by avoiding the middleman and simply calling the box office directly to purchase your tickets (international phone calls are cheap, and credit cards make booking a snap).

Theater Lingo: It's helpful to know these terms when booking tickets—stalls (ground floor), dress circle (first balcony), upper circle (second balcony), balcony (sky-high third balcony), slips

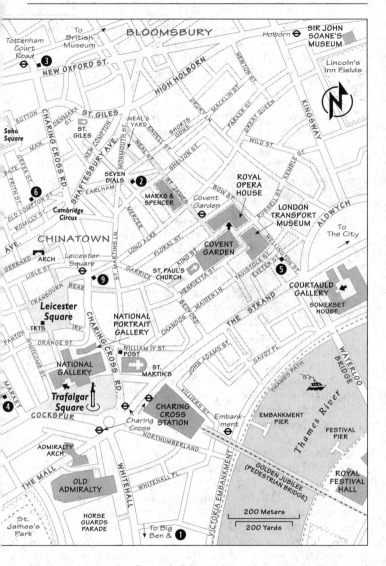

(cheap seats on the fringes). Many cheap seats have a restricted view (behind a pillar).

Cheap Theater Tricks: Most theaters offer cheap returned tickets, standing-room, matinee, and senior or student standby deals. These "concessions" (discounted tickets) are indicated with a "conc" or "s" in the listings. Picking up a late return can get you a great seat at a cheap-seat price. Even if a show is "sold out," there's usually a way to get a seat. Call the theater box office and ask how.

If you don't care where you sit, you can often buy the absolute cheapest seats—those with an obstructed view or in the nosebleed section—at the box office; these tickets generally cost less than £20. Many theaters are so small that there's hardly a bad seat. After the lights go down, scooting up is less than a capital offense. Shakespeare did it.

Half-Price "tkts" Booth: This famous ticket booth at Leicester (LESS-ter) Square sells discounted tickets for top-price

seats to shows on the push list—but only on the day of the performance (generally £3 service charge per ticket, Mon-Sat 10:00-19:00, Sun 11:00-16:00, lines often form early, list of shows available online at www.tkts.co.uk). Most tickets are half-price; other shows are discounted 25 percent. Note that the real half-price booth (with its "tkts" name) is a freestanding kiosk at the edge of the garden in Leicester Square. Several dishonest outfits nearby advertise "official half-price tickets"—avoid these.

Here are sample prices: A top-notch seat to *Chicago* costs £59 if you buy directly from the theater; the same seat costs £32.50 at Leicester Square. The cheapest balcony seat is £25 through the theater. Half-price tickets can be a good deal, unless you want the cheapest seats or the hottest shows. But check the board; occasionally they sell cheap tickets to good shows.

Theater Options

West End Theaters: The commercial (nonsubsidized) theaters cluster around Soho (especially along Shaftesbury Avenue) and Covent Garden. With a centuries-old tradition of pleasing the masses, these present London theater at its glitziest (see the sidebar for a sampling of what's playing here).

Royal Shakespeare Company: If you'll ever enjoy Shakespeare, it'll be in Britain. The RSC performs at various theaters around London and in Stratford-upon-Avon year-round. To get a schedule, contact the RSC (Royal Shakespeare Theatre, Stratford-upon-Avon, toll tel. 0844-800-1110, www.rsc.org.uk).

Shakespeare's Globe: To see Shakespeare in a replica of the theater for which he wrote his plays, attend a play at the Globe. In this round, thatch-roofed, open-air theater, the plays are performed much as Shakespeare intended—under the sky, with no amplification.

The play's the thing from late April through early October

(usually Mon 19:30, Tue-Sat 14:00 and 19:30, Sun either 13:00 and/or 18:30, tickets can be sold out months in advance). You'll pay £5 to stand and £15-35 to sit, usually on a backless bench. Because only a few rows and the pricier Gentlemen's Rooms have seats with backs, £1 cushions and £3 add-on back rests are considered a good investment by many. Dress for the weather.

The £5 "groundling" tickets—which are open to rain—are most fun. Scurry in early to stake out a spot on the stage's edge, where the most interaction with the actors occurs. You're a crude peasant. You can lean your elbows on the stage, munch a picnic dinner (yes, you can bring in food), or walk around. I've never enjoyed Shakespeare as much as here, performed as it was meant to be in the "wooden O." If you can't get a ticket, consider waiting around. Plays can be long, and many groundlings leave before the end. Hang around outside and beg or buy a ticket from someone leaving early (groundlings are allowed to come and go). A few non-Shakespeare plays are also presented each year. If you can't attend a show, you can take a guided tour of the theater and museum by day (see page 92).

To reserve tickets for plays, call or drop by the theater box office (Mon-Sat 10:00-18:00, Sun 10:00-17:00, open one hour later on performance days, New Globe Walk entrance, no extra charge to book by phone, tel. 020/7401-9919). You can also reserve online (www.shakespeares-globe.org, £2 booking fee). If the tickets are sold out, don't despair; a few often free up at the last minute. Try calling around noon the day of the performance to see if the box office expects any returned tickets. If so, they'll advise you to show up a little more than an hour before the show, when these tickets are sold (first-come, first-served).

The theater is on the South Bank, directly across the Thames over the Millennium Bridge from St. Paul's Cathedral (Tube: Mansion House or London Bridge). The Globe is inconvenient for public transport, but the courtesy phone in the lobby lets you get a minicab in minutes. (These minicabs have set fees—e.g., £8 to South Kensington—but generally cost less than a metered cab and provide fine and honest service.) During theater season, there's a regular supply of black cabs outside the main foyer on New Globe Walk.

Outdoor Theater in Summer: Enjoy Shakespearean drama and other plays under the stars at the Open Air Theatre, in leafy Regent's Park in north London. Food is allowed: You can bring your own picnic; order à la carte from the theater menu; or pre-order a £25 picnic supper from the theater at least 48 hours in advance (tickets £12-50; season runs late May-mid-Sept, box office open April-late May Mon-Sat 10:00-18:00, closed Sun; late May-mid-Sept Mon-Sat 10:00-20:00, Sun 10:00-until start of play on

ENTERTAINMENT

What's On in the West End

Here are some of the perennial favorites that you're likely to find among the West End's evening offerings. If spending the time and money for a London play, I like a full-fledged, high-energy musical (which all of these are). Generally you can book tickets for free at the box office or for a £2-3 fee by telephone or online. See the map on the previous page for locations.

Billy Elliot—This adaptation of the popular British film is part family drama, part story of a boy who just has to dance, set to a score by Elton John (£20-65, Mon-Sat 19:30, matinees Thu and Sat 14:30, Victoria Palace Theatre, Victoria Street, Tube: Victoria, toll tel. 0844-811-0055, www.billyelliotthemusical.com).

Chicago—A chorus-girl-gone-bad forms a nightclub act with another murderess to bring in the bucks (£26-63, Mon-Thu 20:00, Fri 17:30 and 20:30, Sat 15:00 and 20:00, Cambridge Theatre, Earlham Street, Tube: Covent Garden, booking toll tel. 0844-412-4652, www.chicagothemusical.com).

Jersey Boys—This fast-moving, easy-to-follow show tracks the rough start and rise to stardom of Frankie Valli and the Four Seasons. It's light, but the music is so catchy that everyone leaves whistling the group's classics (£20-65, Mon-Sat 19:30, matinees Tue and Sat 14:30, Prince Edward Theatre, Old Compton Street, Tube: Leicester Square, toll tel. 0844-482-5138, www.jersey boyslondon.com).

Les Misérables—Claude-Michel Schönberg's musical adaptation of Victor Hugo's epic follows the life of Jean Valjean as he struggles with the social and political realities of 19th-century France. This inspiring mega-hit takes you back to the days of France's struggle for a just and modern society (£15-63, Mon-Sat 19:30, matinees Wed and Sat 14:30, Queen's Theatre, Shaftesbury Avenue, Tube: Piccadilly Circus, box office toll tel. 0844-482-5138, www.lesmis.com).

performance days only; order tickets online after mid-Jan or by phone Mon-Sun 9:00-21:00; £1 booking fee by phone, no fee if ordering online or in person; toll tel. 0844-826-4242, www.open airtheatre.org; grounds open 1.5 hours prior to evening performances, one hour prior to 2:30 matinee, and 30 minutes prior to earlier matinees; 10-minute walk north of Baker Street Tube, near Queen Mary's Gardens within Regent's Park; detailed directions and more info at www.openairtheatre.org).

Fringe Theater: London's rougher evening-entertainment scene is thriving, filling pages in *Time Out*. Choose from a wide range of fringe theater and comedy acts (generally £5).

The Lion King—In this Disney extravaganza, Simba the lion learns about the delicately balanced circle of life on the savanna (£21-64, Tue-Sat 19:30; matinees Wed, Sat, and Sun 14:30; Lyceum Theatre, Wellington Street, Tube: Charing Cross or Covent Garden, theater info tel. 020/7420-8100, booking toll tel. 0844-844-0005, www.thelionking.co.uk).

Mamma Mia!—This energetic, spandex-and-platform-boots musical weaves together a slew of ABBA hits to tell the story of a bride in search of her real dad as her promiscuous mom plans her Greek Isle wedding. The production has the audience dancing by the time it reaches its happy ending (£20-67, Mon-Thu and Sat 19:30, Fri 20:30, matinees Fri 17:00 and Sat 15:00, Prince of Wales Theatre, Coventry Street, Tube: Piccadilly Circus, box office toll tel. 0844-482-5115, www.mamma-mia.com).

Phantom of the Opera—A mysterious masked man falls in love with a singer in this haunting Andrew Lloyd Webber musical about life beneath the stage of the Paris Opera (£20-62.50, Mon-Sat 19:30, matinees Tue and Sat 14:30, Her Majesty's Theatre, Haymarket, Tube: Piccadilly Circus or Leicester Square, US toll-free tel. 800-334-8457, London booking toll tel. 0844-412-2707, www.thephantomoftheopera.com).

We Will Rock You—Whether or not you're a Queen fan, this musical tribute (more to the band than to Freddie Mercury) is an understandably popular celebration of their work (£30-62, Mon-Sat 19:30, matinee Sat 14:30, Dominion Theatre, Tottenham Court Road, Tube: Tottenham Court Road, Ticketmaster toll tel. 0844-847-1775, www.wewillrockyou.co.uk).

Wicked—This lively prequel to *The Wizard of Oz* examines how the Witch of the West met Glinda the Good Witch, and later became so, you know...(£15-65, Mon-Sat 19:30, matinee Wed and Sat 14:30, Apollo Victoria Theatre, just east of Victoria Station, Tube: Victoria, Ticketmaster toll tel. 0844-826-8000, www.wickedthemusical.co.uk).

Classical Music
Concerts at Churches
For easy, cheap, or free concerts in historic churches, ask the TI (or check *Time Out*) about **lunch concerts,** especially:
- St. Bride's Church, with free lunch concerts twice a week at 13:15 (generally Tue, Wed, or Fri—confirm by phone or online, church tel. 020/7427-0133, www.stbrides.com).
- St. James's at Piccadilly, with 50-minute concerts on Mon, Wed, and Fri at 13:10 (suggested £3.50 donation, info tel. 020/7381-0441, www.st-james-piccadilly.org).
- St. Martin-in-the-Fields, offering concerts on Mon, Tue, and

ENTERTAINMENT

Fri at 13:00 (suggested £3.50 donation, church tel. 020/7766-1100, www.smitf.org).

St. Martin-in-the-Fields also hosts fine **evening concerts** by candlelight (£8-26, several nights a week at 19:30) and live jazz in its underground Café in the Crypt (£5-10 tickets, Wed at 20:00).

Evensong and Organ Recitals at Churches

Evensong services are held at several churches, including:
- St. Paul's Cathedral (Mon-Sat at 17:00, Sun at 15:15).
- Westminster Abbey (Mon-Tue and Thu-Fri at 17:00, Sat-Sun at 15:00 except Sat at 17:00 in summer; there's a service on Wed, but it may be spoken, not sung).
- Southwark Cathedral (Mon-Tue and Thu-Fri at 17:30, Sat at 16:00, Sun at 15:00, no service on Wed or alternate Mon, tel. 020/7367-6700, www.southwark.anglican.org/cathedral).
- St. Bride's Church (Sun at 17:30, tel. 020/7427-0133, www.stbrides.com).

Free **organ recitals** are often held on Sunday at 17:45 in Westminster Abbey (30 minutes, tel. 020/7222-5152). Many other churches have free concerts; ask for the *London Organ Concerts Guide* at the TI.

Performances

Prom Concerts: For a fun classical event (mid-July-mid-Sept), attend a Prom Concert (shortened from "Promenade Concert") during the annual festival at the Royal Albert Hall. Nightly concerts are offered at give-a-peasant-some-culture prices to "Promenaders"—those willing to stand throughout the performance (£5 standing-room spots sold at the door, £7 restricted-view seats, most £20-54 but depends on performance, Tube: South Kensington, toll tel. 0845-401-5045, www.bbc.co.uk/proms).

Opera: Some of the world's best opera is belted out at the prestigious Royal Opera House, near Covent Garden (box office tel. 020/7304-4000, www.roh.org.uk), and at the London Coliseum (English National Opera, St. Martin's Lane, Tube: Leicester Square, box office toll tel. 0871-911-0200, www.eno.org). Or consider taking in an unusual opera at King's Head Pub in Islington, home of London's Little Opera House (11 Upper Street, Tube: Angel, tel. 020/7478-0160, www.kingsheadtheatre.com).

Dance: Sadler's Wells Theatre features both international and UK-based dance troupes (Rosebery Avenue, Islington, Tube: Angel, info tel. 020/7863-8198, box office toll tel. 0844-412-4300, www.sadlerswells.com).

Sightseeing

Evening Museum Visits: Many museums are open an evening or two during the week, offering fewer crowds. See the list on page 74.

Tours: Guided walks are offered several times a day. **London Walks** is the most established company. Daytime walks vary by theme: ancient London, museums, legal London, Dickens, Beatles, Jewish quarter, Christopher Wren, and so on. In the evening, expect a more limited choice: ghosts, Jack the Ripper, pubs, or literary-themed. Get the latest from their brochure or website, or call for a recorded listing of that day's walks. Show up at the listed time and place, pay the guide, and enjoy the two-hour tour (£8, cash only, tel. 020/7624-3978, recorded info tel. 020/7624-9255, www.walks.com).

To see the city illuminated at night, consider a bus tour. A two-hour **London by Night Sightseeing Tour** leaves every evening from Victoria Station and other points (see page 40).

Cruises: During the summer, boats sail as late as 19:00 between Westminster Pier (near Big Ben) and the Tower of London. (For details, see page 44.)

A handful of outfits run Thames River evening cruises with four-course meals and dancing. **London Showboat** offers the best value (£75, April-Oct Wed-Sun, March and Nov-Dec Thu-Sat, Jan-Feb Fri-Sat, 3.5 hours, departs at 19:30 from Westminster Pier and returns by 23:00, reservations necessary, tel. 020/7740-0400, www.citycruises.com). Dinner cruises are also offered by **Bateaux London** (£75-125, tel. 020/7695-1800, www.bateauxlondon.com). For more on cruising, get the *River Thames Boat Services* brochure from a London TI.

Summer Evenings Along the South Bank

If you're visiting London in summer, consider hitting the South Bank after hours.

Take a trip around the **London Eye** while the sun sets over the city (the wheel spins until late—last ascent at 21:30 July-Aug, 21:00 April-June, 20:00 Sept-March). Then cap your night with an evening walk along the pedestrian-only **Jubilee Walkway,** which runs east-west along the river. It's where Londoners go to escape the heat. This pleasant stretch of the walkway—lined with pubs and casual eateries—goes from the London Eye past Shakespeare's Globe to Tower Bridge (you can walk in either direction).

If you're in the mood for a movie, take in a flick at the **BFI Southbank,** located just across the river, alongside Waterloo Bridge. Run by the British Film Institute, the state-of-the-art theater shows mostly classic films, as well as art cinema (£9, £5 on Tue and weekday matinees, Tube: Waterloo or Embankment, box office tel. 020/7928-3232, check www.bfi.org.uk for schedules).

Farther east along the South Bank is **The Scoop**—an outdoor amphitheater next to City Hall. It's a good spot for outdoor movies, concerts, dance, and theater productions throughout the summer—with Tower Bridge as a scenic backdrop. These events are free, nearly nightly, and family-friendly. For the latest event schedule, see www.morelondon.com and click on "The Scoop" (next to City Hall, Riverside, The Queen's Walkway, Tube: London Bridge).

Winter Diversions

London dazzles year-round, so consider visiting in winter, when airfares and hotel rates are generally cheaper and there are fewer tourists. Despite drearier weather and shorter days, London's museums, theaters, concert halls, and pubs offer a warm, cozy welcome.

London at Christmas is especially appealing, with its buildings dressed in their holiday best. Many holiday traditions have their roots in 19th-century Victorian Britain. Beginning in the 1840s, Queen Victoria's German husband, Prince Albert, popularized the decorating of Christmas trees and the sending of Christmas cards. And what could be more traditional than seeing the setting of Charles Dickens' *A Christmas Carol* come to life? God bless us, every one.

November to January

Pantomimes, or "pantos," are a British holiday tradition. Though they have nothing to do with silent mimes—and they don't mention Christmas—these campy fairy-tale plays entertain with outrageous costumes, sets, and dance numbers. Verbal participation is definitely encouraged, and it doesn't take long to learn the lines. Adults will laugh at the more risqué jokes; kids will giggle at the slapstick. Two London theaters that usually stage pantos are the Hackney Empire (northeast London, Tube: Bethnal Green, then 10 minutes on #106 or #254 bus, tel. 020/8985-2424, www.hackney empire.co.uk) or the Old Vic (southeast of Waterloo Station, Tube: Waterloo, toll tel. 0844-871-7628, www.oldvictheatre.com). For a rundown of all theater events, see www.timeout.com or www .officiallondontheatre.co.uk. For more about pantos and their traditions, see www.its-behind-you.com.

Get some exercise at the **outdoor ice rinks** at Somerset House, Tower of London, Natural History Museum, and Hampton Court Palace, among other locations (£10-15/session, includes skates, generally mid-Nov-mid-Jan 10:00-22:00, can be smart to drop in ahead of time to make reservations).

The **Hyde Park Winter Wonderland** offers kitschy carnival

ENTERTAINMENT

Christmas Travel Strategies

- If arriving at Heathrow Airport on Christmas Day, arrange transport from the airport to your hotel in advance. Try SkyShuttle door-to-door shuttle vans (£21.50/person one-way, toll tel. 0845-481-0960 between 6:00 and 22:00, www.skyshuttle.co.uk, reservations@skyshuttle.co.uk).

- Pick a central location if staying over December 25. There is no public transit (Tube, train, or bus) at all on Christmas Day, and reduced services on Christmas Eve and Boxing Day (Dec 26). For specifics, see www.tfl.gov.uk. Taxis are scarce, so be prepared for a long wait (£4 holiday surcharge, toll tel. 0871-871-8710). Better yet, bundle up and walk.

- To save money and avoid transportation difficulties, stay someplace with a kitchen (such as an apartment, hostel, or hotel room with kitchenette) so you can prepare some of your own meals. Don't forget to buy groceries before stores close on Christmas Eve. For tips on finding apartment rentals, see the Sleeping in London chapter.

- If you plan to eat out December 24-26 without reservations, go ethnic: Indian, Chinese, and Middle Eastern restaurants are usually open in Soho, Chinatown, along Edgware Road, or near the East End's Brick Lane.

- Expect closures. Museums are generally closed December 24-26, and smaller shops are usually closed December 26.

fun with a Ferris wheel, carousel, and other rides, as well as an ice rink and vendors selling silly hats and plenty of food and drink (free entry, rides £2-10, late Nov-early Jan, southeast corner of park, Tube: Hyde Park Corner, www.hydeparkwinterwonderland.com).

Stroll around and enjoy the elaborate **light displays** and store windows on major shopping streets from mid-November to early January, especially on Oxford Street, Bond Street, Regent Street, and Brompton Road. Post-holiday sales start December 26 for many stores; the famous Harrods winter sale begins a day or two later.

The Trafalgar Square **Christmas tree** is given to London every year from the people of Oslo, Norway, in appreciation for British help during World War II (lighting ceremony first Thu in Dec, stays up until Jan 6, www.london.gov.uk). Free carol concerts are also held beneath the tree in December.

The **Geffrye Museum's** 11 historic rooms are decorated for Christmas every year, highlighting holiday customs from the 17th century to today (free, see page 86).

Take in a seasonal concert at the grand red-velvet-draped **Royal Albert Hall;** ask about "carols by candlelight" events (tickets as cheap as £12, Tube: South Kensington, box office toll tel. 0845-401-5034, www.royalalberthall.com).

Instead of visiting Santa Claus at the North Pole, British children see **Father Christmas** in his grotto. In London, the poshest Santas are at Harrods and Selfridges, and it may be worth reserving in advance to avoid long lines (late Nov-Christmas Eve, reservation fee about £2, photos-£10-15; Harrods, Tube: Knightsbridge, tel. 020/7730-1234; Selfridges, Tube: Bond Street or Marble Arch, toll-free tel. 0800-123-400).

Nibble your way through **Borough Market,** where you'll find lots of seasonal and gourmet treats (Thu 11:00-17:00, Fri 12:00-18:00, Sat 8:00-17:00; closed Sun-Wed except open daily week before Christmas, closed Dec 25-26; south of London Bridge, where Southwark Street meets Borough High Street; Tube: London Bridge, tel. 020/7407-1002, www.boroughmarket.org.uk). While at the market, be sure and sample traditional favorites such as mulled wine, mince pie, Christmas cake, and Christmas pudding (see page 283).

Don't forget to pick up some **Christmas crackers** to give your holiday meals some extra bang. Not to be confused with something you eat, these fun party favors contain a paper crown, a teeny gift, and a corny joke. Buy them at grocery or department stores, find a friend, and pull hard.

Another popular holiday food event is the German **Cologne Market,** on the South Bank between the London Eye and the Royal Festival Hall (late Nov-late Dec Sun-Thu 11:00-20:00, Fri-Sat 10:00-22:00, Tube: Waterloo, www.xmas-markets.com).

Christmas Day

Spending December 25 in London? While almost everything is closed, and there is no public transit (not even the Tube), there are still a few options for getting out.

Popular **church services** are held both Christmas Eve and Christmas Day at Westminster Abbey, Westminster Cathedral, St. Paul's, and St. Martin-in-the-Fields, among other places. Warning: These draw large crowds, so ask in advance about when to arrive. (For example, you may need to wait in line several hours for the Abbey's 16:00 service on Christmas Eve.)

The Peter Pan Cup **swim race,** held in Hyde Park every Christmas morning since 1864, is named in honor of *Peter Pan* playwright J. M. Barrie, who presented the first cup. You must be a member of the local swimming club to compete, but spectators are welcome (9:00, south side of The Serpentine—a lake in the center of the park). Break the ice by asking a local where to find the nearby Peter Pan statue.

London Walks offers two guided **walking tours** on December 25, with appropriate themes such as "Christmas Morning 1660" and "Charles Dickens' *A Christmas Carol*" (£8, 11:00 & 14:00, meet at Trafalgar Square Christmas tree, tel. 020/7624-3978 or recorded info tel. 020/7624-9255, www.walks.com).

Watch the Queen's annual **Christmas message** on the BBC at 15:00. If you miss it, you can watch it online on Her Majesty's Royal YouTube channel (www.youtube.com).

If your visit extends through the **New Year,** here are two events to be aware of: New Year's Eve **fireworks** from the London Eye attract at least 400,000 revelers to Trafalgar Square and the nearby riverbank, with good viewing spots staked out hours in advance. Public transport is free after the festivities (generally 23:45-04:00). The next day, a **parade** featuring 10,000 performers snakes from Big Ben to Piccadilly Circus (free, grandstand seats-£18, 12:00-15:00, tel. 020/8566-8586, www.londonparade.co.uk).

LONDON CONNECTIONS

By Plane

Phone numbers and websites for London's airports and major airlines are listed in the appendix. For accommodations at or near the major airports, see page 372.

Heathrow Airport

Heathrow Airport is one of the world's busiest airports. Think about it: 68 million passengers a year on 470,000 flights from 180 destinations riding 90 airlines, like some kind of global maypole dance. Read signs, ask questions. For Heathrow's airport, flight, and transfer information, call the switchboard at toll tel. 0844-335-1801, or visit the helpful website at www.heathrow airport.com.

Heathrow has five terminals: T-1 (mostly domestic and Irish flights, with some service to Europe and the US); T-2 (closed for renovation, should reopen in 2013); T-3 (North and South American, Asian, and some European flights); T-4 (European and US flights); and T-5 (British Airways flights only). You can walk between T-1 and T-3. To travel between the other terminals, you can take the Heathrow Express trains (free), buses (free), or the Tube (requires a ticket). Unlike most American airports, there is no train that links all the terminals together on one line, so you may have to transfer if you're going to T-4 or T-5.

If you're flying out of Heathrow, it's critical to confirm which terminal your flight will use (check the Web or call your airline

in advance)—because if it's T-4 or T-5, you'll need to allow extra time. Taxi drivers generally know which terminal you'll need, but bus drivers may not.

Services: Each terminal has an airport information desk (generally daily 6:00-22:00), car-rental agencies, exchange bureaus, ATMs, a pharmacy, a VAT refund desk (tel. 020/8910-3682; you must present the VAT claim form from the retailer here to get your tax rebate on items purchased in Britain—see page 14 for details), and baggage storage (£8.50/item for 24 hours, hours vary by terminal but generally daily 5:30-23:00, www.left-baggage.co.uk). Get online 24 hours a day at Heathrow's Internet access points (at each terminal—T-4's is up on the mezzanine level) or with your laptop (pay Wi-Fi provided by Boingo, www.boingo.com). A post office is on the first floor of T-3. Each terminal has cheap eateries.

Heathrow's small **"TI"** (tourist info shop), even though it's a for-profit business, is worth a visit to pick up free information: a simple map, the *London Planner,* and brochures (daily 6:30-22:00, 5-minute walk from T-3 in Tube station, follow signs to Underground; bypass queue for transit info to reach window for London questions).

Getting to London from Heathrow Airport

You have five basic options for traveling the 14 miles between Heathrow Airport and downtown London: Tube (£5/person), bus (£5/person), direct shuttle bus (£21.50/person), express train with connecting Tube or taxi (about £20/person), or taxi (about £55 per group).

By Tube (Subway): For £5, the Tube takes you from any Heathrow terminal to downtown London in 50-60 minutes on the Piccadilly Line (6/hour; depending on your destination, may

require a transfer, buy ticket at the Tube station ticket window). If you plan to use the Tube for transport in London, it may make sense to buy a Travelcard or pay-as-you-go Oyster card at the Tube station ticket window at the airport. (For information on these passes, see page 29.) If your Travelcard covers only Zones 1-2, it does not include Heathrow (Zone 6); however, you can pay a small supplement for the initial trip from Heathrow to downtown.

If you're taking the Tube from downtown London *to* the airport, note that the Piccadilly Line trains don't stop at every terminal. Trains either stop at T-4, then T-1/T-3 (also called Heathrow Central), in that order; or T-1/T-3 and T-5. When leaving central London on the Tube, allow extra time if going to T-4 or T-5; since you have to be sure you get on a train going to your terminal, carefully check the destination information before you board.

By Bus: Most buses depart from the outdoor common area in the heart of the Heathrow complex called the Central Bus Station. It serves T-1 and T-3, and is a 5-minute walk from these terminals. To get to T-4 or T-5 from the Central Bus Station, go inside, downstairs, and follow signs to take Heathrow Express trains to your terminal (free, but only runs every 15-20 minutes to those terminals); or catch one of the free buses that circulate between terminals.

National Express has regular service from Heathrow's Central Bus Station to Victoria Coach Station in downtown London, near several of my recommended hotels. While slow, the bus is affordable and convenient for those staying near Victoria Station (£5, 1-2/hour, less frequent from Victoria Station to Heathrow, 45-60 minutes depending on time of day, toll tel. 0871-781-8181, www.nationalexpress.com).

By Shuttle: SkyShuttle operates buses about every half-hour between all Heathrow terminals and hotels in central London (£21.50/person one-way, £34.40/person round-trip; reservations toll tel. 0845-481-0960, call between 6:00-22:00; www.skyshuttle.co.uk).

By Train: Two different trains (slow for £8.50, fast for £16.50) run between Heathrow Airport and London's Paddington Station. At Paddington Station, you're in the thick of the Tube system, with easy access to any of my recommended neighborhoods—my Paddington hotels are just outside the front door, and

Notting Hill Gate is just two Tube stops away. The **Heathrow Connect** train is the slightly slower, much cheaper option, serving T-1 and T-3 at one station called Heathrow Central; use free transfers if you're coming from either T-4 or T-5 (£8.50 one-way, 2/hour, 30 minutes, toll tel. 0845-678-6975, www.heathrowconnect.com). The **Heathrow Express** train is fast (15 minutes to downtown from T-1 and T-3; 21 minutes from T-5; transfer required from T-4) and runs more frequently (4/hour), but it's pricey (£16.50 "express class" one-way, £32 round-trip, ask about discount promos at ticket desk, buy ticket before you board or pay a £3 surcharge to buy it on the train, covered by BritRail pass, daily 5:10-23:25, toll tel. 0845-600-1515, www.heathrowexpress .co.uk). At the airport, you can use Heathrow Express as a free transfer between terminals.

By Taxi: Taxis from the airport cost about £45-70 to west and central London (one hour). For four people traveling together, this can be a deal. Hotels can often line up a cab back to the airport for about £30-40. For the cheapest taxi to the airport, don't order one from your hotel. Simply flag down a few and ask them for their best "off-meter" rate. Locals refer to hired cars that do the trip off-meter as "mini-cabs." These are reliable and generally cost about what you'd pay for a taxi in good traffic, but—with a fixed price—they can save you money when taxis are snarled in congestion with the meter running.

Getting to Bath from Heathrow Airport

By Bus: Direct buses run daily from Heathrow to Bath (£19-42, 10/day direct, 2-4 hours, more frequent but slower with transfer in London, toll tel. 0871-781-8181, www.nationalexpress.com). BritRail passholders may prefer the 2.5-hour Heathrow-Bath bus/train connection via Reading (BritRail passholders just pay £15 for bus; otherwise £50-65 depending on time of day, about £10 cheaper when bought in advance; tel. 0118-957-9425, buy bus ticket from www.railair.com, train ticket from www.firstgreatwestern.co.uk). First catch the RailAir Link shuttle bus (2/hour, 45 minutes) to Reading (RED-ding), then hop on the express train (2/hour, 1 hour) to Bath. Factoring in the connection in Reading—which can add at least an hour to the trip—the train is a less convenient option than the direct bus to Bath.

Gatwick Airport

More and more flights land at Gatwick Airport, which is half-way between London and the South Coast (toll tel. 0844-335-1802, www.gatwickairport.com). Gatwick has two terminals, North and South, which are easily connected by a free mono-rail (two-minute trip, runs 24 hours daily). Note that boarding passes say "Gatwick N" or "Gatwick S" to indicate your terminal. British Airways flights generally use Gatwick North. The Gatwick Express trains (described next) stop only at Gatwick South. Schedules in each terminal show only arrivals and departures from that terminal.

Getting to London: Gatwick Express trains are clearly the best way into London from this airport. They shuttle conveniently between Gatwick South and London's Victoria Station, with many of my recommended hotels close by (£18, £31 round-trip, 10 percent discount online, 4/hour, 30 minutes, runs 5:00–24:00 daily, purchase tickets on train at no extra charge, toll tel. 0845-850-1530, www.gatwickexpress.com). If you buy your tickets at the station before boarding, ask about their deal where three adults travel for the price of two, or four for the price of three. (If you see others in the ticket line, suggest buying your tickets together—you'll save more than £5 each.)

You can save a few pounds by taking Southern Railway's slower and less frequent **shuttle train** between Gatwick South and Victoria Station (£11, up to 4/hour, 45 minutes, toll tel. 0845-127-2920, www.southernrailway.com).

A train also runs from Gatwick South to **St. Pancras International Station** (£9, 8/hour, 1 hour, www.firstcapital connect.co.uk)—useful for travelers taking the Eurostar train (to Paris or Brussels) or staying in the St. Pancras/King's Cross neighborhood.

Even slower, but cheap and handy to the Victoria Station neighborhood, you can take the **bus** from Gatwick to Victoria (£7.50, hourly, 1.5 hours, toll tel. 0871-781-8181, www.national express.com).

Getting to Bath: To get to Bath from Gatwick, you can catch a bus to Heathrow and take the bus to Bath from there (10/day, 4-5 hours total, £25 one-way, transfer at Heathrow Airport, www.nationalexpress.com—see "Getting to Bath from Heathrow Airport," previous page). By train, the best Gatwick-Bath connection involves a transfer in Reading (£48-58 one-way depending on time of day, cheaper in advance, hourly, 2.5 hours, www.first greatwestern.co.uk; avoid transfer in London, where you'll have to change stations).

London's Other Airports

Stansted Airport: If you're using Stansted (toll tel. 0870-0000-303, www.stanstedairport.com), you have several options for getting into or out of London. Two different **buses** connect the airport and downtown London's Victoria Station neighborhood: National Express (£10, £17 round-trip, every 20 minutes, 1.75 hours, runs 24 hours a day, picks up and stops throughout London, ends at

Victoria Coach Station, toll tel. 0871-781-8181, www.national express.com) and Terravision (£9, 2-3/hour, 1.25 hours, ends at Green Line Coach Station just south of Victoria Station). Or you can take the faster, pricier Stansted Express **train** (£18-20 one-way, £25-27 round-trip, connects to London's Tube system at Tottenham Hale and Liverpool Street, 4/hour, 45 minutes, 5:00-23:00, toll tel. 0845-850-0150, www.stanstedexpress.com). Stansted is expensive by **cab;** figure £120 one-way from central London.

Luton Airport: For Luton (airport tel. 01582/405-100, www .london-luton.co.uk), there are two choices into or out of London. The fastest way to go is by **rail** to London's St. Pancras International Station (£12 one-way, 1-5/hour, 25-45 minutes—check schedule to avoid the slower trains, toll tel. 0845-712-5678, www.eastmidlands trains.co.uk); catch the 10-minute shuttle bus (£1) from outside the terminal to the Luton Airport Parkway Station. The Green Line express **bus** #757 runs to Buckingham Palace Road, just south of London's Victoria Station (£13 one-way, £16 round-trip, small discount for easyJet passengers who buy online, 2-4/hour, 1.25-1.5 hours, 24 hours a day, toll tel. 0844-801-7261, www.greenline .co.uk). If you're sleeping at Luton, consider easyHotel (see listing on page 370).

London City Airport: There's a slim chance you might use London City Airport (tel. 020/7646-0088, www.londoncity airport.com). To get into London, take the Docklands Light Railway (DLR) to the Bank Tube station, which is one stop east of St. Paul's on the Central Line (£4 one-way, covered by Travelcard, £2.50-2.90 on Oyster card, 22 minutes, tel. 020/7222-1234, www .tfl.gov.uk/dlr).

Connecting London's Airports by Bus

More and more travelers are taking advantage of cheap flights out of London's smaller airports. A handy **National Express bus** runs between Heathrow, Gatwick, Stansted, and Luton airports— easier than having to cut through the center of London—although traffic can be bad and can increase travel times (toll tel. 0871-781-8181, www.nationalexpress.com).

From Heathrow Airport to: Gatwick Airport (1-4/hour, 1-1.5 hours, £21.50 one-way, £40 round-trip, allow at least three hours between flights), **Stansted Airport** (1-2/hour, 1.5-1.75 hours, £24 one-way, £31 round-trip), **Luton Airport** (hourly, 1-1.5 hours, £21 one-way, £31 round-trip).

Discounted Flights from London

London is the hub for many cheap, no-frills airlines, which afford- ably connect the city with other destinations in the British Isles and throughout Europe. Although bmi has been around the longest, the other small airlines generally offer cheaper flights. A visit to www.skyscanner.net, www.mobissimo.com, www.kayak .com, or www.wegolo.com sorts the numerous options offered by the many discount airlines, enabling you to see the best schedules for your trip and find the best deal.

Be aware of the potential drawbacks of flying on the cheap: nonrefundable and nonchangeable tickets, rigid baggage restrictions (and fees if you have more than what's officially allowed), use of airports far outside town, tight schedules that can mean more delays, little in the way of customer assistance if problems arise, and, of course, no frills. To avoid unpleasant surprises, read the small print—especially baggage policies—before you book. If you're traveling with lots of bags, a cheap flight can quickly become a bad deal, due to per-piece baggage fees.

With **bmi,** you can fly inexpensively from London to destinations in the UK and beyond (fares start at about £53 one-way to Edinburgh or Dublin). Call toll tel. 0844-848-4888 or US tel. 800-788-0555, or check www.flybmi.com. Book in advance. Although you can book right up until the flight departs, the cheap seats will have sold out long before, leaving the most expensive seats for latecomers.

Another low-cost airline, **easyJet,** flies from Gatwick, Luton, and Stansted. Prices are based on demand, so the least popular routes make for the cheapest fares, especially if you book early (toll tel. 0871-244-2366, www.easyjet.com).

Ryanair flies from London (mostly Stansted airport, though also Gatwick and Luton) to often obscure airports near Dublin, Glasgow, Frankfurt, Stockholm, Oslo, Venice, Turin, and many other cities. Sample fares: London-Dublin—£50 round-trip (sometimes as low as £30), London-Frankfurt—£45 round-trip (Irish toll tel. 0818-303-030, British toll tel. 0871-246-0000, www .ryanair.com). However, be warned that Ryanair charges additional fees for nearly everything. They require a mandatory online-only check-in (£5 charge) from 15 days to four hours before your flight (no airport check-in). When checking in, you must also print out your boarding pass; if you show up at the airport without it, there's an additional £40 charge. You can carry on only a small day bag; you'll pay a fee for each checked bag (price depends on number of bags; up to three bags allowed per passenger).

Brussels Airlines is a Brussels-based company with good rates (toll tel. 0905-609-5609, US tel. 516/740-5200, www.brussels airlines.com). Brussels Airlines flies from Heathrow to its hub in Brussels, where you can connect cheaply to many cities in Europe.

By Train

Britain is covered by a myriad of rail systems (owned by different companies), which together are called National Rail. London, the country's major transportation hub, has a different train station for each region. There are nine main stations (see the map above):

Euston—Serves northwest England, North Wales, and Scotland.

King's Cross—Serves northeast England and Scotland, including York and Edinburgh.

Liverpool Street—Serves east England, including Essex and Harwich.

London Bridge—Serves south England, including Brighton.

Marylebone—Serves southwest and central England, including Stratford-upon-Avon.

Paddington—Serves south and southwest England, including Heathrow Airport, Windsor, Bath, South Wales, and the Cotswolds.

St. Pancras International—Serves north and south England, plus the Eurostar to Paris or Brussels (see "Crossing the Channel," later).

Victoria—Serves Gatwick Airport, Canterbury, Dover, and Brighton.

Waterloo—Serves southeast England, including Salisbury.

In addition, there are other, smaller train stations in London that you are not likely to use, such as **Charing Cross** or **Blackfriars.**

Any train station has schedule information, can make reservations, and can sell tickets for any destination. Most stations offer a baggage-storage service (£8/bag for 24 hours, look for *left luggage* signs); because of long security lines, it can take a while to check or pick up your bag (www.excess-baggage.com). For more details on the services available at each station, see www.nationalrail.co.uk /stations.

Buying Tickets: For general information, call 0845-748-4950 (or visit www.nationalrail.co.uk or www.eurostar.com; £5 booking fee for telephone reservations). If you book far enough ahead, you might find discounted train tickets on certain routes at www .megatrain.com (toll tel. 0871-266-3333; as they also sell bus tickets, be careful to specify that you want to take the train).

Railpasses: For train travel outside London, consider getting a BritRail pass. Options include passes that cover England as well as Scotland and Wales, England-only passes, England/Ireland passes, "London Plus" passes (good for travel in most of southeast England but not in London itself), and BritRail & Drive passes

CONNECTIONS

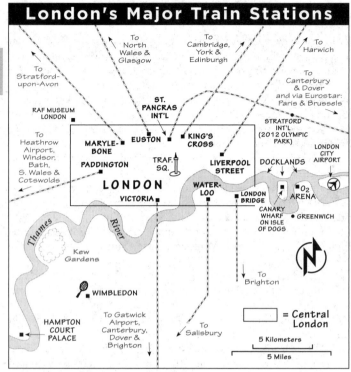

London's Major Train Stations

To North Wales & Glasgow

To Cambridge, York & Edinburgh

To Harwich

To Stratford-upon-Avon

To Canterbury & Dover and via Eurostar: Paris & Brussels

RAF MUSEUM LONDON

ST. PANCRAS INT'L

STRATFORD INT'L (2012 OLYMPIC PARK)

To Heathrow Airport, Windsor, Bath, S. Wales & Cotswolds

MARYLE-BONE

EUSTON

KING'S CROSS

LONDON CITY AIRPORT

PADDINGTON

TRAF. SQ.

LIVERPOOL STREET

DOCKLANDS

LONDON

WATER-LOO

LONDON BRIDGE

O2 ARENA

VICTORIA

CANARY WHARF ON ISLE OF DOGS

GREENWICH

Thames River

Kew Gardens

WIMBLEDON

To Brighton

HAMPTON COURT PALACE

To Gatwick Airport, Canterbury, Dover & Brighton

To Salisbury

= Central London

5 Kilometers

5 Miles

(which offer you some rail days and some car-rental days). For specifics, contact your travel agent, or see www.ricksteves.com/rail.

Train Connections from London

To Points West

From Paddington Station to: Bath (2/hour, 1.5 hours; also consider a guided Evan Evans tour by bus—see page 438), **Oxford** (2/hour direct, 1 hour, more possible with transfer in Reading), **Penzance** (every 1-2 hours, 5-5.5 hours, possible change in Plymouth), and **Cardiff** (2/hour, 2 hours).

To Points North

From King's Cross Station: Trains run at least hourly, stopping in **York** (2 hours), **Durham** (3 hours), and **Edinburgh** (4.5 hours). Trains to **Cambridge** also leave from here (3/hour, 45-60 minutes).

    From Euston Station to: Conwy (nearly hourly, 3.25 hours, transfer in Chester), **Liverpool** (hourly, 2 hours, more with transfer), **Blackpool** (hourly, 3 hours, transfer at Preston), **Keswick**

Public Transportation near London

To North England & Scotland

To York & Scotland

King's Lynn • Norwich

Coventry •

ENGLAND

Stratford-upon-Avon Warwick • Long Buckby • Hunt. • Ely
Leam. Spa Bedford • Cambridge •
Worcester • Moreton • Banbury • Luton
Stow • To Hoek van Holland
Chelten-ham • Blenheim Oxford • Stansted Harwich •
To Cardiff Swindon Didcot •
Avebury Reading **London** London City Greenwich
Bristol Ramsgate To Ostende
Bath • Bedwyn • Windsor Canterbury • Dover
Wells • Stonehenge Heathrow Ashford • (CHUNNEL) Calais •
Glaston-bury South-ampton Gatwick Rye •
Salisbury • Brighton • East-bourne Hastings Calais-Fréthun
To Cornwall Poole • To Paris
Weymouth • Bourne-mouth Portsmouth •
Isle of Wight *English Channel*

Rail
Bus
Boat

Area covered by London Plus Pass

30 Kilometers
30 Miles (approx. scale)

Note: Bus Lines Follow Most Rail Lines

FRANCE

CONNECTIONS

(hourly, 4.5 hours, transfer to bus at Penrith), and **Glasgow** (1-2/hour, 4.5-5 hours).

From London's Other Stations

Trains run between London and **Canterbury,** leaving from St. Pancras International Station and arriving in Canterbury West (1-2/hour, 1 hour), as well as from London's Victoria Station and arriving in Canterbury East (2/hour, 1.5 hours).

Direct trains leave for **Stratford-upon-Avon** from Marylebone Station, located near the southwest corner of Regents Park (5/day direct, more with transfers, 2.25 hours).

To Other Destinations: Dover (hourly, 1.25 hours, from St. Pancras International Station), **Brighton** (4-5/hour, 1 hour, from Victoria Station and London Bridge Station), **Portsmouth** (3/hour, 1.5-2 hours, most from Waterloo Station, a few from Victoria Station), and **Salisbury** (2/hour, 1.5 hours, from Waterloo Station). For trains to **Windsor, Cambridge,** or **Bath,** check transportation connections for each destination, all covered in this book.

By Bus

Buses are slower but considerably cheaper than trains for reaching destinations around Britain, and beyond. Most depart from **Victoria Coach Station,** which is one long block south of Victoria Station (near many recommended accommodations and Tube: Victoria). Inside the station, you'll find basic eateries, kiosks, and a helpful information desk stocked with schedules and ready to point you to your bus or answer any questions.

Most domestic buses are operated by **National Express** (toll tel. 0871-781-8181, www.nationalexpress.com); their international departures are called **Eurolines** (toll tel. 0871-781-8177, www.euro lines.co.uk). A newer, smaller company called **Megabus** undersells National Express with deeply discounted promotional fares—the further ahead you buy, the less you pay (some trips for just £1.50, tend to be slower than National Express, toll tel. 0900-160-0900, www.megabus.com). They also sell discounted train tickets on selected routes.

Try to avoid bus travel on Friday and Sunday evenings, when weekend travelers are more likely to make buses sell out.

To ensure getting a ticket—and to save money with special promotions—you can book your ticket in advance online (see websites above). The cheapest pre-purchased tickets can be changed (for a £5 fee), but they're nonrefundable. If you have a British mobile phone, you can buy an "M-Ticket," which sends your paperless confirmation number right to your phone.

If you're planning to buy your ticket at the station, try to arrive an hour before the bus departs—or drop by the day before. (For buses to Stansted Airport and Oxford, you can buy the ticket on board; otherwise you'll buy it at a ticket window.) Watch your bags carefully—luggage thieves thrive at the station.

To Bath: The National Express bus leaves from Victoria Coach Station (nearly hourly, 2.5-3.75 hours, avoid those with layover in Bristol, sample fares: one-way-£22, round-trip-£29).

To get to Bath via Stonehenge, consider taking a guided bus tour from London to Stonehenge, Salisbury, and Bath, and abandoning the tour in Bath (be sure to confirm that Bath is the last stop on that particular tour). **Evan Evans'** tour is £74 and includes admissions. The tour leaves from Victoria Coach Station every morning at 8:45 (you can stow your bag in a compartment under the bus), stops in Salisbury (for a look at its magnificent cathedral) and Stonehenge, and then stops in Bath before returning to London (offered year-round; they also offer another tour to Stonehenge and Bath via Windsor Castle). You can book the tour at the Victoria Coach Station or the Evan Evans office (258 Vauxhall Bridge Road, near Victoria Coach Station, tel. 020/7950-1777, US tel.

209/830-1521, www.evanevans.co.uk). **Golden Tours** also runs a Stonehenge-Bath tour (£59, check website for seasonal tour days; departs from Fountain Square, located across from Victoria Coach Station, US tel. 800-548-7083, toll tel. 0844-880-5050, www.goldentours.com).

To Other Destinations: Oxford (2-4/hour, about 1.5 hours), **Cambridge** (hourly, 2-2.5 hours), **Canterbury** (about hourly, 2-2.5 hours), **Dover** (about hourly, 2.5-3.25 hours), **Penzance** (5/day, 9 hours, overnight available), **Cardiff** (hourly, 3.25 hours), **Liverpool** (8/day direct, 5.25-6 hours, overnight available), **Blackpool** (4/day direct, 6.25-7 hours, overnight available), **York** (4/day direct, 5.25 hours), **Durham** (4/day direct, 6.5-7.5 hours), **Glasgow** (3/day direct, 8-9 hours, train is a much better option), **Edinburgh** (2/day direct, 8.75-9.75 hours, go by train instead).

To Dublin, Ireland: This bus/boat journey, operated by National Express, takes 10-12 hours (£26-48, 1/day, departs Victoria Coach Station at 18:00, check in with passport one hour before). Consider a cheap 1.25-hour Ryanair flight instead (www.ryanair.com).

To the Continent: Especially in summer, buses run to destinations all over Europe, including Paris, Amsterdam, Brussels, and Germany (sometimes crossing the Channel by ferry, other times through the Chunnel). For any international connection, you need to check in with your passport one hour before departure. For details, call toll tel. 0871-781-8177 or visit www.eurolines.co.uk. For information on crossing the Channel by bus, see the end of this chapter.

Crossing the Channel

By Eurostar Train

The fastest and most convenient way to get from Big Ben to the Eiffel Tower is by rail. Eurostar, a joint service of the Belgian, British, and French railways, is

the speedy passenger train that zips you (and up to 800 others in 18 sleek cars) from downtown London to downtown Paris or Brussels (15+/day, 2.25-2.5 hours) faster and more easily than flying. The actual tunnel crossing is a 20-minute, silent, 100-mile-per-hour nonevent. Your ears won't even pop. Get ready for more high-speed connections: Eurostar's monopoly expired at the beginning of 2010, and Germany's national railroad wants to run its bullet trains to London by 2013.

CONNECTIONS

Eurostar Fares

Channel fares are reasonable but complicated. Prices vary depending on how far ahead you reserve, whether you can live with restrictions, and whether you're eligible for any discounts (children, youths, seniors, round-trip travelers, and railpass holders all qualify).

Fares can change without notice, but typically a **one-way, full-fare ticket** (with no restrictions on refundability) runs about $425 first-class and $300 second-class. **Cheaper seats** come with more restrictions and can sell out quickly (figure $100-160 for second-class, one-way). Those traveling with a railpass that covers France or Britain should look first at the **passholder** fare ($85-130 for second-class, one-way Eurostar trips). For more details, visit my *Guide to Eurail Passes* (www.ricksteves.com/eurostar), Rail Europe (www.raileurope.com), or go directly to Eurostar (www.eurostar.com).

Buying Eurostar Tickets

Because only the most expensive (full-fare) ticket is fully refundable, don't reserve until you're sure of your plans. But if you wait too long, the cheapest tickets will get bought up.

Once you're confident about the time and date of your crossing, you can check and book fares by phone or online. Ordering online through Eurostar or major agents offers a print-at-home e-ticket option. You can also order by phone through Rail Europe at US tel. 800-EUROSTAR for home delivery before you go, or through Eurostar (toll tel. 0870-518-6186, priced in euros) and pick up your ticket at the train station. In continental Europe, you can buy your Eurostar ticket at any major train station in any country or at any travel agency that handles train tickets (expect a booking fee). In Britain, tickets can be issued only at the Eurostar office in St. Pancras International Station. You can purchase passholder discount tickets at Eurostar departure stations, through US agents, or by phone with Eurostar, but they may be harder to get at other train stations and travel agencies, and are a discount category that can sell out.

Remember that Britain's time zone is one hour earlier than

Eurostar Routes

ENGLAND

London
Ebbsfleet
Ashford

English Channel

Calais-Fréthun

Amsterdam

NETH

Brussels

Lille-Europe

BELG.

FRANCE

50 Kilometers
50 Miles

Paris

---- Eurostar
······ Channel Tunnel
------ Other Rail

Building the Chunnel

The toughest obstacle to building a tunnel under the English Channel was overcome in 1986, when longtime rivals Britain and France reached an agreement to build it together. Britain began in Folkestone, France in Calais, planning a rendezvous in the middle.

By 1988, specially made machines three football fields long were boring 26-foot-wide holes under the ground. The dirt they hauled out became landfill in Britain and a hill in France. Crews crept forward 100 feet a day until June 1991, when French and English workers broke through and shook hands midway across the Channel—the tunnel was complete. Rail service began in 1994.

The Chunnel is 31 miles long (24 miles of it underwater) and 26 feet wide. It sits 130 feet below the seabed in a chalky layer of sediment. It's segmented into three separate tunnels—two for trains (one in each direction) and one for service and ventilation. The walls are concrete panels and rebar fixed to the rock around it. Sixteen-thousand-horsepower engines pull 850 tons of railcars and passengers at speeds up to 100 mph through the tunnel.

The ambitious project—the world's longest undersea tunnel—helped to show the European community that cooperation between nations could benefit everyone.

France or Belgium. Times listed on tickets are local times (departure from London is British time, arrival in Paris in French time).

Departing from London: Eurostar trains depart from and arrive at London's St. Pancras International Station. Check in at least 30 minutes in advance for your Eurostar trip. It's very similar to an airport check-in: You pass through airport-like security, show your passport to customs officials, and find a TV monitor to locate your departure gate. There are a few airport-like shops, newsstands, horrible snack bars, and cafés (bring food for the trip from elsewhere), pay-Internet terminals, and a currency-exchange booth with rates about the same as you'll find on the other end.

Cheap Passage by Tour: A tour company called Britain-Shrinkers sells one- or two-day tours to Paris, Brussels, or Bruges, enabling you to side-trip to these cities from London for less than most train tickets alone. For example, you'll pay £109 for a one-day Paris "tour" (unescorted Mon-Sat day trip with Métro pass; tel. 020/7713-1311 or www.britainshrinkers.com). This can be a particularly good option if you need to get to Paris from London on short notice, when only the costliest fares are available.

Crossing the Channel Without Eurostar

The old-fashioned ways of crossing the Channel are cheaper than Eurostar (taking the bus is cheapest). They're also twice as romantic, complicated, and time-consuming.

By Train and Boat

To Paris: You'll take a train from London to the port of Dover, then catch a ferry to Calais, France, before boarding another train for Paris. Trains go from London's St. Pancras International to **Dover's** Priory Station (hourly, 1.25 hours; bus or taxi from train station to ferry dock). P&O Ferries sail from Dover to Calais; TGV trains run from Calais to Paris. You'll need to book your own train tickets to Dover and from Calais to Paris. The prices listed here are for the ferry only (from £35 one-way or £60 round-trip online, more at dock or by phone, book early for best fares; 22/day, 1.5 hours, toll tel. 08716-642-020, www.poferries.com).

To Amsterdam: Stena Line's Dutchflyer service combines train and ferry tickets between London and Amsterdam via the ports of Harwich and Hoek van Holland. Trains go from London's Liverpool Street Station to **Harwich** (hourly, 1.75 hours, most transfer in Manningtree). Stena Line ferries sail from Harwich to Hoek van Holland (7.75 hours), where you can transfer to a train to Amsterdam or other Dutch cities (ferry—from £34, from £63 with cabin, book at least 2 weeks in advance for best price, 13 hours total travel time, Dutchflyer toll tel. 0844-576-2762, www.stenaline .co.uk, Dutch train info at www.ns.nl).

For additional European ferry info, visit www.aferry.to. For UK train and bus info, go to www.traveline.org.uk.

By Bus

You can take the bus from London direct to **Paris** (4/day, 8.25-9.75 hours), **Brussels** (3-4/day, 12 hours), or **Amsterdam** (4/day, 12 hours) from Victoria Coach Station (via ferry or Chunnel, day or overnight). You'll pay the same to Paris, Brussels, or Amsterdam. The price depends on when you book (for example: £28 one-way, £38 round-trip if purchased at least a week ahead; £40 one-way, £55 round-trip if purchased the day before; £44 one-way, £61 round-trip if purchased same day; no discounts and £5 more for any ticket during peak times such as holiday weekends; toll tel. 0871-781-8177; visit www.eurolines.co.uk and look for "funfares").

By Plane

Check with budget airlines for cheap round-trip fares to Paris or Brussels (see "Discounted Flights from London," earlier).

DAY TRIPS

Greenwich • Windsor •
Cambridge • Stonehenge • Bath

Greenwich, Windsor, Cambridge, Stonehenge, and Bath are five of the best day-trip possibilities near London. Any one of these very different but equally enjoyable destinations makes for an entertaining day out from London.

Greenwich is famous as Britain's capital of timekeeping (home of Greenwich Mean Time and the prime meridian) and of all things maritime. The nearest day-trip option from London, Greenwich is a quick Tube or Thames boat ride from downtown, and it's affordable—most sights are free. You can see it in a few hours, and it pairs perfectly with a visit to the Docklands (see previous chapter).

The primary residence of Her Majesty the Queen, **Windsor** hosts a castle that's regally lived-in, yet open to the public. This is simply a charming town to relax in—and its proximity to Heathrow

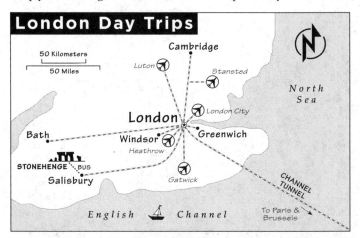

Airport (45-60 minutes by train west of London) makes Windsor easy to combine with a flight into or out of London. Nearby is an oddball collection of intriguing sights, including Legoland Windsor, Eton College (Britain's most elite high school), and Ascot Racecourse (for horse racing).

Of Britain's many university towns, **Cambridge** (an hour north of London by train) is one of the best known—and, for travelers, simply the best. Combining a mellow, fun-to-explore townscape with a big-league university that churns out famous grads (from Charles Darwin to Isaac Newton), Cambridge delights.

Stonehenge, the world's most famous rock group, sits lonesome yet adored in a mysterious field 90 miles southwest of London. Though some consider it overrated, for others, this intricately arranged ring of boulders is a must-see.

The elegant spa town of **Bath** is as historic and genteel as it is fun—from the ancient Roman bath ruins in the heart of town, to the fine rows of Georgian townhouses gracefully arcing across well-tended lawns, to an array of specialized museums covering fashion, circa-1900 industry, and one-time local Jane Austen. An hour and a half by train west of London, Bath can be done as a day trip but is best enjoyed by staying overnight.

Although these five destinations are my top picks, London's convenient public transit can easily whisk you to a wealth of day-trip destinations not covered in this book: Canterbury (cathedral), Dover (castle-crowned chalk cliffs), Portsmouth (treasure trove of maritime history), Stratford-upon-Avon (all things Shakespeare), Warwick (fine medieval castle), Oxford (another classic university town), and Brighton (beach and pier). For details, see *Rick Steves' England.*

GREENWICH, WINDSOR, CAMBRIDGE & STONEHENGE

Four of the best day-trip possibilities are Greenwich, Windsor, Cambridge, and Stonehenge. Greenwich, technically within London's city limits, is England's maritime capital; Windsor, west of the city, has a very famous castle; Cambridge, an hour to the north, is England's best university town; and Stonehenge, to the southwest, is one of the ancient world's most famous sights.

Getting Around

By Train: The British rail system uses London as a hub and normally offers same-day round-trip fares that cost virtually the same as one-way fares. For day trips, these "off-peak day return" tickets, available if you depart London outside rush hour (usually after 9:30 on weekdays and anytime Sat-Sun), are best. Note that a "day return" (round-trip within a single day) is different—and cheaper—than a "return," so be sure to buy the right ticket. You can also save a little money if you purchase tickets before 18:00 the day before your trip.

By Train Tour: London Walks offers a variety of "Explorer Days" tours year-round by train, including a Salisbury and Stonehenge tour (see page 480), as well as a Cambridge itinerary (£14 plus transportation and admissions costs, pick up their brochure at the TI or hotels, tel. 020/7624-3978, www.walks.com).

GREENWICH

Greenwich

Tudor kings favored the palace at Greenwich (GREN-ich). Henry VIII was born here. Later kings commissioned architects Inigo Jones and Christopher Wren to beautify the town and palace, and William and Mary built a grand hospital to care for retired seamen (which later became a college for training naval officers).

Greenwich is England's maritime capital, and visitors come here for all things salty. (The *Cutty Sark* clipper ship, the area's premier attraction, is slated to reopen in the spring of 2012 after a long restoration.) The town is synonymous with timekeeping and astronomy, and at the Royal Observatory Greenwich, you can learn how those pursuits relate to seafaring. Greenwich also has stunning Baroque architecture, appealing markets, a fleet of nautical shops, plenty of parks, kid-friendly museums, and hordes of tourists. Since many of the major sights here are free to enter, and you can travel between central London and Greenwich on a cheap Tube ticket, it's a wonderfully inexpensive day out. And where else can you set your watch with such accuracy?

Planning Your Time

Upon arrival, stroll past the *Cutty Sark* dry dock to the Discover Greenwich exhibit and TI, then drop into the grand buildings of the Old Royal Naval College and walk the shoreline promenade. Enjoy lunch or a drink in the venerable Trafalgar Tavern before heading to the National Maritime Museum, and then through the park up to the Royal Observatory Greenwich. The town's sights are open daily, but its popular market is closed Monday and Tuesday.

If you like to mix and match public transit, I'd suggest taking the boat to Greenwich for the scenery and commentary, and the Docklands Light Railway (DLR) back, especially if you want to stop at the Docklands on the way home. To visit the Docklands— the glittering forest of skyscrapers rising from a once-derelict port— hop off the train at the Canary Wharf stop for a quick stroll (see the Docklands Walk chapter). From there, you can tack on a small detour to check out the 2012 Olympic Park site (see page 104).

Getting to Greenwich

It's a joy by boat or a snap by DLR.

By Boat: From central London, you can cruise scenically down the Thames to Greenwich. Various tour boats—with commentary and open-deck seating up top—leave from the piers at Westminster, Waterloo, and the Tower of London (2/hour, about 1 hour); note that most boats have commentary only on the way to Greenwich, not on the way back.

Thames Clippers offers faster trips, with no commentary and only a small deck at the stern (departs every 20 minutes from several piers in central London, 45 minutes). Thames Clippers also connects Greenwich to the Docklands' Canary Wharf Pier (3/hour, 10 minutes).

For cruising details, see page 44.

By DLR: From Bank station (also accessible from the Monument Tube station) in central London, take the DLR to Cutty Sark station in central Greenwich; it's one stop before the main—but less central—Greenwich station (departs at least every 10 minutes, 20 minutes, all in Zone 2, covered by any Tube pass). Many DLR trains terminate at Canary Wharf, so make sure you get on one that continues to Lewisham or Greenwich. Some DLR trains terminate at Island Gardens—you can generally catch another train to Greenwich's Cutty Sark station within a few minutes, though it may be more memorable to walk under the river through the long Thames pedestrian tunnel.

By Train: Mainline trains also go from London (Cannon Street and London Bridge stations) several times an hour to Greenwich station (10-minute walk from the sights). Although the train is fast and cheap, the DLR is preferable because it drops you right in the heart of town.

By Bus: Catch bus #188 from Russell Square near the British Museum (about 45 minutes to Greenwich).

Orientation to Greenwich

(area code: 020)

Still well within the city limits of London, Greenwich feels like a small town all its own. Covered markets and outdoor stalls make

for lively weekends. Save time to browse the town. Wander beyond the touristy Church Street and Greenwich High Road to where flower stands spill onto the side streets and antique shops sell brass nautical knickknacks. King William Walk, College Approach, Nelson Road, and Turnpin Lane (all in the vicinity of Greenwich Market) are all worth a look. If you need pub grub, Greenwich has almost 100 pubs, with some boasting that they're mere milliseconds from the prime meridian.

Markets: Thanks to its markets, Greenwich throbs with day-trippers on weekends. The **Greenwich Market** is an entertaining mini-Covent Garden, located in the middle of the block

GREENWICH

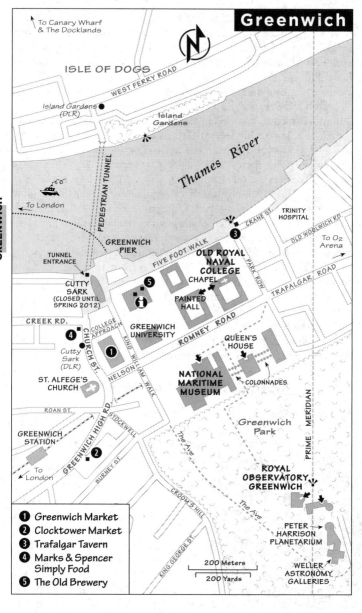

Greenwich

To Canary Wharf & The Docklands

ISLE OF DOGS

WEST FERRY ROAD

Island Gardens (DLR)

Island Gardens

Thames River

To London

PEDESTRIAN TUNNEL

GREENWICH PIER

TUNNEL ENTRANCE

CUTTY SARK (CLOSED UNTIL SPRING 2012)

FIVE FOOT WALK

CRANE ST.

TRINITY HOSPITAL

OLD WOOLWICH RD.

To O2 Arena

❸

OLD ROYAL NAVAL COLLEGE

CHAPEL

PARK ROW

TRAFALGAR ROAD

❺

PAINTED HALL

CREEK RD.

❹

COLLEGE APPROACH

GREENWICH UNIVERSITY

ROMNEY ROAD

QUEEN'S HOUSE

Cutty Sark (DLR)

CHURCH ST.

KING WILLIAM WALK

❶

NELSON RD.

NATIONAL MARITIME MUSEUM

COLONNADES

ST. ALFEGE'S CHURCH

ROAN ST.

STOCKWELL

GREENWICH STATION

GREENWICH HIGH RD.

❷

BURNEY ST.

Greenwich Park

The Ave

PRIME MERIDIAN

To London

CROOM'S HILL

ROYAL OBSERVATORY GREENWICH

The Ave

KING GEORGE ST.

PETER HARRISON PLANETARIUM

200 Meters

200 Yards

WELLER ASTRONOMY GALLERIES

❶ Greenwich Market
❷ Clocktower Market
❸ Trafalgar Tavern
❹ Marks & Spencer Simply Food
❺ The Old Brewery

between the Cutty Sark DLR station and the Old Royal Naval College—right on your way to the sights (Wed-Sun 10:00-17:30, closed Mon-Tue; farmers' market on Wed, food court on Thu-Sun, antiques on Thu-Fri, arts and crafts on Fri-Sun; tel. 020/7515-7153, www.greenwichmarket.net). The **Clocktower Market** sells old odds and ends at high prices on Greenwich High Road, near the post office (Sat-Sun and bank holidays only 10:00-17:00, www .clocktowermarket.co.uk).

Tourist Information

The TI is inside the Discover Greenwich visitors center (described later, under "Sights in Greenwich"). From the DLR station, exit straight ahead to the monumental gateway for the Old Royal Naval College complex; Discover Greenwich is just inside the gate on the left (daily 10:00-17:00, Pepys House, 2 Cutty Sark Gardens, toll tel. 0870-608-2000, www.visitgreenwich.org.uk).

Guided walks, which depart from the TI, offer an overview of the town and go past most of the big sights (£6, daily at 12:15 and 14:15, 1.5 hours; the only sights you enter are the Painted Hall and Chapel of St. Peter and St. Paul, and only on the 14:15 tour).

Sights in Greenwich

I've organized these listings as a handy sightseeing walk through town, starting right next to the Cutty Sark DLR station.

▲▲*Cutty Sark*—The Scottish-built *Cutty Sark* was the last of the great China tea clippers, and was the queen of the seas when first launched in 1869. With 32,000 square feet of sail, with favorable winds she could travel 300 miles in a day. After a five-year-long restoration, the ship is scheduled to open again to the public in the spring of 2012. The new display space allows visitors to walk above and below the suspended ship.

Cost and Hours: Call or look online for the latest information, tel. 020/8858-2698, www.cuttysark.org.uk.

Discover Greenwich—This visitors center (which also houses the TI) is located at the corner of the Old Royal Naval College closest to the *Cutty Sark*. While it's hardly a museum, it offers a decent introduction to Greenwich and some fun exhibits for kids. In the center, a model of the town lights up to tell its history. Surrounding the model are displays and artifacts from various people who have left their mark on the town, along with exhibits about the architecture and construction of Greenwich's fine buildings. Adjoining Discover Greenwich are the TI and a recommended pub, The Old Brewery.

Cost and Hours: Free, daily 10:00-17:00, tel. 020/8269-4747, www.oldroyalnavalcollege.org.

▲**Old Royal Naval College**—The college was originally a hospital founded by Queen Mary II and King William III in 1692 as a charity to care for retired or injured naval officers (called pensioners). William and Mary spared no expense, hiring the great Christopher Wren to design the complex (though other architects completed it). Its days as a hospital ended in 1869, and it served as a college for training naval officers from 1873 to 1998. Now that the Royal Navy has moved out, the public is invited to view the college's elaborate Painted Hall and Chapel of St. Peter and St. Paul, which are in symmetrical buildings that face each other overlooking a broad riverfront park.

Cost and Hours: Free, daily 10:00-17:00, sometimes closed for private events, service Sun at 11:00 in chapel—all are welcome. Guides give 1.5-hour tours covering the hall and chapel, along with other areas not open to the general public (£6, daily at 14:00, departs from TI, call ahead to check availability). Tel. 020/8269-4799, www.oldroyalnavalcollege.org.

● **Self-Guided Tour:** Good descriptions are free to borrow in each building, or you can buy the fun *Nasty Naval College* brochure, with offbeat facts about the place (£1). Guides called Yeoman Warders are often standing by to answer questions.

Here's an overview of what you'll see:

Painted Hall: Originally intended as a dining hall for pen-

sioners, this sumptuously painted room was deemed too glorious (and, in the winter, too cold) for that purpose. So almost as soon as it was completed, it became simply a place to impress visitors.

Enter the hall, climb the stairs, and gape up at one of the largest painted ceilings in Europe—112 feet long. It's a big propaganda scene, glorifying the building's founders, Queen Mary II and King William III (who, as a Protestant monarch, had recently trounced the Catholic French King Louis XIV in a pivotal battle). Crane your neck—or

use the clever wheeled mirrors—to examine the scene. In the center are William and Mary. Under his foot, William is crushing a dark figure with a broken sword... Louis XIV. He is handing a red cap (representing liberty) to the woman on the right, who holds the reins of a white horse (symbolizing Europe). On the left, a white-robed woman hands him an olive branch, a sign of peace. The message: William has granted Europe liberty by saving it from the tyranny of Louis XIV. Below the royal couple, the Spirit of Architecture shows them the plans for this very building (commemorating the sad fact that Mary died before its completion). Ringing the central image are the four seasons (represented by Zodiac signs), the four virtues, and—at the top and bottom—a captured Spanish galleon and a British man-of-war battleship.

Up the steps at the end of the room, along the wall of the **upper hall,** is a portrait of the family of King George I. On the right is the artist who spent 19 years of his life painting this hall, James Thornhill (he finally finished it in 1727). He's holding out his hand—reportedly, he didn't feel he was paid enough for this Sistine-sized undertaking.

• *Exit the hall, and cross the field to enter the...*

Chapel of St. Peter and St. Paul:
Not surprisingly, you'll sense a nautical air in this fine chapel. Notice the rope motif in the floor tiles down the aisle. The painting above the altar, by American Benjamin West, depicts the shipwreck of St. Paul on the island of Malta. According to the

Bible, Paul disturbed a poisonous viper but managed to throw it in a fire, miraculously without being harmed. Soon after the chapel was completed, it was gutted by a fire and had to be redecorated all over again. The plans were too ambitious, so the designers cut corners. Some of the columns and capitals are fake, and the "sculptures" lining the nave high above are actually *trompe l'oeil*—3-D paintings meant to look real. But some items, such as the marble frame around the main door, are finely crafted from expensive materials.

• *Leave the chapel, and walk straight down to the water—enjoying the sweeping views across to the Docklands. When you hit the river, turn right for the...*

Thames to Trafalgar Tavern Stroll—Wander east along the Thames on Five Foot Walk (named for the width of the path). Notice that the Old Royal Naval College is split into two parts; reportedly, Queen Mary didn't want the view from the Queen's House blocked. Looking up from the river, you'll see the college's twin-domed towers (one giving the time, the other the direction of the wind) framing the Queen's House, and the Royal Observatory Greenwich crowning the hill beyond.

Continuing downstream, just past the college, you'll find the **Trafalgar Tavern**. Dickens knew the pub well, and he used it as the setting for the wedding break-fast in *Our Mutual Friend*. Built in 1837 in the Regency style to attract Londoners downriver, the tavern is popular with locals (and tourists) for its fine lunches. The upstairs Nelson Room is still used for weddings. Its formal moldings and elegant windows with balconies over the Thames are a step back in time. In addition to the  casual pub, the tavern also has an elegant ground-floor dining room (£6-11 pub grub; £6-8 starters and £11-17 main courses in restaurant; food served Mon-Sat 12:00-22:00, Sun 12:00-17:00, Park Row, tel. 020/8858-2909).

A mile downstream from the pub, the **O2** (a.k.a. "the Dome") languished for nearly a decade after its controversial construction and brief life as the Millennium Dome. Intended to be a world's

fair-type site and the center of London's year 2000 celebration, it ended up being the topic of heated debates about cost over-runs and its controversial looks. While post-2000 plans for a casino and hotel project fell through, it's come in handy as an emergency homeless shelter. The site was finally bought by a developer a few years ago and rechristened "The O_2" in honor of the telecommunications company that paid for the naming rights. Currently, it hosts sporting events and concerts (at the time of his death, Michael Jackson was planning a massive concert series here), and will see action during the 2012 Summer Olympics.

• *From the Trafalgar Tavern, walk two long blocks up Park Row, and turn right (through the gate near the corner) into the park. The palatial buildings in the middle of the park are the Queen's House and the National Maritime Museum; the Royal Observatory Greenwich is on the hilltop beyond.*

Queen's House—This building, the first Palladian-style villa in Britain, was designed in 1616 by Inigo Jones for James I's wife, Anne of Denmark. All traces of the queen are long gone, and the Great Hall and Royal Apartments now serve as an art gallery for the National Maritime Museum. Predictably, most of the art is nautical-themed, with plenty of paintings of ships and sea battles, and portraits of admirals and captains. The Orangery is home to various Christ-like paintings depicting the death of Admiral Horatio Nelson—the maritime hero who is so adored here in England's naval capital. Among these is the great J. M. W. Turner painting *Battle of Trafalgar* (1824), the artist's only royal commission. The painting is often out on loan, so ask at the entry before you look for it.

Cost and Hours: Free, daily 10:00-17:00, free audioguide, last entry 30 minutes before closing, tel. 020/8858-4422, www.nmm .ac.uk.

▲**National Maritime Museum**—Great for anyone interested in the sea, this museum holds everything from a giant working pad-

dlewheel to the uniform Admiral Nelson wore when he was killed at Trafalgar (look for the bullet hole, in the left shoulder). A big glass roof tops three levels of slick, modern, kid-friendly exhibits about all things seafaring.

The Explorers exhibit covers early expeditions and an ill-fated Arctic trip, complete with a soundtrack of creaking wooden ships and crashing waves. One room displays stained-glass windows honoring members of London's Baltic Exchange (an important shipping consortium) killed in World War I. Kids like the All Hands and Bridge galleries, where they can send secret messages by Morse code and operate a miniature dockside crane. Along with displays of lighthouse technology and a whaling cannon, you'll see model ships, nautical paintings, and various salty odds and ends. Note that some parts of the museum are closed for renovation until 2012, though there's still plenty to see.

Cost and Hours: Free, daily 10:00-17:00, last entry 30 minutes before closing; look for family-oriented events posted at entrance—singing, treasure hunts, storytelling—particularly on weekends; tel. 020/8312-6608, www.nmm.ac.uk.

• *The final sight in town—the Royal Observatory Greenwich—is at the top of the hill just behind the National Maritime Museum. To reach it, cross through the colonnade connecting the museum and the Queen's House, then follow the crowds as they huff up the steep hill (allow 10-15 minutes).*

▲▲**Royal Observatory Greenwich**—Located on the prime meridian (0° longitude), the observatory is famous as the point from which all time is measured. The observatory's early work,

The Longitude Problem

Around 1700, as the ships of seafaring nations began to venture farther from their home bases, the alarming increase in the number of shipwrecks made it clear that navigational tools had to be improved. Determining latitude—the relative position between the equator and the North or South Pole—was straightforward; sailors needed only to measure the angle of the sun at noon. But figuring out longitude, or their east-west position, was not as easy without a fixed point (such as the equator) from which to measure.

In 1714, the British government offered the £20,000 Longitude Prize. Two successful solutions emerged, and both are tied to Greenwich.

The first approach was to map the stars in the night sky over Greenwich. Then, sailors at sea could compare the stars overhead to the Greenwich map and calculate their east-west position. Visitors to the Royal Observatory can still see the giant telescopes—under retractable roofs—that were used to carefully chart the movement of the stars night after night.

The second approach was to create a clock that would remain completely accurate on voyages—no easy feat back then, when turbulence and changes in weather and humidity made timepieces notoriously unreliable at sea. John Harrison spent 45 years working on this problem, finally succeeding in 1760 with his fourth effort, the H4 (which won him the Longitude Prize). All four of his attempts are on display at the Royal Observatory.

So, how can a clock determine longitude? Every 15° of longitude equals an hour when comparing the difference in sunrise or sunset times between two places. For example, the time gap between Greenwich and New York City is five hours, which translates into a longitudinal difference of 75°. Equipped with an accurate timepiece set to Greenwich Mean Time, sailors could figure out their longitude by comparing sunset time at their current position with sunset time back in Greenwich.

Notice that both approaches use Greenwich as a baseline—either on an astral map or on a clock. That's why, to this day, the prime meridian and official world time are both centered in this unassuming London suburb.

GREENWICH

however, had nothing to do with coordinating the world's clocks to Greenwich Mean Time (GMT). The observatory was founded in 1675 by Charles II for the purpose of improving navigation by more accurately charting the night sky. Today, the Greenwich time signal is linked with the BBC (which broadcasts the famous "pips" worldwide at the top of the hour). A visit here gives you a taste of the sciences of astronomy, timekeeping, and seafaring—and how they all meld together—along with great views over Greenwich and the distant London skyline.

Cost and Hours: £10, includes astronomy galleries, ticket good for re-entry for one year; daily 10:00-17:00, later in summer—can be as late as 19:00, courtyard sometimes open later than buildings, last entry 30 minutes before closing; tel. 020/8858-4422, www.nmm.ac.uk.

Planetarium: Shows cost £6.50, last 30 minutes, and generally run every hour (usually Mon-Fri 13:00-16:00, Sat-Sun 11:00-16:00, fewer shows in winter, schedule can change from day to day). Confirm times by calling ahead, checking online, or picking a flier (which you'll see around the observatory). As these shows can sell out, consider calling ahead to order tickets (see phone number above).

GREENWICH

◐ Self-Guided Tour: As you hike up the hill to the observatory, look along the roof for the orange **Time Ball**—also visible from the Thames—which drops daily at 13:00. Nearby, under the analog clock just outside the courtyard, see how your foot measures up to the foot where the public standards of length are cast in bronze.

Entering the observatory, you're directed to choose between two routes: the meridian route, to the right, and the astronomy route, to the left. Since the meridian route is more interesting, do that first.

Meridian Route: Following signs, you'll have the chance to rent an audioguide (£3.50, 1 hour), then enter the courtyard.

Running through the middle of this space is The Line—the **prime meridian.** Visitors wait patiently to have their photographs taken as they straddle the line in front of the monument, with one foot in each hemisphere. While watching all this fuss over a little line, consider that—unlike the equator—the placement of the prime meridian is totally arbitrary. It could well have been at my house, in Timbuktu, or just a few feet over—as, for a time, it was (the trough along the building's roofline shows where one astronomer had placed it). While waiting for your turn, set your wristwatch to the digital clock showing GMT to a tenth of a second.

Three different attractions are scattered around this courtyard. First, hiding in a corner is a **camera obscura.** This thrillingly low-tech device projects a live image from Greenwich onto a flat disc in a darkened room simply by manipulating light, without electricity or machinery. Bizarre as this seems today, imagine how astonishing it was in the days before television.

The smaller building is the **Flamsteed House,** named for John Flamsteed, the first king-appointed Astronomer Royal (in 1675). It contains the apartments that he lived in and the Wren-designed Octagon Room, where he carried out some of his work. Downstairs is a fascinating exhibit on the "Longitude Problem" and how it was solved (see sidebar, earlier). Also on display are all four of John Harrison's sea clocks. Compared to his other contraptions, the fourth and final attempt looks like an oversized pocket watch. But, in terms of its impact, this little timepiece is right up there with the printing press, the cotton gin, the telegraph, and the money belt on the scale of human achievement.

Finally, the **Telescopes Exhibition,** in the larger house, has a wide assortment of historical telescopes, including a couple of room-sized ones.

• *Now head out back for the...*

Astronomy Route: Walk past the giant rusted-copper cone top of the planetarium. The building beyond houses the **Weller Astronomy Galleries,** where interactive, kid-pleasing displays allow you to guide a space mission and touch a 4.5-billion-year-old meteorite. You can also buy tickets for and enter the state-of-the-art, 120-seat **Peter Harrison**

Planetarium from here (for details, see "Planetarium," earlier).

Before you leave the observatory grounds, enjoy the **view** from the overlook—the symmetrical royal buildings, the Thames, the Docklands and its busy cranes (including the prominent Canary

Wharf Tower, with its pyramid cap), the huge O2 dome, and the square-mile City of London, with its skyscrapers and the dome of St. Paul's Cathedral. At night (17:00-24:00), look for the green laser beam the observatory

projects into the sky (best viewed in winter), which extends along the prime meridian for 15 miles.

Eating in Greenwich

If you're in town on a weekend, be sure to drop by the **Greenwich Market,** which hosts a sprawling food court (Thu-Sun 10:00-17:30, directly in front of Cutty Sark DLR station). Another handy place to pick up ready-made food is **Marks & Spencer Simply Food,** between the DLR station and the *Cutty Sark* dry dock (Mon-Sat 8:30-21:00, Sun 10:00-21:00, 55 Greenwich Church Street, tel. 020/8853-1840).

The **Trafalgar Tavern,** described on page 452, is good (Mon-Sat 12:00-22:00, Sun 12:00-17:00, Park Row, tel. 020/8858-2909).

The **Old Brewery,** in the Discover Greenwich center on the Old Royal Naval College grounds, is an upscale gastropub decorated with all things beer. A brewery on this site once provided the daily ration of four pints of beer for pensioners at the hospital. Today it's a microbrewery offering 50 different beers, while a beer sommelier suggests the right pairings with food on the menu (£6-15 pub grub; part of the pub becomes a fancier restaurant in the evenings with £5-6 starters and £11-17 main courses; daily 10:00-23:00, lunch 12:00-17:00, dinner from 18:00, tel. 020/3327-1280).

WINDSOR

Windsor

Windsor, a compact and easy walking town of about 30,000 people, originally grew up around the royal residence. In 1070, William the Conqueror continued his habit of kicking Saxons out of their various settlements, taking over what the locals called "Windlesora" (meaning "riverbank with a hoisting winch")—which eventually became "Windsor." William built the first fortified castle on a chalk hill above the Thames; later, kings added on to his early designs, rebuilding and expanding the castle and surrounding gardens.

By setting up their primary residence here, modern monarchs increased Windsor's popularity and prosperity—most notably, Queen Victoria, whose stern statue glares at you as you approach the castle. After her death, Victoria rejoined her beloved husband, Albert, in the Royal Mausoleum at Frogmore House, a mile south of the castle in a private section of the Home Park (house and mausoleum rarely open). The current Queen considers Windsor her primary residence, and the one where she feels most at home. You can tell if Her Majesty is in residence by checking to see which flag is flying above the round tower: If it's the royal standard (a red, yellow, and blue flag) instead of the Union Jack, the Queen is at home.

While 99 percent of visitors just come to tour the castle and go, some enjoy spending the night. Windsor's charm is most evident when the tourists are gone. Consider overnighting here—parking and access to Heathrow Airport are easy, and an evening at the horse races (on Mondays) is hoof-pounding, heart-thumping fun.

Getting to Windsor

By Train: Windsor has two train stations—Windsor & Eton Central (5-minute walk to palace; TI in adjacent shopping center) and Windsor & Eton Riverside (5-minute walk to palace and TI). First Great Western trains run between London's Paddington Station and Windsor & Eton Central (3/hour, 35 minutes, change at Slough; £8 one-way standard class, £8.50-11 same-day return, www.firstgreatwestern.co.uk). South West Trains run between London's Waterloo Station and Windsor & Eton Riverside (2/hour, 1 hour; £8.60 one-way standard class, £9-15 same-day return, info toll tel. 0845-748-4950, www.nationalrail.co.uk).

If you're day-tripping into London from Windsor, ask at the train station about combining a same-day return train ticket with a One-Day Travelcard—you'll end up with one ticket that covers rail transportation to and from London and doubles as an all-day Tube and bus pass in town (£12-21, lower price for travel after 9:30, rail ticket may also qualify you for half-price London sightseeing discounts—ask or look for brochure at station, or go to www.days outguide.co.uk).

By Bus: Green Line buses #701 and #702 run from London's Victoria Colonnades (between the Victoria train and coach stations) to the Parish Church stop on Windsor's High Street, before continuing on to Legoland (£1-9 one-way, £9.50-13.50 round-trip, prices vary depending on time of day, 1-2/hour, 1.25 hours to Windsor, tel. 01344/782-222, www.rainbowfares.com).

By Car: Windsor is about 20 miles from London and just off Heathrow Airport's landing path. The town (and then the castle and Legoland) is well-signposted from the M4 motorway. It's a convenient first stop if you're arriving at and renting a car from Heathrow, and saving London until the end of your trip.

From Heathrow Airport: Buses #71 and #77 run between Terminal 5 and Windsor, dropping you in the center of town on Peascod Street (about £7, 1-2/hour, 45 minutes, toll tel. 0871-200-2233, www.firstgroup.com). London black cabs can (and do) charge whatever they like from Heathrow to Windsor; avoid them by calling a local cab company, such as Windsor Radio Cars (£25, tel. 01753/677-677, www.windsorcars.com).

Orientation to Windsor

(area code: 01753)

Windsor's pleasant pedestrian shopping zone litters the approach to its famous palace with fun temptations. You'll find most shops and restaurants around the castle on High and Thames Streets, and down the pedestrian Peascod Street (PESS-cot), which runs perpendicular to High Street.

Tourist Information

The TI is immediately adjacent to Windsor & Eton Central Station, in the Windsor Royal Shopping Centre's Old Booking Hall (May-Sept Mon-Fri 9:30-17:30, Sat 9:30-17:00, Sun 10:00-16:00; Oct-April Mon-Sat 10:00-17:00, Sun 10:00-16:00; tel. 01753/743-900, www.windsor.gov.uk). The TI sells discount tickets to Legoland (see "More Sights in Windsor," later).

Arrival in Windsor

By Train: The train to Windsor & Eton Central Station from Paddington (via Slough) will spit you out into the Windsor Royal shopping pavilion (which houses the TI), only a few minutes' walk from the castle. If you arrive instead at Windsor & Eton Riverside Station (from Waterloo Station), you'll see the castle as you exit—just follow the wall to the castle entrance.

By Car: Follow signs from the M4 motorway for pay-and-display parking in the center. River Street Car Park is closest to the castle, but pricey and often full. The cheaper, bigger Alexandra Car Park (near the riverside Alexandra Gardens) is farther west. To walk to the town center from the Alexandra Car Park, head east through the tour-bus parking lot toward the castle. At the souvenir shop, walk up the stairs (or take the elevator) and cross the overpass to the Windsor & Eton Central Station. Just beyond the station, you'll find the TI in the Windsor Royal Shopping Centre.

Helpful Hints

Internet Access: Get online at the **library,** located on Bachelors' Acre, between Peascod and Victoria Streets (£1.50 for 30 minutes, Mon and Thu 9:30-17:00, Tue 9:30-20:00, Wed 14:00-17:00, Fri 9:30-19:00, Sat 9:30-15:00, closed Sun, tel. 01753/743-940, www.rbwm.gov.uk).

Supermarkets: Pick up picnic supplies at **Marks & Spencer** (Mon-Sat 9:00-18:00, Sun 11:00-17:00, 130 Peascod Street, tel. 01753/852-266) or at **Waitrose** (Mon-Tue and Sat 8:30-19:00, Wed-Fri 8:30-20:00, Sun 11:00-17:00, King Edward Court Shopping Centre, just south of the Windsor & Eton

WINDSOR

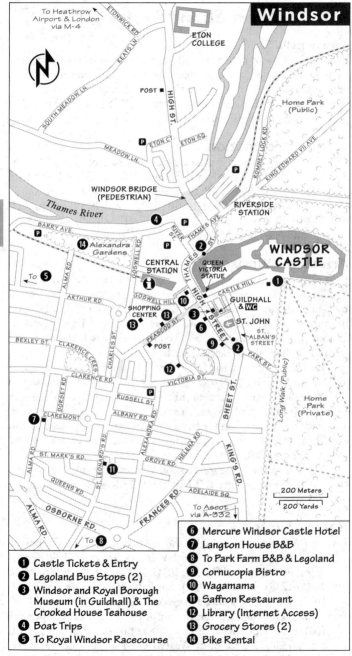

Windsor

To Heathrow Airport & London via M-4

ETON COLLEGE

ETONWICK RD.

KEATS LN.

POST

HIGH ST.

SOUTH MEADOW LN.

MEADOW LN.

ETON CT. ETON SQ.

P

P

WINDSOR BRIDGE (PEDESTRIAN)

RIVER ST.

P

Thames River

4

BARRY AVE.

P

14 Alexandra Gardens

GOSWELL RD.

CENTRAL STATION

i

QUEEN VICTORIA STATUE

2

THAMES ST.

THAMES AVE.

RIVERSIDE STATION

ROMNEY LOCK RD.

KING EDWARD VII AVE.

Home Park (Public)

WINDSOR CASTLE

1

CASTLE HILL

GUILDHALL & **WC**

ST. JOHN

ST. ALBAN'S STREET

To **5**

ALMA RD.

ARTHUR RD.

GOSWELL HILL

10

13
SHOPPING CENTER
13

PEASCOD ST.

3

6

9

HIGH STREET

BEXLEY ST.

CLARENCE CRES.

CHARLES ST.

CLARENCE RD.

POST

12

VICTORIA ST.

2

PARK ST.

SHEET ST.

DORSET RD.

RUSSELL ST.

P

ALBANY RD.

KING'S RD.

Home Park (Private)

CLAREMONT

7

ALEXANDRA RD.

HELENA RD.

GROVE RD.

Long Walk (Public)

ALMA RD.

ST. MARK'S RD.

11

ST. LEONARD'S RD.

QUEENS RD.

FRANCES RD.

ADELAIDE SQ.

OSBORNE RD.

ALMA RD.

To **8**

To Ascot via A-332

200 Meters

200 Yards

1 Castle Tickets & Entry
2 Legoland Bus Stops (2)
3 Windsor and Royal Borough Museum (in Guildhall) & The Crooked House Teahouse
4 Boat Trips
5 To Royal Windsor Racecourse
6 Mercure Windsor Castle Hotel
7 Langton House B&B
8 To Park Farm B&B & Legoland
9 Cornucopia Bistro
10 Wagamama
11 Saffron Restaurant
12 Library (Internet Access)
13 Grocery Stores (2)
14 Bike Rental

Central Station, tel. 01753/860-565). Just outside the castle, you'll find long benches near the statue of Queen Victoria—great for people-watching while you munch.

Bike Rental: Extreme Motion, near the river in Alexandra Gardens, rents 21-speed mountain bikes as well as helmets (£12/4 hours, £17/day, helmets £1-1.50, £100 credit-card deposit required, bring passport as ID, summer daily 10:00-22:00, closed off-season, tel. 01753/830-220).

Sights in Windsor

▲▲Windsor Castle

Windsor Castle, the official home of England's royal family for 900 years, claims to be the largest and oldest occupied castle in the world. Thankfully, touring it is simple. You'll see immense

grounds, lavish staterooms, a crowd-pleasing dollhouse, an art gallery, and the chapel.

Cost and Hours: £16.50, family pass £43.50, ticket good for re-entry for one year if stamped at exit; to skip the lines, purchase tickets in advance online or at the Buckingham Palace ticket office, then go in through a fast entry door; daily March-Oct 9:45-17:15, Nov-Feb 9:45-16:15, last entry 1.25 hours before closing, often closed for special events such as the Garter Service in mid-June—call or check website to make sure it's open when you want to go.

Information: As you enter, ask about the warden's free 30-minute guided walks around the grounds (2/hour). They cover the grounds but not the castle, which is well described by the included audioguide (skip the official guidebook); tel. 020/7766-7304, www.royalcollection.org.uk.

Other Activities: The **Changing of the Guard** takes place Monday through Saturday at 11:00 (April-July) and on alternating days the rest of the year (check website to confirm schedule; ceremonies begin a little earlier—get there by 10:45). There is no Changing of the Guard on Sundays or in very wet weather. An **evensong** takes place in the chapel nightly at 17:15—free for worshippers.

Touring the Castle: Immediately upon entering, you pass through a simple modern building housing a **historical overview** of the castle. This excellent intro is worth a close look—you're basically on your own after this. Inside, you'll find the motte (artificial mound) and bailey (fortified stockade around it) of William the Conqueror's castle. Dating from 1080, this was his first castle in England.

Follow the signs to the staterooms/gallery/dollhouse. **Queen Mary's Dollhouse**—a palace in miniature (1:12 scale, from 1924) and "the most famous dollhouse in the world"—often has the longest wait. If dollhouses aren't your cup of tea, you can skip that line and go immediately into the lavish **staterooms.** Strewn with history and the art of a long line of kings and queens, they're the best I've seen in Britain—and well restored after a devastating 1992 fire. Take advantage of the talkative docents in each room, who are happy to answer your questions.

The adjacent gallery is a changing exhibit featuring the **royal art collection** (and some big names, such as Michelangelo and Leonardo). Signs direct you (downhill) to **St. George's Chapel.** Housing numerous royal tombs, it's a fine example of Perpendicular Gothic, with classic fan-vaulting spreading out from each pillar (dating from about 1500). The simple chapel containing the tombs of the current Queen's parents, King George VI and "Queen Mother" Elizabeth, and younger sister, Princess Margaret, is along the church's north aisle.

Next door is the sumptuous 13th-century **Albert Memorial Chapel,** redecorated after the death of Prince Albert in 1861 and dedicated to his memory.

More Sights in Windsor

Legoland Windsor—Paradise for Legomaniacs under 12, this huge, kid-pleasing park has dozens of tame but fun rides (often with very long lines) scattered throughout its 150 acres. The impressive Miniland has 40 million Lego pieces glued together to create 800 tiny buildings and a minitour of Europe; the Creation Centre boasts an 80 percent scale-model Boeing 747 cockpit, made of two million bricks. Several of the more exciting rides involve getting wet, so dress accordingly or buy a cheap disposable poncho in the gift shop. While you may be tempted to hop on the Hill  Train at the entrance, it's faster and more convenient to walk down into the park. Food is available in the park, but you can save money by bringing a picnic.

Cost: Adults-£41.40, £37.20 in advance online, £36 from Windsor TI; children-£31.20, £27.60 online, £26 from TI, 2-for-1 deals sometimes available; free for ages 3 and under; optional Q-Bot or Q-Bot Express ride-reservation gadget allows you to bypass lines (£10-40 depending on when you go and how much time you want to save); coin lockers-£1.

Hours: Convoluted schedule, but generally mid-March-July Mon-Fri 10:00-17:00, Sat-Sun 10:00-18:00, sometimes closed Tue-Wed in spring; Aug daily 9:30-20:00; Sept-Oct Thu-Mon 10:00-17:00, until 18:00 Sat-Sun, closed Tue-Wed; closed Nov-mid-March. Call or check website for exact schedule, toll tel. 0871-222-2001, www.legoland.co.uk.

Getting There: A £4.50 round-trip shuttle bus runs from opposite Windsor's Theatre Royal on Thames Street, and from the Parish Church stop on High Street (2/hour). If day-tripping from London, ask about rail/shuttle/park admission deals from Paddington or Waterloo train stations. For drivers, the park is on B3022 Windsor/Ascot road, two miles southwest of Windsor and 25 miles west of London. Legoland is clearly signposted from the M3, M4, and M25 motorways. Parking is easy and free.

Eton College—Across the bridge from Windsor Castle you'll find many post-castle tourists filing toward the most famous "public" (the equivalent of our "private") high school in Britain. Eton was founded in 1440 by King Henry VI; today it educates about 1,300 boys (ages 13-18), who live on campus. Eton has molded the characters of 19 prime ministers as well as members of the royal family, most recently princes William and Harry. The college is sparse on sights, but the public is allowed into the schoolyard, chapel, cloisters, and the Museum of Eton Life

Cost and Hours: £6.50, access only by one-hour guided tour at 14:00 and 15:15; tours available late March-Sept, usually Wed and Fri-Sun but daily during spring and summer holiday; closed Oct-late March and about once a month for special events, so call ahead; no photos in chapel, no food or drink allowed; tel. 01753/671-177, www.etoncollege.com.

Windsor and Royal Borough Museum—Tucked into a small space beneath the Guildhall, this little museum does its best to give some insight into the history of Windsor and the surrounding area. Ask at the desk if visits are being allowed to the Guildhall itself (where Prince Charles remarried); if not, it's probably not worth the admission.

Cost and Hours: £3, £1 audioguide, Tue-Sat 10:00-16:00, Sun 12:00-16:00, closed Mon, located in the Guildhall on High Street, tel. 01628/796-846, www.rbwm.gov.uk.

Boat Trips—Cruise up and down the Thames River for classic views of the castle, the village of Eton, Eton College, and the Royal Windsor Racecourse. Choose from a 40-minute or two-hour tour, then relax onboard and nibble a picnic. Boats leave from the riverside promenade adjacent to Barry Avenue.

Cost and Hours: 40-minute tour—£5.40, family pass from £13.50, mid-Feb-Oct 1-2/hour daily 10:00-17:00, Nov Sat-Sun hourly 10:00-16:00; 2-hour tour—£8.60, April-Oct only, 1-2/day;

closed Dec-mid-Feb; tel. 01753/851-900, www.frenchbrothers .co.uk.

Horse Racing—The horses race near Windsor every Monday at the Royal Windsor Racecourse (£10-23 entry, online discounts, those under 18 free with an adult, April-Oct, no races in Sept, off A308 between Windsor and Maidenhead, tel. 01753/498-400, www.windsor-racecourse.co.uk). The romantic way to get there from Windsor is by a 10-minute shuttle boat (£6 round-trip, www .frenchbrothers.co.uk). The famous Ascot Racecourse (described below) is also nearby.

Near Windsor

Ascot Racecourse—Located seven miles southwest of Windsor and just north of the town of Ascot, this royally owned track is one of the most famous horse-racing venues in the world. The horses first ran here in 1711, and the course is best known for June's five-day Royal Ascot race meeting, attended by the Queen and 299,999 of her loyal subjects. For many, the outlandish hats worn on Ladies Day (Thursday) are more interesting than the horses. Royal Ascot is usually the third week in June (likely June 19-23 in 2012); the pricey tickets go on sale the preceding November but are often available close to the date (see website for details). In addition to Royal Ascot, the racecourse runs the ponies year-round—funny hats strictly optional.

   Cost: Regular tickets generally £10-29, Royal Ascot £17-69, online discounts, those 17 and under free; parking £5-7, more for special races; dress code enforced in some areas and on certain days, toll tel. 0870-727-1234, www.ascot.co.uk.

Sleeping in Windsor

(area code: 01753)
Most visitors stay in London and do Windsor as a day trip. But here are a few suggestions for those staying the night.

   $$$ Mercure Windsor Castle Hotel, with 108 business-class rooms, is as central as can be, just down the street from Her Majesty's weekend retreat (Db-£120-165, nonrefundable online deals, breakfast-£16, air-con, free Wi-Fi, 18 High Street, tel. 01753/851-577, www.mercure.com, h6618@accor.com).

   $$ Langton House B&B is a stately Victorian home with four well-appointed rooms lovingly maintained by Paul and Sonja Fogg (Sb-£70, Db-£99, Tb-£119, Qb-£145, 5 percent extra if paying by credit card, lower prices off-season, family-friendly, guest kitchen, free Internet access and Wi-Fi, 46 Alma Road, tel. 01753/858-299, www.langtonhouse.co.uk, paul@langtonhouse.co.uk).

Sleep Code

(£1 = about $1.60, country code: 44)
S = Single, **D** = Double/Twin, **T** = Triple, **Q** = Quad, **b** = bathroom,
s = shower only. Unless otherwise noted, credit cards are
accepted.
    To help you sort through these listings easily, I've divided
the rooms into three categories based on the price for a
standard double room with bath:

  $$$ **Higher Priced**—Most rooms £100 or more.
   $$ **Moderately Priced**—Most rooms between £60-100.
    $ **Lower Priced**—Most rooms £60 or less.

    Prices can change without notice; verify the hotel's
current rates online or by email. For other updates, see www
.ricksteves.com/update.

WINDSOR

$$ Park Farm B&B, bright and cheery, is convenient for
drivers visiting Legoland (Sb-£65, Db-£89, Tb-£105, Qb-£120,
ask about family room with bunk beds, cash only—credit card
solely for reservations, free Wi-Fi, access to shared fridge and
microwave, free off-street parking, 1 mile from Legoland on St.
Leonards Road near Imperial Road, 5-minute bus ride or 1-mile
walk to castle, £4 taxi ride from station, tel. 01753/866-823, www
.parkfarm.com, stay@parkfarm.com, Caroline and Drew Youds).

Eating in Windsor

Elegant Spots with River Views: Several places flank Windsor
Bridge, offering romantic dining after dark. The riverside prom-
enade, with cheap take-away stands scattered about, is a delightful
place for a picnic lunch or dinner with the swans.

    Touristy Places Around the Palace: Strolling the streets and
lanes around the palace entrance, you'll find countless trendy and
inviting eateries. **Cornucopia Bistro** serves tasty international
dishes (£11 two-course lunches, £10-14 main courses at dinner,
daily 12:00-14:30 & 18:00-21:30, Fri-Sat until 22:00, closed Sun
night, 6 High Street). **The Crooked House** is a touristy 17th-
century timber-framed teahouse, serving fresh, hearty £8-10
lunches and cream teas in a tipsy interior or outdoors on its cobbled
lane (daily 10:30-18:00, 51 High Street). **Wagamama** offers mod-
ern Asian food, mostly in the form of noodle soups, in an informal
and communal setting (£7-10 dishes, daily 12:00-23:00, on the left
as you face the Windsor Royal Shopping Centre).

Ethnic Food Along St. Leonards Road: Residents enjoy the vast selection of unpretentious little eateries (including a fire-station-turned-pub) just past the end of pedestrian Peascod Street. You'll also find a handful of ethnic eateries. **Saffron Restaurant** is the local choice for South Indian cuisine, with a modern interior and attentive waiters who struggle with English but are fluent at bringing out tasty dishes. Their vegetarian *thali* is a treat (open daily for lunch from noon, dinner 17:30-23:00, 99 St. Leonards Road, tel. 01753/855-467).

Cambridge

Cambridge, 60 miles north of London, is world famous for its prestigious university. Wordsworth, Isaac Newton, Tennyson, Darwin, and Prince Charles are a few of its illustrious alumni. The university dominates—and owns—most of Cambridge, a historic town of 100,000 people. Cambridge is the epitome of a university town, with busy bikers, stately residence halls, plenty of bookshops, and proud locals who can point out where DNA was originally modeled, the atom first split, and electrons discovered.

In medieval Europe, higher education was the domain of the Church and was limited to ecclesiastical schools. Scholars lived in "halls" on campus. This academic community of residential halls, chapels, and lecture halls connected by peaceful garden courtyards survives today in the colleges that make up the universities of Cambridge and Oxford. By 1350 (Oxford is roughly 100 years older), Cambridge had eight colleges, each with a monastic-type courtyard, chapel, library, and lodgings. Today, Cambridge has 31 colleges, each with its own facilities. In the town center, these grand old halls date back centuries, with ornately decorated facades that try to one-up each other. While students' lives revolve around their independent colleges, the university organizes lectures, presents degrees, and promotes research.

The university schedule has three terms: Lent term from mid-January to mid-March, Easter term from mid-April to mid-June, and Michaelmas term from early October to early December. During exam time (roughly the month of May), the colleges are closed to visitors, which can impede access to all the picturesque little corners of the town. But the main sights—King's College

Chapel and Trinity Library—stay open, and Cambridge is never sleepy.

Planning Your Time

Cambridge is worth most of a day. Start by taking the TI's walking tour, which includes a visit to the town's only must-see sight, the King's College Chapel (first tour at 11:00, later on Sun, call ahead to confirm and reserve—see "Tours in Cambridge," later). Spend the afternoon touring the Fitzwilliam Museum (closed Mon), or simply enjoying the ambience of this stately old college town.

Getting to Cambridge

By Train: It's an easy trip from London and less than an hour away. Catch the train from London's King's Cross Station (3/hour, fast trains leave at :15 and :45 past the hour and run in each direction, 45 minutes, £20 one-way standard class, £21 same-day return after 9:30, make sure to ask for "day return" and not the more expensive "return" ticket, operated by First Capital Connect, toll tel. 0845-748-4950, www.firstcapitalconnect.co.uk or www.nationalrail .co.uk). Trains also run from London's Liverpool Street Station— though more frequent, they take longer (4/hour, 1.25 hours).

By Bus: National Express coaches run from London's Victoria Coach Station to the Parkside stop in Cambridge (hourly, 2-2.5 hours, £11.50, toll tel. 08717-818-181, www.nationalexpress.co.uk).

Orientation to Cambridge

(area code: 01223)

Cambridge is congested but small. Everything is within a pleasant walk. There are two main streets, separated from the Cam River by the most interesting colleges. The town center, brimming with tearooms, has a TI and a colorful open-air market square. The train station is about a mile to the southeast.

Tourist Information

Cambridge's TI is well run and well signposted, just off Market Square in the town center. They book rooms for £5, offer walk- ing tours (see "Tours in Cambridge," later), and sell bus tickets, a £0.60 town map, and a bigger £1 map/guide (Mon-Sat 10:00-17:00, Easter-Sept also Sun 11:00-15:00—otherwise closed Sun, phones answered from 9:00, Peas Hill, toll tel. 0871-226-8006, room-booking tel. 01223/457-581, www.visitcambridge.org).

Arrival in Cambridge

By Train: Cambridge's train station doesn't have baggage storage, but you can pay to leave your bags at the nearby bike-rental shop (see "Helpful Hints," below). The station does not have a TI, but it does have automated machines that dispense city maps for a £1 coin.

To get from the station to downtown Cambridge, you have several options. You can **walk** for about 25 minutes (exit straight ahead on Station Road, bear right at the war memorial onto Hills Road, and follow it into town); take public **bus** #1, #3, or #7 (note that buses are referred to as "Citi 1," "Citi 3," and so on in print and online, but only the number is marked on the bus; £1.30, pay driver, runs every 5-10 minutes, get off at Emmanuel Street stop—look for Grand Arcade shopping mall on the left); pay about £5 for a **taxi;** or ride a City Sightseeing **bus tour** (described later, buy ticket at kiosk next to bus stop).

By Car: Drivers can follow signs from the M11 motorway to any of the handy and central short-stay parking lots. Or you can leave the car at one of five park-and-ride lots outside the city, then take the shuttle into town (free parking, shuttle costs £2.30 round-trip if you buy ticket from machine, or £2.60 from driver).

Helpful Hints

Festival: The **Cambridge Folk Festival** gets things humming and strumming (July 26-29 in 2012, www.cambridgefolkfestival .co.uk).

Bike Rental: Station Cycles, located about a block to your right as you exit the station, rents bikes (£7/4 hours, £10/day, helmets 50p, £60 deposit, cash or credit card) and stores luggage (£3-4/bag depending on size; Mon-Fri 8:00-18:00, Wed until 19:00, Sat 9:00-17:00, Sun 10:00-16:00, tel. 01223/307-125, www.stationcycles.co.uk). They have a second location near the center of town (inside the Grand Arcade shopping mall, Mon-Fri 8:00-19:00, Wed until 20:00, Sat 9:00-18:00, Sun 10:00-18:00, tel. 01223/307-655).

Tours in Cambridge

▲▲Walking Tour of the Colleges—A walking tour is the best way to understand Cambridge's mix of "town and gown." The walks can be more educational (read: dry) than entertaining. But they do provide a good rundown of the historic and scenic highlights of the university, some fun local gossip, and plenty of university trivia. For example, why are entering students called "undergraduates"? Because long ago, new students at Cambridge were assigned to a mentor who already had a degree...so they were "under" the supervision of a "graduate."

The TI offers **daily walking tours** that include the King's College Chapel, as well as another college—usually Queen's

Cambridge

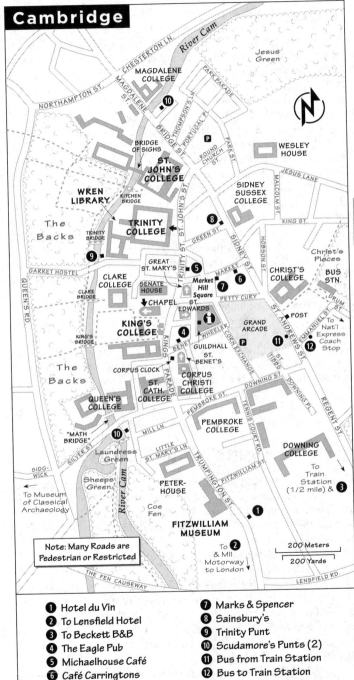

CAMBRIDGE

Note: Many Roads are Pedestrian or Restricted

200 Meters
200 Yards

1 Hotel du Vin
2 To Lensfield Hotel
3 To Beckett B&B
4 The Eagle Pub
5 Michaelhouse Café
6 Café Carringtons
7 Marks & Spencer
8 Sainsbury's
9 Trinity Punt
10 Scudamore's Punts (2)
11 Bus from Train Station
12 Bus to Train Station

College (£14.50, 2 hours, includes admission fees; July-Aug daily at 11:00, 12:00, 13:00, and 14:00, no 11:00 tour on Sun; Sept-June Mon-Sat at 11:00, 13:00, and another time—likely at 12:00, Sun only at 13:00 and possibly at 12:00; tel. 01223/457-574, www.visit cambridge.org). It's smart to call ahead to reserve a spot (they'll take your credit-card number), or you can drop by in person (try to arrive 30 minutes before the tour). Notice that the 12:00 tour overlaps with the limited opening times of the Wren Library—so you'll miss out on the library if you take the noon tour.

Private guides are available through the TI (basic 1-hour tour-£4/person, £60 minimum; 1.5-hour tour-£4.50/person, £67.50 minimum; 2-hour tour-£5/person, £75 minimum; does not include individual college entrance fees, tel. 01223/457-574, tours @cambridge.gov.uk).

Walking and Punting Ghost Tour—If you're in Cambridge on the weekend, consider a £6 ghost walk to where spooky sightings have been reported, Friday evenings at 18:00, or a creepy £17.50 trip on the River Cam followed by a walk, most Saturdays at dusk (20:00 in summer; book ahead for either tour, organized by the TI, tel. 01223/457-574).

Bus Tours—City Sightseeing hop-on, hop-off bus tours are informative and cover the outskirts, including the American WWII Cemetery. But keep in mind that buses can't go where walking tours can—right into the center (£13, 80 minutes for full 21-stop circuit, cash only, departs every 20 minutes in summer, every 40 minutes in winter, first bus leaves train station at 10:06, last bus at 17:46, recorded commentary, tel. 01223/423-578, www.city-sight seeing.com). If arriving by train, you can buy your ticket from the kiosk directly in front of the station, then ride the bus into town.

Sights in Cambridge

Cambridge has many impressive old college buildings to explore, with fancy facades and tranquil grassy courtyards. I've featured the two most interesting (King's and Trinity), but feel free to wander beyond these. You might notice several bricked-up windows on the old buildings around town. This practice dates from a time when taxes were calculated per window...so filling them in saved money.

▲**King's Parade and Nearby**—The lively street in front of King's College, called King's Parade, seems to be where everyone in Cambridge gathers. Looming across the street from the college is **Great St. Mary's Church,** with a climbable bell tower (£3, Mon-Sat 9:30-17:00, Sun 12:30-16:00, 123 stairs). On the street out front, students hawk punting tours on the Cam River (see "Punting on the Cam," later).

Behind the church is the thriving **Market Square.** The big

market is on Sunday (9:30-16:30) and features produce, arts, and crafts. On other days, you'll find mostly clothes and food (Mon-Sat 9:30-16:00).

The imposing Neoclassical building at the top (north) end of King's Parade is the **Senate House,** the meeting place of the university's governing body. In June, you might notice green boxes lining the front of this house. Traditionally at the end of the term, students would come to these boxes to see whether or not they'd earned their degree; if a name was not on the list, the student had flunked. Amazingly, until 2010 this was the only notification students received about their status. (Now they also get an email.)

In the opposite direction (south), at Benet Street, look for the strikingly modern **Corpus Clock.** Designed and commissioned by alum John Taylor, the clock was ceremonially unveiled by Stephen Hawking in 2008. It uses concentric golden dials with blue LED lights to tell the time, but it's precise only every five minutes; its otherwise-irregular timekeeping mimics the unpredictability of life. Perched on top is Chronophage, the "eater of time"—a grotesque giant grasshopper that keeps the clock moving and periodically winks at passersby. Creepy and disturbing? Exactly, says Taylor...so is the passage of time.

Just down Benet Street on the left is the recommended **Eagle Pub**—Cambridge's oldest pub and a sight in itself; it's worth poking into the courtyard to learn about its dynamic history, even if you don't eat or drink here. Across the street from the pub stands the oldest surviving building in Cambridgeshire, **St. Benet's Church.** The Saxons who built the church included circular holes in its bell tower, to encourage owls to roost there and keep the mouse population under control.

▲▲**King's College Chapel**—Built from 1446 to 1515 by Henrys VI through VIII, England's best example of Perpendicular Gothic architecture is the single most impressive building in town.

Cost and Hours: £6.50, erratic hours depending on school schedule and events; during academic term usually Mon-Fri 9:30-15:30, Sat 9:30-15:15, Sun 13:15-14:30; during breaks (see page 466) usually Mon-Sat 9:30-16:00, Sun 10:00-17:00; tel. 01223/331-212, recorded info tel. 01223/331-155, www.kings.cam.ac.uk/chapel.

Evensong: When school's in session, you're welcome to enjoy an evensong service in this glorious space, with a famous choir made up of men and boys (free, Mon-Sat at 17:30, Sun at 15:30).

Getting There: You'll see the regal front facade of King's

College along King's Parade. To enter the chapel, curl around the back: Facing the college on King's Parade, head right and take the first left possible (just after the Senate House, on Senate House passage); at the dead end, bear left on Trinity Lane to reach the gate where you can pay to enter the chapel.

◐ Self-Guided Tour: Stand inside, look up, and marvel, as Christopher Wren did, at what was the largest single span of

vaulted roof anywhere—2,000 tons of incredible fan vaulting, held in place by the force of gravity (a careful balancing act resting delicately on the buttresses visible outside the building).

While Henry VI—who began work on the chapel—wanted it to be austere, his descendants decided it should glorify the House of Tudor (of which his son, Henry VII, was the first king). Lining the walls are giant **Tudor coats-of-arms.** The shield includes a fleur-de-lis because an earlier ancestor, Edward III, woke up one day and—citing his convoluted lineage—somewhat arbitrarily declared himself king of France. The symbols on the

left (a rose and the red dragon of Wales, holding the shield) represent the Tudors, the family of Henry VII's father. On the right, the greyhound holding the shield and the portcullis (the iron grate) symbolize the family of Henry VII's mother, Lady Margaret Beaufort, who prodded her son for years to complete this chapel.

The 26 **stained-glass windows** date from the 16th century. It's the most Renaissance stained glass anywhere in one spot. (Most of the stained glass in English churches dates from Victorian times, but this glass is much older.) The lower panes show scenes from the New Testament, while the upper panes feature correspond-

ing stories from the Old Testament. Considering England's turbulent history, it's miraculous that these windows have survived for nearly half a millennium in such a pristine state. After Henry VIII separated from the Catholic Church in 1534, many such windows and other Catholic features around England were destroyed. (Think of all those ruined abbeys dotting the English countryside.) However, since Henry had just paid for these windows, he couldn't bear to get rid of them. A century later, in the days of Oliver Cromwell, another wave of iconoclasm destroyed more windows around England. Though these windows were slated for removal, they stayed put. (Historians speculate that Cromwell's troops, who were garrisoned in this building, didn't want the windows removed in the chilly wintertime.) Finally, during World War II, the windows were taken out and hidden away to keep them safe, and then painstakingly replaced after the war ended.

The **choir screen** that bisects the church was commissioned by King Henry VIII to commemorate his marriage to Anne Boleyn. By the time it was finished, so was she (beheaded). But it was too late to remove her initials, which were carved into the screen (look for *R.A.*, for *Regina Anna*—"Queen Anne").

Behind the screen is the **choir** area, where the King's College Choir performs a daily evensong (see details earlier). On Christmas Eve, a special service is held here and broadcast around the world on the BBC—a tradition near and dear to the hearts of Brits.

Finally, walk to the altar and admire Rubens' masterful *Adoration of the Magi* (1634). It's actually a family portrait: The admirer in the front (wearing red) is a self-portrait of Rubens, Mary looks an awful lot like his much-younger wife, and the Baby Jesus resembles their own newborn at the time.

▲▲**Trinity College and Wren Library**—More than a third of Cambridge's 83 Nobel Prize winners have come from this richest and biggest of the town's colleges, founded in 1546 by Henry VIII. The college has three sights to see: the entrance gate, the grounds, and the magnificent Wren Library (due to renovation, parts or all of the college may be closed until November 2011).

Cost and Hours: Grounds—£3, daily 9:30-17:00, last entry 45 minutes before closing; library—free, Mon-Fri 12:00-14:00, Nov-mid-June also Sat 10:30-12:30, closed Sun; only 19 people allowed in at a time; to see Wren Library without paying for the grounds, enter from the riverside entrance, located by the Garret Hostel Bridge; tel. 01223/338-400, www.trin.cam.ac.uk.

Trinity Gate: You'll notice gates like these adorning facades of colleges around town. Above the door is a statue of **King Henry VIII,** who founded Trinity because he feared that Cambridge's existing colleges were too cozy with the Church. Notice Henry's right hand holding a chair leg instead of the traditional crown jewels scepter. This is courtesy of Cambridge's Night Climbers, who first replaced the scepter a century ago, and continue to periodically switch it out for other items. According to campus legend, decades ago some of the world's most talented mountaineers enrolled at Cambridge... in one of the flattest parts of England. (Cambridge was actually a seaport until Dutch engineers drained the surrounding swamps.) Lacking opportunities to practice their skill, they began scaling the frilly facades of Cambridge's college buildings under cover of darkness (if caught, they'd have been expelled). In the 1960s, climbers actually managed to haul an entire automobile onto the roof of the Senate House. The university had to bring in the army to cut it into pieces and remove it. Only 50 years later, at a class reunion, did the guilty parties finally 'fess up.

In the little park to the right, notice the lone **apple tree.** Supposedly, this tree is a descendant of the very one that once

stood in the garden of Sir Isaac Newton (who spent 30 years at Trinity). According to legend, Newton was inspired to investigate gravity when an apple fell from the tree onto his head. This tree stopped bearing fruit long ago; if you do see apples, they've been tied on by mischievous students.

• *If you like, head through the gate into the...*

Trinity Grounds: The grounds are enjoyable to explore, if not quite worth the cost of admission. Inside the **Great Court,**

the clock (on the tower on the right) double-rings at the top of each hour. It's a college tradition to take off running from the clock when the high noon bells begin (it takes 43 seconds to clang 24 times), race around the courtyard, touching each of the four corners without setting foot on the cobbles, and return to the same spot by the time the ringing ends. Supposedly only one student (a young lord) ever managed the feat—a scene featured in *Chariots of Fire* (but filmed elsewhere).

The **chapel** (entrance under clock)—which pales in comparison to the stunning King's College Chapel—feels like a shrine to thinking, with statues honoring great Trinity minds both familiar (Isaac Newton, Alfred Lord Tennyson, Francis Bacon) and unfamiliar. Who's missing? The poet Lord Byron, who was such a hellraiser during his time at Trinity that a statue of him was deemed unfit for Church property; his statue stands in the library instead.

Wren Library: Don't miss the 1695 Christopher Wren-designed library, with its wonderful carving and fascinating original manuscripts. Just outside the library entrance, Sir Isaac Newton clapped his hands and timed the echo to measure the speed of sound as it raced down the side of the cloister and back. In the library's 12 display cases (covered with cloth that you flip back), you'll see handwritten works by Sir Isaac Newton and John Milton, alongside A. A. Milne's original *Winnie the Pooh* (the real Christopher Robin attended Trinity College).

▲▲**Fitzwilliam Museum**—Britain's best museum of antiquities and art outside of London is the Fitzwilliam, housed in a grand Neoclassical building a 10-minute walk south of Market Square. The Fitzwilliam's broad collection is like a mini-British Museum/National Gallery rolled into one. The ground floor features an extensive range of antiquities and applied arts—everything from Greek vases, Mesopotamian artifacts, and Egyptian sarcophagi to Roman statues, fine porcelain, and suits of armor.

Upstairs is the painting gallery, with works that span art history: Italian Venetian masters (such as Titian and Canaletto), a worthy English section (featuring Gainsborough, Reynolds, Hogarth, and others), and a nice array of French Impressionist art (including Manet, Renoir, Pissarro, and Sisley). Rounding out the collection are old manuscripts, including some musical compositions from Handel. Watch your step—in 2006, a visitor tripped and accidentally smashed three 17th-century Chinese vases. Amazingly, the vases were restored (with donations from the community) and are now on display in Gallery 17...in a protective case.

Cost and Hours: Free, but suggested £3 donation, audio/videoguide-£3, Tue-Sat 10:00-17:00, Sun 12:00-17:00, closed Mon except bank holidays, no photos, Trumpington Street, tel. 01223/332-900, www.fitzmuseum.cam.ac.uk.

Museum of Classical Archaeology—Although this museum contains no originals, it offers a unique chance to study accurate copies (19th-century casts) of virtually every famous ancient Greek and Roman statue. More than 450 statues are on display. If you've seen the real things in Greece, Istanbul, Rome, and elsewhere, touring this collection is like a high school reunion..."Hey, I know you!" But since it takes some time to get here, this museum is best left to devotees of classical sculpture.

Cost and Hours: Free, Mon-Fri 10:00-17:00, Sat 10:00-13:00 during term, closed Sun, Sidgwick Avenue, tel. 01223/335-153, www.classics.cam.ac.uk/museum.

Getting There: The museum is a five-minute walk west of Silver Street Bridge; after crossing the bridge, continue straight until you reach a sign reading *Sidgwick Site*. The museum is in the long building on the corner to your right; the entrance is on the opposite side, and the museum is upstairs.

▲**Punting on the Cam**—For a little levity and probably more exercise than you really want, try hiring one of the traditional flat-

bottom punts at the river and pole yourself up and down (or around and around, more likely) the lazy Cam. Once you get the hang of it, it's a fine way to enjoy the scenic side of Cambridge. It's less crowded in late afternoon (and less embarrassing).

Several companies rent punts and offer tours. Hawkers try to snare passengers in the thriving people zone in front of King's College. Prices are soft in slow times—try talking them down a bit before committing.

Trinity Punt, just north of Garret Hostel Bridge, is run by Trinity College students (£14/hour, £40 deposit, 45-minute tours-£30/boat, can share ride and cost with up to 2 others, cash only, ask for quick and free lesson, Easter-mid-Oct Mon-Fri 11:00-17:30, Sat-Sun 10:00-17:30, return punts by 18:30, no rentals mid-Oct-Easter, tel. 01223/338-483). **Scudamore's** has two locations: Mill Lane, just south of the central Silver Street Bridge, and the less convenient Quayside at Magdalene Bridge, at the north end of town (£16-18/hour, £80 deposit required—can use credit card; 45-minute tours-£15/person, £12.50 if you book at the TI; open daily June-Aug 9:00-22:00 or later, Sept-May at least 10:00-16:00, weather permitting, tel. 01223/359-750, www.scudamores.com).

Near Cambridge

Imperial War Museum Duxford—This former airfield, nine miles south of Cambridge, is nirvana for aviation fans and WWII buffs. Wander through seven exhibition halls housing 200 vintage aircraft (including Spitfires, B-17 Flying Fortresses, a Concorde, and a Blackbird) as well as military land vehicles and special displays on Normandy and the Battle of Britain. On many weekends, the museum holds special events, such as air shows (extra fee)—check the website for details.

Cost and Hours: £16.50 (includes small donation), show local bus ticket for discount, daily mid-March-late Oct 10:00-18:00, late Oct-mid-March 10:00-16:00, last entry one hour before closing; Concorde interior open until 17:00, 15:00 off-season; tel. 01223/835-000, http://duxford.iwm.org.uk.

Getting There: The museum is located off A505 in Duxford. From Cambridge, take bus #7 from the train station (45 minutes) or from Emmanuel Street's Stop A (55 minutes, bus runs 2/hour Mon-Sat, www.stagecoachbus.com/cambridge). On Sundays and bank holidays, catch the #132 bus, run by private bus operator Myalls, from the train station or the Drummer Street bus station (40 minutes, first bus around 10:00, then every 2 hours until 18:00, tel. 01763/243-225).

Sleeping in Cambridge

(£1 = about $1.60, country code: 44)
While Cambridge is an easy side-trip from London, its subtle charms might convince you to spend the night. Cambridge has very few accommodations in the city center, and none in the tight maze of colleges and shops where you'll spend most of your time. These recommendations are about a 10- to 15-minute walk south of the town center, toward the train station.

$$$ Hotel du Vin blends France, England, and wine. This worthwhile splurge has 41 comfortable, spacious rooms above a characteristic bistro that offers good deals for guests and nonguests alike. This mod place manages to be classy yet unpretentious (Db-£120-150, fancier suites available, check online for special offers, breakfast-£10 if booked ahead, air-con, elevator, pay Wi-Fi, just down the street from the Fitzwilliam Museum at Trumpington Street 15-17, tel. 01223/227-330, fax 01223/227-331, www.hoteldu vin.com, reception.cambridge@hotelduvin.com).

$$$ Lensfield Hotel, popular with visiting professors, has 30 old-fashioned rooms (Sb-£69, Db-£105, pricier rooms also available, pay Wi-Fi, 53 Lensfield Road, tel. 01223/355-017, fax 01223/312-022, www.lensfieldhotel.co.uk, enquiries@lensfield hotel.co.uk).

$ Debbie and Michael Beckett rent one room in their modern home, next door to a big church halfway between downtown and the train station. The room, with a private bathroom on the hall, makes you feel like a houseguest (S-£40, D-£55, includes breakfast, 15 St. Paul's Road, tel. 01223/315-832, debbie.beckett2 @googlemail.com).

Eating in Cambridge

While picnicking is scenic and saves money, the weather may not always cooperate. Here are a few ideas for fortifying yourself with a lunch in central Cambridge.

The Eagle Pub, near the TI, is the oldest pub in town, and a Cambridge institution with a history so rich that a visit here practically qualifies as sightseeing. Find your way into the delightful courtyard, with outdoor seating and a good look at the place's past.

The second-floor windows were once guest rooms, back when this was a coachmen's inn as well as a pub. Notice that the window on the right end is open; any local will love to tell you why. Follow the signs into the misnamed "RAF Bar," where US Air Force pilots signed the ceiling while  stationed here during World War II. Science fans can celebrate the discovery of DNA—Francis Crick and James Watson first announced their findings here in 1953 (£6-8 lunches, £6-11 dinners, food served daily 10:00-22:00, drinks until 23:00, 8 Benet Street, tel. 01223/505-020).

The **Michaelhouse Café** is a heavenly respite from the crowds, tucked into the repurposed St. Michael's Church, just north of Great St. Mary's Church. At lunch, choose from salads, soups, and sandwiches, as well as a few hot dishes and a variety of tasty baked goods (£5-10 light meals, Mon-Sat 8:00-17:00, breakfast served 8:00-11:00, lunch served 11:30-15:30, hot drinks and baked goods always available, closed Sun, Trinity Street, tel. 01223/309-147). Near the end of the day—after 14:30—you can pay £4 to fill your plate with whatever they have left.

Café Carringtons is a cozy cafeteria that serves traditional British food at reasonable prices, including a Sunday roast lunch (£6-8 meals, £5 sandwiches, Mon-Sat 8:00-17:00, Sun 10:00-16:00, down the stairs at 23 Market Street, tel. 01223/361-792).

Supermarkets: There's a **Marks & Spencer Simply Food** at the train station and a larger Marks & Spencer department store on Market Square (Mon-Thu 9:00-18:00, Wed until 19:00, Fri 9:00-19:00, Sat 9:00-18:30, Sun 11:00-17:00, tel. 01223/355-219). **Sainsbury's** supermarket has longer hours (Mon-Sat 8:00-23:30, Sun 11:00-17:00, 44 Sidney Street, at the corner of Green Street).

A good picnic spot is Laundress Green, a grassy park on the river, at the end of Mill Lane near the Silver Street Bridge punts. There are no benches, so bring something to sit on. Remember, the college lawns are private property, so walking or picnicking on the grass is generally not allowed. When in doubt, ask at the college's entrance.

Cambridge Connections

From Cambridge by Train to: York (1-2/hour, 2.5 hours, transfer in Peterborough), **Oxford** (2/hour, 2.5 hours, change in London involves Tube transfer between train stations), **London** (King's Cross Station: 3/hour, 45-60 minutes; Liverpool Street Station:

4/hour, 1.25 hours). Train info: Toll tel. 0845-748-4950, www .nationalrail.co.uk.

By Bus to: London (hourly, 2-2.5 hours), **Heathrow Airport** (1-2/hour, 2-3 hours). Bus info: Toll tel. 08717-818-181, www .nationalexpress.com.

Stonehenge

As old as the pyramids, and older than the Acropolis and the Colosseum, this iconic stone circle amazed medieval Europeans, who figured it was built by a race of giants. And it still impresses visitors today. As one of Europe's most famous sights, Stonehenge does a valiant job of retaining an air of mystery and majesty (partly because cordons, which keep hordes of tourists from trampling all over it, foster the illusion that it stands alone in a field). Although some people are underwhelmed by Stonehenge, most of its almost one million annual visitors find that it's worth the trip. And the ancient site continues to reveal its mysteries: In 2010, within sight

of Stonehenge, archaeologists discovered another 5,000-year-old henge, or ditch, which they believe once encircled a wooden "twin" of the famous circle.

Getting to Stonehenge

Stonehenge is about 90 miles southwest of central London. To reach it from London, you can take a bus tour; go on a guided tour that uses public transportation; or do it on your own using public transport, connecting via Salisbury. It's not worth the hassle or expense to rent a car just for a Stonehenge day trip.

By Bus Tour from London: Several companies offer big-bus day trips to Stonehenge from London, often with stops in Bath, Windsor, Salisbury, and/or Avebury. These generally cost about £45-75, last 8-12 hours, and pack a 45-seat bus. Some include hotel pickup, admission fees, and meals; understand what's included before you book. The more destinations listed for a tour, the less time you'll have at any one stop. Well-known companies are **Evan Evans** (their bare-bones Stonehenge Express gets you there and back for £22, entry fee not included, tel. 020/7950-1777 or US tel.

866-382-6868, www.evanevanstours.co.uk) and **Golden Tours** (tel. 020/7233-7030 or US toll-free tel. 800-548-7083, www.golden tours.co.uk). **International Friends** runs pricier but smaller 16-person tours (£85, tel. 01223/244-555, www.international friends.co.uk). If Bath is your next destination after London, consider taking a multiple-destination bus tour and abandoning it in Bath (for details, see page 438).

By Bus Tour from Other Cities: For tours of Stonehenge from Bath, see page 493 (Mad Max is best).

By Guided Tour on Public Transport: London Walks offers a weekly guided "Explorer Day Tour" to Salisbury and Stonehenge by train and bus from April through October (£55, includes all transportation, Salisbury walking tour, and entry fees and guided tours of Stonehenge and Salisbury Cathedral; buy all tickets from guide; cash only, likely Tue at 9:15 but occasionally at 9:45, a few Sat at 9:45, meet at Waterloo Station's main ticket office, opposite Platform 16, call or check website to verify price and schedule, advance booking not required, tel. 020/7624-3978, recorded info tel. 020/7624-9255, www.walks.com).

On Your Own on Public Transport: Catch a train to Salisbury, then go by bus or taxi to Stonehenge. Trains to Salisbury run from London's Waterloo Station (around £33 for same-day return fare leaving weekdays after 9:30, 1-2/hour, 1.5 hours, toll tel. 0845-600-0650 or 0845-748-4950, www.southwesttrains.co.uk or www.nationalrail.co.uk).

Once in Salisbury, you can take **The Stonehenge Tour** bus to the site. Their distinctive red-and-black double-decker buses leave from the Salisbury train station (also stops at bus station) and make a circuit to Stonehenge and Old Sarum, with lovely scenery and a decent light commentary along the way (£11, £18 with Stonehenge and Old Sarum admission; tickets good all day; buy ticket from driver; daily June-Aug 9:30-17:00, 1-2/hour; may not run on June 21 due to solstice crowds, shorter hours off-season, 30 minutes from station to Stonehenge, tel. 01983/827-005, check www.thestonehengetour.info for timetable).

By Taxi: A local cabbie named Brian will take you between Salisbury and Stonehenge, including an hour at the site (£40-50, 5-6 people max, best to reserve, contact for exact price, entry fee not included). He also offers a three-hour Stonehenge visit, which includes Old Sarum, Woodhenge, Durrington Walls, and Woodford's thatched cottages (£80, entry fee not included, tel. 01722/339-781, briantwort@ntlworld.com).

By Car: Stonehenge is well-signed just off A303. It's about 15 minutes north of Salisbury, an hour east of Glastonbury, and an hour south of Avebury.

Stonehenge is about 70 miles and 1.5 hours west of **London**

Heathrow (barring traffic). From the M25 ring road, connect with M3 toward Southampton. Past Basingstoke, exit to A303. Continue west past Andover to Amesbury and follow "From Salisbury" directions from that point (see below).

From **Salisbury,** head north on A345 (Castle Road) through **Amesbury,** go west on A303 for 1.5 miles, veer right onto A344, and it's just ahead on the left, with the parking lot on the right.

Orientation to Stonehenge

Cost: £7.50, covered by English Heritage Pass and Great British Heritage Pass (see page 17).

Hours: Daily June-Aug 9:00-19:00, mid-March-May and Sept-mid-Oct 9:30-18:00, mid-Oct-mid-March 9:30-16:00, last entry 30 minutes before closing.

When to Go: Shorter hours and possible closures June 20-22 due to huge, raucous solstice crowds; £3 parking fee likely in summer—refundable with paid admission.

Information: Entry includes a worthwhile hour-long audioguide. Tel. 01980/623-108 or toll tel. 0870-333-1181, www.english-heritage.org.uk/stonehenge.

Reaching the Inner Stones: Special one-hour access to the stones' inner circle—before or after regular visiting hours—costs an extra £15.30 and must be reserved well in advance. Details are on the English Heritage website (go to "Explore Stonehenge," then click on the Stone Circle Access link), or call 01722/343-834.

Planned Changes: Future plans for Stonehenge call for the creation of a new visitors center and museum, designed to blend in with the landscape and make the stone circle feel more pristine. Visitors will park farther away and ride a shuttle bus to the site. Construction may begin in 2012.

Self-Guided Tour

The entrance fee includes a good audioguide, but this commentary will help make your visit even more meaningful.

Walk in from the parking lot, buy your ticket, pick up your included audioguide, and head through the ugly underpass beneath the road. On the way up the ramp, notice the artist's rendering of what

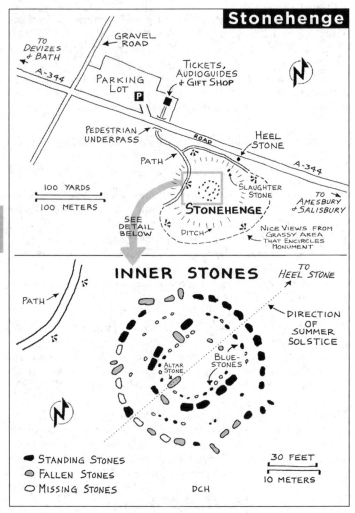

Stonehenge

INNER STONES

- STANDING STONES
- FALLEN STONES
- MISSING STONES

DCH

Stonehenge once looked like. As you approach the massive structure, walk right up to the knee-high cordon and let your fellow
21st-century tourists melt away. It's just you and the druids...

England has hundreds of stone circles, but Stonehenge—
which literally means "hanging stones"—is unique. It's the only
one that has horizontal cross-pieces (called lintels) spanning the
vertical monoliths, and the only one with stones that have been
made smooth and uniform. What you see here is a bit more than
half the original structure—the rest was quarried centuries ago for
other buildings.

Now do a slow counterclockwise spin around the monument,

and ponder the following points. As you walk, mentally flesh out the missing pieces and re-erect the rubble. Knowledgeable guides posted around the site are happy to answer your questions.

This was a hugely significant location to prehistoric peoples. There are some 500 burial mounds within a three-mile radius of Stonehenge—most likely belonging to kings and chieftains. Built in phases between 3000 and 1500 B.C., Stonehenge originally was used as a cremation cemetery (so goes one recently popular theory). But that's not the end of the story, as the monument was expanded over the millennia.

Stonehenge still functions as a remarkably accurate celestial calendar. As the sun rises on the summer solstice (June 21), the "heel stone"—the one set apart from the rest, near the road—lines up with the sun and the altar at the center of the stone circle. A study of more than 300 similar circles in Britain found that each was designed to calculate the movement of the sun, moon, and stars, and to predict eclipses in order to help early societies know when to plant, harvest, and party. Even in modern times, as the summer solstice sun sets in just the right slot at Stonehenge, pagans boogie.

In addition to being a calendar, Stonehenge is built at the precise point where six ley lines intersect. Ley lines are theoretical lines of magnetic or spiritual power that crisscross the globe. Belief in the power of these lines has gone in and out of fashion over time. They are believed to have been very important to prehistoric peoples, but then were largely ignored until the New Age movement of the 20th century. Without realizing it, you follow these ley lines all the time: Many of England's modern highways, following prehistoric paths, and churches, built over prehistoric monuments, are located where ley lines intersect. If you're a skeptic, ask one of the guides at Stonehenge to demonstrate the ley lines with a pair of L-shaped divining rods...it's creepy and convincing.

Notice that two of the stones (facing the entry passageway) are blemished. At the base of one monolith, it looks like someone has pulled back the stone to reveal a concrete skeleton. This is a clumsy repair job to fix damage done long ago by souvenir seekers, who actually rented hammers and chisels to take home a piece of Stonehenge. Look to the right of the repaired stone: The back of another stone is missing the same thin layer of protective lichen that covers the others. The lichen—and some of the stone itself—was sandblasted off to remove graffiti. (No wonder they've got Stonehenge roped off now.)

Stonehenge's builders used two different types of stone. The tall, stout monoliths and lintels are sandstone blocks called sarsen stones. Most of the monoliths weigh about 25 tons (the largest is 45 tons), and the lintels are about 7 tons apiece. These sarsen stones were brought from "only" 20 miles away. The shorter stones in the middle, called bluestones, came from the south coast of Wales—240 miles away (close if you're taking a train, but far if you're packing a megalith). Imagine the logistical puzzle of floating six-ton stones up the River Avon, then rolling them on logs about 20 miles to this position...an impressive feat, even in our era of skyscrapers.

Why didn't the builders of Stonehenge use what seem like perfectly adequate stones nearby? This, like many other questions about Stonehenge, remains shrouded in mystery. Think again about the ley lines. Ponder the fact that many experts accept none of the explanations of how these giant stones were transported. Then imagine congregations gathering here 5,000 years ago, raising thought levels, creating a powerful life force transmitted along the ley lines. Maybe a particular kind of stone was essential for maximum energy transmission. Maybe the stones were levitated here. Maybe psychics really do create powerful vibes. Maybe not. It's as unbelievable as electricity used to be.

BATH

The best city to visit within easy striking distance of London is Bath—just a 1.5-hour train ride away. Two hundred years ago, this city of 85,000 was the trendsetting Hollywood of Britain. If ever a city enjoyed looking in the mirror, Bath's the one. It has more "government-listed" or protected historic buildings per capita than any other town in England. The entire city, built of the creamy warm-tone limestone called "Bath stone," beams in its cover-girl complexion. An architectural chorus line, it's a triumph of the Neoclassical style of the Georgian era—named for the four Georges who sat as England's kings from 1714 to 1830. Proud locals remind visitors that the town is routinely banned from the "Britain in Bloom" contest to give other towns a chance to win. Bath's narcissism is justified. Even with its mobs of tourists (2 million per year) and greedy prices, Bath is a joy to visit.

Bath's fame began with the allure of its (supposedly) healing hot springs. Long before the Romans arrived in the first century, Bath was known for its warm waters. Romans named the popular spa town Aquae Sulis, after a local Celtic goddess. The town's importance carried through Saxon times, when it had a huge church on the site of the present-day abbey and was considered the religious capital of Britain. Its influence peaked in 973 with King Edgar's sumptuous coronation in the abbey. Later, Bath prospered as a wool town.

Bath then declined until the mid-1600s, wasting away to just a huddle of huts around the abbey, with hot, smelly mud and 3,000 residents, oblivious to the Roman ruins 18 feet below their dirt floors. In fact, with its own walls built upon ancient ones, Bath was no bigger than that Roman town. Then, in 1687, Queen Mary, fighting infertility, bathed here. Within 10 months she gave birth to a son...and a new age of popularity for Bath.

The revitalized town boomed as a spa resort. Ninety percent of the buildings you'll see today are from the 18th century. The classical revivalism of Italian architect Andrea Palladio inspired a local father-and-son team—both named John Wood (the Elder and the Younger)—to build a "new Rome." The town bloomed in the Neoclassical style, and streets were lined not with scrawny sidewalks but with wide "parades," upon which women in their stylishly wide dresses could spread their fashionable tails.

Beau Nash (1673-1762) was Bath's "master of ceremonies." He organized the daily social regimen of aristocratic visitors, and he made the city more appealing by lighting the streets, improving security, banning swords, and opening the Pump Room. Under his fashionable baton, Bath became a city of balls, gaming, and concerts—the place to see and be seen in England. This most civilized place became even more so with the great Neoclassical building spree that followed.

These days, modern tourism has stoked the local economy, as has the fast morning train to London. (A growing number of Bath-based professionals catch the 7:13 train to Paddington Station every morning.) With renewed access to Bath's soothing hot springs at the Thermae Bath Spa, the venerable waters are in the spotlight again, attracting a new generation of visitors in need of a cure or a soak.

Planning Your Time

Bath can be done as a day trip from London, but it certainly warrants one to two nights, even on a quick trip. There's plenty to do, and it's a delight to do it. On a one-week trip to London, consider spending two nights in Bath, using it as your jet-lag recovery pillow (by flying into Heathrow and taking the bus to Bath from the airport; or maybe even flying into Bristol) before moving on to London for the rest of your trip.

Consider starting a London vacation this way:

Day 1: Land at Heathrow. Connect to Bath by National Express bus—the better option—or the less convenient bus/train combination (for details, see page 431). Take an evening walking tour.

Day 2: 9:00-Tour the Roman Baths; 10:30-Catch the free city walking tour; 12:30-Picnic on the open deck of a tour bus; 14:00-Free time in the shopping center of old Bath; 15:30-Tour the Fashion Museum or Museum of Bath at Work. At night, consider seeing a play, enjoy the Bizarre Bath comedy walk, or go for an evening soak in the Thermae Bath Spa.

Day 3: Early train into London.

Getting to Bath

Trains from London to Bath depart frequently from Paddington Station (2/hour, 1.5 hours). You can also catch a National Express **bus** from Victoria Coach Station (nearly hourly, 2.5-3.75 hours, avoid those with layover in Bristol). To travel from London to Bath, and see Stonehenge en route, consider an all-day organized **bus tour** from London (and skip out on the return trip if you want to stay overnight; see page 438). To get to Bath from Heathrow Airport, see page 431 for details or consider taking a minibus with Alan Price (see "Celtic Horizons" on page 494).

Orientation to Bath

(area code: 01225)

Bath's town square, three blocks in front of the bus and train station, is a cluster of tourist landmarks, including the abbey, Roman and Medieval Baths, and the Pump Room. Bath is hilly. In general, you'll gain elevation as you head north from the town center.

Tourist Information

The TI is in the abbey churchyard (Mon-Sat 9:30-18:00, Sun 10:00-16:00, closes one hour earlier Mon-Sat Oct-May, pricey toll tel. 0906-711-2000—50p/minute, www.visitbath.co.uk). The TI sells various visitor guides and maps—survey your options before buying one (£1-1.50). Only the most basic visitor guide, with a very rudimentary map, is free. The TI books rooms and theater tickets for no extra fee (booking tel. 0844-847-5256). If you're a Jane Austen fan, ask about the walking tours that leave from the abbey square on weekends. Entertainment listings from the local paper are posted on the bulletin board. You can also buy the Great British Heritage Pass here (see page 17).

Arrival in Bath

The Bath Spa **train station** has a national and international ticket desk and a privately run travel agency masquerading as a TI. Directly in front of the train station is Bath's brand-new SouthGate Bath shopping center. To get from the train station to the TI, exit straight ahead, walk two blocks up Manvers Street, and turn left at the triangular "square" overlooking the riverfront park, following the small TI arrow on a signpost.

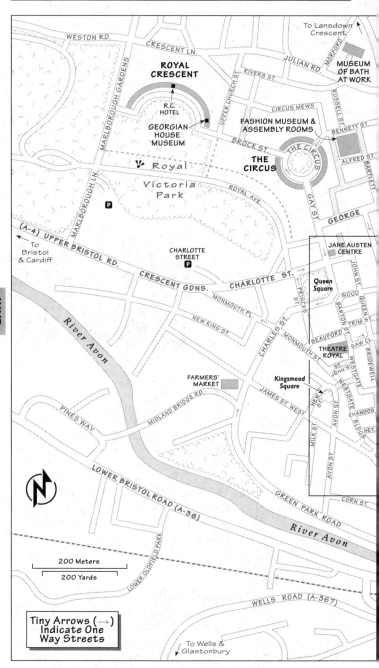

To Lansdown Crescent

WESTON RD.

CRESCENT LN.

MARLBOROUGH GARDENS

JULIAN RD.

MOREFORD

MUSEUM OF BATH AT WORK

ROYAL CRESCENT

UPPER CHURCH ST.

RIVERS ST.

RUSSELL ST.

R.C. HOTEL

CIRCUS MEWS

FASHION MUSEUM & ASSEMBLY ROOMS

BENNETT ST.

GEORGIAN HOUSE MUSEUM

BROCK ST.

THE CIRCUS

ALFRED ST.

BARTLETT

THE CIRCUS

Royal

Victoria Park

ROYAL AVE.

GAY ST.

GEORGE

MARLBOROUGH LN.

P

(A-4) UPPER BRISTOL RD.

To Bristol & Cardiff

JANE AUSTEN CENTRE

CHARLOTTE STREET

P

CRESCENT GDNS.

CHARLOTTE ST.

Queen Square

JOHN ST.

WOOD

QUEEN ST.

MONMOUTH PL.

PRINCES ST.

BARTON ST.

TRIM ST.

BEAUFORD SQ.

SAW CL.

NEW KING ST.

CHARLES ST.

MONMOUTH ST.

THEATRE ROYAL

WESTGATE ST.

BRIDEWELL

River Avon

FARMERS' MARKET

Kingsmead Square

JOHN ST.

JAMES ST. WEST

NEW ST.

AVON ST.

CHANDOS

PINES WAY

MIDLAND BRIDGE RD.

MILK ST.

WESTGATE BLDGS.

HET.

N

LOWER BRISTOL ROAD (A-36)

GREEN PARK ROAD

CORN ST.

River Avon

LOWER OLDFIELD PARK

200 Meters

200 Yards

WELLS ROAD (A-367)

Tiny Arrows (→) Indicate One Way Streets

To Wells & Glastonbury

BATH

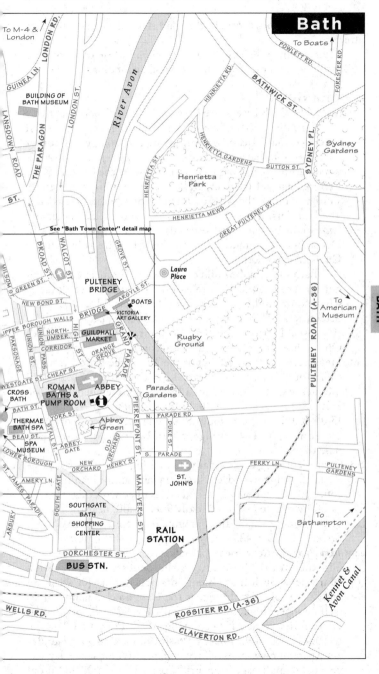

To M-4 & London

GUINEA LN

LONDON RD.

BUILDING OF BATH MUSEUM

LANSDOWN ROAD

THE PARAGON

ST.

LONDON ST.

River Avon

To Boats

POWLETT RD.

FORESTER RD.

HENRIETTA RD.

BATHWICK ST.

SYDNEY PL.

Sydney Gardens

HENRIETTA GARDENS

SUTTON ST.

Henrietta Park

HENRIETTA ST.

HENRIETTA MEWS

GREAT PULTENEY ST.

See "Bath Town Center" detail map

BROAD ST.

WALCOT ST.

GROVE ST.

MILSOM ST.

GREEN ST.

NEW BOND ST.

PULTENEY BRIDGE

Laura Place

ARGYLE ST.

BOATS

UPPER BOROUGH WALLS

BRIDGE ST.

HIGH ST.

GRAND PARADE

VICTORIA ART GALLERY

PARSONAGE

UNION ST.

NORTH-UMBER CORRIDOR

GUILDHALL MARKET

Rugby Ground

ST. JAMES PARADE

WESTGATE ST.

CHEAP ST.

ORANGE GROVE

CROSS BATH

ROMAN BATHS & PUMP ROOM

ABBEY

Parade Gardens

PULTENEY ROAD (A-36)

To American Museum

BATH

BATH ST.

PIERREPONT ST.

THERMAE BATH SPA

BEAU ST.

YORK ST.

Abbey Green

N. PARADE RD.

DUKE ST.

SPA MUSEUM

STALL ST.

LOWER BOROUGH

ABBEY GATE

OLD ORCHARD

S. PARADE

FERRY LN

PULTENEY GARDENS

AMERY LN.

NEW ORCHARD

HENRY ST.

ST. JOHN'S

MANVERS ST.

To Bathampton

SOUTH GATE

SOUTHGATE BATH SHOPPING CENTER

ASBURY

DORCHESTER ST.

RAIL STATION

BUS STN.

Kennet & Avon Canal

WELLS RD.

ROSSITER RD. (A-36)

CLAVERTON RD.

The **bus station** is west of the train station, along Dorchester Street.

My recommended B&Bs are all within a 10- to 15-minute walk or a £4-5 taxi ride from the train and bus stations.

Helpful Hints

Festivals: The **Bath Literature Festival** is an open book February 25-March 6 in 2012 (www.bathlitfest.org.uk). The **Bath International Music Festival** bursts into song every spring (classical, folk, jazz, contemporary; May 23-June 3 in 2012, www.bathmusicfest.org.uk), overlapped by the eclectic **Bath Fringe Festival** (theater, walks, talks, bus trips; generally similar dates to the Music Festival, www.bathfringe.co.uk). The **Jane Austen Festival** unfolds genteelly in late September (www.janeausten.co.uk/festival). And for three weeks in December, the squares around the abbey are filled with a **Christmas market.**

Bath's festival **box office** sells tickets for most events (but not for those at the Theatre Royal), and can tell you exactly what's on tonight (a block down from the TI at 2 Church Street, tel. 01225/463-362, www.bathfestivals.org.uk). The city's weekly paper, the *Bath Chronicle,* publishes a "What's On" events listing (www.thisisbath.com).

Internet Access: Ask your hotel or the TI for the closest Internet café. You can also get online at the Bath **library** (£1.20/20 minutes, slightly cheaper with free library membership, Mon 9:30-18:00, Tue-Thu 9:30-19:00, Fri-Sat 9:30-17:00, Sun 13:00-16:00, in the Podium Shopping Centre on Northgate Street near Pulteney Bridge, tel. 01225/394-041, www.bath nes.gov.uk).

Bookstore: Topping & Company, an inviting bookshop, has posters in the windows advertising frequent author readings, free coffee and tea for browsers, and tables filled with tidy stacks of carefully selected volumes (daily 9:00-20:00, near the bottom of the street called "The Paragon"—where it meets George Street, tel. 01225/428-111, www.toppingbooks.co.uk).

Laundry: The **Spruce Goose Launderette** is between the Circus and the Royal Crescent, on the pedestrian lane called Margaret's Buildings. Bring lots of £1 coins for washing and £0.20 coins for drying, as there are no change machines (self-service: about £4-5/load, daily 8:00-20:00, last load at 19:30; full-service: £12/load, Mon, Wed, Fri-Sat 8:00-12:00; tel. 01225/483-309). **Speedy Wash** can pick up your laundry anywhere in town on weekdays before 11:00 for same-day service (£12/small bag, Mon-Fri 7:30-17:30, Sat 8:30-13:00 but no pickup, closed Sun, no self-service, most hotels work with them, 4 Mile End, London Road, tel. 01225/427-616).

Car Rental: Enterprise provides a pickup service for customers to and from their hotels (extra fee for one-way rentals, at Lower Bristol Road outside Bath, tel. 01225/443-311, www .enterprise.com). Others include **Thrifty** (pickup service and one-way rentals available, in the Burnett Business Park in Keynsham—between Bath and Bristol, tel. 01179/867-997, www.thrifty.co.uk), **Hertz** (one-way rentals possible, at Windsor Bridge, tel. 0870-850-2691, www.hertz.co.uk), and **National/Europcar** (one-way rentals available, £7 by taxi from the train station, at Brassmill Lane—go west on Upper Bristol Road, tel. 01225/481-982 or 01761/479-205). Skip **Avis**—it's a mile from the Bristol train station; you'd need to rent a car to get there. Most offices close Saturday afternoon and all day Sunday, which complicates weekend pickups. Ideally, take the train or bus from downtown London to Bath, and rent a car as you leave Bath.

Parking: Parking in the city center is difficult. Short-term street parking is available but pricey (about £2.50/hour, 2-hour maximum, buy pay-and-display tickets from machine). You'll pay less per hour in long-stay lots (figure £9/24 hours; the Charlotte Street car park is handy). For more info on parking, visit www.bathnes.gov.uk/bathnes.

Tours in Bath

▲▲▲**Walking Tours**—Free two-hour tours are led by **The Mayor's Corps of Honorary Guides,** volunteers who want to share their love of Bath with its many visitors (as the city's mayor first did when he took a group on a guided walk back in the 1930s). These chatty, historical, and gossip-filled walks are essential for your understanding of this town's amazing Georgian social scene. How else would you learn that the old "chair ho" call for your sedan chair evolved into today's "cheerio" farewell? Tours leave from outside the Pump Room in the abbey churchyard (free, no tips, year-round Sun-Fri at 10:30 and 14:00, Sat at 10:30 only; additional evening walks May-Sept Tue and Fri at 19:00; tel. 01225/477-411, www.bathguides.org .uk). Tip for theatergoers: When your guide stops to talk outside the Theatre Royal, skip out for a moment, pop into the box office, and see about snaring a great deal on a play for tonight.

For a **private tour,** call the local guides' bureau, Bath Parade Guides (£60/2 hours, tel. 01225/337-111, www.bathparadeguides .co.uk, bathparadeguides@yahoo.com). For **Ghost Walks** and **Bizarre Bath** tours, see "Nightlife in Bath," later.

▲▲**City Bus Tours**—City Sightseeing's hop-on, hop-off bus tours zip through Bath. Jump on a bus anytime at one of 17

Bath at a Glance

▲▲▲**Walking Tours** Free top-notch tours, helping you make the most of your visit, led by The Mayor's Corps of Honorary Guides. **Hours:** Sun-Fri at 10:30 and 14:00, Sat at 10:30 only; additional evening walks offered May-Sept Tue and Fri at 19:00. See page 491.

▲▲▲**Roman and Medieval Baths** Ancient baths that gave the city its name, tourable with good audioguide. **Hours:** Daily July-Aug 9:00-22:00, March-June and Sept-Oct 9:00-18:00, Nov-Feb 9:30-17:30. See page 495.

▲▲**The Circus and the Royal Crescent** Stately Georgian (Neoclassical) buildings from Bath's late-18th-century glory days. **Hours:** Always viewable. See page 502.

▲▲**Fashion Museum** 400 years of clothing under one roof, plus the opulent Assembly Rooms. **Hours:** Daily March-Oct 10:30-18:00, Nov-Feb 10:30-17:00. See page 503.

▲▲**Museum of Bath at Work** Gadget-ridden circa-1900 engineer's shop, foundry, factory, and office, best enjoyed with a live tour. **Hours:** April-Oct daily 10:30-17:00, Nov and Jan-March weekends only, closed in Dec. See page 504.

▲**Pump Room** Swanky Georgian hall, ideal for a spot of tea or a taste of unforgettably "healthy" spa water. **Hours:** Daily 9:30-12:00 for coffee and breakfast, 12:00-14:30 for lunch, 14:30-16:30 for afternoon tea (open for dinner during Bath International Music Festival, July-Aug, and Christmas holidays only). See page 498.

signposted pickup points, pay the driver, climb upstairs, and hear recorded commentary about Bath. City Sightseeing has two 45-minute routes: a city tour (unintelligible audio recording on half the buses, live guides on the other half—choose the latter), and a "Skyline" route outside town (all live guides, stops near the American Museum—15-minute walk). On a sunny day, this is a multitasking tourist's dream come true: You can munch a sandwich, work on a tan, snap great photos, and learn a lot, all at the same time. Save money by doing the bus tour first—ticket stubs get you minor discounts at many sights (£11.50, ticket valid for 2 days and both tour routes, generally 4/hour daily in summer 9:30-18:30, in winter 10:00-15:00, tel. 01225/444-102, www.city-sightseeing.com).

Taxi Tours—Local taxis, driven by good talkers, go where big buses can't. A group of up to four can rent a cab for an hour (about £20) and enjoy a fine, informative, and—with the right cabbie—

▲**Thermae Bath Spa** Relaxation center that put the bath back in Bath. **Hours:** Daily 9:00-22:00. See page 499.

▲**Bath Abbey** 500-year-old Perpendicular Gothic church, graced with beautiful fan vaulting and stained glass. **Hours:** April-Oct Mon-Sat 9:00-18:00, Sun 13:00-14:30 & 16:30-17:30; Nov-March Mon-Sat 9:00-16:30, Sun 13:00-14:30 & 16:30-17:30. See page 500.

▲**Pulteney Bridge and Parade Gardens** Shop-strewn bridge and relaxing riverside gardens. **Hours:** Bridge—always open; gardens—Easter-Sept daily 11:00-17:00, shorter hours off-season. See page 501.

▲**Georgian House at No. 1 Royal Crescent** Best opportunity to explore the interior of one of Bath's high-rent Georgian beauties. **Hours:** Mid-Feb-Oct Tue-Sun 10:30-17:00, Nov Tue-Sun 10:30-16:00, closed Mon and Dec-mid-Feb. See page 502.

▲**American Museum** An insightful look primarily at colonial/early-American lifestyles, with 18 furnished rooms and eager-to-talk guides. **Hours:** Mid-March-Oct Tue-Sun 12:00-17:00, closed Mon and Nov-mid-March. See page 506.

Jane Austen Centre Exhibit on 19th-century Bath-based novelist, best for her fans. **Hours:** Mid-March-mid-Nov daily 9:45-17:30, July-Aug Thu-Sat until 19:00; mid-Nov-mid-March Sun-Fri 11:00-16:30, Sat 9:45-17:30. See page 505.

BATH

entertaining private joyride. It's probably cheaper to let the meter run than to pay for an hourly rate, but ask the cabbie for advice.

To Stonehenge, Avebury, and the Cotswolds

Bath is a good launch pad for visiting Wells, Avebury, Stonehenge, and more.

Mad Max Minibus Tours—Operating daily from Bath, Maddy and Paul offer thoughtfully organized, informative tours that run with entertaining guides. Book ahead—as far ahead as possible in summer—for these popular tours. Their **Stone Circles** full-day tour covers 110 miles and visits Stonehenge, the Avebury Stone Circles, and two cute villages: Lacock and Castle Combe. Photogenic Lacock is featured in parts of the BBC's *Pride and Prejudice* and the Harry Potter movies, and Castle Combe, the southernmost Cotswold village, is as sweet as they come (£32.50 plus £7.50 Stonehenge entry, tours run daily 8:45-16:30, arrive 15 minutes early, leaves early to beat the Stonehenge hordes). Their shorter tour of **Stonehenge and Lacock** leaves daily at 13:15 and returns at 17:15; occasionally, it also leaves at 8:45 and returns at 12:45 (£17.50 plus £7.50 Stonehenge entry). Most of their tours are limited to 16 people, though on busy days, the half-day tour might have up to 24.

Mad Max also offers a **Cotswold Discovery** full-day tour, a picturesque romp through the countryside with stops and a cream-tea opportunity in the quainter Cotswolds villages, including Stow-on-the-Wold, Bibury, Tetbury, the Coln Valley, The Slaughters (optional walk between the two villages), and others (£35; runs Sun, Tue, and Thu 8:45-17:15; arrive 15 minutes early). If you ask in advance, you can bring your luggage along and use the tour as transportation to Stow or, for £5 extra, Moreton-in-Marsh, with easy train connections to Oxford.

All tours depart from Bath at the Glass House shop on the corner of Orange Grove, a one-minute walk from the abbey. Arrive 15 minutes before your departure time and bring cash (it's possible to pay with credit card only if you book online at least 48 hours in advance—£1 discount). Online or email reservations are preferable to calling (phone answered daily 8:00-18:00, tel. 07990/505-970, www.madmax.abel.co.uk, maddy@madmax.abel.co.uk). Please honor or cancel your seat reservation.

More Bus Tours—If Mad Max is booked up, don't fret. Plenty of companies in Bath offer tours of varying lengths, prices, and destinations. Note that the cost of admission to sights is usually not included with any tour.

Scarper Tours runs a minibus tour to Stonehenge (£14, 10 percent Rick Steves discount if you book direct, doesn't include £7.50 Stonehenge entry fee, departs from behind the abbey; daily mid-June-Aug at 9:30, 13:00, and 16:30; mid-March-mid-June and Sept-mid-Oct at 10:00 and 14:00; mid-Oct-mid-March at 13:00; tel. 07739/644-155, www.scarpertours.com). The three-hour tour (two hours there and back, an hour at the site) includes driver narration en route.

Celtic Horizons, run by retired teacher Alan Price, offers tours from Bath to a variety of destinations, such as Stonehenge, Avebury, and Wells. Alan can provide a convenient transfer service (to or from London, Heathrow, Bristol Airport, the Cotswolds, and so on), with or without a tour itinerary en route. Allow about £25/hour for a group (his comfortable minivans seat 4, 6, or 8 people) and £150 for Heathrow-Bath transfers (1-4 persons). It's best to make arrangements and get pricing information by email at alan@celtichorizons.com (cash only, tel. 01373/461-784, http://celtichorizons.com).

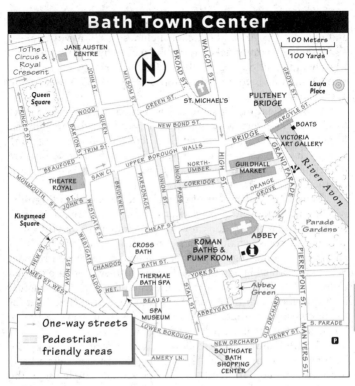

Bath Town Center

To The Circus & Royal Crescent

JANE AUSTEN CENTRE

Queen Square

ST. MICHAEL'S

PULTENEY BRIDGE

Laura Place

BOATS

VICTORIA ART GALLERY

GUILDHALL MARKET

NORTH-UMBER

ORANGE GROVE

THEATRE ROYAL

Kingsmead Square

ABBEY

Parade Gardens

River Avon

CROSS BATH

ROMAN BATHS & PUMP ROOM

THERMAE BATH SPA

Abbey Green

SPA MUSEUM

SOUTHGATE BATH SHOPPING CENTER

S. PARADE

100 Meters
100 Yards

→ One-way streets

Pedestrian-friendly areas

BATH

Sights in Bath

In the Town Center

▲▲▲**Roman and Medieval Baths**—In ancient Roman times, high society enjoyed the mineral springs at Bath. From Londinium—and throughout the empire—Romans traveled so often to Aquae Sulis, as the city was called, to "take a bath" that finally it became known simply as Bath. Today, a fine museum surrounds the ancient bath. With the help of a great audioguide, you'll wander past well-documented displays, Roman artifacts, a temple pediment with an evocative bearded face, a bronze head of the goddess Sulis Minerva, excavated ancient foundations, and the actual mouth of the spring. At the end you'll have a chance to walk around the big pool itself, where Romans once lounged, splished, splashed, and thanked the gods for the gift of naturally hot water.

Cost and Hours: £12.50, £0.75 more in July-Aug, includes audioguide, £15.50 combo-ticket includes Fashion Museum—a £3.50 savings, family ticket available, daily July-Aug 9:00-22:00, March-June and Sept-Oct 9:00-18:00, Nov-Feb 9:30-17:30, last entry one hour before closing, tel. 01225/477-785, www.roman baths.co.uk.

Crowd-Beating Tips: As this is the top sight in this touristy town, it can be very busy on Saturdays and any day in summer (though you'll never wait longer than about 30 minutes to get in). On any day, the least crowded time to visit is before 11:00. If you're here in July or August, the best time is after 19:00, when the baths are romantic, gas-lit, and all yours.

Tours: Take advantage of the included, essential **audioguide,** which will make your visit easy and informative. In addition to the basic commentary, look for posted numbers to key into your audioguide for specialty topics—including a kid-friendly tour and insightful musings from American expat writer Bill Bryson. For those with a big appetite for Roman history, in-depth **guided tours** leave from the end of the museum at the edge of the actual bath (included with ticket, on the hour, a poolside clock is set for the next departure time, 20-40 minutes depending on the guide). You can revisit the museum after the tour.

◑ Self-Guided Tour: Follow the one-way route through the bath and museum complex. This self-guided tour offers a basic overview; for more in-depth commentary, make ample use of the included audioguide.

Begin by walking around the upper **terrace,** overlooking the Great Bath. This terrace—lined with sculptures of VIRs (Very Important Romans)—evokes ancient times but was built in the 1890s. The ruins of the bath complex sat undisturbed for centuries before finally being excavated and turned into a museum in the late 19th century.

Head inside to the **museum,** where exhibits explain the dual purpose of the buildings that stood here in Roman times: a bath complex, for relaxation and for healing; and a temple dedicated to the goddess Sulis Minerva, who was believed to be responsible for the mysterious and much-appreciated thermal springs. Cut-away diagrams and models resurrect both parts of this complex and help establish your bearings among the remaining fragments and foundations.

Peer down into the **spring,** where little air bubbles remind you that 240,000 gallons of water a day emerge from the earth—magically, it must have seemed to Romans—at a constant 115°F.

Go downstairs to get to know the Romans who built and enjoyed these baths. The fragments of the **temple pediment**—carved by indigenous Celtic craftsmen but with Roman themes—

represent a remarkable cultural synthesis. Sit and watch for a while, as a slide projection fills in historians' best guesses as to what once occupied the missing bits. The identity of the circular face in the middle puzzles researchers. (God? Santa Claus?) It could be the head of the Gorgon monster after it was slain by Perseus—are those snakes peeking through its hair and beard? And yet, the Gorgon was traditionally depicted as female. Perhaps instead it's Neptune, the god of water—appropriate for this aquatic site.

The next exhibits examine the importance of Aquae Sulis (the settlement here) in antiquity. Much like the pilgrimage sites of the Middle Ages, this spot exerted a powerful pull on people from all over the realm, who were eager to partake in its healing waters and to worship at the religious site. You'll see some of the small but extremely heavy carved-stone tables that pilgrims hauled here as an offering to the gods.

As you walk through the temple's original foundations, keep an eye out for the sacrificial altar.
The gilded-bronze head of the goddess **Sulis Minerva** (in the display case) once overlooked a flaming cauldron inside the temple, where only priests were allowed to enter. Similar to the Greek goddess Athena, Sulis Minerva was considered to be a life-giving mother goddess. The next room displays some

of the requests (inscribed on sheets of pewter or iron) that visitors made of the goddess. Take time to read some of these—many are comically spiteful and petty, offering a warts-and-all glimpse into day-to-day Roman culture.

Engineers enjoy a close-up look at the spring overflow and the original **drain system**—built two millennia ago—that still carries excess water to the River Avon. Marvel at the cleverness and durability of Roman engineering, created in (what we usually imagine to be) a "primitive" time. A nearby exhibit on pulleys and fasteners lets you play with these inventions.

Head outside to the **Great Bath** itself (where you can join one of the included guided tours—look for the clock with the next start time). Take a slow lap (by foot) around the perimeter, imagining the frolicking Romans who once immersed themselves up to their necks in this five-foot-deep pool. (On busy days, when costumed characters hang out by the bath, you may not have to imagine.) The water is greenish because of algae—don't drink it. The best views are from the west end, looking back toward the abbey. Nearby is a giant chunk of roof span, from a time when this was a cavernous covered swimming hall. At the corner, you'll step over a small canal where hot water still trickles into the main pool. Nearby, find a length of original lead pipe, remarkably well preserved since antiquity.

Symmetrical bath complexes branch off at opposite ends of the Great Bath (perhaps dating from a conservative period when the Romans maintained separate facilities for men and women). The **East Baths** show off changing rooms and various bathing rooms, each one designed for a special therapy or recreational purpose (immersion therapy tub, sauna-like heated floor, and so on), as described in detail by the audioguide.

When you're ready to leave, head for the **West Baths** (including a sweat bath and a *frigidarium*, or "cold plunge" pool) and take another look at the spring and more foundations. After returning your audioguide, exit through the gift shop and dip into the attached **Pump Room** to drink a spot of tea or to gag on the spa water (get a free sample with your bath ticket).

▲**Pump Room**—For centuries, Bath was forgotten as a spa. Then, in 1687, the previously barren Queen Mary bathed here, became

pregnant, and bore a male heir to the throne. A few years later, Queen Anne found the water eased her painful gout. Word of its wonder waters spread, and Bath earned its way back on the aristocratic map. High society soon turned the place into one big pleasure palace. The Pump Room, an elegant Georgian hall just above the Roman Baths, offers visitors their best chance to raise a pinky in Chippendale grandeur. Above the newspaper table and sedan chairs, a statue of Beau Nash himself sniffles down at you. Come for a light meal, or for just the price of a coffee (£3), drop in anytime—except during lunch—to enjoy live music and the atmosphere.

Cost and Hours: Daily 9:30-12:00 for coffee and £6-15 breakfast, 12:00-14:30 for £6-16 lunches, 14:30-16:30 for £17.50 traditional afternoon tea, tea/coffee and pastries also available in the afternoons; open for dinner July-Aug, during Bath International Music Festival, and Christmas holidays only; live music daily—

string trio or piano, times vary; tel. 01225/444-477.

The Spa Water: This is your chance to eat a famous (but forgettable) "Bath bun" and split a drink of the awful curative water (£0.50 or free with your Roman and Medieval Baths ticket—just head to the little alcove on the right and show them your ticket). The water comes from the King's Spring and is brought to you by an appropriately attired server, who explains that the water is 10,000 years old, pumped up from nearly 100 yards deep, and marinated in 43 wonderful minerals. Convenient public WCs (which use plain old tap water) are in the entry hallway that connects the Pump Room with the baths.

▲**Thermae Bath Spa**—After simmering unused for a quarter-century, Bath's natural thermal springs once again offer R&R for

the masses. The state-of-the-art spa is housed in a complex of three buildings that combine historic structures with controversial (and expensive) new glass-and-steel architecture.

Is the Thermae Bath Spa worth the time and money? The experience is pretty pricey and humble compared to similar German and Hungarian spas. The tall, modern building in the city center lacks a certain old-time elegance. Jets in the pools are very limited, and the only water toys are big foam noodles. There's no cold plunge—the only way to cool off between steam rooms is to step onto a small, unglamorous balcony. The Royal Bath's two pools are essentially the same, and the water isn't particularly hot in either—in fact, the main attraction is the rooftop view from the top one (best with a partner or as a social experience).

That said, this is the only natural thermal spa in the UK and your chance to bathe in Bath. Bring your swimsuit and come for a couple of hours (Fri night and all day Sat-Sun are most crowded). Consider an evening visit, when—on a chilly day—Bath's twilight glows through the steam from the rooftop pool.

Cost: The cheapest spa pass is £25 for two hours, which gains you access to the Royal Bath's large, ground-floor "Minerva Bath"; four steam rooms and a waterfall shower; and the view-filled, open-air, rooftop thermal pool. Longer stays are £35/4 hours and £55/day (towel, robe, and slippers are an extra £9). If you arrived in Bath by train, your used rail ticket will score you a four-hour session for the price of two hours (£25, Mon-Fri). The much-hyped £42 Twilight Package includes three hours and a meal (one plate, drink, robe, towel, and slippers). The appeal of this package is not the mediocre meal, but being on top of the building at a magical hour (which you can do for less money at the regular rate).

Thermae has all the "pamper thyself" extras: massages, mud wraps, and various healing-type treatments, including "watsu"—water shiatsu (£40-70 extra). Book treatments at www.thermae bathspa.com.

Hours: Daily 9:00-22:00, last entry at 19:30. No kids under 16 are allowed. It's 100 yards from the Roman and Medieval Baths, on Beau Street, tel. 01225/331-234. There's a salad-and-smoothies café for guests.

The Cross Bath: This renovated, circular Georgian structure across the street from the main spa provides a simpler and less-expensive bathing option. It has a hot-water fountain that taps directly into the spring, making its water hotter than the spa's (£15/1.5 hours, daily 10:00-20:00, last entry at 18:30, check in at the bath's main office across the street and you'll be escorted to the Cross Bath, changing rooms, no access to Royal Bath, no kids under 12).

Spa Visitor Center: Also across the street, in the Hetling Pump Room, this free, one-room exhibit explains the story of the spa (Mon-Sat 10:00-17:00, Sun 10:00-16:00, £2 audioguide).

▲**Bath Abbey**—The town of Bath wasn't much in the Middle Ages, but an important church has stood on this spot since Anglo-Saxon times. King Edgar I was crowned here in 973, when the church was much bigger (before the bishop packed up and moved to Wells). Dominating the town center, today's abbey—the last great medieval church of England—is 500 years old and a fine example of the Late  Perpendicular Gothic style, with breezy fan vaulting and enough stained glass to earn it the nickname "Lantern of the West."

The **facade** (c. 1500, but mostly restored) is interesting for some of its carvings. Look for the angels going down the ladder. The statue of Peter (to the left of the door) lost its head to mean iconoclasts; it was recarved out of Peter's once supersized beard. Take a moment to appreciate the abbey's architecture from the Abbey Green square.

Going **inside** is worth the small suggested contribution. The glass, red-iron gas-powered lamps, and the heating grates on the floor are all remnants of the 19th century. The window behind the altar shows 52 scenes from the life of Christ. A window to the left of the altar shows Edgar's coronation.

Cost and Hours: £2.50 suggested donation; April-Oct Mon-Sat 9:00-18:00, Sun 13:00-14:30 & 16:30-17:30; Nov-March

Mon-Sat 9:00-16:30, Sun 13:00-14:30 & 16:30-17:30; handy flier narrates a self-guided 19-stop tour, schedule of events—including concerts, services, and evensong—posted on the door and online, tel. 01225/422-462, www.bathabbey.org.

Climbing the Tower: You can reach the top of the tower but only with an official 50-minute guided tour. You'll hike up 212 steps for views across the rooftops of Bath and down into the Roman and Medieval Baths (£5, sporadic schedule but generally at the top of each hour Mon-Sat April-Oct 10:00-16:00, Nov-March 11:00-14:00, more often during busy times, no tours Sun, buy tickets in abbey gift shop).

▲**Pulteney Bridge, Parade Gardens, and Cruises**—Bath is inclined to compare its shop-lined Pulteney Bridge to Florence's Ponte Vecchio. That's pushing it. But to best enjoy a sunny day, pay

£1 to enter the Parade Gardens below the bridge (Easter-Sept daily 11:00-17:00, shorter hours off-season, includes deck chairs, ask about concerts held some Sun at 15:00 in summer, entrance a block south of bridge, www.bath nes.gov.uk). Relaxing peacefully at the riverside provides a wonderful break (and memory).

Across the bridge at Pulteney Weir, tour boat companies run **cruises** (£8 round-trip, £4 one-way, up to 7/day if the weather's good, one hour to Bathampton and back, WCs on board, tel. 01225/312-900). Just take whatever boat is running—all stop in Bathampton—allowing you to hop off and walk back (about 45-60 minutes; for details on the walk, see "Activities in Bath," later). Boats come with picnic-friendly sundecks.

Guildhall Market—The little, old-school shopping mall located across from Pulteney Bridge is a frumpy time warp in this affluent town. It's fun for browsing and picnic shopping, and its recommended Market Café is a cheap place for a bite.

Victoria Art Gallery—This gallery, next to Pulteney Bridge, has two parts: The ground floor houses temporary exhibits, while the upstairs is filled with paintings from the late 17th century to the present, along with a small collection of decorative arts.

Cost and Hours: Free, Tue-Sat 10:00-17:00, Sun 13:30-17:00, closed Mon, WC, tel. 01225/477-233, www.victoriagal.org.uk.

Northwest of the Town Center

Several worthwhile public spaces and museums can be found a slightly uphill 10-minute walk away.

▲▲**The Circus and the Royal Crescent**—If Bath is an architectural cancan, these are its knickers. These first Georgian "condos"—built in the mid-18th century by the father-and-son John Woods (the Circus by the Elder, the Royal Crescent by the Younger)—are well explained by the city walking tours. "Georgian" is British for "Neoclassical." These two building complexes, conveniently located a block apart from each other, are quintessential Bath.

Circus: True to its name, this is a circular housing complex. Picture it as a coliseum turned inside out. Its Doric, Ionic, and Corinthian capital decorations pay homage to its Greco-Roman origin, and are a reminder that Bath (with its seven hills) aspired to be "the Rome of England." The frieze above the first row of columns has hundreds of different panels representing the arts, sciences, and crafts. The ground-floor entrances were made large enough that aristocrats could be carried right through the door in their sedan chairs, and women could enter without disturbing their sky-high hairdos. The tiny round windows on the top floors were the servants' quarters. While the building fronts are uniform, the backs are higgledy-piggledy, infamous for their "hanging loos" (bathrooms added years later). Stand in the middle of the Circus among the grand plane trees, on the capped old well. Imagine the days when there was no indoor plumbing, and the servant girls gathered here to fetch water—this was gossip central. If you stand on the well, your clap echoes three times around the circle (try it).

Royal Crescent: A long, graceful arc of buildings—impossible to see in one glance unless you step way back to the edge of the big park in front—evokes

the wealth and gentility of Bath's glory days. As you cruise the Crescent, pretend you're rich. Then pretend you're poor. Notice the "ha ha fence," a drop-off in the front yard that acted as a barrier, invisible from the windows, for keeping out sheep and peasants. The refined and stylish **Royal Crescent Hotel** sits unmarked in the center of the Crescent (with the giant rhododendron growing over the door). You're welcome to (politely) drop in to explore its fine ground-floor public spaces and back garden, where a gracious and traditional tea is served (£14 cream tea, £23.50 afternoon tea, daily 15:00-17:00, sharing is OK, reserve a day in advance in summer, tel. 01225/823-333).

▲**Georgian House at No. 1 Royal Crescent**—This museum (corner of Brock Street and Royal Crescent) offers your best look into a period house. Your visit is limited to four roped-off rooms, but it's worth the admission to get behind one of those classy

Georgian facades, especially if you take the time to talk with the docents stationed in each room. The docents know all the fascinating details of Georgian life...like how high-class women shaved their eyebrows and pasted on carefully trimmed strips of furry mouse skin in their place. On the bedroom dresser sits a bowl of black beauty marks and a head-scratcher from those pre-shampoo days. Fido spent his days in the kitchen treadmill powering the rotisserie.

Cost and Hours: £6.50, mid-Feb-Oct Tue-Sun 10:30-17:00, Nov Tue-Sun 10:30-16:00, closed Mon and Dec-mid-Feb, last entry 30 minutes before closing, £2 guidebook available, no photos, "no stiletto heels, please," tel. 01225/428-126, www.bath-preservation-trust.org.uk. Its WC is accessible from the street (under the entry steps, across from the exit and shop).

▲▲**Fashion Museum**—Housed underneath Bath's Assembly Rooms, this museum displays four centuries of fashion on one floor. It's small, but the fact-filled, included audioguide can stretch a

visit to an informative and enjoyable hour. Like fashion itself, the exhibits change all the time. A major feature is the "Dress of the Year" display, for which a fashion expert anoints a new frock each year. Ongoing since 1963, it's a chance to view nearly a half-century of fashion trends in one sweep of the head. (The menswear version—awarded sporadically—shows a bit less variation, but has flashes of creativity.) Many of the exhibits are organized by theme (bags, shoes, underwear, wedding dresses). You'll see how fashion evolved—just like architecture and other arts—from one historical period to the next: Georgian, Regency, Victorian, the Swinging '60s, and so on. If you're intrigued by all those historic garments, go ahead and lace up your own trainer corset (which looks more like a lifejacket) and try on a hoop underdress.

Cost and Hours: £7.25, £15.50 combo-ticket also covers Roman Baths, family ticket available, daily March-Oct 10:30-18:00, Nov-Feb 10:30-17:00, last entry one hour before closing, self-service café, Bennett Street, tel. 01225/477-789, www.fashionmuseum.co.uk.

Assembly Rooms: Whether or not you're touring the Fashion Museum, poke into the building that houses it, where you can wander the big, grand, empty Assembly Rooms. Card games, concerts, tea, and dances were held here in the 18th century, before the advent of fancy hotels with grand public spaces made them obsolete. Note the extreme symmetry (pleasing to the aristocratic eye) and the high windows (assuring privacy). After the Allies bombed the historic and well-preserved German city of Lübeck, the Germans picked up a Baedeker guide and chose a similarly lovely city to bomb: Bath. The Assembly Rooms—gutted in this wartime tit-for-tat by WWII bombs—have since been restored to their original splendor. (Only the chandeliers are original.)

Nearby: Below the Fashion Museum (to the left as you leave, 20 yards away, at the door marked *14* and *Alfred House*) is one of the few surviving sets of **iron house hardware.** "Link boys" carried torches through the dark streets, lighting the way for big shots in their sedan chairs as they traveled from one affair to the next. The link boys extinguished their torches in the black conical "snuffers." The lamp above was once gas-lit. The crank on the left was used to hoist bulky things to various windows (see the hooks). Few of these sets survived the dark days of the WWII Blitz, when most were collected and melted down, purportedly to make weapons to feed the British war machine. (Not long ago, these well-meaning Brits finally found out that all of their patriotic extra commitment to the national struggle had been for naught, since the metal ended up in junk heaps.)

Shoppers head down **Bartlett Street,** just below the Fashion Museum, to browse the antique shops.

▲▲Museum of Bath at Work—This modest but lovable place explains the industrial history of Bath. The museum is a vivid reminder that there's always been a grimy, workaday side to this spa town.

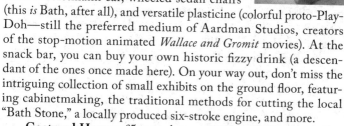

The core of the museum is the well-preserved, circa-1900 fizzy-drink business of one Mr. Bowler. It includes a Dickensian office, engineer's shop, brass foundry, and factory floor. It's just a pile of meaningless old gadgets—until the included audioguide resurrects Mr. Bowler's creative genius. Each item has its own story to tell.

Upstairs are display cases featuring other Bath creations through the years, including a 1914 Horstmann car, wheeled sedan chairs (this *is* Bath, after all), and versatile plasticine (colorful proto-Play-Doh—still the preferred medium of Aardman Studios, creators of the stop-motion animated *Wallace and Gromit* movies). At the snack bar, you can buy your own historic fizzy drink (a descendant of the ones once made here). On your way out, don't miss the intriguing collection of small exhibits on the ground floor, featuring cabinetmaking, the traditional methods for cutting the local "Bath Stone," a locally produced six-stroke engine, and more.

Cost and Hours: £5, people over 60 pay £3.50, April-Oct

daily 10:30-17:00, Nov and Jan-March weekends only, closed Dec, last entry at 16:00, Julian Road, 2 steep blocks up Russell Street from Assembly Rooms, tel. 01225/318-348, www.bath-at-work .org.uk.

Sightseeing Tip: Notice the proximity of this museum to the very different Fashion Museum (described earlier). Museum attendants told me that—while open-minded spouses appreciate both places—it's standard for husbands to visit the Museum of Bath at Work while their wives are touring the Fashion Museum. Maybe it's time to divide and conquer?

Jane Austen Centre—This exhibition focuses on Jane Austen's tumultuous, sometimes troubled five years in Bath (circa 1800, during which time her father died) and the influence the city had on her writing. There's little of historic substance here. You'll walk through a Georgian townhouse that she didn't live in (one of her real addresses in Bath was a few houses up the road, at 25 Gay Street), and you'll see mostly enlarged reproductions of things associated with her writing, but none of that seems to bother the steady stream of happy Austen fans touring through the house.

The museum does describe various places from two novels set in Bath (*Persuasion* and *Northanger Abbey*). Guides give an intro talk (15 minutes, 2/hour, starts at :15 and :45 past the hour) about the romantic but down-to-earth Austen, who skewered the silly, shallow, and arrogant aristocrats' world, where "the doing of nothing all day prevents one from doing anything." They also show a 15-minute video; after that, you're free to wander through the rest of the exhibit. The well-stocked gift shop—with "I love Mr. Darcy" tote bags and Colin Firth's visage emblazoned on teacups, postcards, and more—is a shopping spree in the making for Austen fans.

Cost and Hours: £7.50; mid-March-mid-Nov daily 9:45-17:30, July-Aug Thu-Sat until 19:00; mid-Nov-mid-March Sun-Fri 11:00-16:30, Sat 9:45-17:30; between Queen's Square and the Circus at 40 Gay Street, tel. 01225/443-000, www.janeausten .co.uk.

Tea: Upstairs, the award-winning **Regency Tea Rooms** (free entrance) hits the spot for Austenites, with costumed waitstaff and themed teas (£6-10), including the all-out "Tea with Mr. Darcy" for £12 (also £6 sandwiches, same hours as the Centre, last orders 45 minutes before closing).

Sightseeing Tip: Jane Austen-themed **walking tours** of the city begin at the KC Change shop in the abbey square and end at the Centre (£5, buy tickets at KC Change shop, 1.5 hours, Sat-Sun at 11:00, July-Aug also Fri-Sat at 16:00, no reservation necessary).

Building of Bath Collection—This unique collection offers an intriguing behind-the-scenes look at how the Georgian city was actually built (£4, mid-Feb-Nov Sat-Mon 10:30-17:00, last entry 30 minutes before closing, closed Tue-Fri and Dec-mid-Feb, a short walk north of the city center on a street called "The Paragon," tel. 01225/333-895, www.bath-preservation-trust.org.uk).

Outer Bath

▲**American Museum**—I know, you need this in Bath like you need a Big Mac. The UK's sole museum dedicated to American history, this may be the only place that combines Geronimo and Groucho Marx. It has thoughtful exhibits on the history of Native Americans and the Civil War, but the museum's heart is with the decorative arts and cultural artifacts that reveal how Americans lived from colonial times to the mid-19th century. Each of the 18 completely furnished rooms (from a plain 1600s Massachusetts dining/living room to a Rococo Revival explosion in a New Orleans bedroom) is hosted by eager guides waiting to fill you in on the everyday items that make domestic Yankee history surprisingly interesting. (In the Lee Room, look for the original mouse holes, strategically backlit, in the floor boards.) One room is a quilter's nirvana. You could easily spend an afternoon here, enjoying the surrounding gardens, arboretum, and trails.

Cost and Hours: £9, mid-March-Oct Tue-Sun 12:00-17:00, closed Mon and Nov-mid-March, last entry one hour before closing, at Claverton Manor, tel. 01225/460-503, www.american museum.org.

Getting There: The museum is outside of town and a headache to reach if you don't have a car, involving a 10-15-minute walk from bus #18 or the hop-on, hop-off bus stop.

Activities in Bath

Walking—The Bath Skyline Walk is a six-mile wander around the hills surrounding Bath (leaflet at TI). Plenty of other scenic paths are described in the TI's literature. For additional options, get *Country Walks around Bath,* by Tim Mowl (£4.50 at TI or bookstores).

Hiking the Canal to Bathampton—An idyllic towpath leads two miles from the Bath Spa train station, along the Kennet and Avon Canal, to the sleepy village of Bathampton. Immediately behind the station in Bath, cross the footbridge, turn left, and find where the canal hits the River Avon. Head northeast along the small canal, noticing the series of Industrial Age locks and giving thanks that you're not a horse pulling a barge. After the path crisscrosses the canal a few times, you'll mostly walk with the water on your right. You'll be in Bathampton in less than an hour, where The George, a classic pub, awaits with a nice meal and cellar-temp beer (reservations smart, tel. 01225/425-079).

Boating—The Bath Boating Station, in an old Victorian boat-house, rents rowboats, canoes, and punts (£7/person for first hour, then £3/additional hour, Easter-Sept daily 10:00-18:00, closed off-season, intersection of Forester and Rockcliffe roads, one mile northeast of center, tel. 01225/312-900, www.bathboating.co.uk).

Swimming and Kids' Activities—The Bath Sports and Leisure Centre has a fine pool for laps as well as lots of waterslides. Kids have entertaining options in the mini-gym "Active Club" area, which includes a rock wall and a "Zany Zone" indoor playground (swimming: £3.80 for adults, £2.40 for kids; kids and their parents pay £4 each to use "Active Club" plus pool; Mon-Fri 6:30-22:00, Sat 6:30-19:00, Sun 8:00-20:00, kids' hours limited, call for open-swim times, just across the bridge on North Parade Road, tel. 01225/486-905, www.aquaterra.org).

Shopping—There's great browsing between the abbey and the Assembly Rooms (Fashion Museum). Shops close at about 17:30, and many are open on Sunday (11:00-16:00). Explore the antique shops lining Bartlett Street, below the Fashion Museum.

Nightlife in Bath

For an up-to-date list of events, pick up the local weekly newspaper, the *Bath Chronicle,* which includes a "What's On" schedule (www.thisisbath.com). Younger travelers may enjoy the party-ready bar, club, and nightlife recommendations at www.itchybath.co.uk.

▲▲**Bizarre Bath Street Theater**—For an entertaining walking-tour comedy act "with absolutely no history or culture," follow Dom, J. J., or Noel Britten on their creative and lively Bizarre Bath walk. This 1.5-hour "tour," which combines stand-up comedy with cleverly executed magic tricks, plays off unsuspecting passersby as well as tour members. It's a belly laugh a minute (£8, or £7 if you show your Rick Steves book, April-Oct nightly at 20:00, smaller groups Mon-Thu, promises to insult all nationalities and sensitivities, just racy enough but still good family fun, leaves from The Huntsman pub near the abbey, confirm at TI or call 01225/335-124, www.bizarrebath.co.uk).

▲**Theatre Royal Performance**—The 18th-century, 800-seat Theatre Royal, recently restored and one of England's loveliest, offers a busy schedule of London West End-type plays, including many "pre-London" dress-rehearsal runs (£15-39, shows generally start at 19:30 or 20:00, matinees at 14:30, box office open Mon-Sat 10:00-20:00, Sun 12:00-20:00 if there's a show, £3 extra to book online or by phone with a credit card, on Saw Close, tel. 01225/448-844, www.theatreroyal.org.uk).

Forty nosebleed spots on a bench (misnamed "standbys") go on sale at noon Monday through Saturday for that day's evening performance (£6, 2 tickets maximum, can book ahead but subject to £3 fee; no fee if bought at box office but cash only). If the show is sold out, same-day "standing places" go on sale at 18:00 (12:00 for matinees) for £4 (2 tickets maximum, cash only). Also at the box office, you can snatch up any "last minute" seats for £10-15 a half-hour before "curtain up" (cash only).

Sightseeing Tip: During the free Bath walking tour, your guide stops here. Pop into the box office, ask what's playing, and see if there are many seats left for that night. If the play sounds good and plenty of seats remain unsold, you're fairly safe to come back 30 minutes before curtain time to buy a ticket at the cheaper price. Oh...and if you smell jasmine, it's the ghost of Lady Grey, a mistress of Beau Nash.

Evening Walks—Take your choice: comedy (Bizarre Bath, described earlier), history, or ghost tour. The free **city history walks** (a daily standard described on page 491) are offered on some summer evenings (2 hours, May-Sept Tue and Fri at 19:00, leave from Pump Room). **Ghost Walks** are a popular way to pass the after-dark hours (£7, cash only, 1.5 hours, year-round Thu-Sat at 20:00, leave from The Garrick's Head pub—to the left and behind Theatre Royal as you face it, tel. 01225/350-512, www.ghostwalksofbath.co.uk). The cities of York and Edinburgh—which have houses thought to be actually haunted—are better for these walks.

Pubs—Most pubs in the center are very noisy, catering to a rowdy twentysomething crowd. But on the top end of town, you can still find some classic old places with inviting ambience and live music. These are listed in order from closest to farthest away:

The Old Green Tree, the most convenient of all these pubs, is a rare traditional pub right in the town center (locally brewed real ales, no children, 12 Green Street; also recommended for lunch—see "Eating in Bath," later).

The Star Inn is much appreciated by local beer-lovers for its fine ale and "no machines or music to distract from the chat." It's a spit 'n' sawdust place, and its long bench, nicknamed "death row," still comes with a complimentary pinch of snuff from tins on the ledge. Try the Bellringer Ale, made just up the road (Mon-Fri 12:00-14:30 & 17:30-24:00, Sat-Sun 12:00-24:00, no food served, 23 The Vineyards, top of The Paragon/A4 Roman Road, tel. 01225/425-072, generous and friendly welcome from Paul, who runs the place).

The Bell has a jazzy, pierced-and-tattooed, bohemian feel, but with a mellow older crowd. Some kind of activity is brewing nearly every night, usually live music (£2.50 sandwiches, pizza Fri-Sat only, Mon-Sat 11:30-23:00, Sun 12:00-22:30, 103 Walcot Street, tel. 01225/460-426, www.walcotstreet.com).

Summer Nights at the Baths—In July and August, you can stretch your sightseeing day at the Roman Baths, open nightly until 22:00 (last entry 21:00), when the gas lamps flame and the baths are far less crowded and more atmospheric. To take a dip yourself, consider popping over to the Thermae Bath Spa (last entry at 19:30).

Sleeping in Bath

Bath is a busy tourist town. Accommodations are expensive, and low-cost alternatives are rare. By far the best budget option is the

YMCA—it's central, safe, simple, very well-run, and has plenty of twin rooms available. To get a good B&B, make a telephone reservation in advance. Competition is stiff, and it's worth asking any of these places for a weekday, three-nights-in-a-row, or off-season deal. Friday and Saturday nights are tightest (with many rates going up by about 25 percent)—especially if you're staying only one night, since B&Bs favor those lingering longer. If staying only Saturday night, you're very bad news to a B&B hostess. If you're driving to Bath, stowing your car near the center will cost you (though some less-central B&Bs have parking)—see "Parking" on

Sleep Code

(£1 = about $1.60, country code: 44, area code: 01225)
S = Single, **D** = Double/Twin, **T** = Triple, **Q** = Quad, **b** = bathroom, **s** = shower only. Unless otherwise noted, credit cards are accepted.

To help you sort easily through these listings, I've divided the rooms into three categories based on the price for a standard double room with bath:

$$$ Higher Priced—Most rooms £100 or more.
$$ Moderately Priced—Most rooms between £60-100.
$ Lower Priced—Most rooms £60 or less.

Prices can change without notice; verify the hotel's current rates online or by email. For other updates, see www.ricksteves.com/update.

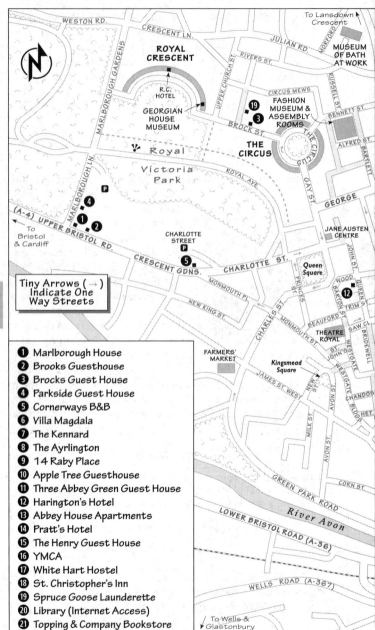

BATH

WESTON RD.
CRESCENT LN.
JULIAN RD.
MOREFORD
To Lansdown Crescent
MUSEUM OF BATH AT WORK
ROYAL CRESCENT
RIVERS ST.
RUSSELL ST.
MARLBOROUGH GARDENS
R.C. HOTEL
UPPER CHURCH ST.
CIRCUS MEWS
BENNETT ST.
GEORGIAN HOUSE MUSEUM
FASHION MUSEUM & ASSEMBLY ROOMS
BROCK ST.
ALFRED ST.
THE CIRCUS
BARTLETT
Royal
Victoria Park
MARLBOROUGH LN.
ROYAL AVE.
THE CIRCUS
GAY ST.
GEORGE
(A-4) UPPER BRISTOL RD.
To Bristol & Cardiff
JANE AUSTEN CENTRE
CHARLOTTE STREET
Queen Square
JOHN ST.
CRESCENT GDNS.
CHARLOTTE ST.
MONMOUTH PL.
WOOD ST.
QUEEN ST.
TRIM ST.
BEAUFORD SQ.
SAW CL.
NEW KING ST.
CHARLES ST.
MONMOUTH ST.
PRINCES ST.
THEATRE ROYAL
ST. JOHN'S PL.
WESTGATE BLDGS.
BRIDEWELL LN.
Tiny Arrows (→) Indicate One Way Streets
FARMERS' MARKET
Kingsmead Square
JAMES ST. WEST
NEW ST.
CHANDOS
BILBURY CL.
AVON ST.
MILK ST.
GREEN PARK ROAD
CORN ST.
LOWER BRISTOL ROAD
River Avon
To Wells & Glastonbury
LOWER BRISTOL ROAD (A-36)
WELLS ROAD (A-367)

1 Marlborough House
2 Brooks Guesthouse
3 Brocks Guest House
4 Parkside Guest House
5 Cornerways B&B
6 Villa Magdala
7 The Kennard
8 The Ayrlington
9 14 Raby Place
10 Apple Tree Guesthouse
11 Three Abbey Green Guest House
12 Harington's Hotel
13 Abbey House Apartments
14 Pratt's Hotel
15 The Henry Guest House
16 YMCA
17 White Hart Hostel
18 St. Christopher's Inn
19 Spruce Goose Launderette
20 Library (Internet Access)
21 Topping & Company Bookstore

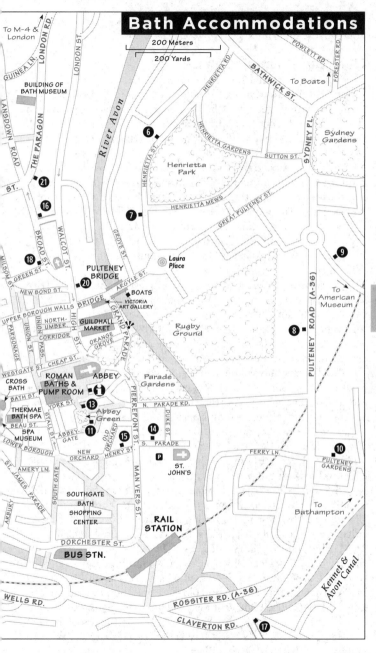

Bath Accommodations

200 Meters
200 Yards

To M-4 & London

GUINEA LN.

LONDON RD.

LONDON ST.

LANSDOWN ROAD

THE PARAGON

BUILDING OF BATH MUSEUM

River Avon

POWLETT RD.

FORESTER RD.

BATHWICK ST.

To Boats

HENRIETTA RD.

6

HENRIETTA ST.

Henrietta Park

HENRIETTA GARDENS

SUTTON ST.

SYDNEY PL.

Sydney Gardens

ST.

21

16

WALCOT ST.

GROVE ST.

7

HENRIETTA MEWS

GREAT PULTENEY ST.

BROAD ST.

18

GREEN ST.

NEW BOND ST.

PULTENEY BRIDGE

ARGYLE ST.

20

BRIDGE

Laura Place

BOATS

VICTORIA ART GALLERY

9

PULTENEY ROAD (A-36)

To American Museum

MILSOM ST.

UPPER BOROUGH WALLS

UNION ST.

HIGH ST.

GUILDHALL MARKET

NORTH-UMBER.

GRAND PARADE

Rugby Ground

8

PARSONAGE

CORRIDOR

ORANGE GROVE

CHEAP ST.

WESTGATE ST.

CROSS BATH

BATH ST.

ROMAN BATHS & PUMP ROOM

ABBEY

Parade Gardens

PIERREPONT ST.

N. PARADE RD.

THERMAE BATH SPA

BEAU ST.

YORK ST.

13

Abbey Green

DUKE ST.

14

SPA MUSEUM

LOWER BOROUGH

ABBEY GATE

11

STALL ST.

OLD ORCHARD

15

S. PARADE

FERRY LN.

10

PULTENEY GARDENS

ST. JAMES'S PARADE

AMERY LN.

SOUTH GATE

NEW ORCHARD

HENRY ST.

MAN VERS ST.

P

ST. JOHN'S

ARBURY

SOUTHGATE BATH SHOPPING CENTER

RAIL STATION

To Bathampton

DORCHESTER ST.

WELLS RD.

BUS STN.

Kennet & Avon Canal

ROSSITER RD. (A-36)

CLAVERTON RD.

17

BATH

page 491, or ask your hotelier. Almost every place provides Wi-Fi at no charge to its guests.

Near the Royal Crescent

These listings are all a 15-minute uphill walk or an easy £4-5 taxi ride from the train station. Or take any hop-on, hop-off bus tour from the station, get off at the stop nearest your accommodation (likely Royal Avenue—confirm with driver), check in, then finish the tour later in the day. The Marlborough Lane places have easier parking but are less centrally located.

$$$ Marlborough House, exuberantly run by Peter, mixes modern style with antique furnishings and features a welcoming breakfast room with an open kitchen. Each of the six rooms comes with a sip of sherry (Sb-£70-95, Db-£85-125, Tb-£95-135, organic vegetarian breakfasts and toiletries, free Wi-Fi, free parking, some street noise, 1 Marlborough Lane, tel. 01225/318-175, fax 01225/466-127, www.marlborough-house.net, mars@manque .dircon.co.uk).

$$$ Brooks Guesthouse is the biggest of the bunch, with 21 modern rooms and classy Victorian public spaces (Sb-£59-89, Db-£80-120, Tb-£109-150, great breakfasts with non-traditional and vegetarian options, free Wi-Fi, 1 Crescent Gardens, Upper Bristol Road, tel. 01225/425-543, www.brooksguesthouse.com, info@brooksguesthouse.com, Andrew and Carla).

$$ Brocks Guest House has six rooms in a Georgian townhouse built by John Wood in 1765. Located between the prestigious Royal Crescent and the courtly Circus, it has been redone in a way that would make the great architect proud (standard Db-£79-85, superior Db-£87-95, family room-£115-125, higher rates are for Fri-Sat, free Wi-Fi, little top-floor library, 32 Brock Street, tel. 01225/338-374, fax 01225/334-245, www.brocksguesthouse.co.uk, brocks@brocksguesthouse.co.uk, Richard).

$$ Parkside Guest House has five large, thoughtfully appointed Edwardian rooms. It's tidy, clean, homey, and well priced—and has a spacious back garden (Sb-£60, Db-£80, these prices are for Rick Steves readers, free Wi-Fi, limited free parking, 11 Marlborough Lane, tel. & fax 01225/429-444, www.parkside bandb.co.uk, post@parksidebandb.co.uk, kind Inge Lynall).

$$ Cornerways B&B, located on a noisy street, is simple and well worn, with three rooms and old-fashioned homey touches (Sb-£45-55, Db-£65-75, 15 percent discount with this book and 3-night stay in 2012, free Wi-Fi, DVD library, free parking, 47 Crescent Gardens, tel. 01225/422-382, www.cornerwaysbath.co.uk, info @cornerwaysbath.co.uk, Sue Black).

East of the River

These listings are a 10-minute walk from the city center. While generally a better value, they are not quite as conveniently located.

$$$ Villa Magdala rents 18 stately, hotelesque rooms in a freestanding Victorian townhouse opposite a park. In a city that's so insistently Georgian, it's fun to stay in a mansion that's Victorian (Db-£120-140 depending on size and demand, family rooms, inviting lounge, free Wi-Fi, free parking, in quiet residential area on Henrietta Street, tel. 01225/466-329, fax 01225/483-207, www .villamagdala.co.uk, enquiries@villamagdala.co.uk).

$$$ The Kennard, with 12 rooms immaculately maintained by proud owners Giovanni and Mary Baiano, is a short walk through a genteel neighborhood from the Pulteney Bridge. Each of the rooms is different, but all are colorfully and elaborately decorated (prices are for Sun-Thu/Fri-Sat: S-£65/£70, Sb-£89/£120, Db-£110/£130, Tb-£150/£180, free Wi-Fi, free street parking permits, thoughtfully planned Georgian garden out back, 11 Henrietta Street, tel. 01225/310-472, fax 01225/460-054, www .kennard.co.uk, reception@kennard.co.uk).

$$$ The Ayrlington, next door to a lawn-bowling green, has 16 attractive rooms with Asian decor and hints of a more genteel time. Though this well-maintained hotel fronts a busy street, it's reasonably quiet and tranquil. Rooms in the back have pleasant views of sports greens and Bath beyond. For the best value, request a standard top-floor double with a view of Bath (twin Db-£80-100, standard Db-£100-125, superior Db-£120-150, big deluxe Db-£130-170, higher price is for Fri-Sun, free Wi-Fi, fine garden, free and easy parking, 24-25 Pulteney Road, tel. 01225/425-495, fax 01225/469-029, www.ayrlington.com, mail@ayrlington.com, Ling Roper).

$$ 14 Raby Place is a good value, mixing Georgian glamour with homey warmth and modern, artistic taste within its five rooms. Muriel Guy keeps things simple and endearingly friendly. She's a fun-loving live wire who serves organic food for breakfast (S with private bathroom on the hall-£35, Db-£75, Tb-£80, cash only; 14 Raby Place—go over bridge on North Parade Road, left on Pulteney Road, cross to church, Raby Place is first row of houses on hill; tel. 01225/465-120, murieljean guy@gmail.com).

$$ Apple Tree Guesthouse offers six comfortable rooms near a shady canal (Sb-£55-66, Db-£85-110, Tb-£120-132, 2-night minimum Fri-Sat nights, free Wi-Fi, free parking, 7 Pulteney Gardens, tel. 01225/337-672, www.appletreeguesthouse.com, enquiries@appletreeguesthouse.co.uk, Les and Lynsay Redwood).

In the Town Center

You'll pay a premium to sleep right in the center. And, since Bath is so pleasant and manageable by foot, a downtown location isn't essential. Still, these are particularly well located.

$$$ Three Abbey Green Guest House, with seven rooms, is bright, cheery, and located in a quiet, traffic-free courtyard only 50 yards from the abbey and the Roman Baths. Its spacious rooms are a fine value (Db-£95-145, four-poster Db-£145-180, family rooms-£140-200, price depends on season and size of room, 2-night minimum on weekends, free Internet access and Wi-Fi, tel. 01225/428-558, www.threeabbeygreen.com, stay@threeabbey green.com; Sue, Derek, and daughter Nicola). They also rent self-catering apartments (Db-£140-160, Qb-£170-200, 2-night minimum).

$$$ Harington's Hotel rents 13 fresh, modern rooms on a quiet street in the town center. This stylish place feels like a boutique hotel, but with a friendlier, laid-back vibe (Sb-£79-155, standard Db-£88-145, superior Db-£98-155, large superior Db-£108-165, Tb-£138-195, prices vary substantially depending on demand, free Wi-Fi, 10 Queen Street, tel. 01225/461-728, fax 01225/444-804, www.haringtonshotel.co.uk, post@haringtons hotel.co.uk). Melissa and Peter offer a 5 percent discount with this book for two-night stays except on Fridays, Saturdays, and holidays. They also rent two self-catering apartments down the street—one can sleep up to three (Db-£125, Tb-£145), and the other can sleep up to eight (prices on request; for apartments: 2-night minimum on weekdays, 3-night minimum on weekends).

$$$ Abbey House Apartments consist of five flats on Abbey Green and several others scattered around town—all tastefully restored by Laura (who, once upon a time, was a San Francisco rock musician). The apartments called Abbey View and Abbey Green (which comes with a washer and dryer) have views of the abbey from their nicely equipped kitchens. These are especially practical and economical if you plan on cooking. Laura provides everything you need for simple breakfasts, and it's fun and cheap to stock the fridge or get take-away for a meal in your flat. When Laura meets you to give you the keys, you become a local (Sb-£90, Db-£100-175, price depends on size, 2-night minimum, rooms can sleep four with Murphy and sofa beds, apartments clearly described on website, free Wi-Fi, Abbey Green, tel. 01225/464-238, www.laurastownhouseapartments.co.uk, laura@laurastown houseapartments.co.uk).

$$$ Pratt's Hotel is as proper and olde English as you'll find in Bath. Its creaks and frays are aristocratic, and even its public places make you want to sip a brandy. The 46 rooms show their age a bit, but are comfy and spacious. Since it's near a busy street,

BATH

occasionally it can get noisy—request a quiet room, away from the street (Sb-£60-100, Db-£90-140, price depends on demand, breakfast-£10, check website for current rates and specials, dogs £7.50—but children under 15 free with 2 adults, elevator, pay Wi-Fi, attached restaurant-bar, 4-6 South Parade, tel. 01225/460-441, fax 01225/448-807, www.forestdale.com, pratts@forestdale .com).

$$$ The Henry Guest House is a simple, vertical place, renting eight clean rooms. It's friendly, well run, and just two blocks from the train station (Sb-£60-65, Db-£100-110, higher prices are for bigger "premier" rooms, extra bed-£15, family room-£155, 2-night minimum on weekends, free Wi-Fi, 6 Henry Street, tel. 01225/424-052, www.thehenry.com, stay@thehenry.com). Steve and Liz also rent two self-catering apartments nearby that sleep up to eight with roll-away beds and a sleeper couch (email them for rates).

Bargain Accommodations

Bath's Best Budget Beds: **$** The **YMCA**, centrally located on a leafy square, has 210 beds in industrial-strength rooms—all with sinks and minimal furnishings. Although it smells a little like a gym, this place is a godsend for budget travelers—safe, secure, quiet, and efficiently run. With lots of twin rooms and no double beds, this is the only easily accessible budget option in downtown Bath (rates for Sun-Thu/Fri-Sat: S-£31/£35, twin D-£53/£59, T-£65/£74, Q-£76/£88, dorm beds-£18/£20, WCs and showers down the hall, includes continental breakfast, cooked breakfast-£2.50, cheap lunches, free linens, rental towels, lockers, pay Internet access, free Wi-Fi, laundry facilities, down a tiny alley off Broad Street on Broad Street Place, tel. 01225/325-900, fax 01225/462-065, www .bathymca.co.uk, stay@bathymca.co.uk).

Sloppy Backpacker Dorms: **$ White Hart Hostel** is a friendly and colorful nine-room place offering adults and families good, cheap beds in two- to six-bed dorms (£15/bed, S-£25, D-£40, Db-£50-70, kitchen, fine garden out back, 5-minute walk behind the train station at Widcombe—where Widcombe Hill hits Claverton Street, tel. 01225/313-985, www.whitehartbath .co.uk). The White Hart also has a pub with a reputation for good, although not cheap, food. **$ St. Christopher's Inn,** in a prime central location, is part of a chain of low-priced, high-energy hubs for backpackers looking for beds and brews. Their beds are so cheap because they know you'll spend money on their beer. The inn sits above the lively, youthful Belushi's pub, which is where you'll find the reception (54 beds in 6- to 12-bed rooms-£15-25, D-£52-60, higher prices are for weekends and walk-ins—it's always cheaper to book online, check website for specials, no guests under 18, pay

Internet access, free Wi-Fi, laundry facilities, lounge, 9 Green Street, tel. 01225/481-444, www.st-christophers.co.uk).

Eating in Bath

Bath is bursting with eateries. There's something for every appetite and budget—just stroll around the center of town. A picnic dinner of deli food or take-out fish-and-chips in the Royal Crescent Park or down by the river is ideal for aristocratic hoboes. The restaurants I recommend are small and popular—reserve a table on Friday and Saturday evenings. Most pricey little bistros offer big savings with their two- and three-course lunches and "pre-theatre" specials. In general, you can get two courses for £10 at lunch or £12 in the early evening (compared to £15 for a main course after 18:30 or 19:00). Restaurants advertise their early-bird specials, and as long as you order within the time window, you're in for a cheap meal.

Romantic, Upscale French and English

Tilleys Bistro serves healthy French, English, and vegetarian meals with candlelit ambience. Owners Dawn and Dave make you feel as if you are guests at a dinner party in their elegant living room. Their fun menu lets you build your own meal, beginning with an interesting array of £6-9 starters. Cap things off with the cheese plate and a glass of the house port, a passion of Dave's. While it's pricey and the portions are modest, this is a memorable splurge (£10-19 main courses; lunch specials: £12.50/2 courses, £15/3 courses; Mon-Sat 12:00-14:30 & 18:00-22:30, Sun 18:00-21:00 only, reservations smart, 3 North Parade Passage, tel. 01225/484-200).

The Garrick's Head is an elegantly simple gastropub right around the corner from the Theatre Royal, with a pricey restaurant on one side and a bar serving affordable snacks on the other. You're welcome to eat from the bar menu, even if you're in the fancy dining room or outside enjoying some great people-watching. The word on the street: The fish-and-chips here are the best in town (£6-10 pub grub, £11-16 main courses on the fancier menu, Mon-Sat 11:00-22:00, Sun 12:00-22:00, drinks until later, 8 St. John's Place, tel. 01225/318-368).

The Circus Café and Restaurant is a relaxing little eatery serving well-executed English cuisine with European flair. Choose between the minimalist modern interior—with seating on the main floor or in the cellar—and the four tables on the peaceful street connecting the Circus and the Royal Crescent (£8 lunches, £7 starters and £13 main courses at dinner, open Mon-Sat 10:00-24:00, closed Sun, reservations smart, 34 Brock Street, tel. 01225/466-020).

Casanis French Bistro-Restaurant is a local hit. Chef Laurent, who hails from Nice, cooks "authentic Provençal cuisine" from the south of France, while his wife, Jill, serves. The decor matches the cuisine—informal, relaxed, simple, and top quality. The intimate Georgian dining room upstairs is a bit nicer and more spacious than the ground floor (lunch specials: £13.50/2 courses, £17/3 courses; dinner special available 18:00-19:00: £17/2 courses, £21/3 courses; open Tue-Sat 12:00-14:00 & 18:00-22:00, closed Sun-Mon, immediately behind the Assembly Rooms at 4 Saville Row, tel. 01225/780-055).

Casual Alternatives

Whether ethnic food or vegetarian, there are plenty of ways to get some fun culinary variation in this town.

Demuths Vegetarian Restaurant is highly rated and ideal for the well-heeled vegetarian. Its tight, stark, understated interior comes with a vegan vibe (£6-11 lunches, £7 starters and £13-15 main courses at dinner, daily 12:00-15:30 & 17:00-21:30, 2 North Parade Passage, tel. 01225/446-059).

Yen Sushi is your basic little sushi bar—plain and sterile, with stools facing a conveyor belt that constantly tempts you with a variety of freshly made delights on color-coded plates. When you're done, the waitstaff will tally your plates and give you the bill (£1.50-4 plates, you can fill up for £12 or so, daily 12:00-15:00 & 17:30-22:30, 11 Bartlett Street, tel. 01225/333-313).

Martini Restaurant, a hopping, purely Italian place, has class and jovial waiters (£9-12 pastas and pizzas, £14-19 meat and fish dishes, daily 12:00-14:30 & 18:00-22:30, open all day long on Sat, plenty of veggie options, daily fish specials, extensive wine list, reservations smart on weekends, 9 George Street, tel. 01225/460-818; Nunzio, Franco, and chef Luigi).

Rajpoot Tandoori serves—by all assessments—the best Indian food in Bath. You'll hike down deep into a sprawling cellar, where the plush Indian atmosphere and award-winning cooking make paying the extra pounds palatable. The seating is tight and the ceilings low, but it's air-conditioned (£8.25 three-course lunch special, £9-11 main courses; figure £20 per person with rice, naan, and drink; daily 12:00-14:30 & 18:00-23:00, 4 Argyle Street, tel. 01225/466-833, Ali).

Thai Balcony Restaurant's open, spacious interior is so plush, it'll have you wondering, "Where's the Thai wedding?" While locals debate which of Bath's handful of Thai restaurants serves the best food or offers the lowest prices, there's no doubt that Thai Balcony's fun and elegant atmosphere makes for a memorable and enjoyable dinner (£9 two-course lunch special, £8-10 plates, daily 12:00-14:00 & 18:00-22:00, reservations smart on weekends, Saw Close, tel. 01225/444-450).

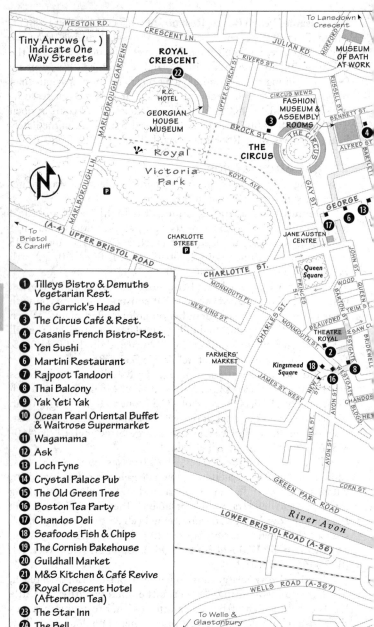

Tiny Arrows (→)
Indicate One
Way Streets

BATH

1. Tilleys Bistro & Demuths
   Vegetarian Rest.
2. The Garrick's Head
3. The Circus Café & Rest.
4. Casanis French Bistro-Rest.
5. Yen Sushi
6. Martini Restaurant
7. Rajpoot Tandoori
8. Thai Balcony
9. Yak Yeti Yak
10. Ocean Pearl Oriental Buffet
    & Waitrose Supermarket
11. Wagamama
12. Ask
13. Loch Fyne
14. Crystal Palace Pub
15. The Old Green Tree
16. Boston Tea Party
17. Chandos Deli
18. Seafoods Fish & Chips
19. The Cornish Bakehouse
20. Guildhall Market
21. M&S Kitchen & Café Revive
22. Royal Crescent Hotel
    (Afternoon Tea)
23. The Star Inn
24. The Bell

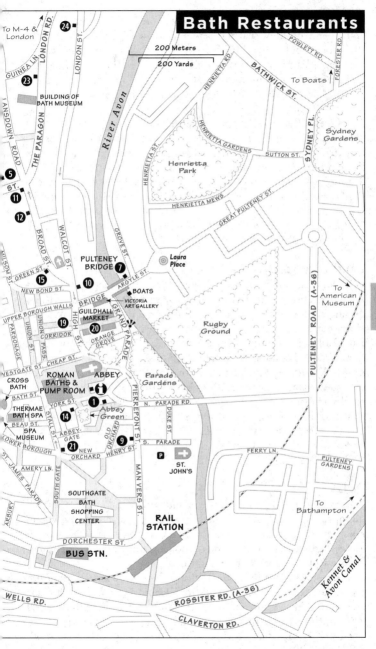

Bath Restaurants

To M-4 & London

200 Meters

200 Yards

GUINEA LN.

LONDON RD.

LONDON ST.

THE PARAGON

❷❹

❷❸

BUILDING OF
BATH MUSEUM

LANSDOWN ROAD

River Avon

POWLETT RD.

FORESTER RD.

BATHWICK ST.

To Boats

HENRIETTA RD.

HENRIETTA GARDENS

SUTTON ST.

SYDNEY PL.

Sydney
Gardens

HENRIETTA ST.

Henrietta
Park

HENRIETTA MEWS

GREAT PULTENEY ST.

❺

❶❶

❶❷

ST.

BROAD ST.

WALCOT ST.

GROVE ST.

Laura
Place

UNION ST.

GREEN ST.

❶❺

NEW BOND ST.

PULTENEY
BRIDGE ❼

❶❶

ARGYLE ST.

BRIDGE ST.

BOATS

VICTORIA
ART GALLERY

UPPER BOROUGH WALLS

HIGH ST.

GUILDHALL
MARKET

GRAND PARADE

PULTENEY ROAD (A-36)

To
American
Museum

PARSONAGE

UNION PASS.

❶❾

CORRIDOR

❷⓿

ORANGE
GROVE

Rugby
Ground

VESTGATE ST.

CHEAP ST.

ROMAN
BATHS &
PUMP ROOM

ABBEY

❶

Parade
Gardens

CROSS
BATH

BATH ST.

YORK ST.

STALL ST.

❶❹

Abbey
Green

PIERREPONT ST.

N. PARADE RD.

THERMAE
BATH SPA

BEAU ST.

SPA
MUSEUM

LOWER BOROUGH

ABBEY
GATE

OLD ORCHARD ST.

❾

DUKE ST.

S. PARADE

FERRY LN.

PULTENEY
GARDENS

❷❶

NEW
ORCHARD

HENRY ST.

MANVERS ST.

P

ST.
JOHN'S

ST. JAMES PARADE

AMERY LN.

SOUTH GATE

SOUTHGATE
BATH
SHOPPING
CENTER

To Bathampton

ARBURY

DORCHESTER ST.

RAIL
STATION

BUS STN.

WELLS RD.

ROSSITER RD. (A-36)

CLAVERTON RD.

Kennet &
Avon Canal

BATH

Yak Yeti Yak is a fun Nepalese restaurant, with both Western and sit-on-the-floor seating. Sera and his wife, Sarah, along with their cheerful, hardworking Nepali team, cook up great traditional food (and plenty of vegetarian plates) at prices that would delight a sherpa (£7-9 lunches, £5 veggie plates, £8-9 meat plates, daily 12:00-14:30 & 17:00-22:30, downstairs at 12 Pierrepont Street, tel. 01225/442-299).

Ocean Pearl Oriental Buffet, inside a shopping mall food court, is famous for being the restaurant Asian tourists eat at repeatedly. It offers a practical, 40-dish, all-you-can-eat buffet in the modern Podium Shopping Centre and spacious seating in a dining hall overlooking the river. You'll pay £6.50 for lunch and £11.50 for dinner. But it's best for take-away—fill up a box for just £3.50 at lunch or £4.50 at dinner (daily 12:00-15:00 & 18:00-22:30, in the Podium Shopping Centre on Northgate Street, tel. 01225/331-238).

Chain Restaurants

With so many homegrown favorites, I see little reason to frequent a chain restaurant in Bath. But if you're a fan, you'll find three decent choices (all of which can be found throughout Britain): **Wagamama** specializes in pan-Asian cuisine (£7-9 meals, Mon-Sat 12:00-23:00, Sun 12:00-22:00, 1 York Buildings, corner of George and Broad streets, tel. 01225/337-314, www.wagamama .com); **Ask** dishes up Italian comfort food (£8-10 pizzas and pastas, good salads, daily 12:00-23:00, George Street but entrance on Broad Street, tel. 01225/789-997); and **Loch Fyne,** a bright, youthful, high-energy place serves fresh fish at reasonable prices in what was once a lavish bank building (£10-18 meals, £10 two-course special from lunch until 19:00 on weekdays, daily 12:00-22:30, 24 Milsom Street, tel. 01225/750-120).

Pubs

Bath is not a good pub-grub town, and with so many other tempting options, eating at a pub here isn't as appealing as elsewhere. For the best pub grub, head for **The Garrick's Head** gastropub (described earlier). But if you're looking for a more traditional, lowbrow place, consider these options.

Crystal Palace Pub is an inviting place just a block away from the abbey, facing the delightful little Abbey Green. With a focus on food rather than drink, they serve "pub grub with a Continental flair" in three different spaces, including a picnic-table back patio (£9-12 meals, food served Mon-Fri 11:00-21:00, Sat 11:00-20:00, Sun 12:00-20:00, last orders for drinks at 23:00, no kids after 16:30, Abbey Green, tel. 01225/482-666).

The **Old Green Tree,** in the old town center, serves satisfying lunches to locals in a characteristic pub setting (real ales on tap, £6-7 sandwiches, £9 meals, lunch served Mon-Sat 12:00-15:00 only, open daily for drinks, no children, can be crowded on weekend nights, 12 Green Street, tel. 01225/448-259).

For a pub to drink and hang out in, rather than eat at, check out **The Star Inn** or **The Bell** (described on page 508).

Simple Options

For a fast, handy, and tasty meal on the go, try one of these easy places. If you get take-away (possible at most of these), you can munch your picnic while watching street musicians from a bench on the abbey square.

The **Boston Tea Party** chain is what Starbucks aspires to be—the neighborhood coffeehouse and hangout. Its extensive breakfasts, light lunches, and salads are fresh and healthy. The outdoor seating overlooks a busy square. They also host musical events, and their walls are decorated with works by local artists (£3-7 breakfasts, £5-7 lunches, Mon-Sat 7:30-19:00, Sun 9:00-19:00, free Wi-Fi, 19 Kingsmead Square, tel. 01225/313-901).

Chandos Deli has good coffee and tasty £3-5 sandwiches made on artisan breads. This upscale but casual five-table place serves breakfast pastries and lunch to dedicated foodies who don't want to pay too much (Mon-Sat 9:00-17:30, Sun 11:00-17:00, 12 George Street, tel. 01225/314-418).

Seafoods Fish & Chips is respected by lovers of greasy fried fish in Bath. There's diner-style and outdoor seating, or you can get your food to go for a bit cheaper (£4-5 take-away meals, Mon-Sat 11:30-22:00, closed Sun, 38 Kingsmead Square, tel. 01225/465-190).

The **Cornish Bakehouse,** tucked down a shopping gallery across from the Guildhall Market, has freshly baked £3 take-away pasties (Mon-Sat 8:30-17:30, Sun 10:00-17:00, off High Street at 11A The Corridor, tel. 01225/426-635).

Produce Market and Café: **Guildhall Market,** across from Pulteney Bridge, has produce stalls with food for picnickers. At its inexpensive **Market Café,** you can slurp a curry or sip a tea while surrounded by stacks of used books, bananas on the push list, and honest-to-goodness old-time locals (£3-5 traditional English meals including fried breakfasts all day, Mon-Sat 8:00-17:00, closed Sun, tel. 01225/461-593 a block north of the abbey, on High Street).

Supermarkets: **Waitrose,** at the Podium Shopping Centre, is great for picnics and has a good salad bar (Mon-Fri 8:30-20:00, Sat 8:30-19:00, Sun 11:00-17:00, just west of Pulteney Bridge and across from post office on High Street). **Marks & Spencer,** near the train station, has a grocery at the back of its department store and two eateries: **M&S Kitchen** on the ground floor and the pleasant, inexpensive **Café Revive** on the top floor (Mon-Fri 8:30-19:00, Sat 8:30-18:00, Sun 11:00-17:00, 16-18 Stall Street).

Bath Connections

Bath's train station is called Bath Spa (toll tel. 0845-748-4950). The National Express bus station is just west of the train station (bus info toll tel. 0871-781-8181, www.nationalexpress.com). For all public bus services in southwestern England, see www.travelinesw.com.

From Bath to London: You can catch a **train** to London's Paddington Station (2/hour, 1.5 hours, best deals for travel after 9:30 and when purchased in advance, www.firstgreatwestern.co.uk), or save money—but not time—by taking the National Express **bus** to Victoria Coach Station (direct buses nearly hourly, 2.5-3.75 hours, sample fares: one-way-£22, round-trip-£29).

From Bath to London's Airports: You can reach **Heathrow** directly and easily by National Express bus (10/day, 2-4 hours, £19-42 one-way, toll tel. 0871-781-8181, www.nationalexpress.com) or by a train-and-bus combination (take twice-hourly train to Reading, catch twice-hourly airport shuttle bus from there, allow 2.5 hours total, £50-65 depending on time of day, about £10 cheaper when bought in advance, BritRail passholders just pay £15 for bus). Or take the Celtic Horizons minibus to Heathrow (see page 494).

You can get to **Gatwick** by train (about hourly, 2.5 hours, £48-58 one-way depending on time of day, cheaper in advance, transfer in Reading) or by bus (10/day, 4-5 hours, £25 one-way, transfer at Heathrow Airport).

Between Bristol Airport and Bath: Located about 20 miles west of Bath, this airport is closer than Heathrow, but they haven't worked out good connections to Bath yet. From Bristol Airport, your most convenient options are to take a taxi (£35) or call Alan Price (see "Celtic Horizons" on page 494). Otherwise, at the airport you can hop aboard the Bristol Airport Flyer (bus #A1), which takes you to the Temple Meads train station in Bristol (£7, 2-6/hour, 30 minutes, buy bus ticket at airport info counter or from driver, tell driver you want the Temple Meads train station). At the Temple Meads Station, check the departure boards for trains going to the Bath Spa train station (4/hour, 15 minutes, £6). To get from Bath to Bristol Airport, take the train to Temple Meads, then catch the Bristol Airport Flyer bus.

GREAT BRITAIN PAST AND PRESENT

Britain was created by force and held together by force. It's really a nation of the 19th century, when this rich Victorian-era empire reached its financial peak. Its traditional industry, buildings, and the popularity of the notion of "Great" Britain are a product of its past wealth.

To best understand the many fascinating tour guides you'll encounter in your travels, have a basic handle on the sweeping story of this land and its capital, London. (Generally speaking, the nice and bad stories guides tell are not true...and the boring ones are.)

London's Major Historical Periods

Invasions (2000 B.C.-A.D. 1066)

The mysterious Stonehenge builders were replaced by the Celts,  whose druid priests made human sacrifices and worshipped nature.

The Romans brought 500 years of peace and stability, establishing London (Londinium) as a major city. Then civilization fell for a thousand years to German pirates (Angles and Saxons), Danish Vikings, and, finally, William the Conqueror (A.D. 1066). During these Dark Ages, Christians battled pagans for supremacy on the island.

Notables

People: Boadicea, Julius Caesar, "King Arthur," "Beowulf," Alfred the Great

Sights: Boadicea statue, Roman Wall, Lindisfarne Gospels

Wars with France, Wars of the Roses (1066-1500)

French-speaking kings ruled England, and English-speaking kings invaded France as the two budding nations defined their modern borders. In the 1400s, feuding English nobles duked it out for control of the country.

Notables

People: Richard the Lionhearted, Robin Hood, Eleanor of Aquitaine, Geoffrey Chaucer, Joan of Arc

Sights: Tower of London, Magna Carta at the British Library, Westminster Abbey, Temple Church

The Tudor Renaissance (1500s)

Powerful Henry VIII thrust England onto the world stage by defying the pope and sparking a century of Protestant/Catholic warfare. His daughter, Elizabeth I, reigned over a cultural renaissance of sea exploration, scientific discovery, and literature known as the "Elizabethan Age."

Notables

People: Anne Boleyn, Thomas More, Bloody Mary, William Shakespeare, Sir Francis Drake, Sir Walter Raleigh

Sights: Shakespeare First Folio at the British Library, Shakespeare's Globe, Tower of London execution site, Chapel of Henry VII and Elizabeth I's tomb in Westminster Abbey, portraits of Henry VIII's wives and daughter Elizabeth in the National Portrait Gallery, King's College Chapel in Cambridge

Kings vs. Parliament (1600s)

The "Virgin Queen" Elizabeth died without heirs, and the Crown passed to the Stuart family. Their arrogant, divine-right management style sparked a civil war, led by the commoner Oliver Cromwell, who beheaded the king and briefly established a republic called the Commonwealth of England. The monarchy returned, along with back-to-back disasters—first the Great Plague (1665) and then the Great Fire (1666) that leveled London.

Notables

People: King James I (Bible), Charles I (headless), Christopher Wren (St. Paul's Cathedral), Isaac Newton (apple)

Sights: St. Paul's and other Wren churches, the Monument, City of London, Banqueting House, crown jewels, King James Bible at the British Library

Colonial Expansion (1700s)

Britannia ruled the waves and became a world power, exploiting the wealth of India, Africa, Australia, and America...at least until the Yanks revolted in the "American War."

Notables

People: King George III, James Cook, George Frideric Handel, Admiral Nelson, Duke of Wellington

Sights: Portraits by Reynolds and Gainsborough in the Tate Britain, Royal Observatory Greenwich, Georgian architecture in Bath

Victorian Gentility and the Industrial Revolution (1800s)

Britain under Queen Victoria reigned supreme, steaming into the modern age with railroads, factories, electricity, telephones, and the first Underground. Meanwhile, Romantic poets longed for the innocence of nature, Charles Dickens questioned the social order, and Rudyard Kipling criticized the colonial system.

Notables

People: Lord Byron, William Wordsworth, John Keats, Percy Shelley, Samuel Taylor Coleridge, William Blake, the Brontë sisters, Jane Austen, James Watt, Charles Darwin, Alfred Lord Tennyson, "Sherlock Holmes," Jack the Ripper

Sights: Big Ben and Houses of Parliament, Buckingham Palace,

The Mall, Hyde Park, the Tube, writers' manuscripts in the British Library, Poets' Corner in Westminster Abbey

World Wars and Recovery (20th Century)

Two world wars whittled Britain down from a world empire to an island chain struggling to compete in a global economy. The German Blitz in World War II leveled eastern London. Colonies rebelled and gained their independence, then flooded London with immigrants. Longtime residents fled on the Tube for London's suburbs.

In the 1960s, "Swinging London" became a center for rock music, film, theater, youth culture, and Austin Powers-style joie de vivre. The 1970s brought massive unemployment and a conservative reaction in the 1980s and early 1990s.

Notables

People: T. E. Lawrence (of Arabia), Winston Churchill, Edward VIII and Wallis Simpson, George VI ("Bertie" of *The King's Speech* fame), T. S. Eliot (American-turned-British), Virginia Woolf, "James Bond," Dylan Thomas, C. S. Lewis, John/Paul/George/Ringo, the Rolling Stones, the Who, Elton John, David Bowie, Michael Caine, Douglas Adams, Stephen Hawking, Margaret Thatcher, John Major, Tony Blair, Martin Amis

Sights: Churchill War Rooms, Cenotaph, Westminster Abbey's Poets' Corner, Blitz photos at St. Paul's, Beatles memorabilia in the British Library, Imperial War Museum

London Today

London is one of the world's major cultural capitals, an exporter of art, science, and technology. In 2012, the city hosts the Olympics for the third time.

Notables

People: David Cameron, Helen Mirren, Judi Dench, J. K. Rowling, Tom Stoppard, Prince William and Kate, Daniel Radcliffe, Richard Branson, Emma Thompson, Nick Hornby, Ian McEwan, Zadie Smith, Rachel Whiteread, Jude Law, Stephen Fry, Ricky Gervais, Helena Bonham Carter, Amy Winehouse, Robert Pattinson, Russell Brand

Sights: The London Eye, West End theaters, Tate Modern contemporary art exhibits, the Docklands skyscraper zone, Olympics 2012 facilities in Stratford district

Timeline of London History

c. 1700 B.C. Stone slabs erected to create ceremonial site...
Stonehenge (90 miles southwest of London).

A.D. **43** Romans defeat the Celtic locals and establish
Londinium as a seaport. They build the original
London Bridge and a city wall, encompassing one
square mile, which sets the city boundaries for 1,500
years.

c. 60 Boadicea defies the Romans and burns Londinium
before the revolt is squelched.

c. 200 London is the thriving, river-trading, walled, Latin-
speaking capital of Roman-dominated England.

410 The city of Rome is looted by invaders, and the
Europe-wide Roman infrastructure crumbles.
England is soon overrun by "barbarian" Anglo-
Saxon invaders from Germany. This begins 500 years
of Viking invasions, poverty, ignorance, superstition,
and hand-me-down leotards—the Dark Ages.

886 King Alfred the Great liberates London from
Danish Vikings; he helps reunite England,
re-establish Christianity, and encourage learning.

1052 King Edward the Confessor builds his palace
and abbey a mile and a half from London at
Westminster.

1066 England is conquered by Norman invaders under
William the Conqueror, beginning two centuries
of rule by French-speaking kings. London reasserts
itself as a trade center.

1209 London Bridge—the famous stone version, topped
with houses—is built. It stands until 1832.

1215 King John, under pressure from barons and London's
powerful trade guilds, signs the Magna Carta,
establishing that even kings must follow the rule of
law.

1280 Old St. Paul's Cathedral is finished.

1337 Start of the Hundred Years' War with France.

1348 The Black Death (bubonic plague) kills half of
London.

1415 British victory over the French at Battle of
Agincourt.

1455-1485 Prosperous London plays kingmaker in the Wars of
the Roses, helping determine which noble becomes
king.

1500 London's population swells to 50,000.

1534 Henry VIII breaks with Rome and dissolves

monasteries, bringing religious strife. Generally speaking, London leans to the Protestant side.

1558 Elizabeth I is crowned, with London's backing. Her reign brings a renaissance of theater (Shakespeare), literature, science, discovery, and manners to the city.

1588 England's navy defeats the powerful Spanish Armada and starts to rule the waves. Overseas trade brings the world's wealth directly to London's wharves.

1600 London, population 200,000, is Europe's largest city, expanding beyond the medieval walls, stretching westward along the river to Charing Cross.

1649 King Charles I is beheaded outside Whitehall as London backs the Protestant Parliament in England's Civil War (1642-1648). Oliver Cromwell heads a democratic commonwealth (1649-1653) and then becomes Lord Protector (1653-1659).

1660 Charles II, son of Charles I, is invited to restore the monarchy.

1665 The Great Plague kills 100,000.

1666 The Great Fire rages for four days, destroying the wooden city. The city is rebuilt in stone, including Christopher Wren's new St. Paul's Cathedral and other churches.

1700 London's population is 500,000 and growing fast. One in seven Brits lives in London.

1702 London's first daily newspapers hit the streets.

1776 Britain fights 13 of its colonies—and France—in the American War of Independence (1775-1783).

1789 The French Revolution sparks more decades of war between Britain and France.

1805 Admiral Nelson defeats the French navy at Trafalgar (Spain), ending the threat of invasion by Napoleon.

1815 The Duke of Wellington defeats Napoleon for good at Waterloo (Belgium). Britain becomes Europe's No. 1 power.

c. 1830 Railroads begin to lace the country together. The Industrial Revolution kicks into high gear.

1837 Eighteen-year-old Victoria becomes queen, soon marries Prince Albert, and presides over an era of peace and middle-class values.

1851 With Britain at the peak of prosperity from its worldwide colonial empire, London—population one million—hosts a Great Exhibition in Hyde Park, trumpeting the latest triumphs of science and technology.

1863   First Underground (Tube) line is built.

1914-1918   World War I. Britain, France, and other allies battle Germany mainly from trenches dug in the open fields of France and Belgium. Nearly a million British men die.

1936   King Edward VIII abdicates to marry an American commoner.

1939-1945   World War II.

1940-1941   The Blitz. Preparing to invade, Nazi Germany bombs Britain, particularly London. Despite enormous devastation, Britain holds firm.

1945   Postwar recovery begins, aided by the United States. Many cheap, concrete (ugly) buildings rise from the rubble. Britain begins granting independence to many foreign colonies.

1964   The Beatles tour America, spreading "Swinging London" hipness to the world.

1970s   Labor strikes, unemployment, and recession.

1973   Britain joins what is now called the European Union, but maintains her distance.

1980s   The Conservative administration of Margaret Thatcher rules.

1981   Prince Charles marries Lady Diana Spencer.

1982   Britain defeats Argentina, expelling the invaders from the Falkland Islands.

1994   Channel Tunnel ("Chunnel") opens, linking London with Paris and Brussels.

1997   Tony Blair becomes prime minister, signaling a shift toward moderate liberalism. Princess Diana dies in a car crash in Paris. The nation—and the world—mourns.

2002   Many EU nations adopt the euro currency, but Britain sticks with the pound sterling.

2003   Britain joins America's "Coalition of the Willing," and invades Iraq, dividing the British people.

2005   Four terrorist bombs rock London on "7/7."

2007   Tony Blair steps down as prime minister, and Gordon Brown takes over. A bank run on Northern Rock, the country's fifth-biggest mortgage lender, marks the beginning of an economic downturn.

2010   After an extremely close election, embattled PM Gordon Brown loses his job to Conservative David Cameron.

2011   Prince William marries Kate Middleton—the first royal wedding in a generation, watched by billions around the world.

2012 London hosts the Summer Olympics, Queen Elizabeth II celebrates her 60-year Diamond Jubilee...and you visit Britain to make your own history.

Basic British History for the Traveler

When Julius Caesar landed on the misty and mysterious isle of Britain in 55 B.C., England entered the history books. The primitive Celtic tribes he conquered were themselves invaders (who had earlier conquered the even more mysterious people who built Stonehenge). The Romans built towns and roads, establishing their capital at Londinium. The Celtic natives in Scotland and Wales—consisting of Gaels, Picts, and Scots—were not easily subdued. The Romans built Hadrian's Wall near the Scottish border as protection against their troublesome northern neighbors. Even today, the Celtic language and influence are strongest in these far reaches of Britain.

As Rome fell, so fell Roman Britain—a victim of invaders and internal troubles. Barbarian tribes from Germany and Denmark, called Angles and Saxons, swept through the southern part of the island, establishing Angle-land. These were the days of the real King Arthur, possibly a Christianized Roman general who fought valiantly—but in vain—against invading barbarians. In 793, England was hit with the first of two centuries of savage invasions by barbarians from Norway, called the Vikings or Norsemen. The island was plunged into 500 years of Dark Ages—wars, plagues, and poverty—lit only by the dim candle of a few learned Christian monks and missionaries trying to convert the barbarians. The sightseer sees little from this Anglo-Saxon period.

Modern England began with yet another invasion. William the Conqueror and his Norman troops crossed the English Channel from France in 1066. William crowned himself king in Westminster Abbey (where all subsequent coronations would take place) and began building the Tower of London. French-speaking Norman kings ruled the country for two centuries. Then followed two centuries of civil wars, with various noble families vying for the crown. In the bitterest feud, the York and Lancaster families fought the Wars of the Roses, so-called because of the white and red flowers the combatants chose as their symbols. Rife with battles, intrigues, and kings, nobles, and ladies imprisoned and executed in the Tower, it's a wonder the country survived its rulers.

England was finally united by the "third-party" Tudor family. Henry VIII, a Tudor, was England's Renaissance king. He was handsome, athletic, highly sexed, a poet, a scholar, and a musician. He was also arrogant, cruel, gluttonous, and paranoid. He went through six wives in 40 years, divorcing, imprisoning, or behead-

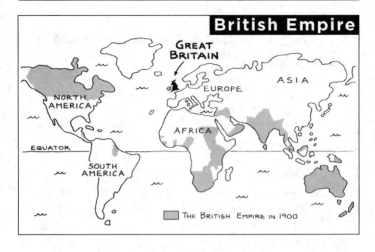

THE BRITISH EMPIRE IN 1900

ing them when they no longer suited his needs.

Henry "divorced" England from the Catholic Church, establishing the Protestant Church of England (the Anglican Church) and setting in motion years of religious squabbles. He also "dissolved" the monasteries (circa 1540), left just the shells of many formerly glorious abbeys dotting the countryside, and pocketed their land and wealth for the crown.

Henry's daughter, Queen Elizabeth I, who reigned for 45 years, made England a great trading and naval power (defeating the Spanish Armada) and presided over the Elizabethan era of great writers (such as William Shakespeare) and scientists (such as Sir Francis Bacon). But Elizabeth never married, so the English Parliament asked the Protestant ruler to the north, Scotland's King James (Elizabeth's first cousin twice removed), if he'd like to inherit the English throne. The two nations have been tied together ever since.

The longstanding quarrel between England's divine-right kings and Parliament's nobles finally erupted into a civil war (1643). Parliament forces under the Protestant Puritan farmer Oliver Cromwell defeated—and beheaded—King Charles I. This civil war left its mark on much of what you'll see in Britain. Eventually, Parliament invited Charles' son to take the throne. This "restoration of the monarchy" was accompanied by a great colonial expansion and the rebuilding of London (including Christopher Wren's St. Paul's Cathedral), which had been devastated by the Great Fire of 1666. Parliament gained ultimate authority over the throne when it deposed Catholic James II in 1688, guaranteeing a Protestant succession.

Britain grew as a naval superpower, colonizing and trading with all parts of the globe (although it lost its most important

Royal Families: Past and Present

Royal Lineage

802-1066	Saxon and Danish kings
1066-1154	Norman invasion (William the Conqueror), Norman kings
1154-1399	Plantagenet (kings with French roots)
1399-1461	Lancaster
1462-1485	York
1485-1603	Tudor (Henry VIII, Elizabeth I)
1603-1649	Stuart (civil war and beheading of Charles I)
1649-1653	Commonwealth, no royal head of state
1653-1659	Protectorate, with Cromwell as Lord Protector
1660-1714	Restoration of Stuart dynasty
1714-1901	Hanover (four Georges, Victoria)
1901-1910	Saxe-Coburg (Edward VII)
1910-present	Windsor (George V, Edward VIII, George VI, Elizabeth II)

The Royal Family Today

It seems you can't pick up a British newspaper without some mention of the latest scandal, event, or oddity involving the royal family. Here is the cast of characters:

Queen Elizabeth II wears the traditional crown of her great-great grandmother Victoria. (Elizabeth's late father, George VI, was the subject of the Oscar-winning film *The King's Speech*.) Elizabeth's husband is Prince Philip, who's not considered king.

Their son, Prince Charles (the Prince of Wales), is next in line to become king. But it's Prince Charles' sons who generate the tabloid buzz these days—especially Prince William (b. 1982). A graduate of Scotland's St. Andrews University and an officer in both the Royal Air Force and Royal Navy, William married Catherine "Kate" Middleton, his longtime girlfriend, on April 29, 2011. The TV audience was estimated at one-quarter of the world's population—more than two billion people. Kate—a commoner he met at university—now is the Duchess of Cambridge and will eventually become Britain's queen.

colony to ungrateful Americans in 1776). Admiral Horatio Nelson's victory over Napoleon's fleet at the Battle of Trafalgar secured her naval superiority ("Britannia rules the waves"), and 10 years later, the Duke of Wellington stomped Napoleon on land at Waterloo. Nelson and Wellington—both buried in London's St. Paul's Cathedral—are memorialized by many arches, columns, and squares throughout England.

William's brother, redheaded Prince Harry (b. 1984), made a media splash as a bad boy when he wore a Nazi armband (as an ill-advised joke) to a costume party. Since then, he's proved his mettle as a career soldier, serving two months in Afghanistan (early 2008). In 2008, he and his regiment did charity work in Africa, and since then he's been training to become a pilot with the Army Air Corps. Harry's love life—especially his relationship with on-again, off-again girlfriend, Chelsy Davy—is a popular topic for the tabloids.

For years their father's love life was also fodder for the British press. In 1981, Charles married Lady Diana Spencer (Princess Di) who, after their bitter 1996 divorce, died in a car crash in 1997. In 2005, Charles married his longtime girlfriend, Camilla Parker Bowles, who is trying to gain respectability with the Queen and the public. But she doesn't call herself a princess—she uses the title "Duchess of Cornwall." Even when Charles becomes king, she will not use "Queen" as her title—instead she plans to call herself the "Princess Consort."

Charles' siblings are occasionally in the news: Princess Anne, Prince Andrew (who married and divorced Sarah "Fergie" Ferguson), and Prince Edward (who married Di look-alike Sophie Rhys-Jones).

For more on the monarchy, see www.royal.gov.uk.

Royal Sightseeing

You can see the trappings of royalty at Buckingham Palace (the Queen's residence) with its Changing of the Guard; Kensington Palace, where members of the extended royal family keep apartments; Clarence House, the London home of Prince Charles and sons; Althorp Estate (80 miles from London), the childhood home and burial place of Princess Diana; Windsor Castle, a royal country home near London; and the crown jewels in the Tower of London.

Your best chances to actually see the Queen are on three public occasions: Opening of Parliament (late October), Remembrance Sunday (early November, at the Cenotaph), or Trooping the Colour (one Saturday in mid-June, parading down Whitehall and at Buckingham Palace).

Otherwise, check the "Latest news and diary" section of www.royal.gov.uk, where you can search for future royal events.

Economically, Britain led the world into the Industrial Age with her mills, factories, coal mines, and trains. By the time of Queen Victoria's reign (1837-1901), Britain was at its zenith of power, with a colonial empire that covered one-fifth of the world.

The 20th century was not kind to Britain. After decades of rebellion, Ireland finally gained its independence—except for the more Protestant north. Two world wars devastated the population.

The Nazi Blitz reduced much of London to rubble, although the freedom-loving world was inspired by Britain's determination to stand up to Hitler. Britain was rallied through difficult times by two leaders: Prime Minister Winston Churchill, a remarkable orator, and King George VI, who overcame a persistent stutter. After the war, the colonial empire dwindled to almost nothing, and Britain lost its superpower economic status.

One post-Empire hot spot—Northern Ireland, plagued by the "Troubles" between Catholics and Protestants—heated up, and then finally started cooling off. In the spring of 2007, the unthinkable happened when leaders of the ultra-nationalist party sat down with those of the ultra-unionist party. London returned control of Northern Ireland to the popularly elected Northern Ireland Assembly. Perhaps most important of all, after almost 40 years, the British Army withdrew from Northern Ireland that summer. Three years later, the British government formally apologized for the 1972 shooting of 26 civilians in Derry by British soldiers—a day of infamy known as "Bloody Sunday."

The tradition (if not the substance) of greatness continues, presided over by Queen Elizabeth II, her husband, Prince Philip, and their son Prince Charles. With economic problems, the marital turmoil of Charles and Diana, Princess Di's untimely death in 1997, and a relentless popular press, the royal family has had a tough time over the past few decades. But the Queen has stayed above it all, and most British people still jump at an opportunity to see royalty. With the worldwide hubbub surrounding the 2011 wedding of the Queen's grandson, Prince William, to commoner Kate Middleton, it's clear that the concept of royalty is still alive and well in the third millennium.

Queen Elizabeth, who turns 86 in 2012, will also mark her 60th year on the throne—her Diamond Jubilee. Only her great-great-grandmother, Queen Victoria, had a longer reign. While many wonder who will succeed her—and when—the situation is fairly straightforward: The Queen sees her job as a lifelong position, and legally, Charles (who wants to be king) cannot be skipped over for his son William. Given the longevity in the family (the Queen's mum, born in August of 1900, made it to a ripe old age of 101), Charles might be in for a long wait.

Thumbnail Sketches of Famous Brits

Albert, Prince (1819-1861)—German-born husband of Queen Victoria, whose support of the arts and sciences enriched London. (See National Portrait Gallery Tour chapter.)

Arthur, King (c. 600?)—A character of legend, perhaps based on a Roman Christian general battling barbarians after the Fall of Rome.

Beatles (1960s)—Rock music quartet (John Lennon, Paul McCartney, George Harrison, Ringo Starr) whose worldwide popularity brought counterculture ideas to the middle class. (See British Library Tour chapter.)

Boadicea (d. 61)—A queen of the Isle's indigenous people, who defied Roman occupation, burning Londinium to the ground before being defeated. (See Westminster Walk chapter.)

Charles I (1600-1649)—King beheaded after England's Civil War, which pitted a Catholic aristocracy against a Protestant Parliament. Parliament won. (See Westminster Walk, National Gallery Tour, and National Portrait Gallery Tour chapters.)

Charles II (1630-1685)—Son of Charles I who was invited to restore the monarchy under supervision by the Parliament. (See National Portrait Gallery Tour chapter.)

Chaucer, Geoffrey (c. 1340-1400)—Poet, author of *The Canterbury Tales*, which popularized common English. (See Westminster Abbey Tour and Bankside Walk chapters.)

Churchill, Sir Winston (1874-1965)—Prime minister during World War II, whose resolve and charismatic speeches rallied Britain during its darkest hour. (See "Churchill War Rooms" on page 55, plus Westminster Walk, St. Paul's Tour, and The City Walk chapters.)

Constable, John (1776-1837)—Painter of the English countryside, specializing in cloudy skies. (See Tate Britain Tour and National Gallery Tour chapters.)

Cromwell, Oliver (1599-1658)—Leader of the Protestant Parliament that deposed the king in England's Civil War, briefly establishing a Parliament-run commonwealth. (See National Portrait Gallery Tour and Westminster Walk chapters.)

Dickens, Charles (1812-1870)—Popular novelist who brought literature to the masses, educating them about Britain's harsh social and economic realities. (See Bankside Walk, National Portrait Gallery Tour, and Westminster Abbey Tour chapters.)

Edward the Confessor (c. 1002-1066)—English king who built Westminster Abbey. His death prompted the Norman invasion by William the Conqueror. (See Westminster Abbey Tour chapter.)

Elizabeth I (1533-1603)—Daughter of Henry VIII and Anne Boleyn and ruler of England when its navies gained mastery of the seas, bringing prosperity and a renaissance of the arts (Shakespeare). (See National Portrait Gallery Tour and Tower of London Tour chapters.)

Garrick, David (1717-1779)—Actor and theater manager whose naturalism on the stage—and business sense off it—greatly enhanced the blossoming theater scene. (See National Portrait Gallery Tour and The City Walk chapters.)

Henry VIII (1491-1547)—Charismatic king during an era of expansion, whose marital choices forced a break with the pope in Rome, leading to centuries of religious division. (See National Portrait Gallery Tour and Tower of London Tour chapters.)

Hogarth, William (1697-1764)—Painter of realistic slices of English life. (See Tate Britain Tour chapter.)

Holmes, Sherlock (late 1800s)—Fictional detective living at 221b Baker Street, who solved fictional crimes that the real Scotland Yard couldn't.

Jack the Ripper (late 1800s)—Serial killer of prostitutes in east London; his or her identity remains unknown.

Johnson, Samuel (1709-1784)—Writer of a magazine column on everyday London life, compiler of the first great English dictionary, known to us today for witty remarks captured by his friend and biographer, James Boswell. (See The City Walk and Westminster Abbey Tour chapters.)

Keats, John (1795-1821)—Romantic poet (in the company of Percy Shelley, Lord Byron, and William Wordsworth) who pondered mortality before dying young. (See National Portrait Gallery Tour chapter.)

Nelson, Horatio (1758-1805)—Admiral who defeated the French navy at Trafalgar (Spain), ending Napoleon's plans to invade England. (See Westminster Walk, National Portrait Gallery Tour, and St. Paul's Tour chapters; and National Maritime Museum in Greenwich—on page 453.)

Pepys, Samuel (1633-1701)—Chronicler of London life and the Great Fire. Not a famous man himself, Pepys' (pronounced "peeps") diary, even today, makes his times come alive. (See The City Walk chapter.)

Richard the Lionhearted (1157-1199)—Not-so-great king who preferred speaking French and spent his energy on distant Crusades.

Robin Hood (1100s)—Legendary (perhaps real) bandit.

Shakespeare, William (1564-1616)—Earth's greatest playwright. Born in Stratford, he lived most of his adult life in London, writing and acting. (See Bankside Walk, British Library Tour, National Portrait Gallery Tour, and Westminster Abbey Tour chapters.)

Thatcher, Margaret (b. 1925)—Prime minister during the conservative 1980s, known as the "Iron Lady." (See Westminster Walk and National Portrait Gallery Tour chapters.)

Victoria, Queen (1819-1901)—Britain's longest-reigning monarch and great-great-grandmother of Elizabeth II (and her husband). During her 64-year rule, the worldwide British Empire reached its height of power and prosperity. "Victorian" has come to describe the prim middle-class morality of the time. (See National Portrait Gallery Tour chapter.)

Wellington, Duke of (1769-1852)—General who defeated Napoleon at Waterloo and later served as a domineering prime minister. (See National Portrait Gallery Tour and St. Paul's Tour chapters.)

William the Conqueror (c. 1027-1087)—Duke of Normandy in northern France who invaded England (1066), then built the Tower of London and initiated two centuries of rule by French-speaking kings. (See Tower of London Tour chapter.)

Wren, Christopher (1632-1723)—Architect who rebuilt London after the Great Fire of 1666, designing more than 20 churches, including his masterpiece, St. Paul's Cathedral. (See St. Paul's Tour and The City Walk chapters.)

Architecture in Britain

From Stonehenge to Big Ben, travelers are storming castle walls, climbing spiral staircases, and snapping pictures of 5,000 years of architecture. Let's sort it out.

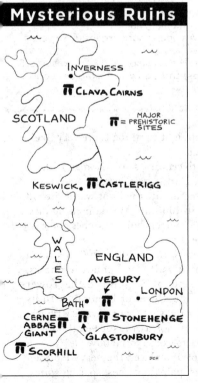

Mysterious Ruins

The oldest ruins—mysterious and prehistoric—date from before Roman times back to 3000 B.C. The earliest sites, such as Stonehenge and Avebury, were built during the Stone and Bronze ages. The remains from these periods are made of huge stones or mounds of earth, even man-made hills, and were created as celestial calendars and for worship or burial. Britain is crisscrossed with lines of these mysterious sights (ley lines). Iron Age people (600 B.C.-A.D. 50) left desolate stone forts. The Romans thrived in Britain from A.D. 50 to 400, building cities, walls, and roads. Evidence of Roman greatness can be seen in lavish villas with ornate mosaic floors, temples uncovered beneath great English churches, and Roman stones in medieval city walls. Roman roads sliced across the island in

Typical Castle Architecture

Castles were fortified residences for medieval nobles. Castles come in all shapes and sizes, but knowing a few general terms will help you understand them.

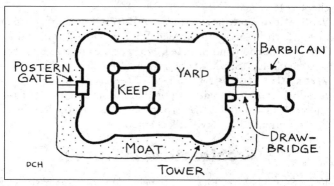

The Keep (or Donjon): A high, strong stone tower in the center of the castle complex that was the lord's home and refuge of last resort.

Great Hall: The largest room in the castle, serving as throne room, conference center, and dining hall.

The Yard (or Bailey or Ward): An open courtyard inside the castle walls.

Loopholes: Narrow slits in the walls (also called embrasures, arrow slits, or arrow loops) through which soldiers could shoot arrows at the enemy.

straight lines. Today, unusually straight rural roads are very likely laid directly on these ancient roads.

As Rome crumbled in the fifth century, so did Roman Britain. Little architecture survives from Dark Ages England, the Saxon period from 500 to 1000. Architecturally, the light was switched on with the Norman Conquest in 1066. As William earned his title "the Conqueror," his French architects built churches and castles in the European Romanesque style.

English Romanesque is called Norman (1066-1200). Norman churches had round arches, thick walls, and small windows; Durham Cathedral and the Chapel of St. John in the Tower of London are prime examples. The Tower of London, with its square keep, small windows, and spiral stone stairways, is a typical Norman castle. You'll see plenty of Norman castles—all built to secure the conquest of these invaders from Normandy.

Gothic architecture (1200-1600) replaced the heavy Norman style with light, vertical buildings, pointed arches, soaring spires,

Towers: Tall structures serving as lookouts, chapels, living quarters, or the dungeon. Towers could be square or round, with either crenellated tops or conical roofs.

Turret: A small lookout tower projecting up from the top of the wall.

Moat: A ditch encircling the wall, often filled with water.

Wall Walk (or Allure): A pathway atop the wall where guards could patrol and where soldiers stood to fire at the enemy.

Parapet: Outer railing of the wall walk.

Crenellation: A gap-toothed pattern of stones atop the parapet.

Hoardings (or Gallery or Brattice): Wooden huts built onto the upper parts of the stone walls. They served as watch towers, living quarters, and fighting platforms.

Machicolation: A stone ledge jutting out from the wall, fitted with holes in the bottom. If the enemy was scaling the walls, soldiers could drop rocks or boiling oil down through the holes and onto the enemy below.

Barbican: A fortified gatehouse, sometimes a stand-alone building located outside the main walls.

Drawbridge: A bridge that could be raised or lowered, using counterweights or a chain-and-winch.

Portcullis: A heavy iron grille that could be lowered across the entrance.

Postern Gate: A small, unfortified side or rear entrance used during peacetime. In wartime, it could become a "sally-port" used to launch surprise attacks, or as an escape route.

and bigger windows. English Gothic is divided into three stages. Early English Gothic (1200-1300) features tall, simple spires; beautifully carved capitals; and elaborate chapter houses (such as the Wells Cathedral). Decorated Gothic (1300-1400) gets fancier, with more elaborate tracery, bigger windows, and ornately carved pinnacles, as you see at Westminster Abbey. Finally, the Perpendicular Gothic style (1400-1600, also called "rectilinear") returns to square towers and emphasizes straight, uninterrupted vertical lines from ceiling to floor, with vast windows and exuberant decoration, including fan-vaulted ceilings (King's College Chapel at Cambridge). Through this evolution, the structural ribs (arches meeting at the top of the ceilings) became more and more decorative and fanciful (the most fancy being the star vaulting and fan vaulting of the Perpendicular style).

As you tour the great medieval churches of Britain, remember that almost everything is symbolic. For instance, on the tombs of knights, if the figure has crossed legs, he was a Crusader. If his

Typical Church Architecture

History comes to life when you visit a centuries-old church. Even if you wouldn't know your apse from a hole in the ground, learning a few simple terms will enrich your experience. Note that not every church has every feature, and that a "cathedral" isn't a type of church architecture, but rather a designation for a church that's a governing center for a local bishop.

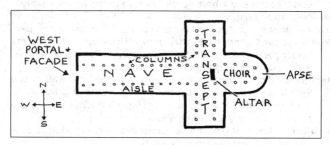

Aisles: The long, generally low-ceilinged arcades that flank the nave.

Altar: The raised area with a ceremonial table (often adorned with candles or a crucifix), where the priest prepares and serves the bread and wine for Communion.

Apse: The space beyond the altar, often bordered with small chapels.

Choir: A cozy area, often screened off, located within the church nave and near the high altar where services are sung in a more intimate setting.

Cloister: A square-shaped series of hallways surrounding an open-air courtyard, traditionally where monks and nuns got fresh air.

Facade: The outer wall of the church's main (west) entrance, viewable from outside and usually highly decorated.

Groin Vault: An arched ceiling formed where two equal barrel vaults meet at right angles. Less common usage: term for a medieval jock strap.

Narthex: The area (portico or foyer) between the main entry and the nave.

Nave: The long, central section of the church (running west to east, from the entrance to the altar) where the congregation stood through the service.

Transept: The north-south part of the church, which crosses (perpendicularly) the east-west nave. In a traditional Latin cross-shaped floor plan, the transept forms the "arms" of the cross.

West Portal: The main entry to the church (on the west end, opposite the main altar).

feet rest on a dog, he died at home; but if the legs rest on a lion, he died in battle. Local guides and books help us modern pilgrims understand at least a little of what we see.

Wales is particularly rich in English castles, which were needed to subdue the stubborn Welsh. Edward I built a ring of powerful castles in Wales, including Conwy and Caernarfon.

Gothic houses were a simple mix of woven strips of thin wood, rubble, and plaster called wattle and daub. The famous black-and-white Tudor (or "half-timbered") look came simply from filling in heavy oak frames with wattle and daub.

The Tudor period (1485-1560) was a time of relative peace (the Wars of the Roses were finally over), prosperity, and renaissance. Henry VIII broke with the Catholic Church and "dissolved" (destroyed) the monasteries, leaving scores of Britain's greatest churches as gutted shells. These hauntingly beautiful abbey ruins (Glastonbury, Tintern, Whitby, Rievaulx, Battle, St. Augustine's in Canterbury, St. Mary's in York, and lots more) surrounded by lush lawns are now pleasant city parks.

Although few churches were built during the Tudor period, this was a time of house and mansion construction. Heating a home was becoming popular and affordable, and Tudor buildings featured small square windows and many chimneys. In towns, where land was scarce, many Tudor houses grew up and out, getting wider with each overhanging floor.

The Elizabethan and Jacobean periods (1560-1620) were followed by the English Renaissance style (1620-1720). English architects mixed Gothic and classical styles, then Baroque and classical styles. Although the ornate Baroque never really grabbed Britain, the classical style of the Italian architect Andrea Palladio did. Inigo Jones (1573-1652), Christopher Wren (1632-1723), and those they inspired plastered Britain with enough columns, domes, and symmetry to please a Caesar. The Great Fire of London (1666) cleared the way for an ambitious young Wren to put his mark on London forever with a grand rebuilding scheme, including the great St. Paul's Cathedral and more than 50 other churches.

The celebrants of the Boston Tea Party remember Britain's Georgian period (1720-1840) for its lousy German kings. "Georgian" is English for "Neoclassical." Its architecture was rich and showed off by being very classical. Grand ornamental doorways, fine cast-ironwork on balconies and railings, Chippendale furniture, and white-on-blue Wedgwood ceramics graced rich homes everywhere. John Woods Sr. and Jr. led the way, giving the trendsetting city of Bath its crescents and circles of aristocratic Georgian row houses.

The Industrial Revolution shaped the Victorian period (1840-1890) with glass, steel, and iron. Britain had a huge new erector set (so did France's Mr. Eiffel). This was also a Romantic period, reviving the "more Christian" Gothic style. London's Houses of Parliament are Neo-Gothic—they're just 140 years old but look 700, except for the telltale modern precision and craftsmanship. Whereas Gothic was stone or concrete, Neo-Gothic was often red brick. These were Britain's glory days, and there was more building in this period than in all previous ages combined.

The architecture of the mid-20th century obeyed the formula "form follows function"—it worried more about your needs than your eyes. Britain treasures its heritage and takes great pains to build tastefully in historic districts and to preserve its many "listed" (government-protected) buildings. With a booming tourist trade, these quaint reminders of its past—and ours—are becoming a valuable part of the British economy.

Britain Today

Regardless of the revolution we had 230-some years ago, many American travelers feel that they "go home" to Britain. This most popular tourist destination has a strange influence and power over us. The more you know of Britain's roots, the better you'll get in touch with your own.

What's So Great About Britain?

Geographically, the Isle of Britain is small (about the size of Uganda or Idaho)—600 miles long and 300 miles at its widest point. England occupies the southeastern part of Britain (with about 60 percent of its land—similar in size to Louisiana—and 80 percent of its population). England's highest mountain (Scafell Pike in the Lake District) is 3,206 feet, a foothill by our standards. The population is a fifth that of the United States. At its peak in the mid-1800s, Britain owned one-fifth of the world and accounted for more than half the planet's industrial output. Today, the Empire is down to the Isle of Britain itself and a few token, troublesome scraps, such as the Falklands, Gibraltar, and Northern Ireland.

Economically, Great Britain's industrial production is about 5 percent of the world's total. After emerging from a recession in 1992, Britain's economy enjoyed its longest period of expansion on record. But in 2008, the global economic slowdown, tight credit, and falling home prices pushed Britain back into a recession.

Culturally, Britain is still a world leader. Her heritage, culture, and people cannot be measured in traditional units of power. London is a major exporter of actors, movies, and theater; of rock

Get It Right

Americans tend to use "England," "Britain," and the "United Kingdom" (or "UK") interchangeably, but they're not quite the same:

- **England** is the country occupying the southeast part of the island.
- **Britain** is the name of the island.
- **Great Britain** is the political union of the island's three countries: England, Scotland, and Wales.
- The **United Kingdom (UK)** adds a fourth country, Northern Ireland.
- The **British Isles** (not a political entity) also includes the independent Republic of Ireland.
- The **British Commonwealth** is a loose association of possessions and former colonies (including Canada, Australia, and India) that profess at least symbolic loyalty to the Crown.

    You can call the modern nation either the United Kingdom ("the UK"), "Great Britain," or simply "Britain."

and classical music; and of writers, painters, and sculptors.

Ethnically, the British Isles are a mix of the descendants of the early Celtic natives (in Scotland, Ireland, Wales, and Cornwall), the invading Anglo-Saxons who took southeast England in the Dark Ages, and the conquering Normans of the 11th century...not to mention more recent immigrants from around the world. Cynics call the United Kingdom an English Empire ruled by London, whose dominant Anglo-Saxon English (50 million) far outnumber their Celtic brothers and sisters (10 million).

Politically, Britain is ruled by the House of Commons, with some guidance from the mostly figurehead Queen and House of Lords. Just as the United States Congress is dominated by Democrats and Republicans, Britain's Parliament is dominated by two parties: left-leaning Labour and right-leaning Conservative ("Tories"). Recently the center-left Liberal Democrats ("Lib Dems") have made some inroads, but still remain a distant third.

Strangely, Britain's "constitution" is not one single document; the government's structures and policies are based on centuries of tradition, statutes, and doctrine, and much of it is not actually in writing. While this might seem potentially troublesome—if not dangerous—the British body politic takes pride in its ethos of civility and mutual respect, which has long made this arrangement work.

The prime minister is the chief executive. He or she is not elected directly by voters; rather, he or she assumes power as the head of the party that wins a majority in Parliamentary elections. (If no party wins a clear majority—as none did in the 2010 election—it's a "hung parliament," and is usually resolved by at least two parties forming a coalition that adds up to a majority.) In the interest of protocol, the Queen symbolically invites the winner to form a "government" (administration). Instead of imposing term limits, the Brits allow their prime ministers to choose when to leave office. The ruling party also gets to choose when to hold elections, as long as it's within five years of the previous one—so prime ministers carefully schedule elections for times that (they hope) their party will win. (Breaking with tradition, the current coalition government has already announced an election for May 7, 2015.) When an election is announced, the Queen dissolves the Parliament so the parties can focus on a short-and-sweet, one-month campaign.

In the 1980s, Conservatives were in charge under Prime Minister Margaret Thatcher and Prime Minister John Major. As proponents of traditional, Victorian values—community, family, hard work, thrift, and trickle-down economics—they took a Reaganesque approach to Britain's serious social and economic problems.

In 1997, a huge Labour victory brought Tony Blair to the prime ministership. Labour began shoring up a social-service system (health care, education, minimum wage) undercut by years of Conservative rule. Blair started out as a respected and well-liked PM. But after he followed US President George W. Bush into war with Iraq, his popularity took a nosedive. In May of 2007, Blair announced that he would resign; a few weeks later, his Chancellor of the Exchequer and longtime colleague, Gordon Brown, was sworn in as Britain's new prime minister. Burdened with an economic crisis and lacking his predecessor's charisma, Brown never achieved a level of popularity anywhere near Blair's.

Elections in May of 2010 pitted Brown against a Conservative opponent, David Cameron, and a third-party Liberal Democrat challenger, Nick Clegg. Brown, Cameron, and Clegg participated in a series of three television debates—the first in UK history. Thanks to the economic crisis—and his own, characteristic stumbles (such as being caught on tape referring to a voter he'd just met as a "bigoted woman")—Brown failed to win a clear majority for his Labour Party. No party won the number of seats needed for a majority—resulting in the first "hung parliament" since 1974. After a few days of wrangling, the Conservatives and the Lib Dems formed a coalition government (the first since World War II), Gordon Brown stepped down, and David Cameron became prime minister.

Because of a huge—and growing—budget deficit, Cameron

announced a program right after the election that would dramatically cut back spending and increase the VAT (Value-Added Tax—the national sales tax) from 17.5 to 20 percent. It remains to be seen whether these bold steps will return Britain to its previous prosperity, or douse the spark of economic recovery.

In the meantime, visitors to England might begin to notice the country's economic woes (locals grumbling about tax hikes or sudden closures of a tourist office or minor sight). However, Britain remains stronger, economically, than many of its fellow EU nations. And Brits are turning their attention to the summer of 2012, when the world's eyes will be on their capital city as London hosts the 30th Olympiad. As the city and country spiff up even more than usual for the Olympics, the people of Britain can look forward to an even brighter future.

Current Challenges

Great as Britain is, the country faces many challenges. You'll likely hear people talking about some of the following hot-button topics during your visit: the economy, the war in Afghanistan, terrorism, immigration, and binge-drinking.

From early 2008 to late 2009, the British economy shrank more than 6 percent—the largest decline since the Great Depression. In this era of uncertainty, British consumers don't seem to be spending much as they try to gauge the effects of Cameron's budget cuts.

While British forces ended combat operations in Iraq in April of 2009, troops remain in Afghanistan, and every new casualty reinvigorates public debate about the merits and possible outcomes of this war.

Like the US, Britain has been coping with its own string of terrorist threats and attacks. On the morning of July 7, 2005, London's commuters were rocked by four different bombs that killed dozens across the city. In the summer of 2006, authorities foiled a plot to carry liquid bombs onto a plane (resulting in the liquid ban air travelers are still experiencing today). On June 29, 2007, two car bombs were discovered (and defused) near London's Piccadilly Circus, and the next day, a flaming car drove into the baggage-claim level at Glasgow Airport. Most Brits have accepted that they now live with the possibility of terrorism at home—and that life must go on.

Britain has taken aggressive measures to prevent future attacks, such as installing "CCTV" (closed-circuit) surveillance cameras everywhere, in both public and private places. (You'll frequently see signs warning you that you're being filmed.) As Brits trade their privacy for security, many wonder if they've given up too much.

The terrorist threats have also highlighted issues relating to Britain's large immigrant population (nearly 4 million). Second-generation Muslims—born in Britain, but who strongly identify with other Muslims rather than their British neighbors—were responsible for the July 2005 bombs. Some Brits reacted to the event known as "7/7" as if all the country's Muslims were to blame. At the same time, a handful of radical Islamic clerics began to justify the bombers' violent actions. Unemployment and the economic downturn have further stretched the already strained relations between communities within Britain.

The large Muslim population is just one thread in the tapestry of today's Britain. While nine out of ten Brits are white, the country has large minority groups, mainly from Britain's former overseas colonies: India, Pakistan, Bangladesh, Africa, the Caribbean, and many other places. But despite the tensions between some groups, for the most part Britain is well integrated, with minorities represented in most (if not all) walks of life.

Recently another wave of immigration has hit Britain. Throughout the British Isles, you'll see many Eastern Europeans (mostly Poles, Slovaks, and Lithuanians) working in restaurants, cafés, and B&Bs. These transplants—who started arriving after their home countries joined the EU in 2004—can make a lot more money working here than back home. British small-business owners have found these new arrivals to be polite, responsible, and affordable. While a few Brits complain that the new arrivals are taking jobs away from the natives, and others are frustrated that their English can be far from perfect, for the most part Britain has absorbed this new set of immigrants gracefully.

Over the last several years, Britain has seen an epidemic of binge-drinking among young people. A 2007 study revealed that one out of every three British men, and one out of every five British women, routinely drink to excess. It's become commonplace for young adults (typically from their mid-teens to mid-20s) to spend weekend nights drinking at pubs and carousing in the streets. (And they ratchet up the debauchery even more when celebrating a "stag night" or "hen night"—bachelor and bachelorette parties.) While sociologists and politicians scratch their heads about this phenomenon, tourists are complaining about weekend noise and obnoxious (though generally harmless) young drunks on the streets.

British TV

Although it has its share of lowbrow reality programming, much British television is still so good—and so British—that it deserves a mention as a sightseeing treat. After a hard day of castle climbing, watch the telly over tea in the living room of your village B&B.

There are currently five free channels that any television can receive. BBC-1 and BBC-2 are government-regulated and commercial-free. Broadcasting of these two channels (and of the five BBC radio stations) is funded by a mandatory £145.50-per-year-per-household television and radio license (hmmm, 65 cents per day to escape commercials and public-broadcasting pledge drives). Channels 3, 4, and 5 are privately owned, are a little more lowbrow, and have commercials—but those commercials are often clever and sophisticated, providing a fun look at British life. In addition, about 85 percent of households now receive digital cable or satellite television, which offer dozens of specialty channels, similar to those available in North America.

Whereas California "accents" fill our airwaves 24 hours a day, homogenizing the way our country speaks, Britain protects and promotes its regional accents by its choice of TV and radio announcers. See if you can tell where each is from (or ask a local for help).

Commercial-free British TV, while looser than it used to be, is still careful about what it airs and when. But after the 21:00 "watershed" hour, when children are expected to be in bed, some nudity and profanity are allowed, and may cause you to spill your tea.

American programs (such as *Mad Men, CSI,* and trash-talk shows) are very popular. But the visiting viewer should be sure to tune the TV to more typically British shows, including a dose of British situation- and political-comedy fun, and the top-notch BBC evening news. British comedies have tickled the American funny bone for years, from sketch comedy *(Monty Python's Flying Circus)* to sitcoms (*Are You Being Served?, Fawlty Towers, Absolutely Fabulous,* and *The Office*). Quiz shows and reality shows are taken very seriously here (*Who Wants to Be a Millionaire?, American Idol, Dancing with the Stars,* and *The X Factor* are all based on British shows). Jonathan Ross is the David Letterman of Britain for sometimes edgy late-night talk. For a tear-filled, slice-of-life taste of British soaps dealing in all the controversial issues, see the popular and remarkably long-running *Emmerdale, Coronation Street,* or *EastEnders.*

PAST AND PRESENT

APPENDIX

Contents

Tourist Information

London has a fine tourist information office, called the **Britain and London Visitors Centre** (will move after March 2012; see page 25). Note that tourist information offices are abbreviated "TI" in this book.

TIs are good places to get a city map, advice on public transportation (including bus and train schedules), walking-tour information, tips on special events, and recommendations for nightlife. For all the help TIs offer, steer clear of their room-finding services (bloated prices, booking fee up to £4, no opinions, and they take a 10 percent cut from your host).

Websites: Start with the TI's official website, www.visit london.com. Other helpful sites include www.timeout.com /london and www.londontown.com. For information on London and beyond, try www.visitbritain.com.

European Calling Chart

Just smile and dial, using this key:
AC = Area Code, LN = Local Number.

European Country	Calling long distance within ...	Calling from the US or Canada to ...	Calling from a European country to ...
Austria	AC + LN	011 + 43 + AC (without the initial zero) + LN	00 + 43 + AC (without the initial zero) + LN
Belgium	LN	011 + 32 + LN (without initial zero)	00 + 32 + LN (without initial zero)
Bosnia-Herzegovina	AC + LN	011 + 387 + AC (without initial zero) + LN	00 + 387 + AC (without initial zero) + LN
Britain	AC + LN	011 + 44 + AC (without initial zero) + LN	00 + 44 + AC (without initial zero) + LN
Croatia	AC + LN	011 + 385 + AC (without initial zero) + LN	00 + 385 + AC (without initial zero) + LN
Czech Republic	LN	011 + 420 + LN	00 + 420 + LN
Denmark	LN	011 + 45 + LN	00 + 45 + LN
Estonia	LN	011 + 372 + LN	00 + 372 + LN
Finland	AC + LN	011 + 358 + AC (without initial zero) + LN	999 (or other 900 number) + 358 + AC (without initial zero) + LN
France	LN	011 + 33 + LN (without initial zero)	00 + 33 + LN (without initial zero)
Germany	AC + LN	011 + 49 + AC (without initial zero) + LN	00 + 49 + AC (without initial zero) + LN
Gibraltar	LN	011 + 350 + LN	00 + 350 + LN
Greece	LN	011 + 30 + LN	00 + 30 + LN
Hungary	06 + AC + LN	011 + 36 + AC + LN	00 + 36 + AC + LN
Ireland	AC + LN	011 + 353 + AC (without initial zero) + LN	00 + 353 + AC (without initial zero) + LN

European Country	Calling long distance within ...	Calling from the US or Canada to ...	Calling from a European country to ...
Italy	LN	011 + 39 + LN	00 + 39 + LN
Montenegro	AC + LN	011 + 382 + AC (without initial zero) + LN	00 + 382 + AC (without initial zero) + LN
Morocco	LN	011 + 212 + LN (without initial zero)	00 + 212 + LN (without initial zero)
Netherlands	AC + LN	011 + 31 + AC (without initial zero) + LN	00 + 31 + AC (without initial zero) + LN
Norway	LN	011 + 47 + LN	00 + 47 + LN
Poland	LN	011 + 48 + LN (without initial zero)	00 + 48 + LN (without initial zero)
Portugal	LN	011 + 351 + LN	00 + 351 + LN
Slovakia	AC + LN	011 + 421 + AC (without initial zero) + LN	00 + 421 + AC (without initial zero) + LN
Slovenia	AC + LN	011 + 386 + AC (without initial zero) + LN	00 + 386 + AC (without initial zero) + LN
Spain	LN	011 + 34 + LN	00 + 34 + LN
Sweden	AC + LN	011 + 46 + AC (without initial zero) + LN	00 + 46 + AC (without initial zero) + LN
Switzerland	LN	011 + 41 + LN (without initial zero)	00 + 41 + LN (without initial zero)
Turkey	AC (if there's no initial zero, add one) + LN	011 + 90 + AC (without initial zero) + LN	00 + 90 + AC (without initial zero) + LN

- The instructions above apply whether you're calling a land line or mobile phone.
- The international access codes (the first numbers you dial when making an international call) are 011 if you're calling from the US or Canada, or 00 if you're calling from virtually anywhere in Europe (except Finland, where it's 999 or another 900 number, depending on the phone service you're using).
- To call the US or Canada from Europe, dial 00, then 1 (the country code for the US and Canada), then the area code and number. In short, 00 + 1 + AC + LN = Hi, Mom!

Communicating

Telephones

Smart travelers get comfortable using the telephone to reserve or reconfirm rooms, get tourist information, reserve restaurants, confirm tour times, or phone home. Generally the easiest, cheapest way to call home is to use an international phone card purchased in Britain. This section covers dialing instructions, phone cards, and types of phones (for more in-depth information, see www .ricksteves.com/phoning).

How to Dial

Calling from the US to Britain, or vice versa, is simple—once you break the code. The European calling chart on the previous page will walk you through it.

Dialing Domestically Within Britain

Britain, like much of the US, uses an area-code dialing system. To make local calls, if you're within an area code, just dial the local number to be connected; but if you're calling outside your area code, you have to dial both the area code (which starts with a 0) and the local number.

Area codes are listed in this book and by city on phone-booth walls, and are available from directory assistance (dial 118-500, £0.64/minute). It's most expensive to call within Britain between 8:00 and 13:00, and cheapest between 17:00 and 8:00. Still, a short call across the country is inexpensive, so don't hesitate to call long distance.

Dialing Internationally to or from Britain

If you want to make an international call, follow these steps:

• Dial the international access code (00 if you're calling from Europe, 011 from the US or Canada).

• Dial the country code of the country you're calling (44 for Britain, or 1 for the US or Canada).

• Dial the area code (London's area code is 020) and the local number, keeping in mind that if you're calling Britain, drop the initial zero of the area code. The European calling chart lists specifics per country.

Calling from the US to Britain: To call a recommended London hotel from the US, dial 011 (the US international access code), 44 (Britain's country code), 20 (London's area code without its initial 0), then 7730-8191 (the hotel's number—in this example, the Lime Tree Hotel).

Calling from any European country to the US: To call my office in Edmonds, Washington, from anywhere in Europe, I dial

The English Accent

In the olden days, an English person's accent indicated his or her social standing. Eliza Doolittle had the right idea—elocution could make or break you. Wealthier families would send their kids to fancy private schools to learn proper pronunciation. But these days, in a sort of reverse snobbery that has gripped the nation, accents are back. Politicians, newscasters, and movie stars are favoring deep accents over the Queen's English. While it's hard for American ears to pick out all of the variations, most English people can determine where a person is from based on their accent...not just the region, but often the village, and even the part of a town.

00 (Europe's international access code), 1 (the US country code), 425 (Edmonds' area code), and 771-8303.

Note: You might see a + in front of a European number. When dialing the number, replace the + with the international access code of the country you're calling from (00 from Europe, 011 from the US or Canada).

Public Phones and Hotel-Room Phones

British public pay phones are easy to find and easy to use, but relatively expensive. They take major credit cards (which you insert into the phone—minimum charge for a credit-card call is £0.50) or coins (have a bunch handy). Phones clearly list which coins you can use (usually from 10p to £1, with a minimum toll of £0.40; some new phones even accept euro coins), and a display shows how your money supply's doing. Only completely unused coins will be returned, so put in biggies with caution. (If money's left over, rather than hanging up, push the "make another call" button.)

The only tricky public pay phones you'll use are the expensive, coin-op ones in bars and B&Bs. Some require money before you dial, while others wait until after you're connected. Many have a button you must push before you begin talking. And some might just eat your money.

International Phone Cards: These are the cheapest way to make international calls from Britain—with the best cards, it costs less than 10 cents a minute to the US, as long as you don't call from a phone booth. British Telecom levies a hefty surcharge for using international phone cards from a pay phone (so instead of 100 minutes for a £5 card, you'll get less than 10 minutes—a miserable deal). But they're still a good deal if you use them when calling from mobile phones or fixed-line phones such as hotel-room phones.

To use the card, dial a toll-free access number, then enter your scratch-to-reveal PIN code. (If you have several access numbers listed on your card, you'll save money overall if you choose the toll-free one starting with 0800, rather than 0845, 0870, or 0871, which cost around £0.10 per minute.) To call the US or Britain, see "How to Dial," above. To make calls within Britain using an international calling card, you need to dial the area code even if you're calling across the street. These cards, which are sold at newsstands, work only within the country of purchase (e.g., one bought in Britain won't work in France). Buy a lower denomination in case the card is a dud.

Hotel-Room Phones: Calling from your room can be cheap for local calls (ask for the rates at the front desk first), but is often a rip-off for long-distance calls, unless you use an international phone card (explained above). Some hotels charge a fee for dialing supposedly "toll-free" numbers, such as the one for your international phone card—ask before you dial. Incoming calls are free, making this a cheap way for friends and family to stay in touch (provided they have a good long-distance plan for calls to Britain—and a list of your hotels' phone numbers).

US Calling Cards: These cards, such as the ones offered by AT&T, Verizon, or Sprint, are the worst option. You'll save money by using an international phone card you've purchased in Britain.

Mobile Phones

Many travelers enjoy the convenience of traveling with a mobile phone.

Using Your Mobile Phone: Your US mobile phone works in Britain if it's GSM-enabled, tri-band or quad-band, and on a calling plan that includes international calls. Phones from AT&T and T-Mobile, which use the same GSM technology that Europe does, are more likely to work overseas than Verizon or Sprint phones (if you're not sure, ask your service provider). Most US providers charge $1.29-1.99 per minute while roaming internationally to make or receive calls, and 20-50 cents to send or receive text messages.

You'll pay cheaper rates if your phone is electronically "unlocked" (ask your provider about this); then in Britain, you can simply buy a tiny **SIM card,** which gives you a British phone number. SIM cards are available at mobile-phone stores and some newsstand kiosks for $5-15, and generally include several minutes' worth of prepaid domestic calling time. When you buy a SIM card, you may need to show ID, such as your passport. Insert the SIM card into your phone (usually in a slot on the side or behind the battery), and it'll work like a British mobile phone. When buying a SIM card and prepaid credit, always ask about fees for domestic and international calls, roaming charges, and how to check your credit balance and buy more time.

Many **smartphones,** such as the iPhone, Android, and BlackBerry, work in Britain (note that you can use the AT&T iPhone—but not the Verizon model—in Britain). For voice calls and text messaging, smartphones work the same as other US mobile phones (explained earlier). But beware of sky-high fees for data downloading (checking email, browsing the Internet, streaming videos, and so on). To avoid this expense, disable data roaming entirely, and get online at Wi-Fi hotspots instead. You can ask your mobile-phone service provider to cut off your account's data roaming capability, or you can manually turn it off on your phone (look under the "Network" menu). If you want Internet access without being limited to Wi-Fi, you'll need to keep data roaming on—but you can take steps to reduce your charges. Consider paying extra for a limited international data-roaming plan through your carrier, then use data roaming selectively (if a particular task gobbles bandwidth, wait until you're on Wi-Fi). In general, ask your provider in advance how to avoid unwittingly roaming your way to a huge bill. If your smartphone is on Wi-Fi, you can use certain apps to make cheap or free voice calls (see "Calling over the Internet," later).

Buying a British Mobile Phone: Mobile-phone shops all over Europe sell basic phones. (For example, Britain's Carphone Warehouse sells pay-as-you-go mobile phones for as little as £10 plus £10 for calling time.) The mobile phone desk in a big department store is another good place to check. Phones that are "locked" to work with a single provider start around £10; "unlocked" phones (which allow you to switch out SIM cards to use your choice of provider) start around £35. You'll also need to get a SIM card and prepaid credit for making calls. If you remain in Britain, incoming calls are generally free, and outgoing domestic calls to a fixed line generally run about 15-20p per minute—less than from a pay phone. (It's more expensive to call a mobile phone or a toll number.) You'll pay more if you're roaming in another country.

Renting a British Mobile Phone: Car-rental companies and mobile-phone companies offer the option to rent a mobile phone with a British number. Some hotels even rent or loan phones. While this seems convenient, hidden fees (such as high per-minute charges or expensive shipping costs) can really add up—which usually makes it a bad value. One exception is Verizon's Global Travel Program, available only to Verizon customers.

Borrowing a Phone: Americans, who generally pay the same no matter how many local calls they make, think nothing of asking a stranger (or B&B owner) if they can use their phone. But most British people pay for each local call (whether from a fixed line or a mobile phone), and rates are expensive. To be polite, ask to use someone's phone only in an emergency—and offer to use an international calling card or to pay for the call.

Calling over the Internet

Some things that seem too good to be true...actually are true. If you're traveling with a laptop, you can make calls using VoIP (Voice over Internet Protocol). With VoIP, two computers act as the phones, and the Internet-based calls are free (or you can pay a few cents to call from your computer to a telephone). If both computers have webcams, you can even see each other while you chat. The major providers are Skype (www.skype.com), followed by Google Talk (www.google.com/talk).

For people traveling with a smartphone, various apps allow you to make VoIP calls from a Wi-Fi hotspot. A Skype app is available for most smartphones (including the iPhone, Android, and BlackBerry), while Fring (www.fring.com) allows you to use other VoIP providers—including Google Talk—on your smart-phone. These apps also work on the iPod Touch (if you have an older model, you'll need to attach an external microphone).

Useful Phone Numbers

Understand the various prefixes—numbers starting with 09 are telephone-sex-type expensive. Numbers beginning with 0800 are toll-free, but numbers with prefixes of 0844, 0845, 0870, and 0871 cost about £0.10 per minute from a fixed line (and can be much more expensive if calling from a mobile phone). If you have questions about a prefix, call 100 for free help.

Emergency Needs
Police and Ambulance: tel. 999

Embassies and Consulates
US Consulate and Embassy: tel. 020/7499-9000, passport info tel. 020/7894-0563, passport services available Mon-Fri 8:30-11:30 plus Mon, Wed, and Fri 14:00-16:00 (24 Grosvenor Square, Tube: Bond Street, www.usembassy.org.uk)
Canadian High Commission: tel. 020/7258-6600, passport services available Mon-Fri 9:30-13:30 (Trafalgar Square, Tube: Charing Cross, www.unitedkingdom.gc.ca)

Travel Advisories
US Department of State: tel. 202/647-5225, www.travel.state.gov
Canadian Department of Foreign Affairs: Canadian tel. 800-267-6788, www.dfait-maeci.gc.ca

US Centers for Disease Control and Prevention: tel. 800-CDC-INFO (800-232-4636), www.cdc.gov/travel

Directory Assistance
Operator Assistance: tel. 100 (free)
Directory Assistance: toll tel. 118-500 (£0.64/minute, plus £0.23/minute connection charge from fixed lines)
International Directory Assistance: toll tel. 118-505 (£1.99/minute, plus £0.69 connection charge)

Trains
Train Information for Trips Within England: tel. 0845-748-4950 (www.nationalrail.co.uk)
Eurostar (Chunnel Info): tel. 08705-186-186 (www.eurostar.com)
Trains to All Points in Europe: tel. 08705-848-848 (www.raileurope.com)

Airports
For online information on the first three airports, check www.baa.co.uk.
Heathrow (flight info): tel. 0870-000-0123
Gatwick (general info): tel. 0870-000-2468 for all airlines, except British Airways—tel. 0870-551-1155 (flights) or 0870-850-9850 (reservations)
Stansted (general info): tel. 0870-000-0303
Luton (general info): tel. 01582/405-100 (www.london-luton.com)
London City Airport (general info): tel. 020/7646-0088 (www.londoncityairport.com)

Airlines
Aer Lingus: tel. 0870-876-5000 (www.aerlingus.com)
Air Canada: tel. 0871-220-1111 (www.aircanada.com)
Alitalia: tel. 08714-241-424, (www.alitalia.com)
American: tel. 020/7365-0777 (www.aa.com)
bmi: toll tel. 0870-607-0555 (www.flybmi.com)
British Airways: tel. 0844-493-0787, flight info tel. 0844-493-0777 (www.ba.com)
Continental Airlines: tel. 0845-607-6760 (www.continental.com)
easyJet: tel. 0905-821-0905 (www.easyjet.com)
KLM Royal Dutch/Northwest Airlines: tel. 0870-507-4074 (www.klm.com)
Lufthansa: tel. 0871-945-9747 (www.lufthansa.com)
Ryanair: tel. 0871-246-0000 (www.ryanair.com)
Scandinavian Airlines (SAS): tel. 0871-521-2772 (www.flysas.com)
United Airlines: tel. 0845-844-4777 (www.unitedairlines.co.uk)
US Airways: tel. 0845-600-3300 (www.usairways.com)

Public Transportation Routes in Britain

-----	Rail
———	Eurostar
– – –	Bus
(8H) ·········	Ferry with crossing time

Ferry Note:
Dover - Calais–1.5 H
Dover - Boul–1.5 H

50 Kilometers

50 Miles

Orkney Islands

Lewis

Burwick

Thurso • John o' Groats

Skye
Portree

Elgin

Inverness

Culloden

Kyle • Loch Ness • Aviemore • Aberdeen

Mallaig

SCOTLAND

Fort William

Pitlochry

Mull
Iona

Oban

Perth • Dundee
Leuchars
• St. Andrews

Stirling

Edinburgh

Glasgow

Berwick

Cairnryan

Hexham

Larne (2H)

Stranraer

Newcastle

To Amsterdam (15H)

Belfast (2-3H)

Carlisle

Durham

NORTHERN
IRELAND

Keswick • Penrith

Windermere

ENGLAND

North
Sea

Isle
of Man

Irish
Sea

Blackpool

Leeds • York • Hull

Dublin (7H)

Preston

Dun
Laoghaire (2-3H)

Holyhead Conwy

Liverpool

Manchester • Lincoln

Bangor

Chester

Grimsby

Caernarfon

Betws-y-Coed

Stoke

Peter-borough

King's Lynn

Norwich

REPUBLIC
OF
IRELAND

Bed.

Blaenau
Ffest.

Derby

Pwlheli

Telf.

Ely

Harlech

Wolv. • Birmingham

Cambridge

To Esbjerg (18 H)

Aberystwyth

Iron Bridge
Gorge

Coventry

Warwick

Harwich

Rosslare (3.5H)

Stratford

To Hoek van
Holland (6H)

WALES

Cheltenham

Moreton

Ebbs-fleet

Fishguard

Carmarthen

Stow • Oxford

Canterbury

Newport

Swansea

Cardiff

London

Dover

To Cork (12H)

Bath

Reading

Woking

Ashford

Calais

Bristol

Stone-henge

Wells

Atlantic
Ocean

Exeter

Salisbury

Southampton

Brighton

Newhaven

EUROSTAR (2.5H)

Dartmoor

Portsmouth

To
Dieppe (4H)

To Paris
& Brussels

St. Ives

Truro

Plymouth

English
Channel

To
Ouistreham (6H)

Penzance

Falmouth

To Roscoff (6H)

To Cherbourg (3H)

FRANCE

Heathrow Airport Car-Rental Agencies
Avis: tel. 0844-544-6000 (www.avis.co.uk)
Budget: tel. 0844-544-4600 (www.budget.co.uk)
Enterprise: tel. 020/8897-2100 (www.enterprise.co.uk)
Europcar: tel. 020/8564-3500 (www.europcar.co.uk)
Hertz: tel. 0870-846-0006 (www.hertz.co.uk)

Internet Access

It's useful to get online periodically as you travel—to confirm trip plans, check train or bus schedules, get weather forecasts, catch up on email, blog or post photos from your trip, or call folks back home (explained earlier, under "Calling over the Internet").

Some hotels and B&Bs offer a computer in the lobby with Internet access for guests. If you ask politely, smaller places may sometimes let you sit at their desk for a few minutes just to check your email. If your hotel doesn't have access, ask your hotelier to direct you to the nearest place to get online. Internet cafés are easy to find in London; for specific listings, see page 28.

Traveling with a Laptop or Tablet: You can get online if your hotel has Wi-Fi (wireless Internet access) or a port in your room for plugging in a cable. Some hotels offer Wi-Fi for free; others charge by the minute or hour. A cellular modem—which lets your laptop access the Internet over a mobile phone network—provides more extensive coverage, but is much more expensive than Wi-Fi.

Mail

Get stamps at the neighborhood post office, newsstands within fancy hotels, and some mini-marts and card shops. While you can arrange for mail delivery to your hotel (allow 10 days for a letter to arrive), phoning and emailing are so easy that I've dispensed with mail stops altogether.

You can mail one package per day to yourself worth up to $200 duty-free from Europe to the US (mark it "personal purchases"). If you're sending a gift to someone, mark it "unsolicited gift." For details, visit www.cbp.gov and search for "Know Before You Go."

Resources

Resources from Rick Steves

Rick Steves' London 2012 is one of many books in my series on European travel, which includes country guidebooks (including Great Britain), city and regional guidebooks (including England), Snapshot guides (excerpted chapters from my country guides), Pocket Guides (full-color little books on big cities), and my budget-travel skills handbook, *Rick Steves' Europe Through the Back Door.* Some of my books are available in electronic format.

My phrase books—for French, Italian, German, Spanish, and Portuguese—are practical and budget-oriented. My other books include *Europe 101* (a crash course on art and history), *Mediterranean Cruise Ports* (how to make the most of your time in port), and *Travel as a Political Act* (a travelogue sprinkled with tips for bringing home a global perspective). For a list of my books, look near the end of this book.

Video: My public television series, *Rick Steves' Europe,* covers European destinations in 100 shows, with 10 episodes on Great Britain. To watch episodes, visit www.hulu.com/rick-steves-europe; for scripts and other details, see www.ricksteves.com/tv.

Audio: My weekly public radio show, *Travel with Rick Steves,* features interviews with travel experts from around the world. I've also produced free, self-guided audio tours of the top sights in London, based on tours in this book: Westminster Walk, British Museum, British Library, St. Paul's, and The City Walk. All of this audio content is available for free at Rick Steves Audio Europe, an extensive online library organized by destination. Choose whatever interests you, and download it for free to your computer or mobile device via www.ricksteves.com/audioeurope, iTunes, or the Rick Steves Audio Europe smartphone app.

Maps

The black-and-white maps in this book are concise and simple, designed to help you locate recommended places and get to local TIs, where you can pick up more in-depth maps of cities and regions (usually free). The color city maps and Tube map at the front of this book are also useful.

For more detail, buy a city map at a London newsstand—the red *Bensons Mapguide* (£2.50) is excellent. Even the vending-machine maps sold in Tube stations are good. The *Rough Guide* map to London is well-designed (£5, sold at London bookstores). The *Rick Steves' Britain, Ireland & London City Map* has a good map of London ($6, www.ricksteves.com). Many Londoners, along with obsessive-compulsive tourists, rely on the highly detailed *London A-Z* map book (generally £5-7, called "A to Zed" by locals,

APPENDIX

Begin Your Trip at www.ricksteves.com

At ricksteves.com, you'll discover a wealth of free information on European destinations, including fresh monthly news and helpful tips from thousands of fellow travelers. You'll find my latest guidebook updates (www.ricksteves.com/update), a monthly travel e-newsletter (easy and free to sign up), my personal travel blog, and my free Rick Steves Audio Europe smartphone app (if you don't have a smartphone, you can access the same content via podcasts). You can even follow me on Facebook and Twitter.

Our **online Travel Store** offers travel bags and accessories specially designed by Rick Steves to help you travel smarter and lighter. These include Rick's popular carry-on bags (roll-aboard and backpack versions), money belts, totes, toiletries kits, adapters, other accessories, and a wide selection of guidebooks, journals, planning maps, and DVDs.

Choosing the right **railpass** for your trip—amidst hundreds of options—can drive you nutty. We'll help you choose the best pass for your needs and ship it to you for free, plus give you a bunch of free extras.

Rick Steves' Europe Through the Back Door travel company offers **tours** with more than three dozen itineraries and more than 400 departures reaching the best destinations in this book...and beyond. We offer several tours that include London, such as our seven-day in-depth London city tour and our 14-day England tour. You'll enjoy great guides, a fun bunch of travel partners (with small groups of around 20-24), and plenty of room to spread out in a big, comfy bus. You'll find European adventures to fit every vacation length. For all the details, and to get our Tour Catalog and a free Rick Steves Tour Experience DVD (filmed on location during an actual tour), visit www.ricksteves.com or call the Tour Department at 425/608-4217.

APPENDIX

available at newsstands). Before you buy a map, look at it to be sure it has the level of detail you want.

Other Guidebooks

If you're like most travelers, this book is all you need. But if you're heading beyond my recommended neighborhoods and destinations, $40 for extra maps and books can be money well spent.

The following books are worthwhile, though not updated annually; check the publication date before you buy. The scholarly *Michelin Green Guide to London*, which is somewhat dry, and the more readable Access guide for London, are both well-researched. *Let's Go: London* is youth-oriented, with good coverage of nightlife, hosteling, and cheap transportation deals. *Secret London* by Andrew Duncan leads the reader on unique walks through a less-touristy London.

London's TIs hand out a useful, free monthly *London Planner* (includes a listing of sights and lots of London tips). Newsstands sell the excellent weekly entertainment magazine *Time Out*, which has good maps and a concise and opinionated rundown on sightseeing, shopping, entertainment, and eats (£3, www.timeout.com /london).

If you'll be traveling elsewhere in Britain, consider *Rick Steves' England 2012* or *Rick Steves' Great Britain 2012.*

Recommended Books and Movies

To learn more about London past and present, check out a few of these books or films.

Nonfiction

A History of London (Inwood), topping out at 1,000 pages, covers 2,000 years. *London* (Ackroyd) takes the form of a biography rather than a conventional history. *Elizabeth's London* (Picard) re-creates 16th-century life in the era of England's first great queen.

Originally published in the *New Yorker* magazine, *Letters from London* (Barnes) captures life in the city in the early 1990s. The book *84, Charing Cross Road* is a collection of letters between a stiff-upper-lip London bookseller and a witty writer, Helene Hanff, in the post-WWII years. (Also worth reading is the sequel, *The Duchess of Bloomsbury Street*.) Although not specific to London, consider *Notes from a Small Island*, which is chock-full of Bill Bryson's witty observations about Great Britain. Dava Sobel's *Longitude* tells the story of the clockmaker who solved a problem that had thwarted previous geniuses. Kids of all ages enjoy the whimsical and colorful impressions of the city in Miroslav Sasek's classic picture-book *This Is London*.

Fiction

Describing the classics of British literature is a book in itself. But some favorites that feature London include *Pygmalion* (Shaw), the story of a young Cockney girl groomed for high society; *Persuasion*, a beloved Jane Austen book partially set in Bath; and Charles Dickens' tale of a workhouse urchin, *Oliver Twist*.

Dating from the turn of the century, P. G. Wodehouse's Jeeves series, with a problem-solving valet as the lead character, have endured. *A Study in Scarlet* (Doyle) introduced the world to detective Sherlock Holmes.

Edward Rutherfurd's *London*, which begins in ancient times and continues through to the 20th century, is as big and sprawling as its namesake. *The Jupiter Myth* (Davis) takes place in the days when the city was called Londinium. In *The Great Stink* (Clark), the sewer system is also a metaphor for the blight that plagued the city.

Lucia in London (Benson) sends the protagonist of this 1920s series to the big city. Helen Fielding created another well-loved heroine in her *Bridget Jones* books, which began in the late 1990s as a newspaper column (and inspired two fun films). *Confessions of a Shopaholic* (Kinsella) continues the Bridget Jones formula. Nick Hornby explores a young male perspective of life and love in *Fever Pitch, High Fidelity,* and *About a Boy.*

London's movers and shakers commit bad deeds in the detective story *In the Presence of the Enemy* (George). *Murder in Mayfair* (Barnard) is based on a true crime from the 1980s. *Rumpole of the Bailey,* created by Sir John Mortimer, is a popular detective series, spawning both books and television shows.

Ian McEwan's highly praised post-9/11 novel, *Saturday,* takes place over the course of a day all over the sprawling city. Many recent works feature the city's thriving immigrant communities, including *The Buddha of Suburbia* (Kureishi), *White Teeth* (Smith), and *Brick Lane* (Ali, also a 2007 film).

Films

For a taste of Tudor-era London, try *Shakespeare in Love* (1999), which is set in the original Globe Theatre. In *A Man for All Seasons* (1966), Sir Thomas More faces down Henry VIII. Showtime's racy, lavish series *The Tudors* (2007-2010) is an entertaining, loosely accurate chronicle of the marriages of Henry VIII. For equally good portraits of Elizabeth I, try *Elizabeth* (1998), its sequel *Elizabeth: The Golden Age* (2007), and *Elizabeth I* (2005, a BBC/HBO miniseries).

Written and set in the early 19th century, the works of Jane Austen have fared well in film. *Persuasion* (1995) was partially filmed in Bath.

Equally genteel was the Edwardian era of the early 20th century. *Howard's End* (1992) captures the stifling societal pressure underneath the gracious manners. In *The Elephant Man* (1980), the cruelty of Victorian London is starkly portrayed in a black-and-white film.

Wartime London was captured in many fine movies, including *Waterloo Bridge* (1940), a story of lost love between a woman and a WWI officer. In *Passport to Pimlico* (1949), an explosion in a Tube station is the source of riches and comedy in a time of post-WWII rationing.

In the 1960s, two blockbuster Hollywood musicals were set in London: *Mary Poppins* (1964) and *My Fair Lady* (1964). British acts were all the rage in the States, thanks to a little band called the Beatles, whose *A Hard Day's Night* (1964) is filled with wit and charm.

During this time, "swinging London" also exploded on the international scene, with films such as *Alfie* (1966), *Blowup* (1966), and *Georgy Girl* (1966). (For a swinging spoof of this time, try the Austin Powers comedies.) In *To Sir, with Love* (1967), Sidney Poitier brings order to his undisciplined students.

You can watch Hugh Grant charming the ladies in *Four Weddings and a Funeral* (1994) and *Notting Hill* (1999); Gwyneth Paltrow living two lives in *Sliding Doors* (1998); and *A Fish Called Wanda* (1988), in which John Cleese is embroiled in love, revenge, and exotic fish.

For something completely different from the typical Hollywood fare, see *My Beautiful Laundrette* (1986), a gritty story of two gay men (one of whom is played by Daniel Day-Lewis). For another portrayal of urban London—and the racial tensions found in its multiethnic center—look for *Sammy and Rosie Get Laid* (1987). *Lock, Stock and Two Smoking Barrels* (1998) is a violent crime caper set in the city.

Billy Elliot (2000), about a young boy ballet dancer, and *Bend It Like Beckham* (2003), about a young Punjabi soccer player, were both huge crowd-pleasers. In *The Queen* (2006), Helen Mirren channels Elizabeth II during the days after Princess Diana's death. *The King's Speech* (2010) won the Academy Award for Best Picture, and Colin Firth was named Best Actor for his portrayal of King George VI on the cusp of World War II.

Shaun of the Dead (2004) combines comedy and horror, when the city's residents turn into zombies. The same moviemaking team later merged cop/action films and comedy in *Hot Fuzz* (2007). *V for Vendetta* (2006), based on a British graphic novel, shows a sci-fi future of a London ruled with an iron fist. *Sweeney Todd* (2007) captures the gritty Victorian milieu, as does the highly stylized *Sherlock Holmes* (2009).

If you're traveling to London or Great Britain with children, consider watching *Mary Poppins* (1964), *My Fair Lady* (1964), *A Little Princess* (1995), the *Wallace & Gromit* movies, Rowan Atkinson's *Mr. Bean* television series and movies, and the *Harry Potter* films.

Holidays and Festivals

This list includes many—but not all—major festivals in London, plus national holidays observed throughout Great Britain. Many sights and banks close on national holidays—keep this in mind when planning your itinerary. Before planning a trip around a festival, make sure to verify its dates by checking the festival's website or TI sites (www.visitlondon.com and www.visitbritain.com).

In London, hotels get booked up on major holidays—New Year's Day, Good Friday through Easter Monday, Christmas, and Boxing Day—and on Fridays and Saturdays year-round. Some hotels require you to book the full three-day weekend around Bank Holiday Mondays (there's one apiece in May, June, and Aug).

Included in this list are events in the nearby towns of Bath, Windsor, and Cambridge. Each of these towns is an easy train ride from London.

Here are some major holidays in 2012:

Jan 1	New Year's Day
Feb (one week)	London Fashion Week (www.london fashionweek.co.uk)
March 2-March 11	Literature Festival, Bath (www.bathlit fest.org.uk)
April 6	Good Friday
April 8-9	Easter Sunday and Monday
May 7	Early May Bank Holiday (first Monday in May)
Late May	Chelsea Flower Show, London (book tickets ahead for this popular event at www.rhs.org.uk/chelsea)
May 23-June 3	International Music Festival, Bath (www.bathmusicfest.org.uk)
Late May-early June	Fringe Festival, Bath (alternative music, dance, and theater; www.bathfringe .co.uk)
Early-Mid-June	Trooping the Colour, London (military bands and pageantry, Queen's birthday parade; www.trooping-the-colour .co.uk)
June 4	Spring Bank Holiday (first Monday in June)

2012

JANUARY

S	M	T	W	T	F	S
1	2	3	4	5	6	7
8	9	10	11	12	13	14
15	16	17	18	19	20	21
22	23	24	25	26	27	28
29	30	31				

FEBRUARY

S	M	T	W	T	F	S
			1	2	3	4
5	6	7	8	9	10	11
12	13	14	15	16	17	18
19	20	21	22	23	24	25
26	27	28	29			

MARCH

S	M	T	W	T	F	S
				1	2	3
4	5	6	7	8	9	10
11	12	13	14	15	16	17
18	19	20	21	22	23	24
25	26	27	28	29	30	31

APRIL

S	M	T	W	T	F	S
1	2	3	4	5	6	7
8	9	10	11	12	13	14
15	16	17	18	19	20	21
22	23	24	25	26	27	28
29	30					

MAY

S	M	T	W	T	F	S
		1	2	3	4	5
6	7	8	9	10	11	12
13	14	15	16	17	18	19
20	21	22	23	24	25	26
27	28	29	30	31		

JUNE

S	M	T	W	T	F	S
					1	2
3	4	5	6	7	8	9
10	11	12	13	14	15	16
17	18	19	20	21	22	23
24	25	26	27	28	29	30

JULY

S	M	T	W	T	F	S
1	2	3	4	5	6	7
8	9	10	11	12	13	14
15	16	17	18	19	20	21
22	23	24	25	26	27	28
29	30	31				

AUGUST

S	M	T	W	T	F	S
			1	2	3	4
5	6	7	8	9	10	11
12	13	14	15	16	17	18
19	20	21	22	23	24	25
26	27	28	29	30	31	

SEPTEMBER

S	M	T	W	T	F	S
						1
2	3	4	5	6	7	8
9	10	11	12	13	14	15
16	17	18	19	20	21	22
23/30	24	25	26	27	28	29

OCTOBER

S	M	T	W	T	F	S
	1	2	3	4	5	6
7	8	9	10	11	12	13
14	15	16	17	18	19	20
21	22	23	24	25	26	27
28	29	30	31			

NOVEMBER

S	M	T	W	T	F	S
				1	2	3
4	5	6	7	8	9	10
11	12	13	14	15	16	17
18	19	20	21	22	23	24
25	26	27	28	29	30	

DECEMBER

S	M	T	W	T	F	S
						1
2	3	4	5	6	7	8
9	10	11	12	13	14	15
16	17	18	19	20	21	22
23/30	24/31	25	26	27	28	29

June 19-23	Royal Ascot Horse Race (www.ascot.co.uk), Ascot (near Windsor)
Late June-early July	Wimbledon Tennis Championship, London (www.wimbledon.org)
Late July-early Aug	Cambridge Folk Festival, Cambridge (buy tickets early at www.cambridge folkfestival.co.uk)
Late Aug	Notting Hill Carnival, London (costumes, Caribbean music, www.thenottinghillcarnival.com)
Aug 27	Late Summer Bank Holiday (last Monday in August; England only, not Scotland)
Sept (one week)	London Fashion Week (www.londonfashionweek.co.uk)
Late Sept	Jane Austen Festival, Bath (www.janeausten.co.uk)

Nov 5	Bonfire Night (bonfires, fireworks, effigy burning of 1605 traitor Guy Fawkes)
Nov 10	Lord Mayor's Show, London (second Saturday in November; huge parade in The City with fireworks, www .lordmayorsshow.org)
Nov 11	Remembrance Sunday (royals lay wreaths at Cenotaph for WWI dead)
Mid-Nov-early Dec	State Opening of Parliament (Queen travels by carriage in parade from Buckingham Palace to Houses of Parliament, www.parliament.uk)
Dec 24-26	Christmas holidays (many sights close; limited or no public transport)

Conversions and Climate

Britain uses a mix of the metric system and "our" Imperial system. That, and a few other little differences, can cause visitors to stumble. Here are the basics, along with a snapshot of the weather you can expect.

Numbers and Stumblers

- The British write a few of their numbers differently than we do. 1 = 1, 4 = 4, 7 = 7.
- In Europe, dates appear as day/month/year, so Christmas is 25/12/12.
- What Americans call the second floor of a building is the first floor in Britain.
- On escalators and moving sidewalks, Brits keep the left "lane" open for passing. Stand to the right.
- When pointing, use your whole hand, palm down.
- When counting with fingers, start with your thumb. If you hold up your first finger to request one item, you'll probably get two.
- To avoid the British version of giving someone "the finger," don't hold up the first two fingers of your hand with your palm facing you. (It looks like a reversed victory sign.)
- And please...don't call your waist pack a "fanny pack" (see the British-Yankee Vocabulary list at the end of this appendix).

Metric Conversions (approximate)

Weight and volume are typically calculated in metric: A kilogram is 2.2 pounds, and a liter is about a quart. The weight of a person is measured by "stone" (one stone equals 14 pounds). On the road, Brits use miles instead of kilometers. Temperatures are generally given in both Celsius and Fahrenheit.

1 foot = 0.3 meter	1 square yard = 0.8 square meter
1 yard = 0.9 meter	1 square mile = 2.6 square kilometers
1 mile = 1.6 kilometers	1 ounce = 28 grams
1 centimeter = 0.4 inch	1 quart = 0.95 liter
1 meter = 39.4 inches	1 kilogram = 2.2 pounds
1 kilometer = 0.62 mile	32°F = 0°C

Weights and Measures

1 British pint = 1.2 US pints
1 imperial gallon = 1.2 US gallons or about 4.5 liters
1 stone = 14 pounds (a 168-pound person weighs 12 stone)

Clothing Sizes

When shopping for clothing, use these US-to-UK comparisons as general guidelines (but note that no conversion is perfect).

- Women's dresses and blouses: Add 4
  (US women's size 10 = UK size 14)
- Men's suits and jackets: US and UK use the same sizing
- Men's shirts: US and UK use the same sizing
- Women's shoes: Subtract 2½
  (US size 8 = UK size 5½)
- Men's shoes: Subtract about ½
  (US size 9 = UK size 8½)

London's Climate

First line, average daily high temperature; second line, average daily low; third line, average days without rain. For more detailed weather statistics for destinations throughout England (as well as the rest of the world), check www.worldclimate.com.

J	F	M	A	M	J	J	A	S	O	N	D
43°	44°	50°	56°	62°	69°	71°	71°	65°	58°	50°	45°
36°	36°	38°	42°	47°	53°	56°	56°	52°	46°	42°	38°
16	15	20	18	19	19	19	20	17	18	15	16

Temperature Conversion: Fahrenheit and Celsius

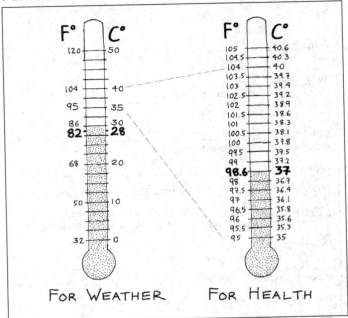

Britain uses both Celsius and Fahrenheit to take its temperature. For a rough conversion from Celsius to Fahrenheit, double the number and add 30. For weather, remember that 28°C is 82°F—perfect. For health, 37°C is just right.

Hotel Reservation

To: _____   _____
                 hotel   *email or fax*

From: _____   _____
                 name   *email or fax*

Today's date: _____ / _____ / _____
                   day   *month*   *year*

Dear Hotel _____ ,
Please make this reservation for me:

Name: _____

Total # of people: _____   # of rooms: _____   # of nights: _____

Arriving: _____ / _____ / _____   My time of arrival (24-hr clock): _____
              day *month* *year*   (I will telephone if I will be late)

Departing: _____ / _____ / _____
               day *month* *year*

Room(s): Single____   Double ____   Twin ____   Triple ____   Quad____

With: Toilet ____   Shower ____   Bath ____   Sink only____

Special needs: View____   Quiet____   Cheapest ____   Ground Floor____

Please email or fax confirmation of my reservation, along with the type of room reserved and the price. Please also inform me of your cancellation policy. After I hear from you, I will quickly send my credit-card information as a deposit to hold the room. Thank you.

Name _____

Address _____

City _____ **State** _____ **Zip Code** _____ **Country** _____

Before hoteliers can make your reservation, they want to know the information listed above. You can use this form as the basis for your email, or you can photocopy this page, fill in the information, and send it as a fax (also available online at www.ricksteves.com/reservation).

Packing Checklist

Whether you're traveling for five days or five weeks, here's what you'll need to bring. Pack light to enjoy the sweet freedom of true mobility. Happy travels!

❏ 5 shirts: long- and short-sleeve
❏ 1 sweater or lightweight fleece
❏ 2 pairs pants
❏ 1 pair shorts
❏ 1 swimsuit
❏ 5 pairs underwear and socks
❏ 1 pair shoes
❏ 1 rainproof jacket with hood
❏ Tie or scarf
❏ Money belt
❏ Money—your mix of:
   ❏ Debit card (for ATM withdrawals)
   ❏ Credit card
   ❏ Hard cash (in easy-to-exchange $20 bills)
❏ Documents plus photocopies:
   ❏ Passport
   ❏ Printout of airline eticket
   ❏ Driver's license
   ❏ Student ID and hostel card
   ❏ Railpass/car rental voucher
   ❏ Insurance details
❏ Daypack
❏ Electronics—your choice of:
   ❏ Camera (and related gear)
   ❏ Mobile phone or smartphone
   ❏ iPod (or other MP3 player)
   ❏ Laptop/netbook
   ❏ ebook reader
   ❏ Chargers for each of the above
   ❏ Plug adapter

❏ Empty water bottle
❏ Wristwatch and alarm clock
❏ Earplugs
❏ Toiletries kit
   ❏ Toiletries
   ❏ Medicines and vitamins
   ❏ First-aid kit
   ❏ Glasses/contacts/sunglasses (with prescriptions)
❏ Sealable plastic baggies
❏ Laundry soap
❏ Clothesline
❏ Small towel
❏ Sewing kit
❏ Travel information (guidebooks and maps)
❏ Address list (for sending postcards)
❏ Postcards and photos from home
❏ Notepad and pen
❏ Journal

If you plan to carry on your luggage, note that all liquids must be in 3.4-ounce or smaller containers and fit within a single quart-size sealable baggie. For details, see www.tsa.gov/travelers.

APPENDIX

British–Yankee Vocabulary

advert-advertisement

afters-dessert

anticlockwise-counterclockwise

Antipodean-An Australian or New Zealander

aubergine-eggplant

banger-sausage

bangers and mash-sausage and mashed potatoes

bank holiday-legal holiday

bap-small roll

bespoke-custom-made

billion-a thousand of our billions (a million million)

biro-ballpoint pen

biscuit-cookie

black pudding-sausage made from dried blood

bloody-damn

blow off-fart

bobby-policeman ("the Bill" is more common)

Bob's your uncle-there you go (with a shrug), naturally

boffin-nerd, geek

bollocks-testicles (used in many colorful expressions)

bolshy-argumentative

bomb-success or failure

bonnet-car hood

boot-car trunk

braces-suspenders

bridle way-path for walkers, bikers, and horse riders

brilliant-cool

brolly-umbrella

bubble and squeak-cabbage and potatoes fried together

builder-construction worker

bum-butt

candy floss-cotton candy

caravan-trailer

car boot sale-temporary flea market, often for charity

car park-parking lot

cashpoint-ATM

casualty-emergency room

cat's eyes-road reflectors

ceilidh (KAY-lee)-informal evening of song and folk fun (Scottish and Irish)

cheap and cheerful-budget but adequate

cheap and nasty-cheap and bad quality

cheers-good-bye or thanks; also a toast

chemist-pharmacist

chicory-endive

chippie-fish-and-chip shop; carpenter (see also "joiner")

chips-French fries

chock-a-block-jam-packed

chuffed-pleased

cider-alcoholic apple cider

clearway-road where you can't stop

coach-long-distance bus

concession-discounted admission

concs (pronounced "conks")-short for "concession"

cos-romaine lettuce

cot-baby crib

cotton buds-Q-tips

council estate-public housing

courgette-zucchini

craic (pronounced "crack")-fun, good conversation (Irish and spreading to England)

crisps-potato chips

cuppa-cup of tea

curry-any Indian meal flavored with curry, popular with all Brits

dear-expensive

dicey-iffy, risky

digestives-round graham cookies

dinner-lunch or dinner

diversion-detour

donkey's years-ages, long time

draughts-checkers

draw-marijuana

dual carriageway-divided highway (four lanes)

dummy-pacifier

elevenses-coffee-and-biscuits break before lunch

elvers-baby eels

engaged tone-busy signal

estate car-station wagon

face flannel-washcloth

faff-bumble (about)

fag-cigarette

fagged-exhausted

faggot-meatball

fairy cake-cupcake

fancy-to like, to be attracted to (a person)

fanny-vagina

fell-hill or high plain (Lake District)

first floor-second floor

fixture-sports schedule

fizzy drink-pop or soda

flat-apartment

flutter-a bet

football-soccer

force-waterfall (Lake District)

fortnight-two weeks

fringe-hair bangs

Frogs-French people

fruit machine-slot machine

full Monty-whole shebang; everything

gallery-balcony

gammon-ham

gangway-aisle

gaol-jail (same pronunciation)

gateau (or gateaux)-cake

gear lever-stick shift

geezer-dude (slang for young man)

ginger-haired-redhead

give way-yield

glen-narrow valley (Scotland)

goods wagon-freight truck

green fingers-green thumbs

grizzle-grumble, fuss (especially by a baby)

gutted-deeply disappointed

half eight-8:30 (not 7:30)

hash sign-pound sign, as on a phone

heath-open treeless land

hen night-bachelorette party

High Street-Main Street (in a generic sense)

hire-rent, as in a car or bike

hire car-rental car

hob-stove burner

holiday-vacation

homely-homey or cozy

hoover-vacuum cleaner

ice lolly-Popsicle

interval-intermission

ironmonger-hardware store

ish-more or less

jacket potato-baked potato

jelly-Jell-O

Joe Bloggs-John Q. Public

joiner-carpenter (see also "chippie")

jumble sale-rummage sale

jumper-sweater

just a tick-just a second

kipper-smoked herring

knackered-exhausted (Cockney: cream crackered)

knickers-ladies' panties

knocking shop-brothel

knock up-wake up or visit (old-fashioned)

ladybird-ladybug

lady fingers-flat, spongy cookie

lady's finger-okra

lager-light, fizzy beer

left luggage-baggage check

lemon squash-lemonade, not fizzy

lemonade-lemon-lime pop, fizzy

let-rent, as in property

licenced-restaurant authorized to sell alcohol

lie-in, having a-sleeping in late

lift-elevator

listed-protected historic building

loo-toilet or bathroom

lorry-truck

mac-mackintosh raincoat

mangetout-snow peas

main-entrée

mains-electrical outlet

Marmite-yeast paste, spread on sandwiches

marrow-summer squash

mate-buddy (boy or girl)

mean-stingy

mental-wild, memorable

mews-former stables converted to two-story rowhouses (London)

mince-hamburger meat

mobile (MOH-bile)-cell phone

moggie-cat

M.O.T.-mandatory annual car safety certificate

motorway-freeway

naff-dorky

nappy-diaper

natter-talk on and on

neep-Scottish for turnip

newsagent-corner store

nought-zero

noughts & crosses-tic-tac-toe

O.A.P.-old-age pensioner, retiree

off-licence-liquor store

on offer-for sale

one-off-unique; one-time event

panto, pantomime-fairy-tale play performed at Christmas (silly but fun)

pants-underwear, briefs

paracetamol-acetaminophen, Tylenol

pasty (PASS-tee)-crusted savory (usually meat) pie from Cornwall

pavement-sidewalk

people mover-minivan

pear-shaped-messed up, gone wrong

pensioner-senior citizen, retiree

petrol-gas

pillar box-mailbox

pissed (rude), **paralytic, bevvied, wellied, popped up, merry, trollied, ratted, rat-arsed, pissed as a newt**-drunk

pitch-playing field

plaster-Band-Aid

pram-baby carriage

publican-pub manager (old-fashioned)

public school-private "prep" school (e.g., Eton)

pudding-dessert in general

pull, to be on the-looking for love

punter-customer, especially in gambling

pushchair-stroller

put a sock in it-shut up

queue-line

queue up-line up

quid-a pound (money)

randy-horny

rasher-slice of bacon

redundant, made-laid off

Remembrance Day-Veterans' Day

return ticket-round-trip

revising; doing revisions-studying for exams

ring up-call (telephone)

rocket-arugula

roundabout-traffic circle

rubber-eraser

rubbish-bad

salad cream-mayo, mustard, and vinegar dressing

Sat Nav-GPS device

sausage roll-sausage wrapped in a flaky pastry

Scotch egg-hard-boiled egg wrapped in sausage meat

scrumpy-type of hard cider

self-catering-accommodation with kitchen

Sellotape-Scotch tape

services-freeway rest area

serviette-napkin

settee-couch

shag-intercourse (cruder than in the US)

shandy-lager and 7-Up

silencer-car muffler

single ticket-one-way ticket

skip-Dumpster

sleeping policeman-speed bumps

smalls-underwear

snogging-kissing, making out

sod-mildly offensive insult

sod it, sod off-screw it, screw off

soda-soda water (not pop)

solicitor-lawyer (a.k.a. barrister)

spanner-wrench

sparkie-electrician

spend a penny-urinate

stag night-bachelor party

starkers-buck naked

starters-appetizers

state school-public school

sticking plaster-Band-Aid

sticky tape-Scotch tape

stone-14 pounds (measurement of weight)

stroppy-bad-tempered

subway-underground walkway

suet-fat from animal rendering (sometimes used in cooking)

sultanas-golden raisins

surgical spirit-rubbing alcohol

suspenders-garters

suss out-figure out

swede-rutabaga

ta-thank you

take the mickey-tease

tatty-worn out or tacky

taxi rank-taxi stand

telly-TV

tenement-stone apartment house (not necessarily a slum)

tenner-£10 bill

theatre-live stage

tick-a check mark

tight as a fish's bum-cheapskate (watertight)

tights-panty hose

tin-can

tip-public dump

tipper lorry-dump truck

top hole-first rate

top up-refill a drink

torch-flashlight

towel, press-on-panty liner

towpath-path along a river

trainers-sneakers

Tube-subway

twee-quaint, cute

twitcher-bird watcher

Underground-subway

verge-grassy edge of road

verger-church official

way out-exit

wee (adj)-small (Scottish)

wee (verb)-urinate
Wellingtons, wellies-rubber boots
whacked-exhausted
whinge (rhymes with hinge)-whine

wind up-tease, irritate
witter on-gab and gab
yob-hooligan
zebra crossing-crosswalk
zed-the letter *Z*

INDEX

MAP INDEX

Audio Europe

RICK STEVES
AUDIO
EUROPE

Rick's free app and podcasts

The FREE **Rick Steves Audio Europe**™ app for iPhone, iPad and iPod Touch gives you 29 self-guided audio tours of Europe's top museums, sights and historic walks—plus more than 200 tracks filled with cultural insights and sightseeing tips from Rick's radio interviews—all organized into geographic-specific playlists.

Let **Rick Steves Audio Europe**™ amplify your guidebook.

With Rick whispering in your ear Europe gets even better.

Thanks Facebook fans for submitting photos while on location! From top: John Kuijper in Florence, Brenda Mamer with her mother in Rome, Angel Capobianco in London, and Alyssa Passey with her friend in Paris.

Find out more at ricksteves.com